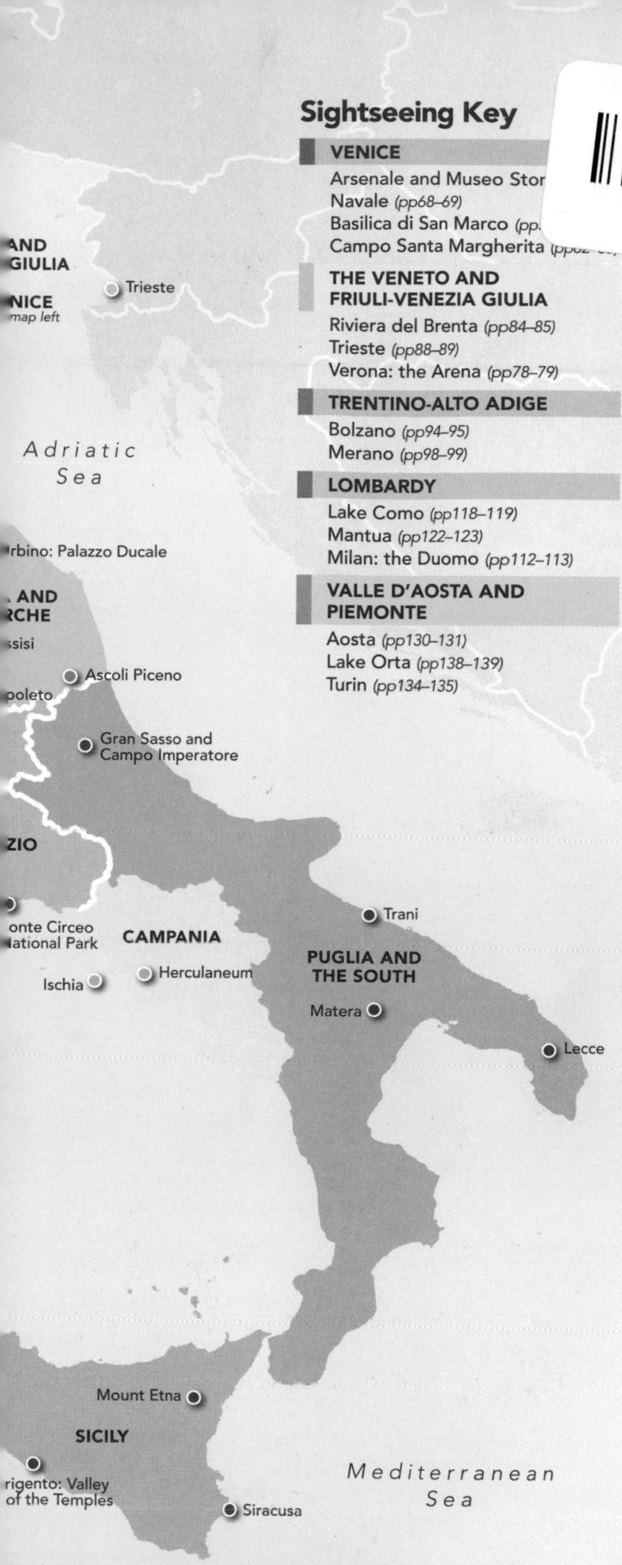

Sightseeing Key

AND
GIULIA
NICE
map left
Trieste

Adriatic
Sea

rbino: Palazzo Ducale

. AND
RCHE
ssisi
poleto
Ascoli Piceno

Gran Sasso and
Campo Imperatore

ZIO

onte Circeo
lational Park

Ischia

CAMPANIA

Herculaneum

PUGLIA AND
THE SOUTH

Matera

Trani

Lecce

Mount Etna

SICILY

rigento: Valley
of the Temples

Siracusa

Mediterranean
Sea

EYEWITNESS TRAVEL

FAMILY GUIDE

ITALY

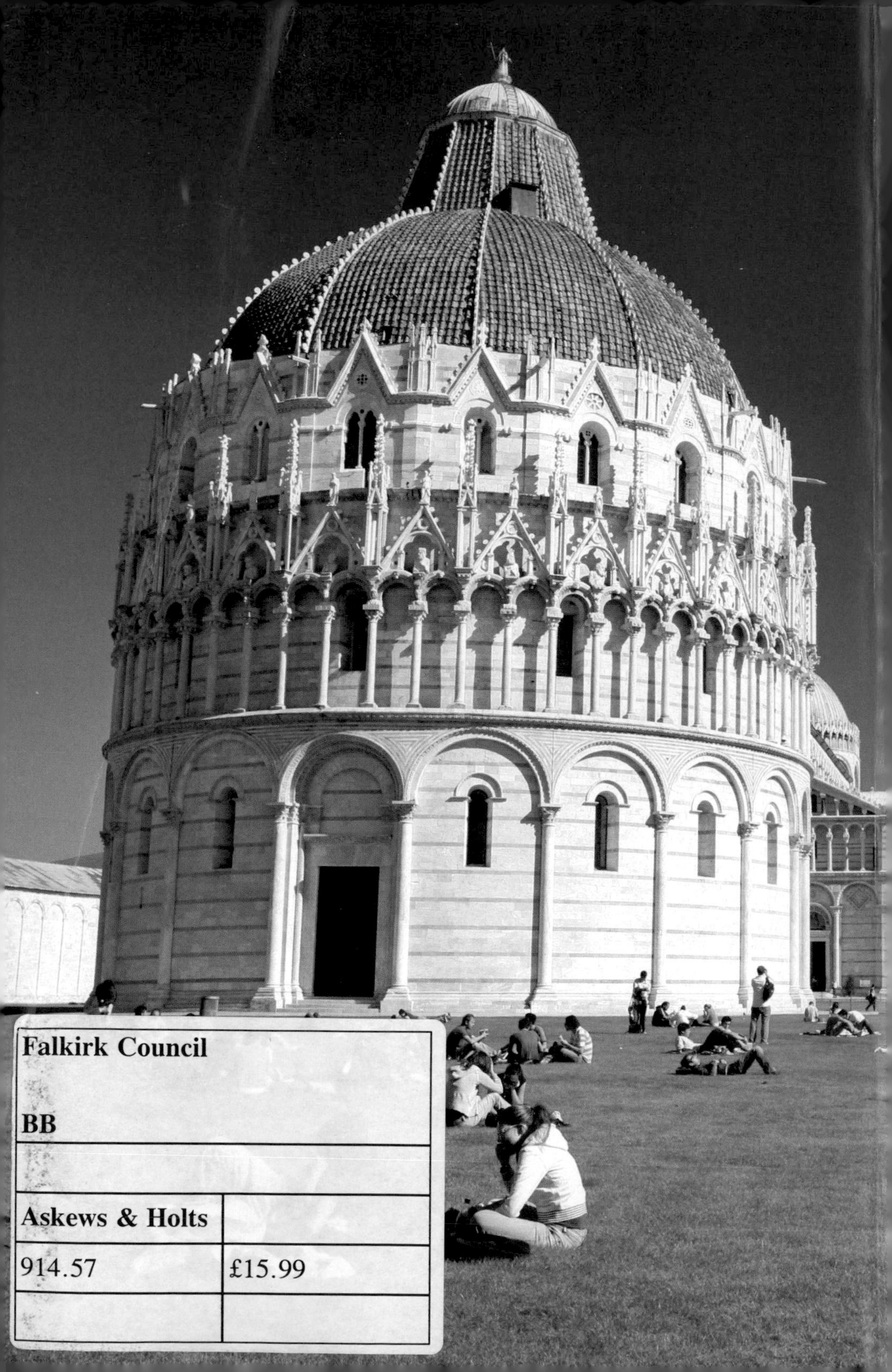

EYEWITNESS TRAVEL

FAMILY GUIDE

ITALY

DK

LONDON, NEW YORK,
MELBOURNE, MUNICH AND DELHI
WWW.DK.COM

PUBLISHER Vivien Antwi

LIST MANAGER Christine Stroyan

MANAGING ART EDITOR Mabel Chan

SENIOR EDITORS Michelle Crane,
Sadie Smith

PROJECT EDITOR Georgina Palffy

EDITORS Vicki Allen, Claire Bush,
Fay Franklin, Rada Radojicic

DESIGNERS Shahid Mahmood,
Tracy Smith

PICTURE RESEARCH Ellen Root,
Marta Bescos

SENIOR DTP DESIGNER Jason Little

SENIOR CARTOGRAPHIC MANAGER
Casper Morris

PHOTOGRAPHY Nick Bonetti,
Nigel Hicks, Anna Mockford,
Helena Smith

CARTOONS Tom Morgan-Jones

ADDITIONAL ILLUSTRATIONS Arun
Pottirayil, Stephen Conlin, Donati
Giudici Associati srl, Stephen
Gyapay, Roger Hutchins,
Maltings Partnership, Simon
Roulstone, Paul Weston,
John Woodcock

PRODUCTION CONTROLLER
Rebecca Short

DESIGN CONCEPT
Keith Hagan at www.
greenwichdesign.co.uk

Printed and bound in China by South
China Printing Co. Ltd, China

First published in Great Britain in 2012 by
Dorling Kindersley Limited, 80 Strand,
London WC2R 0RL. A Penguin Company

12 13 14 15 10 9 8 7 6 5 4 3 2 1

A CIP catalogue record is available from
the British Library.

ISBN 978-1-4053-6800-1

Contents

Tuscan landscape with poppies and cypress trees

*Gondolas by the Rialto Bridge,
Venice, in the moonlight*

How to Use this Guide

This guide is designed to help families to get the most from a visit to Italy, providing expert recommendations for sightseeing with kids, along with detailed practical information. The opening section contains an introduction to Italy and its highlights, as well as all the essentials required to plan a family holiday (including how to get there, getting around, health, insurance, money and communications), a guide to family-friendly festivals through the year and a brief historical overview.

The main sightseeing section is divided into regions. A "best of" feature is followed by the key sights and other attractions to visit in each region, as well as options for where to eat, drink and stay. At the back of the book are detailed maps of Italy and Rome, and a language section listing essential words and phrases for family travel.

INTRODUCING THE REGION
Each regional chapter is opened by a double-page spread setting it in context, with a brief introduction, locator map and a selection of regional highlights.

Locator map locates the region.

Highlights give a flavour of what to see in the area.

THE BEST OF...
A planner to show at a glance the best things for families to see and do in the region, with themed suggestions ranging from seasonal visits to short stays, cultural holidays and the great outdoors.

Themed suggestions for the best things to see and do with kids.

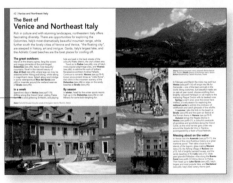

WHERE TO STAY
Our expert authors have compiled a wide range of recommendations for places to stay with families, from hotels and B&Bs that welcome children to self-catering, *agriturismi* and camping.

Easy-to-use symbols show the key family-friendly features of places to stay, such as family rooms, gardens, swimming pools, beaches and kitchens.

Price Guide box gives details of the price categories for a family of four.

SIGHTSEEING IN ITALY

Each regional chapter is divided into 2–4 smaller regions, all of which are shown on the regional map at the start of the chapter. These feature a number of "hub" destinations (see below): pragmatic and enjoyable plans for a half-day or day's visit, giving both adults and children a real insight into the destination, balanced with chances for kids to let off steam, "take cover" options for rainy days, suggestions for where to eat, drink and shop as a family, ideas for where to continue sightseeing, and all the practicalities, including transport.

Introductory text describes the key characteristics and geography of the region, and gives information on the transport infrastructure.

The regional map shows the regions covered and all the hubs, colour-coded by area.

The Lowdown gives all the practical information you need to visit the area.

Kids' Corner is featured on all sightseeing pages (see below).

The "hub" destinations pick out the best places to visit in each region, using lively and informative text to engage and entertain both adults and children.

The Lowdown provides comprehensive practical information, including transport, opening times, costs, activities, age range suitability and how long to allow for a visit.

Key Features/Sights uses illustrated artworks to show the most interesting features of each destination, highlighting elements most likely to appeal to children.

Next stop... suggests other places to visit, either near the key destination, thematically linked to it, or a complete change of pace for the rest of the day.

Letting off steam suggests a place to take children to play freely following a cultural visit.

Eat and drink lists family-friendly places to eat and drink, from picnics and snacks to full meals and gourmet dining in settings that can accommodate children.

Find out more gives suggestions for downloads, games, apps or films to enthuse children about a place and help them to learn more about it.

Further sights around each hub destination are described on the following pages. Each sight or destination is selected to appeal to both adults and children.

Kids' Corner is designed to involve children with the destination, with things to look out for, games to play, cartoons and fun facts. Answers to quizzes are at the bottom of the panel.

Town or sight gives details of the places of interest to visit, with an emphasis on the aspects most likely to attract children, incorporating quirky stories and unusual facts.

The Lowdown provides the usual comprehensive practical and transport information for each sight.

The ideal Renaissance town of Pienza in the Val d'Orcia, Tuscany

Introducing
ITALY

The Best of Italy

Stretching from the snow-capped Alps to the sun-baked orange groves of Sicily, and with more UNESCO heritage sites than anywhere else in the world, Italy is perhaps the most richly varied country in Europe. Child-focused museums may be rare, activities for kids in galleries and museums in their infancy and children's menus virtually unheard of, but this is a family-centred society in which youngsters are adored and welcomed everywhere.

Travel back in time

Centuries before Rome established itself as the centre of the civilized world, there was plenty happening around the Italian peninsula.

In **Bolzano** (see pp94–5), at the archaeological museum, visitors can pay their respects to the oldest known Italian, 5,300-year-old Ötzi, whose well-preserved mummified remains were found on the Similaun Glacier in 1991. Analysis of Ötzi has revealed many details about life in the Copper Age – what people ate, what they wore, how they lived.

Some 2,800 years after Ötzi's icy death, Sicily was the centre of the ancient Greek world, with the city of **Siracusa** (see pp362–3) the most powerful in the Mediterranean. There are dramatic relics of this time throughout Sicily – magnificently preserved temples at **Agrigento** (see pp352–3) and **Selinunte** (see p353), and fine theatres at **Siracusa** (see p362) and **Taormina** (see p360) that are still used today.

In central Italy, at around the same time, Etruscan civilization was at its peak. There are marvellous frescoes to be seen in the Etruscan museum and haunting necropolis at **Tarquinia** (see pp304–5), and fantastic sculptures and objects from everyday life at **Villa Giulia** (see p286), Rome's Etruscan museum.

However, it is for its ancient Roman monuments that Italy is best known. The Romans left traces throughout the peninsula – the amphitheatre at **Verona** (see pp78–9) and the splendid villa at **Piazza Armerina** (see p354) in Sicily are the most impressive – but the most exciting of all the ancient sites are the buried cities of **Pompeii** (see p327) and **Herculaneum** (see pp324–5) – plus **Rome** itself, of course (see pp261–301).

For most children, the top site in Rome is the **Colosseum** (see pp266–7), where gladiators fought to the death against wild animals and each other, but there are also palaces, temples, baths, catacombs, a market and, in the nearby town of **Ostia** (see pp302–3), a 20-seater toilet.

Medieval majesty

Italy is full of perfectly preserved castles and fortresses whose turreted fortifications, arrow-slit windows, moats and drawbridges bring the world of medieval chivalry and battle magically to life.

Castel del Monte (see p341) in Puglia, **Castello Caetani** at Sermoneta (see p312), **Castello di Fénis** near Aosta (see pp130–31), and the fortress at **San Leo** (see p246) in central Italy are among the most impressive, while at the heart of modern **Milan** (see pp112–15) is the magnificent **Castello Sforzesco** (see p115). But castle living was not all about defence against attack. For a glimpse of the lavish lifestyle of medieval lords and ladies, visit the beautiful palaces of **Venice** (see pp47–73).

Another part of Italy's medieval heritage is its walled towns. Many of these are virtually traffic-free, with sights to see, labyrinthine streets to explore, local crafts to buy, and plenty of cafés and restaurants with terraces where parents can relax while the children play. **Lucca** (see pp190–91), where it is possible to walk or cycle round the walls, **San Gimignano** (see pp200–1) with its forest of towers and **Montalcino** (see pp194–5) with its relaxed vibe and magnificent fortress are among the best.

Below Fresoced walls of a room in Herculaneum, near Naples

Cities of culture

Italy's world-famous art cities – **Rome**, **Venice**, **Florence** (see pp161–81), **Pisa** (see p192), **Siena** (see pp186–7) and **Assisi** (see pp228–9) – have fantastic architecture, fine art and a lively cultural scene. They can be great for a family visit, particularly with slightly older children. Historical centres tend to be compact, making it easy to combine a visit to a church, gallery or museum with relaxing in a park or piazza.

Lesser-known cities are well worth exploring, too, and the choice is vast and wide-ranging. There is the spectacular cave-city of **Matera** (see pp346–7) and the Sicilian towns of **Noto** (see p364), **Scicli** (see p364) and **Modica** (see p365), where children can seek out stone monsters on Baroque *palazzi*, sample the best ice cream in Italy and watch chocolate being made.Less-visited but up-and-coming destinations include **Turin** (see pp134–5), with its breathtaking Egyptian museum and elegant boulevards that date from its years as capital of the Savoy kings.

The great outdoors

Italy covers a huge variety of landscapes. There are vast, deep lakes; networks of caves; dramatic river gorges; rolling hills and rugged mountains. Well-marked walking, horseriding and mountain-biking trails in national parks and nature reserves offer the chance to spot wildlife, from golden eagles to flamingos, brown bears to wolves.

For most kids, a volcano is the ultimate natural wonder, and the island of **Stromboli** (see p361), off the Sicilian coast, is the most active one in Europe. Hikers can watch eruptions from the summit, but to see the spectacle at night from a boat is an equally unforgettable experience. Italy's volcanic activity has created some unique landscapes as well – notably the fume-filled, spongy sulphur fields of **Pozzuoli** (see p326), near Naples. For walking enthusiasts, the beautiful **Parco Nazionale d'Abruzzo** (see p337) offers an extensive network of hiking trails, as does the **Parco Nazionale del Gran Paradiso** (see p132), an area of outstanding natural beauty where kids can really run free.

Of northern Italy's famous and beautiful lakes, family favourites are **Como** (see pp118–21), **Orta** (see pp138–141), and **Garda** (see p82), with its watersports and lively theme parks to keep active kids entertained and happy.

Top *The Filarete Tower of Castello Sforzesco in Milan*
Centre *Villas clinging to the wooded sides of Lake Como*
Below *The magnificent Basilica di San Marco in Venice*

Beside the seaside

Italy's coastline ranges from rocky coves to wind-swept dunes, and from dramatic swathes of black volcanic pebbles to the endless ribbon of golden sand that runs along the Adriatic seaboard.

Italians like to be comfortable on holiday: in summer many beaches are given over to orderly grids of sun umbrellas and loungers. These are, however, sociable places, and can be a good option for giving children a chance make friends. And for families with young children, a little comfort and plenty of shade are ideal.

The family-friendly beach resort of **Rimini** (see p221) and **Grado** (see p90), with a wetland nature reserve, make good choices. Other good destinations for families are **Camogli** (see p151) and the towns of the **Cinque Terre** (see p148) on the Ligurian Riviera, and Monte Argentario, a peninsula on the Tuscan coast near **Pitigliano** (see pp210–11).

The volcanic **Aeolian Islands** (see p361), off the coast of Sicily, are great for families, with strange pumice and lava landscapes. **Sardinia** (see pp369–77) has some of the best beaches in Europe, along with offshore islands to explore, such as **Asinara** (see p371) and the **Maddalena Islands** (see p374). Back on the mainland, Puglia has some lovely beaches too, especially **Ostuni** (see p344) and **Otranto** (see p344).

For families who like wild, unspoiled beaches, Italy has several coastal nature reserves. Among the finest are the Parco dell'Uccellina, near **Pitigliano** (see pp210–11) in Tuscany, the **Riserva Naturale dello Zingaro** (see p356) and the **Riserva Naturale Oasi Faunistica di Vendicari** (see p364) in Sicily, and Lazio's **Parco Nazionale del Circeo** (see pp310–11).

City breaks

Any number of Italian cities and towns are ideal for a short family break. Spending a long weekend or a few days off the beaten tourist track will give adults and children alike a real sense of discovery. Among the most rewarding are medieval **Bergamo** (see p116); Italy's gourmet capital **Bologna** (see pp218–19); **Genoa** (see pp144–7), with its amazing aquarium; **Lecce** (see pp342–3) with its exuberant Baroque buildings; **Verona** (see pp78–81), the city of Romeo and Juliet; **Trieste** (see pp88–9), where central Europe meets the Mediterranean; and **Bolzano** (see pp94–5) in the Sud Tirol or **Cagliari** (see pp374–5) in Sardinia.

If time is limited in which to see one of the big-name cities, **Venice** (see pp47–73) is both easy and appealing, with plenty to do and see on foot and by hopping on and off water buses, which children love. **Rome** (see pp261–301) is another good option, especially if the kids are interested in gladiators. Although it is a smaller city, **Florence** (see pp161–81) is a little more demanding with young children, as its principal attractions are fine art treasures hidden away inside palaces and museums. Three to five days in any of these cities makes for an excellent family break, and is an ideal taster for kids.

Italy in a week

With a whole week at their disposal, families with older children might choose to visit one or more of Italy's great "art cities". **Venice**, **Florence** and **Rome** (see above) all have more than enough to keep the family interested for a

Below Beautiful La Speranza beach, Sardinia

week. However, excellent train services make it feasible to combine any two of Venice, Florence and Rome. It is even possible to cover all three, by sticking to the main sights.

Italy's plethora of small provincial airports make it easy to create a tailor-made short break. To visit the Roman sites of **Pompeii** *(see p327)* and **Herculaneum** *(see pp324–5)*, fly to **Naples** *(see p326)* but stay on the island of **Ischia** *(see p328–9)*, from which both can be visited on day trips. In between, spend lazier days exploring the gardens of La Mortella, snorkelling off the rocks of Sant'Angelo and cooking lunch in the volcanically hot sands of Maronti beach.

To explore Tuscany, take a flight to **Pisa** *(see p192)* but stay in civilized **Lucca** *(see pp190–91)*, or pick a farmhouse or villa as a base from which to discover some of this region's fabulous cities of art and history such as **Siena** *(see pp186–7)*

Below The Rialto Bridge, spanning the Grand Canal in Venice
Bottom Neptune fountain on Piazza Navona Rome

Above Fountain in Florence's Boboli Gardens

and **Arezzo** *(see pp204–5)* or fairy-tale hill towns like **San Gimignano** *(see pp200–201)*. Spring and autumn are the perfect times to visit.

Umbria and Le Marche are also good to tackle from a country house, with a pool. From there, jewel-like little cities such as **Urbino** *(see pp244–5)*, **Orvieto** *(see pp240–41)* and **Ascoli Piceno** *(see pp248–9)* can be visited for the day, and villages like **San Leo** *(see p246)* explored.

Sicily's west coast is ideal for a late autumn or early spring break. Fly into **Trapani** *(see p356)*. From a seaside base, it is possible to explore the beaches and paths of the **Riserva Naturale dello Zingaro** *(see p356)*; visit the ancient Greek temples at **Agrigento** *(see pp352–3)*; take a cable car up from Trapani to the medieval hilltop village of **Erice** *(see p356)*; and hop on a hydrofoil to the **Egadi Islands** *(see p357)*.

For a week in northern Italy, fly into **Bergamo** *(see p116)*, staying in the town's atmospheric Città Alta. Ferry-hop along **Lake Como** *(see pp118–21)* and make a day trip to nearby **Milan** *(see pp112–15)*, where kids will love to clamber around the rooftops of the Duomo and see Leonardo da Vinci's *Last Supper*. Style-savvy teens are sure to adore the super-chic shops. For a more rural northern week, fly to **Verona** *(see pp78–81)* and stay on a farm outside **Bolzano** *(see pp94–5)* or **Merano** *(see pp98–9)* in the mountains. Visit Ötzi, a Copper Age man *(see p94)*, take a chairlift to the dizzy peaks of the **Cinque Torri** *(see p97)* and bask in the warm waters of Merano's thermal spa *(see p98)*.

Italy Through the Year

Italy is a country for all seasons, thanks partly to its geographical diversity – it is possible to be be skiing in Val d'Aosta one day and swimming in the warm seas off Sicily the next – and partly to its busy calendar of festivals and other events, celebrating everything from food to flowers. Add the fact that it has more internationally acclaimed cities of art, architecture and history than anywhere else in the world, and any month is a great time to visit.

Spring

The Italian spring (*primavera*) starts very early, particularly in the south, where the first blossoms can be seen already in February, and where swimming in the sea is no more bracing than it would be during summer in northern Europe.

The weather can be unpredictable, and often wet, in the centre and north of the country, but eerie mists make **Venice** (*see pp47–73*) especially atmospheric and – except during Carnevale – it is less crowded than at other times. The **Italian Lakes** (*see pp118–21 & pp138–41*) are lovely from Easter onwards, and late spring weather is usually gorgeous everywhere.

MARCH

Carnevale (Carnival) festivities take place throughout Italy in the run-up to the beginning of Lent. The most famous celebrations are in Venice, but kids will enjoy themselves just as much in any small town, where it is traditional for them to wear fancy dress on **Shrove Tuesday** (*Martedì Grasso*) and the weekend before. There are often parades, followed by communal street parties featuring delicious local dishes. **Viareggio** (*Map 5 B2*), **Foiano della Chiana** (*Map 5 D4*), and **Acireale** in Sicily (*Map 14 G4*), are all famous for their celebrations. **Ivrea** (*Map 1 C2*), hosts one of the most unusual events, the **Battle of the Oranges**, in which its citizens pelt each other with the fruit until the streets flow with juice.

The **Festa di San Giuseppe** (Feast of St Joseph), on 19 March, is celebrated in towns throughout Sicily. Elaborate altars are made of bread, locals dress up as the Holy Family and great vats of bean soup are cooked up on streets and in piazzas. There are lively festivities at **Malfa** (*Map 14 F2*) and **Alcamo** (*Map 13 C3*).

APRIL

Easter (*Pasqua*) is hugely important in Italy, and especially in Sicily. The faithful flock in droves to Rome for **Holy Week** (*Settimana Santa*).

There are haunting processions in many towns on **Good Friday** (*Venerdì Santo*), some of which, particularly in the south and Sicily, may be disturbing for children, with re-enactments of the Crucifixion and parades of masked, hooded figures.

Far more joyous is the festival of **Scoppio del Carro** in **Florence** (*see pp166–7*) on **Easter Sunday**, with a splendid firework display lit by a mechanical dove. The pope's Easter Sunday address takes place in Rome's **St Peter's Square** (*see pp294–5*).

Below left *Elaborately dressed participants at the Venice Carnevale*
Below right *Children playing on the beach in the historic seaside town of Grado*

Other family-friendly events in April include the **Festa degli Aquiloni**, a kite festival held on the first Sunday after Easter in the Tuscan town of **San Miniato** (Map 5 C3), and the **Festa di San Marco**, on 25 April, when the patron saint of **Venice** is celebrated with gondola races.

MAY

This month sees some particularly quirky events that kids will love. In the first week, the village of **Cocullo** (Map 8 E2) celebrates its patron saint, San Domenico Abate, by draping his statue with hundreds of live and wriggling snakes and parading it through the streets.

On the first Sunday, the citizens of **Gubbio** (see p232), dressed in medieval garb, race three massive 3.5-m (20-ft) wooden "candles" (ceri) through the old town in the **Corsa dei Ceri**.

On the second Sunday, San Fortunato, the patron saint of fishermen, is honoured in **Camogli** (see p151) with fried fish feasts, fireworks and bonfires.

Flowers are everywhere in May. On **Mother's Day**, the second Sunday of the month, children give mimosa to their mothers. For the **Infiorata**, over the third weekend, the streets of **Noto**, Sicily (see p364), are carpeted with petals.

Summer

Italian schoolchildren have long holidays – from early or mid-June until mid-September. Most families leave town for the coast, so prices rise and accommodation should definitely be booked in advance.

Summer (estate) is a time of food and cultural festivals galore, while the feast days of patron saints in seaside and lakeside towns are particularly spectacular, featuring elaborate firework displays.

JUNE

La Sagra del Cappero (Festival of the Caper) takes place in early June in the remote village of Pollara on the island of **Salina** (see p361). Kids can have fun learning how to collect and salt the capers. Youngsters with a sweeter tooth might prefer one of this month's many strawberry festivals, however. Two of the best are at **Borgo San Martino** (Map 1 D3) in Piedmont and **Maletto** on the slopes of Etna (see pp358–9).

On **Lake Como** (see pp118–21), festivals take place throughout the month at lakeside villages, ending in huge firework displays and torchlit boat processions on 24 June. In the lovely seaside town of **Amalfi** (see p330), the **Festa di Sant'Andrea** on 27 June honours the local saint with yet more fantastic fireworks.

On 24 June, **Florence** (see pp166–7) hosts the **Calcio Storico Fiorentino**, featuring a medieval-style football match along with other festivities in celebration of San Giovanni, the city's patron saint.

Cultural festivals with plenty of child-friendly events include the **Estate Romana**, Rome's summer festival, and the **Festival dei Due Mondi** in **Spoleto** (see p234).

JULY

At the beginning of the month, one of Italy's most famous and popular events takes place – the **Palio** of **Siena** (see pp186–7). This daring bareback horse race in the town square dates back to medieval times and is accompanied by splendid pageantry.

In southern Italy, the town of **Matera** (see pp346–7) celebrates the **Festa della Madonna della Bruna**, at which a statue of the town's patron saint is paraded on an elaborate float and then burned. The fireworks over the town's cave dwellings (sassi) are exceptional. The **Festino di Santa Rosalia** in **Palermo** (see p354) is a crazy, chaotic five-day street party; Rome's equally colourful street festival, the **Festa de' Noantri**, takes place in the **Trastevere** district (see pp298–9).

Below left Bareback riders in medieval costume race in the Palio around Siena's main square
Below right The village of Bellagio on the shores of Lake Como, popular with Italians in summer

AUGUST

Ferragosto, or Assumption Day, is celebrated on 15 August, with local festivals, water fights and fireworks all over Italy. Its religious significance is honoured with famous processions in **Messina**, Sicily *(Map 14 H2)*. The next day, **Siena** stages its second **Palio** of the summer *(see pp186–7)*.

Autumn

Autumn *(autunno)* is a lovely time to visit Italy's historic cities, cooler and quieter now than in high summer.

Gastronomic festivals celebrate the fruits of the season, such as chestnuts, truffles, olives and mushrooms... to say nothing of the wine.

In the south the weather remains warm into November, while in the mountains bordering Austria and Switzerland, October is a golden time of settled weather during which Italians and tourists alike go in for *Törggelen* – cable-car assisted rambles culminating in long rest stops at wayside farms and inns.

SEPTEMBER

On the first Sunday of the month, **Venice** *(see pp40–73)* holds its **Regata Storica**. A spectacular flotilla makes it way along the Grand Canal, and gondola teams in medieval dress compete in rowing races.

Naples *(see pp326–7)* honours its patron saint at the **Festa di San Gennaro** on 15 September. At its climax, crowds gather in the cathedral to witness the saint's dried blood turn miraculously to liquid. In **Verona** *(see pp78–81)*, 16 September sees entertainment and general street partying to celebrate the (alleged) birthday of Juliet.

The **Palio** of **Asti** *(Map 1 D4)* is not as crowded as those of Siena, and provides another chance to see splendid medieval processions and a dramatic bareback horse race.

OCTOBER

Marino *(Map 7 C3)* celebrates its **Sagra dell'Uva** on the first weekend of the month. Although staged in a tiny hilltop town, this is one of the most famous wine festivals in the country. Even if the kids are too young for wine, they will be amazed to see fountains literally flowing with the stuff.

Alba *(Map 1 C4)* and **Acqualagna** *(Map 6 F3)* are both famed for their **Fiera del Tartufo Bianco** but many other towns in northern Italy hold smaller festivals of the prized white winter truffle. But truffles of another kind will appeal more to children, so **Eurochocolate**, held in **Perugia** *(see p230)*, is the perfect place to tickle young tastebuds.

NOVEMBER

La Festa dei Morti (the Day of the Dead), on 2 November, is celebrated more in the south than the north, and is usually a holiday there. Children leave shoes under their beds overnight, to be filled with sweets and gifts by their "late" relatives, and families visit cemeteries to place flowers on the graves of loved ones.

Winter

Christmas fairs and markets pop up in towns and cities throughout the country, selling crafts and presents. Winter *(inverno)* is a good time to visit **Naples** *(see p326)*, famous for its Christmas crib scenes, or **Bolzano** *(see pp94–5)* and other South Tyrolean towns with their Germanic heritage.

It is the start of the winter sports season in the Alps and Dolomites, and Italy has plenty of child-friendly ski resorts. **Val Gardena** *(Map 4 E2)* is especially popular with families.

DECEMBER

Presepi Viventi ("living nativities") are an Italian tradition, in which townsfolk play out roles from the Christmas story in the streets. Of the small-town *presepi*, those in **Barga** *(Map 2 G6)* and **Pietrelcina** *(Map 8 G4)* are particularly charming.

Below left *Marmolada cable-car in the Dolomites, used by walkers in summer and skiers in winter*
Below right *Christmas market in Piazza Mercanti, Milan*

The cave complex of **Stiffe** (Map 7 D2) in Abruzzo is home to a different type of nativity. Life-size statues are carried down into a 650-m (2,130-ft) deep grotto to shelter for the month among stalagmites beside a waterfall.

La Vigilia di Natale (Christmas Eve) sees a family meal of seafood being eaten before Midnight Mass, and on **Natale** (Christmas Day) itself the pope gives a public blessing in St Peter's Square in **Rome**.

JANUARY

Capodanno (New Year) is celebrated with fireworks and, in rural regions, volleys of gunshots fired by hunters.

On 6 January, **La Befana**, the Epiphany witch, brings toys and sweets to good children, and coal (these days made of sugar) to naughty ones. In **Milan** (see pp112–13), the Three Kings lead a splendid costumed parade from the Duomo to Sant'Eustorgio, the supposed resting place of the Magi.

FEBRUARY

In Sicily, the **Festa di Sant'Agata** of **Catania** (see p360) is a spectacular but serious event; while the **Sagra del Mandorlo in Fiore** of Agrigento (see pp352–3) celebrates the first almond blossom with music, dancing and a parade of painted carts.

The Lowdown

Public holidays
New Year's Day (1 Jan)
Epiphany (6 Jan)
Easter (late Mar/Apr)
Liberation Day (25 April)
Labour Day (1 May)
Republic Day (2 Jun)
Ferragosto (15 Aug)
All Saints' Day (1 Nov)
Immaculate Conception (8 Dec)
Christmas Day (25 Dec)
Santo Stefano (26 Dec)

Events
For a full list of events, visit:
Italian State Tourist Board http://web.italiantouristboard.co.uk/it/ind/i24.html

Spring
Battle of the Oranges www.carnevalediivrea.com
Camogli San Fortunato www.prolococamogli.it/penglish/esagra.htm
Cocullo Snake Festival www.lifeinabruzzo.com/cocullo-snake-festival
Corsa dei Ceri www.argoweb.it/gubbio/ceri.uk.html
Festa degli Aquiloni www.festadegliaquiloni.it
Festa di San Giuseppe www.italiannotebook.com/events/festa-di-san-giuseppe
Festa di San Marco www.veneziasi.it/tradizioni-venezia/festa-san-marco.html
Scoppio del Carro www.duomofirenze.it/feste/pasqua_eng.htm
Venice Carnevale www.venice-carnival-italy.com

Summer
Calcio Storico Fiorentino www.visitflorence.com
Estate Romana www.estateromana.comune.roma.it
Sagra del Cappero www.salinalive.it/home/eventi-e-tradizioni.html
Festa de' Noantri www.festadenoantri.it
Festival dei Due Mondi www.festivaldispoleto.com
Festa della Madonna della Bruna www.festadellabruna.it
Festa di Santa Rosalia www.festedisicilia.it/santa-rosalia.htm
Festa di Sant'Andrea www.incampania.com
Palio di Siena www.ilpalio.org

Autumn
Asti Palio www.palio.asti.it
Eurochocolate www.eurochocolate.com
Festa di San Gennaro www.portanapoli.com/Eng/Culture/blood_miracle.html
Fiera del Tartufo Bianco www.fieradeltartufo.org
Regata Storica www.regatastoricavenezia.it
Sagra dell'Uva http://italianwinehub.com/news08/marino.html

Winter
Festa di Sant'Agata www.ragusaonline.com/santagata/_index.htm
Sagra del Mandorlo in Fiore www.sagradelmandorlo.net
Stiffe www.grottedistiffe.it

Below left Banners representing the rival teams competing in the Palio at Asti
Below right Gondolas and barges make their way down the Grand Canal in Venice's Regata Storica

Getting to Italy

Italy is well connected with major cities across the world, and prices for flights are competitive. There are two intercontinental airports, dozens of smaller provincial ones, fast motorway and train links with the rest of Europe and ferries all around the Mediterranean. Fly-drive holidays are an attractive option for families, making the most of well-located regional airports, while travelling by train can feel like a big adventure for children.

Arriving by air

As well as the Italian national airline, **Alitalia**, many European carriers (including **British Airways, KLM** and **Lufthansa**) fly to Italy via their country capitals. The country is also served by North American airlines (such as **American Airlines, Air Canada** and **Delta**) and Asia-Pacific companies (among them **Malaysia Airlines, Qantas** and **Thai Airways**). Intercontinental flights arrive at Rome Fiumicino (Leonardo da Vinci) and Milan Malpensa airports, but for travellers from Europe there are dozens of smaller airports dotted across the country, from Bergamo to Brindisi. These are usually served by "no-frills" airlines (notably **easyJet, Jet2** and **Ryanair**).

Fares vary according to season. Peak season for most of Italy stretches from Easter to mid-September, though December too is a popular month to visit the cities of Florence, Rome and Venice. The best deals can be obtained by booking well in advance.

There is transport from all airports to the closest town, but check with your airline or on the airport website as at small airports this could be just one bus a day. Car hire companies have offices at all but the smallest airports. For more on internal flights in Italy, *see p21*.

Arriving by rail

Rail travel is an attractive option for families, offering ever-changing scenery as well as space to move around. Direct trains (including many sleepers) link Italy with France, Germany, Austria, Spain and Switzerland. From the UK, take **Eurostar** to Paris and change to a sleeper with cabins, convenient for family travel. There are also direct motorail train services from the Netherlands and Germany to northern Italy and Tuscany. All routes into northern Italy pass through Alpine scenery, although many of the journeys are scheduled through the night.

Train prices are becoming more competitive. The best deals can be found by booking through an agency or online around three months before travel (four months for Eurostar), when the tickets are first released. Conditions vary depending on the type of train and the rail company, but in general under-6s travel free (sharing a bunk or a seat) and under-12s pay around half the adult fare. Remember that the European train network is very busy on Friday evenings, just before the Christmas holidays and at the start and end of August.

Below left Rome's Fiumicino (Leonardo da Vinci) airport *Below centre* Train travelling along the scenic Cinque Terre coastline

If you are intending to travel frequently and far in Italy by train it may be worth considering an Inter-rail (for European residents) or Eurail pass (non-European residents) for each member of the family, but compare prices first as Italian rail prices are economical, so individual fares may be just as cost efficient. For more on travelling by train in Italy see p21.

Arriving by road

For families travelling from elsewhere in Europe, driving may be a practical option, especially if visiting a region where a car is the best means for getting around. But it is worth weighing the convenience and possible cost savings against the distance travelled and your children's capacity to endure long road journeys. In July and August roads are likely to be clogged with traffic. Add in snacks, meals and overnight stays, and costs mount up. It may be worth investing in audiobooks and an in-car DVD player to keep kids entertained. Motorail trains are a good way to avoid some driving.

Most roads into Italy pass through the Alps by tunnel or mountain pass. The exceptions are the approach from Slovenia in the northeast (on the A4 motorway) and the route along the French Riviera that enters Italy as the A10 motorway at Ventimiglia. The most popular route from Geneva and southeast France is via the Mont Blanc tunnel and A5 motorway, entering Italy by Aosta and Turin. Another approach (from Switzerland) uses the St Bernard Pass and tunnel. The main route from Austria and southern Germany crosses the Brenner Pass and heads to Verona on the A22 motorway via Trento and the Adige valley. Most motor- ways are toll roads; pay with cash or credit card as you exit. The **AA** and **Michelin** both offer reliable route planners and alternative routes.

Car owners must carry their vehicle insurance policy, ideally with a statement of cover in Italian (usually provided by the insurer), plus the vehicle's registration document and a valid driving licence. Italian law requires drivers also to carry spare bulbs, a red warning triangle and a fluorescent jacket, in the event of a breakdown. The headlights of right-hand drive cars will need to be adjusted for left-hand driving.

Roadside service stations vary, but are decent. In Italy you will find child-friendly catering, but

baby-chang
guaranteed. F
in Italy, see p2

Arriving by

Ferries link mainland   with Spain, Greece, Turkey, Albania, Croatia and Tunisia, as well as Corsica and Malta. Boats can be very crowded in summer and their frequency is greatly reduced outside the summer season, but that is the best time to look for special offers. For services to Sicily, Sardinia and the smaller Italian islands, see p21.

The Lowdown

By air
Air Canada www.aircanada.com
Alitalia www.alitalia.com
American Airlines www.aa.com
British Airways www.ba.com
Delta www.delta.com
easyJet www.easyjet.com
Jet2 www.jet2.com
KLM www.klm.com
Lufthansa www.lufthansa.com
Malaysia Airlines www.malaysiaairlines.com
Qantas www.qantas.com
Ryanair www.ryanair.com
Thai Airways www.thaiair.com

By rail
Artesia www.artesia.eu
Autoslaap Trein www.autoslaaptrein.nl
Deutsche Bahn www.dbautozug.de
Eurail www.eurail.com
European Rail www.europeanrail.com
Eurostar www.eurostar.com
Eurotunnel www.eurotunnel.com
Inter-rail www.interrail.net
The Man in Seat 61 www.seat61.com
Raileurope www.raileurope.co.uk

By road
AA www.theaa.com
Michelin www.viamichelin.com

By sea
Channel crossings www.ferrycheap.com
Mediterranean ferries www.traghettionline.com

Below right Airport arrivals and departures board

...tting Around Italy

While a car may be the most convenient way to get around rural areas of Italy, driving on overcrowded motorways and in congested cities with few or expensive parking options can be fraught. Rail is an efficient and affordable way to travel from one city to another, but infrequent buses may be the only means to reach smaller villages. Within towns, there are all kinds of public transport options, in some places even funiculars, gondolas or bike-share schemes.

By car

Driving can be a useful way to tour parts of Italy, but it is worth taking into account high petrol prices, parking difficulties and driving restrictions in cities.

RULES OF THE ROAD

Drive on the right and, unless road signs indicate otherwise, give way to traffic from the right. Speed limits are 50kph (30mph) in built-up areas, 110kph (70mph) on highways and 130kph (80mph) on motorways. Dipped headlights must be used at all times outside built-up areas. Children aged 4–12 are forbidden from travelling in the front seat. Under-4s must be in a child seat.

ROADS

Most motorways (autostrade) operate toll systems. Take a ticket when you enter and pay when you leave (for cash payment follow the white signs; for payment by credit card look for the blue signs).

PETROL

Petrol (benzina) stations are common, and most are open from early morning until lunchtime and from around 3pm to 7pm. Outside these hours you will often find an automatic pump that takes either credit/debit cards or bank notes (these are less common in rural areas). Motorway petrol stations tend to be open 24 hours a day.

IN TOWNS

Driving among the complicated one-way systems and ancient narrow streets of Italy's towns is best avoided. Many towns and villages have restricted traffic areas (zone traffico limitato), marked by signs with a black "ZTL" on a yellow background and controlled with cameras. Milan also has a congestion charge. On-street pay-and-display parking spaces are marked with blue paint, and car parks (parcheggi) are common. Make sure you park legitimately – saying you are a visitor will be no defence against a parking fine.

CAR HIRE

International car-hire (autonoleggio) companies have offices at most airports and in town centres around Italy. You will need to be over 21 and carry a valid driver's licence (and passport if your driving licence does not have a photo) and credit card to hire a car. Fly-drive deals can save money. Book your car well in advance and reserve any child seats as car-hire firms frequently run out. For more information about driving in Italy, see p19.

Below left Passengers disembarking from a ferry on Lake Maggiore

CAMPER VAN HIRE

Camper vans or mobile homes are popular in Italy and the number of rental companies is increasing. They offer freedom for families, and facilities are generally good, with free overnight parking at service stations and in tourist areas (see p27).

By bus

Buses are sometimes the only form of public transport to rural areas, but services are infrequent at weekends and in school holidays. Towns usually have bus stations. Tickets can usually be bought from bars or newsagents, but rarely on the bus.

By rail

Italy's rail network is an efficient way of getting around. It may be worth considering an Inter-rail or Eurail pass (see p19), but **Trenitalia** prices are competitive. All train tickets must be validated in the yellow machines on the platform before boarding your train; failure to do so will lead to heavy fines.

By air

Competitive "no-frills" airfares mean that for long distances within Italy or trips to the islands, you may want to consider a short internal flight. There are more flights in summer; book ahead to get the best deal.

By ferry and hydrofoil

Passenger and car ferries serve Sicily, Sardinia and the smaller Italian islands and there is also a hydrofoil service between Reggio di Calabria and Messina in Sicily. These need to be booked in advance for peak periods. On the larger lakes in the north of Italy, ferry services are efficient and offer good value.

City transport

Towns and cities all have their own characteristic forms of public transport, from clattering trams to funicular railways, lifts, buses and metro systems. Most famous of all are Venice's water buses (vaporetti) and gondola ferries (traghetti). The less traditional but increasingly ubiquitous open-top tourist buses are also a popular way for families to see a city's sights without too much planning or legwork.

Carnets of tickets or day passes can prove economical if you plan to use public transport a lot. Depending where you are in the country, children under 5 or 10 travel free; ask before buying tickets.

The Lowdown

Roads and breakdown
Autostrade per l'Italia
www.autostrade.it
Roadside assistance 800 116 800
(free from mobile phones)

Car hire
Avis www.avis.com
Europcar www.europcar.com
Hertz www.hertz.com
Maggiore www.maggiore.com
National www.nationalcar.com
Sixt www.sixt.com

Camper van hire
Blurent www.blurent.com
Como Caravan www.comocaravan.it

Rail
Trenitalia www.trenitalia.it

Domestic airlines
Air One www.flyairone.it
Meridiana www.meridiana.it
Windjet www.windjet.it

Ferry services
Lake ferries www.navigazionelaghi.it
Sea ferries www.traghettionline.com

Many towns have bike-share schemes accessible to visitors. The bikes are a great way for confident cyclists to get around, but helmets are not provided. Bicycle hire is common in the north, with child seats and children's bikes available.

Below centre A city bus in the centre of Verona *Below right* Travelling by camper van, a fun and convenient way of getting around Italy for families

Practical Information

In many respects Italy is a fully modern European country, but it still suffers from some age-old practical problems, especially where the state or bureaucracy is involved. The north still tends to be much more efficient than the south, but if visiting a bank or post office or the police or a doctor, be sure to take ID and plenty of books and games for the children, and be prepared for a long wait.

Passports and visas

EU citizens need a valid passport to enter Italy and can stay for an unlimited period. Nationals of the USA, Canada, Australia and New Zealand need a valid passport, with which they can stay in Italy for up to 3 months – for longer stays a visa is required. Citizens from other countries should consult their local Italian consulate. Children travelling without one or both parents may be asked to provide written travel consent from the absent parent.

Customs information

For EU citizens there are no limits on goods taken into or out of Italy provided they are for personal use only. Non-EU residents can claim back sales tax on purchases over €155 by filling in a tax-free form (www.global-blue.com).

Insurance

It is advisable to take out insurance against medical emergencies, travel cancellations or delays (transport strikes are fairly common in Italy), emergency repatriation and legal expenses, theft and loss. Make sure that any planned activities such as skiing, wind-surfing or scuba-diving are included and check individual limits for valuable items.

Health

EU citizens have access to Italian emergency health care under the same rules as residents, which means that a small fee may be payable for some treatment but treatment will always be given. UK residents should apply for a free European Health Insurance Card (EHIC) for each family member, available online at www.ehic.org.uk or at a post office. The Australian Medicare system also has a reciprocal agreement with Italy (www.medicareaustralia.gov.au). All other travellers should make sure they are adequately covered by medical insurance.

PHARMACIES

For minor ailments, an Italian pharmacy (farmacia) is a good first port of call. Staff usually give good advice or can direct you to a doctor (medico) if necessary. A list of duty pharmacies open out of hours is displayed outside all pharmacies.

WATER

Tap water is drinkable in Italy and water from the many taps and fountains found in parks and squares throughout the country is safe to drink. Water not for drinking is marked "acqua non potabile".

Below left Window of a pharmacy
Below right Beware of pickpockets in crowded places such as markets, especially in large cities

MINOR HAZARDS

No vaccinations are required and there are no specific health hazards in Italy beyond sun and heat, but do go prepared with hats and sun screen and think about adapting your family's routine to stay in the shade during the hottest hours of the day in summer. Take insect repellent and cream for treating insect (especially mosquito) bites.

Swimmers in the Mediterranean need to watch out for jellyfish, which have become increasingly prevalent. If stung, relieve the pain and swelling by washing the wound with sea water (never fresh water) and put a bag of ice on for 5 or 10 minutes before disinfecting it. In severe cases or with adverse reactions, seek medical attention.

Personal safety

Italy is a relatively safe country but tourist-focused petty crime does occur in the larger cities. Beware of pickpockets around tourist sights, at crowded markets and on public transport; distraction techniques by children and women while your pockets and bags are lightened are not uncommon. Be careful not to leave anything on display in parked cars, especially if you have foreign number plates.

Be very careful when crossing the road in Italy. Drivers rarely stop for pedestrians at crossings and motorists and moped riders often jump traffic lights. Remind children to look both ways before crossing.

Adults need to carry ID at all times, and should make sure children have some sort of ID and know how to get in contact by mobile phone in case they get lost. Some beach resorts, such as Rimini, have tagging systems for small children.

POLICE

If you are a victim of any crime, report the incident within 24 hours to the nearest police station. Thefts can be reported to either the Carabinieri or the Polizia Statale, who will issue a crime report; this is essential for any insurance claim.

Money

Italy is one of the many European countries using the euro, which is split into 100 cents. The seven euro notes (€5, €10, €20, €50, €100, €200 and €500) are identical within the eurozone but the eight coins (€2, €1, and 50, 20, 10, 5, 2 and 1 cents) show the country of origin, although they are valid in all countries. Country-spotting on euro coins can be a fun holiday activity.

CREDIT AND CASH CARDS

Italy is still a largely cash society so it is always advsiable to carry some with you. Credit and debit cards are still useful, however, for accessing your money. ATMs (Bancomat) are common in all but the smallest Italian towns. Make sure to notify your bank and credit card providers before you leave for Italy. Some banks forbid foreign transactions for security reasons unless they have been notified ahead of time. Cards usually have a maximum daily withdrawal limit (typically €250) and credit cards will start charging interest on cash withdrawals from the first day. Check your bank's rates and charges before travelling.

CHANGING MONEY, TRAVELLER'S CHEQUES AND CASH PASSPORT

The best exchange rates are at banks and larger post offices, while bureaux de change (cambio) offer the convenience of extended opening hours but are far less competitive. Traveller's cheques are not always accepted in Italy. Consider opting instead for a Cash Passport (www.cashpassport.com), a prepaid currency card that is loaded before travelling and can be used in ATMs. It gives more control over commission charges and provides greater security.

Below left *Two Carabinieri policemen in uniform*
Below right *Motorists and moped riders in Italy cannot be relied upon to stop at crossings*

Communications and media

MOBILE PHONES

European mobile phones will work in Italy, but travellers from North America, Australia and New Zealand will need a tri-band or 3G phone. Coverage is generally good, but can be patchy near mountains or in thick-walled old buildings. Check roaming options with your provider. Make sure that your handset is unlocked – some operators lock their phones to specific networks. It is impossible to buy a local SIM without an Italian address and a *codice fiscale* (tax number).

INTERNATIONAL AND LOCAL CALLS

Italians are rarely parted from their state-of-the-art mobile phones (*cellulari* or *telefonini*), so public phone booths are increasingly hard to find. Few take coins, some will accept credit cards, but most operate by phone card (*scheda telefonica*), bought from bars, newsagents and tobacconists. Alternatively, the many call centres around railway stations, mostly used by migrant workers to phone home, offer competitive international rates. To call Italy from abroad, first dial +39. To call abroad from Italy, dial 00 followed by the country code.

INTERNET AND EMAIL

Internet access is widely available in Italy. Many urban hotels and bars have free Wi-Fi and there are internet cafés in all but the smallest towns and villages. Libraries, too, often offer public access.

TV AND PRESS

Newspaper kiosks in major cities and tourist destinations stock the international press. They also have an eye-catching selection of children's magazines, the more colourful of which could entertain kids through a long meal or on a train journey. Most hotels have satellite TV, which usually offers at least one kids' channel; Rai Yo-yo and K2 are favourites with under-10s.

Opening hours

Banks open 8:30am–1:30pm and usually 2:30–4pm Monday–Friday. Many shops open 8am–1pm and 4–7pm Monday–Saturday, but can be closed on Saturday afternoons and Monday mornings. Supermarkets open all day, and Sunday shopping is common in larger cities.

In restaurants lunch tends to be served noon–3pm and dinner 7–11pm, with regional variations. Restaurants often close one day a week and in cities many close in August, while in rural tourist areas many shut for part of the winter.

Museums generally close on Mondays. In summer some stay open into the late evening.

Post offices open 8:30am–7:30pm Monday–Saturday (until 1pm in small towns).

Disabled facilities

Facilities for the disabled are few and far between in Italy. Toilets for disabled people in bars and restaurants are now more common and some hotels have adapted rooms, but access to sights is frequently stepped, with lifts often unattended or in disrepair. Cobbled streets, randomly parked cars and scooters, and high kerbs can make it hard going for the visually and mobility impaired. Public transport is only slightly better, with many trams, trains, metro systems and buses still not wheelchair accessible.

Italian time

Italy is 1 hour ahead of Greenwich Mean Time (GMT) or British Summer Time (BST), 7 hours ahead of US Eastern Standard or Daylight Time and 10 hours ahead of Pacific Standard or Daylight Time.

Below left Post office sign **Below right** A branch of Prenatal, a children's clothing shop, in Milan

Toilets

There are few public toilets in Italy. If you find one you will need small change to pay the attendant. If not, café-bars are required by law to let anyone use their facilities.

Electricity

The voltage in Italy is 220 volts. Plugs have either two or three round pins. It is advisable to take a multi-plug adapter as the size of pins depends on the age of electrical installation.

What to pack

Italians have smart-casual style off to a fine art. You will rarely need formal clothes, but being presentable will help you to fit in. Take a cardigan or shawl to cover bare shoulders if visiting churches. Sun hats are useful and comfortable shoes can take the pain out of sightseeing.

What to expect

Supplies for babies are pricey in Italy: nappies (*pannolini*) and milk formula (*latte formulato*) cost more than double their price in neighbouring countries. Supermarket baby food often contains sugar, but health-food shops have sugar-free

alternatives. High chairs are unusual in restaurants. Breastfeeding is generally accepted, but be sensitive in conservative rural areas. Nappy-changing facilities are rare. Prenatal, a chain of maternity and children's clothing shops, offers feeding and changing areas (*www.prenatal.it*).

Etiquette and attitudes

Children are fêted in Italy, but that does not mean that they are not expected to respect others. Make sure they do not get under the feet of waiters in restaurants, and take crying babies outside to calm them. Italian children are always kept clean, so tomato-sauce faces or sticky ice-cream hands should be wiped. A few words of Italian will always be appreciated: teach children to say *buon giorno* (good morning), *ciao* (hello/goodbye) and *grazie* (thank you).

Babysitting

In larger cities, hotels and apartment complexes may well have access to agencies with English-speaking babysitters. Otherwise, it will be down to the good will of hotel managers, who may be able to recommend someone suitable, but security checks will be non-existent.

Below left Sign for a public toilet *Below right* Newspaper and magazine kiosk in Piazza del Comune, Cremona

Where to Stay

Italy has a fabulous range of places to stay, from historic palaces to converted farmhouses. Although children are very welcome, Italy does not specialize in family-friendly hotels. The Italian ethos celebrates children rather than catering specifically for them, but there are great family options in rural *agriturismi*, self-catering city apartments and country villas and farmhouses, while religious institutions and camp sites offer budget choices.

Hotels

Italian hotels range from patrician villas to purpose-built towers, as well as everything in between. The Italian terms *albergo*, *locanda* and *pensione* are interchangeable translations of "hotel". There is an official grading system from one to five stars, although this indicates the presence of facilities such as lifts or TVs rather than overall quality and charm. Prices vary between the south and north of the country, as well as between tourist hotspots (cities are more expensive) and less-visited areas. Air conditioning is not always available. Some cheaper hotels in cities may not have lifts.

Most hotels close between October and Easter outside the cities and main tourist locations. Many hotels insist that stays are a minimum of two or three nights during August and some may insist on full board or half board in peak season. A large room may be sold as a family room (*camera familiare*), and an extra bed (*letto extra*) or cot (*lettino*) can usually be added for a supplement, but it is important to notifiy the hotel about this at the time of reservation. Many hotels and most B&Bs will mainly have showers not bathtubs. Parents with small children for whom "bathtime" is important should ask for a bath (*vasca da bagno*).

Online agency **Italy Family Hotels** has a list of hotels on the coast offering child-friendly facilities such as kids' clubs, children's menus and play areas. In Trentino, **Gioco Vacanza** member hotels cater for families, with facilities including children's dressing gowns, potties and bottle-warming equipment in the rooms, well-designed play areas and creative workshops.

B&Bs

There are a large number of bed and breakfasts across the country. Rooms in homes, they range from cosy bedrooms with a shared bathroom in a historic city centre palazzo to self-contained apartments.

Agriturismi

The *agriturismo* scheme covers a multitude of rural farmstay options, from a bedroom in a farmhouse to a converted outhouse with kitchen on a working wine estate. They are a wonderful way to relax into Italian rural life and a truly family-friendly experience. Grounds may extend from a garden with a play area to olive groves and mountain pastures, and many have pools. Often the hospitable owners grow and cook delicious food and can organize horse-riding and other activities.

Below left The tranquil garden and swimming pool of Costantinopoli 104 hotel in Naples *Below right* Tents pitched on a camp site in the shadow of Monte Brione, near Lake Garda

Self-catering

The freedom of self-catering is attractive to families: not only to save on restaurants and have more flexibility, but also to enjoy shopping at local markets and supermarkets, which is fun for all. Converted farmhouses, mansions and villas are available for rent across the country, particularly on the islands, along the coasts and in rural Puglia, Tuscany, Umbria and Le Marche, although bargains are hard to find.

For families planning to holiday together, sharing a large villa may be more economical. Weekly rental prices can be as much as double in high season (July and August). It is a good idea to book well in advance, although there are sometimes last-minute deals available. A hire car is almost always a necessity with rural self-catering.

City-centre apartments are a popular way for families to enjoy hectic cities such as Rome, Florence and Venice. A minimum stay of three nights may be required.

Residenze ("residences") can be a good alternative option in holiday areas, where several small, well-equipped apartments share facilities such as gardens, a pool or a private beach. They are a perfect blend of the independence of self-catering and the facilities of a hotel, and often have delivery arrangements with local food shops and *pizzerie*. They may also offer children the chance to make holiday friends.

Monasteries

A budget alternative is to take advantage of the hundreds of religious properties across Italy that now rent out en-suite rooms. They tend to be quite basic, but very clean, and are sometimes in stunning old monasteries and convents in hard-to-beat locations. A good one-stop shop is the online agency **Monastery Stays**.

Camping

On the whole, camping in Italy is a highly structured experience; while it may offer a cheap and relaxed way to stay in some stunning locations, by the waterside or near historic cities, it is usually far from wilderness camping. On the coast and around the lakes most camp sites are mini-resorts boasting cafés, supermarkets, pools and, more often than not, cabaret entertainment. Apart from the all-in-one convenience, kids' clubs are an added attraction for some families and there are usually plenty of other children around for company. Language barriers tend to melt away pretty quickly. In the mountainous areas of Italy, camp sites are often much more low key, offering a better chance to enjoy the landscape undisturbed.

Camper vans are popular in Italy. A four-bed van with unlimited mileage will cost around €900 per week in high season (see also p21).

The Lowdown

Hotels and self-catering
www.bridgewater-travel.co.uk
www.friendlyrentals.com
www.giocovacanza.it
www.guestinitaly.com
www.i-escape.com
www.iliostravel.com
www.italian-connection.co.uk
www.italyfamilyhotels.it
www.long-travel.co.uk
www.venere.com

B&Bs
www.bbitalia.it

Agriturismi
www.agriturismo.it
www.agriturismo.com

Monasteries
www.monastorystays.com

Camping
www.camping.it

Below left Hotel La Residenza, housed in a historic palazzo in Venice **Below right** The charming tree-lined courtyard of Buonanotte B&B in Trastevere, Rome, a pleasant refuge from the hustle and bustle of the city outside

Where to Eat

You can't go too far wrong when eating out with children in Italy, the home of pasta, pizza and ice cream. Myriad pasta shapes and sauces should keep even fussy eaters happy; for those who like to experiment, Italian children's favourites such as *polpette* (meat balls), *polenta* and *arancini* (deep-fried rice balls) may attract new fans. Add the welcoming attitude to children among hosts, and the chances are all members of the family will enjoy eating out.

Practical information

Lunch *(pranzo)* is usually served noon–3pm, depending on where you are in the country – everything happens about an hour later in summer in the south. In resort areas a few restaurants stay open until the evening. Dinner *(cena)* is usually served 7pm–midnight. Most eateries close one day a week, although in popular tourist areas many open seven days in summer.

In many restaurants a cover charge *(coperto)* will be added to the bill *(conto)* and, in some, a service charge will be included too. Where it is not, it is usual to leave a small tip (usually up to 10 per cent).

Types of restaurant

Traditionally a *trattoria* and an *osteria* offered simple, economical home-style cooking (*cucina casalinga*), but today the names are also used by smarter establishments to illustrate their interest in reviving traditions and sourcing quality ingredients. A *ristorante* was once a smart restaurant, but this has become a pretty generic term. An *enoteca* is a wine bar, which may also serve snacks or meals. If you are heading to a *pizzeria* look out for one with a *forno a legna* (wood-burning oven), which makes crispier and tastier pizzas than standard ovens. Anywhere with a garden or terrace will of course appeal to children – and their parents.

In cafés and bars it is cheapest to eat and drink standing at the bar. You will pay a little extra to sit at a table. There are also substantial supplements for eating outside at tables on a pavement terrace or in a piazza, especially in famous locations such as Piazza San Marco in Venice.

Courses

Italian meals traditionally have four courses, beginning with an *antipasto*, or starter. This is followed by the *primo*, or first course (pasta, risotto or soup). The *secondo* is the meat or fish course, with a *contorno* (vegetable or salad) served on a separate plate. Last course is the *dolce* (dessert), unless you opt for *formaggi* (cheeses). House wines vary, but a *quarto* (quarter), *mezzo* (half) or one-litre *caraffa* (carafe) will always be drinkable. For children, order *aqua minerale*, *con* or *senza gas* (fizzy or still mineral water), or *spremuta* (freshly squeezed juice).

Catering for children

All but the very smartest restaurants will be happy to welcome children, even late into the evening. Children are often fussed over and special

Below left *A theatrical pizzettaro making pizza in a wood-burning oven at Gustapizza in Florence*
Below centre *Stalls laden with fresh fruit and vegetables at Testaccio market in Rome, great for picnic supplies*

requests, such as heating up baby food and asking for food to share (*da dividere*), will usually be catered for. However, highchairs (*seggiolini*) and changing facilities (*fasciatoi*) are uncommon outside tourist spots. Although welcome, children will be expected to sit at the table and not to run around, so it is best to warn them in advance.

Pasta al pomodoro (pasta with tomato sauce) is the fail-safe Italian alternative to a children's menu, which rarely exists, but *carbonara* (bacon and egg), *amatriciana* (bacon and tomato) and *pesto* are just some of the other child-friendly sauces. Those with an aversion to tomato can choose rice or pasta *in bianco* (white), which comes plain with grated cheese, or *pizza bianca*. Food allergies other than gluten-intolerance (*celiachia*) are less readily understood, so be prepared with the right vocabulary to explain. Download a free translation card from *www.celiactravel.com/cards*.

Breakfast

Breakfast (*prima colazione*) in Italy usually consists of a bowl of milk, milky coffee or hot chocolate, orange juice and a choice of pastries, including croissants (*cornetti*) or *brioches*, plain or filled with jam (*marmellata*), custard (*crema*) or chocolate (*cioccolato*). Most milk served will be UHT, not fresh. In some hotels there is likely to be a buffet that also includes hams and cheeses. If breakfast is not included in your hotel stay, a good alternative is to eat at a local bar, an enjoyable Italian institution.

Picnics

Putting together a picnic is one of the best ways to try local produce. Find a delicatessen (*alimentari*) to buy cheese, ham or olives; often they will put together filled rolls (*panini*) for you. Bakeries (*il forno*) usually offer *focaccia* and little pizzas as well as bread. Greengrocers (*fruttivendolo*) are packed with seasonal fruits and vegetables. Weekly markets offer stall upon stall of fresh vegetables and fruit plus local smallholders with cheese and home-cured salami. There is often also a van or two selling roast chicken, *porchetta* (roast pork) or *arancini* (deep-fried rice balls). Italian supermarkets (*see p31*) also stock good-quality fresh produce.

Mountain regions may offer picnic areas with outside grills, and around lakes there are free beaches. In towns there are benches in shady corners of piazzas or parks.

Below right Outdoor tables on a sunny day at a café on Campo Santo Stefano, Venice

Shopping

Milan is famous for its designer fashion stores, Turin for its chocolate, and Sicily for its roadside stalls selling mouthwatering fruit, while across the country markets tempt visitors with local produce and crafts. Traditionally, textiles, leather, ceramics and glassware are strong in Italy, and many manufacturing businesses are family-run. Apart from street markets it is not a country for bargains, but window-shopping will offer plenty of family fun.

What to buy

It is worthy checking out local specialities: Turin is famous for chocolate; Milan is renowned for designer clothes and furniture; Venice for lace and Murano glassware; Florence for leather goods such as coats, belts, bags and wallets as well as marbled paper and jewellery; Naples for its Christmas market selling crib characters; and Tuscany, Sicily and Perugia for ceramics and pottery. Sicily has great puppets too, and marzipan.

Rural areas often sell good basketware and local terracotta or ceramic items, as well as a feast of locally produced olive oils, cheeses, truffles, hams, capers and salamis.

For clothes – both children's and adults' – you could blow any budget, but bargains can be found at designer factory outlet shops.

Top-brand furniture and homeware is often designed and even made in Italy, but that does not make it cheaper than buying at home.

Staff can be snooty in smart shops, so make sure kids are on best behaviour and keep sticky fingers off high-priced merchandise. Younger children may be best excluded from a trip around the designer fashion shops of Milan or the glassware shops in Venice.

Markets and stalls

Most villages and towns across the country have at least one weekly street market, which can be a great place for kids to practise a few words of Italian and perhaps buy a small keepsake to take home. The fruit and vegetable stalls are usually bursting with colourful local produce (fresher and less expensive than in shops) – it is easy to spot the best stalls as there will be a queue of local people. Other stalls may sell basketwork, ceramics, plastic toys, sweets of every shape and hue, as well as cheap household goods, clothes and shoes.

Some larger towns have equally colourful permanent markets. The Mercato Centrale in Florence (see p167) and the Vucciria in Palermo (see p354) are bigger, noisier versions of weekly street markets, where it is usually possible to pick up a good, cheap lunch while browsing the stalls.

Many villages, particularly in tourist areas, have monthly antiques or bric-a-brac markets (tourist offices will have details), although true antiques are hard to find. In December, Christmas markets spring up in town centres selling gifts and items to make nativity

Below left Window-shopping at Gucci in Portofino, Liguria **Below right** Colourful Christmas market in Bressanone, Alto Adige

scenes. They continue until 6 January when the Befana, a kindly witch, brings sweets for good children and coal for naughty ones. The stalls are full of sugar imitation coal and other sweet treats.

Roadside stalls selling anything from watermelons or mozzarella to baskets and flowerpots are common. Prices are usually good, but check the goods before buying them as there will be no redress.

In wine-growing areas visit vineyard shops, where prices are lower and it is often possible to taste before buying.

Food shops and supermarkets

National and international supermarkets such as **Esselunga**, **Coop**, **Conad**, **Carrefour** and **Billa** provide good-quality produce. They often have extended opening hours, with larger branches closing at 10pm, and may open on Sundays. There is a wide choice of goods and kids will enjoy spotting the differences from supermarkets at home. For a more authentic experience, pop into an *alimentari* or delicatessen. The variously shaped pastas, fresh cheeses, hams and salamis are irresistible.

Department and chain stores

There are several department store chains – **la Rinascente**, **Coin** and **Upim** – with branches in cities across Italy. La Rinascente's flagship store is in Piazza Duomo in Milan and it is a designer heaven, while Coin is less glitzy but strong on well-priced, stylish menswear. Upim offers a wide variety of goods at reasonable prices.

Prenatal, which has about 200 branches throughout Italy, is a useful chain of shops specializing in merchandise for younger children, including clothes for under-11s and toys. It also has changing facilities.

Sales and factory outlets

Sales (*saldi*) are held in early January and July on state-appointed dates. Outside these periods, keep an eye out for factory outlets (there are more than 700 of them across Italy), often on the outskirts of towns. Italy's industry is traditionally based on small, family-run manufacturing concerns, many of which have opened shops to sell off seconds or old stock. Ask at tourist offices or check the internet for particular

brands. Gucci and Dolce & Gabbana have outlets near Florence, while homeware brand Alessi has a factory shop near Lake Maggiore and there is a Prada outlet near Lake Como.

Cards and tax refunds

Although debit and credit cards are accepted in larger stores, they are not always welcome in small shops. Visitors resident outside the EU are entitled to a rebate on sales tax (IVA) paid on items over €155. Ask for a receipt at the time of purchase and allow goods to be checked at the airport and the receipt stamped when you depart *(see p22)*.

The Lowdown

Supermarkets
www.billa.it
www.carrefouritalia.it
www.conad.it
www.coop.it
www.esselunga.it

Department and chain stores
www.coin.it
www.prenatal.it
www.rinascente.it
www.upim.it

Factory outlets
www.factory-outlet-italy.com

Below left Galleria Vittorio Emanuele II, a 19th-century arcade, in Milan Below right Stall selling children's toys and puppets at Santo Spirito market in Florence

Entertainment and Activities

The best music in Italy can be heard in stunning settings, at international festivals of opera, classical music and jazz and rock, but it is in regional folk traditions that home-grown talent is most evident. Every town in Italy boasts a theatre, the art of puppetry is going strong, and open-air cinemas spring up in summer. Football, of course, is a national obsession, but it is local street festivals that provide the best entertainment for families.

Practical information

Italy's tourist board, the **Agenzia Nazionale del Turismo** (ENIT) has up-to-date information on what's on in Italy, and regional newspapers carry local listings. Most venues have online booking facilities or a booking line to call. Major events sell out quickly, so book ahead.

Opera, dance and music

Italy is best-known for its opera, with seasons of international repute held at **La Scala** in Milan (see pp112–15) and **La Fenice** in Venice (see p57), and a renowned summer festival at the **Arena di Verona** (see pp78–9) . There is also opera in summer at the **Baths of Caracalla** in Rome (see p268), and one-off events are held in spectacular venues such as the Greek theatres of Siracusa (see pp362–3) and Taormina (see p360).

Italy's most famous home-grown ballet company is that of **La Scala**, but international dance troupes often tour the country too.

Some enchanting music festivals are held over the summer. The most off-beat, and family-friendly, is **I Suoni delle Dolomiti**, a series of jazz, folk, classical and world music concerts by artists from all over the world, held in the mountains of the Sud Tirol. Audiences hike to unusual locations – in woods and rocky gullies – to listen to the concerts. Performances are in the evenings and sometimes at dawn.

The **Ravello Festival** is a more traditional classical music festival, held in the gardens of Villa Rufolo and Villa Cimbrone (see pp330–31),

and in a fabulous auditorium designed by Oscar Niemeyer (late Jun–late Aug). An excellent chamber music festival, **Incontri in Terra di Siena**, is held on the La Foce estate near Pienza in Tuscany (late Jul), and every year Florence hosts **Maggio Musicale**, a festival of music, dance and opera (May–Jun).

Italy's most famous jazz event is **Umbria Jazz**, which attracts world-class artists to Perugia in summer. The most trendy rock festivals of recent years have been **Italia Wave Love Festival**, in Lecce (mid-Jul), and the **Heineken Jammin Festival**, in Mestre, Venice (early Jun). To hear some of Italy's fabulous folk music, look out for posters advertising concerts locally.

Theatre and puppetry

Italy has the biggest concentration of theatres in Europe, with mixed programmes incorporating classical and popular culture. There is little children's theatre, but puppetry is alive, punching and kicking, notably in Sicily, where plays often tell the story of battles between Saracens and Normans. Children's interest may be stirred by a visit to a puppet workshop. The best puppet companies are in **Palermo** (see p354) and **Siracusa** (see pp362–3).

Sagre and religious festivals

Some of the best family days out in Italy are to be had at the festivals held in almost every town and

village. *Sagre*, celebrating food and drink, from wine and capers to truffles and strawberries, are held all over rural Italy to coincide with the harvest. There is usually plenty of free food and the festivals often end with music, dancing and fireworks.

Religious festivals often include food as well – bean soup for San Giuseppe, bone-like white biscuits for the Day of the Dead, deep-fried pastries for Carnival – but it is the processions that make most impact. For more on festivals, see pp14–17, and for festivals held at specific destinations see individual entries.

Sports

Italy's most popular spectator sport is, of course, football (soccer). The annual season starts in mid-August, with matches normally played on Sunday afternoons. The **Lega Calcio** (football league) has a

Below Colourful puppet play in Piazza Maggiore, Bologna

Above Windsurfers on Lake Garda in Lombardy *Below* Hikers on the Punta Gnifetti in Piedmont *Bottom* An audience gathers at the Arena in Verona

calendar of events and information on where and how to buy tickets.

Basketball is also popular. Most cities have a team, and Italy is now one of the top-ranked nations in the world. **Eurobasket** has details of leagues and fixtures.

Motor-racing events are held year-round at the **Autodromo di Monza**, and the annual **Giro d'Italia** *(late May)* attracts scores of cyclists and cheering, excited crowds.

Outdoor activities

Skiing, snowboarding and sledging are all favourite winter activities, and sailing, windsurfing, diving and snorkelling are popular in summer. **Mark Warner** offers sailing and windsurfing courses in Sardinia,

while **Club Med** has resorts with activities in Sicily, Calabria and Puglia. The **Adventure Company** runs family hiking and pizza-making holidays to Naples, Vesuvius and Pompeii, and **Backroads** arranges cooking, biking and hiking holidays.

For more activities at specific destinations, see individual entries.

The Lowdown

Agenzia Nazionale del Turismo www.enit.it

Adventure Company www.adventurecompany.co.uk

Arena di Verona www.arena.it

Autodromo di Monza www.monzanet.it

Backroads www.backroads.com

Baths of Caracalla www.operaroma.it

Club Med www.clubmed.co.uk

Eurobasket www.eurobasket.com

La Fenice www.teatrolafenice.it

Giro d'Italia www.gazzetta.it

Heineken Jammin Festival www.heineken.it

Incontri in Terra di Siena www.itslafoce.org

Italia Wave Love Festival www.italiawave.com

Lega Calcio www.lega-calcio.it

Maggio Musicale www.maggiofiorentino.com

Mark Warner www.markwarner.co.uk

Ravello Festival www.ravellofestival.com

La Scala www.teatroallascala.org

I Suoni delle Dolomiti www.isuonidelledolomiti.it

Umbria Jazz www.umbriajazz.com

A Brief History of Italy

The modern nation of Italy is a relatively recent invention – it celebrated its 150th anniversary in 2011. Famous for the Roman Empire, the Renaissance and its Roman Catholic religion, for most of the past two thousand years the boot-shaped peninsula and its two main islands have been a diverse collection of warring states, often under foreign rule – but their history and culture have affected every aspect of Western culture for at least two millennia.

Etruscans and Greeks

By around 700 BC the Etruscans, an ancient people who had settled in central Italy, had a flourishing civilization. Little writing has survived, but from their tombs historians have deduced that the Etruscans had an advanced society with developed trade, agriculture and urban centres. Further south, sea trade and agriculture were also flourishing in the Greek settlements known as Magna Graecia, on the mainland and on the island of Sicily.

A statue of Rome's most famous Republican ruler, Julius Caesar

The Romans

The small town of Rome – according to legend founded in 753 BC by twin orphans Romulus and Remus on the site where they were suckled by a she-wolf – slowly rose in importance, taking over both Etruscan and Greek territory and much more besides. After two hundred years a Republic was founded, with expansionist aims and a sophisticated system of taxes to fund its military expeditions. The main power rival of the day was Carthage, on the north African coast, and for one hundred years the Romans were engaged in the Punic Wars, before finally defeating and annexing the city and its territories. Julius Caesar, the most famous of the Republican rulers, conquered much of Rome's territory across the rest of northern Africa, the Iberian peninsula and most of modern-day France. Caesar's murder in 44 BC signalled the end of the Republic and paved the way for Imperial Rome and a cast of emperors. In AD 312, Emperor Constantine converted to Christianity.

The Middle Ages

Over the ensuing centuries, the Roman Empire was invaded by civilizations from all sides, including the Goths, Franks, Huns, Visigoths and Byzantines, leading to a slow decline, and in 476 the Western Roman Empire officially came to an end. In the 8th and 9th centuries Charlemagne brought centralized government back to northern and central Italy, during which time the Christian Church in Rome gained in strength and political influence. The late 11th and 12th centuries saw southern Italy and Sicily flourish under Norman rule. When Charlemagne's dynasty died out, Italy's central geographical location in the Mediterranean and on trade routes from the east led to the emergence of commerce-based city states – most notably Florence, Genoa, Milan and Venice.

The Renaissance

Although power struggles continued, relative peace and booming trade in the late 14th

Timeline

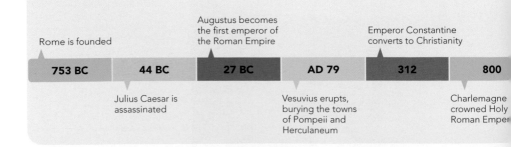

753 BC	44 BC	27 BC	AD 79	312	800

Rome is founded

Augustus becomes the first emperor of the Roman Empire

Emperor Constantine converts to Christianity

Julius Caesar is assassinated

Vesuvius erupts, burying the towns of Pompeii and Herculaneum

Charlemagne crowned Holy Roman Emper

The Army of Charlemagne (742–814), from an illuminated Venetian manuscript

and 15th centuries financed the great cultural flowering of the Renaissance. This "rebirth" grew out of the humanist movement of intellectuals who studied the scholarship of ancient Greece and Rome. The Medicis, a wealthy banking family, ruled Florence from 1434 on, and commissioned artists and architects such as Donatello and Brunelleschi to construct a city to reflect the family's power and learning. At the same time, city states such as Milan, Ferrara and Mantua employed Renaissance artists such as Leonardo da Vinci and Leon Battista Alberti. As the fortunes of the noble families waned, it was the turn of the papacy in Rome to become the centre of artistic Europe. Splendid churches and palaces were built, decorated with works of art by men such as Raphael, Michelangelo and Bramante, in an attempt to re-establish Rome as the cultural centre of the world. In the 16th century the maritime republic of Venice was another focal point of the Italian Renaissance, nurturing artists like Bellini, Titian, and Tintoretto. Meanwhile, humanist ideas continued to spread and affect art, literature, architecture and learning across the whole of Europe.

Michelangelo's frescoed ceiling of the Sistine Chapel, a Renaissance masterpiece

HEROES & VILLAINS

Nero
Roman Emperor Nero (AD 37–68) is famous for fiddling while Rome burned. In fact, he couldn't have, as fiddles hadn't been invented then, but he was callous. He is said to have ordered the death of his father, his half-brother and two wives (probably) and his mother (definitely) – although it is hard to know how much contemporary historians exaggerated as they didn't like him much.

Cesare Borgia
Nastiness ran in the Borgia family: Cesare's father, Pope Alexander VI (remember popes are not meant to have children), was one of the most corrupt popes ever. Cesare himself (1475–1507) was a successful soldier but treacherous and cruel.

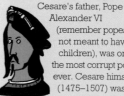

Isabella d'Este
Isabella d'Este (1474–1539) was a powerful Renaissance woman who made her husband, the Duke of Mantua, jealous because she ruled so wisely while he was away at war. She supported some of the most important artists of her day, such as Titian and Raphael, and set fashion trends that were copied across Italy and France.

Giuseppe Garibaldi
In 1860, Giuseppe Garibaldi (1807–1882) led an army of a thousand red-shirted volunteers ("I Mille") to Sicily, beginning the Unification of Italy. Known as the Risorgimento ("Resurgence"), the movement led to the creation of a united country, rather than separate states ruled by foreign powers and local kings.

Marco Polo returns from China to Venice

The Medicis come to rule Florence

1298   **1347–9**   **1434**   **1498**

Italy is devastated by the Black Death

Leonardo da Vinci paints *The Last Supper* in Milan

Foreign powers

In the 16th and 17th centuries, instead of uniting against invading foreign powers, the city states divided their allegiances and most of the territories were split between the French and Spanish. The papacy in Rome remained independent and powerful, and life in the peninsula was characterized by the Church's intolerance of dissent leading to the Counter Reformation – an attempt to combat the rise of Protestantism – and the vicious torture of the Inquisition against "heretics."

The 17th century witnessed the peak of papal power in Rome, while poverty, plague and decline swept across the rest of the country. The 18th century saw territory-swapping between the French, Austrians and Spanish and in the first years of the 19th century much of the peninsula was ruled by French emperor Napoleon and his brother, and the power of the Church was reduced.

Mussolini heads a parade to inaugurate the Via dei Fori Imperiali, in Rome

War of Unification

With the decline of France in 1815, popular uprisings and revolution throughout the territory characterized the next sixty years. Backed by the political ideology of Giuseppe Mazzini, the military know-how and revolutionary conviction of Giuseppe Garibaldi (*see p35*) galvanized popular opinion in support of the Kingdom of Piemonte and its reforming Prime Minister, the Count of Cavour. Garibaldi led an army of a thousand volunteers, known as "I Mille", to support an uprising in Sicily, and from there headed back up the boot of Italy, gaining support as he went, to meet Cavour in Naples. Vittorio Emanuele II of Piemonte was declared King of Italy in March 1861.

World War I

Italy hesitated before becoming involved in World War I, but sided with Britain, France and Russia in 1915 and finally, after three years of heavy casualties, defeated Austria at Vittorio Veneto, for which the country was rewarded with the territory of Trentino-Alto Adige and the Adriatic port of Trieste.

Fascism

Post-war disillusionment, national debt and social unrest led to massive support for the rising ex-Socialist politician, Benito Mussolini. In October 1922, as

Mussolini marched on Rome with his Blackshirts, the king made him prime minister. Within three years a dictatorship had been declared, the Socialist leader G. Matteotti assassinated, political opposition outlawed, the press censored and all dissension brutally repressed. In an attempt to provide employment and make the country self-sufficient, the regime embarked on a massive construction programme, as well as agricultural reforms and foolhardy military campaigns in north Africa; Mussolini is still remembered as the man who made the trains run on time. In the Lateran Pact of 1929, he did a deal with the papacy and, for the first time, the Vatican became a formally recognized state within the Kingdom of Italy.

World War II

Mussolini provided support for Franco's Fascist party in the Spanish Civil War (1936–8) and in 1938 anti-Semitic laws were passed prohibiting Jews from marrying non-Jews, owning land or holding public jobs. In 1940, Italy joined World War II on the side of Nazi Germany. Italian troops were eventually defeated on all fronts – in France, northern Africa, Greece and, most disastrously, in Russia. Italian industry was razed to the ground by Allied bombs.

In September 1943, two months after the Allies had landed in Sicily, the king took constitutional power away from Mussolini and Italy

Italy timeline

Napoleon is crowned King of Italy in Milan

Italy enters World War I on the side of Britain, France and Russia

Italians vote for a republic and an end to the monarchy

| 1805 | 1861 | 1915 | 1940 | 1946 | 1994 |

Italy becomes a unified nation under King Emanuele II

Italy declares war on France and Britain, and invades Greece

Silvio Berlusconi's centre-right Forza Italia party wins the general election

officially swapped sides in the war. Mussolini was arrested, only to be rescued from his mountain-top prison in Gran Sasso by the Germans and set up as the head of a puppet government, called the Republic of Salò, on the banks of Lake Garda. A bloody hand-to-hand battle between retreating German soldiers and Italian partisans continued the length and breadth of the country. In April 1945, two days after Milan was liberated, Mussolini was captured and executed while attempting to escape to Switzerland with his mistress, Clara Petacci.

Modern-day Italy

Italy was in chaos after the war, with the infrastructure destroyed by bombing and resistance groups settling old scores with violence. However, financed and politically guided by the United States under the Marshall Plan, and with the conscious aim of keeping the Communists from power, post-war Italy became a prosperous place in the main, particularly in the manufacturing towns of northern Italy. However, destructive politics and internal terrorism held the country to ransom in the 1970s, embodied in the kidnap and murder of former prime minister Aldo Moro in 1978, and murky goings-on continued in the 1980s and early 1990s, with backhanders and shady deals the norm between politicians, business and organized crime.

A church badly damaged in the 2009 earthquake in L'Aquila

The 90s saw the rise of Italy's modern day antihero – Silvio Berlusconi – a cruise-ship crooner and business man who turned to politics to protect his own interests. Famous for his gaffes, scandals and bad jokes, he was, however, the longest serving prime minister in the history of the nation. Accusations ranged from abuse of power and press censorship, to corruption and involvement with the Mafia and under-age prostitutes, but with all the focus on Berlusconi and his personal life, the country sank to the brink of bankruptcy and Berlusconi was finally forced to quit. An emergency government of technocrats was hurriedly put together under the esteemed economist Mario Monti to steer Italy through yet another crisis, albeit one that affects the rest of Europe more directly than ever before.

FACTS & FIGURES

Mafia, 'Ndrangheta and Camorra

The Sicilian Mafia is a mentality and a way of life that dates from the end of the 19th century. The island of Sicily is divided among families who control everything in their region through a brutal culture of honour and obedience. The 'Ndrangheta in Calabria and the Camorra in Campania are similar regional organizations.

The world's smallest country

A triangle less than half a square kilometre (0.2 square miles) in the heart of Rome, with a population of around 800, is the smallest country in the world. The Vatican City is ruled by the bishop of Rome – the pope – and was established in 1929 as an independent state within Italy. It has its own stamps, postboxes and euro coins.

Pasta-eaters

Italians eat on average 30 kg (66 lbs) of pasta a year each. First brought by Arab invaders to Sicily in the 8th century in the form of noodles, it now comes in 350 different shapes.

Flying houses and kings' bones

Italy has some vivid links with Christianity; the Virgin Mary's house apparently "flew" to Loreto in Le Marche; the blood-stained shroud said to have been used to wrap the dead body of Christ is in Turin; Milan houses the bones of the Three Kings; and in Naples, the blood of San Gennaro liquefies three times a year.

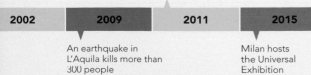

The euro replaces the lira as Italy's currency		With Italy on the verge of bankruptcy, Prime Minister Berlusconi resigns	
2002	**2009**	**2011**	**2015**
	An earthquake in L'Aquila kills more than 300 people		Milan hosts the Universal Exhibition

The village of Vernazza on its promontory in the Cinque Terre, Liguria.

Exploring
ITALY

Venice and
Northeast Italy

This varied area encompasses the natural beauty of sparkling lakes and lagoons, soaring mountains and the golden beaches of the Adriatic Sea, as well as the man-made beauty of magnificent towns such as Verona and the artistic treasures of Padua. And then there is Venice, the unique city built on water, a sublime capital of carnivals and art, with all the fun of exploring its hidden nooks and crannies by boat.

Highlights

Venice
The romantic city has plenty to offer kids too, from the joy of travelling along its watery "streets" by boat to the riot of colours at Carnival (see pp47–76).

Verona
The home of Romeo and Juliet and a gladiatorial Roman arena, this is one of northern Italy's most splendid cities (see pp78–83).

Riviera del Brenta
The River Brenta stretches between Padua and the Venetian lagoon, and a boat trip between the two reveals magnificent villas (see pp84–5).

Grado's beach resorts
Nicknamed the "island of the sun", Grado boasts a fine wetlands reserve, with the long sandy beaches of Lignano nearby (see pp90–91).

Bolzano
Worth visiting for Ötzi the "Ice Man" alone, a 5,300-year-old mummified man found near the Austrian border (see pp94–5).

The Dolomites
Designated a UNESCO World Heritage Site for the spectacular scenery, these mountains are great for hiking in summer and for winter sports too (see p96).

Left The Rialto Bridge, Venice, reflected in the moonlit Grand Canal
Above right Views across to Bolzano from the Messner Mountain Museum

The Best of
Venice and Northeast Italy

Rich in culture and with stunning landscapes, northeastern Italy offers fascinating diversity. There are opportunities for exploring the Dolomites, Italy's most dramatically beautiful mountain range, while further south the lovely cities of Verona and Venice, "the floating city", are steeped in history, art and intrigue. Garda, Italy's largest lake, and the Adriatic Coast beaches are the best places for cooling off.

The great outdoors

Marvel at the dreamy spires, fang-like towers and craggy pinnacles of the pink-tinged **Dolomites** (see p96), Italy's most beautiful mountains. Revel in the natural beauty of **Alpe di Siusi** (see p96), where legs can truly be stretched either hiking and biking, whilst taking in magnificent views. Splash about and indulge in some watersports at **Riva del Garda** (see p83) or meander around the wetland reserves of **Grado** (see p90).

In a week

Spend two days in **Venice** (see pp47–76), drifting along the Grand Canal, visiting Piazza San Marco and glittering St Mark's, and playing hide and seek in the back streets of the colourful Rialto district, the city's oldest area.

Travel on to **Padua** (see p86), one of Italy's most popular pilgrimage sites, and **Vicenza** (see p86), to admire the work of brilliant Renaissance architect Andrea Palladio. Continue to romantic **Verona** (see pp78–9), known since ancient times as "Little Rome", then drink in the mountain scenery of the **Dolomites** (see p86) or relax on the sandy beaches at **Grado** (see p90).

By season

In **winter**, head for the winter sports resorts high up in the **Dolomites** (see p96) or visit Merano for some bob-sleighing fun.

Below Colourful houses lining the canals of the lagoon island of Burano, Venice

In February and March the mists may swirl but **Venice** (*see pp47–76*) will erupt into life for Carnevale – one of the best carnivals in the world. Bring costumes, but beautiful masks are on sale all year round: choose anything from brightly coloured Harlequin or cat masks to the menacing Plague Doctor with its beaked nose.

Spring is warm and, once the snows have melted, a lovely season for exploring the **national parks** to admire the profusion of wildflowers and catch glimpses of the wildlife.

In **summer**, take the kids to the beach at **Grado** (*see p90*) and the open-air festival at the Roman Arena in **Verona** (*see pp78–9*).

Autumn brings the Regata Storica in **Venice** (*see pp48–51*), a colourful cavalcade of gondolas and gondoliers along the Grand Canal, as the wine harvest gets under way around the Strada del Vino in Trentino, accompanied by a feast of food festivals.

Messing about on the water

In Venice visit the **Arsenale** (*see pp70–71*), the centre of the city's illustrious history as a great maritime power. Then take a boat to the islands of the lagoon, glass-making **Murano** (*see p72*), the fishing village of **Burano** (*see p72*), full of brightly painted houses, and the sandy beaches of the **Lido** (*see p73*). Glide past splendid Palladian villas along the **Brenta Canal** (*see pp84–5*) linking Venice to Padua. Then head up to **Lake Garda** (*see p82*), Italy's largest and most popular lake, and **Gardaland** (*see p83*), Italy's best watery theme park.

Venice and Northeast Italy

The area fanning out to the west of Venice is a fertile plain traversed by three rivers: the Po, the Adige and the Brenta, which all flow into the Adriatic Sea. Water has always been part of people's lives in the Veneto, and this is especially true of Venice, which is built on it. To the east along the coast is the cultural melting pot of Trieste, while to the north, in Trentino-Alto Adige, is the stunning Dolomite mountain range.

The lion of St Mark on the Basilica di San Marco, Venice

Places of Interest

- ⬜ **VENICE** *(See pp 47–76)*
- ⬜ **VENETO AND FRIULI-VENEZIA GIULIA**
  1. Verona: the Arena
  2. Casa di Giulietta (Verona)
  3. Teatro Romano (Verona)
  4. San Zeno Maggiore (Verona)
  5. Lake Garda
  6. Gardone Riviera
  7. Riva del Garda
  8. Riviera del Brenta
  9. Padua
  10. Vicenza
  11. Treviso
  12. Trieste
  13. Aquileia
  14. Grado
  15. Udine

- ⬜ **TRENTINO-ALTO ADIGE**
  1. Bolzano (Bozen)
  2. Alpe di Siusi (Seiser Alm)
  3. Great Dolomites Road
  4. Passo di Falzàrego and the Cinque Torri
  5. Merano (Meran)
  6. Archeoparc
  7. MuseoPassiria
  8. Juval Castle

A gondola gliding under the Rialto Bridge on the Grand Canal in Venice

Messner Mountain Museum Firmian,
in Sigmundskron, near Bolzano

The Lowdown

Getting there and around
Air to Venice, Treviso or Verona (see p46). **Car** essential for Trentino-Alto Adige and Lake Garda, but congestion common around cities on the plain. **Car hire** from all major firms at airports and main train stations, or Morini Rent (www.morinirent.com) in Verona. **Train** between towns efficient, reliable and good value (www.trenitalia.it). **Buses** connect airports to towns (see p46). **Ferry** to Venice (www.alilaguna.it). **Vaporetto** or waterbus around Venice (www.actv.it)

Supermarkets Billa (open daily until 8pm) and Coop in several locations around Venice. In Verona, Vicenza, Padua and Treviso, look for Famila stores (www.famila.it). **Markets** Venice: Rialto (Tue–Sat am) and Tronchetto island, near the station (Mon–Sat). Verona: various locations (Wed–Sat). Padua: Piazza delle Erbe (Mon–Sat am). Treviso: Viale Burchiellati (Tue and Sat am)

Festivals Venice: Carnival (Feb–Mar; www.carnevale.venezia.it); San Marco (25 Apr); Festa della Sensa (mid-May); Festa del Redentore (third Sun in Jul); Regata Storica (first Sun in Sep). Padua: San Antonio (13 Jun). Verona: San Zeno (21 May).

Opening hours Restaurants mostly open 12:30–3pm for lunch and 7:30–10pm for dinner, and pizzerias for dinner only until midnight. Many shops close on Sundays and at lunchtime. Major museums now tend to be open all day, but some still close for lunch, so check. Many museums close on Mondays.

Pharmacies To find an all-night pharmacy, check servizio notturno listings on pharmacy doors or in the local papers.

Public toilets There are 19 public toilets in Venice, eight with baby-change facilities. Buy a WC card to use them, or the service is included with the Venice Card, both available from the Hello Venezia kiosks. Elsewhere, buy a drink in a café-bar to use facilities.

Venice and Northeast Italy Airports

Three airports serve the Veneto and northeastern Italy, with connections to many European and some American destinations, and plenty of low-cost options. Venezia Marco Polo (about 7 km/4 miles north of Venice) and Treviso (about 30 km/19 miles inland) are not far from each other. Verona, further west, has its own airport, to cater not only for tourism, but also for visitors and business people drawn by the wine trade.

Venezia Marco Polo

The largest of the Veneto's airports is **Venezia Marco Polo**. Flights operate to and from various regional airports in the UK, and Dublin in Ireland. As well as catering for domestic internal flights, the airport also serves Belgium, Finland, Germany, Greece, Norway, Portugal, Spain, Tunisia, Morocco, Egypt, Israel, Turkey, Ukraine, a couple of Russian cities, and US hubs such as Atlanta, New York and Philadelphia.

The airport is a 20-minute bus ride by **ATVO** bus (buy tickets at the ATVO ticket office or ticket machine at the airport) or **ACTV** bus 5 (buy tickets from a newsagent at the airport) to Piazzale Roma, beside Venice railway station. Buses run every 30 minutes. An alternative is the **Alilaguna** waterbus, which has various drop-off points in Venice, from where travellers can connect with ACTV *vaporetti* (waterbuses) to their final destination. The Alilaguna desk is near arrivals on the ground floor. Another (expensive) way to travel is by water taxi.

In the airport there are cafés, a family area on the first floor, and a large circular shopping precinct.

Treviso

Various budget airlines, including Ryanair and Germanwings, use little Treviso airport. Treviso operates

Jet taking off from Venezia Marco Polo airport

flights to and from Bristol, East Midlands, Leeds, Stansted and Dublin in the UK and Ireland, as well as France, Belgium, Spain, Malta, Sweden, Norway, Holland, the Czech Republic, Romania, Bulgaria and Ukraine.

ATVO and ACTV run a bus service from the airport to Treviso railway station that takes 20 minutes. Buy tickets at the airport ticket office. From Treviso, trains run to Venice in 30–40 minutes. There is also an ATVO Eurobus connection to Venice Mestre, on the mainland, and from there it is a 5-minute train ride to Venice proper. If arriving in the evening, consider staying a night in Treviso to enjoy a lovely small town with waterways of its own.

Verona Valerio Catullo

Smallish but quite busy, the airport at Verona offers flights to London Gatwick (British Airways) and Stansted (Ryanair), to other Italian destinations and to Amsterdam, Athens, Barcelona, Berlin, Brussels, Frankfurt, Vienna, Istanbul, Crete, Tunis, Tel Aviv and Moscow.

A shuttle bus runs to and from Verona station from 6:30am to 11:30pm. Verona is well worth a visit in its own right. To reach Venice by fast train takes just over an hour; by slow train, at a fraction of the cost, just over 2 hours.

There are kids' play areas in both arrivals and departures, plus there is a bar-restaurant area.

The Lowdown

Airports
Treviso 0422 315 111;
www.trevisoairport.it
Venezia Marco Polo 041 260 9260; *www.veniceairport.it*
Verona Valerio Catullo 045 809 5666; *www.aeroportoverona.it*

Airport transport
ACTV *www.actv.it*
Alilaguna *www.alilaguna.it*
ATVO 0421 594 671
Trains *www.trenitalia.it*

ACTV vaporetto (waterbus), which connects with Alilaguna services from the airport

Venice

Venice is a unique jewel sparkling in its lagoon, home to precious works of art representing the wealth and power of a great seafaring republic. Fascinating for adults, it is exciting and mysterious for children, a city where everyone goes by water or on foot and where Carnival has made disguise *de rigueur*: wear a cloak and a mask and play hide and seek.

Below *The Grand Canal with Santa Maria della Salute in the background*

The Grand Canal: Ponte degli Scalzi to Rialto
Stately parade of canalside palaces

Shaped like a back-to-front "S", the Grand Canal snakes through the heart of Venice, connecting its various districts. From the earliest times it was a key trade and transport route, which is why the city's wealthy families built their palaces along its banks. More than 170 of these splendid residences remain, revealing a thousand years of history. The *vaporetto* (waterbus) gives a great view of these buildings, reflected in the shimmering water.

Ponte degli Scalzi to Rialto

Cannaregio

Santa Croce

San Polo

San Marco

Dorsoduro   *see next page*

③ **The Cannaregio Canal** This waterway connects the Grand Canal with the Cannaregio district, which was once densely populated and contained the original Jewish Ghetto.

① **Ponte degli Scalzi** Built in 1858 to provide access to the city's then recently constructed railway station, this is one of four bridges crossing the Grand Canal. The original version was made in iron; it was later replaced with stone.

Riva di Biaiso

San Marcuola

Ferrovia

② **Palazzo Labia** Built between the 17th and 18th centuries, this huge residence, in the ornate Baroque style, contains a ballroom decorated with scenes from the life of Cleopatra, painted by Giambattista Tiepolo between 1745 and 1750.

The Lowdown

Address Palazzo Labia: Fondamenta Labia (entrance on Campo San Geremaia). Fondaco dei Turchi (Natural History Museum): Santa Croce 1730; www.msn.ve.it. Ca' Pesaro: Santa Croce 2076; www.capesaro.visit muve.it. Ca' d'Oro: Canal Grande (Calle Ca' d'Oro); www.cadoro.org

Visitor information Stazione Santa Lucia, 30121, Venezia; 041 529 8711; www.turismovenezia.it

Vaporetto (waterbus) ACTV (www.actv.it) line 1 makes frequent stops, including Ca' d'Oro, Rialto and Accademia; (€3 per person for one stop, €6.50 for 60 minutes' travel, €16 for 12 hours).

Gondola trips are expensive (€80 for 40 minutes for a six-person gondola, or €100 for 40 minutes after 7pm). *Traghetti* (gondola ferries) across the Grand Canal are more affordable

(50 cents a crossing). The boats are slightly larger, and all gondoliers take a turn working them once a year. Locals ride standing up. Crossings include San Marcuola to Fondaco dei Turchi, Santa Sofia to Rialto-Pescheria, Santa Maria del Giglio to Salute, and Carbon to Riva del Vin.

Private boat tours Canal Grande; 041 971 692; www.canalgrande.it

④ **Fondaco dei Turchi** Originally built in the 13th century as a warehouse and lodging for Turkish traders, this once-splendid building underwent a brutal restoration last century. Today it houses the Natural History Museum.

⑤ **Palazzo Vendramin Calergi** With its double tier of arched windows, this palazzo, built in the late 1400s, is one of the finest Renaissance buildings in Venice. The great German composer Richard Wagner died here in 1883, and there is a museum devoted to him on the first floor. Today, Venice's casino is housed in the palace.

⑧ **The Pescheria** has been the site of a busy fish market for six centuries. Held in a striking mock-Gothic market hall, the Pescheria is best visited early in the morning, when the colourful catch makes quite a show.

San Stae

⑥ **Ca' Pesaro** This stately palace was built for the wealthy Pesaro family in the late 17th century. It now houses the Gallery of Modern Art, with glittering works by Austrian artist Gustav Klimt.

Ca' d'Oro

⑨ **Rialto Bridge** Built in 1591 to replace an earlier wooden bridge that had collapsed under the weight of crowds watching a wedding procession, the Rialto Bridge was designed by the aptly named Antonio da Ponte – *ponte* means "bridge" in Italian (see p58).

⑦ **Ca' d'Oro** The most famous of Venetian Gothic palaces, and perhaps the most beautiful on the canal, houses paintings, frescoes and sculpture from the collection of Baron Giorgio Franchetti, who bequeathed the palace to the state.

Rialto Mercato

(minimum 5 people; departures at 11am and 4pm; €42 per person)

Open Museum of Natural History: Jun–Oct 10am–6pm daily, 9am–5pm Tue–Fri, Nov–May 10am –6pm Sat & Sun. Ca' Pesaro: Apr–Oct 10am–6pm daily, Nov–Mar 10am–5pm. Ca' d'Oro:8:15am–2pm Mon, 8:15am–7:15pm Tue–Sun.

Price Museum of Natural History: €16–32. Ca' Pesaro €8–16. Ca' d'Oro: €16–32; EU under-18s free

Grand Canal continued ▶

The Grand Canal cont: Rialto to San Marco

Rialto to San Marco

Cannaregio
see previous page

Santa Croce

San Polo

San Marco

Dorsoduro

⑩ **View to the Rialto Bridge** This bridge was built to span the Grand Canal in what was, and still is, the most commercial quarter of the city.

⑪ **Riva del Ferro** German trading barges once offloaded iron *(ferro)* at this quayside.

⑫ **The Riva del Vin** A good place for watching canal life, this stretch of quayside is where wine – *vin* in Venetian dialect – used to be unloaded. The best wines came from near Verona, and travelled all the way here by boat.

⑬ **Palazzo Garzoni** This grand renovated Gothic palace is now part of the university. The traghetto service, which links neighboring Calle Garzoni to San Tomà on the other side of the canal is one of the oldest in Venice.

Sant' Angelo ⑬

San Toma

⑭

⑮ ⑯

⑰

⑱

San Samuele

Ca' Rezzonico

⑭ **Palazzo Balbi** Built in the 16th century, this handsome palace has two main reception areas one above the other, with arched windows overlooking the canal, and two curious obelisk-shaped pinnacles on the roof.

Accademia

⑲

⑮ **Ca' Foscari** Built in 1437 for Doge Francesco Foscari, this is now part of the University of Venice.

⑯ **La Volta** The point where the canal doubles back on itself is known as "La Volta" (meaning "the bend"). This splendid curve was long ago established as the finishing stretch for the annual Regata Storica. Following the curve, the views widen and become more spectacular as it heads towards San Marco.

San Silvestro

Rialto

The Lowdown

🌐 **Address** Palazzo Balbi: Calle del Remer 3901, Dorsoduro. Ca' Foscari: Calle Foscari 3246, Dorsoduro. Palazzo Moro Lin: Calle Moro Lin 3242, San Marco. Gallerie dell'Accademia: Campo della Carità 1050, Dorsoduro; 041 520 0345; www.gallerie accademia.org, Palazzo Dario: Calle Barbaro 352, Dorsoduro. Santa Maria della Salute: Campo de la Salute 1, Dorsoduro; Palazzo Garzoni: San Marco 3417; Palazzo Grassi: Campo San Samuele, 041 271 9039

🕐 **Open** Gallerie dell' Accademia: 8:15am–2pm Mon, 8:15am–7:15pm Tue– Sun. Palazzo Grassi: 10am–7pm daily (except Tues). Santa Maria della Salute: 9am–noon & 3–5:30pm daily

€ **Price** Gallerie dell'Accademia: €13–26. Palazzo Grassi: €50 (children under 11 free)

⑰ **Palazzo Moro Lin** Created out of two Gothic houses in the 17th century for a painter who obviously understood the importance of light, this residence is known as the "palace of the 13 windows". How many can actually be seen from the water?

⑱ **Palazzi Grasso** This noble looking palace was built in the 1730s and has a beautiful Neo-Classical façade. In 1984 it was bought by Fiat, and turned into a venue for art exhibitions.

⑲ **Gallerie dell'Accademia** Once a monastery, this building houses the world's greatest collection of Venetian paintings (see p65).

⑳ **Palazzo Dario** Coloured marble inlay makes the façade so pretty that it is hard to believe that murder, suicide and bankruptcy have all befallen the building's owners.

㉑ **Santa Maria della Salute** (St Mary of Health) was built in thanksgiving for the city's deliverance from the plague in 1630. Once a customs house, the building now contains a contemporary art collection (see p67).

㉒ **Giardinetti Reali** These royal gardens were created by Napoleon, and lead through to Piazza San Marco.

San Marco
Vallaressa

Santa Maria
del Giglio

Salute

San Marco and Rialto

San Marco has been considered the true heart of Venice since 829, when St Mark's remains were brought here from Alexandria and housed in a magnificent basilica, which was consecrated in 1094. Today the area is also home to upmarket hotels and shops and a wealth of handsome palazzos. A short walk away is the city's busiest and oldest quarter, the Rialto, home to one of Venice's most famous sights, the Rialto Bridge. The grand structure standing here today was finished in 1591 and always throngs with people.

San Marco and Rialto

Rialto • Basilica di San Marco

Campo Santa Margherita p60 • Arsenale p68

Places of Interest

SIGHTS

1. Basilica di San Marco
2. Doge's Palace
3. Teatro La Fenice
4. The Rialto

● EAT AND DRINK

1. Rosticceria San Bartolomeo
2. Trattoria do Forno
3. Caffè Florian
4. Black Jack
5. Osteria ai Assassini
6. Vino Vino
7. La Fenice Café
8. Osteria da Carla
9. Casa del Parmigiano
10. Moscacieka
11. Naranzaria
12. Poste Vecie

● SHOPPING

1. Sole Luna
2. Paolo Olbi

● WHERE TO STAY

1. Ateneo
2. Casa Querini
3. Antica Locanda Sturion
4. Hotel Flora
5. Locanda Fiorita

The impressive entrance to Basilica di San Marco

Displays of fresh fish and seafood at the pescheria, Rialto | Gold lion of St Mark on the façade of Basilica di San Marco

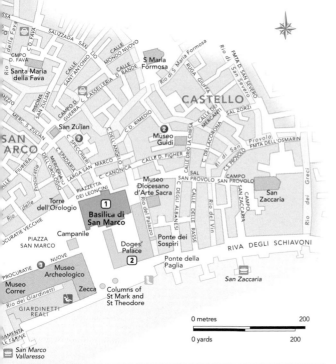

The Lowdown

🚤 **Vaporetto** (waterbus) lines 1 or 2, both of which stop at San Marco, and 51, which stops at San Zaccaria, just round the corner from Piazza San Marco. **On foot** It takes about 30–40 minutes to walk to San Marco from the railway station. To reach Rialto from San Marco, walk along the shop-lined Mercerie quarter, on the left as you face the Basilica di San Marco.

ℹ️ **Visitor information** San Marco, 71/f, 9am–3:30pm; 041 529 8711; www.turismovenezia.it

🛒 **Supermarkets** In Rialto, Su. Ve. has a branch on Calle de la Fava, Castello 5601. More of a boutique food store is I Tre Mercanti (www.itremercanti.it), Campo della Guerra, 5364 Castello. **Markets** Rialto fruit and vegetable market, and adjoining Fish Market (7:30am–noon, Tue–Sat)

🎭 **Festivals** Carnival (Feb–March); patron saint San Marco (25 Apr); Festa della Sensa, Ascension Day (mid May); Regata Storica (1st Sun in Sep)

➕ **Pharmacies** San Marco: Farmacia Italo–Inglese, Calle della Mandola 3717; 041 5224837; Farmacia Internazionale, Via XXII Marzo 2067, 041 522 2311. Rialto: Farmacia Morelli, San Marco 5310; 041 5224196

🛝 **Nearest play area** Giardinetti Reali, south of Piazza San Marco

View of Il Salute from the quayside of the Doge's Palace

① Basilica di San Marco
Onion domes, glittering mosaics and stolen booty

Piazza San Marco was once the epicentre of the wealthiest, most powerful city in Europe, a maritime power at the crossroads of the medieval world between Byzantium and Rome. Like something out of *Aladdin*, the Oriental splendour of the Basilica di San Marco (St Mark's) is like almost nothing else in Western Europe. Founded in AD 828, its interior surfaces are covered by more than 4 square kilometres (1½ square miles) of beautiful mosaics – the fruit of 600 years of labour.

St Mark and angels, façade

Key Features

Façade mosaics A 17th-century mosaic shows the body of St Mark being smuggled out of Alexandria in Egypt.

Ascension Dome

Horses of St Mark

Domes San Marco has five bulbed domes; the Ascension Dome has a lavish 13th-century mosaic of Christ, Mary and the apostles inside.

Mosaic floor Inside the Basilica, multi-coloured patterns of marble and glass depict flowers, birds and allegorical beasts in the style of an Oriental carpet.

Pala d'Oro

St Mark's body The saint's remains lie in a green marble sarcophagus behind the main altar – or do they? They were destroyed by a fire in AD 976, but miraculously reappeared just as the new church was consecrated in 1094.

Treasury The Basilica is known as "the world's greatest stolen property office" and its *tesoro* (treasury) is filled with booty from Venice's far-flung empire.

Horses of St Mark On the central balcony are replicas of the four 2nd-century AD gilded bronze horses, brought here from Constantinople (modern Istanbul) in 1204. The originals are inside.

Pala d'Oro A dazzling golden medieval altarpiece, its enamel panels are encrusted with 2,500 precious gems. The left side depicts the story of Christ, the right side the story of St Mark.

Letting off steam

Kids will love chasing the pigeons in Piazza San Marco, but do note that feeding the birds here has been forbidden since 2008. Alternatively walk towards the waterfront and turn left over the Ponte della Paglia to the quayside at Riva degli Schiavoni, which is much less crowded. It once thronged with merchants and slave dealers; now it is busy with souvenir sellers.

Prices given are for a family of four

Eat and drink

Picnic: under €25; Snacks: €25–40; Real meal: €40–80; Family treat: €80 or more (based on a family of four)

PICNIC Rialto (see pp58–9) has some of the best market stalls to shop for a picnic. Alternatively, stock up at one of the **Billa** supermarkets before heading to the **Giardinetti Reali** (former Royal Gardens), a cool oasis just around the corner from Piazza San Marco.

SNACKS Rosticceria San Bartolomeo (Calle della Bissa 5424, San Marco, 30124; 041 522 3569) prepares good food to take away, displayed under a glass counter at this bustling *tavola calda*.
REAL MEAL Trattoria Do Forni (Calle dei Specchieri 457/468, San Marco, 30124; 041 523 2148; www.doforni.it) is a historic, rustic-style restaurant serving traditional and local specialities –

The Lowdown

🌐 **Address** Piazza San Marco, 30124 San Marco; 041 270 8311; www.basilicasanmarco.it

🚢 **Vaporetto** (waterbus) 1, 2, 41, 42, 51 or 52 to Piazza San Marco

ℹ️ **Visitor information** Piazza San Marco 71f, 30124 San Marco; 041 529 7811; www.turismovenezia.it

🕐 **Open** 9:45am–5pm Mon–Sat; 2–4pm Sun; sightseeing restricted during services

€ **Price** Basilica: free. Pala d'Oro: €5–7. Treasury: €6–9

👥 **Skipping the queue** Visit in the early morning or late afternoon to avoid the worst queues and book ahead at www.venetoinside.com (€1 booking fee) for the Basilica's paying attractions. Note that it is less crowded in winter months.

🚩 **Guided tours** 11am Mon–Sat; check calendar in the Basilica's atrium for languages, or call 041 241 3817 (10am–noon Mon–Fri) for information.

👫 **Age range** 5 plus

⏱️ **Allow** 2 hours

♿ **Wheelchair access** Yes, ask guards for ramp in the afternoon.

☕ **Café** Caffè Florian in Piazza San Marco (see below)

🚻 **Toilets** Yes, by the tourist office, or in the cafés and bars

Good family value?
The gleaming gold interior, rearing horses and views bring to life Venice's former role as gateway to the Orient, most of it for free.

Venetian *pasticcio di verdure* (vegetable pie), seafood risotto, steak and pasta – served in cosy interlinked rooms, each of which has a different atmosphere.
FAMILY TREAT Caffè Florian *(Piazza San Marco, San Marco, 30124; 041 520 5641; www. caffeflorian.com)* was established in 1720 and is Venice's oldest café. For the grown-ups, it is the place to come for a cocktail or a prosecco. It is rather pricey, but the ambience is unbeatable.

Shopping

Sole Luna *(Calle Frezzeria, San Marco 1503, 30124; 041 528 7543)* sells *papier mâché* and leather carnival masks, hand-crafted here.

Western end of the Riva degli Schiavoni, off Piazza San Marco

There is also a great display of masks worn by characters in the Commedia dell'Arte – traditional Venetian masked theatre.

The Gothic Doge's Palace, as viewed from a gondola

Find out more

FILM In the classic James Bond film *Moonraker* (1979), Bond is chased by villain Drax's henchmen along the Grand Canal. His motorized gondola turns into a hovercraft and he escapes across Piazza San Marco.

Next stop...

DOGE'S PALACE Continue to the adjoining palace (see p56) and cross the famous Bridge of Sighs. Or climb the **Campanile** or the **Torre dell' Orologio** with its astrological clock, for bird's eye views of the piazza.

② Doge's Palace

Lacework made of stone, with a cold heart

The seat of Venetian government from the 9th century until the fall of the Republic in 1797, the Doge's Palace (Palazzo Ducale) was the official residence of the Venetian ruler, known as the doge. An airy Gothic masterpiece of the 14th and 15th centuries, the bulk of the pink Veronese marble building appears perched on loggias and arcades of white Istrian stone. It is full of superb paintings and sculpture, but as well as being a showcase for Venetian supremacy, it also had a sinister side as a hotbed of spies and inquisitors.

Take the 15th-century Giants' Stairway (Scala dei Giganti) to the upper loggia, passing lavish sculptures of *Neptune* and *Mars* – symbols of Venice's power – by the influential Venetian architect and sculptor Jacopo d'Antonio Sansovino (1486–1570). In the gloomy Sala del Consiglio dei Dieci, the loathed Council of Ten, set up in 1310, would assemble to decide who it wanted to execute. In the antechamber were lions' heads, where citizens could post anonymous bills denouncing others for their crimes, real or imaginary. In the Sala del Maggior Consiglio, the meeting place for Venice's Grand Council, hangs Tintoretto's *Paradise* (1590), said to be the world's largest oil painting.

Linking the Doge's Palace to its prisons is the covered Bridge of Sighs (Ponte dei Sospiri). It takes its

Venice's most famous bridge, the Bridge of Sighs, passing over the Rio di Palazzo

name from the laments of prisoners forced to walk across it to certain torture and probable death in prison; through its tiny windows they could catch a glimpse of the lagoon – and freedom. The "Terrible Ten" inquisitors were notorious for their severe sentences. The bridge allowed them to slip back and forth unobserved from the "old" prisons in the Doge's Palace to the "new" prisons and torture chambers. Adventurer and seducer Giacomo Casanova was imprisoned here in 1755, but managed to escape using an iron bar and a piece of polished marble.

For those with strong stomachs, a Secret Itineraries (Itinerari Segreti) tour follows a murky maze to parts of the palace normally out of bounds to visitors, including the torture chambers and the cell from which Casanova escaped.

Letting off steam

Bounded by the Doge's Palace and the Basilica di San Marco, the **Piazzetta San Marco**, with the columns of St Theodore and St Mark *(see p53)*, overlooks the Molo San Marco (quay). It is a great spot to cool off and watch the boats gliding by.

The Lowdown

🌐 **Address** San Marco 1, 30124 (entrance on Piazzetta San Marco); www.museicivicivenezian.it

🚤 **Vaporetto** 1, 2, 41, 42, 51, 52 to Piazza San Marco

🕐 **Open** Daily Apr–Oct 8:30am–7pm, Nov–Mar 8:30am–5:30pm

💶 **Price** €32–52; under-6s free

🙋 **Skipping the queue** Book in advance online or by phone (041 520 9070 or 041 291 5911)

🚩 **Guided tours** Fri–Mon 9:30am, 11:30am and 12:30pm in English, 12:30pm in Italian (€16, plus cost of entry). Itinerari Segreti tours: 9:55am, 10:45am and 11:35am in English, 9:30am and 11:10am in Italian (€60, including entry to rest of palace; pre-booking essential, online, by phone or in person)

👫 **Age range** 5 plus

⏱ **Allow** 45 minutes; Itinerari Segreti tour 1 hour and 15 minutes

♿ **Wheelchair access** Partial

🍴 **Eat and Drink** *Snacks* Black Jack *(Campo San Luca, 30124, San Marco; 041 522 2518)* is a little bar with excellent and inexpensive snacks. *Real meal* Osteria Ai Assassini *(San Marco 3695, 30124; 041 528 7986; closed Sun; www. osteriaaiassassini.it)* specializes in traditional and innovative dishes made with seasonal produce, while Vino Vino *(Calle delle Veste, 30124, San Marco 2877; 041 241 7688; www.vinovinowinebar.com)* is utterly Venetian: rub shoulders with gondoliers over *cicchetti* (Venetian tapas) of sweet and sour sardines and polenta.

🎉 **Festivals** Festa di San Marco (saint's day, culminating in a gondola race): 25 Apr. Vogalonga (Long Row across the lagoon to Burano): May

The lacy look of the Doge's Palace, typical of Venetian Gothic architecture

③ Teatro La Fenice

Phoenix risen from the ashes

In classical mythology, a *fenice* (phoenix) was a bird resembling an eagle that lived for 500 years in the Arabian desert and then burned itself to death on a funeral pyre, rising from the ashes with renewed youth to live through another cycle – and so it is with La Fenice.

Originally built to replace the San Benedetto theatre, which burned down in a devastating fire in 1774, it was abandoned during construction due to a legal dispute between the opera company and the theatre's owners. La Fenice finally opened in 1792, only to be engulfed in flames in 1836. It was brought back to its original glory within a year, but tragedy struck again in 1996 when arson destroyed the theatre, with fire brigades fighting the blaze for the entire night of 29 January. Two electricians were later found guilty of maliciously starting the fire to avoid fines for not finishing their work in time. The theatrical world was in mourning for the loss of one of its most beautiful theatres, known for its outstanding acoustics. It remained closed for eight long years.

In November 2004, La Fenice officially re-opened with a celebratory performance of Romantic composer Giuseppe Verdi's *La Traviata*, which had premiered at this very theatre in 1853. If a night at the opera with kids is impractical, take a tour of this delightful jewel-box of a theatre to see the ornate Foyer and Sala Grande (auditorium).

Ornate sign at the Teatro La Fenice, showing a phoenix rising from the ashes

Letting off steam

If the joys of pigeon-chasing and boat-watching in crowded Piazza San Marco and its less crowded Piazzetta begin to wear thin, **Campo Santo Stefano** by the Accademia bridge (5–10 minutes' walk away) is a good place to run around. Until 1802 it was a location for bull-baiting, but it is now lined with cafés and has a playground.

The Lowdown

- 🌐 **Address** Campo San Fantin 1965, 30124, San Marco; 041 786 511; www.teatrolafenice.it
- 🚤 **Vaporetto** 1 to Santa Maria del Giglio
- 🕐 **Open** 9:30am–6pm daily, depending on performances
- 💶 **Price** Tours: €32; under-6s free; ticket price includes audio guide
- 👫 **Age range** 8 plus
- ⏱ **Allow** 45 minutes
- 🍵 **Eat and drink** *Snacks* La Fenice Café in the courtyard is a stylish place for coffee and a sandwich. *Real meal* Osteria da Carla (Corte Contarina 1535, 30124, San Marco; 041 523 7855; closed Sun) is a typical Venetian inn serving local specialities and *cicchetti* (tapas) in a quiet square.

The grand façade of the venerable Teatro La Fenice

④ Rialto
What's new on the Rialto?

Venice's oldest district, tucked into the Grand Canal's middle bend, the Rialto was the original crossroads between East and West, where spices and silks were traded; the Rialto Bridge was the only bridge linking the two banks of the Grand Canal until 1854. Its alleyways are filled with hole-in-the-wall *bacari* (hostelries) and markets that have changed little since the time of Shakespeare's *Merchant of Venice* (1596–8). In that play, merchant Antonio enquires, "What's new on the Rialto?" The answer is, not much.

Clock face, San Giacomo di Rialto

Key Sights

Rialto di quà, Rialto di là The San Marco right bank is known as the Rialto di quá (this side), while the left bank is called Rialto di là (that side).

Ponte Storico Like many bridges in Venice, Ponte Storico is crooked. It leads under a portico to Calle Stretta, a narrow alley that is only 1 m (3 ft) wide in places.

Rialto Bridge A beloved landmark of the Grand Canal, this bridge was designed by architect Antonio da Ponte. Its 7.5 m (24 ft) arch was created to allow ships to travel under it.

Markets

CAMPO DELLA PESCHERIA

RUGA DEGLI ORETICI

RUGA VECCHIA SAN GIOVANNI

RIVA DEL VIN

GRAND CANAL

Rialto Bridge

Rialto Markets Traders have hawked their wares in the guttural Venetian dialect at the Erberia (fruit and vegetable market) and Pescheria (fish market) on this site for centuries.

San Giacomo di Rialto

San Giacomo di Rialto This stone church was the only building left after a terrible fire engulfed the area in 1514 – Venice was once as prone to fire as it is to flooding today.

Letting off steam

Five to ten minutes' walk from the Rialto Bridge, **Campo San Polo** – Venice's largest square after Piazza San Marco – is a great spot to picnic on a bench or run around with a ball. There are plenty of cafés where adults can enjoy a drink on the terrace while kids play.

For the more adventurous, hop on a *vaporetto* to Punta della Dogana and try *voga veneta* (Venetian rowing) or canoeing at the **Reale Società Canottieri Bucintoro** (*Fondamenta Dogana e Salute 15, 30123, Dorsoduro; 335 667 3851; www.bucintoro.org*), with lessons available for all ages.

Prices given are for a family of four

Eat and drink

Picnic: under €25; Snacks: €25–40; Real meal: €40–80; Family treat: €80 or more (based on a family of four)

PICNIC Pick up fruit and vegetables from the Erberia and perhaps a seafood snack from the Pescheria. Next to the Pescheria, the **Casa del Parmigiano** (*San Polo 214/215, 30125, Rialto; 041 520 6525*) is great not just for cheeses, but also for cold meats. Then head for nearby Campo San Polo, which has a good array of grocery stores.
SNACKS Moscacieka (*Calle dei Fabbri 4717, 30124, San Marco; 041 520 8085*) is a fun, upbeat place between Rialto and Piazza San

Marco, serving grilled sandwiches, lasagna and salads at lunchtimes.
REAL MEAL Naranzaria (*San Polo 130, 30125, Rialto; 041 724 1035; www.naranzaria.it; closed Mon*) is a lovely spot to drink in the views of the Rialto Bridge and Grand Canal. Traditional and modern dishes and the chef's Mediterranean take on sushi, using fresh fish from the Pescheria, are all on offer.
FAMILY TREAT Poste Vecie (*Rialto Pescheria 1608, 30125, Rialto; 041 721 822; closed Mon and Tue lunch*) claims to be the oldest restaurant in the city. The entrance is from the fish market at the Rialto, and the homemade pastas are excellent.

The Lowdown

🌐 **Address** Ponte di Rialto, Sestiere San Polo 125, 30125

🚤 **Vaporetto** to San Tomà/Sant'Angelo: no 1, 2, N (night boat); San Silvestro/Riva del Carbon: no 1; Rialto Mercato/Santa Sofia: no 1, N (www.venice.nu/vapmap/vapomapLatest.jpg)

ℹ **Visitor information** Piazza San Marco 71f, 30124, San Marco; 041 529 7811; www.turismovenezia.it

🕐 **Open** Erberia and Pescheria markets: Tue–Sat dawn–noon

👥 **Skipping the queue** The Rialto markets are always busy, but the bustle is part of the attraction.

👫 **Age range** 5 plus, but it is a tiring place to keep track of young children and the bridges are challenging with pushchairs.

⏱ **Allow** 1 hour

☕ **Café** Plenty in the alleys

🚻 **Toilets** In the cafés and bars

Good family value?
The Rialto is an atmospheric area to wander around, with lots to see. The historical attractions here are free, and it is a good area to picnic, if you don't mind sitting on benches in the squares.

Shopping
Paolo Olbi (Calle della Mandola, San Marco 3653; 041 528 5025; Mon–Fri 9am–1pm) specializes in beautiful Venetian marbled paper, with every type of hand-crafted stationery imaginable: luxurious notebooks, travel journals and calfskin covered diaries; notepaper with Venetian scenes; and inexpensive notebooks and bookmarks. Everything here is of the finest quality; a leather-bound photo album makes the perfect gift.

Find out more
FILM Michael Radford's 2004 film of The Merchant of Venice closely follows Shakespeare's original text and stars Al Pacino as Shylock the moneylender and Jeremy Irons as Antonio the merchant. It was filmed on location in the city, including scenes shot around the Rialto.

Elegant façade of Museo di Storia Naturale on the Grand Canal

Next stop...
MUSEO DI STORIA NATURALE
There are over two million fossils and ferocious beasts in this natural history museum in Santa Croce, and a brand new aquarium for getting up close to fish from the Adriatic Sea. The star of the collection is the skeleton of the dinosaur *Ouranosaurus nigeriensis*, discovered in the Sahara Desert by the explorer Giancarlo Ligabue in 1973 (www.msn.ve.it).

Tree-shaded benches in Campo San Polo, perfect for a picnic

Campo Santa Margherita and around

Lively Campo Santa Margherita is the heart of the *sestiere* of Dorsoduro. Surrounded by a spider's web of little streets, it is spacious and airy, with cafés, shops and eateries around the perimeter, plus a fish, fruit and vegetable market. Also among the Dorsoduro's attractions are the wide-embracing lagoon views, both from the eastern tip near the Salute and from the Zattere across to the island of Giudecca. To discover the quieter part of the *sestiere*, travel east of the Peggy Guggenheim Collection for pretty shaded squares and picturesque residences.

Campo Santa Margherita and around

Rialto *p58*

Basilica di San Marco *p52*

Campo Santa Margherita

Arsenale *p68*

Places of Interest

SIGHTS

1. Campo Santa Margherita
2. Ponte dei Pugni
3. Campo San Barnaba
4. Gallerie dell'Accademia
5. Peggy Guggenheim Collection
6. I Gesuati
7. Santa Maria della Salute

● EAT AND DRINK

1. Barozzi Gianfranco & Co
2. Pizza Al Volo
3. L'Osteria alla Bifora
4. Ristoteca Oniga
5. Enoteca Bar Ai Artisti
6. Quattro Feri
7. Il Caffè
8. Agli Alboretti
9. Gelateria Nico
10. Trattoria Borghi
11. Bar da Gino
12. Antica Osteria al Pantalon
13. La Rivista
14. Al Chioschetto
15. Linea d'Ombra

● SHOPPING

1. La Botttega dei Mascareri

● WHERE TO STAY

1. Ai Carmini
2. Antica Locanda Montin
3. Locanda San Barnaba
4. Ca' San Trovaso
5. De Zorzi

Pretty buildings and street life in Campo Santa Margherita

Floating barge selling fruit and vegetables, a permanent sight in Campo San Barnaba

Ponte dei Pugni, spanning the Rio San Barnaba

Gesuati church on the Zattere, as seen from Giudecca

The Lowdown

🚤 **Vaporetto** The nearest *vaporetto* stop for Campo Santa Margherita is Ca' Rezzonico (nos. 1 and 2). The area's main sights are all within easy walking distance. For sights to the east of Campo Santa Margherita, take the *vaporetto* to Accademia or Salute.

🛒 **Supermarkets** Biga mini market, San Polo 2605. Billa supermarket, Dorsoduro 1491. **Markets** For fruit and vegetables, the most convenient option is the street market in the square (which runs from 7am to 7:30pm every day), or the barge on Rio San Barnaba.

🎭 **Festivals** Carnival: Feb–Mar. Patron saint San Marco: 25 Apr. Festa della Sensa, Ascension Day: mid May. Festa del Redentore: 3rd Sun in Jul. Regata Storica:1st Sun in Sep

➕ **Pharmacies** Farmacia Santa Margherita, Dorsoduro 3692; 041 5223 872. Farmacia Solveni, Dorsoduro 993; 041 5220 840

🐛 **Nearest play area** The gardens at Ca' Rezzónico have a small corner equipped as a playground.

Hand-crafted carnival masks on display in a workshop

① Campo Santa Margherita
A playful oasis for people-watching

This picturesque square is the social heart of the Dorsoduro district and a hive of activity. One of Venice's largest *campi*, it was part of an ambitious project in the 19th century to open up the south end of the island by filling in canals. The church that gave the square its name, Santa Margherita, was deconsecrated under Napoleon and is now a university auditorium. The square is always crowded with students, market stalls and children playing, and is lined with some excellent cafés.

Santa Margherita and dragon

Key Sights

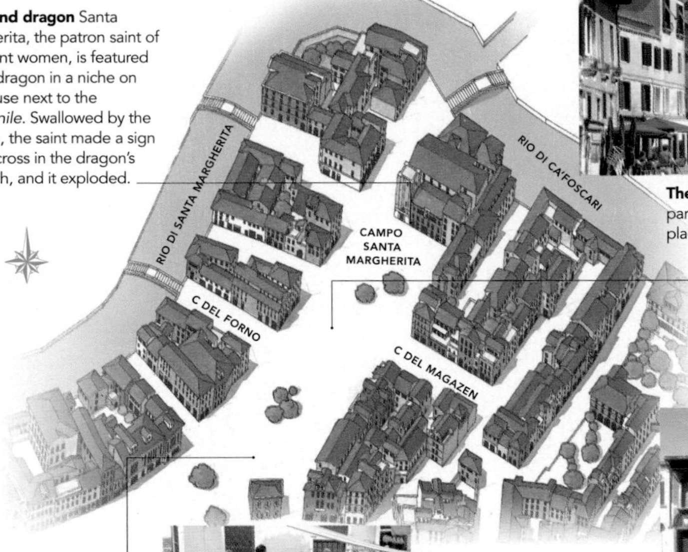

Saint and dragon Santa Margherita, the patron saint of pregnant women, is featured with a dragon in a niche on the house next to the *campanile*. Swallowed by the dragon, the saint made a sign of the cross in the dragon's stomach, and it exploded.

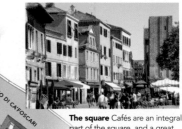

The square Cafés are an integral part of the square, and a great place for people-watching.

Fish scales An ancient stone in a kiosk prescribes the minimum size of fish sold in the *campo*: eels must be over 25 cm (10 in) long.

Architecture Byzantine mansions line the west of the *campo* at numbers 2961, 2962 and 2496, and there are Gothic palazzos at 2927–2935. The beautiful Palazzetto Foscolo-Corner is at 2931–33.

Mermaid fountain In the middle of the *campo* is a fountain with a mermaid carved on it. Perhaps a symbol of the square's fishmongers, it is a source of fresh drinking water.

Market fare Fish and vegetable markets grace the *campo* Monday to Saturday; on Saturdays there is plenty of bric-a-brac to browse.

Map labels: RIO DI SANTA MARGHERITA, RIO DI CA'FOSCARI, CAMPO SANTA MARGHERITA, C DEL FORNO, C DEL MAGAZEN

Letting off steam

A popular game in Campo Santa Margherita is *frullo*, which involves skipping over a rope with a ball on the end, attached to the ankle (ankle-skipping). The cafés around the *campo* attract students from the nearby university, and adults may wish to join them on the terraces of **Café Rosso** (*Campo Santa Margherita 2963, 30123*), while children can enjoy a delicious *gelato* from **GROM** (*2 minutes' walk away at Campo San Barnaba 2761, 30123*), in a *campo* famous for film shoots and greengrocers' barges.

Prices given are for a family of four

Eat and drink

Picnic: under €25; Snacks: €25–40; Real meal: €40–80; Family treat: €80 or more (based on a family of four)

PICNIC Pick up supplies from the Campo Santa Margherita market or the little supermarket and wine shop on the *campo*. **Barozzi Gianfranco & Co** (*Dorsoduro 3662, 30123; 041 522 5424*) bakery starts serving delicious freshly baked bread at 7am every day. Look out for the *ciabattini con olive* – small, crusty loaves studded with black olives. There is also a big **Billa** supermarket on the Fondamenta Zattere. Tuck into a feast on the *campo*: there are benches and even a few trees for shade.

SNACKS Pizza Al Volo (*Campo Santa Margherita 2944, Dorsoduro, 30123; 041 522 5430; open noon–1am*) serves excellent, huge, thin pizzas. They also come "*al taglio*" (by the slice) to take away.

REAL MEAL L'Osteria alla Bifora (*Campo Santa Margherita 2930, Dorsoduro 30123; 041 523 6119*) is a charming restaurant specializing in *cicchetti* (Venetian tapas) and plates of ham, salami and cheeses. There are also tables outside.

The Lowdown

🌐 **Address** Campo Santa Margherita, 30123 Dorsoduro

🚤 **Vaporetto** to Cà Rezzonico, then follow signs to Campo Santa Margherita

ℹ **Visitor information** Piazza San Marco 71f, San Marco, 30124; 041 529 7811; www.turismovenezia.it

👫 **Age range** All

⏲ **Allow** 1 hour

☕ **Café** Cafés ring the square.

🚻 **Toilets** In the cafés and bars

Good family value?
Without any heavyweight sights, the campo is a fun and inexpensive place for a bit of downtime in a fabulously authentic setting.

FAMILY TREAT Ristoteca Oniga (Campo San Barnaba 2852, 30123 Dorsoduro; 041 522 4410; www.oniga.it; closed Tue) is set in charming, rustic-style surroundings with an outdoor terrace. The seafood platters here are legendary, but there are plenty of options for carnivores too, including delectable duck. Leave room for the delicious home-made puddings.

Shopping

Venice's best mask shop has donned a different disguise and transformed itself into the Museo Mondonovo Maschere, now located near Vicenza, in the Veneto (Palazzo Corielli, Via Cardinal de Lai 2, 36034 Malo; www.mondonovomaschere.it). A good alternative is **La Bottega dei Mascareri**, 5 minutes' walk away (Calle dei Saoneri, San Polo 2720; 041 524 2887), which produces papier-mâché masks from casts.

Display of beautiful Venetian carnival masks for sale

Find out more

FILM Campo San Barnaba (see p64) was a location in Steven Spielberg's Indiana Jones and the Last Crusade (1989). It is the place where Indiana Jones sneaks out of the sewers after finding the secret catacombs, and the Ponte dei Pugni (see p64) is the bridge towards which Professor

Schneider and Indy walk. In the Bond film Casino Royale (2006), Vespa Lynd walks from the bridge to the campo and the Toletta bookshop.

Take cover

The **Peggy Guggenheim Collection** (see p66), 15 minutes' walk away, has a fabulous display of modern art. Every Sunday, from 3 to 4:30pm, children aged 4–10 can take part in a workshop and make art inspired by the collection.

Courtyard of the Peggy Guggenheim Collection with Giacometti sculpture

Next stop...

SQUERO DI SAN TROVASO
Walk to the waterfront, on the corner of Rio Trovaso and Rio Ognissanti, to see a picturesque gondola repair yard (Dorsoduro 1077, 30123). One of three traditional boatyards still surviving in Venice, this is the oldest, dating back to the 17th century.

Gondola repair workshops in Squero di San Trovaso

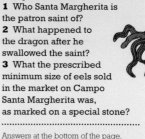

The Ponte dei Pugni, spanning the peaceful Rio San Barnaba

② Ponte dei Pugni

Fisticuffs on the bridge

Venice has several Ponti dei Pugni ("bridges of fists"), but this is the most famous. Until the 18th century it was the site of fights ("*pugni*" means clenched fists) between rival clans of Venetians – the Castellani, who wore red caps, and the Nicolotti, who donned black caps. From the Castello district on the west side and San Nicolò district on the east, respectively, the lads would wrestle each other bare-fisted into the water from the bridge during ritual, often bloody, fights. They were cheered on by baying crowds and frequently the competition would degenerate into a general battle. The brawls either finished with the winning side

dunking its opponents and taking possession of the bridge or were ended by the police, but not before bloodshed that left many casualties and even some dead. Formerly there were no balustrades and contenders hurled each other straight into the water. Fights on the bridge were finally banned in 1705 when gangs started using knives and it all became too violent, but four footprints embedded in the stonework on the crown of the bridge – marking the starting point for the fights – are reminders of those bloodthirsty days.

Letting off steam

Walk across the bridge to **Campo San Barnaba** to cool off with an ice cream from GROM (*Campo San Barnaba 2761, Dorsoduro 30123*), where children are spoiled for choice with a huge selection of mouthwatering flavours.

Boats and barges moored along picturesque Rio San Barnaba

③ Campo San Barnaba

Indiana Jones and the church of San Barnaba

The parish of San Barnaba, with its canalside square at the centre, was known in the 18th century as the home of impoverished Venetian patricians. They were attracted by the cheap rents and, while some relied on state support or begging, others worked in the state gambling house. Today the square and canal are quietly appealing. The delightful Rio San Barnaba is best viewed from the Ponte dei Pugni, near the floating barge crammed with crates of fruit and vegetables. The church here is unremarkable, apart from a Tiepolesque ceiling and a *Holy Family* attributed to Paolo Veronese. It was, however, famously used as a location for the 1989 film *Indiana Jones and the Last Crusade*. Fondamenta Gherardini runs beside the Rio San Barnaba, and is one of the prettiest canals in the area.

Letting off steam

Just a short walk from San Barnaba, over the Ponte dei Pugni, are the lovely little gardens at **Ca' Rezzonico** (*Fondamenta Rezzonico 3136*). There are stone benches for the weary, small lawns, some statues, a fountain with fish and tortoises, and a corner equipped as a playground.

The Lowdown

- 🌐 **Address** Ponte dei Pugni, 30123 Dorsoduro
- 🚤 **Vaporetto** to Ca' Rezzonico
- 👫 **Age range** Any
- ⏱ **Allow** 20 minutes
- ☕ **Eat and drink** *Snacks* Enoteca Ai Artisti (*Fondamenta della Toeletta 1169, 30123 Dorsoduro; 041 523 8944; www.enotecaartisti.com*) is a historic establishment which serves good light meals, including pasta and salads. *Real meal* Quattro Feri (*Calle Lunga San Barnaba 2754, 30123 Dorsoduro; 041 520 6978*), set in a narrow alley just off Campo San Barnaba, is a buzzing *osteria* serving traditional Venetian cuisine in an equally traditional, cosy setting.

The Lowdown

- 🌐 **Address** Campo San Barnaba, 30123 Dorsoduro
- 🚤 **Vaporetto** to Ca' Rezzonico
- 👫 **Age range** Any
- ⏱ **Allow** 20 minutes
- ☕ **Eat and drink** *Snacks* Il Caffè (*Campo San Toma 2963, 30123 Dorsoduro; 041 528 7998*), also known as Caffé Rosso because of its bright red interior, is a great spot for a snack and a drink in the area. *Real meal* Agli Alboretti (*Rio Terrá Antonio Foscarini 884, 30123 Dorsoduro; 041 523 0058*) is a hotel restaurant offering a warm welcome in winter and outdoor dining in summer. Serves great speciality risotto.

The Tempest by Giorgione, Gallerie dell'Accademia

④ Gallerie dell'Accademia

Venetian red and blue lapis lazuli

The city's most precious artworks from the 14th to the 18th centuries are displayed here, including masterpieces by Canaletto, Tintoretto, Veronese, Giorgione, Bellini and Mantegna. The order of the collection is more or less chronological, with the exception of the final rooms, which take visitors back to the Renaissance.

The gallery houses the largest collection of Venetian art in existence, and the basis of the collection was the Accademia di Belle Arti, founded in 1780 by the painter Giovanni Battista Piazzetta. In 1807 Napoleon moved the academy to these premises, and the collection was greatly enlarged by works of art from the churches and monasteries he suppressed. Housed in three former religious buildings, the gallery is naturally lit, so try to visit on a bright day.

If there is one thing that distinguishes Venetian painting, it is the vibrant colours. It is no coincidence that the city was long the centre of Europe's pigment trade – this was the place to buy blue lapis lazuli, imported from Afghanistan and prominent in the works of Titian and Bellini. The famous Venetian red, a pigment extracted from the iron-oxide-rich countryside of the Veneto, is characteristic of 15th-century Venetian painting.

Letting off steam

Campo Santo Stefano, near the Accademia bridge, is the closest open space for a run around in this area. It has nice cafés too.

The Lowdown

🌐 **Address** Campo della Carità, Dorsoduro 1050, 30125; 041 520 0345; www.gallerieaccademia.org

🚤 **Vaporetto** 1 or 2 to Accademia

🕐 **Open** 8:15am–2pm Mon; 8:15am–7:15pm Tue–Sun

💶 **Price** Family €13–19.50, adult €6.50, EU citizens aged 18–25 €3.25, under-18s free

👫 **Skipping the queue** Book in advance by phone or online (€1 booking fee).

👨‍👩‍👧 **Age range** 8 plus

⏱ **Allow** 45 minutes to see carefully selected highlights

♿ **Wheelchair access** Difficult: there are steps to the entrance and stairs to the first-floor gallery; call 041 522 2247 to use stairlift.

🍽 **Eat and drink** Snacks Gelateria Nico (Fondamenta Zattere, Dorsoduro 922, 30123; 041 522 5293; www.gelaterianico.com) is famous for its home-made ice creams and boasts great views of the Giudecca island. *Real meal* Trattoria Borghi (San Basilio 1516, Dorsoduro, 30123; 041 521 0028; open Tue–Sat) offers a friendly welcome in a family-run inn popular with locals. Venetian specialities include liver, grilled fish and spaghetti with seafood.

⑤ Peggy Guggenheim Collection

Lions, dogs and amazing modern art

Named after the American art collector and millionairess who lived here in the Palazzo Venier dei Leoni until 1979, the collection showcases modern art and is a treasure trove of the European avant-garde. The quirky 18th-century palazzo was built for the Veniers, among the oldest Venetian dynasties, and its nickname "*dei leoni*" (meaning "of the lions") comes from the Veniers' habit of keeping a pet lion chained in the courtyard. Peggy herself is buried in the delightful grounds overlooking the Grand Canal, alongside her 14 dogs, which she called "my beloved babies".

Sculptures great and small adorn the garden, including Alexander Calder's *Three-Coloured Dog* (1973). An entire room is devoted to Peggy's own discovery, American Abstract Expressionist Jackson Pollock; and Max Ernst, her second husband, is also well represented. Other artists featured include Picasso, Kandinsky, Klee, Mondrian, Magritte and Moore.

Letting off steam

There is a bit of space to run around in the museum gardens, or head down to the **Zattere**, the long promenade facing the Giudecca island – the Venetians' favourite walk – with spectacular views.

The Lowdown

- 🌐 **Address** Calle San Cristoforo, Dorsoduro 701, 30123; 041 240 5411; www.guggenheim-venice.it
- 🚤 **Vaporetto** 1 or 2 to Accademia or Salute
- 🕐 **Open** 10am–6pm Wed–Mon
- 💲 **Price** €24–38; under-10s free
- 🚹 **Skipping the queue** Buy tickets in advance online or by phone
- 🎧 **Guided tours** Audioguides in English and Italian €7
- 👫 **Activities** Kids' workshops 3–4:30pm Sun (*see p63*)
- 🚻 **Age range** 5 plus

- 🕐 **Allow** 1 hour
- ♿ **Wheelchair access** Partial, with a wheelchair lift to the entrance; for information call 041 240 5440.
- ☕ **Eat and drink** *Snacks* Excellent museum café and restaurant overlooking the sculpture garden (*041 522 8688*), with good-value children's menus. *Real meal* La Rivista (*Dorsoduro 979a, 30123; 041 240 1425*), behind the Accademia, is a good wine and cheese bar, which also serves hams and salami, in a designer setting.

Yoko Ono's Wish Tree, Peggy Guggenheim Collection

⑥ I Gesuati

Cardinal virtues and optical illusions

Dedicated to Santa Maria del Rosario, this church is a lovely example of 18th-century Venetian architecture was the work of Giorgio Massari in 1724–36. On the façade, look for the statues representing the four cardinal virtues: *Prudence*, *Justice*, *Strength* and *Temperance*. The interior is harmonious and graceful, with works created by the greatest masters of Venetian 18th-century art. In the first altar on the right there are splendid paintings by Giambattista Tiepolo (1696–1770) in their original setting: look for the magnificent altarpiece of the *Madonna* (1749). Also by Tiepolo are ceiling frescoes showing the *Feast of the Rosary* (1739), surrounded by medallions that appear to be carved stucco but are in fact a painted optical illusion. Mirrors reflect the ceiling for ease of viewing. The oldest painting in the church is Tintoretto's *Crucifixion* (1560), remarkable for the richness of its colour.

Letting off steam

I Gesuati fronts onto the **Zattere** (*see previous entry*), the best place for a walk in this part of Venice.

The Lowdown

- 🌐 **Address** Fondamenta delle Zattere ai Gesuati, Dorsoduro, 30123
- 🚤 **Vaporetto** Zattere
- 🕐 **Open** 10am–5pm Mon–Sat, from 1pm Sun
- 💲 **Price** €6–12, under-10s free; Chorus Pass: entry to I Gesuati and 15 other churches for 1 year €20 (www.chorusvenezia.org)
- 🚻 **Age range** 8 plus
- 🕐 **Allow** 30 minutes
- ☕ **Eat and drink** *Snacks* Bar da Gino (*San Vio, Dorsoduro 853a, 30123; 041 528 5276; closed Sun*) has a nice terrace and serves *cicchetti* and sandwiches. *Real meal* Antica Osteria al Pantalon (*Dorsoduro 3958, 30123; 041 710 849; www.osteriaalpantalon. it*) prides itself on its friendly service and typical fish dishes.

The pretty gardens of the Peggy Guggenheim Collection, full of sculptures

Prices given are for a family of four

and Titian's altarpiece (1511–12) with the martyred St Sebastian shot through with arrows.

Letting off steam
Picnic on the dramatic flight of steps leading up to La Salute or play in the open space at Punta della Dogana, in front of the church.

The Lowdown

🌐 **Address** Campo della Salute, Dorsoduro, 30123

🚤 **Vaporetto** to Salute or **traghetto** from Santa Maria del Giglio on the far bank of the Grand Canal

🕐 **Open** 9am–noon and 3–5:30pm

👫 **Age range** 8 plus for the plague history and views

⏱ **Allow** 30 minutes

☕ **Eat and drink** *Snacks* Al Chioschetto *(by the Capitaneria di Porto, Fondamenta Zattere, Dorsoduro, 30123)*, a kiosk-bar on the waterfront, serves good snack lunches. *Real meal* Linea d'Ombra *(Ponte dell'Umiltà, Fondamenta Zattere, Dorsoduro, 30123; 041 241 1881; www.ristorantelineadombra.com; closed Tue)* is a wine bar and restaurant with a floating terrace (fenced), which serves fish and Venetian classics with an innovative twist.

🎉 **Festivals** Festa della Madonna della Salute – thanksgiving for the city's deliverance from plague, with a procession on pontoons across the Grand Canal and gondoliers bringing their oars to be blessed by a priest on the steps of the church: 21 Nov.

People strolling along the Zattere, beside I Gesuati church

⑦ Santa Maria della Salute
Plague church

Built by the people of Venice in gratitude for being saved from the plague of 1630 (*"salute"* means health and salvation), this imposing Baroque church stands guard at the end of the Grand Canal – writer Henry James likened it to "some great lady on the threshold of her salon". Architect Baldassare Longhena spent half a century working on the monumental building, dying five years before the job was completed in 1687. The majestic dome, built in the shape of a crown, dominates the Venetian skyline. In the dark octagonal interior look out for Jacopo Tintoretto's *Wedding at Cana* (1551)

The great Baroque church of Santa Maria della Salute

KIDS' CORNER

Spot the painting
See if you can spot the following examples of different modern art movements in the Peggy Guggenheim Collection:
1 Cubism: Pablo Picasso's *The Poet* (1911) and Georges Braque's *The Clarinet* (1912), both of which use cubes, cones and cylinders to show all sides of an object at once.
2 Surrealism: Max Ernst's *The Forest* (1927–8), made by rubbing and scraping paint until an image appeared, and René Magritte's *Empire of Light* (1953–4), a bizarre night-time scene with a daylit sky.

SPLAT!
American artist Jackson Pollock developed the "action painting" technique, which involved pouring, dripping and splattering gloss paint on huge floor-sized canvases.

Spot the painting (cont)
3 European Abstraction: Wassily Kandinsky's *White Cross* (1922), composed of geometric elements, and Piet Mondrian's *Composition No 1* (1938), a grid of black lines and red squares.
4 Abstract Expressionism: Willem de Kooning's *Untitled* (1958) uses "free expression" to create an abstract urban landscape of light and colour.

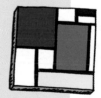

Arsenale and the Lagoon Islands

The Arsenale was the great shipyard of Venice, and it's a good place for setting out on a short lagoon voyage. To set the scene, it is well worth visiting the Museo Storico Navale to learn how Venice ruled the waves in the name of trade. A *vaporetto* to the Lido will give everyone a feeling for fin-de-siècle luxury and lassitude. And from here, it is a pleasant trip across the lagoon to quiet but colourful Burano, followed by a visit to Murano, which bustles with activity revolving around its time-honoured prowess in glass-blowing.

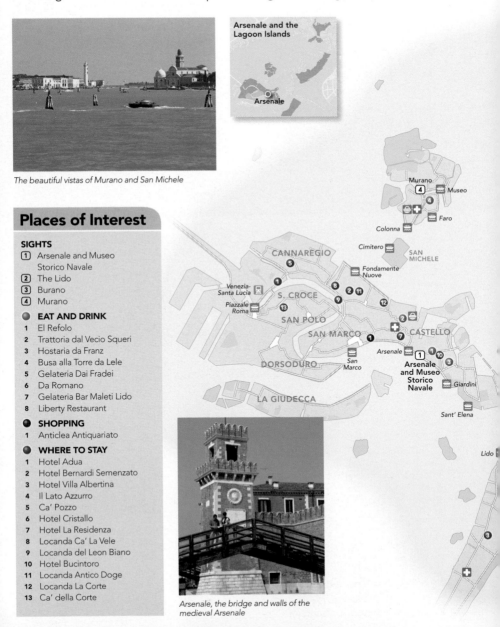

Arsenale and the Lagoon Islands

The beautiful vistas of Murano and San Michele

Places of Interest

SIGHTS
1. Arsenale and Museo Storico Navale
2. The Lido
3. Burano
4. Murano

EAT AND DRINK
1. El Refolo
2. Trattoria dal Vecio Squeri
3. Hostaria da Franz
4. Busa alla Torre da Lele
5. Gelateria Dai Fradei
6. Da Romano
7. Gelateria Bar Maleti Lido
8. Liberty Restaurant

SHOPPING
1. Anticlea Antiquariato

WHERE TO STAY
1. Hotel Adua
2. Hotel Bernardi Semenzato
3. Hotel Villa Albertina
4. Il Lato Azzurro
5. Ca' Pozzo
6. Hotel Cristallo
7. Hotel La Residenza
8. Locanda Ca' La Vele
9. Locanda del Leon Biano
10. Hotel Bucintoro
11. Locanda Antico Doge
12. Locanda La Corte
13. Ca' della Corte

Arsenale, the bridge and walls of the medieval Arsenale

0 kilometre   1

0 mile   1

TORCELLO
Torcello

Mazzorbo
MAZZORBO

Burano
Burano
③
⑤ ⑥

Punta Vela

Chiesa

SANT'
ERASMO

Capannone

④

VIGNOLE

LIDO
⑦
⑧
②
Lido

Colourful canalside buildings and boats in Burano

Glass-blowing in Murano

The idyllic setting of the Lido canal, perfect for a stroll

The Lowdown

🚃 **Train** to Santa Lucia station, then 50 mins on foot. **Vaporetto** (waterbus) to Arsenale: 1, 52; from Arsenale to the Lido 1; Murano: 41, 42; from the Lido to Burano, then Murano: LN Line

🛒 **Supermarkets** None in the Arsenale district. Closest is New Venice Come, Castello 3199. There are Incoop stores on the Lido, including one at Via Doge Domenico Michiel 16. On Murano there is an Incoop at Fondamenta Riva Longa 27; plus Despar on Fondamenta dei Vetrai.

🎌 **Festivals** Carnival: Feb–Mar. Patron saint San Marco: 25 April. Festa della Sensa (Ascension Day): mid-May. Festa del Redentore: 3rd Sun in Jul. Regata Storica: 1st Sun in Sep. The Arsenale itself is only open to the public for special events and exhibitions, often as part of the art Biennale: late summer–autumn. The Venice Film Festival occupies the Lido for ten days: late Aug and early Sep.

➕ **Pharmacies** No pharmacy in the Arsenale district. The closest is Farmacia Croce di Malta, Castello 3470; 041 2411 262. On the Lido: Farmacia Baldassirotto, Viale S. Maria Elisabetta 55/a; 041 5260 117; plus three in the Via Gallo Sandro. On Murano: Farmacia Comunale, Fondamenta dei Vetrai 139; 041 739 046

① Arsenale and Museo Storico Navale
Lions, galleys and gondolas

This area symbolizes Venetian maritime might, with impressive docks and warehouses guarded by crenellated brick towers, fortifications, Baroque statues and great stone lions. Founded in 1104, the Arsenale became Europe's largest medieval shipyard, employing 16,000 people at its height and making Venice the leading maritime power in the Mediterranean. The Naval History Museum is crammed full of model ships and naval artifacts, among them the Doge's ceremonial barge, gondolas and lagoon boats.

Gilded detail of the Bucintoro

Key Features

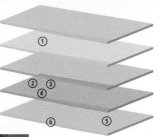

■ **Fourth floor**
Shell collection and Swedish room, with models of Viking ships and polar expeditions

■ **Third floor**
Gondolas, Venetian lagoon boats and marine ex-votos of the 16th to 19th centuries

■ **Second floor**
Displays on the Italian Unification Navy (1859–70), and naval uniforms and flags

■ **First floor**
Models of the Bucintoro, *Galeazza* and square-sailed sailing ships of the 1660s

■ **Ground floor**
History of ships, starting with the Egyptians, Phoenicians, Etruscans and Romans

① **Historic gondolas**
The display of historic gondolas includes heiress Peggy Guggenheim's private vessel. The art collector made a splash as she rode down the Grand Canal with her little dogs. Antique ceremonial gondolas are also on show (*see left*).

② **Square riggers**
A whole room is dedicated to models of the square-sailed ships that developed after 1660. One of the biggest, with 64 cannons, was created for Napoleon, but by the time it was launched in 1815 he had been sent into exile.

③ **Bucintoro**
The Doge's ceremonial barge, the Bucintoro, resembled a gilded dragon, with the winged lion of St Mark on the prow. Napoleon destroyed the last one in 1797, but the museum has a scale model.

④ **Three-masted galley**
A model of a three-masted galley, of the type used as a warship by the victorious Holy League fleet against the Ottoman Turks at the Battle of Lepanto (1571), is shown with captured Turkish standards.

⑤ **Stern lanterns**
Just inside the main entrance is a marvellous collection of *fanali di poppa*, the stern lanterns used to light 16th-century Venetian galleys at night.

Arsenale
The lion of St Mark holding a closed book (symbolizing war) stands over the gate of the Arsenale, enclosed by 3 km (2 miles) of walls and crenellated towers. Two stone lions and a smaller pair on the right, dating from the 6th century BC, guard the entrance. The Museo Storico Navale is right next door.

The Lowdown

🌐 **Address** Museo Storico Navale, Riva San Biasio, Castello 2148, 30122; 041 520 0276; www.marina.difesa.it/storiacultura/ufficiostorico/musei/museo storicove/Pagine/default.aspx

🚤 **Vaporetto** to Arsenale, Giardini

ℹ **Visitor information** San Marco 71/f, 30124; 041 529 8711; www.turismovenezia.it

🕐 **Open** Museo Storico Navale: 8:45am–1pm Mon–Sat

€ **Price** Museo Storico Navale: €6–12; under-10s free

👥 **Skipping the queue** Queues unlikely; Venice Card discount

👫 **Age range** 5 plus

⏱ **Allow** 1 hour

♿ **Wheelchair access** No

☕ **Café** In nearby Via Garibaldi

🚻 **Toilets** In the museum

🏷 **Shop** Postcards and guidebooks

Good family value?
It is cheap to get in and there is stacks to see, but most families will be satisfied with a few highlights.

⑥ **Entrance**
The museum is housed in old grain warehouses, its entrance flanked by two massive anchors seized by the Italian Navy from Austrian battleships in World War I.

Letting off steam

Via Garibaldi was once a canal. Now filled in, it is the widest street in Venice, lined with cafés and cake shops and good for a stroll. Nearby are the **Giardini Pubblici**, or Giardini della Biennale, where the Art Biennale, a major international contemporary art show, is held every other year. The gardens, dotted with designer pavilions, are a pleasant place to roam and picnic year-round.

The lush green Giardini Pubblici, also known as the Giardini della Biennale

Eat and drink

Picnic: under €25; Snacks: €25–40, Real meal: €40–80; Family treat: €80 or more (based on a family of four)

PICNIC Stock up at one of the shops on Via Garibaldi or pick up produce at the floating market at the eastern end of Rio di Sant'Anna, which sells mainly vegetables and fruit. Feast in the Giardini Pubblici.
SNACKS El Refolo *(Via Garibaldi, Castello 1580; 32110)* is a little hole-in-the-wall café-bar with good filled rolls and sandwiches and a varied selection of pasta dishes and delicious salads.

Cafés with outdoor seating and shops along broad Via Garibaldi

REAL MEAL Trattoria dal Vecio Squeri *(Castello 6533, 32110; 041 520 8379; www.dalveciosqueri.com; closed Sun)*, near the Giardini Pubblici, is a historic Venetian inn with a cosy atmosphere. Dishes include *sarde in saor* (sweet and sour sardines) and excellent pasta.

FAMILY TREAT Hostaria da Franz *(Fondamenta San Giuseppe 754, Castello, 30122; 041 522 0861; www.hostariadafranz.com)* is also close to the Giardini Pubblici. Set in a former rope-making shop, the canalside *trattoria* was opened in 1842 by an Austrian soldier who fell for a Venetian girl, and boasts a star-studded clientele. The fish and seafood menu combines Venetian tradition with creative twists.

Shopping

Anticlea Antiquariato *(Calle San Provolo, Castello 4719/a)* is a little treasure trove of antique glass beads, earrings, necklaces and hat pins.

Find out more

DIGITAL Visit *www.cogandgalleyships.com* to look at different kinds of ships or go to *explorethemed.com/Venice.asp?c=1* to see maps of Venice's maritime republic from the Middle Ages until the 16th century.

Next stop...

SCUOLA DI SAN GIORGIO DEGLI SCHIAVONI It is a 10-minute walk from the Arsenale to the old guild-hall of St George *(Calle dei Furlani 3259/a, Castello, 30122; 041 522 8828; open Tue–Sat, and Sun am; €16)*. Entering it is like stepping into a jewel box: the ground floor was decorated by Venetian painter Vittore Carpaccio with paintings of *St George and the Dragon* (1502–1507). Look for the knight in shining armour slaying the monster.

Scuola di San Giorgio degli Schiavoni, home to a fresco cycle by Carpaccio

Façade of the Museo del Vetro (glass museum), on Murano

② The Lido
Sun, sand and the world's first lido

Only 15 minutes by boat from Venice, the Lido (pronounced "Leedo") is another world, busy with cars and big department stores. For centuries it was little more than a sandbar that protected Venice. In 1818 English Romantic poets Percy Bysshe Shelley and Lord Byron put their horses through their paces along the empty sands. Then in 1857 the first "bathing facility" was set up – a wooden platform on stilts. Soon wooden huts popped up all over the Lido, used as family retreats for changing, eating and playing. By the end of the 19th century the name Lido had become a byword for a beach resort and its fame spread worldwide. The Lungomare (seaside promenade) on the Adriatic Sea side has several elegant hotels, including the Hôtel des Bains, the setting for German writer Thomas Mann's lugubrious novel *Death in Venice* (1912). Nearby are the neo-Moorish Hotel

Excelsior and the 1930s Palazzo del Cinema, the main location of the Venice Film Festival.

Letting off steam
Get to know the Lido by pedalling around on a bike from **Venice Bike Rental** (*Gran Viale 79a; www.venicebike rental.com; open Mar–Oct, closed in bad weather*). All sizes of bike are available. If it rains, take cover in the historic deli, bakery and pastry shop **Rizzo Pane** (*Gran Viale 16; 041 5260 0011*).

The Lowdown

- **Address** 30126 Lido di Venezia
- **Vaporetto** 1, from any stop along the Grand Canal; 51 or 52, from Piazzale Roma; 61 or 62, from the Zattere; or N, from San Zaccaria. **Car ferry** 17 (from Tronchetto)
- **i Visitor information** Gran Viale 69, Lido di Venezia, 30126; 041 529 8711; open Jun–Sep only
- **Age range** All
- **Activities** Rent a bike from Venice Bike Rental (*see above*).
- **Allow** Half a day
- **Eat and drink** *Snacks* Gelateria Bar Maleti Lido (*Gran Viale 47, 30126 Lido di Venezia; 041 526 9273*), just by the jetty, is a good spot for snacks and ice creams. *Real meal* Liberty Restaurant (*Hôtel des Bains, Via Lungomare Marconi 17, 30126 Lido di Venezia; 041 526 5921*) is worth a visit for the Art Deco setting of this famous hotel alone.
- **Festivals** Venice Film Festival (*www.labiennale.org*): 10 days in early Sep

③ Burano
Colourful lace-making island

Tiny Burano is one of the most photogenic of the lagoon islands, with the vibrant blues, pinks, reds, yellows, lilacs and greens of the little houses reflected in the narrow canals. It is said that the fishermen's wives painted their houses in different colours so that the men could instantly recognize their homes from out at sea; nowadays paint colours have to be approved by the authorities. Look out for the tower of San Martino, its alarmingly tilted *campanile* adding charm to the scene.

There is a strong tradition of lace-making on the island dating back to the 15th century. The **Museo del Merletto** (Lace Museum) displays historic lace designs. Most of the lace for sale in the *calli* (alleys) is imported from China – real Burano lace is as light and delicate as tulle, and also very expensive, as it can take ten women up to three years to produce a single tablecloth.

Letting off steam
There is not a lot of space on Burano, so hop on *vaporetto* T to neighbouring **Torcello** instead: its overgrown paths and lost canals are charming to wander.

The Lowdown

- **Address** 30142 Burano; Museo del Merletto: Piazza Galuppi 187, 30012 Burano; www.museiciveveneziani.it
- **Vaporetto** 12, 14 or LN (Laguna Nord) from Fondamente Nuove, or DM to Murano Faro then 12, 14
- **Open** Museo del Merletto: 10am–6pm Tue–Sun (until 5pm Nov–Mar)
- **Price** Museo del Merletto: €10–17, under-6s free
- **Age range** 8 plus
- **Allow** Half a day
- **Eat and drink** *Snacks* Gelateria Dai Fradei (*Via Galuppi 380, 30012 Burano; 041 735 630*) is a good stop for ice cream or the local biscuits, *bussolai buranelli*. *Real meal* Da Romano (*Via San Martino, 30142 Burano; 041 730 030; www.daromano.it*) is hung with paintings and has a terrace. Fish and seafood are specialities.
- **Festivals** Regata di Burano: third Sun in Sep

Sun-worshippers on the Lido, Venice's famous seaside resort

Prices given are for a family of four

Brightly painted houses in a canalside street in Burano

④ Murano
Island of glass

The famous glass-making island of Murano is like a miniature Venice, less than 2 km (1 mile) across, with canals, bridges, handsome houses and even a scaled-down Grand Canal. The art of glass-making came to medieval Venice from the Orient, but the wooden city around Rivo Alto (modern Rialto) and Dorsoduro was at huge risk from fires, and in 1291 the Venetian Republic ordered

glass-makers and their furnaces to move to Murano. The Murano glass-blowers were the only craftsmen in Europe who knew how to make mirrors, multi-coloured and enamelled glass, and historically the island owes its prosperity entirely to the Industry.

Murano is still the best place to watch glass-blowing and buy Venetian glass beads, but beware of counterfeit glass and always look for the trademark – a heart with Vetro Murano Artistico emblazoned upon it.

Take cover
The **Museo del Vetro** (Glass Museum), in the Palazzo Giustinian near the Museo *vaporetto* stop, tells the story of Venetian glass-blowing – children will be fascinated to see how objects are made here. It also displays a collection of antique glass pieces.

Pretty glass beads made at a glass foundry in Murano

The Lowdown

🌐 **Address** 37121 Murano; Museo del Vetro: Fondamenta Giustinian 8, 30121 Murano; *www. muselcivicivenezlani.it*

🚤 **Vaporetto** 41, 42 or DM (Diretto Murano) from Fondamente Nuove to Museo, Navagero, Colonna or Faro

ℹ️ **Visitor information** Promovetro, Calle Marco da Murano 4, 30141 Murano; 041 527 5074; *www.promovetro.com*

🕐 **Open** Museo del Vetro: daily 10am–6pm Apr–Oct, 10am–5pm Nov–Mar

ⓒ **Price** €13–21; under-6s free

🚹 **Age range** 8 plus

⏱️ **Allow** 2 hours

🍴 **Eat and drink** *Picnic* Pick up a picnic at the Incoop supermarket *(Fondamenta Riva Longa 27, 30100 Murano)* near the Glass Museum and eat it in Murano's public garden, Parco Navaghero. *Real Meal* Busa alla Torre da Lele *(Campo Santo Stefano 3, 30100 Murano; 041 739 662; lunch only)* is a pleasant rustic *trattoria* set in a tree-shaded square, renowned well beyond the lagoon for its fish dishes and friendly service.

🎪 **Festivals** Regata di Murano: Jul

Where to Stay in Venice

Accommodation in Venice is notoriously expensive. The unique location means that hotel prices can be about 30 per cent higher than on the mainland. A room with a view will always cost more. Try to book early, check website offers, and shop around.

AGENCY

Bianco Holidays
San Polo 3101, 31025; 345 294 8255; www.apartmentinvenice.it
This Venetian agency offers apartments within the city's historic centre. The smallest have one bedroom and, unlike other apartment agencies, which often require a one-week minimum stay, accommodation can be booked per night.

San Marco and Rialto

HOTELS

Ateneo
Calle Minelli, San Marco 3673, 30124; 041 520 0777; www.ateneo.it
Very close to La Fenice opera house, this hotel is set in a small courtyard overlooking the *canal dei barcaioli*, reserved for gondolas. Rooms, on four floors, are furnished in classic Venetian style. Standard rooms are very small.
✳   €€

Casa Querini
Campo San Giovanni Novo, Castello 4388, 30122; 041 241 1294; www. locandaquerini.com
A warm welcome awaits in this family-run inn set in a 16th-century palazzo only 5 minutes' walk from Piazza San Marco. The rooms are comfortable and spacious, with Venetian-style furnishings.
𝄞   €€

Antica Locanda Sturion
Calle del Sturion, San Polo 679, 30125; 041 523 6243; www. locandasturion.com
This family-friendly hotel oozes opulence. Once home to merchants, ambassadors and navigators, it is depicted in Carpaccio's *Miracle of the Cross* (1494) in the Accademia. Check website for frequent special offers, including quads at the triple-room rate.
⇆ 🍴 ✳ 🍽   €€€

Hotel Flora
Via XXII Marzo/Calle Bergamaschi, San Marco 22283/a, 30124; 041 520 5844; www.hotelflora.it
Tucked behind Piazza San Marco, this charming family-run hotel, housed in a 17th-century palazzo, is also exceptionally family-friendly. It has elegant period furniture, Murano glass chandeliers, fine fabrics and oriental carpets, as well as a beautiful, large courtyard garden for breakfast and play. There are several family rooms, and the first child under 12 stays free in the parents' room. Children's tea is included. Check the website for frequent special offers.
⇆ 🅿 🍴 🍽 ⛶   €€€

One of the comfortable, spacious rooms at Casa Querini, near Piazza San Marco

Locanda Fiorita
Campiello Novo, San Marco 3457, 30124; 041 523 4754; www.locandafiorita.com
Set a in rosy-red palazzo draped with wisteria, this charming, popular hotel is just off Campo Santo Stefano. It has exposed beams, is decorated with Venetian flair and benefits from a great children's play area on the square that it overlooks. There are additional rooms in nearby annexes.
🅿 🍴 𝄞 ✳   €€€

Campo Santa Margherita and around

HOTELS

Ai Carmini
Fondamenta del Soccorso 2604, Dorsoduro, 30123; 041 099 0213; www.venere.com
A serviced apartment-hotel set on a canal 5 minutes' walk from the Accademia. The lobby is typically Venetian, the rooms are spacious and functional, but the great bonus is the central, canalside location.
⇆ 🍴 ✳ 🍽   €€

Antica Locanda Montin
Fondamenta di Borgo, Dorsoduro 1147, 30125; 041 522 7151; www.locandamontin.com
Close to the Accademia, this is a cosy Venetian inn with a well-loved adjoining restaurant. Rooms tend to be on the small side, and only a few have private bathrooms, but the hotel is full of atmosphere, and has its own terrace.
🅿 ✳ 🍽   €€€

Locanda San Barnaba
Calle del Traghetto 2785–6, Dorsoduro, 30123; 041 241 1233; www.locanda-sanbarnaba.com
This 16th-century frescoed palazzo close to Ca' Rezzonico, is run by its ancestral owner. The very pleasant

The elegant exterior of the Locanda Fiorita hotel

bedrooms are decorated in elegant, traditional Venetian style; some are frescoed. Junior suites for families.

€€€

B&Bs

De Zorzi

Fondamenta San Giacomo, Giudecca 197, 30100; 041 528 6380

An apartment and rooms in a family-run B&B with a terrace, garden, sun room and sitting room for guests, on the quiet island of Giudecca, a 5-minute ferry ride from Piazza San Marco. Formerly part of an ancient church, De Zorzi has great views across the Bacino di San Marco to Venice proper.

€

Ca' San Trovaso

Fondamenta delle Eremite, Dorsoduro 1350–51, 30123; 041 277 1146; www.casantrovaso.com

Set on a quiet canal, this small, unpretentious B&B is only a short walk from the Peggy Guggenheim Museum, the Accademia and La Salute. Damask wallpaper decorates the terracotta-floored rooms, and the bathrooms are reasonably sized. There is a roof terrace, but no television or phone.

€€

Arsenale, Lagoon Islands and beyond

HOTELS

Hotel Adua

Lista di Spagna, Cannaregio 233, 30121; 041 716 184; www.aduahotel.com

Very convenient for Santa Lucia train station, and set among many shops and restaurants, the Adua dates from the 17th century and has traditional charm, blended with modernity. This small hotel also has a delightful terrace, but not all rooms have en-suite bathroom.

€

Hotel Bernardi Semenzato

Calle de l'Oca 4363–66, Cannaregio, 30121; 041 522 7257; www.hotelbernardi.com

A very good-value hotel close to the Rialto Bridge, with attractive hand-painted Venetian furnishings, tapestries and exposed beams; the overall effect is bright and clean. The nearby annexe's rooms are more spacious, some with views over the Canal Grande. Quad rooms are available with or without bathroom. Family-run, the hotel positively welcomes children.

€

Hotel Villa Albertina

Via Vallaresso 1/a, Venice Lido, 30126; 041 526 0879; www.villalbertina.com

A pretty ochre-coloured villa on the Lido di Venezia, close to the Palazzo dei Congressi (where the Venice Film Festival takes place) and the beach. This family-run hotel has a cosy lounge and comfortable, sunny rooms, as well as a pretty garden. Only 20 minutes by boat to Piazza San Marco. Mountain bikes for hire.

P €

Il Lato Azzurro

Via Forti 13, Isola di Sant'Erasmo, 30141; 041 523 0642; www.latoazzurro.it

A simple, sporty hotel on Venice's market garden island, Sant'Erasmo, with good-value rooms that are clean and functional and vary in size. A good restaurant serves only local produce. There is a beach nearby, and bicycles and kayaks are available for hire. Popular with families. Ferries to central Venice.

€

Ca' Pozzo

Sottopergo Ca' Pozzo, Cannaregio 1279; 30123; 041 524 0504; www.capozzoinn.com

This small boutique hotel in the Old Ghetto area is designed in modern, minimalist style with plenty of pastel hues, marble-effect walls, exposed beams and contemporary art. There is a charming internal courtyard for breakfast in summer, and kosher breakfasts are available for guests year-round. A short walk from Piazzale Roma and the Ponte delle Guglie *vaporetto* stop on the Grand Canal, for San Marco and the rest of Venice.

€€

The breakfast room of minimalist Ca' Pozzo in the Old Ghetto district

Hotel Cristallo

Gran Viale Santa Maria Elisabetta 51, Venice Lido, 30126; 041 526 5293; www.cristallovenezia.com

A pink, Renaissance-style property offering good-value accommodation on the Lido. Large rooms and inter-connecting family rooms are available, and there is also a small garden where guests can enjoy breakfast alfresco in summer. There are bathing huts for guests on the private beach.

€€

Hotel La Residenza

Campo Bandiera e Moro, Castello 3608, 30122; 041 528 5315; www.venicelaresidenza.com

Gothic palazzo on a quiet campo very close to the Arsenale and San Marco. Some rooms are ornately stuccoed and hung with Venetian drapes and damask, while others have been refurbished in a lighter, more modern style. Some family rooms are available.

€€

Locanda Ca' Le Vele

Ca' Le Vele, Cannaregio 3969, 30121; 041 241 3960; www.locandalevele.com

Overlooking the Santa Sofia Canal and the old sailmakers' street, 5 minutes' walk from the Rialto Bridge and close to Ca' d'Oro, this little inn is run by two brothers and has a welcoming atmosphere. The traditional Venetian charm of damasks, marble and Murano glass chandeliers is matched by every modern comfort. Quadruple rooms, useful for large families or families travelling together, are available.

€€

Price Guide

The following price ranges are based on one night's accommodation in high season for a family of four, inclusive of service charges and any additional taxes.

€ Under €200 **€€** €200–350 **€€€** over €350

Key to symbols *see back cover flap*

Locanda del Leon Bianco

Corte Leon Bianco, Cannaregio 5629, 30131; 041 523 3572; www.leonbianco.it;

Tucked away in an inner courtyard, this unpretentious but atmospheric hotel in a 13th-century palazzo overlooks the Grand Canal between Ca' d'Oro and the Rialto Bridge. Some rooms have ornate mahogany and Murano chandeliers, others are less opulent. During high season stays of more than one night are compulsory. Cots on request.

€€

Hotel Bucintoro

Riva degli Schiavoni, Castello 2135/a, 30122; 041 528 990; www.hotelbucintoro.com

This popular, family-run hotel prides itself on the stunning views from all the bedrooms, especially from the top floors. Rooms look out directly onto the Molo di San Marco, with sweeping vistas across the lagoon to San Giorgio. It is a short walk from here to both Piazza San Marco and the attractions of the Arsenale area. Suites for three people and inter-connecting rooms for four are available.

€€€

Locanda Antico Doge

Campo Santi Apostoli, Cannaregio 5643, 30131; 041 241 1570; www.anticodoge.com

Set on a busy but pleasant square, this elegant hotel is located in a palazzo that once belonged to the 14th-century Doge Marin Falier. The bedrooms are richly decorated with silk, brocade, damask, and gilt mirrors, and almost all have views of the Canal Grande. The breakfast room is equally grand.

€€€

Locanda La Corte

Calle Bressana, Castello 6317, 30122; 041 241 1300; www.locandalacorte.it

A small Gothic palazzo set off Campo Santi Giovanni e Paolo, a short walk from San Marco and the Rialto Bridge, this hotel is decorated in a muted version of traditional Venetian style. Bedrooms, in three separate buildings, overlook either a charming inner courtyard or the canal. Breakfast is served in the courtyard in summer.

€€€

The elegant Locanda Antico Doge, former residence of a notorious doge

SELF-CATERING
Ca' della Corte

Corte Surian, 3560 Dorsoduro; 30123; 041 715 877; www. cadellacorte.com

Close to the station, this stylish inn has apartments housing from two to eight people in a modernized period palazzo. The decor is very Venetian in style, with masks and oriental rugs. A daily cleaning service is included, plus free use of cots, pushchairs and bottle-warmers for families with young children.

€€€

Around Venice

CAMPING
Alba d'Oro   Map 4 F5

Via Triestina 214/b, Ca'noghera, 30030; 041 541 5102; www.camping.com

A range of accommodation is on offer here, from private rooms to house tents. The fully-serviced campsite, run by friendly owners has an on-site pizzeria, restaurant, pool, beach volleyball, internet café, and activities such as toga parties. It is a good alternative for younger children who can only take small doses of culture. Regular shuttle buses from the site to Venice (20 minutes).

€

Camping Village Cavallino   Map 4 F5

Via delle Batterie 164, Cavallino, 30013; www.baiaholiday.com

On the Venetian coast between Lido di Jesolo and Punta Sabbioni, close to Venice, this is a well-equipped complex set among pine trees, fronting a large, sandy beach.

Bungalows, mobile homes and caravans are available to rent, and there is a swimming pool, mini-golf, playground and other entertainment for families, as well as a pizzeria.

€

Treviso   Map 4 F4

Within easy reach, Treviso *(see p87)* is very convenient for Venice. Low-cost airlines fly into its airport, and accommodation is considerably cheaper than on the islands of Venice, a 30-minute train or bus ride away. See *www.bbitalia.it/en/bed-breakfast:treviso.html*.

B&Bs
19 Borgo Cavour Design

Borgo Camillo Benso Conte di Cavour 19, 31100; 0422 419 145; www.19borgocavourtreviso.it

In the centre of Treviso, close to the Duomo, this is a haven of art, design and creativity, presided over by the most welcoming owner, Marta. It is set in a tastefully modernized 17th-century property, with every creature comfort offered in its spacious bedrooms. It has its own library, too.

€

Dolce Vita

Via Parenzo,14, 31100; 328 768 9094; www.dolcevitatreviso.com

A "home from home" set in a pleasant house in a peaceful spot close to the historic centre. Family-friendly, with ample bedrooms and private or shared bathrooms. Self-catering apartments are an option. Bicycle hire available.

€

Veneto and Friuli-Venezia Giulia

The Veneto countryside embraces canals and waterways, lakes, beaches, soaring pink-tinged mountains, and great art cities, while Italy's easternmost region, Friuli-Venezia Giulia, is a sliver of coastline with an intriguing cultural mix.

Below Waterfront promenade at Riva del Garda on Lake Garda, near Verona

Verona
p78

Riviera
del Brenta
p84

Trieste
p88

① Verona: the Arena
Gladiatorial games and dazzling musical performances

Completed in AD 30, this is the world's third largest Roman amphitheatre, after the Colosseum and the one outside Capua, near Naples, and it is still in superb condition. Originally, it could hold the entire population of Roman Verona, and visitors came from all across the Veneto to watch the mock battles and gladitorial combats held here. Today it is used for opera shows in summer, and the cries of "*jugula!*" (slit his throat!) have been replaced by "*bravo!*" (good!).

The monster balcony in the Giardino Giusti

Key Features

Stone seats in 44 tiers

Remains of the outer circle

Dungeons and underground passages

Original extent of the arena's exterior

Arches
The arena is 139 m (500 ft) long and 110 m (400 ft) wide and can seat 15,000 people. Two of its three original rings of arches are still intact.

Top tier
An earthquake in the 12th century destroyed the top tier of seats, but four arches still remain of the outer circle.

The interior
The interior of the arena has survived virtually intact. Gladiators and animals occupied a maze of passages and dungeons underground.

Façade
The arena was clad in pink and white marble from Valpolicella, almost all of which was later scavenged for use on other buildings; only a fragment remains.

The Lowdown

Map reference 3 C5
Address Piazza Brà, 37121 Verona, Veneto; 045 800 3204; www.arena.it

Train to Verona Porta Nuova, on Milan–Venice or Rome–Brennero lines. **Bus** 11,12,13,14, 72 and 73 to Piazza Brà

Visitor information Palazzo Barbieri, Piazza Brà, 37121; 045 807 7774; www.comune.verona.it

Open 8:30am–7:30pm Tue–Sun, 1:30–7:30pm Mon; may close early for opera performances in festival time (mid-Jun–early Sep).

Price €9–11, children aged 8–13 €1, under-8s free

Skipping the queue VeronaCard gives free access to the Arena and 14 other sights in Verona, discounted admission to other museums and free travel on city buses. On sale at major sights, tobacconists, hotels and travel agents. €15 per adult for two days, €20 for five days; 045 807 7774; www.comune.verona.it

Guided tours Walking tours 5:30pm Mon–Fri, 11:30am Sat, Mar–Oct; one and a half hours; €10 per person; 045 806 8680

Age range 5 plus

Activities Performances at the Opera Festival (mid-Jun–early Sep); prices from €15 to €200, with discounts for under- 26s; performances start at 9 or 9:15pm, so get children to take a siesta.

Allow 45 minutes

Wheelchair access Stalls only

Café Several on Piazza Brà

Toilets In the cafés

Good family value?
Entry is cheap, and it is a great place to let imaginations run wild.

The shady lawns and topiary hedges of the Renaissance Giardino Giusti

Letting off steam

The Arena itself has plenty of space for kids to clamber around, but for a greener, shadier place to play, take a 20-minute walk to the **Giardino Giusti** (*Via Giardino Giusti 2, 37121; 045 803 4029; open daily 9am–8pm Apr–Sep, until dusk Oct–Mar; €20*) on the far side of the Adige river. One of Italy's most beautiful Renaissance gardens, it has fountains, statues and a maze. Follow a cypress-tree avenue up the hill to the "monster balcony" for views of the city. There are wild woodlands and mossy caves too.

Eat and drink

Picnic: under €25; Snacks: €25–40; Real meal: €40–80; Family treat: €80 or more (based on a family of four)

PICNIC Piazza delle Erbe (*Mon–Sat am*) is Verona's most colourful market, with all kinds of tempting food from local cheeses, hams and salamis, to fresh fruit, vegetables and juices. The **Antica Salumeria Albertini** (*Corso Santa Anastasia 41, 37100; 045 803 1074; www.salumeriaalbertini.it*) is close to the piazza, with a great selection of food and wines, while the **Pam** supermarket (*Via dei Mutilati 3, 37122*), close to the Arena, is open every day including Sunday and has everything needed for an alfresco feast. Take a picnic to the Giardino Giusti.

SNACKS Caffè alle Fogge (*Via Fogge 10, 37121; 045 800 6831*) is a little café just off Via Mazzini with a great range of snacks, *panini* and light lunches.

REAL MEAL Ristorante Pizzeria Liston (*Via Dietro Listone 19, 37121; 045 803 4003*) is tucked away in a small street near the Arena, offering excellent pizzas and *antipasti*, as well as more substantial meals. It also has outdoor tables.

FAMILY TREAT Greppia (*Vicolo Samaritana 3, 37121; 045 800 4577; www.ristorantegreppia.it*), hidden in a little street close to Juliet's House, is a deservedly popular restaurant, with local traditional dishes on the menu, and a lovely courtyard for alfresco dining.

Shopping

Via Mazzini is lined with designer stores, great for window-shopping, and near Piazza delle Erbe there are several teen fashion shops. **Coin** (*Via Cappello 30, 37121*) is a useful department store, while **Gulliver** bookshop (*Via Stella 16/b, 37121; www.gullivertravelbooks.it; closed Sun and Mon am*) is all about travel, with plenty of books in English.

Via Mazzini, a lively street full of designer shops in Verona

Find out more

FILM *Letters to Juliet* (2010) is set in Verona and based on the letters sent to Juliet's House (*see p80*).

Next stop...

MUSEO ARCHEOLOGICO Cross the River Adige to the **Teatro Romano** (*see p80*), and take the lift up the cliffs to the Museo Archeologico to see a bronze bust of the first Roman emperor, Augustus (63 BC–AD 14).

Verona cont ▶

The balcony of Casa di Giulietta, said to be the inspiration for Romeo and Juliet

② Casa di Giulietta

On the trail of star-crossed lovers and romance

The tragic story of Romeo and Juliet, two young lovers from rival families, was written by Luigi da Porto of Vicenza in the 1520s, and has inspired countless dramas, films, operas and ballets – the most famous of which is English dramatist William Shakespeare's *Romeo and Juliet*. Romeo is said to have climbed up to Juliet's balcony in this house in Verona. In reality it is a restored 13th-century inn, but why allow that to get in the way of a good story? As well as the balcony (in fact an old sarcophagus), Juliet's House has a much-loved bronze statue of Juliet. It is traditional to give her right breast a rub for good luck in love and life – it is highly burnished! The walls of the house are covered in graffiti declarations of undying love, and it is possible to get married on Juliet's balcony.

A few streets away in Via Arche Scaligeri is the **Casa di Romeo**, a run-down 14th-century house. While there, take a look at the **Tombs of the Scaligeri**, which house the remains of the Della Scala family that ruled Verona in the 13th and 14th centuries. Look out for the tombs of Cangrande I (died 1329), topped by an equestrian statue, Mastino II (died 1351) and Cansignorio (died 1375).

Letting off steam
The 15-minute walk along the river to the so-called **Tomba di Giulietta** (Juliet's Tomb), displayed in a crypt below the cloister of San Francesco al Corso on Via del Pontiere, provides a chance for children to let off some steam. The red marble sarcophagus lies in an atmospheric setting, next door to the church where the star-crossed lovers' marriage is said to have taken place.

The Lowdown

🌐 **Map reference** 3 C5
Address Casa di Giulietta, Via Cappello 23, Verona 37121; 045 803 4303. Casa di Romeo, Via Arche Scaligeri 2, 37121. Tombs of the Scaligeri, Via Arche Scaligeri. Tomba di Giulietta, Via del Pontiere 9, 37122, 045 25361

🚌 **Bus** 11, 12, 13, 72 (Mon–Sat), 90, 92, 93, 96,97 (Sun) to Piazza Brà

🕐 **Open** Casa di Giulietta and Tomba di Giulietta: 1:30–7:30pm Mon, 8:30am–7:30pm Tue–Sun

💶 **Price** Casa and Tomba: €16–24, children aged 8–13 €1; first Sun of month (not Jun–Aug) €1 each

👫 **Age range** All, but the romance will appeal more to older children

⏱ **Allow** 2 hours for all sights

🍴 **Eat and drink** *Snacks* Balu (57/b Corso Porta Borsari, 37121; 045 803 6341), just off Piazza Brà, is one of the best *gelaterie* in Verona. *Real meal* Caffè Liston (Piazza Brà12; 045 803 1168) has tables spilling out onto the piazza, and offers a wide range of meals.

🎭 **Festivals** Juliet's birthday: 16 Sep

③ Teatro Romano

Verona's oldest Roman venue

The Arena was used for gladiatorial games but this theatre – the city's oldest Roman monument – was for the tamer variety of plays and spectacles; no wild beasts or executions here. Built in the 1st century BC, it later fell into oblivion, buried under the city until 1830, when a local archaeologist began painstaking excavations. From its largely intact semicircular seating area it enjoys splendid views over the city. It stages regular open-air performances of Shakespeare's *Two Gentlemen of Verona* and *Romeo and Juliet*, and concerts in summer.

A lift carries visitors from the theatre up the cliffs to an interesting little **Museo Archeologico** above.

Letting off steam
Continue up to **Castel San Pietro**, built by the Austrians over Roman fortifications. It has fabulous views over the town at sunset.

The Lowdown

🌐 **Map reference** 3 C5
Address Teatro Romano and Museo Archeologico, Rigaste Redentore 2, 37121 Verona; 045 800 0360

🚌 **Bus** 31, 32, 33 (Mon–Sat), 91 (Sun) from Castelvecchio

🕐 **Open** 1:30–7:30pm Mon, 8:30am–7:30pm Tue–Sun; theatre closes early on performance days

💶 **Price** €11–15, children aged 8–13 €1

👫 **Age range** All

⏱ **Allow** 1 hour

♿ **Wheelchair access** Yes

🍴 **Eat and drink** *Snacks* Caffè Filippini (Piazza delle Erbe 26, 37121; 045 800 4549) is a 20–minute walk from the theatre, overlooks the market piazza, and is a great spot for snacks. *Real meal* Trattoria Al Pompiere (Vicolo Regina d'Ungheria 5, 37121; 045 803 0537; www.alpompiere.com) is very popular, especially for its hams, large selection of cheeses and tasty home-made pasta. It was originally opened by a retired fireman, whose hat is on the wall.

🎭 **Festivals** Shakespeare Festival at the Teatro Romano, including performances in English, concerts and ballet: Jun–Aug

The Teatro Romano against the backdrop of Castel San Pietro

④ San Zeno Maggiore

A church of artist marvels

A 20-minute walk to the west of Verona's centre and the Arena, San Zeno, built in 1120–38, is northern Italy's most ornate Romanesque church. Dedicated to San Zeno, Verona's patron saint, who died in 380, it was originally built over his tomb. Between the 9th and 13th centuries this was one of the most powerful abbeys in the Veneto, but it had to be rebuilt after it was destroyed by the shattering earthquake of 1117.

At the centre of the stone façade, which is adorned with marble reliefs and a graceful porch canopy, is the impressive 13th-century rose window known as the Ruota della Fortuna (Wheel of Fortune). The West Doors are made of wood, but each has 24 bronze plates nailed on to make them look like solid metal. Primitive but forceful, they depict scenes from the Old and New Testaments and scenes from the life of San Zeno. Especially arresting are Salome dancing for the head of John the Baptist and a Descent into Limbo. Inside the church, on the high altar, is Andrea Mantegna's famous Madonna con Bambino e Santi triptych (1457–9), a masterpiece of perspective. In

the vaulted crypt, 49 columns lead to the shrine of San Zeno, where the saint's remains are kept.

Letting off steam

Walk by the river to **Castelvecchio** (1355), the fortress of nobleman Cangrande, and the **Arco dei Gavi**, a Roman arch by Vitruvius, reconstructed by the Fascists in the 1930s. Continue along **Corso Cavour** for the evening *passeggiata*.

The Lowdown

- 🌐 **Map reference** 3 C5
  Address Piazza San Zeno, 37123 Verona; 045 800 6120
- 🚌 **Bus** 31 from Porta Borsari or Corso Cavour (near the Arena)
- 🕐 **Open** Apr–Oct 8:30am–6pm Mon–Sat, 1–6pm Sun. Nov–Mar 10am–1pm Tue–Sat, 1–5pm Sun
- 💶 **Price** €12
- 👫 **Age range** 8 plus
- ⏱ **Allow** 45 minutes
- 🍴 **Eat and drink** *Real meal* Trattoria al Calmiere *(Piazza San Zeno 10, 37123; 045 803 0765; www. calmiere.com)*, right on the piazza devoted to Verona's patron saint, is a welcoming *trattoria* which offers traditional Veronese specialities and a good selection of wines from the Veneto.
- 🎏 **Festivals** Bacanal del Gnocco; one of Italy's oldest carnivals, culminating in a parade of 4,000 masked dancers, over 500 floats and giant figures including the Papa dello Gnoco, named after the nobleman considered to be father of the carnival – free plates of *gnocchi* (dumplings) are handed out at carnival time: (Feb/Mar).

The Gothic interior of San Zeno Maggiore, with its vaulted ceiling

A thrilling roller coaster at Gardaland, Italy's top amusement park

⑤ Lake Garda

Alpine landscapes and thrilling theme parks

This is the largest of the Italian lakes and also the most popular. It is 52 km (32 miles) long and 19 km (12 miles) at its widest – a round trip by road covers 144 km (90 miles). The countryside ranges from the gentle plains, vines, olives and citrus trees of the south to the untamed north, ringed by dramatic snow-capped peaks. **Sirmione**, in the south, has a fairy-tale turreted castle, the **Rocca Scaligera**, with drawbridge, moat and spectacular views from its towers. The Della Scala family ruled Verona and this area for over 100 years from the late 13th century. At the tip of the Sirmione peninsula is the **Grotte di Catullo**, remains of a Roman villa that once belonged to Catullus, ancient Rome's greatest and raunchiest lyric poet, dating to the 1st century BC.

Letting off steam

Gardaland (well signposted from Peschiera del Garda at the southern tip of the lake, and connected to its train station by a shuttle bus), is Italy's largest theme park. It has all the thrills and spills: wild-water rides, loop-the-loop roller coasters and a Fantasy Kingdom. Alternatively head for **Movieland** in Lazise sul Garda (6 km/4 miles up the east side of the lake from Peschiera) for Peter Pan pirate fights at its Parco Studios, and the watery delights of its Parco Aqua. Otherwise, the **Parco Natura Viva** drive-through safari park (also in the vicinity of Peschiera), is rated as one of Europe's top zoos.

⑥ Gardone Riviera

King of kitsch and a mystical garden

Once a magnet for European royalty, heads of state and writers, the resort of Gardone is lined with vast *belle époque* hotels. It is still the site of the most famous villa-museum on Lake Garda, **Il Vittoriale**. Dictator Mussolini presented this villa to the controversial Fascist sympathizer, soldier, poet and womanizer Gabriele d'Annunzio (1863–1938) in 1925. This Art Deco kitsch kingdom is full of bizarre objects such as his death mask, embalmed pet tortoise, grandiose mausoleum and a coffin where he would retire, in life, to think in peace. Outside, the grounds are awash with fountains and symbols of d'Annunzio's wartime exploits, including the battleship *Puglia* and a biplane that he used to fly over Vienna in memory of Italy's victory over Austria in 1918.

The **Heller Garden** (Giardino Botanico Fondazione André Heller) is a fascinating bohemian botanical garden, laid out in 1900 but

The Lowdown

🌐 **Map reference** 3 C4
Address Veneto/Lombardy. Rocca Scaligera: Piazza Castello, 25019 Sirmione; 030 916 468. Grotte di Catullo: Piazzale Orti Manala 4, 25019 Sirmione; 030 916 157. Gardaland: Via Derna 4, 37014 Castelnuovo del Garda; www.gardaland.it. Movieland: Località Fossaltà 58, 37017 Lazise sul Garda; www.movieland.it. Parco Natura Viva: Località Figara 40, 37012 Bussolengo; www.parconaturaviva.it

🚗 **Boat** Paddle steamers, high-speed hydrofoils and ferries ply the lake (Navigazione Lago di Garda: 030 914 9511, 800 551 801; www.navigazionelaghi.it)

ℹ️ **Visitor information** Viale Marconi 2; 030 916 245; www.bresciaholiday.com

🕐 **Open** Rocca Scaligera: 8:30am–7:30pm Tue–Sat; Grotte di Catullo: Mar–Oct 8:30am–7pm Tue–Sat, 9am–2pm Sun, 9am–2pm Tue–Sun Nov–Feb; Gardaland: check website; Parco Natura Viva: Apr–Oct 9am–6pm, Nov–Mar subject to weather. Movieland: check website

💶 **Price** Rocca Scaligera: €8–16; Grotte di Catullo: €8–12; Gardaland: €73–132; Parco Natura Viva: €55–76. Movieland: €86–96

👫 **Skipping the queue** Check theme park websites for promotions.

🚻 **Age range** All

⏱️ **Allow** 1–3 days

🍴 **Eat and drink** *Snacks* Gardaland (25019 Castelnuovo del Garda; 045 644 977) serves ice cream, *panini*, pizza and pasta. *Real meal* Trattoria La Fiasca (Via Santa Maria Maggiore 1, 25019 Sirmione; 0309 906 111) has good, unfussy food.

🎉 **Festivals** Centomiglia Regatta (www.centomiglia.it): Sep

A stone sculpture in the gardens of D'Annunzio's museum home, Il Vittoriale

redesigned in the 1990s by the Austrian artist André Heller. It is full of mystical contemporary sculptures, huge tree ferns and waterfalls.

Letting off steam
The gardens of Il Vittoriale (gardens-only tickets available) are a great place to play among extravagant monuments. The amphitheatre has fine views.

The Lowdown

🌐 **Map reference** 3 C4
Address 25083 Gardone Riviera. Il Vittoriale: Via Vittoriale 12; *www. vittoriale.it*. Heller Garden: Via Roma 2; *www.hellergarden.com*

🚃 **Train** to Brescia, then bus *(www. sia-autoservi.it)*. **Ferry** *www. navigazionelaghi.it*

ℹ️ **Visitor information** Corso della Repubblica 8, 25083; 0365 374 8736

🕐 **Open** Il Vittoriale: Apr–Sep 8:30am–8pm daily, Oct–Mar 9am–5pm daily. Heller Garden: Mar–Oct 9am–7pm daily

💷 **Price** Il Vittoriale: €16–28; Heller Garden: €18–28

👫 **Age range** All

⏱️ **Allow** Half a day

🍴 **Eat and drink** *Snacks* Pasticceria Vassalli *(Via di San Carlo 82, 25083 Salò; 0365 20752)* has sweet treats. *Real meal* Locanda agli Angeli *(Via Dosso 7, 25083 Gardone Riviera; 0365 20991; www.agliangeli.com)* is a rustic trattoria close to Il Vittoriale, with a delightful terrace. Specialities include lake fish and risotto.

🎭 **Festivals** Stagione al Vittoriale (dance, music and theatre at the Teatro del Vittoriale): Jun–Aug

⑦ Riva del Garda
The untamed north

Lively Riva del Garda is Lake Garda's northernmost resort, guarded by the soaring cliffs of mountainous Trentino Alto-Adige. It has a lovely medieval square, Piazza III Novembre, a long waterfront and a 12th-century castle, **La Rocca**. Inside is a museum displaying finds from the Bronze Age as well as an armoury collection, and next to it is the Torre Apponale – climb up its 165 steps to be rewarded with great views of the mountains and lake. Both Riva and picturesque Torbole, nearby, are splendid for windsurfing

and dinghy sailing. On a clear day it is possible to see the whole length of the lake from Torbole.

Letting off steam
Behind Riva is the **Grotta Cascata Varone**, a spectacular waterfall cascading through a narrow canyon. Try windsurfing, kayaking or biking at Riva del Garda or the **Marco Segnana Surf Centre** in Torbole *(0464 505 963; www. surfsegnana.it)*, which offers lessons for all abilities.

The lakeside waterfront at Riva del Garda, lined with restaurants and cafés

The Lowdown

🌐 **Map reference** 3 C4
Address 38066 Riva del Garda. La Rocca: Piazza C Battisti

🚃 **Train** to Desenzano, then bus *(www.aptv.it)* or train to Rovereto, then bus *(www.ttesercizio.it)*. **Ferry** *www.navigazionelaghi.it*

ℹ️ **Visitor information** Largo Medaglie d'Oro 5, 38066; 0464 554 444; *www.gardatrentino.it*

🕐 **Open** La Rocca: Apr–Nov Tue–Sun, Jul–Sep daily

💷 **Price** La Rocca: €4–8

👫 **Age range** All

⏱️ **Allow** 1 day, with windsurfing

🍴 **Eat and drink** *Snacks* Birreria Spaten *(Via Maffei 7, 38066; 0464 553 670)* serves dumplings, pasta, sausage, sauerkraut and pizza, in an indoor beer garden. *Real Meal* Al Volt *(Via Fiume 73, 38066; 0464 552 570)* is a highly acclaimed restaurant in a 17th-century palazzo.

Picnic under €25; **Snacks** €25–40; **Real meal** €40–80; **Family treat** €80 or more (based on a family of four)

⑧ Riviera del Brenta
Boat trip among magnificent villas and gardens

Catching a *burchiello* (river boat) from Padua to Venice is a fun way for kids and adults to enjoy the palatial villas of the Riviera del Brenta. Originally an ornate wooden boat for ferrying wealthy Venetians down the Brenta canal to their magnificent country retreats, *burchiello* is the name now given to any of the modern boats that make trips through ingenious locks and revolving bridges past the villas. Visit some of the finest to appreciate the lavish scale of their architecture and gardens.

Atlas statue, Villa Pisani

Key Sights

⑤ Chiusa di Dolo
There has been a lock here since 1625, rebuilt in 1934. It allow boats to negotiate changes in water level.

⑥ Antichi Molini di Dolo
Built in the 16th century, a flourmill complex near the pretty village of Dolo harnessed the water flow to turn the stones to grind the wheat used for bread.

① Ponte dei Graissi
The beautiful medieval bridge that boats pass under as they leave Padua sits low over the water and is built of pinkish brick, like many of Padua's buildings.

② Villa Giovanelli
The fine Villa Giovanelli, built on the site of Padua's former river port, has an impressive central flight of steps leading up to a colonnaded entrance.

③ River Brenta
The river flows down from the Trentino mountains to the Adriatic Sea via Venice's lagoon. As its estuary silted up between the 13th and 16th centuries it was channelled into a network of canals.

④ Villa Pisani
Begun in 1720, the villa's 114 rooms were a showpiece for the aristocratic Pisani family and later Napoleon. It is now a museum, with amazing frescoes and a maze.

⑦ Villa Foscari (La Malcontenta)
Close to the Venetian lagoon, this villa was designed in 1560 by Andrea Palladio, one of the most influential architects of all time. It is decorated with magnificent frescoes.

The Lowdown

🌐 **Map reference** 4 E5
Address 30031 Riviera del Brenta, Veneto

🚗 **Train** to Padua from Venice or Milan. **Boat** along the Brenta Canal from Padua: Il Burchiello (www.ilburchiello.it), I Battelli del Brenta (www.battellidelbrenta.it), Delta Tour Navigazione Turistica (www.deltatour.it)

ℹ️ **Visitor information** Via Mazzini, 76, 30031 Dolo; 041 510 2341; www.rivieradelbrentaturismo.com

🕑 **Open** Half-day boat tours start at 9am and 2:30pm, whole day tours at 8:30am, but check with

individual companies for details; Villa Pisani: Apr–Sep 9am–7pm, Oct–Mar 9am–4pm, maze Apr–Sep 9am–1:30pm & 2:15–7:15pm, except in bad weather; Villa Foscari (La Malcontenta): May–Oct 9am–noon Tue & Sat, at other times by prior booking

💶 **Price** Boat tours: check with individual companies, but estimate €180–248 for a family for a full-day tour, including lunch but not villa entrance tickets, with under-5s usually free. Villa Pisani and maze: €20–40, under-18s free. Villa Foscari (La Malcontenta): €40

🧍 **Skipping the queue** It is advisable to book online.

🚩 **Guided tours** All boat tours have English-speaking guides.

👫 **Age range** Any for boat trips

⏲️ **Allow** Half a day or a full day

☕ **Café** Boats serve refreshments; Villa Pisani museum café

🚻 **Toilets** On boats and at villas

Good family value?
The boat trips are expensive, but are a child-friendly way to see the villas. Travelling by car is cheaper, but the kids may enjoy this less.

Trying to find the way out of the box-hedge maze at Villa Pisani

Letting off steam

Designed by Gerolamo Frigimelica in 1720, the **maze at Villa Pisani** is one of the most famous and best preserved in Europe. Its nine concentric circles were originally hornbeam hedges, but have been replanted with box hedges, with a spiralling tower in the centre. Climb up to the top and retrace the route out. Small children are probably best accompanied by an older sibling or adult, but there are helpers to find the way out.

Eat and drink

Picnic: under €25; Snacks: €25–40; Real meal: €40–80; Family treat: €80 or more (based on a family of four)

PICNIC Franchin (*Via del Santo 95, 35123 Padua; 049 875 0532; www.franchin-pd.it*), a deli in the heart of Padua, has a sumptuous selection of salami, ham, cheese and wine. Picnic on the riverbank.
SNACKS Brek (*Piazza Cavour 20, 35123 Padua; 049 875 3788*), in the centre of Padua, is one of a chain of popular northern Italian self-service restaurants, good for hot snacks. For a quick bite to eat that is more typical of the region, try one of the traditional *folpari* stalls that are dotted around Padua in autumn, which sell fresh shellfish cooked in a variety of ways.
REAL MEAL Il Burchiello (*Via Venezia 40, 30034 Oriago di Mira; 041 472 244; www.burchiello.it; closed Mon and Tue lunch*) is a restaurant in a hotel at Oriago di Mira, in a lovely position by the River Brenta. It offers a moderately priced lunch menu of pasta and fish.

FAMILY TREAT Villa Alberti (*Via Ettore Tito 90, 30031 Dolo; 041 426 6512; www.villalberti.it*), at Dolo, half an hour by bus from Venice, is an 18th-century villa surrounded by lush gardens overlooking the River Brenta. It houses an inn with an elegant restaurant featuring quality local produce.

Brek, a popular self-service restaurant in the centre of Padua

Shopping

Add a spring to your step at luxury shoe factory outlets near Padua: two good ones are **Rossimoda** (*Via Muggia 4, 35010 Vigonza; 049 828 4101*) and **Ballin** (*Vicolo B. Cellini 4, 30032 Fiesso d'Artico; 041 513 7211*). The tourist office can supply a full list of outlets and a map.

Find out more

DIGITAL To understand how locks take boats up and down hills, go to *www.canals.com/locks.htm* or *www.rideau-info.com/canal/lock.html*.

Take cover

Torronificio Scaldaferro (*Via Ca' Tron 31, 30031 Dolo; 041 410 467; www.scaldaferro.it*) in Dolo has been making honey and almond nougat, some with candied fruit or chocolate, since 1919. Visit the workshop, taste the delicious nougat and buy some to take home.

Next stop...

BOAT TOUR For a change from architecture, take a guided nature tour by boat on the lagoon south of Venice with ATN Laguna Sud (*www.atnlagunasud.it; €112–136 for a full day with a guide*). There is a wealth of birdlife to discover, and the guide narrates interesting history and tales of hunting and fishing in the swamplands.

KIDS' CORNER

Q&A
1 How many circles of hedges are there in the maze at Villa Pisani?
2 What was the original *burchiello*?
3 Why do you think the Venetians built their villas along the Brenta?
4 What is a lock gate for?

Answers at the bottom of the page.

Exciting villas
Venetian villas were designed to provide entertainment. Each area of the gardens created a different mood: shady, wooded parts to make visitors thoughtful, and flowery parts to make them joyful. Bushes shaped to look like animals or birds were created and small lakes and little temples would be built at the focal point of a view. Some of the villas even had theatres made from clipped hedges, where musical comedies would be staged. The maze gave the illusion of getting lost while always knowing there is a way out. Take a sketchbook and draw some of these elements, then design your own garden with fun features.

LOCK UP, LOCK DOWN
The locks on the Brenta Canal allow boats to navigate up- and downstream. Lock gates let water in between two gates to raise the level, and then let it out to lower the level.

Answers: 1 Nine. 2 The ornate wooden boat used by Venetians to reach their country villas on the banks of the Brenta. 3 There was not enough land in Venice itself for such large gardens and villas. 4 To control water flow and levels.

⑨ Padua
A patron saint of lost things

Padua (Padova in Italian) is a busy city with an arcaded centre and three handsome market squares: Piazza delle Erbe sells fruit and vegetables, Piazza dei Signori supplies household goods and Piazza dei Frutti offers both. Padua's famous university, founded in the 13th century, accounts for the town's youthful population. The city also attracts five million pilgrims a year, to revere St Anthony at the **Basilica di Sant'Antonio**; the saint is believed to help restore lost people and property. Apart from his sanctuary, the main attraction is the **Cappella degli Scrovegni**, a chapel home to a remarkable fresco cycle completed in two years by Giotto, the early 14th-century artist who gave a new sense of realism to painting. It was commissioned in 1303 by Enrico Scrovegni, a rich banker who wished to appease God when his father was accused of lending money at unfair interest rates. In the *Last Judgment*, Scrovegni offers the Virgin Mary a model of the chapel. The Paduans must have been sensitive to money matters, because the **Palazzo della Ragione**, which boasts a vast hall

St Anthony's basilica in Padua, where millions of pilgrims visit every year

decorated with astrological frescoes, also houses a "Stone of Shame" where the bankrupt were ridiculed in public before being exiled.

Letting off steam
Founded in 1545 by the Senate of the Republic of Venice, for the cultivation of medicinal plants, the **Orto Botanico** is the world's oldest university botanical garden. The wall that surrounds it was added in 1552 to stop the Paduans popping in to help themselves from this natural pharmacy. Rhubarb and potatoes were first grown in Italy here.

⑩ Vicenza
Buildings inspired by Rome and a fun park

This lovely town is famous for the buildings of Andrea Palladio (1508–1580), Italy's most influential architect. Inspired by the style and proportion of the buildings of ancient Rome, in 1580 Palladio designed the **Teatro Olimpico**, the oldest roofed theatre in the world. The scenery, designed by Vincenzo Scamozzi for the first production in 1585, creates an illusion of long streets receding to a distant horizon through trompe l'oeil effects. The same visual harmony on a more imposing scale can be seen in **Palazzo Chiericati**, which houses the **Pinacoteca**, with a fine collection of paintings and Palladio drawings, and in the **Basilica Palladiana**, also by Palladio.

The Lowdown

🌐 **Map reference** 4 E5
Address 35100 Padua, Veneto. Basilica di Sant'Antonio: Piazza del Santo 11, 35123; 049 875 1244; *www.basilicadelsanto.org*. Cappella degli Scrovegni: Piazza Eremitani 8, 35100; 049 820 4551; *www.cappelladegliscrovegni.it*. Palazzo della Ragione: Via VIII Febbraio, 35100; 049 820 5006. Orto Botanico: Via Orto Botanico 15, 35100; 049 827 2119; *www. ortobotanico.unipd.it*

🚗 **Train** from Venice, Vicenza, Florence, Milan, Rome or Turin. **Car** A4 Milan–Venice or A13 Bologna–Padua motorway

ℹ️ **Visitor information** Galleria Pedrocchi, Via VIII Febbraio 15, 35100; 049 876 7927; *www. turismopadova.it*; 9am–1:30pm and 3–7pm Mon–Sat

🕐 **Open** Basilica: 9am–1pm and 2–6pm daily. Cappella: 9am–7pm daily. Palazzo: 9am–6pm daily (until 7pm Apr–Oct) Orto: 9am–1pm and 3–7pm daily (am only Nov–Mar)

💶 **Price** Basilica: free. Cappella and Palazzo: Museums Family Card €25, plus €1 per person chapel booking fee. Orto: €10, students and children €1

🧍 **Skipping the queue** Cappella: booking essential, six weeks to 24 hours in advance, online or call 049 201 0020; collect tickets 1 hour before visit from adjacent Museo Civici agli Eremitani; visits restricted to 30 minutes.

🚩 **Guided tours** Cappella: in Italian, €2 (book with ticket). Orto: audio-guide in Italian or English, €3

👫 **Age range** 8 plus

⏱️ **Allow** 1 day

🍴 **Eat and drink** *Snacks* Caffè Pedrocchi (*Via VIII Febbraio 15, 35100; 049 878 1231; www. caffepedrocchi.it*) was founded in 1831. Pop into this famous café for a coffee or an ice cream. *Real meal* L'Anfora (*Via dei Soncin 13, 35100; 049 656 629; closed Sun*) is great for hearty soups and pastas.

Piazza dei Signori, Vicenza, with columns topped by St Mark the Lion and Christ

Letting off steam
Central **Parco Querini**, off Via Rodolfi (dawn–dusk daily), has space to run around and an open-air **Parco delle Scienze** (Science Park) for children aged 6–14, where they can play with optical illusions and sound.

The Lowdown

- 🌐 **Map reference** 3 D4
  Address 36100 Vicenza, Veneto. Teatro Olimpico: Piazza Matteotti, 36100; 0444 222 800; www. teatrolimpicovicenza.it. Palazzo Chiericati and Pinacoteca: Piazza Matteotti 37–39, 36100; 0444 222 811; www.museicivicivicenza. it. Basilica Palladiana: Piazza dei Signori, 36100

- 🚗 **Train** from Venice and Padua **Car** A4 Milan–Venice motorway.

- ℹ️ **Visitor information** Piazza Matteotti 12, 36100; 0444 320 854; open 9am–1pm and 2–6pm

- 🕐 **Open** Teatro, Palazzo and Pinacoteca: 9am–5pm Tue–Sun

- 💶 **Price** Combined three-day family ticket €12, under-14s free

- 👫 **Age range** 8 plus

- ⏱ **Allow** 1 day

- 🍽 **Eat and drink** Snacks Self-Service Righetti (Piazza Duomo 3, 36100; 0444 543 135; www.selfrighetti.it; open Mon–Fri) has a good choice. Real meal Antica Osteria al Bersagliere (Contrà Pescheria 11, 36100; 0444 323 507; open Mon–Sat) serves gnocchi, polenta, rabbit and other local classics.

⑪ Treviso
Waterways, bridges and painted houses
Often nicknamed "Little Venice", this attractive medieval town features buildings with decoratively

One of the canals that flow through Treviso's medieval core

painted façades and a network of waterways deriving from the River Sile. There is an excellent fish market (Tue–Sat mornings) on the Pescheria, an artificial island created in the town centre in 1856. There is also a general market in Piazza Burchiellati and the surrounding area (Tue and Sat mornings). The long, white-ribbed, deep red vegetable stacked on stalls is radicchio rosso, a local speciality.

Letting off steam
The River Sile is part of a regional park offering plenty of space for walking, running and biking, starting in the town centre and heading out towards the countryside. Download a map of walking and bike routes with explanations in English at www.parcosile.it.

A fish scupIture in Treviso's fish market on the Pescheria island in the River Sile

The Lowdown

- 🌐 **Map reference** 4 E4
  Address 31100 Treviso

- 🚗 **Train** from Venezia Santa Lucia or Mestre, with connections from Padua and Vicenza. **Car** A27 motorway from Venice, connecting with A4 from Padua and Vicenza.

- ℹ️ **Visitor information** Piazzetta Monte di Pietà 8, 31100; 0422 547 632

- 👫 **Age range** All

- ⏱ **Allow** 1 day

- 🍽 **Eat and drink** Real meal Osteria Muscoli (Via Pescheria 23, 31110; 0422 583 390; open 7am–11pm Mon–Sat) just opposite the fish market, offers classic pasta dishes, wine (prosecco, for instance) and snacks. Family treat Il Basilisco (Via Bison 34, 31100; 0422 541 822; closed Sat lunch and Sun), a little out of the centre, towards the trade fair, is renowned for its tagliatello with guinea-fowl sauce, leg of lamb and calf's liver.

⑫ Trieste
Little Europe on sea

The Romans called it Tergeste (marketplace) in the 2nd century BC and Trieste was the main harbour of the Habsburg Empire until 1918, when it was given to Italy. Today's commercial port is the largest in the Adriatic, and the Mediterranean's main importer of coffee beans. Perched on a natural balcony overlooking the Gulf of Trieste, the cosmopolitan city is a blend of Slavic, Italian and German-speaking peoples. It is also home to grand cafés, once frequented by writers such as James Joyce and Italo Svevo.

Statue of James Joyce

Key Sights

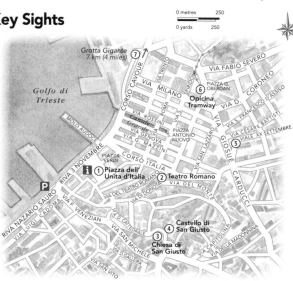

0 metres 250
0 yards 250

① Piazza dell'Unità d'Italia
The biggest sea-facing piazza in Italy, built as a perfect rectangle and surrounded by splendid buildings and monuments. This is the place to see and be seen in Trieste.

② Teatro Romano
Built during Trajan's reign in the first and second centuries, this theatre is still remarkably intact.

③ Chiesa di San Giusto
Up hundreds of steps, this church is dedicated to Trieste's patron saint, who was martyred by drowning by Emperor Diocletian. Built in the 1300s, it incorporates two older churches.

④ Castello di San Giusto
Next door, this 15th-century castle was built by the Venetians and has panoramic views. A small museum displays arms and armour.

⑤ Viale XX Settembre
Location of an ancient Roman aqueduct, this is now a pedestrianized walkway where Trieste's best *gelaterie* are found.

⑥ Opicina Tramway
Take the electric tramway, built in 1902, from the city centre to the top of Trieste's plateau. Enjoy amazing views of the city and the Gulf of Trieste.

⑦ Grotta Gigante
Sitting up above Trieste, this gigantic cave is full of impressive stalagmites and stalactites in weird and wonderful shapes.

The Lowdown

🌐 **Map reference** 4 H4
Address 34100 Trieste, Friuli -Venezia Giulia. Chiesa and Castello di San Giusto: Piazza della Cattedrale 3, 34100; 040 309 362; *www.reticivica.trieste. it/triestecultura/new*. Teatro Romano: Via Giuseppe Mazzini, 34121. Grotta Gigante: Borgo Grotta Gigante 42/a, 34100, Sgonico; 040 327 312; *www. grottagigante.it*.

🚗 **Train** from Venice and Udine to Trieste Centrale, bus to centre. **Bus** 42 to Grotta Gigante, 24 to Castello di San Giusto

ℹ️ **Visitor information** Via dell' Orologio 1, 34121; 040 347 8312; *www.turismofvg.it*

🕐 **Open** Grotta Gigante: 10am–6pm Tue–Sun, daily Jul– Aug. Chiesa di San Giusto: 7am–noon and 4–7pm Mon–Sat, 7:30am–1pm and 3:30–8pm

Sun. Castello di San Giusto: 9am–1pm daily

💶 **Price** Grotta Gigante: €22–38, under-6s free. Chiesa di San Giusto: free. Castello di San Giusto: €14, children and students €3

🚶 **Skipping the queue** Avoid the first week of October unless there for La Barcolana regatta.

🚩 **Guided tours** Itineraries and audio gudies available in English from the tourist office.

👪 **Age range** 8 plus

⏱️ **Allow** At least 1 day

🚻 **Toilets** At Grotta Gigante, Castello di San Giusto and cafés.

Good family value?
There is plenty to see for free with children old enough to enjoy roaming the atmospheric streets and piazzas.

Letting off steam

Take the **Opicina Tramway** up to Villa Opicina to enjoy amazing views of the city and the Gulf of Trieste *(leaves from Piazza Guglielmo Oberdan every 20 minutes; €2.20–4.40, children under 1 m (3 ft) tall free)*. At the top, take a walk or stop at one of the cafés in the village for a drink or ice cream.

View down over Trieste from the Opicina Tramway

Eat and drink

Picnic: under €25; Snacks: €25–40; Real meal: €40–80; Family treat: €80 or more (based on a family of four)

PICNIC Pick up supplies at the daily **market** in Piazza Ponterosso, right next to the Canale Grande. To eat it, walk up to the Giardino Pubblico, a tranquil oasis on Via Battisti, near Viale XX Settembre, which has a small playground.
SNACKS Sandwich Club *(Via Economo 10/b, 34100; 335 662 5130; closed Sat–Sun afternoons)* offers a good range of rolls and open sandwiches, washed down with wine by the glass for adults.

The interior of Caffè Tommaseo, once frequented by Joyce and Svevo

REAL MEAL Caffè Tommaseo *(Via Tre Novembre 5, 34100; 040 362 666; www.caffetommaseo.com)*, the oldest and most luxurious café in Trieste, opened in 1825 and was a great favourite of Italian nationalists and intellectuals and writers – among them Joyce and Svevo. It still serves delicious food in fabulous *belle époque* surroundings.

FAMILY TREAT Al Bagatto *(Via Cadorna 7, 34124; 040 301 771; www.albagatto.it; open Tue–Sat)* is considered by many to be the best seafood restaurant in the entire Friuli-Venezia Giulia area.

Shopping

Borgo Teresiano is best for clothes and shoes. In the *centro storico*, the **Umberto Saba Antiquarian Bookshop** has been at Via San Nicolò 30 since 1914, when James Joyce was teaching at the Berlitz school next door. An **antiques and flea market** is held on the third Sunday of the month near Piazza dell'Unità d'Italia.

Find out more

DIGITAL Trieste has museums devoted to Joyce and Svevo *(both Via Madonna del Mare 13, 34121; www.museojoycetrieste.it and www.museo sveviano.it)*. Their websites have interesting facts about the two writers, their friendship and Trieste, as well as guides to their old haunts.

Next stop...

CASTELLO DI MIRAMARE Built by the Habsburgs in 1856–60 on a promontory 10 km (6 miles) northwest of Trieste, surrounded by the beautiful Parco di Miramare, the castle *(www.castello-miramare.it; open daily 9am–6pm; €12–20, under-18s free)* has a dark history *(see Kids' Corner)*. Visit its richly decorated interior.

The supposedly haunted Castello di Miramare on its promontory

Exterior of the Basilica of Aquileia, which has 4th-century Roman foundations

⑬ Aquileia

Epic battles between cockerels and tortoises

Once one of the great towns of the Roman Empire, Aquileia's highlight is its **Basilica**, originally built in AD 314 – a year after Emperor Constantine first granted official status to Christians. A fabulous, well-preserved swathe of richly coloured and patterned 4th-century mosaic pavement stretches the entire length of its nave. Created between AD 314 and 319, the designs are a mix of geometric patterns, biblical stories and scenes from everyday life in ancient Aquileia. It is full of symbols including fish, symbolic of Christ; cockerels, representing the Church of Rome; lowly tortoises, depicting heresy; and colourful birds such as peacocks, symbolizing immortality. The tale of Jonah and the whale, portrayed as a sea monster, is recounted in sparkling, still-vibrant colours. The mosaics were only uncovered 100 years ago, under an 11th-century floor, and a major restoration took place in 2000, when they were painstakingly polished, stone by stone.

Letting off steam

Climb to the top of the bell tower, which is right next to the Basilica. Stroll by the river, just behind the Basilica, and find the wharfs where the Roman boats used to dock. While walking, count the number of pillars left by the Romans.

Prices given are for a family of four

The Lowdown

Map reference 4 G4
Address Basilica: Piazza Capitolo, 33051 Aquileia, Friuli Venezia-Giulia; 0431 91067; *www.aquileia.net*

Train to Cervignano, then bus to Aquileia (*www.saf.ud.it*)

Visitor information Via Iulia Augusta, 33051; 0431 919 491; *www.turismo.fvg.it*

Open 9am–1pm and 2–5pm daily (until 7pm Jul–Aug)

Price Basilica: free. Crypt €11, under-10s free

Age range All

Activities Download from *www.aquileiaforum.org.*

Allow 2 hours

Wheelchair access Partial: to main church but not to crypt

Eat and Drink *Snacks* A café and a *gelateria* opposite the Basilica offers a good range of snacks. *Real meal* Antico Monastero di Beligna *(Località Beligna 4, 33051; 340 530 0162; www.beligna.com)*, serves good homemade pasta.

Toilets Next to the Basilica

⑭ Grado

It's all about the beach!

Grado, or the Golden Island as it was called, was famous as an official health resort for the Habsburg Empire at the end of the 19th century. Tubercular children were brought here to be cured by the freshwater spring. The **Terme Marine** are as popular now as they were then, as are the beaches lapped by warm waters. Like Venice, Grado is in the Adriatic lagoon, surrounded by small islands that provide a haven for birdlife. On a clear day it is possible to see the snow-capped peaks of the Dolomites. Take a stroll around the picturesque old town, visit the Duomo and compare the mosaics with those of Aquileia – less colourful, but more geometric.

The Lowdown

Map reference 4 G4
Address 34073 Grado, Friuli Venezia-Giulia. Terme Marine: Largo San Grisogono 3, 34073; 0431 876 375; *www.gradoit.it*

Train to Cervignano, then bus (25 minutes; *www.saf.ud.it)* to Piazza Carpaccio, near the port

Visitor information Viale Dante 72, 34073; 0431 877 111; *www.grado.it*

Open Terme Marine: 8:30am–7:30pm daily.

Price Terme Marine: check website for details.

Age range All, but the Terme Marine are aimed at adults.

Activities Boat trips depart daily from Canale della Schiusa; €17, under-4s free *(www.motoscafigradesi.it)*

Eat and drink *Real meal* Agli Artisti *(Campiello Porta Grande 2; 34073; 0431 83081; www.agliartistigrado.com; closed Tue)* is a fabulous fish restaurant near the market, with delicious desserts. Spaghetti House *(Via Gradenigo 33, 34073; 0431 84361)* serves good pasta.

Festivals Festival Laguna Golosa (food and wine): early Sep

The Spiaggia Costa Azzurra in Grado, a popular buckets-and-spades beach

Letting off steam

Swim and sunbathe on the free beaches or take the boat trip out to **Barbana**, a pretty little island in the lagoon with a resident community of Franciscans. There is plenty of room to play and picnic here. Miniclub entertainment is offered for children on the main beach, or visit the bouncy castle play parks in the centre, next to the main entrance to the beach.

⑮ Udine

The city of Tiepolo

Udine is a charming city with lagoons to its south and the Carnic Alps to the north. It has a lovely old centre surrounded by canals and is also the capital of Friuli nationalism – the language spoken around town is the Friuli dialect. From 1420 to 1797 Udine was under Venetian rule, and the lion of St Mark is visible everywhere. The Venetian influence is also apparent in the city's pretty squares and loggias, and in the splendid frescoes by Venetian artist Giambattista Tiepolo (1696–1770).

The best way to appreciate the city is to wander around the old centre and the portico-lined piazzas between Piazza Libertà – "the most beautiful Venetian piazza on the mainland," according to the proud Udinese – and Piazza Matteotti. They were built in the 15th and 16th centuries to create the atmosphere of an open-air *salotto* (sitting room). Then visit the buildings that house the great Tiepolo frescoes painted for Udinese patron Dionisio Delfino between 1726 and 1728: the

Red-and-white striped Loggia del Lionello in Piazza Libertà, Udine

Galleria del Tiepolo, **Duomo** and **Oratorio della Purità**. Young Tiepolo was a celebrity of his day for his sunny Rococo style.

Letting off steam

Pick up a bike from the tourist office and ride around the city, perhaps heading to Udine's Castello, set in grassy parkland perfect for picnicking, with views from the Alps to the Adriatic Sea. For a real splash-out, drive to **Aquasplash** at Lignano Sabbiadoro *(1 hour south; open 10am–6pm daily Jun–Aug; €70; www.aquasplash.it)*. While there, stop off to talk to the many species of parrots at the **Parco dei Pappagalli** in Latisana *(open daily 9:30am–7pm Mar–Oct, 10am–5pm Nov–Feb; €26; www.parcodeipappagalli.com)*.

Piazza Matteotti, also known as Piazza delle Erbe or Piazza San Giacomo, Udine

The Lowdown

🌐 **Map reference** 4 G3
   Address 33100 Udine, Friuli Venezia-Giulia. Galleria del Tiepolo: Piazza Patriarcato 1, 33100; 0432 298 056; *www.musdioc-tiepolo.it*. Duomo: Piazza del Duomo, 33100. Oratorio della Purità: Via del Pozzo, 33100

🚃 **Train** from Venice or Trieste

ℹ **Visitor information** Piazza I Maggio 7, 33100; 0432 295 972; *www.turismo.fvg.it*

🕐 **Open** Galleria del Tiepolo: 10am–noon and 3:30–6:30pm Wed–Sun, Oratorio: 9–noon and 4–6pm Mon–Sat, 4–6pm Sun

💶 **Price** Galleria del Tiepolo: €10, under-6s free

👫 **Age range** All

⏱ **Allow** At least 1 day

☕ **Eat and drink** *Real meal* Al Vecchio Stallo *(Via Viola 7, 33100; 0432 21296)* serves local cuisine in a shady courtyard. *Family treat* Hostaria alla Tavernetta *(Via di Prampero 2, 33100; 0432 501 066)*, by the Duomo, prepares local dishes made with top-quality ingredients.

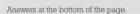

Where to stay in the Veneto and Friuli-Venezia Giulia

Accommodation is plentiful at every price level. In the cities, simple B&Bs and boutique establishments are found alongside luxury five-star hotels, while in the countryside some of the best options are farms, set in attractive surroundings.

AGENCIES

fvg.info
www.friuliveneziagiulia.info/
Offers details of B&Bs, farms and hotels in the region.

Agriturismo
www.agriturismofriulivg.it/
A great website for farm stays.

Aquileia
Map 4 G4

HOTEL

Hotel Patriarchi
Via G Augusta12, 33051; 0431 919 595; www.hotelpatriarchi.it
Family-run hotel with 23 modern rooms and an excellent restaurant serving traditional Fruili cuisine (half-board an option). Bikes available for hire, and staff can give suggestions for trails to explore in the area.

€€

Grado
Map 4 G4

HOTEL

Locanda Ambriabella
Riva Sant'Andrea 36, 34073 Isola della Schiusa; 0431 84753; www.ambriabella.it
A charming hotel, with just six spacious, airy rooms in an idyllic position, facing out over the lagoon. The suite is good for families.

€

Lignano Sabbiadoro
Map G5 6

AGRITURISMO

Tenuta Regina Agriturismo
Via Tenuta Regina 8, Palazzolo dello Stella, 33056; 0431 587 971; www.adriabella.com/tenutaregina
Ten elegantly renovated apartments in idyllic countryside, with a pool, table tennis, a big garden and a playground – an ideal spot for a family holiday.

€€

Padua
Map 4 E5

B&B

Casa Ciriani
Via Guazzi 1, 35031 Abano Terme; 0497 15272; www.casaciriani.com
An appealing B&B set in extensive grounds, with just three large rooms, furnished with antiques. Family-run, with personal service.

€

Clean, modern interior of a room in Due Mori, Vicenza

Treviso see p76

Trieste
Map 4 H4

HOTEL

Albero Nascosto
Via Felice Venezian 18, 34124; 040 300 188; www.alberonascosto.it
This beautifully renovated building has studio apartments.

€€€

Udine
Map 4 G3

HOTEL

Hotel Ristorante Allegria
Via Grazzano 18, 33100; 0432 201 116; www.hotelallegria.it
An attractive, small hotel with large rooms and excellent bathrooms.

€€

AGRITURISMO

La Faula Agriturismo
Via Faula 5, 33040 Ravosa di Povoletto; 334 399 6734; www.faula.com
A working farm set in beautiful countryside within easy driving

distance of Udine. Its nine rooms are characterful, and the restaurant serves up farm-fresh produce.

€€

Verona
Map 3 C5

HOTEL

Hotel Giulietta e Romeo
Vicolo Tre Marchetti 3, 37121; 045 800 3554; www.giulietta eromeo.com
A centrally located hotel just a block from the Arena and Verona's main shopping street. Large, comfortable rooms with modern bathrooms. Friendly staff. Ideal for a city stay.

P €€

Vicenza
Map 3 D5

HOTEL

Due Mori
Corso Giuseppe Mazzini 73/75, 36063 Marostica; 0424 471 777; www.duemori.it
An 18th-century townhouse in the heart of medieval Marostica (about 30 km/20 miles from Vicenza, near Bassano del Grappa). Beautifully renovated with 12 inviting rooms.

€€

Tenuta Regina Agriturismo, near the sandy beaches of Lignano Sabbiadoro

Price Guide

The following price ranges are based on one night's accommodation in high season for a family of four, inclusive of service charges and any additional taxes.

€ Under €200 €€ €200–350 €€€ over €350

Trentino-Alto Adige

This mountainous, German-speaking frontier region became the Alto Adige after World War I; until then it was part of the Austrian Tyrol. The limestone peaks of the Dolomites are its huge draw, offering winter sports, hiking and wildflower-filled meadows, and the unmissable sight is Ötzi, the mummified remains of a Copper Age man, now on display in Bolzano.

Below The Messner Mountain Museum Firmian, high in the Dolomites

Merano
p98

Bolzano
p94

① Bolzano (Bozen)
Meet Ötzi – he is 5,000 years old!

With its Gothic spires and frescoed houses, this lovely Alpine market town is a mix of Germanic and Italian cultures, and regularly wins polls as the town where Italians would most like to live. Do not miss Ötzi the Ice Man in the Museo Archeologico (archaeological museum) – a chance to come face to face with a 5,000-year-old ancestor – or the Museo Scienze Naturali Alto Adige (Natural History Museum), with examples of sea creatures fossilized in rock from the Dolomites.

Ötzi museum sign, Museo Archeologico

Key Features

① **Museion** Make creative discoveries on Family Sundays at the Museum of Modern and Contemporary Art.

③ **Piazza delle Erbe (Obstplatz)** A fruit and vegetable market is held here Monday–Saturday. The Neptune fountain (1745) is nicknamed Gabelwirt (Innkeeper with a Fork).

⑤ **Piazza Walther (Waltherplatz)** A statue of poet Walther von der Vogelweide reigns over the main square.

⑥ **Via Portici (Lauben)** This is an arcaded medieval street in typical Tyrolean style.

⑦ **Museo Scienze Naturali Alto Adige (Naturmuseum Südtirol)** Experiments, models and games tell the story of the Dolomites.

[Map of Bolzano showing locations: Castel Mareccio, Castel Róncolo (2.5 km/1.5 miles), Museo Scienze Naturali Alto Adige ⑦, Piazza delle Erbe ③, Museo Archaeologico ②, Via Portici ⑥, Funivia del Renon ⑧, Piazza Walther ⑤, Museion ①, Duomo ④. Scale: 0 metres 200 / 0 yards 200]

② **Museo Archeologico**
The major exhibit here is Copper Age man Ötzi's mummified body, which was found in the ice of the Ötztal Alps in 1991 (see p100), and is kept perfectly chilled in a special freezer cabinet.

④ **Duomo (Dom)** Stonemasons from Lombardy began Bolzano's cathedral in Romanesque style in 1295; it was finished by Swabian masons in Gothic style in 1382.

⑧ **Funivia del Renon (Rittner Seilbahn)** The cable car makes the 950-m (3,120-ft) ascent to Renon, on the mountain of the same name, in an incredible 12 minutes.

The Lowdown

🌐 **Map reference** 3 D2
Address 39100 Bolzano (Bozen), Trentino-Alto Adige. Museion: Via Dante, *www.museion.it*; Museo Archeologico: Via Museo 43, *www.iceman.it*; Museo Scienze Naturali Alto Adige: Via Bottai 1, *www.natur museum.it*; Cable car: *www.sii.bz.it*

🚗 **Train** Innsbruck–Verona *(www.sii. bz.it)*. **Car** 1–2 hours from Verona or Innsbruck (A22 motorway from Innsbruck can be very slow).

ℹ **Visitor information** Piazza Walther 8, 39100; 0471 307 000; *www.bolzano-bozen.it*; 9am–6:30pm Mon–Fri, 9am–noon Sat

🕐 **Open** Museion: 10am–6pm Tue–Sun (till 10pm Thu). Museo Archeologico: 10am–6pm Tue–Sun (also Mon Jul, Aug, Dec). Duomo: 10am–noon, 2–5pm Mon–Fri, 10am–noon Sat. Museo Scienze Naturali Alto Adige: 10am–6pm Tue–Sun. Cable car: every 4 mins, option to return by train every 30 mins

💶 **Price** Museion: family ticket €12, free 5–10pm Thu. Museo Archeologico: family ticket €18. Museo Scienze Naturali Alto Adige: family ticket €10, under-6s free. Cable car: individual €3.50 return, €5 for train

👫 **Skipping the queue** Museum Mobilcard allows entry to South Tyrol museums for 3/7 days: adults €20/25, children €10/12.50; from tourist office and museums; *www.mobilcard.info*

👫 **Age range** All

⏱ **Activities** Bike hire from the tourist office (€5 a day). See Museion website for workshops.

⏱ **Allow** At least a day

Good family value?
There is heaps to see in Bolzano, with good family ticket prices and plenty of free attractions.

The 13th-century Castel Roncolo (Schloss Runkelstein) near Bolzano

Letting off steam

The grassy **riverbanks** just north of the Talvera (Talfer) bridge are a peaceful spot for picnicking, and there are two playgrounds, one next to **Mareccio (Maretsch) Castle**. A cycle path on the west bank leads to the **Castel Roncolo (Schloss Runkelstein)**. Alternatively, take the cable car up to Renon and another cable car up to Schwarzseespitze (2,070 m/6,791 ft) and do a signposted, circular panoramic walk (1 hour, easy), or take the narrow-gauge tram from Renon to Collalbo (Klobenstein). In winter, rent sledges from the cable-car ticket office and have fun on the 2-km (1-mile) run (easy to medium).

Eat and drink

Picnic: under €25; Snacks: €25–40; Real meal: €40–80; Family treat: €80 or more (based on a family of four)

PICNIC Coin *(Via Portici 42, 39100, 0471 976352, www.coin.it)* supermarket or the fresh-produce **market on Piazza delle Erbe** are good places to stock up on supplies. **Franziskaner** bakery *(Via dei Franceschi/Franziskanergasse 3, 39100)* sells delicious German-style bread. Head to the Talvera (Talfer) river for a scenic picnic.
SNACKS Stadt Café Città *(Piazza Walther 21, 39100; 0471 975 221)* is a spacious café in the centre of town with outdoor tables on the main square, great for organic sandwiches, delicious Austrian-style cakes and ice cream.
REAL MEAL Hopfen & Co *(Piazza delle Erbe (Obstplatz) 17, 39100; 0471 300 788; www.boznerbier.it)* is a pub-restaurant with outdoor

tables on the cobbled street and a cosy and dark interior. It serves hearty local dishes such as barley pasta and beer dumplings.
FAMILY TREAT Ca' de Bezzi/ Batzenhäusl *(Via Andreas Hofer/ Andreas-Hofer-Strasse 30, 39100; 0471 050 950; www.batzen.it; open 11am–1am)*, a 600-year-old inn with outdoor tables in summer, has good food and music. There are mixed plates of hams and cheeses to share, and the speciality dish is *canederli* (dumplings) in broth.

Shopping

For toys, games and presents try **Creativ** *(Via della Roggia 24, off Via Museo)* or **Gutweniger** *(Via Doktor Streiter 14, 39100)*. Via Doktor Streiter, parallel to Portici (Lauben), has several quirky shops selling cool clothes, chocolate and fun stuff that kids will love to browse.

Find out more

DIGITAL There is plenty of information about Copper Age man Ötzi at *www.iceman.it*. Click on "Kids" on the homepage and choose between three sections for different age groups. For more about knights, troubadours and the medieval code of chivalry, visit *medievaleurope.mrdonn.org*.

A stone figure at the Messner Mountain Museum in Firmiano (Sigmundskron)

Next stop...

MESSNER MOUNTAIN MUSEUM FIRMIAN Pedal to Castel Sigmundskron, 25 minutes by bike on the cycle path from Bolzano. One of the oldest forts in South Tyrol, it dates from AD 945, has walls 5 m (16 ft) thick, and has been restored by mountaineer Reinhold Messner as part of the Messner Mountain Museum *(www. messner-mountain-museum.it)*.

② Alpe di Siusi (Seiser Alm)

On the trail of witch-hunters

A day spent mountain-biking, hiking or picnicking in the wildflower-strewn meadows of the Alpe di Siusi (Seiser Alm) is a breath of fresh air after more strenuous sightseeing elsewhere. To get to the Alpe – Europe's largest Alpine plateau, extending for 60 sq km (23 square miles) and bordered by flat-topped Sciliar (Schlern), the emblem of the Dolomites – park in Siusi (Seis) and take the **cable car** up to Compaccio (Compatsch). A map at the top cable-car station shows walk routes. Try hiking up to the viewpoint at Bullaccia (Puflatsch; one and a half hours), or take the chairlift. A path continues to the throne-like rocks known as the Panche delle Streghe (Hexenbänke) or "witches' benches".

Sciliar was associated with pagan rituals and worship until medieval times, when nine women were

Cable car from Siusi (Seis) to Compaccio (Compatsch) in the Alpe di Siusi

burned at the stake as witches. Chief witch-hunter was Leonhard of Völs (1458–1530), who worked for the bishops of Bressanone (Brixen). Visit **Castel (Schloss) Prösels**, his home, with parts dating back to the 13th century. An early 16th-century peasants' revolt against Leonhard's high taxes suggests that poverty and malnutrition – rather than black magic – were to blame for the high infant mortality rate.

Letting off steam

The wide grassy meadows of the Alpe are perfect for ball games or Frisbee, as well as walking. From Easter to early November, the **Maneggio Unterlanzin** horse-riding stables in Castelrotto (Kastelruth) *(0471 706 575)* can arrange day treks on their Haflinger horses.

③ Great Dolomites Road

Mountains steeped in legend

For the best of the Dolomites, drive on the SS241 and then the SS48 from Bolzano in the direction of Cortina d'Ampezzo. Among the most beautiful mountains in Europe, these vast rocky bastions have been eroded over the last 200 million years into a weird and wonderful array of towers and pinnacles. The valleys that radiate from here have been home for thousands of years to the Ladins – a people whose culture is steeped in legend. Cable cars travel from the small resorts making it possible to walk along

high, well-marked footpaths without the need for anything beyond average fitness. In the Val di Fassa, take the **chairlift** that travels in three stages from Pera di Fassa to Ciampedie at 2,000 m (6,562 ft), where there is a children's playground and a choice of refuges for drinks and meals. An easy forest trail (50 minutes) leads from Ciampedie to the Gardeccia refuge, giving a closer view of the Catinaccio (Rosengarten) range and the Torri di Vajolet peaks, which turn a spectacular rosy red at sunset.

Letting off steam

Walk a section of the **Viel del Pan** ("trail of bread" in Venetian dialect), a grain-smuggling route used to avoid taxes in the 17th century. It is signposted from Albergo Savoia at Passo Pordoi. After the initial rocky, uneven section, a level path cut into the turf traverses the mountainside.

The Lowdown

- 🌐 **Map reference** 4 E3
  Address 38030–38039, Trentino-Alto Adige
- 🚗 **Car** essential for this route
- ℹ️ **Visitor information** Seasonal offices in villages; www.fassa.com
- 🕐 **Open** Pera di Fassa–Ciampedie chairlift: late Jun–early Sep
- 🎫 **Skipping the queue** Avoid August, when roads and hiking trails are very busy.
- 👫 **Age range** 7 plus for easy walks, but wear proper walking boots and check the weather.
- ⏱️ **Allow** A day to a week
- ☕ **Eat and drink** *Picnic* Buy provisions for a barbecue in Bolzano and picnic at Andraz. *Real meal* Ciampedie refuge (38039 Vigo di Fassa; 0462 764 432) has a restaurant serving traditional local cuisine.

Ciampedie refuge and the Catinaccio (Rosengarten) mountains

④ Passo Falzàrego and the Cinque Torri

World War I on the frontline

Do not be alarmed by the World War I soldier standing guard outside the **Tre Sassi fort** on the road to the Passo di Valparola (2,168 m/7,113 ft) – he is just keeping an eye on the museum commemorating the 1914–18 war inside (and is just an actor).

The fortress was built to defend the southern reaches of the Austro-Hungarian empire, and fighting between Italy and Austria broke out here in 1915. The fort was destroyed by Italian missiles; now restored, it contains soldiers' kit, letters and weapons and photographs showing the harsh conditions that soldiers on both sides fought under. The conflict was bitter, and neither side could gain the upper hand: Austrian troops controlled the mountainous ridge overlooking the Falzàrego and Valparola passes, while Italian troops took up a position on the south face of Lagazuoi Piccolo (2,779 m/ 9,117 ft). To get an idea of what fighting in the mountains was like, take the **cable car** up from Passo di Falzàrego to Lagazuoi.

From Falzàrego drive 3 km (2 miles) in the direction of Cortina d'Ampezzo to the Cinque Torri Funivia station. Take the **chairlift** to the top, where Rifugio Scoiattoli lies directly ahead. A gravel path

leads off to the left to the **Cinque Torri** (Five Towers) open-air museum, a fascinating restoration of the Italian mountain artillery unit HQ, complete with armoured trenches and cannon emplacements trained on the Austrian troops at the Tre Sassi fort. Easy, well-marked routes ranging from 15 minutes to 3 hours wind their way along the trenches.

Letting off steam

The grassy slopes around **Rifugio Scoiattoli** are perfect for a run around, and there is the option of walking back down to your car instead of taking the chairlift.

Walkers pausing to look at the war memorials at Passo di Falzàrego

Picnic under €25; **Snacks** €25–40; **Real meal** €40–80; **Family treat** €80 or more (based on a family of four)

5 Merano (Meran)

Spa town with bobsleighs and bikes

Merano's medieval core of narrow, porticoed streets expanded into an elegant spa town in the 19th century; the thermal baths (Terme) make it a great family destination. Towering above town is a superb 12th-century castle owned by the counts of Tyrol. Above this rise the Giogaia di Tessa (Texelgruppe) mountains. An easy, high-level footpath encircles this wild nature park, and a cycle path traces the old Via Claudia Augustus along the River Adige to Malles, at the head of the Val Venosta (Vinschgau).

Castel Tirolo above Merano

Key Features

① **Terme Merano** Merano's family-friendly thermal baths were created by hip architect Matteo Thun in 2005. It has both indoor and outdoor pools.

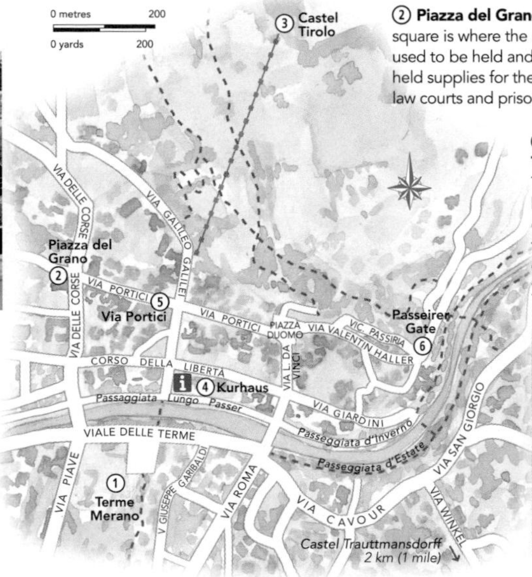

② **Piazza del Grano (Kornplatz)** This square is where the medieval corn market used to be held and warehouses here once held supplies for the whole of Tyrol. Now, the law courts and prison are on this square.

③ **Castel Tirolo (Schloss Tirol)** A chairlift runs to Tirolo (Dorf Tirol) and the huge castle. For an idea of medieval daily life, there are hands-on displays in the kitchen yard.

④ **Kurhaus** During Merano's heyday at the end of the 19th century, the great and the good of the Austro-Hungarian empire came to the town for their winter "cure" at the Art Nouveau Kurhaus.

⑤ **Via Portici (Laubengasse)** Since the early Middle Ages, this arcaded street has been the commercial heart of Merano. The original owners lived above their shops.

⑥ **Passeirer Gate** Merano was surrounded by defensive walls and towers in the 13th century. This ivy-covered, gable-roofed tower is one of the three surviving town gates.

The Lowdown

Map reference 3 D2
Address 39012 Merano. Terme Merano: Piazza Terme 9, *www.thermemeran.it*. Castel Tirolo: Schlossweg 24; *www.schlosstirol.it*. Alpine Bob: *www.meran2000.net*.

Train from Bolzano *(www.sii.bz.it)*. Merano–Tirolo **seggiovia** (chairlift) for Castel Tirolo (9am–6/7pm; €37). Bergbahn **funivia** (cable car; 9am–5/6pm; €72) or Falzeben **cabinovia** (gondola; 9am–5/6pm; €27) to Piffing 1950 lift station for Alpine Bob

Bikemobil Card allows free travel on South Tyrol's trains and cable cars, and free bike rental from Val Venosta stations *(one-day pass €72; www.vinschgauerbahn.it)*.

Visitor information Corso Liberia 45, 0473 272 000, *www.meranerland.com*

Open Terme: 9am–10pm. Castel: Tue–Sun 10am–5pm 15 Mar–11 Dec (until 6pm Aug). Alpine Bob: daily 10am–4:30pm (until 5:30pm Jul–Aug)

Price Terme: all-day ticket €58–63. Castel: €12. Alpine Bob: €12.40 for one run, discounts for more.

Guided tours Castel Tirolo €2

Age range Any

Allow One day to one week

Café In Terme, Castel Tirolo and Touriseum, and around town

Toilets In Castel Tirolo and at Touriseum, and in cafés

Festivals Easter horse races. Grape festival: late Oct. Törggelen (first wine celebration): Oct–Nov

Good family value?
Merano and its environs are great fun for families, but not cheap.

Prices given are for a family of four

Letting off steam

For a real adrenaline rush, try **Alpine Bob** at Merano 2000 – the longest bob run in Italy. Starting 1,900 m (6,234 ft) above the valley, sleds speed along rails through the trees and down the snowy slopes (grassy in summer), for a thrilling 1-km (half-mile) white-knuckle ride (kids under 10 must go with an adult). It is also possible to ski here. Alternatively, head to the **Meraner Höhenweg**, pick up a bike from a train station along the Val Venosta (Vinschgau) and cycle a section of the **Via Claudia Augustus**.

Gourmet wine bar and food shop at the Pur Südtirol farmers' market

Eat and drink

Picnic: under €25; Snacks: €25–40; Real meal: €40–80; Family treat: €80 or more (based on a family of four)

PICNIC Pur Südtirol (Corso Libertà/ Freiheitsstrasse 35, 39012; 0473 012 140; www.pursuedtirol.com; open all day Mon–Sat) is a covered farmers' market, selling South Tyrolean delicacies including cheese, ham, bread and fruit. Take the chairlift from Merano to Tirolo (Dorf Tirol) and on to Hochmuth to picnic on the slopes of the Giogaia di Tessa (Texelgruppe) mountains. **SNACKS Caffé Kunsthaus** (Via Portici/Laubengasse 163, 39012; 0473 427 050; www.kunst meranoartc.org), within Merano's contemporary art gallery in the Cassa di Risparmio (Sparkasse) building, is a lively place to meet, serving pasta at lunchtime. **REAL MEAL Pfefferlechner** (St Martinsweg 4, 39011 Lana; www. pfefferlechner.it) is a place to wine and dine rustic-style, with a beer garden and playground, and medieval dining rooms overlooking the stables. This historic inn brews its own beer and produces its own smoked bacon and trout, as well as hearty Tyrolean dishes and desserts.

FAMILY TREAT Hotel Terme Merano (Piazza Terme/Thermeplatz 1, 39012; 0473 259 000; www. hoteltermemerano.com), a family-friendly hotel in the heart of Merano, has several dining options. At its Wolkenstein restaurant, diners can watch the chefs in the open kitchen as they prepare light South Tyrolean cuisine with a Mediterranean twist, including dishes such as tomato soup with courgette *ravioli* and *gnocchi* with gorgonzola and ratatouille.

Shopping

Visit **Alte Mühle** (Via Cassa di Risparmio, Sparkassenstrasse 11/a, 39012; 0473 274 442) for books and games. **Bimbo** (Corso Libertà 174, 39012; 0473 236 325) and **Exclusive Holz und Spiel** (Corso Libertà 34, 39012; 0473 220 945) both sell toys.

Find out more

Learn more about castles like Castel Tirolo at www.childrensmuseum. org/castles/games.php. Play games to equip a knight ready for battle and protect the kingdom without causing a peasants' revolt to win treasure (for children aged 5–9).

Next stop...

TOURISEUM (Via San Valentino/St Valentin Str 51/a, 39012; www. touriseum.it) Set in beautiful botanical gardens 2 km (1 mile) from Merano, Trauttmansdorff Castle is home to the Touriseum, a fun, interactive museum covering major historic events in the South Tyrol. Exhibits include film footage of troops abseiling down cliffs with cannons and skiing James Bond style down snowy slopes in World War I – the action blockbusters of their day.

Trauttmansdorff Castle, set in vast botanical gardens just outside Merano

① Merano continued ▶

KIDS' CORNER

All in a day's work
Castles were homes for nobles and royalty, and it took many people to keep one running smoothly. See if you can match the job title to the task.
Job titles:
1 Bottler or butler
2 Porter
3 Fletcher
4 Bowyer
5 Man at arms
Tasks:
a Grab weapons and fight at a moment's notice!
b Make bows.
c Guard the gate and decide who to let into the castle.
d Look after fresh water and drinks.
e Make arrows.

Answers at the bottom of the page.

SÜDTIROL BANNED!
After the South Tyrol became part of Italy in 1919, the Fascist Government banned all German names. Resort names were Italianized, and from 1923 on, using Südtirol instead of Alto Adige was a punishable offence.

Scary mountains
Question: What did early travellers to Merano fear?
1 Highwaymen
2 Mountain scenery
3 Falling rocks, landslides and avalanches
4 A coach wheel breaking
Answer: All of them! It was not until the Romantic movement of the early 1800s that wild, rugged landscapes were thought beautiful – until then, travellers would draw their carriage curtains so they did not have to look at the "awful scenery".

Answers: 1 d 2 c 3 e 4 b 5 a

⑥ ArcheoParc

Travel back in time to the Copper Age

In 1991, the 5,000-year-old iceman Ötzi was discovered in a glacier on the Italian-Austrian border. His remains are displayed in Bolzano's archaeological museum (see p94). After visiting Ötzi there, a trip up the wooded Val Senales (Schnalstal) to the ArcheoParc reveals what daily life would have been like for this Copper Age man. The open-air museum is a reconstructed village from 3,500 BC, where visitors can try their hand at archery using flint-tipped arrows, make a fire, bake bread and smelt copper – the metal that lent its name to a whole period in human history. Around the huts, fields have been sown with cereals, fruit, vegetables, poppies and flax – essential Neolithic crops.

Clues from Ötzi's mummified body, and objects found nearby, reveal what he did in the hours before he died. Ötzi's final meal was deer and ibex (wild goat) meat, grain and vegetables. His shoes had woven inner liners and were stuffed with straw to keep his feet warm; and he was hastily carving himself a new bow as he dodged attackers, before an arrow pierced his left shoulder, fatally wounding him.

Letting off steam

Guided glacier tours suitable for children of eight years and up set off from the head of the valley, where the **Grawand cable car** ascends to the Ötztal Alps

The Lowdown

- 🌐 **Map reference** 3 C2
  Address Madonna (Unser Frau) 163, 39020 Val Senales (Schnalstal); 0473 67 60 20; www.archeoparc.it
- 🚌 **Bus** from Merano train station to Naturno (Naturns), then bus to ArcheoParc (www.sii.biz.it)
- ℹ️ **Visitor information** Certosa 42, 39020 Senales; 0473 679 148; www.schnalstal.com; open 8:30am–noon, 2–6pm Mon–Fri, 8:30am–noon Sat
- 🕐 **Open** Easter–Oct 10am–6pm Tue–Sun (also Mon Jul–Aug)
- 💶 **Price** €23
- 🚻 **Age range** All
- ⏱️ **Allow** Half a day to a day
- 🍴 **Eat and drink** Picnic Bring supplies from Merano and picnic on the shores of Lake Vernago (Vernagt), up the valley from the ArcheoParc. Snacks The small café-bar at the ArcheoParc has local fruit juice and wine.

(www.schnalstal.com or www. bergsteiger schule.com/en/ tagestouren.php). Or have a go on the thrilling Flying Fox run at the **Ötzi Rope Park** (www.schnalstal. com/en/activities/high-rope-garden) at Lake Vernago (Vernagt).

⑦ MuseoPassiria

Heroes and firing squads

The Tyrol has been much fought over by neighbouring superpowers, but when Bavarian and Napoleonic troops invaded at the end of the 18th century, the Tyrolean people

fought back. Innkeeper and cattle dealer Andreas Hofer (1767–1810) led rebellions and was hailed as a hero, but ended up being executed by firing squad, on Napoleon's orders. To commemorate his stand, Hofer's birthplace, the Sandhof Inn outside San Leonardo in Passiria (St Leonhard in Passeier), has been turned into a fascinating museum of Tyrolean history and heroism – the MuseoPassiria (MuseumPasseier).

Do not miss the hamlet of chalets that have been transported here from various parts of the valley, with barns and beehives, a mill for making loden (felt fabric) and a schnapps still.

Letting off steam

There is a playground in San Leonardo, below the fire station. Or walk up to **Pfistradalm** at 1,350 m (4,430 ft; 1½ hours), where there is a dairy.

Relief showing the Tyrolean people rebelling against invaders, MuseoPassiria

The Lowdown

- 🌐 **Map reference** 3 D2
  Address MuseoPassiria (MuseumPasseier), Via Passiria (Passeirer Strasse) 72, 39015 San Leonardo in Passiria (St Leonhard in Passeier); 0473 659 086; www.museum.passeier.it
- 🚌 **Bus** from Merano station to Val Passiria (Passeiertal; www.sii.bz.it)
- ℹ️ **Visitor information** Via Passiria 40, 39015 San Leonardo in Passiria; 0473 656 188; www.passeiertal.it
- 🕐 **Open** 10am–6pm Tue–Sun mid-Mar–Oct (daily Aug–Sep)
- 💶 **Price** €14
- 🚻 **Age range** Any
- ⏱️ **Allow** 2 hours
- 🍴 **Eat and drink** Picnic Bio Bergkäserei (Handwerker-zone Lahne 7/1, 39010; 0473 650 139) in St Martin, 2 km (1 mile) along the Merano road, sells mountain cheeses. Picnic next to the river. Real meal Trattoria Lamm (Via Villaggio 36, 39010 San Martino in Passiria; 0473 641 240; www. gasthaus-lamm.it) serves home-made pasta and strudel.

Visitors making a bow at ArcheoParc, which recreates life in the Neolithic age

Prices given are for a family of four

The 13th-century Juval Castle, housing the Messner Mountain Museum

⑧ Juval Castle

Mystery, masks and a mountain zoo

The higher up a mountain you are, the closer you are to heaven, some religions say, and this link between spirituality, mystery and mountains is explored at the magical museum in Castel (Schloss) Juval. Masks from five continents decorate the walls of the castle, which dates back to 1298. One room has been turned into a Tibetan-style Buddhist temple, and the castle courtyard contains statues of Hindu deities.

The museum is the brainchild and summer residence of Reinhold Messner, one of the world's greatest climbers, who grew up in the Dolomites. Messner has got pretty close to heaven himself: he is famous for the first oxygen-free ascent of Everest in 1978, and then for being the first to climb all 14 of the peaks over 8,000 m (26,000 ft) in the world. While here, don't miss the small mountain zoo and the exhibition about Tibetan mythological hero Gesar of Ling.

Letting off steam

Take a trip to the **Parcines (Partschins) waterfall**, one of the highest (97 m/ 318 ft) and most beautiful in the Alps. A shuttle bus runs from Parcines village to the Birkenwald car park, then it is a short walk to a viewing platform overlooking the falls, most impressive from May to July or after heavy rainfall (*www.partschins.com/en*).

The Lowdown

🌐 **Map reference** 3 C2
Address MMM Juval, Castel Juval, Castelbello (Kastelbell) 39020; 348 443 3871; *www.messner-mountain-museum.it*

🚗 **Train** to Stava (Staben) from Merano (Meran) (*www.sii.bz.it*).
Car to castle car park on Naturno (Naturns) to Stava (Staben) road, then shuttle bus (*0473 668 058*) or 1-hour walk along signposted paths beside the Stabner, Tscharser or Schnalser irrigation channels up to the castle.

🕐 **Open** 10am–4pm Thu–Tue, Palm Sunday–Jun and Sep–Oct

🎫 **Price** Family ticket €18

🚩 **Guided tours** Visits by frequent guided tours in German only; tour lasts 1 hour.

👫 **Age range** All

⏱ **Allow** At least 3 hours, including the walk to and from the car park

🍴 **Eat and drink** *Picnic* Vinschger Bauernladen (*Juval, Naturno, 30095; www.bauernladen.it*) is a farm shop at the foot of the hill. Stock up here on cheese, ham and fruit and picnic in the Val Martello, which leads into the heart of the Parco Nazionale dello Stelvio (Stelvio National Park). *Real meal* Schlosswirt (*Juval, 39020 Castelbello-Ciardes (Kastelbell-Tschars); 0473 668 056; www.schlosswirtjuval.it; open Mar–Nov 10am–7pm Sun–Tue, until midnight Thu–Sat*) is a restaurant in a restored farmhouse just below the castle. Enjoy local organic produce and fresh herbs in the delicious traditional Tyrolean dishes here.

Where to Stay in Trentino-Alto Adige

The Dolomites' scenery is matched by warm hospitality. Hotels that have been in the same family for generations are not unusual, and farmstays give an insight into a traditional way of life. But there is also a new breed of hotel, offering a modern take on Alpine style, glamorous but welcoming to children.

FARM HOLIDAYS
Red Rooster
Südtiroler Bauernbund Red Rooster, K M Gamper-Strasse 5, Bolzano (Bozen), 39100; 0471 999 325; www.redrooster.it
An agency that connects visitors to South Tyrol with farmers who offer guesthouse or self-catering accommodation.

Aldino (Aldein)   Map 3 D3

HOTEL
Krone Gasthof
Piazza Principale (Dorfplatz) 3, 39040; 0471 886 825; www.gasthof-krone.it
With wood-burning fires, ornate ceramic stoves and painted furniture, this friendly village inn dating back to 1577 has 13 rooms. It is practical, with a family apartment, as well as historic, with suits of armour guarding the landings.

🛏 🐾 🍽 🍴   €€

Krone Gasthof, a historic village inn with traditional furnishings in Aldino

Bolzano (Bozen)   Map 3 D2

HOTELS
Pension Röllhof
Campegno (Kampenn), 39100 (a 10-minute drive from Bolzano, near Colle/Kohlern); 0471 329 958; www.roellhof.com
At 930 m (3,051 ft) above sea level, this mountainside guesthouse still catches the breeze when the towns on the valley floor are sweltering. It has apartments, as well as double

rooms. Meat grilled over a wood fire, home-cured *speck* (ham) and vegetables from the kitchen garden are specialities. Games include tennis and table tennis.

🛏 🐾 🍽 🍱 🛟   €

Gasthof Kohlern
Via al Colle (Kohlern) 11, 39100; 0471 329 978; www.kohlern.com
In the hills 800 m (2,624 ft) above Bolzano, near the top of the Colle (Kohlern) cable car, this inn offers modern Tyrolean-style rooms with cow-hide rugs. There is a small pool with views (May–Oct). Children can run around in the meadows nearby.

🐾 🍽 🛟   €€

Parkhotel Holzner
Dorf 18, 39059 Soprabolzano Renon (Oberbozen Ritten); 0471 345 231; www.parkhotel-holzner.com
This airy Art Nouveau-style hotel is in a stunning location on Rittner Horn mountain, 18 km (11 miles) from Bolzano, with a large pool in the grounds and activities for children.

🛏 🐾 🍽 🛟   €€

Stadt Hotel Città
Piazza Walther (Waltherplatz) 21, 39100; 0471 975 221; www.hotelcitta.info
On the edge of Bolzano's main square, very near the town's sights, this hote has rooms with original parquet floors and free Wi-Fi. Organic breakfasts, and a choice of family rooms and apartments.

🛏 🍽 🛜 ☕ 🛟   €€€

Parkhotel Holzner, Bolzano, with a large swimming pool in its grounds

Canazei   Map 4 E2

B&B
Garni Stella Alpina
Streda do Ruf de Antermont 6, 38032; 0462 601 127; www.stella-alpina.net
In the historic centre of an attractive ski village in the Val di Fassa, 5 minutes' walk from the cable car, this small B&B has eight cosy, en-suite rooms, decorated in old-fashioned Ladin style. The hotel's busy time is during the winter season, but it also opens for the summer hiking season. There is a big buffet breakfast spread.

☕   €€

Compaccio (Compatsch)   Map 3 D2

HOTEL
Seiser Alm Compatsch
39040 Compaccio (Compatsch); 0471 727 919; www.seiseralm.com
A simple, laid-back hotel, Seiser Alm Compatsch has a cosy *zirbenstube* (snug) and comfortable, no-frills rooms, including three family rooms. With the car-free Alpe di Siusi to run around, children will love this place. Special hiking tours and sessions to learn about mountain plants are offered for kids.

🛏 🐾 🍽   €€

Malles (Mals)   Map 3 C2

HOTEL
Bio-Hotel Panorama
Staatsstrasse 5, 39024 Vinschgau; 0473 831 186; www.hotel-panorama-mals.it
A green hotel in the Val Venosta, Bio-Hotel Panorama serves local, seasonal organic food, including produce from their own garden on a sunny terrace; half-board is available. The bedrooms have balconies with hammocks.

🛏 🐾 🍽   €€

Merano (Meran) Map 3 D2

HOTELS
Pergola Residence
*Kassianweg 40, 39022; 0473 201
435; www.pergola-residence.com*
Named after its vine-covered
pergolas, this hotel with 12 suites
and two villas, 3 km (2 miles) from
the centre of Merano, was designed
by architect Matteo Thun using
larch, stone and silver quartzite. A
healthy breakfast buffet of berrries
and local breads is served until noon.
€€

Hotel Terme Merano
*Piazza Terme 1, 39012; 0473 259 000;
www.hoteltermemerano.com*
Designed by Matteo Thun, this
stunning town-centre hotel offers a
playful take on traditional Tyrolean
style. All rooms have a balcony. It is
a grown-up hotel, but children are
welcome. At certain periods there is
no charge for under-12s (Mon–Thu).
€€€

Miramonti
GranPanorama
*Santa Caterina 14, 39010
Avelengo-Merano; 0473 279 335;
www.hotel-miramonti.com*
In the hills above Merano, this smart,
modern hotel has great food and
fabulous views of the Adige (Etsch)
valley, as well as luxurious family
suites, a children's playroom with
games and an indoor pool. Five-
night minimum stay at peak times.
€€€

SELF-CATERING
Gapphof Apartments
*Weingartnerstrasse 27, 39022
Algund; 0473 449 678;
www.gapphof.com*
A farm with an apartment annexe set
among orchards, this is 4 km (2 miles)
from Merano in the Adige (Etsch)
valley. The apartments are small, but
modern and there is a communal
terrace and a reed-lined swimming
pond. Fresh bread and fruit from
the farm available daily.
€

Residence Aqualis
*Vicolo San Felice 30, 39020
Marlengo; 0473 447 170;
www.residence-aqualis.com*
Run by the Egger family, this stylish
apartment residence is near the
12-km (8-mile) Marlinger Waalweg

irrigation channel, built in 1737 for
vineyard-owning Carthusian monks,
which makes a great start for hikes.
Apartments sleep from two to eight
and have terraces and kitchens.
€€

*Lagació Mountain Residence, with cosy
apartments, in San Cassiano*

San Cassiano Map 4 E2

B&B/SELF-CATERING
Garni Ai Pini
*Strada Glira 4, 39030; 0471 849 541;
www.ai-pini.it*
In the peaceful Cassiano valley, this
guesthouse is a short drive from
Passo Falzàrego, and offers B&B or
small apartments. There are rugs
and benches around a wood-fired
stove in the sunny breakfast room.
€

Lagació Mountain Residence
*Micurá de Rü 48, 39030; 0471 849
503; www.lagacio.com*
A luxury apartment residence,
Lagació has wood fires, animal-hide
rugs and panoramic views over
meadows to the Dolomite peaks.
Each apartment, built in Swiss pine,
larch or spruce and stone, has a
small kitchen and dining area.
€€€

Val Gardena Map 4 E2

HOTEL
Smart Hotel Saslong
*Via Pallua (Soplases), 39047 Santa
Cristina; 0471 774 444; www.saslong.
eu*
In a ski village in the Val Gardena, this
50-room hotel by cutting-edge
furniture and interior designer

Antonio Citterio pioneers a new
concept, combining hip interiors
and South Tyrolean hospitality.
€

Val Senales
(Schnalstal) Map 3 C2

HOTELS
Bella Vista
Mountain Hut
*39020 Kurzras; 0473 662 140;
www.goldenerose.it*
Ride by cable car to this mountain
refuge, ideal for skiing or trips onto
the Hochjochferner glacier (high
altitude kit essential). Rustic-style
bedrooms sleep three or four (plus
there is a dorm option). There is an
outdoor sauna and hot tub from
which to watch the sunset.
€

Schwarzer Adler
*Madonna di Senales 26, 39020; 0473
669 652; www.adlernest.com*
With an emphasis on fun and a
warm welcome, this hotel offers
guided hikes and "nature detective
camps" for 6–12-year-olds; activities
range from farm visits to identifying
edible and poisonous wild plants.
€€

Zur Goldenen Rose
*Karthaus 29, 39020; 0473 679 130;
www.goldenerose.it*
An open fire, cosy dining rooms with
a ceramic stove and bedrooms with
larch floors make this a relaxing
bolt-hole halfway up the Val Senales
(Schnalstal), convenient for the
ArcheoParc and glacier visits.
€€

SELF-CATERING
Palla Bianca (Weisskugel)
*Karthaus 105, 39020; 0473 689130;
www.goldenerose.it*
Well-equipped apartments with
wood-burning stoves sleep from
two to six people, with access to
garden, lawns, barbecue and picnic
area, table tennis table, playground
and football field. Full-board option.
€

Key to symbols *see back cover flap*

Milan
and Northwest Italy

The mountains of northwest Italy have Swiss and French influences, but the region becomes more Italian heading south, via Italy's lake district, to Milan, home of Leonardo da Vinci's *Last Supper* and a super science museum. Turin is chocolate heaven, while harbour city Genoa has Italy's best aquarium. Beaches beckon, from the sandy bays of the Riviera di Ponente to the rugged coves of the Cinque Terre.

Highlights

Milan's Duomo
Climb 150 steps (or take a lift) to the roof and clamber among statues and gargoyles, with dizzying views *(see pp112–3)*.

Lake Como
The most scenic of the lakes, Lake Como is surrounded by lemon trees and lush vegetation; zigzag slowly from shore to shore by lake ferry *(see pp118–19)*.

Mantova
Described by Aldous Huxley as the most romantic city in the world, Mantova has beautiful domes, towers and medieval squares *(see pp122–3)*.

Parco Nazionale del Gran Paradiso
Spot ibex, chamois and the rare *stella alpina* (edelweiss) in Italy's first national park *(see p132)*.

Turin's Museo Egizio
Find out all about papyrus, the pharoahs and scarabs, and see mummies galore in one of the world's most important Egyptian museums *(see p134)*.

Cinque Terre
Five fishing villages are shoe-horned into a steep part of Liguria's coastline, linked by a coastal path with olive groves and vineyards *(see pp148–9)*.

Left The beach at Monterosso, one of the five villages of Liguria's Cinque Terre
Above right Walking among the ornate carvings on the roof of Milan's Duomo

The Best of
Milan and Northwest Italy

This part of Italy offers mountains, sea, lakes and several appealing cities, with an enticing array of activities. Simply travelling around here is an adventure, whether traversing lakes by ferry or getting lost in a maze of narrow alleyways in Genoa's old town. There is exceptional architecture and art in the cities of Bergamo, Mantua, Turin and Milan, while beaches and coves can be found on the Ligurian Riviera.

On the water

Lake Orta (see pp138–9) is small, mystical and romantic, with Orta San Giulio probably the prettiest medieval village in all the lakes. Boats cross to the island, Isola di San Giulio, five minutes' journey across the water. The waters off the **Ligurian coast** (see pp148–50) are home to dolphins and, perhaps surprisingly, 12 species of whale swim the open sea. The thousand-year-old **Abbey of San Fruttuoso** (see p151) is accessible only by boat or on foot: take a ferry from virtually any harbour on the Portofino headland, and enjoy a simple lunch at a *trattoria* on the small pebble beach. To enjoy the charms of **Lake Como** (see pp118–21), catch a ferry – the sweeping shoreline and magnificent villas look their best from the water, and the lake is never more than 5 km (3 miles) wide, so it is easy to harbour-hop. At **Mantua** (see pp122–3), small pleasure boats sail on the River Mincio; take bikes – it is possible to cruise in the morning, picnic at lunchtime and have a leisurely pedal back in the afternoon.

In a week

Begin with a night or two in a city of a manageable size, such as **Turin** (see pp134–5), **Mantua** (see pp122–3) or **Bergamo** (see p116), to get into the swing of sightseeing, *gelato*-eating and the daily *passeggiata* (evening stroll), then home in on two or three key sights on a flying visit to **Milan** (see pp112–15). Next, choose between the mountains – perhaps a trip up **Monte Bianco**, the Italian side of Mont Blanc (see p132) – or the lakes. Alternatively, head for the **Ligurian coast** (see pp148–50), staying in a fishing port such as **Camogli** (see p151), which English writer Charles Dickens called "the saltiest, most piratical little place". Combine beach trips with day trips to **Genoa** (see pp144–5) to visit the attractions of the renovated Porto Antico.

By season

In **spring**, enjoy the lakes, **Lake Como** (see pp118–21) and **Lake Orta** (see pp138–9), where after Easter it is warm enough to eat outdoors, but the crowds have yet to arrive. On the Ligurian Riviera, the Sagra del Pesce, a huge fish fry-up in aid of the patron saint of fishermen, takes place in **Camogli** (see p151) on the second Sunday in May. In late May the Idroscalo in Festa brings picnics, concerts and sporting events to **Milan** (see pp112–15).

Summer is the best time to hike in the **Parco Nazionale del Gran Paradiso** (see p132) in the Valle d'Aosta. The **Ligurian Riviera** (see pp148–50) bursts into life at this time of year and, although busy, this is the most fun time to visit. There are concerts in the **Abbey of San Fruttuoso** and, on the last Saturday in July, a torch-lit boat procession to the Cristo degli Abissi, eight fathoms below on the seabed. It is hot in the big cities, which are best avoided.

Below Cafés lining Piazza Motta in Orta San Giulio, the main resort on the shores of Lake Orta

*Above A view down onto the rooftoops of Varenna from the Castello di Vezio above Lake Como **Below left** The magnificent façade of Milan's Duomo*

place of the Magi. Piazza Duomo is the hub of Milan's Carnevale (Feb–Mar), one of the best times for children in the city. In the mountains, **Courmayeur** (see p132) offers winter sports and the **Parco Avventura Mont Blanc** has a wide range of winter sporting activities on offer, suitable for children and adults of all abilities (see p132).

Eat your way around...

Some well known Italian foods come from northwest Italy. Try fresh pesto, basil pounded with pine nuts, olive oil and Parmesan, in **Liguria** (see pp144–51). The stubby-grained arborio or carnaroli rice grown in the flood plains of the Po, west of **Milan** (see pp112–15), is used to make risotto. If Italians want to insult people from Lombardy, they call them *polentoni* or "polenta eaters"; cornmeal polenta was once the food of the poor, but these days classy restaurants feature it and the Bergamese have formed the Ordine dei Cavalieri della Polenta (Order of the Knights of Polenta). *Taleggio*, a tangy, soft cows' milk cheese, is served at the end of a meal in **Bergamo** (see p116), with tasty farmhouse versions to be found in the countryside of the Lombardy plain. Focaccia, a dimpled flatbread with rosemary and sea salt, comes from **Liguria** (see pp148–50) where it is sold as fast food. Creamy *tiramisù* owes its richness to the soft *mascarpone* cheese from Lodi, southwest of Milan, while **Turin** (see pp134–5) is credited with inventing *zabaglione*, a rich egg-yolk, sugar and dessert wine confection.

Autumn is a glorious time to visit **Mantua** (see pp122–3) and sample the *tortelli di zucca* (pumpkin-stuffed pasta). Violin-makers' town **Cremona** (see p125) is well visited now too. If dry, autumn is ideal for walks in the **Cinque Terre** (see pp148–9). It is also a good time to visit **Milan** (see pp112–15) as the summer heat dies down and families return from the seaside.

In **winter**, more than 30 artists claim a street or piazza in **Turin** (see pp134–5) as their own for the Christmas *Luci d'Artista Torino* (Festival of Lights). Epiphany in **Milan** (see pp112–15) is known as La Befana, after the kind witch who brings presents to good children; on 6 January a costumed procession of the Three Kings travels from the Duomo to the Church of Sant'Eustorgio, said to be the final resting

Milan and Northwest Italy

For northern Italians, Milan is the country's affluent heart. The city is in the low-lying Po Valley, well connected with Turin and Genoa. The urban sprawl of the *pianura* (plain) is foggy in winter and muggy in summer, but the Milanese escape to Lake Como (30 minutes by train) or to the ski resorts of the Valle d'Aosta. Elegant Turin is well placed for hikes in the Gran Paradiso park. And for sun and sea, hop on a train to the balmy Ligurian Riviera.

Bronze doors of Milan's Duomo, fitted in 1965

Places of interest

🔲 LOMBARDY

1. Milan: the Duomo
2. Leonardo da Vinci's *Last Supper*
3. Triennale Design Museum
4. Castello Sforzesco
5. Bergamo
6. Certosa di Pavia
7. Villa Panza, Varese
8. Lake Como
9. Varenna
10. Sacro Monte di Ossuccio
11. Como
12. Mantua
13. Valeggio sul Mincio
14. San Martino della Battaglia
15. Santuario delle Grazie
16. Cremona

🔲 VALLE D'AOSTA AND PIEMONTE

1. Aosta
2. Parco Nazionale del Gran Paradiso
3. Courmayeur
4. Forte di Bard
5. Turin
6. PAV Parco Arte Vivente
7. Castello di Rivoli
8. La Venaria Reale
9. Lake Orta
10. Museo dell'Arte della Tornitura del Legno
11. Santuario della Madonna del Sasso
12. Calderara Collection of Contemporary Art

🔲 LIGURIA

1. Genoa: the Aquarium
2. Galleria Nazionale di Palazzo Spinola
3. Museo Navale di Pegli
4. Museo di Archeologia Ligure
5. Cinque Terre
6. Sestri Levante
7. Rapallo
8. Camogli

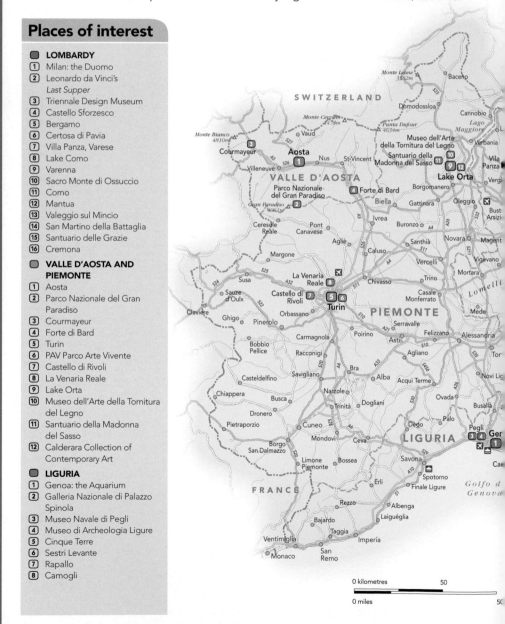

The trenino *taking visitors around Orta San Giulio*

The pretty Cinque Terre village, Manarola, clinging to the cliffs

The gleaming marble façade of Milan's Duomo

The Lowdown

🚗 **Getting there and around**
Air Milan, Turin, Genoa and Bergamo all have airports (see p110). **Car hire** All major firms have offices at airports. Avoid driving in cities and along the Cinque Terre coast, but a car is essential for the Valle d'Aosta and the smaller lakes. **Train** Mainline trains connect all main towns and the Cinque Terre villages (www.trenitalia.it). **Public transport** in Milan, Turin and Genoa is good. **Bus** and train timetables in Lombardy: www.trasporti.regione.lombardia.it; Liguria: www.orariotrasporti.regione.liguria.it; Piemonte: www.comune.torino.it, www.savda.it and www.vitagroup.it

🍴 **Supermarkets** Major chains Auchan, Billa, Carrefour, Conad, Coop, LIDL, Pam and SPAR have branches in all larger towns. Open non-stop and often as late as 10pm.

🕐 **Opening hours** Restaurants open 12:30–3pm for lunch and 7:30–10pm for dinner. Shops usually close at lunchtime and on Sundays. Many museums now open all day, but some still close for lunch, so check. Almost all close on Mondays.

➕ **Pharmacies** To find an all-night pharmacy, check the list on any pharmacy door or in local papers, or call 800 801 185. There is a 24-hour pharmacy at Milan Stazione Centrale (02 669 0735).

🚻 **Public toilets** Café-bars have to let anyone use their toilets, by law, but the cleanest ones are usually in museums.

Milan and Northwest Italy Airports

Milano Malpensa is the main gateway to the region for international flights, with the other airports served mainly by domestic and regional services. The small airports of northern Italy are easy to navigate compared with the major hubs of northern Europe. The flipside is that there are fewer facilities, especially once security has been passed, but there will always be a no-nonsense café-bar to fuel hungry families.

Milano Malpensa

Milano Malpensa airport, 45 km (28 miles) northwest of Milan, is the international gateway to northern Italy. It has two terminals: Terminal 1 serves international and domestic flights and Terminal 2 is used by budget airlines and charter flights. A free bus shuttles between the two.

The airport is served by most major international airlines. There are few direct flights from North America and Asia, with many going via Frankfurt, Paris or the Gulf states. Budget airlines bmi (from Aberdeen, Belfast, East Midlands, Edinburgh, Glasgow, Leeds, London Heathrow and Manchester), easyJet (from London airports, Edinburgh and Rome) and FlyBe (from 13 regional UK airports) also fly into Malpensa.

The Malpensa Express train runs frequently from Terminal 1 to Milan Piazza Cadorna station (30 minutes) and less often to Stazione Centrale. The Malpensa Shuttle bus and other frequent bus services depart from Terminal 1 for Stazione Centrale (50 minutes). High-speed rail links run to Bologna, Florence, Rome and Naples. All major car rental firms operate from the airport.

Malpensa is open 24 hours a day, but most shops and cafés close between 9pm and 9am. There is a playroom for children in Terminal 1, with slides, bricks and mats. Be prepared for relatively long walks from arrivals to baggage reclaim.

Milano Linate

Milano Linate airport is a small, busy airport just 7 km (4 miles) east of Milan, used mainly for short-haul international and domestic flights. It is served by Alitalia (AirOne) and major international airlines including British Airways, Delta, KLM and Iberia, and no-frills easyJet (from London Gatwick and Paris Orly).

Frequent Starfly buses connect Linate to Milan Stazione Centrale as do Milan city buses 73 and X73, and there are several car-hire desks.

There is a restaurant with a good view of take-offs and landings, as well as assorted snack bars. Lack of signage can make it tricky to find your way around, and there is limited seating at boarding gates.

Bergamo Orio al Serio

Bergamo Orio al Serio airport, 4 km (2 miles) southeast of Bergamo, is used mainly by low-cost airlines Jet2 (from Leeds) and Ryanair (from Bristol, Cork, Dublin, East Midlands, Glasgow, Liverpool, London Gatwick and Stansted), and by Alitalia (AirOne) and Lufthansa.

An Airport Bus takes passengers to the Città Alta (20 minutes), and city bus 1C shuttles from the airport to Bergamo train station (10 minutes). The airport is 45 km (28 miles) from

Planes on the tarmac at Bergamo al Serio airport

Milan and several bus services operate to Milan Stazione Centrale (one hour). There can be heavy traffic on the A4 motorway and the small airport gets congested, so leave plenty of time to make your flight. Car hire is reached by shuttle bus from arrivals.

On-site facilities are limited, but the airport is connected by an underground walkway with the Oriocenter shopping mall. There is a good view of the runway from the McDonald's in the Schengen area.

Genova Cristoforo Colombo

Served by major carriers including Alitalia (AirOne), Air France, British Airways (from London Gatwick), Iberia, KLM, Lufthansa and Swiss,

and by Ryanair (from London Stansted), Genova Cristoforo Colombo airport is just 6 km (4 miles) from Genoa's city centre.

The Volabus runs every hour from the airport to Genoa's three main rail stations, and the ticket includes 60 minutes of further travel on the public transport network, including the funicular railway. The 124 shuttle bus connects the airport to the Sestri Ponente district. All major car rental firms are represented at the airport, which has basic facilities, including a selection of cafés.

Torino Caselle Sandro Pertini

Turin's small airport, 15 km (9 miles) north of the city, is served by Alitalia (AirOne) and British Airways (from London Gatwick), low-cost carriers bmi (from Edinburgh and East Midlands), Ryanair (from Dublin, East Midlands, Edinburgh and London Stansted), easyJet (from London Luton) and Thomas Cook charters (from Birmingham, Bristol, London Gatwick and Manchester).

Regular buses travel between the airport and Turin Porta Susa and Porta Nuova train stations (45 minutes). There are good facilities, with a decent selection of café-bars and restaurants and good views of the runway for kids, but the airport gets quite crowded in ski season.

The Lowdown

Airports
Bergamo Orio al Serio 035 326 323; *www.orioaeroporto.it*

Genova Cristoforo Colombo 010 60151; *www.airport.genova*

Milano Linate 02 74851; *www.sea-aeroportimilano.it*

Milano Malpensa 02 7485 2200; *www.sea-aeroportimilano.it*

Torino Caselle Sandro Pertini 011 567 6378; *www.aeroportoditorino.it*

Lombardy

Half the fun of Lombardy is that it is possible to have an entirely car-free holiday, travelling by boat, bike or train. Zigzag by boat between the pretty villages and lidos of Lake Como, meandering and swimming along the way; hop on a train to Mantua and bike to its Renaissance palaces; and then explore the cultural treasures and street life of Milan on foot.

Below View of Lake Como from Moltrasio, its shores crowded with villas and gardens

① Milan: the Duomo
Running on rooftops and grimacing at gargoyles

Milan's massive cathedral has a forest of soaring marble spires dating back to 1386. Although used for worship from 1418, with the builders still hard at work, the cathedral was not officially completed until 1813, under pressure from Napoleon, eight years after he was crowned King of Italy here. Its bronze doors were only fitted in 1965. In the 14th century canals were built to ship marble here on barges from Lake Maggiore, providing the material for some of the best sculptors and architects, including Leonardo da Vinci, to work on.

Gargoyle at the Duomo

Key Features

Madonnina At the highest point of the roof, the symbol of Milan, the "little Madonna," stands over 4.16 m (13 ft 6 in) tall.

Roof terraces Gurning at gargoyles on the roof is the highlight of a cathedral visit.

St Bartholomew The gruesome statue of St Bartholomew skinned alive, by Marco d'Agrate (1562), holds his skin like a toga. The popping-out veins and muscles show Renaissance artists' fascination with anatomy.

Crypt The mummified body of San Carlo Borromeo (1538–84), who tended plague victims and burned Protestants, lies under the altar in a silver death mask.

The Interior The five aisles in the nave are separated by 52 piers, whose capitals are decorated with statues.

Trivulzio Candelabrum Little beasts attack the four winged dragons holding up this giant candle holder. The altar behind was installed to stop sheep being driven through to market.

Palaeochristian Baptistry Remains of the original 4th-century church were uncovered in the 1940s during the digging of an air-raid shelter, and more was uncovered in the 1960s during metro works.

The Lowdown

Address Piazza del Duomo, 20121 Milan; www.duomomilano.it

Metro Duomo. **Tram** The city's iconic trams are not to be missed: the orange 1928 trams are the most atmospheric, number 3 is a useful tramline from the Duomo to the Navigli canal area.

Open 7am–7pm daily. Roof terrace: Apr–Oct 9am–9:45pm, Nov–Feb 9am–4.45pm, Mar 9am–5.45pm. Archaeological areas: 9.30am–5:30pm daily; Treasure: Mon–Fri 9am–1pm & 2–6pm, Sat 9am–1:30pm & 2–5 pm, Sun 1:30–4pm

Price Free. Roof terrace: €24 (stairs), €40 (elevator). Archaeological areas: €16. Treasure: €8. Combined ticket: €40 (stairs), €52 (elevator)

Skipping the queue Book roof terrace tickets online to avoid queues (booking fee applies).

Guided tours 10am Sat in English

Age range All ages: younger children will be awestruck by the size and the candle-lit darkness, older children will be intrigued by the mummy and all children

will enjoy clambering among the roof terraces and gargoyles.

Allow 30–40 minutes inside and the same again for the roof

Café No, but don't miss the organic ice cream at Grom, Via Santa Margherita 16 (off Piazza Duomo), 20121; www.grom.it.

Toilets No. The Rinascente department store is the best bet.

Good family value
The family ticket makes the rooftop experience good value and most of the spectacular inside can be enjoyed for free.

Letting off steam

Chase the pigeons in the piazza: cathedral elders have spent years trying to get rid of them, as their droppings corrode the cathedral's marble. The **Giardini Pubblici** public gardens (Metro Palestro/Porta Venezia) offer shady grass areas and playgrounds. Across the road, behind the **Palazzo Reale** (Royal Palace), is a toddlers' play area and a small lake with carp and turtles. In summer, head for an open-air swimming pool: **Romano** (Via Ampere 20, 20133; 02 7060 0224; Metro Piola) and **Argelati** (Via Segantini 6, 20143; 02 5810 0012; Metro Porta Genova) are the most convenient.

Eat and drink

Picnic: under €25; Snacks: €25–40; Real meal: €40–80; Family Treat: €80 or more (based on a family of four)

PICNIC Luini (Via San Radegonda 16, 20121; 02 8646 1917; www.luini.it; closed Sun and Aug) serves piping hot mozzarella and tomato pastries to take away, perhaps to the benches in nearby Piazza San Fedele.
SNACKS Colonne di San Lorenzo (a 15-minute walk down Corso Torino) is a fun area to enjoy an aperitivo. Bars spill onto the streets, there are nibbles, skateboarders to watch and a playground around the corner in Parco della Vetra.
REAL MEAL Anema e Cozze (Via Casale 7, 20145; 02 837 5459; www.anemaecozze.com) is great for fresh seafood, salads and pizzas. On

Visitors marvelling at the magnificent façade of the Duomo

summer evenings head to the Navigli (canal) district, for a meal at this restaurant amid buzzing streets.
FAMILY TREAT Rinascente department store (Piazza Duomo 12;, 20121 www.rinascente.it) has a good food hall on the top floor with something for everyone, from sushi and designer sandwiches to a three-course meal. There is also an excellent food market, selling fine wines, preserves and olive oils.

Shopping

Ten minutes' wander northeast from the Duomo is Milan's world-famous **Quadrilatero d'Oro**, a rectangle of cobbled lanes and streets housing top designer boutiques, where window-shopping is always fun. Or pop into the 19th-century shopping arcade, the **Galleria Vittorio Emanuele II**, to glory at the glass cupola and mosaics celebrating Italian unification in 1865.

Find out more

DIGITAL The Duomo website, www.duomomilano.it/ground1024_it.html, has a memory game and tells the story of the cathedral through the eyes of the Madonnina.

Next stop...

ART GALLERY AND MUSEUM The **Padiglione d'Arte Contemporanea** (www.comune.milano.it/pac) next door to the Duomo often has good exhibitions in a child-friendly space. The **Museo della Scienza** (Science Museum; www.museoscienza.org) is another good option, with old-school exhibits, hands-on models, steam engines and even a real submarine.

Galleria Vittorio Emanuele II, opened in 1867 by the King of the same name

Last Supper *by Leonardo da Vinci, in the refectory of Santa Maria delle Grazie*

② Leonardo da Vinci's *Last Supper*

Mysterious masterpiece

In 1495 Leonardo da Vinci was commissioned by Lodovico il Moro, the Duke of Milan, to decorate the wall of the refectory (where the monks ate their meals) of the monastery of Santa Maria delle Grazie. Also known as the *Cenacolo Vinciano*, the painting portrays the dramatic moment described in the Gospel of St John when, during a meal with his 12 apostles, Jesus announces that he knows one of them will betray him. Leonardo shows Jesus composed in the centre, and all the disciples around the table stunned and protesting except Judas (five from the left) who drops his bread and recoils in guilty horror. The painting is famous for the gesturing hands of the apostles, so expressive that critics have said they "speak".

The fragility of the blotchy and faded image means that visits are limited to 15 minutes, but it is amazing there is anything left at all. Leonardo painted in tempera rather than the standard, longer-lasting fresco technique in which pigment is mixed with the plaster, and the painting started to deteriorate almost immediately. Later, a door was knocked through the bottom part of the picture, then Napoleon's troops used the wall for target practice and, in 1943, the rest of the monastery was destroyed by a bomb, leaving just this wall standing.

Prices given are for a family of four

Letting off steam

Leonardo da Vinci stayed in the monastery across the road, now the **Palazzo Stelline** (*Corso Magenta 60*), while painting *The Last Supper*. Through the courtyard at the back is a shady garden with enough grass for a game of football or a picnic.

The Lowdown

- 🌐 **Address** Cenacolo Vinciano, Piazza Santa Maria delle Grazie 2, 20100 Milan; 02 9280 0360; www. cenacolovinciano.net
- 🚗 **Metro** Conciliazione or Cadorna. **Tram** 18 and 24
- 🕐 **Open** 8:15am–6:45pm Tue–Sun; collect tickets 20 mins in advance
- 💶 **Price** €16
- 👪 **Skipping the queue** Tickets must be pre-booked online, up to three months ahead.
- 👄 **Guided tours** In English at 9:30am and 3:30pm, €14
- 👫 **Age range** 5 plus
- ⏱ **Allow** 15 minutes (timed visits)
- 🍴 **Eat and drink** *Snacks* Chocolat (*Via Boccaccio 9, 20123; 02 481 005 97; www.chocolatmilano.it*) serves to-die-for hot chocolate and ice cream. *Real meal* Acero Rosso (*Piazza Virgilio 3, 20123; 02 469 0288; www.ristorante acerorosso.it; closed Sun*) for pizzas and *antipasti*.

③ Triennale Design Museum

Art and fancy knick-knacks

From salt cellars to sofas, Milan is one of the world centres of the design industry. The Triennale or,

officially, the Palazzo dell'Arte, was built in 1931 to house a triennial design exhibition. It's a wonderful building, full of light and space, with a monumental staircase and acres of cool marble. Since 2007 it has been home to a permanent collection of some of the most famous furniture design and knick-knacks to come out of Italy, and also hosts stylish temporary exhibitions on contemporary art, architecture and design from around the world.

Letting off steam

An extension of the Parco Sempione, the gardens of the Triennale are home to sculptures by famous artists – sit on, lie in and climb all over them.

Interacting with a garden sculpture, Triennale Design Museum

The Lowdown

- 🌐 **Address** Viale Emilio Alemagna 6, 20121 Milan; www.triennale.org
- 🚗 **Metro** Cadorna
- 🕐 **Open** 10:30am–8:30pm Sat–Wed, closes 11pm Thu & Fri
- 💶 **Price** Free, except exhibitions
- 👫 **Age range** All
- ⏱ **Allow** 1–2 hours
- 🍴 **Eat and drink** *Snacks* The Triennale Design Café (*02 875 441*) is a stylish café and snack bar inside the museum. There is a hip *aperitivo* bar outside in summer that adults will be sure to enjoy. *Real meal* Combattenti e Reduci (*Piazza Sempione 2A, 20154; www.cenemilano.com, Mon–Fri lunch only*), in the toll house by the Arco della Pace, is a family-run trattoria, offering decent home cooking in a set menu.

Grand fountains and the Filarete (central castle tower), Castello Sforzesco

④ Castello Sforzesco

Suits of armour and an ancient mummy

The Sforza dukes of Milan ruled over one of the most mighty and cultured Renaissance courts in Europe from these courtyards, but under later Spanish, Austrian and French occupation the castle was used as barracks. During the Unification of Italy, in 1861 the castle was given back to the city of Milan, restored and converted into a museum. Not much has changed since then, but the displays of gleaming swords, suits of armour and firearms are worth a look. There were many more weapons here before an uprising against the Austrians in 1848, when useful arms were looted. Don't miss the chain mail shoes and spurs on the mounted knight in the middle of the armour room. In the cellars, the Ancient Egyptian collection, with its decorated sarcophagi and a mummy, is a favourite too.

Letting off steam

The castle leads directly onto the dukes' hunting ground, now Milan's biggest park, the **Parco Sempione**. There are acres of paths, grass and trees here with playgrounds to keep children busy and cafés for a refreshing break. If that's not enough, check out the Arco delle Pace, the Art Nouveau **aquarium** (www.acquariocivico milano.eu), and, for a bird's eye view of it all, the **Torre Branca** (www.branca.it/en/mondo/torre-branca.asp).

View across Parco Sempione to Arco delle Pace

The Lowdown

🌐 **Address** Piazza Castello, 20121 Milan; www.milanocastello.it

🚗 **Metro** Cadorna, Cairoli or Lanza. **Tram** 1, 4, 12, 14 and 2–19

🕐 **Open** Castle: 7am–7pm daily; museums: 9am–5:30pm Tue–Sun

€ **Price** €6, free for under-25s and from 2pm on Fridays and 4:30pm on other days

👫 **Age range** 3 plus

⏱ **Allow** 2 hours for castle and park

🍴 **Eat and drink** Snacks Bar Bianco (Viale Ibsen 4, 20121; 02 8699 2026; www.bar-bianco.com) and six café kiosks dotted around the Parco Sempione offer refreshments alfresco. Family treat Da Claudio (Via Cusini 1; 02 8697 5741; www. pescheriadaclaudio.it), top-class fishmongers, serve fresh fish carpaccio and seafood with a glass of prosecco. Eat sitting up at bar stools around the shop counters.

Picnic under €25; Snacks €25–40; Real meal €40–80; Family treat €80 or more (based on a family of four)

⑤ Bergamo
The winged lions of the walled city

Bergamo is a beautiful town with a medieval hilltop centre of narrow lanes and pretty squares. This upper town (Città Alta) is reached from the grand 18th-century lower town (Città Bassa) by a creaking old funicular railway. Just off the central Piazza Vecchia with its ancient buildings and loggias is the Baroque confection of **Santa Maria Maggiore**, while the **Colleoni Chapel** next door is a High Renaissance gem. Huff and puff up the 230 steps of the **Torre Civica** belltower for great views and clamber around the cannons in the ruins of the **Rocca** (castle). The stone winged lions (symbols of Venice) which crouch around town, and the strong **city walls**, are reminders that Bergamo was an important stronghold for the powerful Venetian Republic, which ruled for more than 300 years. The lions guarded this gateway to the Alps as well as keeping an eye on their rivals, Milan.

Letting off steam
On the way up let the two funicular railways do the legwork – they whisk visitors to the top of town at San Vigilio. Then charge back down the steep and panoramic avenues, following the city walls to the lower town through Porta San Giacomo.

The imposing Basilica di Santa Maria Maggiore in Bergamo

⑥ Certosa di Pavia
Magnificent monastery

This spectacular church and monastery, rising out of the rice fields south of Milan, were started in 1396 by Duke of Milan Gian Galeazzo Visconti to house his family's tombs. The church is impressive – the lower part of the façade is lavishly decorated with statues of Roman emperors and saints. The monastery gives a fascinating insight into the daily lives of the Carthusian monks who lived here under a strict vow of silence. In the refectory (dining hall), spot the hidden staircase in the panelling that leads to the pulpit where Bible stories would be read while the monks ate. Leading off the grand cloister are the monks' cells, attractive two-storey cottages with their own gardens for meditation. Note the hatch next to the door so that food could be passed without any human contact.

Letting off steam
There's plenty of space to run around outside the main gate. The energetic could cycle here from Pavia (8 km/5 miles) or Milan (30 km/18 miles). The flat paths follow canals, so take mosquito repellent.

The Lowdown

🌐 **Map reference** 2 E3
Address Viale Monumento, 27012 Pavia ; www. certosadipavia.com

🚗 **Train** Regular direct trains from Milan. **Bus** from Milan (30 min) and Pavia (10 min)

ℹ **Visitor information** Palazzo del Broletto, Piazza della Vittoria, 27100 Pavia; 0382 597 001; www.provincia.pv.it

🕐 **Open** 9–11:30am & 2:30–5:30pm Tue–Sun; Oct–Mar closes 4:30pm; May–Aug closes 6pm

💲 **Price** Free, donations for tour

👫 **Age range** 5 plus

⏱ **Allow** 1–2 hours

🍽 **Eat and drink** Snacks The bar outside has sandwiches and drinks. Family treat Locanda Vecchia Pavia al Molino (Via al Monumento 5, 27012; 0382 925 894; www.vecchiapaviaalmulino. it) is a smart restaurant with a Michelin star.

The Lowdown

🌐 **Map reference** 2 F2
Address Bergamo, 24100; Santa Maria Maggiore, Passaggio Ca' Longa, 24129; Torre Civica, Piazza Vecchia, 24129; Rocca, Piazzale Brigata Legnano, 24129

🚗 **Train** Frequent direct trains from Milan (45 min); regular trains to Como with one change (1hr 45min). **Bus** 1A direct from Bergamo airport (Orio al Serio) to lower town. **Funicular** to Città Alta and peak of San Vigilio

ℹ **Visitor information** Torre del Gombito 13, Città Alta, 24129; 035 242 226; www.provincia.bergamo. it/turismo, www.turismo.bergamo.it

🕐 **Open** Santa Maria Maggiore: 9am–12:30pm and 2:30–5pm Mon–Fri, 9am–1pm and 2–5pm Sat. Colleoni Chapel: Mar–Oct 9am–12.30pm and 2–6:30pm daily, Nov–Feb closes 4:30pm and closed Sun. Torre Civica: Mar–Oct 9:30am–7pm Tue–Fri and 9:30am–4:30pm Sat

and Sun, Nov–Feb 9:30am–4:30pm Sat and Sun. Rocca: Jun–Sep 9:30am–1pm and 3–5:30pm Tue–Fri, 9:30am–7pm Sat and Sun, Oct–May 9:30am–1pm and 2–5:30pm daily

💲 **Price** Santa Maria Maggiore: free. Torre Civica: €20. Rocca: free

👫 **Age range** Any for the funicular, tower, castle and walls; 11 plus for Santa Maria Maggiore

⏱ **Allow** Half a day

🍽 **Eat and Drink** Picnic Il Fornaio (3 Via Colleoni, Città Alta, 24129) serves mouthwatering pizza al taglio. Real meal Cooperativa Città Alta (Vicolo Sant'Agata 19, off Via Colleoni, Città Alta, 24129; 035 218 568) has a large garden and serves pasta, polenta and salami.

🎉 **Festivals** 13 Dec: Santa Lucia brings presents for the children of Bergamo: lights, toys, sweets, and ice skating in the lower town (Via XX Settembre, Città Bassa).

The fine façade of the Church of Our Lady of Graces at Certosa di Pavia

⑦ Villa Panza, Varese

Neon lights and works of art

On the edge of the pretty provincial town of Varese stands the 18th-century villa of the Panza family. In the 1950s, before many people had even noticed them, Count Giuseppe Panza started to build up an enviable collection of contemporary art by American environmental artists such as James Turrell and fluorescent-light artist Dan Flavin. Site-specific installations were created for the wings of the villa, using the colour, light and atmosphere of the setting, and cutting-edge temporary exhibitions are now held in the stables. There are rooms of neon lights and shadows which play games with space, volume and perception. Monochrome canvases are also displayed alongside the Neo-Classical decor of the elegant country villa.

The vast landscaped gardens with their fountains, temple and grotto are perfect for lengthy games of hide and seek.

Letting off steam

Make a day of it and head off to the **Campo dei Fiori**, a natural park just north of Varese with a Via Sacra – a series of chapels which lead steeply up for 2 km (1 mile) through the woods to the church and hamlet of Santa Maria del Monte. Bus C from the hamlet goes to the bottom.

One of the splendid chapels peeping out of the trees on route to Campo dei Fiori

The Lowdown

- 🌐 **Map reference** 2 E2
  Address Villa Panza, Piazza Litta, 1, 21100 Varese; 0332 283 960; *www.fondoambiente.it/beni/villa-e-collezione-panza.asp*
- 🚃 **Trains** link Varese with Milan Porta Garibaldi (55 min). **Bus** A from the train station passes the villa. **Car** Varese is 45 km (28 miles) north of Milan on the A8 motorway
- ℹ️ **Visitor information** Via Carrobbio 2, 21100; 0332 283 604; *www.vareselandoftourism.it*
- 🕐 **Open** 10am–6pm Tue–Sun, last entrance 45 mins before.
- 💶 **Price** €24
- 👪 **Age range** All
- ⏱️ **Allow** 2 hours–1 day
- 🍴 **Eat and drink** *Snacks* Pasticceria Ghezzi (*Corso Matteotti 36, 21100*) is a historic café in the pedestrian lanes of the centre serving delicious pastries such as *Dolce Varese*, a local speciality made with maize flour. *Family treat* Ristorante Luce (*Villa Panza; 033 242 199*) is the Villa's own sophisticated restaurant serving set menus. The weekday lunch bistro is more family-friendly.

Old meets new at Villa Panza: Neo-Classical architecture outside, contemporary art inside

⑧ Lake Como
Celebrities, *Star Wars* and an island curse

The sparkling waters and stunning scenery of Lake Como have inspired poets and artists for centuries. These days the fabulous villas for which the lake is famous are popular with celebrities. There is much to see and do here: explore the pretty lakeside towns or pull on hiking boots and climb up to castles, mount a horse or grab a mountain bike, and then cool down in the shady garden of one of the villas. The best way to see the lake itself is from one of the ferries linking all the main towns on the shore.

Waterfront hotel, Varenna

Key Sights

① **Bellagio** This pretty village makes a good base as it's right at the centre of the lake (though the many steps makes it tricky with pushchairs). Its steep, narrow lanes are full of restaurants and hotels.

④ **Tremezzo** This splendid town is a lakeside tourist resort and home to the 18th-century Villa Carlotta (*above*). The residence was converted into a Neo-Classical villa in the 1800s.

② **Lenno** This town's main draw is the lovely Villa Balbianello and its magnificent gardens. The villa is a favourite with Hollywood: *Star Wars: Episode II* and *Casino Royale* both had scenes shot here.

③ **Como** The lake's largest town has ancient streets and buildings and a fun funicular ride, too (*see p121*).

⑤ **Varenna** This lovely lakeside village (*see p120*) is a warren of narrow lanes, and after a steep trek, a ruined castle with a fossil collection, and the odd ghost or two.

⑥ **Orrido de Bellano** With the water thundering below, walkways squeeze through the narrow crevices of this spectacular gorge.

The Lowdown

 Map reference 2 E2
Address Villa Balbianello: Via Comoedia 5, 22016 Lenno; Orrido di Bellano: Piazza San Giorgio, 23822 Bellano; Villa Carlotta: Via Regina 2b, 23822 Tremezzo 9. www.comoguide.com

Train Como and Varenna are linked directly with Milan by train. **Bus** C10 heads north round the lake and C30 shuttles between Como and Bellagio.

Ferry The most reliable option (www.navigazionelaghi.it)

Open Villa Balbianello: Mar–Nov 10am–6pm Tue and Thu–Sun. Orrido di Bellano: Apr–Sep 10am–1pm and 2:30–7pm daily, Oct–Mar 10am–12:30pm and 2:30–5pm Sat and Sun. Villa Carlotta: Mar–Nov 10am–4pm. Silk Museum: Tue–Fri 9am–12 noon and 3–6pm

Price Villa Balbianello: €38, children aged 4–12 €7. Orrido di Bellano: €14; children aged 5–14

€3. Villa Carlotta: €34, children under 6 free. Silk Museum €21

Age range All ages

Allow At least 2 days.

Festivals Sagra di San Giovanni (a series of music and folk festivals and fireworks), Como: nearest Sat to 24 Jun

Good family value
There's an exciting pick-and-mix of activities on Lake Como to suit everyone, and many are free.

Windsurfers taking advantage of the winds in Domaso, on Lake Como

Letting off steam

The winds around **Domaso** in the north of the lake make windsurfing and dinghy sailing a breeze. **Menaggio** is most fun for hikes into the beautiful countryside, horse treks and mountain-bike riding. There are several **lidos** (Lenno, Cadenabbia, Dongo, Varenna and Menaggio have the nicest), and although the shoreline is a little muddy or shingly you can't beat a paddle in the waters to cool down.

Eat and drink

Picnic: under €25; Snacks: €25–40; Real meal: €40–80; Family treats: €80 or more (based on a family of four)

PICNIC Most lakeside villages boast a weekly market (tourist offices have details of days, with the same stalls popping up in different locations). Put together a wonderful picnic from the fresh produce and hot snacks available, then head for a shady bench by the water to enjoy it.
SNACKS Castiglioni Gastronomia (*Via Cantù 9, 22100 Como; 031 263 388; www.castiglionistore.com*) is a family-run delicatessen in the pedestrian centre of Como, where you can buy snacks to take away or sit in the pretty internal courtyard to enjoy midweek lunchtime specials.
REAL MEAL Il Ristorante di Paolo (*Largo Cavour 5, 22017 Menaggio; 0344 32 133*) offers gourmet cooking at trattoria prices in a relaxed dining room with outside tables on the traffic-free lakeside square. Simple children's dishes are no problem for the friendly staff. Excellent wine list too.
FAMILY TREAT La Pergola (*Piazza del Porto 4, Pescallo, 22021 Bellagio,; 031 950 263; www.lapergolabellagio.it*) is a romantic waterside restaurant in the fishing hamlet of Pescallo. It is a

great spot for tasty local specialities, and has lovely views, but parents need to be attentive, because of the tables' proximity to the water.

Find out more

FILM As well as the films that used Villa Balbianello as a location (see opposite), *Quantum of Solace* and *Ocean's Twelve* both use gorgeous Lake Como villas as a backdrop.

Take cover

Como made its fortune from silk and still supplies Milan's fashion houses. The atmospheric **Silk Museum** (*Via Castelnuovo 9, 22100 Como; www.museo setacomo.com*) will capture young imaginations.

The beautiful Villa Balbianello, overlooking Lake Como in Lenno

Next stop...

ISOLA COMACINA The only island on the lake can be reached by a boat trip, which is a must when visiting Lake Como. The ferry to the island leaves from Sala Comacina (*www.boatservices.it*).

The view to Isola Comacina, the only island on Lake Como

⑨ Varenna
A ruined castle and birds of prey

After a steep, stepped 15-minute climb from the main road, the **Castello di Vezio** high above the pretty village of Varenna offers attractive ruins to clamber over, fantastic views and falconry displays. Back down by the ferry dock on the waterfront, a lakeside walkway leads into the village. Here it is possible to dive down alleyways and get lost along cobbled lanes as there are no cars to worry about. And in the afternoon sun, the shady terraced gardens of **Villa Cipressi** and **Villa Monastero** are perfect for a quiet read or afternoon snooze.

Letting off steam

Opposite the ferry dock there's a low-key lido (*Via al Lido, 1, 23828*) with a bit of shore, sun loungers and a café. There's also a small children's playground, best for younger kids.

The Lowdown

🌐 **Map reference** 2 F1
Address 23829 Varenna. Castello di Vezio, Via del Castellano, 6, 23828; *www.castellodivezio.it.* Villa Cipressi, Via 4 Novembre, 18, 23829; *www.hotelvillacipressi. it.* Villa Monastero, Via Polvani, 4, 23829; *www.villamonastero.it*

🚗 **Trains** from Milan Centrale. **Ferry** Varenna is centrally placed on the lake Como ferry network

ℹ **Visitor information** Via Imbarcadero 1; *www.varennaitaly. com*; open May–Oct

🕐 **Open** Castello di Vezio: Mar–Nov 10am–sunset daily. Villa Cipressi: Mar–mid-Nov 9am–8pm daily. Villa Monastero: mid-Mar–mid-Oct 10am–5pm, May–Sep 9am–7pm daily

💶 **Price** Castello di Vezio: €8–16, under-6s free. Villa Cipressi: free. Villa Monastero: €16–32, under-7s free

👫 **Age range** Something for all

⏱ **Allow** Half a day

☕ **Eat and Drink** *Snacks* Il Ristoro del Castello (*Via al Castello, 23828; 0333 2935667*) serves local specialities. *Real meal* Albergo del Sole (*Piazza San Giorgio 17; www.albergodelsole. lc.it*) has a wood-fired pizza oven.

🎆 **Festivals** Festa del Lago; (fireworks and candlelit boat processions): early Jun

Varenna's colourful houses nestling by the shore of Lake Como

⑩ Sacro Monte di Ossuccio
Life-sized Bible stories in an olive grove

Each of the 14 chapels leading up through the hillside of olive groves high above Lake Como tells a Bible story from the life of Mary, the mother of Christ, with dramatic scenes and life-size plaster statues. They were built by various artists over 25 years beginning in1663.

There are several of these *sacri monti* or sacred mountains in northern Italy, created in an attempt to educate the illiterate in Catholic culture and to stem the spread of Protestantism from north of the Alps. The footpath weaves through the countryside up to the Santuario della Madonna del Soccorso, with unrivalled lake views.

Letting off steam

After climbing all the way to the top of the hill, run down again, seeing who can remember the stories told in each chapel. To cool off, head to the nearby lido at Lenno, or the one slightly further north up the shore at Menaggio (*see pp118–19*).

The Lowdown

🌐 **Map reference** 2 E1
Address Via del Santuario, 22016 Ossuccio

🚗 **Ferries** and **Bus** C10 stops in Ossuccio but then it's a 30-minute uphill walk along roads to the start of the trail. It's easier to reach with a car.

ℹ **Visitor information** *www. comunicare.it/ofmcap/luoghi/ ossuccio.htm*; *www.sacrimonti. net*; *www.ossuccio.com*

🕐 **Open** 24 hours

💶 **Price** Free

👫 **Age range** All ages

⏱ **Allow** 2 hours

☕ **Eat and Drink** *Picnic* Ellemarket (*Via Statale 19, 22010 Ossuccio; 0344 56736*) is a small, basic supermarket on the main lakeside road with supplies for a picnic. Head to the Sacro Monte or the waterside for a great view. *Family treat* Locanda dell'Isola Comacina (*Isola Comacina, 22010 Ossuccio; 0344 55083; open Mar–Oct*), the legendary island restaurant, serves a set menu that ends with an atmospheric fire ritual. The island is reached by boat from Sala Comacina (*www.boatservices.it*).

🎆 **Festivals** San Giovanni, Sagra dei Lumaghitt (*see opposite*): 24 Jun

Santuario della Madonna del Soccorso, on Sacro Monte di Ossuccio

Above *A bird's eye view of Como from the lovely village of Brunate*
Below *The funicular train to Brunate*

⑪ Como
Hydroplanes and fun funicular rides

The bustling traffic-free grid of Roman roads at the centre of Como is full of everyday shops and ancient buildings. Just behind the lake, the façade of the medieval **Duomo** is sculpted with saints and bishops, and the 1215 Broletto (law courts) next door is a pretty pink. Head along the waterfront promenade to see hydroplanes and a monument to physicist Alessandro Volta, with instruments from his electrical experiments. Here too is the Monumento ai Caduti, to the fallen of World War I, built by Como's most famous modern architect, Giuseppe Terragni. Across town, the funicular railway trundles up through gardens to the Art Nouveau village of **Brunate**, which offers a bird's eye view of the town and lake.

Letting off steam
The piazzas in the town centre and the waterfront promenade make for a lovely stroll with plenty of room for kids to run about. For a refreshing dip, head northwest around the waterfront to **Villa Olmo** (*www.lidovillaolmo.it*; open May–Sep), where there is lake access, a beach with umbrellas and deck chairs and two open-air swimming pools.

The Lowdown

🌐 **Map reference** 2 E2
Address 22100 Como. Duomo: Piazza Duomo. Broletto: Via Pietro Boldoni, 3. Funicular: Piazza De Gasperi 4, *www.funicolarecomo.it*. Brunate, 22034

🚗 **Trains** from Milan, and Lugano in Switzerland. **Bus** The C10 heads north along the western shore of the lake and the C30 scuttles round to Bellagio. **Ferries** leave from the docks by Piazza Cavour.

ℹ **Visitor information** Piazza Cavour 17, 22100; 031 269 712; *www.lakecomo.it*

🕐 **Open** Duomo: 7am–noon and 3–7pm. Funicular: 6am–10:30pm

💶 **Price** Duomo: free. Funicular: €10–20; under 1.10m (3ft 7in) free

👫 **Age range** Younger kids will enjoy the funicular, older kids the Volta monument.

🕐 **Allow** Half a day

🍴 **Eat and Drink** *Real meal* Le Colonne (*Piazza Mazzini 12, 22015; 031 264 859; www.albergodelduca.it*) is a friendly family-run restaurant on a pretty central square, serving tasty pasta, pizza and local specialities. *Family treat* Osteria del Gallo (*Via Vitani 16, 22100; 031 272 591*) is a good spot for an *aperitivo* with nibbles and snacks.

🎡 **Festivals** Festa di Sant' Abbondio (fireworks and concerts for Como's patron saint): 31 Aug

⑫ Mantua
Palaces and pumpkins

Almost floating among three lakes, the small fairytale town of Mantua (Mantova) is repeatedly voted the best place to live in Italy. In the 15th and 16th centuries it was an important political and artistic centre ruled by the Gonzaga family. There are two huge palaces, ancient churches, cobbled streets and hundreds of works of art. It is also home to one of the tastiest plates of pasta – *tortelli di zucca*. Best enjoyed fresh in autumn, these pumpkin parcels are usually served simply with melted butter and sage.

Clock tower, Piazza delle Erbe

Key Sights

① **Palazzo Ducale** The highlight of the huge Gonzaga palace is the Camera degli Sposi (Bridal Chamber), frescoed by court artist Mantegna in 1465–74.

② **Sant'Andrea** This church, in the style of a Greek temple, was begun in 1472 by Leon Battista Alberti on a site where a vial of Christ's blood was said to be buried.

③ **Teatro Bibiena** Thirteen-year-old Wolfgang Amadeus Mozart played the theatre's opening concert in 1770. The luxurious Baroque theatre was also used for medical operations.

Map showing central Mantua with streets including VIA ALBERTO PITENTINO, VIA PORTO, VIA CONCEZIONE, VIALE TRENTO, VIALE MINCIO, VIA CAVOUR, VIA G. VERDI, VIA FRATELLI BANDIERA, VIA VITTORIO EMANUELE, VIA ROMA, LUNGOLAGO DEL GONZAGA. Landmarks: Lago di Mezzo, PIAZZA VIRGILIANO, Mantova, Torre della Gabbia, PIAZZA SORDELLO, ① Palazzo Ducale, ② Sant'Andrea, ⑥, ④ Piazza delle Erbe, ⑤ Rotonda di San Lorenzo, ③ Teatro Bibiena, Palazzo Tè (1.5 km (0.9 mile))

0 metres 200
0 yards 200

⑤ **Rotonda di San Lorenzo** Mantua's oldest church is over 1,000 years old. Visitors step down to what was the original street level to enter this round church.

④ **Piazza delle Erbe** The town hall, law courts and clock tower in this picturesque square were so noisy that in 1579 the San Lorenzo church closed as Mass was inaudible.

⑥ **Torre della Gabbia** Medieval criminals would be hung in full public view in a cage from Mantua's highest tower to die of cold, thirst or hunger.

The Lowdown

🌐 **Map reference** 2 H4
Address 46100 Mantua. Palazzo Ducale: Piazza Sordello 40, *www.mantova ducale.it*. Teatro Bibiena: Via Accademia 47, 0376 327 653. Rotonda di San Lorenzo: Piazza delle Erbe. Palazzo Tè: Viale Tè 134, *www.palazzote.it*

🚆 **Train** Direct from Verona, Milan and Cremona. Station is a 15-minute walk from centre.
Bus Route number 1 takes circular route from station to town.

ℹ️ **Visitor information** Piazza Mantegna 6; 0376 432 432;

www.turismo.mantova.it; open 9am–5pm daily

🕐 **Open** Palazzo Ducale: 8:15am–7:15pm Tue–Sun. Teatro Bibiena: 9:30am–12:30pm daily also 3–6pm Tue–Sun; Rotonda di San Lorenzo: 10am–1pm and 3–6pm daily; Palazzo Tè: 1–6pm Mon, 9am–6pm Tue–Sun

💰 **Price** Palazzo Ducale: €13–18.50, EU citizens aged 18–25 €3.25, under-18s free. Teatro Bibiena: €8. San Lorenzo: free. Palazzo Tè: €16–21, under-11s free

👥 **Skipping the queue** Booking essential for Camera degli Sposi

(041 241 1897; www.ducale mantova.org); €1 booking fee

👫 **Age range** Young children may not have stamina for the art, but will enjoy the bustling piazza, the gardens and grotto at Palazzo Tè, biking and boating.

⏱️ **Allow** A day for Mantua, longer to explore the surroundings

🚻 **Toilets** In the Palazzo Ducale

Good family value
With its piazzas, gardens and bike-friendly terrain Mantua can be enjoyed inexpensively. Museums offer good-value family tickets.

A tour boat cruising Lago Superiore, one of the three lakes surrounding Mantua

Letting off steam

The car-free piazzas in Mantua's centre, the playgrounds in **Piazza Virgiliana** and the grassy park by **Palazzo Tè** are ideal for down time.

Mantua and the surrounding countryside can easily be explored on two wheels as they are flat and relatively car-free. There is a bike-sharing initiative in town: register with a passport at **Casa del Rigoletto** *(Piazza Sordello 23)*. For smaller bikes, child seats or trips further afield try **Mantua Bike** *(Viale Piave 22B; 0376 220 909)*. Boat trips on **Lago Superiore**, **Lago di Mezzo** and **Lago Inferiore** vary from one or two hours to day trips to Venice *(www.motonaviandes.it; www.fiume mincio.it)*.

Eat and drink

Picnic: under €25; Snacks: €25–40; Real meal: €40–80; Family treat: €80 or more (based on a family of four)

PICNIC Sma *(Via Giustiziati 15, 46100; 0376 321 244)* is a well-stocked supermarket. Head to the lakeside to enjoy your picnic put together from the Sma.
SNACKS La Masseria *(Piazza Broletto 7, 46100; 0376 365 303)* has tables on the piazza in summer. It serves wood-oven baked pizzas and offers children's portions.
REAL MEAL Trattoria Due Cavallini *(Via Salnitro 5, 46100; 0376 322 084)* dishes up Mantuan specialities including delicious *tortelli di zucca* (pumpkin-stuffed pasta).
FAMILY TREAT Osteria la Porta Accanto *(Vicolo Bonacolsi 4, 46100; 0376 366 751; www.laportaccanto. it)* serves mouthwatering dishes inspired by local traditions. It is run by the son of the owners of Aquila Nigra *(www.aquilanigra.it)*, a Mantuan culinary institution in a frescoed old palace next door.

Take cover

If it is too hot or it rains, an easy indoor option is to spend half a day exploring some of the 500 rooms and 15 courtyards of the **Palazzo Ducale**. Highlights include the Galleria degli Specchi (Hall of Mirrors) and Appartamento dei Nani (Apartment of the Dwarfs), with its low ceiling. **Palazzo Tè** is another fascinating building, where giants crash down on your head in the Camera dei Giganti, frescoed from floor to ceiling in an illusion of chaos.

Arched entrance to Palazzo Tè, built by Giulio Romano for the Gonzaga family

Next stop...

LAKE GARDA Half an hour north of Mantua is Lake Garda with its cooling waters, historic villages and family theme parks (see p82).
VERONA Not much further away is Verona (see pp78–9), another family favourite as the fictional home of Shakespeare's *Romeo and Juliet*. It has a splendid Roman amphitheatre.

Relaxing on the waterfront at Peschiera del Garda, Lake Garda

Restaurants by the river in Borghetto, Valeggio sul Mincio

⑬ Valeggio sul Mincio

Love knots

Valeggio sul Mincio is famous for its little twists of pasta stuffed with meat or cheese, *nodi d'amore* (love knots), which are served in dozens of restaurants here. It was on the border of the Republic of Venice and the Dukedom of Milan for over 300 years and there are impressive remains of the defence systems. The 13th-century Castello Scaligero is said to be haunted on full-moon nights. Down by the river, the hamlet of Borghetto with a watermill and restaurants is towered over by the fortified medieval Ponte Visconteo, part of a defensive wall from the 14th century.

Letting off steam

Explore the pretty gardens and woods of **Parco Giardino Sigurtà** (*www.sigurta.it; open Mar–Nov*

The Lowdown

🌐 **Map reference** 2 H3
Address: 37067 Valeggio sul Mincio

🚌 **Bus** 46 Mantua–Peschiera

ℹ️ **Visitor information** Piazza Carlo Alberto 32; *www.valeggio.com*

👫 **Age range** Pasta, castle, bridge and river will appeal to most ages

⏱️ **Allow** Half a day

🍽️ **Eat and drink** *Snacks* Bar Renzo Martini (*Piazza Carlo Alberto 40, 37067*) serves both cakes and ice cream. *Real meal* San Marco (*Via Raffaello Sanzio 10, 37067; 045 795 0018; closed Mon, Tue*) serves the local pasta dish, and is in a lovely location by the river.

🎉 **Festival** Festa del Nodo d'Amore – tables line the bridge for an alfresco meal for 4,000 people: 15 Jun.

9am–6pm; €24–36; children under 5 free) on the edge of the village, and meet friendly animals including Polpetta the donkey at the children's farm.

The medieval walls and gateway of Borghetto, Valeggio sul Mincio

⑭ San Martino della Battaglia

A bloody battlefield and the Red Cross

This 74-m (243-ft) tower was built in 1893 in memory of those killed in the Italian wars of independence, known as the Risorgimento. The rolling hills seen from the top of the tower were the scene of one of the bloodiest battles of the whole campaign, the Battle of Solferino. On 24 June 1859, soldiers of France and the Kingdom of Sardinia fought the occupying Austrian army here in a bloody hand-to-hand battle for over 9 hours, leaving more than 37,000 men dead, dying or injured. The future Italian alliance won but at terrible cost. A Swiss businessman, Henry Dunant, witnessed the

carnage and was so shocked and moved by the way that the wounded and dying were simply left where they fell, with only the charity of local villagers to help, that he was inspired to found a neutral hospital corps, the Red Cross, in 1863. The museum behind the tower mixes sabres, cannons, singed uniforms and tattered ensigns with tender last letters sent home by soldiers at the battle.

Letting off steam

Head to **Sirmione** (5 km/3 miles away) on Lake Garda, where there is a shingly beach (open May–Oct).

The Lowdown

🌐 **Map reference** 3 C5
Address Via Torre 2, 25015 San Martino della Battaglia; 030 9910 370; *www.solferinoesanmartino.it*

🚗 **Car** Best reached by car

⏱️ **Open** 9am–12:30pm, 2–5:30pm daily (until 7pm Mar–Sep)

💶 **Price** €10–14, under-6s free

👫 **Age range** 5 plus

⏱️ **Allow** 1 hour for tower plus lunch

🍽️ **Eat and drink** *Real meal* Osteria alla Torre (*Via Torre 1, 25015; 030 910 8261; www.osteriaalla torre.it; closed Tue*) serves pasta and good mixed grills under a portico by the tower. *Family treat* Cascina Capuzza (*Località Selva Capuzza, 25015; 030 9910 279*) serves tasty local dishes.

⑮ Santuario delle Grazie

Flying crocodile and buboes

Dangling high above the nave of this 13th-century pilgrimage church dedicated to the Virgin Mary is an

The beach at Sirmione, with the clearest waters for swimming at Lake Garda

The Lowdown

- 🌐 **Map reference** 3 C5
  Address 46010 Curtatone
- 🚌 **Bus** 13 from Mantua
- 🕐 **Open** 7:30am–12:30pm, 3–6:30pm daily
- 💲 **Price** Free
- 🚹🚺 **Age range** All
- ⏱ **Allow** 1 hour plus picnic time
- 🍵 **Eat and drink** *Picnic* Bring a picnic from Mantua or put one together from the counter at the bar at Via del Santuario 1. Eat by the river behind the church.
- 🎪 **Festivals** La Fiera delle Grazie, (see talented pavement artists at work): 15 Aug

embalmed crocodile said to have been killed by a local fisherman after it ate his brother. Pilgrims come here to say *grazie* (thanks) to the Virgin Mary for saving them from life-threatening disease or disaster. Look closely at the wooden niches lining the church; the decorations are small hearts, breasts, eyes, hands and plague buboes (swollen lumps). These offerings, or ex-votos, were left by pilgrims over the centuries as thanks. The 53 wooden statues are in appreciation of bigger miracles, and include figures saved from the noose or the guillotine by the Virgin.

Letting off steam

A ramp leads behind the church to the grassy riverside, and there are boat trips from March until October (0376 349 292; www.fiumemincio.it).

Antonio Stradivari's statue in the public gardens in Piazza Roma, Cremona

⑯ Cremona

Sticky sweets and virtuoso violins

The modern violin was invented in Cremona in 1566 and the best-known violin-maker in the world, Antonio Stradivari (1644–1737), was born and worked here. There are violin workshops all over town and the **Museo Stradivariano** shows Stradivari's tools and working methods. In **Palazzo del Comune**, his and other historic violins are exhibited and played. Opposite is the wonderful **Duomo** with its pink striped marble, statues, arches and rose window. There are zodiac signs on the complicated astronomical clock (1588) on the 113-m (344-ft) medieval bell tower – the **Torrazzo**.

Letting off steam

Climb 502 steps to the top of the **Torrazzo** for a great view, and run around the piazza.

The Lowdown

- 🌐 **Map reference** 3 B5
  Address 26100 Cremona. Museo Stradivariano: Via Ugolani Dati 4; 0372 803 622. Palazzo del Comune: Piazza del Comune 8; 0372 803 618. Duomo: Piazza del Comune. Torrazzo: Piazza del Comune
- 🚗 **Train** Direct trains from Milan
- ℹ **Visitor information** Piazza del Comune 5, 26100; 0372 23233; www.turismocremona.it, www.musei.comune.cremona.it
- 🕐 **Open** Museo Stradivariano: 9am–6pm Tue–Sat, 10am–6pm Sun. Palazzo Comunale: 9am–6pm Tue–Sat, 10am–6pm Sun. Duomo: 8am–noon, 3:30–7pm daily. Torrazzo: 10am–1pm, 2:30–6pm daily

- 💲 **Price** Museo Stradivariano: €14–24, under-7s free. Palazzo Comunale: €12–20, under-7s free, €3 extra to hear violins played, joint museum ticket €11/6. Duomo: free; Torrazzo: €18–20
- 🚹🚺 **Age range** Hearing violins played brings them to life for most ages.
- ⏱ **Allow** Half a day
- 🍵 **Eat and drink** *Snacks* La Piadineria (Via Platina 20, 26100) is a good place to try a tasty *piadina* (flat-bread sandwich). *Real meal* Pizzeria Ristorante Duomo (Via Gonfalonieri 13, 26100) has pavement tables outside the cathedral, a lovely location for an alfresco lunch.

Where to Stay in Lombardy

This varied region offers an equally varied range of places to stay, from simple, traditional hotels with restaurants serving local cuisine to palatial B&Bs, and *agriturismi* in glorious settings with plenty of outdoor activities. For families visiting Milan, renting an apartment is an excellent alternative to city hotels.

B&B, AGRITURISMO AND SELF-CATERING AGENCIES

Agrituristico Mantovano
0376 324 889; www. agriturismomantova.it
Some of Lombardy's best *agriturismi* are along the canals and rivers around Mantua, with opportunity for families to join in with grape-picking, fruit-picking and looking after cattle and horses. Lots of offers for families.

Bed & Bergamo
www.bedandbergamo.it
A good selection of B&Bs and a few self-catering houses and apartments in Bergamo's Città Alta, at the heart of the old town.

Friendly Rentals
069 926 8405; www. friendlyrentals.com
This highly rated, efficient and, yes, friendly agency has a choice of stylish and surprisingly affordable two- to six-bed apartments throughout Milan. Minimum stay three nights. Note that prices are quoted per person on the website.

Bellagio
Map 2 F1

HOTEL
Bellagio
Salita Grandi 6, 22021; 031 950 424; www.hotelbellagio.it
Appealing modern rooms in the heart of the old town, with wonderful views over Lake Como. The hotel offers use of a pool and sports facilities at a sports club.
 €€€

B&B
Alla Torretta
Via Nuova 3, 22021; 031 951272; www.allatorretta.com
This villa outside Bellagio has spacious B&B rooms above a family-run pizzeria and caters well to families, with extra beds, use of the kitchen and a garden with swings.
€

Bergamo
Map 2 F2

HOTELS
Agnello d'Oro
Via Gombito 22, Città Alta, 24129; 035 249 883; www.agnellodoro.it
An old-world, family-run hotel in the cobbled streets of the upper town, with standard, but pristine,

The terrace of La Marianna, on the shores of Lake Como in Cadenabbia di Griante

furnishings and a great location. The cosy, traditional restaurant has an outdoor terrace.
€€

Gombit Hotel
Via Mario Lupo 6, Città Alta, 24129; 035 247 009; www.gombithotel.it
Treat the family to a night in a grown-up "design" hotel that is perfectly located for kids too – in the heart of Bergamo's pedestrianized Città Alta, right next to the medieval Torre del Gombito.
 €€

HOSTEL
Nuovo Ostello di Bergamo
Via Galileo Ferraris 1, 24123; 035 369 2376; www.ostellodibergamo.it
A functional but well-organized hostel with en-suite family rooms, lovely views of Bergamo, and a garden. It is a 10-minute bus ride from the Città Alta, and bikes can be rented. Playground nearby.
€

Como
Map 2 E2

HOTELS
Quarcino
Salita Quarcino 4, 22100; 031 303 934; www.hotelquarcino.it
A quiet, simple hotel on the edge of town near the funicular and close to the lake, this hotel has good-value family rooms and suites, as well as a shady garden.
€€

One of the stylish rooms in the Gombit Hotel in Bergamo's Città Alta

Del Duca
Piazza Mazzini 12, 22100; 031 264 859; www.albergodelduca.it
On a pretty, pedestrianized square in the centre of town, within walking distance of the lake, this hotel has pleasant, if smallish, rooms.

€€€

B&B
La Canarina
Via Manzoni 22, 22100; 031 301 1913; www.bed-and-breakfast-como.it
In a great location, this family home with a lovely garden offers very attractive en-suite twins and doubles. It takes its name – The Canary – from the pet shop that once used to be downstairs.

€€

Cremona
Map 3 B5

HOTEL
Duomo
Via Gonfalonieri 13, 26100; 0372 35 242; www.hotelduomocremona.com
Clean, plain rooms – doubles and triples plus extra beds if needed – in a traditional hotel just off the main square. The hotel has its own pizzeria and restaurant, with tables outside enjoying views of the cathedral square.

€

AGRITURISMO
Cascina Nuova
Via Boschetto 51, 26100; 0372 460 433; www.cascinanuova.it
Bright, comfortable rooms and apartments in a restored farmhouse in the countryside, yet only 30 minutes' stroll from the town. The restaurant serves delicious dishes made using produce grown on the farm.

€

Lake Como
Map 2 E2

HOTELS
Locanda Lauro
Rezzonico, 22010; 0344 500 29; www.hotellauro.com
A small, very simple one-star hotel, run by one family since the 1800s, in a lakeside hamlet away from the crowds. The restaurant serves traditional cuisine. There is a tiny shingle beach but no ferry service.

€

The shady courtyard garden of Armellino, a palazzo B&B in the heart of Mantua

La Marianna
Via Regina 57, 22010 Cadenabbia di Griante; 034 443 111; www.lamarianna.com
A traditional, small hotel above a restaurant on Lake Como's western shore. Most rooms have views of the lake, and there are discounts at the nearby swimming pool for guests at the hotel.

€€

B&B
Casa Pini
Via Brentano 12/f, 22010 Griante; 0344 373 02; www.casapini.com
Bright, airy rooms in a friendly B&B on the western shore of Lake Como. There is an attractive garden, and the lake, a ferry landing stage and pool are all a short walk away. Extra beds available for children.

€

AGRITURISMO
Cascina Borgo Francone
Pian di Spagna, 22010 Gera Lario; 334 6431 783; www.cascinaborgofrancone.com
Comfortable apartments in an agriturismo in a converted farm set among woods and fields at the northern end of the lake. Outdoor activities can be organized.

€€€

Mantua
Map 2 H4

HOTEL
Rechigi
Via P Calvi 30, 46100; 0376 320 781; www.rechigi.com
A comfortable, modern four-star hotel right in the heart of ancient Mantua, with all mod cons including some spa rooms. There is an

inter-connecting family room with a queen bed and its own Jacuzzi. Bikes are available for rent.

€€

B&B
Armellino
Via Cavour 67, 46100; 346 314 8060; www.bebarmellino.it
Treat the family to a night in a 17th-century palazzo with frescoed ceilings and state-of-the-art bathrooms at this impressive B&B in the very centre of Mantua. There is a pretty courtyard garden too.

€€

AGRITURISMO
Corte San Girolamo
Via San Girolamo 1, 46100 Gambarara; 347 800 8505; www.agriturismo-sangirolamo.it
Attractive rustic rooms and spacious grounds for guests at this watermill a 3-km (2-mile) bicycle ride out of Mantua (bikes available for guest use). Horse-riding and swimming nearby, as well as restaurants.

€€

HOSTEL
Ostello del Mincio
Via Porto 23, 46040 Rivalta; 0376 653 924; www.ostellodelmincio.org
A modern youth hostel with family rooms in a lovely spot in a tiny fishing village on the banks of the River Mincio, 10 km (6 miles) from Mantua. Canoes and bikes for hire.

€

Price Guide
The following price ranges are based on one night's accommodation in high season for a family of four, inclusive of service charges and any additional taxes.
€ Under €200 €€ €200–350 €€€ over €350

Key to symbols *see back cover flap*

Milan
Map 2 E3

HOTELS
Euro
*Via Sirtori 24, 20129; 02 2040 4010;
www.eurohotelmilano.it*
Good-value rooms in a modern,
friendly hotel just a 10-minute
walk from the Duomo. The nearby
Giardini Pubblici *(see pp113)* have
playgrounds and lots of space for
kids to let off steam after seeing
the sights. Triple rooms available.
€€

Palazzo delle Stelline
*Corso Magenta 61, 20123; 02 481
8431; www.hotelpalazzostelline.it*
A pleasant business hotel with
standard rooms, ideally located
across the road from Leonardo Da
Vinci's *Last Supper*, near Cadorna
station and with a large garden
where children run around.
€€

Antica Locanda
dei Mercanti
*Via San Tomaso 6, 20121; 02 805
4080; www.locanda.it*
The fresh flowers and charming
homely rooms here are an oasis at
the pedestrianized heart of the city.
Four of the rooms have private
terraces, there are several suites,
and extra beds can be added.
€€€

London
*Via Rovello 3, 20121; 02 7202 0166;
www.hotellondonmilano.com*
Unexciting decor but a clean,
air-conditioned, family-run place in a
very convenient, central location
between Piazza Duomo and the
Castello Sforzesco, and within easy
reach of La Scala. Triple rooms.
€€€

Pavia
Map 2 E3

B&B
Le Betulle
*Frazione Samperone 93, Certosa di
Pavia, 27012; 0382 924 032; www.
lebetullebb.it*
A simple, friendly B&B in the
countryside close to Pavia's Charter-
house, with two-, three- or four-bed
rooms and a small farm to run
around and explore. Guests have
their own entrance.
€

The terrace of the Euro hotel, conveniently located close to Milan's Giardini Pubblici

San Martino
Map 2 E3

SELF-CATERING
Selva Capuzza
*Agriturismo Borgo San Donino,
Desenzano del Garda; 25015; 030
9910 279; www.selvacapuzza.it*
Self-catering apartments in a
converted farmhouse set among
rolling vineyards and olive groves.
There is plenty of outside space
plus a pool and a good restaurant
using home-grown produce.
€€

Valeggio
sul Mincio
Map 2 H4

AGRITURISMO
Il Cigno
*Loc Casa Cogoletto 43, 37067; 0456
371 148; www.agriturismoilcigno.it*
Pleasant, well-furnished rooms and
apartments sleeping up to seven,
deep in the countryside just outside
Valeggio, with an attractive garden,
pool, and bicycles available for hire.
€€

Varenna
Map 2 F1

HOTELS
Albergo del Sole
*Piazza San Giorgio 17, 23829; 0341
815 218; www.albergodelsole.lc.it*
This three-star hotel is located
above a pizzeria-restaurant in the
village centre. It has attractive
rooms including suites with sofa
beds. Lake Como is close by.
€€

Albergo Milano
*Via XX Settembre 29, 23829;
0341 830 298; www.varenna.net*
A lovely boutique hotel right on
the lake, which also offers several
stylish apartments in the village
centre. Its lakeside terrace
restaurant, La Vista, is very popular
for drinks and dinner.
€€

Varese
Map 2 F1

HOTEL
Al Borducan
*Via Beata C Moriggi 43, Sacro
Monte, 21100; 0332 222 916;
www.borducan.com*
In the Sacro Monte natural park on
the edge of Varese, this historic
hotel has large rooms with
breathtaking views, and a good
restaurant serving classic dishes
based on the local cuisine.
€€

SELF-CATERING
I Marroni
*Gaggiolo, Orino, 21030; 0331 631
355; www.imarroni.it*
Two comfortable apartments away
from any hustle or bustle on a berry
farm deep in Campo dei Fiori
regional park. The farm itself has
acres of chestnut woods and lawns
which guests are free to enjoy, and
BBQs are available on request.
Extra beds for children (no charge)
and weekly discounts.
€

Valle d'Aosta and Piemonte

Relatively unspoiled, the mountainous Valle d'Aosta is a great destination for hiking and wildlife-watching in the Gran Paradiso National Park. The vine-clad hillsides of Piedmont around Barolo offer more walking, plus wine-tasting for adults, while Turin has a magnificent Egyptian Museum, arguably the world's best cinema museum and a great chocolate tradition.

Aosta
p130

Lago d'Orta
p138

Turin
p134

Below *A pleasure-boat jetty at Pella on Lake Orta*

① Aosta
Roman remains and curious customs

Encircled by mountains offering great winter and summer activities, Aosta does not feel Italian. Founded in 25 BC by the Roman emperor Augustus, it later spent centuries under French rule, and the locals speak a French dialect as well as Italian. It is an attractive town that has preserved its ancient monuments, its identity and customs, such as the taking of coffee with lemon, grappa and sugar, drunk out of a *grolla* – a wooden friendship goblet with several spouts for communal drinking.

Les Amis du Bois wood-carving

Key Sights

⑥ **Sant'Orso Bell Tower**
The lower part of the tower was a 12th-century lookout. The upper part, with its four tiers of arched openings, was added 100 years later.

⑦ **Arch of Augustus**
This arch was built in 25 BC as an homage to the emperor and a celebration of the Roman troops. The crucifix was added in 1449 as a talisman against flooding.

⑧ **Roman Bridge**
Built of blocks of local stone, this ancient bridge crossed the Buthier stream until it changed its course.

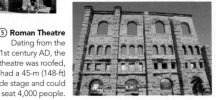

① **Museo Archeologico Regionale**
The ancient artifacts here show how people lived in Aosta from 7000 BC until the fall of the Roman Empire in AD476.

② **Criptoportico**
This underground structure consists of impressive rows of arches cut out of tufa stone. Its original purpose is a mystery: perhaps it was a grain store.

③ **Porta Pretoria**
On the east side of Aosta, this gate controlled access to the city. The opening between two parallel stone walls was patrolled by Roman soldiers.

④ **City Walls**
The handsome stone walls, with their square watchtowers, are some of the best preserved fortifications in the entire Roman world. Walk their 3-km (2-mile) length.

⑤ **Roman Theatre**
Dating from the 1st century AD, the theatre was roofed, had a 45-m (148-ft) wide stage and could seat 4,000 people.

The Lowdown

🌐 **Map reference** 1 B2
Address 11100 Aosta, Valle d'Aosta Museo Archeologico Regionale: Piazza Roncas 12; 0165 275 902. Criptoportico: Piazza Giovanni XXIII. Roman Theatre: Via Porta Pretoria; 0165 275 902

🚗 **Car** 98 km (61 miles) on A5 from Turin. **Train** (www.trenitalia.it) from Turin and up Val d'Aosta. **Bus** from Turin and Milan and up Val d'Aosta (www.savda.it)

ℹ️ **Visitor information** Piazza Chanoux Emile 4; 0165 236 627; www.regione.vda.it

🕐 **Open** Museo Archeologico Regionale: daily 9am–7pm. Criptoportico: 10:30am–12:30pm and 1:30pm–6:30pm Mar–Sep, 11:30am–5pm Oct–Feb. Roman Theatre: daily 9am–5pm in winter, until 6:30pm in spring and 8pm in summer

💰 **Price** Museo Archeologico Regionale, Criptoportico and Roman Theatre: all free

👥 **Skipping the queue** Visit outdoor sites early or late in the day.

🏷️ **Guided tours** Call 0165 239 627 for private guides.

👫 **Age range** 8 plus

⏱️ **Allow** 1 or 2 days

☕ **Café** Caffè Nazionale on Piazza Chanoux

🚻 **Toilets** In the Museo Regionale Archeologico and in café-bars

🐐 **Festivals** Batailles de Reines et de Chèvres (cow-fighting and goat-fighting between local breeds), final in Aosta: Oct

Good family value?
Aosta provides exceptionally good value for families, as all of its attractions are free.

Letting off steam

The town's **Parco Saumont** is a good space for children, and pleasant for adults as well. There are plenty of walking routes, plus a creative play area and artificial lakes, with a focus on learning about nature and local traditions. It has good toilet facilities.

Les Amis du Bois workshop, producing wooden objects typical of local traditions

Eat and drink

Picnic: under €25; Snacks: €25–40; Real meal: €40–80; Family treat: €80 or more (based on a family of four)

PICNIC La Bottega degli Antichi **Sapori** *(Via Porta Praetoria 63; 0165 239 666)* sells lots of goodies; the local cheeses are especially tasty. Then buy fragrant bread made with stone-ground organic flour at **Biopanetteria** *(Via Gilles de Chevrères 21, 11100; 0165 216 101; www.biopanetteria.it).*
SNACKS Bar Roncas *(Piazza Roncas 9; 0165 262 281; open 7am–9pm)* has outdoor tables and all kinds of sandwiches, but also salads, platters of hams and salami, desserts and ice cream.
REAL MEAL Trattoria degli Artisti *(Via Maillet 5–7; 0165 40960; closed Sun and Mon)* serves vegetable flans, cheese fondue, polenta, braised meats, fruit tarts and good local and Piedmontese wines, with outdoor seating.
FAMILY TREAT Hotel La Madonnina del Gran Paradiso *(7 Rue Laydetré, 11012 Cogne; 0165 74078; www.la madonnina. com)*, 27 km/17 miles from Aosta, has a restaurant serving both traditional and innovative cuisine. There is outdoor seating and a playroom for kids and, for those tempted to stay, the comfortable hotel has a new annexe with spa.

Shopping

For hand-painted wooden toys and objects, visit the workshop of **Franco Grobberio** *(Via Bramafan 22, 11100; 348 695 8960; www.grobberio.it).* At Introd, just outside Aosta, **Les Amis du Bois** specializes in local wood-carving, including the *grolla* friend-ship cup *(www.lesamisdubois.com).*

Take cover

At **Fénis**, visit the fairytale castle with turrets, dungeons and frescoes *(11020 Fénis; 0165 764 263; open Wed–Mon 9am–7pm Mar–Sep, 10am–noon and 1:30–5pm Oct–Feb; €10, under-18s free).* Also at Fénis is **MAV**, the **Museo dell'Artigianato Valdostano** *(Chez Sapin 86, 11020 Fénis; 0165 763 912; www.mav.ao.it; open Tue–Sun, 10am–5pm Dec–Mar, until 6pm Apr–Sep; €10–16, children aged 6–18 €3, under-6s free)*, with lots of crafts to see and do, and kids' workshops at 3–5pm on Wednesdays.

Next stop...

ETROUBLES The medieval village of Etroubles, 17 km (10 miles) from Aosta and the same distance from the Swiss border, has become an open-air museum exhibiting works by world-famous artists. Wander down cobbled streets lined with contemporary art, or contact **ArtEtroubles** *(www.expoetroubles. eu)* to arrange a guided tour.

The medieval towers and turreted walls of the pentagonal Castello di Fénis

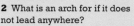

The lovely Paradisia Botanical Gardens, in the Gran Paradiso National Park

② Parco Nazionale del Gran Paradiso

A garden of stones

Made the personal hunting ground of Italy's first king, Vittorio Emanuele II, in 1856, Italy's first national park (created 1922) is now the protected home of many species, including the ibex and golden eagle. It is a perfect place for strolling, hiking or treks. One of the main towns in the park is **Cogne** (1,650 m/5,413 ft above sea level), beyond which is the hamlet of Lillaz. From here it is possible to walk through a stone garden – an open-air museum explaining the rocks in the area – and up to a fantastic waterfall.

Letting off steam

At Valnontey, the other main town in the park, families will enjoy the **Giardino Botanico Paradisia**, an Alpine botanical garden with a network of paths and grassy slopes set against the craggy backdrop of the mountains.

The Lowdown

- 🌐 **Map reference** 1 B2
  Address Parco Nazionale del Gran Paradiso visitor centre, Villaggio Minatori, 11012 Cogne, Valle d'Aosta; 0165 749 264; *www.pngp.it.* Giardino Botanico Paradisia, 11012 Valnontey; 0165 749 264; *www.grand-paradis.it*
- 🚗 **Car** from Aosta, following signs to Cogne. **Bus** to Valle d'Aosta valleys of the park (*www.savda.it*)
- ℹ️ **Visitor information** At the visitor centre; open 2–6pm Sat–Sun Dec–Jun, Thu–Tue Jul–mid-Sep
- 🕐 **Open** Giardino Botanico Paradisia: 10am–5:30pm mid-Jun–mid-Sep, 10am–6pm Jul–Aug
- 💶 **Price** Giardino Botanico: €6–9
- 👫 **Age range** All
- 🕐 **Allow** 1 day to 1 week
- ☕ **Eat and drink** *Real Meal* Les Pertzes (*Via Grappein 93, 11012 Cogne; 0165 749 227; closed Tue–Wed*) does light meals. *Family treat* Lou Tchappé (*11012 Lillaz; 0165 74379; closed Mon*) cooks local *soça* (meat, potatoes, cabbage and *fontina* cheese).

③ Courmayeur

Up, up and away

This attractive town is so close to Monte Bianco (Mont Blanc) – Western Europe's highest mountain, at 4,810 m (15,782 ft) – that it almost feels possible to stretch out and touch it. As well as skiing in winter, there are plenty of chances to trek in beautiful countryside in the summer. Travel by **cable car** to the French side and the Aiguille du Midi at a dizzying 3,642 m (11,948 ft). A family activity that makes a fun alternative to skiing is dog-sledding at Grand Chemin.

Letting off steam

There is a great range of outdoor activities of varying difficulties for children and adults at the **Parco Avventura Mont Blanc**, 11 km (7 miles) south of Courmayeur, past Pré-Saint-Didier towards the Piccolo San Bernardo pass. Bridges over ravines are a thrilling feature – all participants are harnessed and helmeted. The park has its own café.

The Lowdown

- 🌐 **Map reference** 1 B1
  Address 11013 Courmayeur, Valle d'Aosta. Parco Avventura Mont Blanc, 11013 Pré-St- Didier; 335 591 8089; *www. parcoavventuramontblanc.com*
- 🚗 **Car** from Aosta. **Train** to Pré-St-Didier, then bus. **Bus** from Milan, Turin and Aosta (*www.savda.it*)
- ℹ️ **Visitor information** Piazzale Monte Bianco, 11013; 0165 842 060;
- 🕐 **Open** Cable car: 8:25am–5pm. Parco Avventura Mont Blanc: winter (weather permitting): 1–4:30/5pm Sat–Sun (daily Christmas and New Year period); summer 9:30am–4/6:30pm Sat–Sun (daily Jun–Sep)
- 💶 **Price** Cable car: €52–64, under-12s €10 (summer; ski passes in winter). Parco Avventura: €52–84
- 👫 **Age range** All
- 👫 **Activities** Hiking and skiing: ask at the visitor information centre. Dog sledding: *www.dogsledman.com*
- 🕐 **Allow** 1 day to 1 week
- ☕ **Eat and drink** *Real meal* Baita Ermitage (*Ermitage, 11013; 0165 844 351; closed Wed*) has *involtini* of ham and melted cheese. *Family treat* Le Vieux Pommier (*Piazzale Monte Bianco 25, 11013; 0165 842 281; closed Mon*), serves soup and game.

The Alpine Hotel, in a stunning setting at Courmayeur

Prices given are for a family of four

④ Forte di Bard

Life in the mountains

This vast **fortress** above the town of Bard was built in the 1830s to control the route in and out of the valley. It consists of several rather severe-looking buildings, stepped one above the other, which now contain a fantastic museum, the **Museo delle Alpi**, and an activities complex devoted to local mountain culture. There is an interactive section for children, **Le Alpi dei Ragazzi**, which gives an idea of what it is like to be a mountaineer. Excellent exhibitions and concerts are often held, and there is a nice café, a tempting artisan chocolate shop and a bookshop. To get up to the fort, it is worth taking the glass-sided funicular elevator from its foot, which gives stunning views.

Letting off steam

A 10-minute drive away in a clearing surrounded by the chestnut and beech woods known as **Bousc Darè**, 2 km (1 mile) above Pont-Saint-Martin towards Perloz, there is a panoramic picnic spot equipped with tables and barbecue facilities. From here, there is a pleasant track through vineyards.

Back down in **Pont-Saint-Martin**, walk across the bridge. According to legend, it was built by the Devil, who had a pact with St Martin whereby the Devil would take the soul of whoever first crossed the bridge. Once the bridge was ready, the wily saint tricked the Devil by throwing a loaf of bread onto the bridge so that a hungry dog ran after it. The Devil was so upset by not getting the promised human soul that he sank back down to Hell. It is actually a Roman bridge, built around 25 BC, with a span of 30 m (98 ft). Because of its high arch, it has never been damaged by floodwaters.

The Lowdown

🌐 **Map reference** 1 C2
Address 11020 Bard; 0125 833 811; www.fortedibard.it. Bousc Darè, 11026 Pont-St-Martin

🚗 **Car** on SS26 then A5 from Aosta, exit Verrès. **Train** to Pont-Saint-Martin, then bus (0125 966 546)

ℹ️ **Visitor information** At the fort

🕐 **Open** Fort and Museo delle Alpi: 10am–6pm Tue–Fri, 10am–7pm Sat–Sun; Le Alpi dei Ragazzi Sat–Sun only; closed two weeks late Nov–early Dec

💰 **Price** Fort: free. Museo delle Alpi: €24–28. Le Alpi dei Ragazzi: €20–22. Combined ticket: €36–38; discounts for children aged 6–18

👫 **Age range** All

🏃 **Activities** At the fort (check website for programme)

🕐 **Allow** 2 hours; a day for Bousc Darè and Pont-Saint-Martin too

🍽️ **Eat and drink** *Snacks* The Forte di Bard cafeteria has a good range of snacks and light meals. *Real meal* L'Arcadien, in Champagnolaz near Arnad (0125 966 928; closed Mon and Thu) serves local dishes, including soups, cheeses and meats.

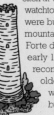

Visitors picnicking on the lawns of the Forte di Bard

Picnic under €25; **Snacks** €25–40; **Real meal** €40–80; **Family treat** €80 or more (based on a family of four)

⑤ Turin

Moving image with bird's eye view

With the Alps in the background, rolling hills close to the handsome city centre, the River Po running through it, plenty of greenery and long tree-lined streets, Turin (Torino) has plenty of natural charm. Yet it is also a dynamic place. The cradle of Fiat automobiles, it boasts a great car museum, the ultimate hands-on cinema museum and one of the most important Egyptian museum outside Cairo.

Star Wars *masks at the Museo del Cinema*

Key Sights

④ Porta Palazzo
Europe's largest outdoor market **(Mon–Fri am)**, located a few steps from the Duomo, sells just about everything: food, clothing, household goods and toys. On Saturday it turns into a fleamarket.

① Lingotto
The old Fiat factory at Lingotto had a test track on its roof. Now an exhibition venue, it includes the Pinacoteca Agnelli old masters and modern art collection.

② MAUTO
The Automobile Museum has a fantastic collection of historic cars, from the first ever self-propelling vehicle (France, 1769) through the classics of early car design to the 1960s.

③ Casa Scaccabarozzi
Known as the Slice of Polenta, this building was designed in 1840 by the same architect as the Mole Antonelliana. It looks fragile, but survived a nearby gunpowder explosion in 1851 and an earthquake in 1887.

Map labels: Parco della Pellerina, CORSO REGINA MARGHERITA, Dora, Porta Palazzo ④, GIARDINI REALI, Museo Egizio ⑦, ⑥ Museo Nazionale del Cinema, ③ Casa Scaccabarozzi, CORSO VITTORIO EMANUELE II, GIARDINO BALBO, Ristocolor ⑤, PARCO DEL VALENTINO, PARCO CAVALIERI DI VITTORIO VENETO, CORSO ROSSELLI, Fiume Po, CORSO 11 NOVEMBRE, CORSO UNIONE SOVIETICA, CORSO BRAMANTE, CORSO MONCALIERI, PAV (see p136), MAUTO ②, Lingotto ①, CORSO UNITÀ D'ITALIA, PARCO GIUSEPPE DI VITTORIO

0 kilometres 2
0 miles 1

⑤ Ristocolor
This extravagantly painted tram snakes around town in the evening. Passengers are served meals while they see the sights. Menus and routes vary.

⑥ Museo Nazionale del Cinema
Fun, hands-on and instructive, the film museum is a must. It is located in the Mole Antonelliana, a soaring tower designed in 1863 by architect Alessandro Antonelli, with fantastic views.

⑦ Museo Egizio
The fabulous collections at the Egyptian Museum include 4,500-year-old mummies and sculptures of kings, queens, goddesses and gods – among them a magnificent portrayal of Ramses the Great. Sphinxes and decorated wooden perfume boxes are on display, too.

The Lowdown

🌐 **Map reference** 1 C3
Address 10121–10156 Turin. Lingotto: Via Nizza 230, 10126; 011 006 2713; www.pinacoteca-agnelli.it. MAUTO: Corso Unità d'Italia 40, 10126; 011 677 666; www.museoauto.it. Casa Scaccabarozzi: Via Giulia Di Barolo 9, 10124. Porta Palazzo: Piazza della Repubblica, 10152. Museo Nazionale del Cinema: Via Montebello 20, 10124; 011 8138 560; www.museonazionaledelcinema.it. Museo Egizio: Via Accademia delle Scienze 6, 10123; 011 561 7776; www.museoegizio.org

🚗 **Car** on A56 motorway. **Train** from Milan and Genoa to Torino Porta Nuova. Good **bus**, **tram** and **metro** network (www.comune.torino.it/gtt/urbana/mappa)

ℹ **Visitor information** Piazza Castello, 10122; 011 535 181; www.turismotorino.org

🕐 **Open** Lingotto: 10am–7pm Tue–Sun. MAUTO: 10am–2pm Mon, 2–7pm Tue, 10am–7pm Wed–Sun (until 9pm Fri–Sat). Museo Nazionale del Cinema: 9am–8pm Tue–Sun (until 11pm Sat). Museo Egizio: 8:30am–7:30pm Tue–Sun

💶 **Price** Lingotto: €8–20, children aged 6–16 €2.50 (€6 for special exhibitions). MAUTO: €16–28, children aged 6–14 €6, under-6s free. Museo Nazionale del Cinema: €14–18, children aged 6–18 €2, under-6s free. Museo Egizio: €15, under-18s free. **Torino+Piemonte Card** gives free admission to sights, and free city transport, to one adult and one child under 12 for two to seven days (€19–35). Two-day Junior Card for under-18s €10. Available from the tourist office.

👥 **Skipping the queue** Museo Nazionale del Cinema: book

Letting off steam

There are a number of playgrounds in city squares and gardens. In the centre is the **Giardino Balbo** (bus 68); along the River Dora is **Parco della Pellerina** (bus 2 and others towards Corso Appio Claudio). A boat trip on the River Po is also fun: boats depart from Murazzi or Borgo Medioevale, a fake medieval village and castle built for the International Expo, 1884 (www.comune.torino.it).

Boat trips on River Po motor cruisers, a fun way to see the city from the water

Eat and drink

Picnic: under €25; Snacks: €25–40; Real meal: €40–80; Family treat: €80 or more (for a family of four)

PICNIC Buy provisions at one of the 60 street markets and head for the **Parco del Valentino** down by the river, or indulge in cheese, ham, salami and prepared dishes at the historic **Steffanone Deli** near Piazza San Carlo (Via Maria Vittoria 2, 10123).
SNACKS Le Fanfaron (Via Principe Amedeo 39/a, 10123; www.fanfaron.it; open Mon–Sat) is great for traditional Piedmontese snacks such as *raclette* (melted cheese served on grilled vegetables).

online. Ristocolor tram: book by email at *servizituristici@gtt.to.it*

Age range 5 plus

Activities Check museum websites

Allow Three days

Wheelchair access Yes, to museums

Café At Lingotto, MAUTO and Museo Nazionale del Cinema

Shop At Lingotto, Museo Nazionale del Cinema and Museo Egizio

Toilets At all the museums

Good family value?
Turin has plenty to see and do for kids at moderate prices.

REAL MEAL Dausin (Via Goito 9, 10121; 011 669 3933; closed Sat lunch and Sun) has a pleasantly informal ambience and cuisine based on locally grown ingredients.
FAMILY TREAT Il Consorzio (Via Monte di Pietà 23, 10121; 011 276 7661; www.ristoranteconsorzio.it; closed Sat lunch and Sun) does a fresh take on Piedmontese cuisine, such as tripe *ravioli* on a bed of beans with glazed onions.

Shopping

Department store **La Rinascente** (Via Lagrange 15, 10121) stocks the essentials. **Baratti & Milano** (Piazza Castello 27, 10121) and **Gobino** (Via Lagrange 1/a, 10121) are legendary chocolate shops. **Paradiso dei Bambini** (Via C. Alberto, 10121) and the **Centro Gioco Educativo** (Via Cernaia 25, 10121) are great for toys.

Find out more

FILM The Italian Job (1969), a comic film starring Michael Caine, is about a plot to steal a gold transport by creating a traffic jam. It features a Mini Cooper chase through Turin.

Take cover

Turin is renowned for its chocolate. A **ChocoPass** (€48 for a family of four for two days, from the tourist office) gains entry to nine tastings in specialist shops and cafés.

The rack tramway at Sassi station, where there is also a Tram Museum

Next stop...
SASSI–SUPERGA RACK

TRAMWAY The unique rack tramway began back in 1884 as a cable railway. It offers breathtaking views of Turin and the Alps. The 3-km (2-mile) track from Sassi station ends up at Superga (650 m/2,000 ft), with a basilica, royal tombs, nature park, café and pizzeria (€8–22, children under 1 m/3 ft tall free).

⑥ Parco Arte Vivente (PAV)

Art comes to life

The Parco Arte Vivente (Living Art Park) is a sort of crossroads between art and biology. Known as PAV, it is a fantastic transformation of an industrial district into a park devoted to living art – not only plants and the environment, but also the whole creative process. There is a permanent exhibition and various installations, as well as temporary shows in the Bioma building. The focus is interactive, with lots of hands-on experiences designed by contemporary artist Piero Gilardi to bring out the creative side in children, and in adults too.

Letting off steam

The gardens of PAV are a work in progress, showing how plants and design can transform what we see. There is plenty of green space, with curious paths, visual surprises and a

The Lowdown

🌐 **Map reference** 1 C3

Address PAV, Via Giordano Bruno 31, 10134 Turin, Piemont; 011 318 2235; www. parcoartevivente.it

🚗 **Metro** from Turin Porta Nuova station to Carducci, then cross the bridge. **Train** 4 to Distretto Militare. **Bus** 1 or 35 to Carducci Nord, then bus 17 towards Rivoli, getting off at Bramante

🕐 **Open** 1pm–6pm Wed–Fri, noon–7pm Sat–Sun

💶 **Price** €6–10, under-25s €2, under-10s free

👫 **Age range** All

🧒 **Activities** Workshops for children (and adults) aged 5 plus 10am–noon and 3–5pm Tue–Fri; €4 for under-18s, €5 for adults; booking mandatory on 011 318 2235 or lab@parcoartevivente.it

⏱ **Allow** Half a day

🍽 **Eat and drink** Snacks Pasticceria Beatrice (Corso Bramante 61, 10134; 011 696 3208), has pastries and sandwiches. Real meal La Mela Stregata (Piazza Carducci 122, 10134; 011 659 8445), opposite Pasticceria Beatrice, has more substantial meals, while Pizzeria La Stadera (Corso Dante 85, 10134; 011 669 8690) serves up pizza and pasta.

family of ducks who have taken up residence here. Friendly English-speaking guides are available to explain it all, but there is also the possibility of roaming freely. Access is via the stunning glasshouse-style lobby building.

⑦ Castello di Rivoli

Weird castle, wacky art

Located on the site of a medieval castle, in 1718 this building was redesigned by Filippo Juvarra, one of Italy's great Baroque architects, to create a grandiose royal palace that could compete with Europe's greatest. Only a third of the original plan was built, and even that was abandoned until the late 20th century, when it was decided to turn the whole edifice into a cutting- edge contemporary art gallery featuring artists from all over the world, including German-born painter and sculptor Anselm Kiefer, British-based duo Gilbert and George and Italian-born humorist Maurizio Cattelan. As well as the permanent collection, there are many temporary exhibitions. The mix of provocative contemporary art with the ornate setting makes quite an impact.

Letting off steam

Alberando Adventure Park, in San Grato park beside the Castello di Rivoli, offers safe tree-climbing activities (338 622 7242; www. parcoalberando.it).

Imposing entrance to the Castello di Rivoli contemporary art museum

The Lowdown

🌐 **Map reference** 1 C3

Address Castello di Rivoli Museo d'Arte Contemporanea, Piazza Mafalda di Savoia, 10098 Rivoli, Piemont; 011 956 5222; www. castellodirivoli.org

🚗 **Metro** from Turin Porta Susa or Porta Nuova station to Paradiso (10 minutes), then bus 36 to the terminus for Rivoli (30 minutes)

🕐 **Open** 10am–5pm Tue–Fri, 10am–7pm Sat–Sun

💶 **Price** €13–26, reductions for 11–14-year-olds, under-11s free

🚩 **Guided tours** Sat 3:30pm and 6pm, Sun 11am, 3pm and 6pm; free

👫 **Age range** All

⏱ **Allow** At least 2 hours

♿ **Wheelchair access** Yes

🍽 **Eat and drink** Real meal La Grotta degli Elfi (Corso Allamano 115, 10098; 011 950 8566, www.lagrottadeglielfi.it; closed Mon) serves simple pasta. Family treat Combal.Zero (0119 565 225; www.combal.org; closed Sun and Mon) is an experimental restaurant inside the Castello di Rivoli museum, with two Michelin stars.

Exploring the sculptural installations in PAV Parco Arte Vivente, Turin's Living Art Park

⑧ La Venaria Reale

Princely palace and gardens

One of the most imposing tributes to hunting ever created, this huge complex consists of an ancient town, an amazing royal palace, large gardens and a park surrounded by 35 km (nearly 22 miles) of walls. It was begun in 1659 by Duke Carlo Emanuele II of Savoy, at a time when the splendour of the hunt was a sign of sovereign power. In 1716 Baroque supremo Filippo Juvarra took over its design. Now a UNESCO World Heritage site, the Venaria has a 2-km (1-mile) long tour covering the "architecture, history and magnificence" of the Reggia (royal palace) and the Savoy dynasty. It also hosts blockbusting exhibitions of fine art and fashion, and monthly "royal dinners" prepared by great chefs from April to November in the Great Gallery. The extensive gardens comprise styles from the 17th century to the present.

La Venaria Reale royal palace, seen from its stylish landscaped gardens

Letting off steam

The 8-hectare (20-acre) **Potager Royal** was the vegetable patch for the palace, and is now a fascinating mixture of flowers, fruit trees, vegetables and cereals typical of the region. There are hands-on tours designed to get children interested in where their food comes from, plus beehives, fountains and benches.

The Lowdown

🌐 **Map reference** 1 C3
Address Piazza della Repubblica, 10078 Venaria Reale, Piemont; 011 499 2333; www.lavenaria.it

🚗 **Car** Follow Venaria signs from Turin's Tangenziale Nord. **Train** GTT Dora–Ceres line to Venaria. **Bus** GTT line 72 or 11 or direct shuttle (www.gtt.to.it)

🕐 **Open** Palace: Nov–Mar 9am–6pm Tue–Fri, 9am–8pm Sat–Sun 9am–6pm Tue–Fri, Apr–Oct 9am–9:30pm Sat, 9am–8pm Sun. Gardens: 9am–dusk

💶 **Price** Palace and gardens: €24–40, under-18s €8, under-12s free. Gardens only: €4 and €1 Sun, under-18s €3, under-12s free

👪 **Age range** All for the gardens, 8 plus for the Reggia

🕐 **Allow** 1 day

♿ **Wheelchair accessible** Yes

🍴 **Eat and drink** *Real meal* Passami il Sale *(Via Andrea Mensa 37a, 10078; 011 459 8387; www.passamiilsale.it; closed Mon–Thu lunch and Tue eve)* has simple, well-made local cuisine. *Family treat* Scacco Matto, *(Via Tessarin 8, 10078; 011 497 769; booking essential)* serves good pizza or a choice of fixed menus.

The sumptuous La Venaria Reale gardens, against a backdrop of the Alps

⑨ Lake Orta
Fairy-tale island on a peaceful lake

Tucked between Lake Maggiore and the Valsesia, 13-km (9-mile) long Lake Orta is surrounded by colourful little towns bathed in soft, watery light. Luxuriant greenery and a wealth of flowers flourish in the mild climate, filling gardens that sweep down to the lakeside. Higher up the hillsides are beech, oak and birch woods, where a range of outdoor activities can be enjoyed. The tiny Isola San Giulio, with its early Christian basilica, adds a touch of mystery to the enchanting scene.

Taking a sailing boat out on Lake Orta

Key Sights

Monte Mottarone
15 km (9 miles) ⑥

Omegna
10 km (6 miles)

Gignese
12 km (7 miles)

⑤ Villa Nigra
MIASINO

Lago d'Orta

'Orta San Giulio ①

Isola San Giulio ②

④ Sacro Monte

③ Legro

AMENO

VACCIAGO

Calderara Collection of Contemporary Art
(see p141)

⑨ SS229

LORTALLO

CORCONIO

Monte Mesma ⑦

⑧ Torre di Buccione

0 kilometres   1
0 miles   1

① **Orta San Giulio** On the east bank of the lake this charming town features fine old houses with lovely gardens. In its centre is the arcaded Piazza Motta, home to many cafés and shops.

③ **Legro** Find painted walls with scenes from films here, in honour of the many directors who were inspired by the location in the early and mid-20th century.

⑥ **Monte Mottarone** Enjoy fabulous views of both Lake Maggiore and Lake Orta, and beyond from here. Winter sports, summer hiking and hang-gliding are popular, as is the Giardino Botanico Alpinia, near Stresa, which is well worth a visit.

⑦ **Monte Mesma** Topped by an impressive 16th-century convent, this nature reserve is great for walks. Woodland paths open up to reveal breathtaking views of Lake Orta.

② **Isola San Giulio** This island seems to exist in another time. Founded in the 4th century, the basilica here houses a silent order of nuns who offer guest accommodation. Take a stroll to enjoy the island's natural beauty.

④ **Sacro Monte** Twenty chapels devoted to St Francis of Assisi and built between the 16th and 18th centuries can be found on this leafy hillside. Nature and mysticism still prevail here.

⑤ **Villa Nigra** Baroque residences overlooking the lake are a feature of Miasino, but this villa is the jewel in the crown. It houses exhibitions, concerts and a restaurant.

⑧ **Torre di Buccione** Overlooking Lake Orta from the southeast, this 23-m (75-ft) tall hilltop watchtower was once part of a medieval castle.

The Lowdown

🌐 **Map reference** 1 2D
Address 28016 Orta San Giulio, Piemonte. Giardino Botanico Alpinia: Piazzale Lido 8, 28838 Stresa; *www. giardinoalpinia.it*. Umbrella and Parasol Museum: Via Golf Panorama 2, 28836 Gignese; 0323 89622; *www.gignese.it/ museo/ombrello*. Giardini Botanici di Villa Taranto: Via Vittorio Veneto 111, 28922 Verbania Pallanza; *www. villataranto.it*

🚗 **Car** On the A26 motorway, exit at Borgomanero or Arona and follow the signs for Lago d'Orta.

Train to Orta San Giulio station on the Novara–Ornavasso and Domodossola–Borgomanero–Novara lines (*www.trenitalia.it*). **Waterbus** to Isola San Giulio from Piazza Motta in Orta San Giulio (*www.navigazionelaghi.it*). **Walk** to Sacro Monte from Orta San Giulio (10 mins). **Cable car** from Stresa to Monte Mottarone, via the Giardino Botanico Alpinia (*www.stresa-mottarone.it*), or by car follow signs from Miasino and Armeno.

ℹ **Visitor information** Corso Italia 18, 28838 Stresa, 0323 30416 *www.distrettolaghi.it*

🕐 **Open** Giardino Botanico Alpinia: Apr–Oct 9:30am–6pm. Parco della Fantasia: check website for family workshops. Umbrella and Parasol Museum: Apr–Sep 10am–noon and 3–6pm Tue–Sun. Giardini Botanici di Villa Taranto: Mar–Nov 8:30am–6:30pm

💰 **Price** Giardino Botanico Alpinia: €6–12, under-4s free. Umbrella and Parasol Museum: €8–10. Giardini Botanici di Villa Taranto: €30–38, under-6s free

👥 **Skipping the queue** Booking is essential for the Parco della Fantasia.

Letting off steam

Pay a visit to the **Parco della Fantasia Gianni Rodari** in Omegna, *(Parco Maulini 1, 28887 Omegna; 0323 887 233; www.rodariparco fantasia.it)* a homage to Gianni Rodari, considered by many to be Italy's most important 20th-century children's author. Few of his books have been translated into English, but the park offers kids a chance to unleash their imaginations with fun workshops and games.

Eat and drink

Picnic: under €25; Snacks: €25–40; Real meal: €40–80; Family treat: €80 or more (based on a family of four)

PICNIC Il Buongustaio *(Piazza Ragazzoni 8/10, 28016 Orta San Giulio)* stocks local delicacies such as *mortadella ortese*, a cured sausage meat found only in this region.

SNACKS Il Pozzo *(Via Panoramica 16, 28016 Orta San Giulio; 0322 90150, closed Thu)* sells a wide range of sandwiches, tarts (sweet and savoury) and pizza.

REAL MEAL L'Ustaria Cà dal Rat *(Via Novara 66, 28016 Orta San Giulio; 0322 905 120; closed Wed)*, overlooks the water and serves excellent sautéed rabbit and *gnocchi* with duck and thyme sauce.

FAMILY TREAT Ristorante **Al Sorriso** *(Via Roma 18, 28010 Soriso; 8km south of Orta San Giulio; 0322 983 228; www.alsorriso. com)* is renowned for its Michelin-starred seasonal menus using locally sourced ingredients, including wild mushrooms and tagliatelle with chives and fresh fish.

Age range All

Activities Mountain-biking, walking, horse-riding, sailing *(www.bicico.it)* and skiing *(www.scuolascimottarone. it)* on Monte Mottarone.

Allow 3 to 5 days

Café On Piazza Motta in Orta San Giulio

Good family value?

As well as organized outdoor activities, there is plenty of scope for walks and wandering around Lake Orta free of charge.

Shopping

Handmade soaps are sold at **Ricordi** in Orta San Giulio *(Piazza Motta 30, 28016; 0322 90337).*

Find out more

FILM Many scenes from the Oscar-winning 1932 film *A Farewell to Arms*, based on Ernest Hemingway's novel and starring Gary Cooper and Helen Hayes, were shot in the vicinity of Legro.

DIGITAL To read Gianni Rodari's story *Polenta Fritta*, translated as *Mashed Potatoes*, in English, go to *www.ibabbleon.com/gianni_rodari_ english_translation.html*

Take cover

There is no place like an **Umbrella and Parasol Museum** for taking cover! This amazing collection of what was once a fashion item for the wealthy is in nearby Gignese, where umbrella-making was a traditional craft, with child apprentices.

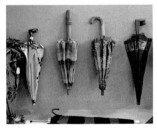

Attractive umbrellas on display at the Umbrella and Parasol Museum

Next stop...

The **Giardini Botanici di Villa Taranto** at Pallanza, stretching down to Lake Maggiore, were begun by a Scotsman in the 1930s and show off 20,000 important botanical species.

Flowers in bloom in the botanical gardens of Villa Taranto

⑩ Museo dell'Arte della Tornitura del Legno

Water-powered wood-turning

Just north of Orta San Giulio on Lake Orta, Pettenasco is a pleasant lakeside town and home of the little museum of the art of wood-turning, devoted to what used to be a typical craft in this area. See what skilled craftsmen turned out here from the mid-19th century until a few decades ago, using machinery powered by five watermills along the Pescone river. Typical products were pestles and mortars, and the first turned pepper mills. Original tools are on display in the old workshops too. Also worth a visit is the church of SS Audenzio e Caterina – its 12th-century Romanesque bell tower is one of the oldest in the area.

Letting off steam

Less than 1 km (half a mile) from town, the Lake Orta beaches at **Riva Pisola** and **Approdo** are good for a splash around. Both have ferry stops.

The Lowdown

- 🌐 **Map reference** 1 2D
  Address Museo dell'Arte della Tornitura del Legno, Via Vittorio Veneto, 28028 Pettenasco, Piemonte; 0323 89622
- 🚗 **Car** 2 km (1 mile) from Orta San Giulio on SR229. **Train** on Novara–Domodossola line to Pettenasco station. **Bus** from Omegna, Orta San Giulio and Arona (www.comazzibus.com).
- 🕐 **Open** mid-Jun–mid-Sep 10am–12:30pm and 2:30pm–6pm; rest of year by appointment
- 💶 **Price** Free
- 👫 **Age range** 8 plus
- ⏱ **Allow** 30 minutes
- 🍴 **Eat and drink** *Real meal* Il Vecchio Forno (*Via Gaetano Fara 3, 28028; 0323 89444; closed Sat and Sun eve and Mon*) offers pizza, vegetarian dishes and local meats. *Family treat* Birrificio di Pettenasco (*Corso Roma, 28028; 0323 89666; May–Oct open eves Wed–Sun, Nov–Apr Fri–Sun*) is a micro-brewery and restaurant set in an old foundry. Service is swift and dishes such as pork shin cooked in beer are on the menu.

Jetties and pleasure boats on the still water of Lake Orta at Pella

⑪ Santuario della Madonna del Sasso

Perfect wedding venue?

According to legend, many centuries ago a soldier in a fit of jealous rage dragged his wife up to this outcrop high above the west side of the lake and hurled her off the edge, then had second thoughts and tried to grab her back. She was so frightened by his anger that she preferred to let herself fall. In time a cross was erected here, then a small chapel and, between 1730 and 1748, the Santuario della Madonna del Sasso church with its frescoed interiors. The fact that today lots of couples choose to wed here speaks volumes for the power of a glorious view. The

The 18th-century church of Madonna del Sasso, a popular wedding venue

The Lowdown

- 🌐 **Map reference** 1 1D
  Address Santuario della Madonna del Sasso, 28894 Verbania, Piemonte
- 🚗 **Car** A26 to Borgomanero or Arona exit. **Train** to Gozzano, 11 km (7 miles) from Madonna del Sasso. **Lake ferry** from Orta San Giulio and Omegna to Pella
- 🕐 **Open** Sanctuary for religious functions, view always accessible
- 💶 **Price** Free
- 👫 **Age range** More interesting for older children, 11 plus
- ⏱ **Allow** 30 minutes
- 🍴 **Eat and drink** *Snacks* Gelateria Antica Torre (*Via Lungo Lago 8, 28028 Pella*) offers fantastic ice cream and sweet and savoury crepes. *Family treat* La Cruna del Lago (*Via Bellosta 1, 28017 San Maurizio d'Opaglio; 0322 967 435*) serves sophisticated cuisine such as delicious rabbit ravioli with peppers, sage and butter sauce.

neighbouring village of Boleto is also pretty, with cobbled streets and great views across to Monte Rosa.

Letting off steam

Just over 1 km (half a mile) downhill is the lakeside village of **Pella**, where the public gardens are equipped with a children's playground and a basketball court, and there is a pretty promenade by the lake. There is also a nice, sandy beach at **Rialaccio** in neighbouring Frazione Roncallo (2 km/1 mile), providing easy access to the water.

Loggias overlooking the courtyard at Antonio Calderara's house

⑫ Calderara Collection of Contemporary Art

How artists see the world

Self-taught painter Antonio Calderara (1903–1978) moved during his career from an almost sculptural realism to total abstraction. Instead of creating a lifelike image of what he saw, he played with the shape of things, making them ever more geometrical. Yet he preserved in his work an atmosphere that suggests the diffused light typical of lakeside areas, where the sun's rays are softened through reflection from the water. Calderara was born in Abbiategrasso near Milan and spent childhood holidays in Vacciago. He lived in this splendid house from the mid-1970s, building up a collection of contemporary art that comprises 56 of his own works, and 271 creations by fellow artists from Italy, Europe, America, Japan and China. Dating back to the late Renaissance, the house itself consists of three storeys with loggias overlooking the lake, a courtyard and a garden. There is something peaceful, yet stimulating, about the collection, which is representative of all the main artistic styles of the mid- to late 20th century.

Letting off steam

Just south of Vacciago, in the hamlet of Lortallo, are three paths offering great walks around the **Riserva Naturale di Monte**

Mesma, a lovely nature reserve with a wooded hill surmounted by a 16th-century convent. There is a paved Via Crucis flanked by little chapels that can be walked to the top in around 20 minutes, another path that leads through chestnut woods to the summit and a third track beside the Rio Membra and Torrente Agogna streams. There are good chances of sighting local fauna, including deer, wild boar, squirrels, foxes and birds of prey.

The Lowdown

🌐 **Map reference** 1 2D
Address La Fondazione Calderara, Via Bardelli 9, 28010 Località Vacciago di Ameno; 0322 998 192; www.fondazionecalderara.it,

🚗 **Car** on A4 or A8, exit Borgomanero, then SS229 to Gravellona Toce and Vacciago. **Train** to Gozzano.

🕐 **Open** May–mid-Oct 3–7pm Tue–Fri, 10am–noon and 3–7pm Sat–Sun

💶 **Price** Free

👫 **Age range** 11 plus

⏱ **Allow** 1 hour

🍽 **Eat and drink** *Real meal* Vecchio Circolo di Fierobecco (*Via Carlo Porta 4, 28010; 0322 998 098; open Wed–Sun*) is located where the tracks up Monte Mesma begin, and serves delicious fish dishes. *Real meal* Ristorante Sant' Antonio at Miasino (*Regione Tortirogno 4, 28010; 0322 911 963*) is in a lovely lakeside setting and serves pizza and fried fish. It is very popular, so book a table in advance.

Where to Stay in Valle d'Aosta & Piemonte

There is great variety here, from sophisticated boutique hotels to friendly farm accommodation; family-run B&Bs to simple but pleasant rooms run by a religious brotherhood. Magnificent views are often part of the package, especially in the mountains, where snow-capped peaks are to be expected.

AGENCY

The Salt Way
0183 930 098; www.saltway.it
Apartments to let in Turin (three-day minimum stay), and farmhouses in southern Piemonte.

Aosta
Map 1 B2

HOTELS
Le Charaban
Loc Saraillon 38, 11100; 0165 238 289; www.lecharaban.it
Just off the SS27 towards Gran San Bernardo, this is a good option with various family rooms, and a nearby apartment that sleeps six, plus a warm, woody interior and restaurant.
€

Milleluci
Loc Porossan Roppoz 15, 11100; 0165 235 278; www.hotelmilleluci.com
A lovely old family farmhouse turned into a quietly elegant hotel in a magnificent hillside location just outside Aosta. Great breakfasts, with local rye bread, jams and hams.
€€€

Courmayeur
Map 1 B1

HOTEL
Hotel Albergo Aigle
Strada La Palud 5, Fraz Entrèves, 11013; 0165 869 700; www.hotelaigle.it
A comfortable, family-run hotel just outside Courmayeur, with balconies facing Mont Blanc, and a garden. Ideal for hiking and river-rafting in summer. Attractive family packages.
€

The nicely furnished interior of Hotel Leon d'Oro on the shores of Lake Orta

Key to symbols *see back cover flap*

Gran Paradiso-Valnontey
Map 1 B1

HOTEL
Hotel Gran Paradiso
Loc Pont Valsavarenche, 11010; 0165 95318; www.hotelgparadiso.com
At 2,000 m (6,561 ft), this is the perfect spot for enjoying the great outdoors and spotting wild animals.
€

CAMPING
Campeggio Lo Stambecco
Fraz Valnontey 6, 11012 Valnontey/ Cogne; 0165 74152; www.campeggiolostambecco.it
In a lovely valley off the Val di Cogne, with 140 pitches, four restaurants and a grocery shop.
€

Lake Orta
Map 1 D2

HOTELS
La Bussola
Via Panoramica 24, 28016 Orta San Giulio; 0322 911 913; www.hotelbussolaorta.it
A comfortable hotel with amazing views down over the town to the lake. Terrace restaurant in summer.
€

Hotel Leon d'Oro
Piazza Motta 42, 28016 Orta San Giulio; 0322 911 991; www.albergoleondoro.it
In a fabulous position right on the lake, with a landing stage. Meals on the garden terrace in summer.
€€

La Salle

HOTEL
Les Combes
Map 1 B2
Fraz Cheverel, 11015; 0165 863 982; www.lescombes.it
Hotel created out of a tiny hamlet, looking out over the Mont Blanc chain. Good family rooms and deals.
€

The elegant Hotel Victoria in the centre of Turin, close to shops and restaurants

Turin
Map 1 C3

HOTELS
Foresteria della Basilica di Superga
Strada della Basilica di Superga, 10132; 011 898 0083; www.basilicadisuperga.com/accoglienza.html
A tranquil spot outside Turin, run by the Servi di Maria brotherhood. Nice old rooms with modern bathrooms.
€

Artuà e Solferino
Via Brofferio 3, 10121; 011 517 5301; www.hotelartuasolferino.it
Near the Museo Egizio, on the top floor of a handsome 19th century residence with a fabulous period lift.
€€

Hotel Victoria
Via Nino Costa 4, 10121; 011 561 1909; www.hotelvictoria-torino.com
Quietly classy accommodation in a pedestrian district of the city centre, with a spa, pool and sauna.
€€€

Price Guide
The following price ranges are based on one night's accommodation in high season for a family of four, inclusive of service charges and any additional taxes.
€ Under €200 €€ €200–350 €€€ over €350

Liguria

Backed by steep hillsides glittering with olive trees, colourful Liguria looks out over the Tyrrhenian Sea. For centuries maritime trade was a mainstay, bringing sugar, salt and fish – the flavours of its cuisine – to the coast, along with prosperity. North of Genoa and its aquarium are sandy beaches, while the south offers walks among Cinque Terre fishing villages.

Below *Vernazza, one of the Cinque Terre villages, seen from the coastal footpath*

Genoa
p144

Cinque Terre
p148

① Genoa: the Aquarium
Something very fishy

At the heart of Genoa's old harbour is the futuristic Aquarium. Built to honour the seafaring city's most famous son, Christopher Columbus, on the 500th anniversary of his discovery of the Americas in 1492, it looks like a ship in full sail and is home to more than 12,000 sea creatures – Europe's second-largest aquarium. Inside, tiny seahorses float, colourful parrotfish and clownfish dart about, jellyfish ripple by, penguins march, seals and dolphins play and sinister sharks glide past in the water.

Emperor angelfish

Key Features

■ **Upper Floor** Tropical Lagoons, Amazonian Rivers, Mangroves and Central American forests, Red Sea and Moluccas' corals

■ **Main Floor** The deep waters of the Mediterranean Sea, Cinque Terre and Micronesian corals, piranhas and discus fish

Entrance

① **Manatees**
These threatened herbivorous marine mammals weigh in at up to 1,500 kg (over 3,300 lb). They make up for bad vision with their sense of touch.

② **Sharks**
The sharks with their big curved mouths can be seen from below. Bold 7–13-year-olds can actually spend a night here.

③ **Dolphins**
The dolphins' tank is open to the sky, so its graceful inmates can practise aerial acrobatics.

④ **Medusas**
There are nine tanks containing different species of jellyfish – ancient creatures that have populated the oceans for the past 650 million years.

⑤ **Seals**
The huge tank allows visitors to view seals in the water and on the rocks. Seal pups born here are suckled by their mothers in a special nursery aquarium.

⑥ **Madagascar Lagoon**
This tank holds various tropical creatures, including a huge Cuban turtle that was smuggled into Italy and dumped near the Aquarium before being rescued.

⑦ **Penguins**
Magellan penguins with white-striped throats and smaller Papua penguins live in a multi-level tank, allowing views of them underwater and on the rocks. Feeding time is always fun to see (9am and 3pm daily).

⑧ **Touch Pool**
Dip hands into the water to stroke the friendly rays that seem to enjoy gentle human contact.

The Lowdown

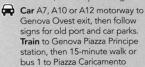

Letting off steam

The **Città dei Bambini** (Children's City) in the old port engages kids of all ages with interactive installations that are both fun and educational. Younger children (3–5-year-olds) can explore the senses in three different settings – building site, hands in the water and the mirror image – while older children (6–12-year-olds) can engage in all sorts of exciting scientific experiments. There is a "digiwall" for climbing, a mini TV studio and a section devoted to the marvels of physics.

An outdoor area at Genoa's Aquarium, with views out over the port

Eat and drink

Picnic: under €25; Snacks: €25–40; Real meal: €40–80; Family treat: €80 or more (based on a family of four)

PICNIC Friggitoria Carega *(Via di Sottoripa 113/r, 16124; closed Sun)*, which serves classic Genoese finger food such as *farinata* (a baked chickpea-flour pancake), savoury tarts and fried seafood. Across the road there are benches to sit on in the old port area.
SNACKS Le Vele, right below the Aquarium *(open 8:30am–6:30pm)*, makes sandwiches and pizza.
REAL MEAL I Tre Merli *(Calata Cattaneo 17, 16128; 010 246 4416; www.itremerli.it)*, just down the road from the Aquarium, offers food ranging from *farinata* and cheese *focaccia* to salads, pasta and fish. Outdoor tables overlooking the water are available in fine weather.
FAMILY TREAT Le Cantine Squarciafico *(Piazza Invrea 3, 16123; 010 247 0823; www. squarciaficolecantine.com)*, near Genoa's cathedral, has an elegant interior dating back to the 16th century, and an interesting new take on Genoese classics such as pesto and salt cod. The menu is strong on both fish and meat and there is an excellent wine list.

Shopping

Tucked away behind Piazza de Ferrari is the **Fabbrica di Cioccolato Viganotti** *(Vicolo dei Castagna 14/r, 16128; 010 251 4061)*, a traditional chocolate shop. Intelligent toys can be found at **Città del Sole** *(Via Luccoli 42, 16128; www.cittadelsole.it)*.

Find out more

DIGITAL For Italian speakers, the website *www.acquariovillage.it* gives a good introduction to the attractions of the old port, including a virtual tour of the Aquarium.

Next stop...

BOATS, BIOSPHERES AND BIGO
An excellent museum in the old port, the **Galata Museo del Mare**, explores the city's seafaring tradition, from rowing boats to sailing ships and vessels devoted to scientific discovery. The third floor focuses on setting sail for America, with an interactive account of emigration. Get an idea of what it was like to leave home and seek a new life across the seas. For more boats, continue to the Museo Navale di Pegli *(see pp146–7)*.

The painted stern of a galleon in the Galata Museo del Mare

The glass globe of the **Biosfera** contains a mini tropical forest, including cacao and rubber trees, pepper and cinnamon plants, and ferns. There are orange ibis and hosts of butterflies in summer too.

For a breathtaking panorama of the port and city, hop aboard the **Bigo**, a rotating glass cabin that rises 40 m (131 ft) above the ground.

② Galleria Nazionale di Palazzo Spinola

All that glitters...

This grandiose palace was built in 1593 by the Grimaldi family, one of Genoa's ruling dynasties from the end of the Crusades in the 12th century until Napoleon's troops entered the city in 1797 – with a few hiccups (a branch of the family still reigns over Monaco, which they seized after being exiled from Genoa in 1270). In the 16th century the family formed one of 28 *alberghi* or governing clans. Their Pallavicini, Doria and Spinola heirs remodelled and redecorated in the 18th century, while the top two floors, destroyed in World War II, were rebuilt in modern style to house the Galleria Nazionale della Liguria art collection. The bottom two floors still feel like a princely residence, adorned with splendid frescoes, mirrors, gold leaf

The lavish, gilt hall of mirrors in the Galleria Nazionale di Palazzo Spinola

and brocades. There is exquisite porcelain from China, and fine examples of Dutch painting include Rubens' charming *Sacra Famiglia della Cesta* (1615), with baby Jesus in a wicker basket, and a Van Dyck portrait of one of the palace's former inhabitants, Ansaldo Pallavicino.

Letting off steam

Less than 10 minutes' walk away are the large, sloping public gardens of the **Villetta Di Negro** *(open daily 8am–sunset)*. Designed in the early 1800s, they feature a waterfall and a pagoda, and offer a great view of the city and coast from the top. A modern building in the gardens houses the excellent **Museo d'Arte Orientale**, one of the best oriental collections in Europe; children will be fascinated by the Japanese Samurai and Chinese mask displays. Afterwards, head to the grounds, where there is room to play.

A rooftop garden fountain at the Galleria Nazionale di Palazzo Spinola

The Lowdown

- 🌐 **Map reference** 2 E5
  Address 16123 Genoa. Palazzo Spinola: Piazza Pellicceria 1, 16123; 010 270 5300; *www. palazzospinola.it.* Museo d'Arte Orientale: Villetta Di Negro, Piazzale Mazzini 4, 16122; 010 542 285; *www.museidigenova.it*
- 🚇 **Metro** Darsena or San Giorgio.
- 🕐 **Open** Palazzo Spinola: 8:30am–7:30pm Tue–Sat, 1:30–7:30pm Sun. Museo d'Arte Orientale: 9am–1pm Tue–Fri, 10am–7pm Sat–Sun
- 💶 **Price** Palazzo Spinola: €8, under-18s free. Museo d'Arte Orientale: €8, under-18s free
- 👫 **Age range** 11 plus
- ⏱ **Allow** 30 minutes
- ☕ **Eat and drink** *Snacks* I Due Truogoli *(Piazza dei Truogoli di Santa Brigida 15–17, 16123; 010 246 2198; closed Sun; booking advised)* is a good place for a quick lunch of dishes such as rice salad or *frittata* (a thick omelette similar to a Spanish *tortilla*), or a more relaxed dinner. *Real meal* La Funicolare *(Corso Magenta, 16122; 010 2513 286; open eves only, from 5pm; booking advised)* is pleasantly informal and serves pizza and *farinata* (a baked chickpea-flour pancake), especially good in spring with artichokes.

③ Museo Navale di Pegli

Setting sail

Located in the 17th-century Villa Doria, originally the abode of another of Genoa's most prominent

The Lowdown

- 🌐 **Map reference** 2 E5
  Address Museo Navale di Pegli: Villa Doria, Piazza Bonavino 7, 16156; 010 696 9885, *www.museidigenova.it.* Parco Avventura Pegli: Viale Modugno 121, 16156; 348 346 3507; *genova-pegli.parcoavventura.it*
- 🚢 **Boat** Navebus from Genoa's old port to Pegli *(www.amt.genova.it).* **Train** from Stazione Principe to Genova-Pegli, then AMT bus 93, 190. **Car** on A10, exit Genova-Pegli
- 🕐 **Open** Museo Navale: 9am–1pm Tue–Fri, 10am–7pm Sat–Sun. Parco Avventura: Mar–mid-Jun and mid-Sep–Nov 10am–5pm Sat–Sun; mid-Jun–mid-Sep 3–6pm Mon–Fri, 10am–6pm Sat–Sun
- 💶 **Price** Museo Navale: €8, children free. Parco Avventura: €50
- 👫 **Age range** 6 plus
- ⏱ **Allow** Half a day
- ☕ **Eat and drink** *Real meal* Antica Via Venti *(Via Martiri della Libertà 63/r, 16156; 010 664 665; www. anticaviaventi.it; open Tue–Sun lunch, Fri–Sat also dinner)* offers a good choice of classic dishes, with a nice outside area. *Real meal* Ristorante La Vetta *(Viale Modugno 62, 16156; 010 697 0066)* is great for pizza or classic seafood dishes with a view.

families, the city's naval museum in Pegli illustrates the Ligurian Riviera's relationship with the sea between the 15th and 19th centuries – the age of sail – complementing the displays of the Museo Galata in Genoa's old port (see p145). The Genoese made a name for themselves as explorers, merchants and fishermen, but also as shipbuilders, and alongside the museum's collections of maps and model ships – in fabulously frescoed rooms – are reconstructions of sail-makers', flag-makers' and lifebuoy-makers' workshops, showing the expertise behind Liguria's nautical adventures.

Letting off steam
Just 2 km (1 mile) from the museum (bus 189) is the fantastic **Parco Avventura Pegli**, a tree-top adventure park with climbing trails on suspended rope bridges, rope ladders and flying foxes (zip wires).

④ Museo di Archeologia Ligure
Giant bears living in caves

The Ligurian archaeological museum is housed in a villa built by another of Genoa's aristocratic families in the 19th century, the Villa Durazzo Pallavicini. The first rooms cover the last Ice Age, from 80,000 to 10,000 BC, when rhinoceroses, lions and bears roamed the Ligurian hillsides and sheltered in caves. By the 5th millennium BC, humans had settled in the area and were making tools and amulets. Huge technical advances followed in the Bronze Age (3600–800 BC). Pride of place in the rooms devoted to the

earliest settlers in Genoa goes to the the Tavola di Polcevera (117 BC), a bronze tablet issued by the Roman Senate resolving a tribal boundary dispute in favour of the Genuati of Genoa, and a sculpture of Cerberus, the three-headed dog who is said to guard the underworld. The style testifies to Roman colonization, but also shows the influence of Celtic culture.

Letting off steam
The villa's gardens were designed by a famous early 19th-century theatrical designer, Michele Canzio, who designed sets for the Carlo Felice opera house. The gardens, which include a lake, temples and bridges, aim to create a series of pleasant surprises for the visitor.

The Lowdown

- **Map reference** 2 E5
  Address Villa Pallavicini, Via Pallavicini 11, 16155; 010 698 1048; www.museidigenova.it
- **Boat** Navebus from Genoa's old port to Pegli (www.amt.genova.it). **Train** to Genova-Pegli. **Car** on A10, exit Genova-Pegli
- **Open** 9am–1pm Tue–Fri, 10am–7pm Sat–Sun
- **Price** €8, children free
- **Age range** 5 plus
- **Allow** 1 hour
- **Eat and drink** Real meal Trattoria da Nanni (Via Zaccaria Benedetto 12/r, 16155; 010 697 5012; www. trattoriadananni.it; closed Tue) has seafood lasagne, grilled fish and great views. Family treat La Rose en Table (Lungomare di Pegli 79/r, 16155; 010 407 4156; open eves, also lunch Sun; closed Mon) offers a new take on fish.

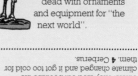

Villa Durazzo Pallavicini in Pegli, home of Museo di Archeolgia Ligure

Picnic under €25; **Snacks** €25–40; **Real meal** €40–80; **Family treat** €80 or more (based on a family of four)

⑤ Cinque Terre
Clifftop trails, colourful villages and a sparkling sea

A rugged stretch of coastline named after five small towns that seem to cling dramatically to the edge of vertiginous cliffs, the UNESCO-listed Cinque Terre is the wildest part of the Ligurian coast. Connected by railway but still unblemished by coastal roads, the area offers walking trails with superb views over terraced vineyards and wooded valleys towards the sea. Other highlights include pretty fishing villages, a cuisine based on vegetables and salted fish, and delectable local wines.

Café beside Vernazza harbour

Key Sights

① **Bonassola** This quiet hamlet is tucked between two rocky outcrops and can be reached by car or train. Be sure to walk to the Punta della Madonna promontory.

② **Monterosso** The largest of the Cinque Terre towns, Monterosso has beaches, a medieval tower, the ruins of a clifftop castle and three 16th-century watchtowers built to protect inhabitants from pirates.

③ **Vernazza** Founded around AD 1000, Vernazza straddles a large rocky promontory. Walk the narrow lanes between colourful houses and visit the remains of a medieval castle.

④ **Corniglia** Perched 100 m (328 ft) above sea level, Corniglia is the only Cinque Terre town inaccessible by boat. Walking from Manarola (1 km/½ mile) or Vernazza (4 km/2½ miles) is well worth the effort.

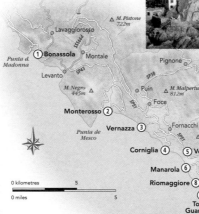

⑤ **Volastra** This pretty hamlet can be reached by bus, though climbing the steps from Manarola is much more rewarding. Volastra is perched on the hillside at 300 m (nearly 1,000 ft) above sea level, and is a fantastic vantage point over the five towns of the Cinque Terre.

⑥ **Manarola** Rustic and quiet, Manarola appears to grow right out of the dark rocks that plunge down to the sea. The hamlet is divided by a road that was once a stream, Il Ponte, which connects the central church of San Lorenzo with the marina.

⑦ **Torre Guardiola** Set on a promontory above Capo Montenero, Torre Guardiola has been transformed from a lookout bunker into a bird-watching and wildlife-observation centre. The café boasts fabulous sea views.

⑧ **Riomaggiore** This village is built on such sheer hillsides that the houses appear piled on top of one another, almost elbowing their way into the sunlight. Take the famous Via dell'Amore footpath from here to Manarola.

Map labels: Lavaggiorosso, M. Pistone 722m, ① Bonassola, Montale, Punta d. Madonna, Levanto, M. Negro 445m, Pignone, Puin, M. Malpertuso 812m, Foce, Monterosso ②, Punta de Mesco, Vernazza ③, Fornacchi, M. Capri 785m, Corniglia ④, ⑤ Volastra, Manarola ⑥, Riomaggiore ⑧, ⑦ Torre Guardiola

0 kilometres 5
0 miles 5

Letting off steam

The waters surrounding the Cinque Terre are clear and inviting, and there are various small beaches that are good for swimming and scampering about on. The only sandy one is Monterosso, where there are rent sun beds and parasols to rent. The small coves at Corniglia and Riomaggiore are pebbly, while at Vernazza and Manarola smooth rocks provide access to the water. The most memorable beach is Guvano, in

a bay between Vernazza and Corniglia. To get there from Corniglia, take the blue path towards Vernazza, heading downhill after 15 minutes and following the sign that reads "Spiaggia Libera", then proceeding for a further 60 minutes. For a 15-minute, non-panoramic alternative, take a torch and use the ex-railway tunnel near Corniglia station (€5 at the exit), which has been restored and is quite impressive.

Eat and drink

Picnic: under €25; Snacks: €25–40; Real meal: €40–80; Family treat: €80 or more (for a family of four)

PICNIC It is a great idea to take a picnic when going out walking, since the trails can be quite long. Stock up on the three Fs, *focaccia* (flat, salty bread, often containing cheese), *farinata* (a pancake made with chickpea flour) and fresh fruit, in any town, and always take water. A drop of fresh Pigato, a local white wine, might also be welcome.

The Lowdown

- **Map reference** 2 F6
  Address 19011 Bonassola. 19016 Monterosso. 19018 Vernazza. 19018 Corniglia. 19017 Volastra. 19017 Manarola. 19017 Torre Guardiola. 19017 Riomaggiore.

- **Train** The La Spezia–Genoa line stops in all the Cinque Terre towns. **Car** A12 to La Spezia, then the SS530 to Portovenere or the SS370 to Manarola; or A12 to Carrodano, then the SS566 to Monterosso and Levanto. **Ferry** from La Spezia (9:15am, 10am, 11:15am and 2:15pm); between Portovenere and Palmaria, see *www. navigazionegolfodeipoeti.it.*

- **i** **Visitor information** Via Telemaco Signorini, Riomaggiore; 0187 92 0113; *www.parconazionale5terre.it*

- **Price** The "5 Terre Card" (€15 for a family of four) is a sensible way to use the park's trails, sustainable transport and sights. Available at the visitor centre and railway stations.

- **Age range** Any

- **Activities** Guided sea-watching for families within the protected marine park; sessions on Tue and Thu; equipment provided. Information at the visitor centre. For walking trails, visit *www. cinqueterreriomaggiore.com.*

- **Allow** 3 days

Good family value?
It is not a cheap place to stay or eat in high season, but most activities (walking, swimming, exploring old towns) are free.

SNACKS Il Pirata delle 5 Terre
(Via Gavino 36/38, 19018 Vernazza; 0187 812047; www.ilpiratarooms. com; open all day), which overlooks the small port of Vernazza, is known for its fresh sandwiches, pastries and other delicious savouries.
REAL MEAL Ristorante Gli Ulivi
(Via N.S. della Salute 114, 19017 Volastra; 0187 760 020; www. ristoranteulivi.it; open all day) serves up well-presented, tasty snacks as well as full meals that often include excellent, home-made pesto – the area's greatest gift to gastronomy.
FAMILY TREAT Ristorante Ripa Del Sole *(Via De Gasperi 282, 19017 Riomaggiore; 0187 920 143; closed Mon),* overlooking the rooftops of Riomaggiore and the bay, specializes in local classics, such as stuffed anchovies and pasta with pesto. The quality of the ingredients used here is excellent, and the wine list is great. This is a popular place, so booking ahead is advisable.

Café life in the picturesque Cinque Terre port of Vernazza

Shopping
Enjoy a range of products, including natural cosmetics and foods made in the Cinque Terre, at the **Laboratorio** *(Via de Gasperi, 19017 Riomaggiore; www. fitocosmeticiparconazionale5terre. com; open 11am–1pm daily).*

Find out more
DIGITAL Many watchtowers overlook the Ligurian coast; pirates were a threat because nearby Genoa was a major trading port. Try the Rise of Pirates game to learn how pirates operated *(www.freeonlinegames. com/game/rise-of-pirates.html).*

Take cover
Photos and multimedia installations at the **Museo della Memoria** *(Via Colombo, 19017 Riomaggiore; 0187 760530)* reveal a Cinque Terre before the days of mass tourism.

Next stop...
PORTOVENERE Named after Venus in Roman times, this town dips its toes into the Gulf of La Spezia. Highlights include the Genoese Castello Doria and the 13th-century Basilica di San Pietro, built on the remains of an early Pagan temple to Venus. Arriving by ferry gives the best view.

---

⑥ Sestri Levante
Beaches and a magical town

One of the few resorts on the Riviera di Levante that has sandy beaches as well as an attractive waterfront, Sestri Levante is perched on a rocky outcrop with the Baia del Silenzio (Bay of Silence) on one side and the Bais delle Favole (Bay of Fables – named after Hans Christian Andersen) on the other. The town does indeed have a magical feel: it is little wonder that the Danish fairy-tale writer was once a regular visitor. A waterfront villa houses the **Museo Galleria Rizzi**, an interesting collection of Ligurian art, furnishings and ceramics from the 18th to 20th centuries which evokes the life of a wealthy middle-class family at the end of the 19th century.

Letting off steam

There is a pleasant, shady **public garden** (open daily 8:30am–7pm) with a children's playground halfway up Via Nazionale, in Via Dante

A colourful esplanade lined with palm trees and cafés at Sestri Levante

Sedini. Pause to look at the fountain, where a mermaid drinks from a shell. For a longer outing, head up the coast to Lavagna, and from there inland towards Graveglia, Ne and finally Reppia for the **Museo Minerario Gambatesa**, an exciting new mining museum that will supply hard hats and a trip down into the bowels of the earth, partly on little trains and partly on foot. Make sure to take a sweater as it can get cold underground.

⑦ Rapallo
A cable car and a magic flute

In a sheltered position overlooking a pretty bay, with green hills at the back that protect the town from cold winter winds, Rapallo enjoys a mild climate. The seaside town was a haven for writers such as D H Lawrence and Ezra Pound in the 1920s. Its most famous landmark is the 16th-century castle that appears

to be paddling in the waters of the port, not far from where yachts are often moored. Take a ride up to the hilltop Santuario di Montallegro by cable car for the views, or hike the

Rapallo's cable car taking passengers up to the Santuario di Montallegro

The Lowdown

🌐 **Map reference** 2 E5
Address 16039 Sestri Levante. Museo Galleria Rizzi: Via Cappuccini 8, 16039; 0185 413 00. Museo Minerario: Loc. Piandifieno 45, 16040, Ne; 0185 338 876; www.minieragambatesa.it

🚗 **Car** A12 motorway, exit Sestri Levante. **Train** to Sestri Levante on coastal Genova–Pisa line

🕑 **Open** Museo Galleria Rizzi: 4–7pm Wed May–Sep and 9:30pm–11:30pm Fri Jul–Aug. Museo Minerario: 9am–5pm Wed–Sun

💶 **Price** Museo Galleria Rizzi: €20. Museo Minerario: €32

👫 **Age range** Any

⏱ **Allow** Half a day

🍴 **Eat and drink** *Real meal* Trattoria Angiolina (Via Rimembranza 49, 16039; 0185 41198; closed Tue) serves superb spaghetti with clams, and zucchini flowers stuffed with ricotta and prawns. *Family treat* Cantine Cattaneo (Via Vicinale della Madonnetta 1, 16039; 0185 487 431; closed Mon) serves irresistible antipasti.

🎊 **Festivals** Hans Christian Andersen Festival: late May. Palio Marinaro del Tigullio (boat challenge): Jun–Aug. Barcarolata (best-decorated boat): last Sun in Jul

The Lowdown

🌐 **Map reference** 2 E5
Address 16035 Rapallo. Museo del Merletto: Villa Tigullio, Parco Casale, 16035 0185 63305. Museo Civico Gaffoglio: ex-Monastero delle Clarisse, Piazzale Josemaria Escrivá, 16035; 0185 234 497. Santuario di Montallegro: www.santuarionsmontallegro.com

🚗 **Car** A12 motorway, exit Rapallo. **Train** to Rapallo on coastal Genova–Pisa line. **Bus** to Santa Margherita Ligure and Camogli (www.tigulliotrasporti.it)

ℹ️ **Visitor information** Lungomare Vittorio Veneto 7, 16035; 0185 230 346; www.turismo.provincia.genova.it; www.comune.rapallo.ge.it

🕑 **Open** Museo del Merletto: 3pm–6pm Tue, Wed, Fri and Sat; 10am–noon Thu and Sun. Museo Civico Gaffoglio: 10:30am–12:30pm and 3–5pm Sat–Sun

💶 **Price** Both museums: €16

👫 **Age range** Any

⏱ **Allow** Half a day

🍴 **Eat and drink** *Real meal* Trattoria Genovese (Corso Roma 19, 16035; 0185 61111; closed Tue) has fresh pasta and seafood on the menu. *Family treat* Osteria Vecchio Mulino (Via Bana 144, 16035; 0185 773 540; closed Mon) serves up hearty dishes.

🎊 **Festivals** Festa di Nostra Signora di Montallegro: 1–3 Jul

old mule tracks over the hills. There is a collection of largely 19th-century paintings and furnishings in the **Museo Civico Gaffoglio**, and the **Museo del Merletto** (Lace Museum) has a collection of beautiful lace dresses.

Letting off steam
Down the road at Santa Margherita Ligure's **Parco Carmagnola** (Viale Rainusso, 16038; 0185 205 423), the great 20th-century set designer Lele Luzzati created a quiet wonderland devoted to the characters in Mozart's Magic Flute (see Kids' Corner). It is whimsical and fun, and children will love it.

⑧ Camogli
Small boats and a castle that was once a prison

The heart of this colourful fishing village – a favourite getaway for Milanese in need of fresh air – is really the port. On the one side are small boats and a few larger ones reflected in the clear water, and on the other, the characteristic carruggi, pebbled lanes that weave their way up between the houses on the hillside. Down on the quay there is a curious monument: an ancient iron crane, built in 1846, when the town was at the height of its maritime prosperity. Overlooking the peaceful scene is the fearsome-looking Castello della Dragonara, built as a fort in the 12th century and later used as a prison. It now houses the **Acquario Tirrenico**, whose 20 tanks display fascinating varieties of local sea life.

Letting off steam
Get ready to battle the enemy – play Saracen invaders on the steps of the **Castello della Dragonara**. Further afield, set out on one of the paths leading up the hillsides of the **Parco Regionale Naturale di Portofino** (www.parcoportofino.it). It is 2 hours' walk to **San Fruttuoso**, accessible only on foot or by boat – a tiny hamlet with an abbey, a church and a tower, on the beach.

The Lowdown
🌐 **Map reference** 2 E5
Address 16032 Camogli
🚗 **Car** A12 motorway, exit Recco. **Train** to Camogli on coastal line. **Bus** from regional towns (www.tigulliotrasporti.it). **Boat** to San Fruttuoso (www.golfoparadiso.it)
ℹ️ **Visitor information** Via XX Settembre 33, 16032; 0185 771 066; www.prolococamogli.it
🕐 **Open** Acquario: daily 10am–noon and 3–7pm Apr–Sep, 10–11:45am and 2–5:45pm Oct–Mar
💶 **Price** Acquario Tirrenico €16
👫 **Age range** Any
⏱️ **Allow** Half a day
🍴 **Eat and drink** Snacks Ristorante Bar Da Nico (Via San Niccolò 36, 16032; 0185 772 072; closed Tue) makes classic Ligurian dishes such as pansoti (stuffed pasta) with nut sauce. Real meal La Bossa di Mario (Via della Repubblica 124, 16032; 0185 772 505; eves only, from 6pm; closed Wed) serves a range of dishes such as baked salt cod.
🎉 **Festivals** Sagra del Pesce: 2nd Sun in May. Festa di Cristo degli Abissi: last Sat in July

Camogli's sliver of pebbly beach, with the Castello della Dragonara in the distance

Picnic under €25; Snacks €25–40; Real meal €40–80; Family treat €80 or more (based on a family of four)

Where to Stay in Liguria

Though Liguria is one of Italy's smaller regions, it offers a remarkably varied range of accommodation. Even in Genoa, there are leafy campsites, B&Bs and boutique hotels as well as big city chains, while the quiet coastal areas offer some lovely, small, family-run options with glorious views.

AGENCY
The Salt Way
0183 930 098; www.saltway.it
Apartments, villas and farmhouses to let along the Ligurian coast and in the back country.

Bonassola
Map 2 E5

HOTEL
Hotel Villa Belvedere
Via Ammiraglio Serra 33, 19011; 0187 813 622; www. bonassolahotelvillabelvedere.com
There are wonderful views over the bay from this nice old villa, which has shady gardens surrounded by pine trees, citrus and olive groves, and a path leading down to the beach. Sea-facing rooms.

€

Camogli
Map 2 E5

HOTELS
La Camogliese
Via Garibaldi 55, 16032; 0185 771 402; www.lacamogliese.it
This traditional hotel right by the water, run by the same family since 1950, has rooms with sea views and a reading room. Half-board deal with nearby restaurant an option.

€€

Cenobio dei Dogi
Via N Cuneo 4, 16032; 0185 7241; www.cenobio.it
Classic comfort and elegance right in town but away from the holiday bustle, in a hotel surrounded by pleasant gardens, with a private beach and a waterfront restaurant.

€€€

Corniglia
Map 2 F6

HOTEL
Pensione Cecio
Via Serra 58, 19010; 0187 812 043; www.cecio5terre.com
A classic, family-run *pensione* of the sort that is becoming rare. Simple, clean rooms with magnificent views.

A perfect stop after a day walking the trails, not least because its restaurant is an attraction in its own right.

€

Genoa
Map 2 E5

HOTELS
Agnello d'Oro
Vico Monachette 6, 16126; 010 246 2084; www.hotelagnellodoro.it
The communicating double rooms make this a good family choice in the city centre, close to the main station and 10 minutes' walk from the Aquarium. Simple but pleasant, with a reading room, a panoramic terrace, bike hire and parking.

€

Villa Bonera
Via Sarfatti 8, Nervi, 16167; 010 372 6164; www.villabonera.com
In a charming old villa surrounded by gardens, 5 minutes' walk from the sea and a stone's throw from the bus stop for transport into the city centre, this hotel has spacious, airy rooms, some with their own terrace, and attractive period detail in floors, stucco and furnishings.

€

Family-run La Camogliese, in a prime spot beside the sea in Camogli

Hotel Metropoli
Piazza Fontane Marose, 16126; 010 246 8888; www.hotelmetropoli.it
This Best Western hotel provides families with lots of extras, from toys to bottle-warming. It is just around the corner from the Opera House and Palazzo Ducale, and a short walk from the Aquarium. Fantastic

breakfasts include fresh fruit, good coffee, *focaccia* from a Slow Food bakery and artisan jams.

€€

B&B
Il Borgo di Genova
Via Borgo degli Incrociati 7, 16137; 010 839 5622; www.ilborgodigenova.com
A pleasant B&B, well positioned for visiting the centre on foot, with four light, airy double rooms, equipped with kettles for making tea or coffee. Italian breakfast with home-made tarts, fresh bread and *focaccia*.

€

CAMPING
Camping Villa Doria
Via al Campeggio Villa Doria 15, 16156 Pegli; 010 696 9600; www. camping.it/liguria/villadoria/
In Pegli, 8 km (5 miles) west of Genoa, well located for the naval and archaeological museums, and less than 1 km (half a mile) from a pebbly beach, this is a quiet, leafy alternative. Wooden bungalows to rent for those without a tent.

€

Levanto
Map 2 F6

HOTEL
L'Antico Borgo
Loc Dosso, 19105; 0187 802 681; www.anticoborgo.net
In a medieval hamlet close to Levanto, the attractive rooms of this handsome dwelling feel like home from home. There is a small library with a fireplace and a terrace where excellent breakfasts are served in summer.

€€

AGRITURISMO
Agriturismo Villanova
Loc Villanova, 19015; 0187 802 517; www.agriturismovillanova.it
This magnificent old residence and farm lies in the hills overlooking the coast, less than 2 km (3 miles)

inland. Spacious, elegant rooms and apartments, with period furniture; organic, locally grown breakfasts; and plenty of outdoor space, with a children's play area. Bike hire.

 €

Manarola
Map 2 F6

HOTEL
Ca' d'Andrean
Via Discovolo 101, 19017; 0187 920 040; www.cadandrean.it
This small, family-run hotel in a village on a terraced hillside occupies a converted olive mill and wine cellar. Clean, comfortable rooms, many of which open onto a terrace. In fine weather, breakfast is served among the lemon trees.

€

L'Antico Borgo offers smart rooms and breakfast on the terrace in summer

Monterosso
Map 2 F6

HOTEL
Hotel Pasquale & Villa Steno
Via Roma 109/Via Fegina 4, 19016; 0187 817 028; www.pasini.com
The Pasini family runs two charming hotels in Monterosso: the Pasquale, down by the sea, and Villa Steno, surrounded by lemon and orange trees and an olive grove, a little further up the hillside. Organic, local breakfasts with home-made jams.

€€

Rapallo
Map 2 E5

HOTEL
Hotel Vesuvio
Lungomare Vittorio Veneto 29, 16035; 0185 234 823; www. hotelvesuviorapallo.it
In a renovated Art Nouveau-style villa on the promenade, this hotel has preserved nice period details, such as a brick-vaulted ceiling in the bar. Rooms with balconies and sea views. Wi-Fi even on the terrace.

€€

Riomaggiore
Map 2 F6

HOTEL
Locanda del Sole
Via Santuario 114, 19017; 0187 920 773; www.locandadelsole.net
A new building set on various levels, with French windows opening onto small areas of terraced garden. Inside the decor is simple but pleasant. Picnic lunches for guests out hiking all day.

€€

Santa Margherita Ligure
Map 2 E5

HOTELS
Hotel Fasce
Via Luigi Bozzo 3, 16038; 0185 286 435; www.hotelfasce.it
A historic, family-run hotel located in two early 20th-century villas surrounded by a pleasant garden. All rooms supplied with kettles. Bicycles available for guests.

€€

Santa Margherita Palace
Via Roma 9, 16038; 0185 287 139; www.santamargheritapalace.com
A stylish new design hotel with an emphasis on minimalist chic in black, white and grey, 100 m (100 yards) from the beach. Rooms include suites with terrace and Jacuzzi. Breakfast served until midday. Special rates for younger children.

€€€

Sestri Levante
Map 2 E5

HOTELS
Marina
Via V Fascie 100, 16039; 0185 41527; www.marinahotel.it
Founded in 1955 by Anselmo Giulin, who had worked as a waiter on transatlantic cruise lines, the hotel is still run by the same family, but has been renovated completely. Five minutes' walk from the sea, it has a sun terrace and a billiards table. Good-value half-board option, and discounts for under-8s.

€

Vis-à-Vis
Via della Chiusa 28, 16039; 0185 480 801; www.hotelvisavis.com
Perched above town, with glorious views across the bay, this classy hotel has it all, including a pool, a

Turkish bath and a crèche to park children in while adults enjoy the spa. In summer, there are restaurants in the garden and on the beach. First child under 12 free with parents. Check website for offers.

€€€

Agriturismo Villanova has loads of romping room including a playground

Vernazza
Map 2 F6

HOTEL
Gianni Franzi
Piazza Marconi 1, 19108; 0187 821 003; www.giannifranzi.it
A historic restaurant in the main square of this charming village, with rooms in a separate building three flights of steps up the hillside. From this rocky promontory, the rooms have fabulous views of the sea and along the coast, with glimpses of the terraced gardens.

€€

Volastra
Map 2 F6

HOTEL
Luna di Marzo
Via Montello 387, 19017; 0187 920 530; www.albergolunadimarzo.com
The hall of this simple modern hotel, perched above the coast, opens out onto a terrace with such a stunning view that visitors may be tempted to spend most of their time there. Breakfasts include the cheese *focaccia* for which this part of Liguria is renowned.

€€

Price Guide
The following price ranges are based on one night's accommodation in high season for a family of four, inclusive of service charges and any additional taxes.
€ Under €200 €€ €200–350 €€€ over €350

Florence
and Central Italy

Famous for its art, history and landscapes, Central Italy is a region where past and present coexist in pleasing harmony. Start in the art-filled city of Florence, before venturing out to discover the medieval hill towns and beautiful countryside of Tuscany and Umbria, and the lesser-known glories of Le Marche. Vibrant Bologna, in gourmet Emilia-Romagna, offers its own culinary and artistic delights.

Highlights

Florence
Birthplace of the Renaissance, Florence is a perfect playground for adults and children, with grand piazzas, awesome art and a beautiful park (see pp161–84).

Siena
The shell-shaped Campo in the heart of the city is ideal for a race around, and is surrounded by tall towers, narrow streets and palaces to explore (see pp186–9).

Montalcino
One of Tuscany's more laid-back hill towns, Montalcino features an intriguing fortress and some great cafés (see pp194–9).

San Gimignano
A forest of impressive towers and mighty town walls make pretty San Gimignano a delight to explore (see pp200–203).

Bologna
The home of *tagliatelle alla bolognese* and other culinary treats, Bologna is full of arcaded streets, making it a wonderful place to wander (see pp218–21).

Perugia
This handsome Umbrian city is ideal for a promenade and features curious subterranean streets and a bird's eye view over Assisi (see p230).

Left The distinctive cupola of Florence's Duomo, seen from the leafy hills above the town **Above right** The pretty village of Fonterutoli, in the wine-producing region of Chianti, Tuscany

The Best of
Florence and Central Italy

The diverse sights of Central Italy are perfect for dawdling around. Florence and smaller Siena are essential stops for art-lovers, while the family-friendly hill towns also boast many art treasures. The countryside is endlessly varied, from the classic lines of cypress trees and olive groves in southern Tuscany to the dense woods of the Monti Sibillini, and a host of vibrant festivals offer year-round entertainment.

Culture vultures

In **Florence** (see pp161–84), book ahead for tickets to the Uffizi and the Accademia and be sure to visit Santa Maria Novella for its ground-breaking works of art. Climb the medieval Torre di Mangia in **Siena** (see pp186–9), a deafening experience if the bells are pealing, and don't miss the Duomo, with its sculpted pulpit. **Arezzo** (see pp204–209) features Piero della Francesca's great narrative fresco cycle, while the Palazzo Ducale in **Urbino** (see pp244–7) impresses visitors with its grand interiors, including an inlaid-wood room decorated with trompe l'oeil shelves and musical instruments.

Left Rolling Tuscan landscape with vineyards and cypress trees
Below Façade of the Duomo and the Baptistry, Florence

Above *Cyclists on one of Tuscany's hilly back roads*

In a week

Spend two days in **Florence** (see pp161–84), visiting the Duomo and its Baptistry, with Lorenzo Ghiberti's beautiful bronze doors, the Uffizi and Accademia, repositories of the best Italian Renaissance painting and sculpture. Other must-see sights include the Boboli Gardens and San Marco, a monastery frescoed by Fra Angelico, where children can easily imagine the life of a 15th-century monk. From there make a day trip by train to **Pisa** (see p192), to see the Leaning Tower, which stands on the open lawns of the Campo Santo. Take another train south to handsome **Cortona** (see p206), whose lively street life and rich art treasures merit a couple of days' stay, then head south again to spend a night in **Orvieto** (see pp240–41), whose decorated cathedral façade is one of the region's unmissable sights. Go inside for Luca Signorelli's *Last Judgment* (1499–1503); it inspired Michelangelo's decoration of the Sistine Chapel in Rome.

The great outdoors

In the rugged hills and valleys of Tuscany's wooded north, explore the caves of the **Grotta del Vento** (see p192) near Barga, picnic in the Orrido di Botri gorge near **Bagni di Lucca** (see p192), and head out to San Pellegrino in Alpe in the **Parco Naturale delle Alpi Apuane** (see p192) for a museum celebrating peasant life. Spoleto is a good base for trips to the **Parco Nazionale dei Monti Sibillini** (see p250), with its woodland hikes, cycle tracks and remote villages. And **Lago Trasimeno** (see p232), a large inland lake, is a great spot for wind-surfing, sailing and swimming.

Right Florentine lion keeping a watchful eye on a copy of Michelangelo's David, Piazza della Signoria, Florence

Events and festivals

Easter Sunday sees Florence celebrating with the **Scoppio del Carro**, a firework display lit by a mechanical dove in front of the Duomo. Perhaps the greatest festival in the whole of Italy is Siena's **Palio** (see pp186–7), a bareback gallop round the shell-shaped Campo. Held on 2 July and 16 August, it is preceded by much flag-throwing and medieval pageantry, and followed by wild celebrations from the winning team. The end of August sees the **Bravio delle Botti**, a boisterous barrel-rolling competition, in Montepulciano (see p198), while in September visitors can enjoy the **Palio della Balestra**, a hotly contested crossbow tournament, in Sansepolcro (see p207); the costumed participants can be seen parading through the streets. Throughout the region, early October is generally the time for the **vendemmia**, or grape harvest: *agriturismi* (farm stays) are great places for families to stay and perhaps help with the grape-picking.

Florence and Central Italy

Central Italy comprises four regions spanning the width of the country. Emilia-Romagna is to the north, with Bologna at its centre; Tuscany sits southwest of here, bordered to the east by landlocked Umbria. East of Umbria is little-visited Le Marche, on the Adriatic coast. Florence, the capital of Tuscany, is bisected by the River Arno, and surrounded by hills. In summer, it is usually hot and humid here.

Winged lion of St Mark, Orsanmichele, Florence

Places of Interest

San Gimignano's distinctive towers dominating the skyline, Tuscany

Ponte Vecchio over the River Arno, Florence, illuminated in the twilight

The Lowdown

Getting there and around
By **air** *(see p160)*. **Train** Florence and Bologna are both major hubs on the international and national rail network. Trains serving the main regional towns are fast, reliable and cheap (www.ferroviedellostato.it). **Buses** run by regional operators connect smaller towns, but are not frequent. **Car hire** Cars can be rented at all the regional airports. For parts of Umbria and Le Marche, in particular, it is much easier to travel by car.

Supermarkets Unicoop has branches throughout central Italy: www.tuscany.net/tourist/tour9.htm lists all branches in Tuscany. **Markets** Markets are aplenty in the region. Particularly famous is the Mercato dell'Antiquariato in Arezzo on the Piazza Grande on the first weekend of every month.

Opening hours Many sights close on Mondays.

Pharmacies Thanks to a night rota (*servizio notturno*) there is always a pharmacy open in all cities and towns across these regions. Information can be found on any pharmacy door and in local papers. In Florence, the Farmacia Aperte helpline (800 420 707) helps people to find an open pharmacy in the city.

Toilets As in the rest of Italy, there are a few public toilets in Florence and the central regions; make use of the facilities in cafés, museums and galleries.

Florence and Central Italy Airports

Most visitors fly to Pisa airport for Tuscany; from the airport there are direct links to Florence, a regional transport hub. An option is to fly to Bologna in Emilia-Romagna, with fast train links to Florence, the Adriatic Coast and Le Marche. For Umbria, fly to one of Rome's airports and take the train or drive. Both Florence and Perugia also have minor airports. The overnight train from Paris to Bologna or Florence is a fun, green alternative.

Pisa Galileo Galilei

There are regular flights between UK and Dublin airports and Pisa Galileo Galilei airport, operated by major carriers British Airways and Alitalia and no-frills airlines easyJet, Ryanair and Jet2.com. There are no direct intercontinental flights to Pisa, so it may be necessary to fly to Milan or Rome and connect.

Trains run from Pisa airport to the city of Pisa itself (10 minutes), and to Florence Santa Maria Novella station (1 hour). Buses connect Pisa airport with Pisa town centre every 10 minutes. A frequent coach service runs to the bus terminus next to Santa Maria Novella station in Florence. There is a taxi rank in front of the airport and major car rental firms have desks inside.

The airport is a manageable size, on two floors and easy for families to negotiate. It has a number of decent cafés and restaurants which serve Tuscan food, and there are a couple of pizzerias and an outlet selling *piadine* (stuffed flatbreads) – a handy snack.

Bologna G Marconi

Located about 6 km (4 miles) to the northwest of the city, Bologna G Marconi airport is served by British

An Alitalia plane flying over the Italian countryside

Airways, Alitalia and Aer Lingus, as well as Ryanair and easyJet. An Aerobus service running every 15 minutes throughout the day connects the airport with the city centre and train station (20 minutes). Tickets can be purchased on board. If continuing to Florence, the best option is to catch a train from Bologna (it is a long drive over the Apennines); Bologna Stazione Centrale is one of Italy's main rail hubs. There are also direct buses from the airport to Modena and Siena. Car-hire firms are well represented at desks in the airport.

The airport is small, on three levels and easy to navigate. Standard cafés and restaurants can be found on all three floors.

Florence Amerigo Vespucci (Peretola)

Meridiana flies from London Gatwick to Florence Amerigo Vespucci airport, about 4 km/2 miles northwest of Florence. Alitalia flights from London Heathrow can be booked on cheapflights.co.uk. CityJet flies from London City airport. A shuttle bus runs to the city centre (30 minutes).

Perugia San Francesco d'Assisi (San Egidio)

Perugia's tiny airport has daily Ryanair flights from London Stansted. There is a regular bus connection to Perugia train station.

Rome airports

For information on Rome Fiumicino and Rome Ciampino, *see p260*.

For information on Rome Fiumicino and Rome Ciampino, *see p260*.

The Lowdown

Bologna G Marconi 051 647 9615; www.bologna-airport.it

Florence Amerigo Vespucci (Peretola) 055 306 1300; www.aeroporto.firenze.it

Perugia San Francesco d'Assisi (San Egidio) 075 592 141; www.airport.umbria.it

Pisa Galileo Galilei 050 849 300; www.pisa-airport.com

Train travel www.raileurope.co.uk; www.seat61.com

Pisa Galileo Galilei, the main airport for Tuscany

Florence

Florence was created in a whirlwind of artistic energy that still makes itself felt more than 500 years later. But it is no museum-piece: street performers entertain the crowds and scrumptious ice cream is always near at hand. The city is sliced through by the River Arno, its north bank packed with art and architectural highlights, while to the south lies more lived-in Oltrarno, with the medieval Ponte Vecchio linking the two.

Below The spectacular red-tiled dome of Florence's Duomo rising above the rooftops

Duomo
p164

The Uffizi
p170

Boboli Gardens
p176

Florence as an Art City

Florence's reputation as an art city is unparalleled. Its galleries have fine medieval works, but the city's artistic revolution came with the Renaissance, inspired by the forms and subject matter of Classical art. Renaissance artists studied anatomy to breathe life into their works and used mathematical principles to introduce perspective into their painting, and the great artists imbued their works, both sacred and secular, with psychological insight.

Bargello

There is more than one *David* in town: Donatello's bronze version, looking rather camp with hand on hip, reintroduced the nude to Western sculpture. It is housed in the **Bargello**, built as the town hall in 1255 and converted into a sculpture gallery in the 19th century. Other treasures here include a panel made by Brunelleschi for the competition to sculpt the Baptistry doors *(see p166)*, and sculptures such as Verrocchio's delicate *Lady with a Posy* and Giambologna's fleet-footed *Mercury*.

Cappella Brancacci

Located in the church of Santa Maria del Carmine in Oltrarno, the **Cappella Brancacci** *(see p180)* is famous for the pioneering *Life of St Peter* frescoes, started by Masolino in 1425, but mainly painted by his great pupil Masaccio. Masaccio died at the age of 27 before the chapel was finished – according to legend he was poisoned by an envious rival – so it was completed by Filippino Lippi. While Masolino's work is elegant and decorative, Masaccio's shocks with its emotional and social realism – Adam and Eve are depicted in anguish and shame, and the sick supplicants to St Peter are shown in starkly realistic, uncompromising poverty.

Michelangelo

One of the ultimate Renaissance men, Michelangelo left a great legacy to Florence in the form of architecture, sculpture, painting and even poetry. His most iconic work is the towering statue of *David* in the **Accademia** *(see p169)*. He also created the magnificent tombs of the **Medici Chapel** in the church of San Lorenzo *(see p168)*; painted the highly charged and coloured *Doni Tondo* which hangs in the **Uffizi** *(see pp172–3)*; and sculpted a *Pietà* which is in the **Museo dell'Opera del Duomo** *(see pp166–7)* – its hooded figure of Nicodemus is said to be a self-portrait.

Palaces

The **Palazzo Pitti** *(see p180)* was the mighty home of the Medicis, and features a vast array of treasures: there are paintings by Raphael, frescoes by Pietro da Cortona, a glittering museum of silverware, a carriage museum and a gallery of modern art. The **Palazzo Medici Riccardi**, home to the family for 1,000 years from 1444, showcases Benozzo Gozzoli's absorbing and colourful *Procession of the Magi*, with plenty of lively detail to interest observant kids.

San Marco

The Dominican church and convent of **San Marco** once housed the infamous preacher Savonarola, who ordered heretical books to be burned in a Bonfire of the Vanities. It was also home to Fra Angelico, whose delicate frescoes make this an unmissable stop for art lovers. Look out for his tender *Deposition*, a still *Annunciation* set in an arcaded loggia, the subdued scene of *Mary Magdalene and St John* mourning Christ at his tomb, and the powerful *Crucifixion*.

Below *Santa Croce, the resting place of Michelangelo*

Above Sculpture-packed courtyard of the Bargello *Left* Crucifixion *fresco by Fra Angelico in San Marco* ***Below left*** *Michelangelo's David in the Accademia*

Santa Croce

Behind the elaborate façade of **Santa Croce** *(see p174)* are some of the city's best-known early artworks: lustrous frescoes painted by Giotto in the early 14th century: look out for the angel stigmatizing a startled St Francis. Also look for the tomb of Michelangelo, designed by artist and biographer Vasari; a fragile 13th-century crucifix by Cimabue; and a mesmerisingly realistic crucifix and *Annunciation* by Donatello.

Santa Maria Novella

In a city renowned for remarkable artworks, Masaccio's *Trinità* in **Santa Maria Novella** *(see p168)* is still arresting in its impact, showcasing the artist's mastery of perspective. The venerable church also features beautiful fresco cycles by Ghirlandaio and Filippino Lippi.

The Uffizi

Vasari designed the **Uffizi** *(see pp166–7)*, which the Medicis adapted in the 1580s to display their magnificent art collection. There are enough masterpieces here to last a week, so tailor the visit in advance. Highlights include

Botticelli's resplendent *Birth of Venus* and *Primavera*; Piero della Francesca's uncompromising portrait of Federico da Montefeltro and Battista Sforza; Giotto's *Ognissanti Madonna*; Raphael's *Madonna of the Goldfinch*; and Fra Filippo Lippi's *Madonna and Child*.

The Lowdown

Accademia Via Ricasoli 58–60, 50122; *www.uffizi.firenze.it*

Bargello Via del Proconsolo 4, 50122; *www.uffizi.firenze.it*

Cappella Brancacci Santa Maria del Carmine, Piazza del Carmine, 50124; *www.museicivicifiorentini.it/brancacci*

Medici Chapel Piazza Madonna degli Aldobrandini 6, 50123; *www.uffizi.firenze.it*

Museo dell'Opera del Duomo Via della Canonica 1, 50122; *www.operaduomo.firenze.it*

Palazzo Medici Riccardi Via Camillo Cavour 1, 50129; *www.palazzo-medici.it*

Palazzo Pitti Piazza Pitti 1, 50125; *www.uffizi.firenze.it*

San Marco Piazza San Marco 3, 50121; *www.uffizi.firenze.it*

Santa Croce Piazza Santa Croce 16, 50122; *www.santacroceopera.it*

Santa Maria Novella Piazza Santa Maria Novella 18, 50123; *www.chiesasantamarianovella.it*

The Uffizi Piazzale degli Uffizi, 50122; *www.uffizi.firenze.it*

Duomo, Baptistry and around

The Duomo (cathedral) is in the heart of Florence, and is easy to locate – just look for the high terracotta dome that dominates the city's roofscape. The area around the Duomo is pedestrianized and usually crammed with visitors. The easiest way to get around this area, with its flat streets and wide pavements, is on foot. There are a few cafés and ice-cream parlours in and around the square, handy for a rest from sightseeing.

Duomo, Baptistry
and around

Duomo

The Uffizi
p170

Boboli Gardens
p176

Detail of the bronze
Baptistry doors

Places of Interest

SIGHTS
1. Duomo and Baptistry
2. Santa Maria Novella
3. San Lorenzo
4. Accademia

EAT AND DRINK
1. Coronas Café
2. Trattoria ZaZa
3. Gilli
4. Bar Deanna
5. Palle d'Oro
6. Pizzeria Il Grande Nuti
7. Ristorante Accademia
8. Oliandolo
9. Taverna del Bronzino

SHOPPING
1. Edison bookshop
2. Via dei Calzaiuoli

WHERE TO STAY
1. Hotel Il Bargellino
2. Hotel Colomba
3. Hotel Giglio
4. Hotel Benivieni
5. Hotel Il Guelfo Bianco
6. Hotel de Lanzi
7. Hotel Loggiato dei Serviti
8. Hotel Perseo
9. Grand Hotel Minerva
10. Hotel Calzaiuoli
11. Panerai & Panerai
12. Antica Dimora Johlea
13. Palazzo Alfani al David

The terracotta dome of Florence's Duomo

Horse-drawn
carriages waiting to
take visitors for a
ride in front of
Florence's Baptistry

Frescoes inside Brunelleschi's cupola by Giorgio Vasari, one of the many
Renaissance painters and sculptors who collaborated on the Duomo

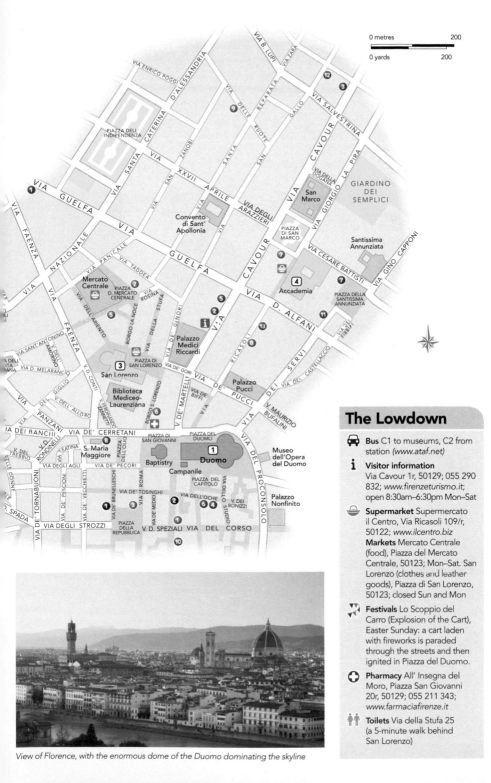

0 metres 200
0 yards 200

PIAZZA DELL'
INDIPENDENZA

VIA ENRICO POGGI
VIA D'ALESSANDRIA
VIA B. LUPI
VIA ZARA

VIA CATERINA
VIA DELLE RUOTE
REFATATA
GALLO
VIA SALVESTRINA
VIA CAVOUR

9

VIA XXVII APRILE
VIA SANTA
VIA SAN ZANOBI
VIA SANTA
VIA SAN

12
3

GIARDINO
DEI
SEMPLICI

San
Marco

VIA DELLA DOGANA
VIA GIORGIO LA PIRA

VIA GUELFA
VIA NAZIONALE
VIA FAENZA

Convento
di Sant'
Apollonia

VIA DEGLI
ARAZZIERI

PIAZZA
DI SAN
MARCO

7

Santissima
Annunziata

VIA GINO CAPPONI

VIA GUELFA
VIA PANICALE
VIA TADDEA

VIA CAVOUR
VIA CESARE BATTISTI

Mercato
Centrale

PIAZZA
D. MERCATO
CENTRALE

2
VIA ROSINA
VIA DELLA STUFA
BORGO LA NOCE

5

5
2

Accademia

7

PIAZZA DELLA
SANTISSIMA
ANNUNZIATA

11

VIA D. ALFANI

VIA DEI GINORI
VIA DEI SERVI

Palazzo
Medici
Riccardi

i
13
8

VIA RICASOLI

VIA SANT'ANTONINO
VIA DELL'ARIENTO
V. DELL'AMORINO

3

San Lorenzo

PIAZZA DI
SAN LORENZO

VIA DE' GORI
VIA DE' MARTELLI

Palazzo
Pucci

VIA DE'
PUCCI

VIA DU. CASTELLACCIO

V. MAURIZIO
BUFALINI

VIA D. MELARANCIO
VIA D. CONTI

Biblioteca
Mediceo-
Laurenziana

BORGO S. LORENZO

6

VIA DE' BIFFI

VIA DE'
PANZANI
VIA DE' CERRETANI

PIAZZA DI
SAN GIOVANNI

PIAZZA DEL
DUOMO

VIA DEL PROCONSOLO

S. Maria
Maggiore

8

Baptistry

1
Duomo

Campanile

Museo
dell'Opera
del Duomo

VIA DEGLI AGLI
VIA DE' PECORI
VIA DE' TOSINGHI
PIAZZA DEL
CAPITOLO

Palazzo
Nonfinito

VIA DE' PESCIONI
VIA DE' VECCHIETTI
VIA ROMA
VIA DE' MEDICI

1
3
2
VIA DELL'OCHE
5
4
V. DEI
BONIZZI

PIAZZA
DELLA
REPUBBLICA

V. D. SPEZIALI
VIA DEL CORSO

1

10

The Lowdown

🚌 **Bus** C1 to museums, C2 from station (www.ataf.net)

ℹ️ **Visitor information** Via Cavour 1r, 50129; 055 290 832; www.firenzeturismo.it; open 8:30am–6:30pm Mon–Sat

🎩 **Supermarket** Supermercato il Centro, Via Ricasoli 109/r, 50122; www.ilcentro.biz
Markets Mercato Centrale (food), Piazza del Mercato Centrale, 50123; Mon–Sat. San Lorenzo (clothes and leather goods), Piazza di San Lorenzo, 50123; closed Sun and Mon

🎆 **Festivals** Lo Scoppio del Carro (Explosion of the Cart), Easter Sunday: a cart laden with fireworks is paraded through the streets and then ignited in Piazza del Duomo.

➕ **Pharmacy** All' Insegna del Moro, Piazza San Giovanni 20r, 50129; 055 211 343; www.farmaciafirenze.it

🚻 **Toilets** Via della Stufa 25 (a 5-minute walk behind San Lorenzo)

View of Florence, with the enormous dome of the Duomo dominating the skyline

① Duomo and Baptistry
The patterned cathedral with the giant dome

Florence's Duomo is unmissable: the huge pink, white and green marble cathedral of Santa Maria del Fiore with the big orange dome can hold 20,000 people. One of the great early Renaissance buildings, its foundation stone was laid in 1296, but the Neo-Gothic patterned marble façade was not completed until 1887; it was inspired by the pretty decoration of Giotto's tall Campanile alongside. The octagonal building nearby is the Baptistry, where Florentines were once baptized.

Detail from the Baptistry doors

Key Features

The dome
Brunelleschi built the impressive cathedral dome (1418–36), at the time the biggest in the world, without scaffolding.

Cupola interior
Frescoes of the *Last Judgment* by Vasari.

East doors, Baptistry
In 1401, Lorenzo Ghiberti won a competition to design the north Baptistry doors. In 1425–52 he designed the east doors; Michelangelo called them the "Gates of Paradise".

Campanile

Campanile
The bell tower (1339) has terracotta panels by Andrea Pisano depicting Bible scenes.

Crypt
The crypt hides the remains of the original 4th-century church of Santa Reparata.

Entrance to crypt

South doors

Baptistry ceiling
Dazzling 13th-century gold mosaics illustrating the Last Judgment cover the ceiling.

Portrait of Dante On the Duomo's north wall, this picture of the poet Dante Alighieri (1265–1321) by Domenico di Michelino shows iconic buildings of mid-15th century Florence. Can you spot the Duomo?

The Lowdown

🌐 **Address** Piazza del Duomo, 50122; 055 230 2885; www.duomofirenze.it, www.operaduomo.firenze.it

🚗 **Bus** 1, 6, 14, 17 and 23

ℹ️ **Visitor information** Via Cavour 1/r, 50129; 055 290 832; firenzeturismo.it; 8:30am–6:30pm Mon–Sat, 8:30am–1:30pm Sun

🕐 **Open** Duomo: 10am–5pm Mon–Sat (May & Oct closes 3:30pm Thu), 1:30–4:45pm Sun. Dome: 8:30am–7pm Mon–Fri, 8:30am–5pm Sat, closed Sun. Baptistry: noon–7pm Mon–Sat,

8:30am–2pm Sun. Campanile: 8:30am–7.30pm daily

💶 **Price** Duomo: free. Dome: €32. Campanile: €24. Baptistry: €16. Santa Reparata: €12; combined tickets available.

🚻 **Skipping the queue** There is room for hordes of visitors in the Duomo, but not in the Baptistry; visit in the evening to see doors.

Guided tours Tours of the Duomo (€36), dome (€44), Santa Reparata (€36) and Baptistry (€28; prices include admission) at 11am and 3pm daily or by

reservation; 055 215 380; www.operaduomo.firenze.it

👫 **Age range** 8 plus

⏱️ **Allow** At least 2 hours

♿ **Wheelchair access** Only to the Duomo and Baptistry

🚻 **Toilets** No

🎉 **Festivals** Scoppio del Carro (Easter Sunday).

Good family value?
There is plenty to see for free in the Duomo, and it is worth paying for the Baptistry's gold ceilings.

Letting off steam

Next to the Duomo is its **Campanile** (bell tower). Climb the 414 steps to the top, breathing in as there is not much space on the narrow stairs to pass people coming down. From the top there is a bird's eye view of the city. Central Florence does not have much green space, but there is room to run around in **Piazza della Signoria**, a 10-minute walk down Via dei Calzaiuoli, or cross over the Arno to the **Boboli Gardens** (see pp178–9); a 20-minute walk or bus C2, 36 or 6.

Candied fruits piled high in the window of Gilli café in Via Roma

Eat and drink

Picnic: under €25; Snacks: €25–40; Real meal: €40–80; Family treat: €80 or more (based on a family of four)

PICNIC The stalls of the **Mercato Centrale** (Piazza Mercato Centrale, 50123; 7am–2pm Mon–Sat) sell cakes and sandwiches. Picnic on the grass of Piazza Santa Maria Novella to avoid crowded Piazza del Duomo. **SNACKS Coronas Café** (corner of Via del Corso and Via dei Calzaiuoli, 50122) is a great place to stop for coffee, drinks, cakes and ice cream.

REAL MEAL Trattoria ZaZa (Piazza Mercato Centrale 26/r, 50123; 055 215 411; www.trattoriazaza.it) is a buzzy, cheerful place near the food market, serving Tuscan cuisine. It is popular with tourists, but still a great location for an outdoor meal, with quirky décor inside.
FAMILY TREAT Gilli (Via Roma 1, 50123; 055 213 896; www.gilli.it), a glamorous 18th-century café, has pretty stucco ceilings, wood panelling, outdoor seating on Piazza della Repubblica and a selection of exquisite cakes and sweets.

Shopping

Good leather sandals and bags, as well as T-shirts and other cheap clothes, can be found at the outdoor stalls of **Mercato San Lorenzo**, 2 minutes' walk from the Duomo. **Edison** bookshop (Piazza della Repubblica 27/r; 50123; www.libreriaedison.it) stocks maps, books and magazines in English.

Find out more

DIGITAL For a fun introduction to the Renaissance, go to www.renaissanceconnection.org/index2.cfm, and for more on Florence and the Renaissance, try www.learner.org/interactives/renaissance/florence.html.

Next stop...

SHOP TILL YOU DROP After a dose of culture, head for the shops of **Via dei Calzaiuoli** and the **Mercato Nuovo**. Visit Il Porcellino, the bronze sculpture of a boar, a modern copy of a Baroque copy of an ancient Greek marble. Rub its nose to ensure a return to Florence.

Rubbing Il Porcellino on its shiny nose ensures a return to Florence

② Santa Maria Novella

Putting art in perspective

Built by Dominican monks between 1279 and 1357, Santa Maria Novella is more than just a pretty façade; inside are some landmark works of art. The lower part of the façade is Romanesque, and was incorporated into one based on Classical proportions by pioneering architect Leon Battista Alberti in 1456–70 – an oddly harmonious combination. On entering, visitors see a fresco of Jesus on the Cross, God the Father behind him and the dove of the Holy Spirit hovering between, all in a trompe l'oeil vaulted chapel in the form of a Classical triumphal arch. This is Masaccio's *Trinità* (1425–6). Its illusion of space and depth was one of the triumphs of Renaissance perspective: Florentines were so amazed when it was unveiled in 1427 that they queued up to see it.

There are plenty more artworks to see. Busy dogs round up lost sheep in frescoes in the Spanish Chapel (off the cloister), symbolizing the Dominican monks' quest for lost souls. Filippino Lippi painted a bizarre fresco of St Philip exorcizing

Piazza Santa Maria Novella, a grassy square that used to be a venue for chariot-racing

a dragon-demon (1502) in the Filippo Strozzi Chapel (in the right transept). Domenico Bigordi, better known as "Ghirlandaio", painted the frescoes of the *Life of St John* (1485) in the Tornabuoni Chapel (behind the altar), which are peopled with Florentine aristocrats in the fashionable dress of the day.

Letting off steam

Grassy **Piazza Santa Maria Novella**, in front of the church, is perfect for a picnic. The two obelisks sitting on tortoises used to mark out chariot races round the square, held from the 1560s until the late 19th century.

③ San Lorenzo

Bankers' mausoleum

Stay more than a day in Florence and the name Medici will become familiar. The Medici family ruled Florence from 1434 until the 18th century. Originally wool-traders, in 1397 they founded the Medici Bank, which became Europe's largest bank in the 15th century, and spent part of the profits commissioning the best artists to create paeans to their

wealth and power. San Lorenzo was the parish church of the Medici family, and in 1419 Brunelleschi was commissioned to rebuild it in the Classical style of the Renaissance. In 1515, Michelangelo submitted a winning design for the façade. It was never built however, perhaps because he was too busy sculpting the muscular figures of Medici family members for their tombs in the Medici Chapel (1520–34),

The Lowdown

- 🌐 **Address** Piazza Santa Maria Novella, 50123; www.chiesasantamarianovella.it
- 🚌 **Bus** A, 6, 11, 36, 37
- 🕐 **Open** 9am–5:30pm Mon–Thu, 11am–5:30pm Fri, 9am–5pm Sat, 12–5pm Sun (longer for prayer)
- 🎫 **Price** €7–14, under-5s free
- 👫 **Age range** 8 plus for perspective, but animal-spotting in frescoes may entertain younger children.
- ⏱ **Allow** 1 hour or more
- ☕ **Eat and drink** *Snacks* The spacious café, Bar Deanna, next to the SITA bus station on Piazza della Stazione is handy for a snack and a drink, with a decent selection of sandwiches and pastries. *Real meal* Palle d'Oro (*Via Sant'Antonino 43–45/r, 50123; 055 288 383; closed Sun*), a vibrant trattoria, serves *antipasti* on wooden boards, pasta and steaks. Head there at the weekend for a quieter and more relaxed atmosphere.
- 🚻 **Toilets** At Santa Maria Novella train station

The Lowdown

- 🌐 **Address** Basilica di San Lorenzo: Piazza di San Lorenzo, 50123; www.operamedicealaurenziana.it. Medici Chapel: Piazza Madonna degli Aldobrandini 6, 50123; www.polomuseale.firenze.it/cappellemedicee
- 🚌 **Bus** A, 6, 11, 36, 37
- 🕐 **Open** Basilica: 10am–5pm Mon–Sat and 1–5pm Sun, Nov–Feb closed Sun. Medici Chapel: 8:15am–1:50pm daily, until 4:20pm Mar–Nov
- 🎫 **Price** Basilica: €14, under-11s free. Medici Chapel: €12, under-18s free
- 👫 **Age range** 8 plus, though younger children may marvel at the overblown sumptuousness
- ⏱ **Allow** At least 1 hour
- ☕ **Eat and drink** *Snacks* Pizzeria il Grande Nuti (*22–24 Borgo San Lorenzo, 50123; 055 210 145; www.ristorantenuti.it*) is the place to go for pizza and *calzoni*. *Real meal* Ristorante Accademia (*Piazza San Marco 7/r, 50121; 055 217 343*) is a popular local option, with delicious soups and pasta.

Salami for sale in San Lorenzo market, also good for leather goods and clothes

or designing the Mannerist staircase (built 1559) that leads to the Biblioteca Mediceo-Laurenziana. A true multi-talented "Renaissance man", he designed the library's inlaid desks, taking time out to oppose his patrons as a military engineer for the Florentine Republic in 1530. Cosimo Il Vecchio (1389–1464), founder of the Medici dynasty, is buried under a simple slab in the basilica, flanked by two bronze pulpits (1460) by Donatello.

Letting off steam
A market is held daily in **Piazza San Lorenzo**, selling leather bags and belts. Play hide and seek among the stalls, or bargain for souvenirs.

④ Accademia
Dazzling *David*

The tall chap with no clothes on and curly hair may be familiar. Originally intended for Piazza della Signoria (where a copy stands) Michelangelo's *David* is now in the Accademia – Europe's first art school, established in 1563. Its artworks were collected for students to copy and *David* (1504), a colossal 5-m (17-ft) nude of the biblical hero who killed the giant Goliath, is the most famous. His hands and arms look oversized – a clever trick, as in his original setting onlookers would have looked up at him, so Michelangelo made his top half bigger to appear proportionate from below. Another Michelangelo masterpiece, the *Quattro Prigionieri* (Four Prisoners)

(1521–3), sculpted for the tomb of Pope Julius II, is also here. The four muscular figures appear to be struggling to break free from the stone. The gallery houses 15th- and 16th-century Florentine paintings and a painted wedding chest too.

Letting off steam
Florence is chock-a-block with buildings. To escape the stone, head for the **Giardino dei Semplici**, created in 1545 and home to some 300-year-old trees. It is a 5-minute walk, past the university.

The Lowdown

- **Address** Via Ricasoli 58–60, 50122; 055 238 8612; www.polomuseale.firenze.it
- **Bus** 1, 17
- **Open** 8:15am–6:50pm Tue–Sun
- **Price** €13, EU under-18s free
- **Skipping the queue** Book tickets in advance online or by phone (€4 booking fee).
- **Age range** 8 plus
- **Allow** 1 hour
- **Wheelchair access** Yes
- **Eat and drink** *Real meal* Oliandolo (*Via Ricasoli 38–40/r, 50122; 055 211 296; closed Sun*) serves good local dishes and is a good option for lunch or dinner. *Family treat* Taverna del Bronzino (*Via delle Ruote 27/r, 50129; 055 495 220; www.tavernadelbronzino.com/*) offers relaxed eating in a 16th-century house.
- **Toilets** By the entrance

Michelangelo's David in the Accademia

The Uffizi and around

The Uffizi art gallery is just off Piazza della Signoria, where a replica of Michelangelo's *David* stands tall over spectacular fountains beside the stately Palazzo Vecchio. The long loggia of the gallery connects the piazza to the River Arno. It's a short walk from the medieval Ponte Vecchio, crammed with jewellery shops. The surrounding streets and squares, though thronged with people, offer plenty of options for meals, drinks and ice creams.

The Uffizi and around

Duomo p164

The Uffizi

Boboli Gardens p176

Places of Interest

SIGHTS

1. The Uffizi
2. Orsanmichele
3. Museo Galileo
4. Ponte Vecchio
5. Palazzo Vecchio

● **EAT AND DRINK**

1. Vivoli
2. Acqua al Due
3. Osteria del Caffè Italiano
4. Paoli
5. Trattoria Antico Fattore
6. Lorenzaccio
7. Trattoria da Benvenuto
8. Le Volpi e l'Uva
9. Casalinga
10. Trattoria Roberto
11. Osteria dei Baroncelli

● **SHOPPING**

1. Rinascente
2. La Bottega dell'Olio

● **WHERE TO STAY**

1. Hotel Alessandra
2. Hotel Davanzati
3. Hotel Berchielli
4. Casa Rovai Guest House
5. Residenza Casanuova
6. Relais Piazza Signoria

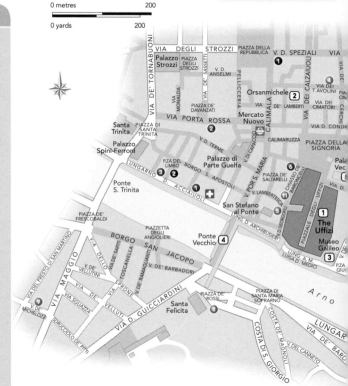

The Ponte Vecchio, the oldest bridge in Florence, lined with jewellery shops

The octagonal Tribuna in the Uffizi, built to house treasures of the Medici family

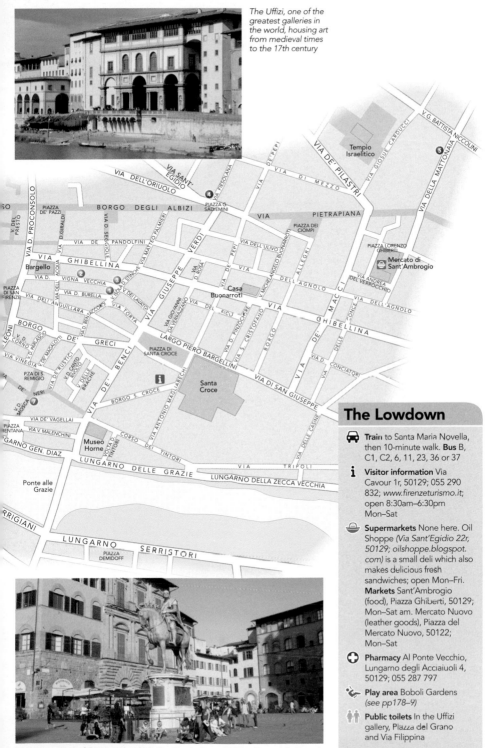

The Uffizi, one of the greatest galleries in the world, housing art from medieval times to the 17th century

Equestrian statue of Cosimo I de' Medici by Giambologna (1594) in Piazza della Signoria

The Lowdown

🚗 **Train** to Santa Maria Novella, then 10-minute walk. **Bus** B, C1, C2, 6, 11, 23, 36 or 37

ℹ️ **Visitor information** Via Cavour 1r, 50129; 055 290 832; www.firenzeturismo.it; open 8:30am–6:30pm Mon–Sat

🍴 **Supermarkets** None here. Oil Shoppe (Via Sant'Egidio 22r, 50129; oilshoppe.blogspot.com) is a small deli which also makes delicious fresh sandwiches; open Mon–Fri. **Markets** Sant'Ambrogio (food), Piazza Ghiberti, 50129; Mon–Sat am. Mercato Nuovo (leather goods), Piazza del Mercato Nuovo, 50122; Mon–Sat

➕ **Pharmacy** Al Ponte Vecchio, Lungarno degli Acciaiuoli 4, 50129; 055 287 797

👟 **Play area** Boboli Gardens (see pp178–9)

🚻 **Public toilets** In the Uffizi gallery, Piazza del Grano and Via Filippina

① The Uffizi
Incredible artists and the wings of angels

The Uffizi is one of Italy's greatest art galleries. It covers the whole sweep of Florentine art, from stylized Byzantine icons to the flowing lines of early medieval art, through Renaissance masterpieces to the colourful complexities of Mannerist art. Do not attempt to see every painting. Instead, see how many animals can be spotted in a painting, or count angel wings. Or stick to highlights by the most famous Italian artists – Giotto, Botticelli, Piero della Francesca, Leonardo and Michelangelo.

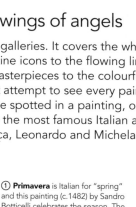

Street performer outside the Uffizi

Gallery Highlights

Second floor Works are hung in chronological order around the horseshoe-shaped galleries.

① **Primavera** is Italian for "spring" and this painting (c.1482) by Sandro Botticelli celebrates the season. The blue figure on the right is Zephyrus, god of the west wind.

Entrance

— **Exit**

⑥

④

⑤

①

③

②

② **The Holy Family** (1505–1506) Perhaps Michelangelo was a bit bored with all those paintings showing Jesus on the Virgin's lap. Here, Mary reaches over her shoulder to cuddle her baby.

③ **The Annunciation** Leonardo da Vinci painted this image of the angel Gabriel appearing to Mary in 1472–5, when he was only about 20. The angel's wings were based on drawings of birds' wings.

④ **Ognissanti Madonna** This precious altarpiece was painted by Giotto in 1310. See how the halos and the background glow with real gold leaf, and how the artist has conveyed spatial depth.

⑤ **The Duke and Duchess of Urbino** (1460–72) This portrait of Federico da Montefeltro and Battista Sforza by Piero della Francesca shows the duke's hooked nose in a realistic way.

⑥ **Rembrandt's self-portraits** There are two self-portraits by famous Dutch artist Rembrandt. One (1639) shows him as a confident young man, the other (1669) as a rather tired old man.

The Lowdown

🌐 **Address** Piazzale degli Uffizi 6, 50122; 055 238 8651; *www.uffizi.firenze.it*

🚌 **Bus** B, 23, A

🕐 **Open** 8:15am–6:50pm Tue–Sun

💶 **Price** €13–26, under-18s free

👪 **Skipping the queue** Buy tickets online or by phone (€4 booking fee), or from Palazzo Pitti or the Orsanmichele booth, where queues are shorter. The Firenze Card, which gives one admission to each of Florence's major museums within 72 hours (€50 per person; under-18s free), allows direct entry.

🔫 **Guided tours** Audio tours in Italian, English, French, German and Japanese; guide booklets in English for children are available at the bookshop.

👫 **Age range** 8 plus; the Uffizi is best for kids old enough to engage with the art on some level, and not run up and down!

♿ **Wheelchair access** Lifts throughout make the gallery wheelchair-friendly.

⏱ **Allow** 2 hours

☕ **Café** On the terrace above the Uffizi loggia, which runs the length of the gallery.

🛍 **Shop** At the entrance and exit, selling books and gifts

🚻 **Toilets** At various locations throughout the museum

Good family value?
The ticket price is not high for such a panoply of fabulous art, but families with toddlers may be better off visiting other attractions.

Prices given are for a family of four

Letting off steam

Pedestrianized **Piazza della Signoria** is the perfect place to run around after the artistic confines of the Uffizi. Among the crowds, visitors can spot mime artists, jugglers and living statues. It is also one of Italy's most beautiful and historic squares, with plenty to look at, from the gigantic copy of Michelangelo's statue *David* to the horses in the fountain.

The Piazza della Signoria, a great place to roam and run

Eat and drink

Picnic: under €25; Snacks: €25–40; Real meal: €40–80; Family treat: €80 or more (based on a family of four)

PICNIC Sant'Ambrogio market *(Piazza Ghiberti, 50122; open 7am–2pm Mon–Sat)* is the best place to grab some delicious bread, cheese, ham, salami and fruit; then enjoy a picnic in nearby Piazza Santa Croce.

SNACKS Vivoli *(Via Isola delle Stinche 7, 50122; 055 292 334; www.vivoli.it)*, open since 1930, is said by some to sell the best ice cream in Italy – though there are plenty of other contenders! Whatever the verdict, it is hard to say no to a cone topped with their chocolate-orange flavour.

REAL MEAL Acqua al Due *(Via della Vigna 40r, 50122; 055 284 170; www.acquaal2.it)*, located near Piazza della Signoria and with a barrel-vaulted ceiling, is a cheerful restaurant to sample filling, traditional Florentine cuisine.

Wafers and biscuits to go with the gelato at the famous Vivoli ice cream parlour

FAMILY TREAT Osteria del Caffè Italiano *(Via Isola delle Stinche 11/13r, 50122; 055 289 368; www.caffeitaliano.it)* is a traditional, smart restaurant that is a good place to try *bistecca alla fiorentina* (T-bone steak from the famous Chianina cattle).

Shopping

Rinascente *(Piazza della Repubblica, 50123; www.rinascente.it)* is a handy, central department store, with something for everyone. **La Bottega dell'Olio** *(Piazza del Limbo 2r, 50123; 055 267 0468)*, a little shop near the Ponte Vecchio, sells anything related to olive trees, including soap and, of course, oil.

Find out more

DIGITAL The website *www.arttrav.com/dblog* features podcasts and pdfs specifically aimed at youngsters exploring the Uffizi. **FILM** *A Room With a View*, the 1985 Merchant Ivory film of E M Forster's 1908 novel, sees heroine Lucy Honeychurch (Helena Bonham Carter) being carried to the Uffizi steps by George Emerson (Julian Sands) when she faints.

Grand Palazzo Vecchio, still fulfilling its role as Florence's town hall

Next stop...

PALAZZO VECCHIO Situated on Piazza Signoria, this is one of the city's grandest palaces. There is a lot to explore, including a Family Museum with fun tours and story-telling for kids *(www.palazzovecchio-familymuseum.it; see p175)*.

KIDS' CORNER

Try your hand...

1 Botticelli's famous picture celebrates the spring. Why not pick another time of year and draw or paint it as you like?
2 Rembrandt drew and painted himself throughout his life. Draw your own self-portrait. Do you need a mirror? Or can you draw yourself from memory?
3 Leonardo liked to draw from life, which means he painted things that were in front of him. Look for interesting details to draw – fruit on a market stall, a flower in a vase or a lamp in the room you are staying in.
4 Piero della Francesca's portraits are very realistic. He didn't try to make people prettier than they really were. Paint a realistic portrait of someone you know!

BONFIRE OF THE VANITIES

This infamous event took place in Piazza della Signoria in 1497, when stern preacher Savonarola burned the musical instruments, art works, cosmetics and even books of the frivolous Florentine rich.

Michelangelo versus Leonardo

These two were rivals and both wanted to be considered the greatest artist of the age. The government in Florence set them a challenge – to create public art works depicting famous battles. Both of the battle pictures were reckoned at the time to be pretty amazing, but neither has survived, leaving the question of who is the champion still unanswered. Which painter do you prefer?

An old-fashioned merry-go-round on Piazza della Repubblica

② Orsanmichele
Statues by star sculptors

Visitors may notice that the church of Orsanmichele does not look much like a church. In fact, it was built in 1337 as a grain market and turned into a church in 1380. The outside was decorated with 14 statues paid for by craftsmen's guilds. Highly competitive, each guild wanted the best and most famous artist to create a statue of its patron saint. The guild of armourers commissioned Donatello to make a statue of St George, the guild of linen-weavers asked him to sculpt St Mark and the guild of farriers had Nanni di Banco create one in honour of St Eligius. Each statue was placed in a niche, creating an extraordinary outdoor gallery of 15th-century sculpture. The statues outside the church today are copies of the originals.

The Lowdown

- **Address** Via dell'Arte della Lana, 50123; 055 284 944; *www. orsanmichele.net, www. museumsinflorence.com*
- **Bus** B, 23
- **Open** Exterior always accessible; interior: 10am–5pm daily (closed Mon in Aug)
- **Price** Free
- **Age range** 5 plus
- **Allow** 30 minutes
- **Wheelchair access** Yes
- **Eat and drink** *Snacks* I Fratellini (*Via dei Cimatori 38r, 50122; 055 239 6096*) serves up great panini. *Real meal* Trattoria Antico Fattore (*Via Lambertesca 1, 50123; 055 288 975; closed Sun*) is a traditional restaurant known for its fresh pasta and beef steaks.

Letting off steam

Head to the grand open space of **Piazza della Repubblica** where parents can sit in one of the historic cafés while kids whirl on "horseback" on the old-fashioned carousel (usually open late spring–late autumn). The square is on the site of a Roman market, and there's a tall column with a statue of Abundance on top.

③ Museo Galileo
Celestial fun for everyone

The Museo Galileo displays more than a thousand scientific objects, including the telescope belonging to Italian scientist Galileo Galilei (1564–1642), through which he identified Jupiter's moons. Florence has a long history of scientific discovery – the ruling Medici family did not only support the arts, they also funded scientific developments such as measuring gravity, temperature and air pressure. Hi-tech video guides show how the most complicated contraptions worked. As well as globes (including an 11th-century Arabic brass one), there are navigation instruments, devices to generate electricity and a beautiful 16th-century armillary sphere, used to map the movements of planets and stars.

Letting off steam

The piazza in front of the pretty church of Santa Croce (*see p162*) is one of Florence's finest. A little off the beaten track, it is a good spot for picnics and chasing pigeons.

The Lowdown

- **Address** Piazza dei Giudici 1, 50122; 055 265 311; *www. museogalileo.it*
- **Bus** B, 23
- **Open** 9:30am–6pm Wed–Mon, 9:30am–1pm Tue
- **Price** €16–28, children aged 7–18 €5, under-7s free
- **Age range** 5 plus
- **Activities** Kids' workshops on topics such as Galileo's instruments (Sat; 90 minutes; drop-off an option; see website for details), and videos to help kids explore the collection
- **Allow** At least 90 minutes
- **Wheelchair access** Yes
- **Eat and drink** *Snacks* Lorenzaccio (*Piazza della Signoria 32, 50122; 055 29 4553; www. ristorantelorenzaccio.com; closed Thu*) on the piazza bakes pizza and *calzoni* in its wood oven. *Real meal* Trattoria da Benvenuto (*Via Mosca 16r, 50122; 055 214 833*) is a simple, satisfying neighbourhood restaurant.

A sundial in front of the Museo Galileo; there are many more inside

Shops and jewellery workshops lining the medieval Ponte Vecchio

④ Ponte Vecchio
Jewels on the bridge

Il Ponte Vecchio ("the old bridge") was built in 1345, making it more than 650 years old. It is lined with jewellery workshops and shops whose windows glisten with gold. In the old days, however, leather tanners and butchers had their workshops here. The smell was pretty bad, especially as the workers threw their rubbish straight into the River Arno. In 1593 Duke Ferdinand I put an end to these stinky trades on the bridge, and the goldsmiths have been goldsmithing here ever since.

Letting off steam
Cross the bridge to Oltrarno, and head for **Boboli Gardens** (see pp178–9), where there are acres of grass to run around and picnic on.

The Lowdown

- **Address** Ponte Vecchio, 50125
- **Bus** B, 23
- **Age range** All: even toddlers will enjoy seeing the river and glittering jewellers' windows
- **Allow** 30 minutes
- **Wheelchair access** Yes
- **Eat and drink** Snacks Le Volpi e l'Uva (Piazza dei Rossi, 50125; 055 239 8132; www.levolpieluva.com; closed Sun) is a simple wine bar on the far side of the Ponte Vecchio – children can enjoy soft drinks and sandwiches. Real meal Casalinga (Via dei Michelozzi 9r, 50125; 055 218 624; closed Sun) is a local restaurant across the bridge in Oltrarno dishing up Florentine fare.

Palazzo Vecchio, a distinctive landmark on the skyline of Florence

⑤ Palazzo Vecchio
Frescoes at the town hall

The battlemented Palazzo Vecchio (meaning "old palace") dominates Piazza della Signoria. Designed by Arnolfo di Cambio and built in the early 14th century, it was both an effective fortress and a graceful creation, with its arched Gothic windows and lines of crenellations. The bell tower, nearly 100 m (328 ft) high, was used to alert citizens to attack, flood or fire. Inside, frescoes by Giorgio Vasari (1555–79) decorate the walls in a hymn to his patron Cosimo de' Medici, and visitors can see Michelangelo's Genius of Victory statue (1533–4), an early Mannerist masterpiece.

Letting off steam
Run around the swirly floral columns and Verrocchio's fountain, with its chubby cherub hugging a diving dolphin, in the entrance courtyard to the palace.

The Lowdown

- **Address** Piazza della Signoria, 50122; 055 276 8325; www.museicivicifiorentini.it
- **Bus** B, 23
- **Open** 9am–7pm Fri–Wed, 9am–2pm Thu
- **Price** Family of four €14, of five €16, under-3s free
- **Guided tours** Tours for children such as the Medieval Palace Revealed and Life at the Medieval Court; pre-book on www.palazzovecchio-familymuseum.it
- **Age range** Special activities for children aged 3 plus or 10 plus make the palazzo palatable to kids
- **Allow** At least 1 hour
- **Activities** Follow a guide around the museum looking for sculpted and painted turtles
- **Wheelchair access** Via dei Gondi
- **Eat and drink** Real meal Trattoria Roberto (Via dei Castellani 4r, 50122; 055 218 822) is a traditional restaurant serving dishes such as Tuscan bean soup and bistecca alla fiorentina (T-bone steak). Family treat Osteria dei Baroncelli (Via Chiasso dei Baroncelli, 50122; 055 288 219; www.osteriadeibaroncelli.it) is tucked away on a narrow street behind Piazza della Signoria, and serves excellent food.

QUI ARRIVÒ L'ARNO
IL 4 NOVEMBRE 1966

FLORENTINE FLOOD
In 1966, Florence suffered the worst floods in a thousand years. The River Arno burst its banks and the Uffizi was badly flooded, but none of the major masterpieces were lost. Look for the plaques that show the level of the floodwaters.

Survival of the bridge
The Ponte Vecchio is the only one of its kind in Florence. During World War II, when the German army was retreating from the city and the Allied armies were advancing, the Germans mined and destroyed all the other bridges. It is said the Ponte Vecchio was saved on German leader Adolf Hitler's own orders.

Boboli Gardens and around

The sprawling Boboli Gardens, adjoining the vast hulk of Palazzo Pitti in the Oltrarno district, are the green lungs of Florence. Laid out in formal glory, they provide a refreshing break from the city streets. After the gardens, the narrow lanes of Oltrarno offer plenty of enticements: great local restaurants and old-fashioned shops and workshops. The area gives an insight into the way the Florentines live, away from the tourist honeypot across the river.

View of Palazzo Pitti, a vast repository for Medici collections of just about everything, including Renaissance art, seen from the grassy slopes of the Boboli Gardens

Places of Interest

SIGHTS

1. Boboli Gardens
2. Palazzo Pitti
3. Cappella Brancacci
4. Santo Spirito

● EAT AND DRINK

1. Gustapanino
2. Gustapizza
3. Borgo Antico
4. Pane e Vino
5. Pitti Gola e Cantina
6. Il Santo Bevitore
7. Hemingway
8. Al Tranvai
9. Bar Richi
10. Osteria Santo Spirito

● SHOPPING

1. Borgo Tegolaio
2. Giulio Giannini & Figlio

● WHERE TO STAY

1. Hotel Palazzo Guadagni
2. Giglio Bianco
3. Home in Florence
4. San Frediano Mansion B&B
5. Istituo Gould

Viottolone, a shady avenue of cypress trees in Boboli Gardens, planted in 1612

An antiquarian fair in Piazza Santo Spirito, with Chiesa di Santo Spirito behind

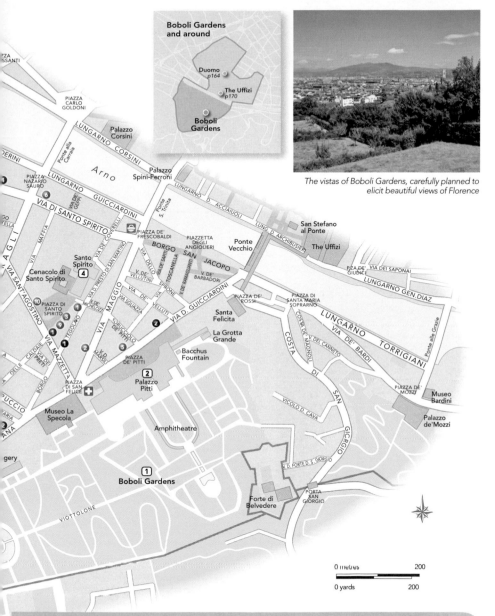

Boboli Gardens and around

PIAZZA SSANTI

PIAZZA CARLO GOLDONI

PIAZZA NAZARIO SAURO

Duomo p164

The Uffizi p170

Boboli Gardens

Palazzo Corsini

Palazzo Spini-Ferroni

Arno

LUNGARNO CORSINI

Ponte alla Carraia

VIA DI SANTO SPIRITO

LUNGARNO GUICCIARDINI

S. Trinita

Ponte S. Trinita

LUNGARNO D. ACCIAIUOLI

LUNG. D. ARCHIBUSIERI

San Stefano al Ponte

The Uffizi

PIAZZA DE' FRESCOBALDI

PIAZZETTA DEGLI ANGIOLIERI

Ponte Vecchio

BORGO SAN JACOPO

Santo Spirito **4**

Cenacolo di Santo Spirito

VIA DE' VELLUTINI

V. DEL PRESTO DI SAN MARTINO

V. DE' RAMAGLIANTI

V. DE' BARBADORI

PIAZZA DEL ROSSI

PIAZZA DI SANTA MARIA SOPRARNO

PZA DE' GIUDEI

VIA DEI SAPONAI

LUNGARNO GEN. DIAZ

10 PIAZZA DI SANTO SPIRITO

Santa Felicita

La Grotta Grande

LUNGARNO TORRIGIANI

COSTA DE' MAGNOLI

VIA DE' BARDI

COSTA SAN GIORGIO

Ponte alle Grazie

PIAZZA DI SAN FELICE

PIAZZA DE' PITTI

Bacchus Fountain

2 Palazzo Pitti

VICOLO D. CAVA

PIAZZA DE' MOZZI

Museo Bardini

Palazzo de'Mozzi

Museo La Specola

Amphitheatre

1 Boboli Gardens

VIOTTOLONE

V. D. FORTE D. S. GIORGIO

Forte di Belvedere

PORTA SAN GIORGIO

The vistas of Boboli Gardens, carefully planned to elicit beautiful views of Florence

0 metres 200
0 yards 200

The Lowdown

🚗 **Bus** D, 11, 36, 37

ℹ️ **Visitor Information** Borgo Santa Croce 29r, 50122; 055 2340 444; summer 9am–7pm, winter 9am–5pm Mon–Sat; all year 9am–2pm Sun; www. firenzeturismo.it (excellent kids' section with information on free kids' activities, parks and playgrounds); www.comune.fi.it

🍴 **Supermarkets** Small grocery stores abound in the area. Alternatively head to the exceptional speciality food and wine store Olio & Convivium: Via Santo Spirito 4, 50124; 055 265 8198; www.conviviumfirenze.it. **Markets** Piazza Santo Spirito (toys and bric-a-brac) Sun, third Sun of month organic produce

🎪 **Festivals** Il Palio dei Renaioli (boat race on the Arno): late Jun (www.renaioli.it); Festa di San Giovanni (fireworks over the Arno): 24 Jun

➕ **Pharmacies** Farmacia Pitti: Piazza San Felice 4r, 50124; 055 22 44 02

🎨 **Nearest play area** Piazza Torquato Tasso

① Boboli Gardens
Florentine fountains and a pretend cave

Florence does not have a lot of green space, but what it does have is the Boboli Gardens. The glorious grounds of the Palazzo Pitti, the gardens were designed for the Medicis in the 1550s, with neat box hedges cut into symmetrical patterns, stretches of wild ilex and cypress trees, and plenty of fountains and statues. Whether to fly a kite, have a picnic or just find space to run and play, the Boboli Gardens are a great place to get out of doors.

Lion relief carving on façade of Palazzo Pitti

Key Sights

① **Palazzo Pitti** The huge palace was built by banker Luca Pitti in 1457, but within 100 years it was acquired by the rival Medici family.

② **Amphitheatre** The first ever opera performances were staged here at the wedding of Marie de' Medici to Henri IV of France in 1600.

③ **Bacchus Fountain** The fat fellow astride a turtle was modelled on a real person – a 16th-century court dwarf – but represents Bacchus, the Roman god of wine.

Palace entrance

④ **Kaffeehaus** In summer, have a drink and enjoy the city views from this coffee house set in a pretty Rococo pavilion.

⑤ **Orangery** A grand glasshouse built to protect rare plants from the cold and wind.

⑥ **Viottolone** This sloping avenue of cypress trees was planted in 1612, and is lined with statues, some of them of ancient Roman origin.

⑦ **La Grotta Grande** Dripping with fake stalactites and crammed with sculptures, including *Venus Bathing* by Giambologna, these caves were built in the 16th century.

⑧ **Isolotto** The "little island" in the gardens' Vasca dell'Isola (Island Pool) features tumbling plants and a tall statue of Neptune, god of the sea.

Eat and drink

Picnic: under €25; Snacks: €25–40; Real meal: €40–80; Family treat: €80 or more (based on a family of four)

PICNIC Gustapanino (*Via de' Michelozzi 13, 50125*), located on Piazza Santo Spirito, is a tiny and justifiably popular place – great for filled *panini* and drinks to have in the piazza – or a picnic to take to the Boboli Gardens.
SNACKS Gustapizza (*Via Maggio 46r, 50125; 055 285 068*) is a fun, buzzy pizza joint. Kids will love watching the chefs swirl the pizza dough high in the air and then

A pizzettaro at Gustapizza swirling the dough around to make a pizza

shovel the topped dough into the wood-fired pizza oven.
REAL MEAL Borgo Antico (*Piazza Santo Spirito 6r, 50125; 055 210 437*) is a trendy *trattoria*, with quieter tables outside in the summer months. It serves Tuscan cuisine, risotto and tasty pizzas that children will be sure to tuck into. Good-sized portions and friendly, attentive staff makes this a favourite dining spot in Florence.
FAMILY TREAT Pane e Vino (*Piazza di Cestello, 50124; 055 247 6956; www.ristorantepaneevino.it*), a former wine shop, is housed in a

The Lowdown

- 🌐 **Address** Piazza Pitti 1, 50125; 055 238 8786; www.firenzemusei.it

- 🚗 **Bus** D, 11, 36, 37 and 68

- 🕐 **Open** Boboli Gardens: daily Nov–Feb 8:15am–4:30pm, Mar and Oct 8:15am–5:30pm, Apr, May, Sep and Oct 8:15am–6:30pm, Jun–Aug 8:15am–7:30pm, closed first and last Mon of the month. Palazzo Pitti: 8:15am–5:50pm Tue–Sun

- 💲 **Price** €12–24; under-18s free; combined with Palazzo Pitti: €23–33 for 3 days, children free

- 👥 **Skipping the queue** The information desk at Palazzo Pitti also sells tickets for the Uffizi and the Accademia (booking fee), so if continuing to the galleries, book ahead here.

- 🪧 **Guided tours** Ask at the desk in Palazzo Pitti about themed garden and museum itineraries.

- 👫 **Age range** All

- 🕐 **Allow** At least 2 hours for a leisurely stroll and a picnic

- ♿ **Wheelchair access** Partial: enter via the archway at the left end of the palace façade; some paths are too steep.

- ☕ **Café** Kaffeehaus (in summer)

- 🎩 **Shop** Bookshop and gift shop in Palazzo Pitti

- 👫 **Toilets** In the Pitti Palace courtyard

Good family value?
For a modest price, the gardens offer Florence's best green space for kids to roll, run and chase each other around.

FLORENTINE FLORINS
Under the Medicis, Florence was Europe's main banking centre. The Florentine coin – the florin – was trusted by everyone to be pure gold, so it became a standard coin all over Europe.

Wedding party
When Cosimo III de' Medici got married in 1661, he ordered a spectacular show for the Boboli Gardens, with 20,000 onlookers crammed into the amphitheatre. It featured a huge construction that showed the Greek god Atlas carrying a globe on his shoulders. The globe was split open and earth spilled out of it to form a mountain. Despite the elaborate party, Cosimo did not have a happy marriage… his pretty French wife Marguerite Louise eventually left him.

---

converted barn. Now a stylish restaurant, Pane e Vino serves elegant Italian dishes and exquisite puddings – a real treat for special-occasion dining.

Interior of smart Pane e Vino restaurant, which serves classic Italian dishes

Shopping
Borgo Tegolaio is famous for its artisan workshops; see gilding and gold-working in action. There is also a fine traditional paper-maker, **Giulio Giannini & Figlio**, on Piazza Pitti (www.giuliogiannini.it).

Find out more
DIGITAL For more on the life and times of the Medici family, visit galileo.rice.edu/gal/medici.html, or

for a chronology of their rise and fall, go to www.channel4.com/history/microsites/H/history/i-m/medici.html.

Take cover
There is plenty to see on a rainy day in **Palazzo Pitti** (see p180): visit the Medici apartments, where every surface gleams with Venetian glass, and galleries displaying costumes and carriages, as well as Renaissance paintings hung one above another.

Next stop…
PIAZZA SANTO SPIRITO This square, with its buzzing cafés, is particularly worth a visit on Sundays, when there is a bric-a-brac market. It has plenty to appeal to children, including a stall selling brightly coloured cloth puppets.

Puppet stall in the Sunday bric-a-brac market on Piazza Santo Spirito

Palazzo Pitti, a former residence of Florentine rulers, now houses several museums

② Palazzo Pitti
Museums full of Medici hoards

This monolithic Renaissance palace was begun in 1457 for the Pitti family of bankers, to outclass the rival Medici family with a display of wealth and power. Ironically, the building costs bankrupted the Pitti, and the Medicis acquired the palace. In 1550 it became the main residence of the Medicis, and all subsequent rulers of Florence lived here. It contains all sorts of lavish treasures. The Palatine Gallery has about 1,000 Renaissance and Baroque paintings from the 16th and 17th centuries by artists such as Botticelli, Perugino, Giorgione, Caravaggio and Van Dyck. There is a whole room full of some of Raphael's best High Renaissance works. There are also museums of silver and porcelain, a carriage museum and a costume museum with sumptuous

18th- and 19th-century garb on display. The Royal Apartments drip with gilt and chandeliers, providing a vivid illustration of how the other half once lived in Florence.

Letting off steam
The enormous sloping square in front of the palace is good for a run around before a reviving ice cream from one of the cafés at the bottom. Alternatively, the **Boboli Gardens** *(see pp178–9)* to the rear of Palazzo Pitti are a great place for a picnic and a leisurely afternoon.

③ Cappella Brancacci
Big and little Thomas

The Cappella Brancacci, in the church of Santa Maria del Carmine, houses famous frescoes of *The Life of St Peter.* Begun by Masolino

("little Thomas") in 1424, they were continued by his pupil Masaccio ("big Thomas") and completed by Filippino Lippi 50 years later. Masaccio's work was revolutionary for its use of perspective, narrative drama and the tragic realism of his figures. In the scene of *St Peter Healing the Sick,* the cripples and beggars are lifelike in their misery. *The Expulsion of Adam and Eve* is a psychological study of the pair expelled from Paradise, who cover their bodies and faces in anguish and shame. In several scenes St Peter (in the orange cloak) is depicted against a background of Florentine buildings, painted using pioneering perspective.

Many great artists, including Michelangelo, later visited the chapel to study Masaccio's ground-breaking work. By contrast, the frescoes by Masolino are less naturalistic and more decorative – look for the two turbaned figures.

Letting off steam
Less than 5 minutes' walk away, **Piazza Torquato Tasso** has gardens and a play area. Medieval city walls, fun to explore, lead to the ancient Porta Romana.

The Lowdown
- **Address** Piazza del Carmine, 50122; 055 238 2195; www.museicivicifiorentini.it
- **Bus** D
- **Open** 10am–5pm Mon and Wed–Sat, 1–5pm Sun
- **Price** Family ticket €9.50 (2 adults and 2 children), €11 (2 adults and 3 children); under-3s free
- **Skipping the queue** Book in advance on 055 276 8224 or info. museoragazzi@comune.fi.it
- **Age range** 8 plus
- **Allow** Chapel visits are limited to 15 minutes, preceded by a 40-minute introductory video *The Eye of Masaccio* (optional).
- **Wheelchair access** No
- **Eat and drink** *Snacks* Hemingway (Piazza Piattellina 9r, 50124; 055 284 781) is chocolate heaven, with home-made ice cream, cakes, crepes and even chocolate soup. *Real meal* Al Tranvai (Piazza Torquato Tasso 14r, 50124; 055 225 197), a little family-run trattoria, serves great pecorino fondue, rabbit, wild boar and delicious fig cake, as well as other Tuscan dishes.

The Lowdown
- **Address** Piazza Pitti 1, 50125; 055 238 8616; www.uffizi.firenze.it/palazzopitti
- **Bus** D, 11, 36, 37 or 68
- **Open** 8:15am–5:50pm Tue–Sun; ticket offices close 45 minutes before the museums.
- **Price** €23–42, EU under-18s free; ticket for all museums, valid 3 days; tickets for single museums may cost less.
- **Skipping the queue** Book online on museum website or by phone on 055 294 883; €3 booking fee
- **Guided tour** Ask at the desk about themed museum itineraries.

Corridoio Vasariano from Palazzo Pitti; call 055 294 883 to book.
- **Age range** 8 plus
- **Allow** At least 2 hours
- **Wheelchair access** Yes
- **Eat and drink** *Real meal* Pitti Gola e Cantina (Piazza Pitti 16, 50125; 055 212 704) is a pleasant eatery for a rest after sightseeing, with good antipasti, salads, gnocchi and pasta. *Family treat* Il Santo Bevitore (Via di Santo Spirito 66r, 50125; 055 211 264; www.ilsantobevitore.com) is a vaulted restaurant with a modern take on Tuscan food.
- **Toilets** In the museum

View of Santo Spirito church, designed by Brunelleschi, among Florence's rooftops

④ Santo Spirito
Splendid church

Brunelleschi, architect of the Duomo's dome, designed this harmonious church in 1440. The plain façade, added in the 18th century, gives no indication of the splendour within. Brunelleschi did not live to see what some consider to be his finest church built, but the colonnaded nave and aisles are faithful to his design. The harmony of the proportions has been slightly spoiled by the elaborate Baroque *baldacchino* and high altar. The 38 side altars are decorated with Renaissance paintings and sculpture, among them Filippino Lippi's *Madonna and Child* (1466). This engaging and complex work, in the Nerli Chapel in the south transept, depicts an arcaded loggia complete with an intriguing Florentine vista in the background.

Letting off steam

Lively **Piazza Santo Spirito** is a fun place to play, enjoy a coffee or ice cream and browse the market stalls.

The Lowdown

- **Address** Piazza Santo Spirito 30, 50125 Florence; 055 210 030; www.basilicasantospirito.it
- **Bus** D, 6, 11, 36, 37 and 68
- **Open** 9:30am–12:30pm & 3–5:30pm Thu–Sat and Mon–Tue, 3–5:30pm Sun
- **Age range** 8 plus
- **Allow** Half an hour
- **Wheelchair access** Yes
- **Eat and drink** *Snacks* Bar Richi (Piazza S. Spirito 9r, 50125; 055 215 864) sells ice cream and does an Italian breakfast. *Real meal* Osteria Santo Spirito (Piazza Santo Spirito 16r, 50125; 055 238 2383) has a lovely location on the square. Try the *gnocchi gratinati* (oven-baked dumplings).

Fresco by Masaccio and Filippino Lippi in the Cappella Brancacci

Picnic under €25; **Snacks** €25–40; **Real meal** €40–80; **Family treat** €80 or more (based on a family of four)

Where to Stay in Florence

Florence has a huge range of accommodation for families, from expensive hotels and apartments to smaller family-run city hotels and some fantastic B&Bs tucked away in mansion blocks. It is possible to camp outside town within walking distance of the Ponte Vecchio or, in the hills of Fiesole.

AGENCIES
Pitcher & Flaccomio
www.pitcherflaccomio.com
A high-end property company, with some handsome, central apartments for rent by the week. Worthwhile for longer stays, with self-catering at markets and delis.

Way to Stay
www.waytostay.com
A huge variety of apartments to rent, ranging from cosy studios to five-bedroom luxury flats decorated with interesting antiques, and also including more affordable options.

Duomo and Baptistry

HOTELS
Hotel Il Bargellino
Via Guelfa 87, 50129; 055 238 2658; www.ilbargellino.com
Owned and run by an American woman and her Italian husband, who are both very hospitable, this hotel is small and cosy, conveniently located five minutes' walk from Santa Maria Novella train station, but quiet. There is no breakfast, but coffee is available on the terrace.

€

Hotel Colomba
Via Cavour 21, 50129; 055 289 139; www.hotelcolomba.com
Located in a handsome 19th-century palazzo, a short stroll away from the Duomo, this welcoming, family-run hotel has single, twin, triple and quadruple rooms that are bright and modern. There are also two rooms equipped for disabled travellers. The breakfasts are generous.

€

Hotel Giglio
Via Cavour 85, 50129; 055 486 621; www.hotelgiglio.fi.it
A pair of helpful brothers own the Hotel Giglio and they will happily give the lowdown to guests on what to see and where to eat nearby. The rooms are comfortable though plainly decorated, with terracotta or wooden floors, and the buffet breakfast is very good.

€

Hotel Benivieni
Via delle Oche 5, 50122; 055 238 2133; www.hotelbenivieni.it
In an early-15th-century historic palazzo close to the Duomo, this hotel has a fine exterior and comfortable rooms. The staff can

help book excursion tickets and offer advice on sightseeing. An additional charge of €70 is made for an extra bed.

€€

Hotel Il Guelfo Bianco
Via Camillo Cavour 29, 50129; 055 288 330; www.ilguelfobianco.it
This gorgeous 16th-century mansion in a great setting just north of the Duomo has a modern art collection and a pretty internal garden for breakfast. The restaurant is supplied by the family's farm.

€€

Hotel de Lanzi
Via delle Oche 11, 50123; 055 288 043; www.hoteldelanziflorence.com
Located close to Piazza del Duomo, some of the rooms here have cathedral views. The decor is plain, but the rooms are comfortable and the bathrooms well equipped. The helpful staff can assist with planning trips around the city.

€€

Hotel Loggiato dei Serviti
Piazza SS Annunziata 3, 50100; 055 289 592; www.loggiato deiservitihotel.it
This historic hotel in the northern part of the city centre is still only a 10-minute walk from the Duomo. It was built in the early 16th century as a monastery, and is full of charm, with original wood-beamed ceilings. There is a suite with views of the Duomo – great for families.

€€

Hotel Perseo
Via Cerretani 1, 50123; 055 212 504; www.hotelperseo.it
A modernized hotel in the centre of the city, Hotel Perseo is very well located for the Duomo and Baptistry, with spacious rooms. The decor is contemporary and plain, but the hotel is well run and impeccably clean.

€€

Hotel Calzaiuoli, conveniently situated right in the heart of the city

Grand Hotel Minerva with a rooftop pool offering views of the Duomo

Grand Hotel Minerva
Piazza Santa Maria Novella 16, 50123; 055 27230; www.grandhotel minerva.net
In an excellent setting right next to Santa Maria Novella church, this grand old hotel has been thoroughly modernized. The rooftop pool has views of the Duomo, and may alone be enough to justify the price. There are two family suites, each of which can accommodate four people.
🛏️ 🖥️ 🍽️ ⚙️   €€€

Hotel Calzaiuoli
Via dei Calzaiuoli 6, 50122; 055 212 456; www.calzaiuoli.it
An upmarket option right in the heart of the city, this hotel is traditionally and unstuffily furnished. Triple rooms make it a good choice for families, and the breakfast buffet will set children up for the day. Despite the very central location, rooms are quiet thanks to the good soundproofing.
🛏️   €€€

B&Bs
Panerai & Panerai
Via dei Servi 49, 50122; 055 264 103; www.soggiornopanerai.it
This warmly welcoming B&B, set in an imposing mansion close to the Duomo, has rooms featuring wonderful wooden beds with colourful quilts, painted ceilings and terracotta floors. There are triple and quadruple family rooms.
🛏️   €

Antica Dimora Johlea
Via San Gallo 80, 50129; 055 463 3292; www.johanna.it
One of a little chain of sumptuously furnished Tuscan B&Bs, this is just north of the historic centre. It is luxurious but homely, with a rooftop terrace, four-poster beds, antique prints and colourful Indian quilts.
🖥️ 🛏️   €€

SELF-CATERING
Palazzo Alfani al David
Via Ricasoli 49, 50122; 055 291 574; www.palazzoalfani.com
A historic 16th-century palazzo opposite the Accademia, this building has been in the owner's family since the early 19th century. It has been carefully converted into apartments, with spacious, comfortable rooms. The suites sleep four to eight guests.
🛏️   €€

The Uffizi

HOTELS
Hotel Alessandra
Borgo SS Apostoli 17, Tornabuoni, 50123; 055 283 438; www.hotel alessandra.com
Housed in a 16th-century building, this hotel is close to the Ponte Vecchio and nicely furnished rooms as well as a large suite. It is family-run with helpful staff, but it is upstairs with no lift.
🛏️   €

Residenza Casanuova, a B&B in a charming family home

Hotel Davanzati
Via Porta Rossa 5, 50123; 055 286 666; www.hoteldavanzati.it
A handsome shuttered building with terracotta-tiled floors and quietly elegant furnishings, this hotel is located in the old city, a short walk from Santa Maria Novella train station.
🛏️   €

Hotel Berchielli
Lungarno Acciaiuoli 14, 50123; 055 264061; www.berchielli.it
Located on the Arno just a few minutes' walk from the Ponte Vecchio, this is a great hotel for getting to the main sights as well as Oltrarno. There is a triple room for families and a roof garden.
🛏️ 🖥️ 📶   €€€

B&Bs
Casa Rovai Guest House
Via Fiesolana 1, 50122; 055 200 1647; www.casarovai.it
There are six lovely, spacious rooms in this quiet apartment building. Despite being elegantly decorated with antiques, ceiling frescoes and lovely fabrics, it is very family-friendly. The hosts are happy to provide guidance for family sight-seeing in Florence.
🛏️   €

Residenza Casanuova
Via della Mattonaia 21, 50121; 055 234 3413; www.residenzacasanuova.it
This charming family home would suit parents travelling with older children who will respect the beautiful furnishings and antiques. It has been in the family for three generations, and the welcoming owners speak good English. In summer it is possible to have an alfresco breakfast on the terrace, with its romantic rooftop views over the city.
✉️ 🖥️   €

Relais Piazza Signoria
Via Vaccherrecia 3, 50122; 055 398 7239; www.relaispiazzasignoria.com
These swish modern apartments are in a plum position overlooking the Piazza della Signoria. There are studio rooms and two attic apartments that can accommodate families, with modern furniture and rugged stone walls.
🛏️ 🍽️   €€€

Boboli Gardens

HOTEL
Hotel Palazzo Guadagni
Piazza di Santo Spirito 9, 50125; 055 265 8376, www.palazzo guadagni.com/
Built in the 16th century, this beautiful, historic palazzo has a beautiful terrace garden with views of the hills. Extra beds for additional family members can be added to the rooms.
🖥️ 🛏️ ❄️   €€

Price Guide
For a family of four per night in high season, in one or more rooms, inclusive of breakfast, service charges and any additional taxes such as VAT.

€ Under €200 **€€** €200–350 **€€€** over €350

Key to symbols *see back cover flap*

B&Bs
Giglio Bianco
Via Romana 28, 50125; 055 225 873; www.gigliobianco.it
Housed in a grand mansion building, this B&B is in a great location for visiting the Boboli Gardens. The two en-suite rooms are comfortable and spacious. Breakfasts are generous and varied, and there is a restaurant that serves dinner with views of the Boboli gardens from the three large windows.
🍴 €

Home in Florence
Via Santa Maria 21, 50125; 055 233 7186; www.homeinflorence.com
With tiled floors, high ceilings and antique furniture, this is a quiet B&B near the Boboli Gardens. There are triple and quadruple rooms, as well as doubles – all are en suite. Book in advance for extra beds and cots; children under 2 stay for free.
🛏 🍴 ⌣ €

San Frediano Mansion
Via Borgo San Frediano 8, 50124; 055 212 991; www.sanfrediano mansion.com
A grand old mansion with an enormous front door. Some of the rooms here are a little spartan, but they offer good value for money. There are family rooms that accommodate three to five people, and a small self-catering apartment. Visitors are given a key and are free to come and go as they please.
🛏 ⌣ ✕ ⟡ €€

HOSTEL
Istituto Gould
Via de' Serragli 49, 50124; 055 212 576; www.istitutogould.it/foresteria
One of the city's best bargains, this beautiful 17th-century palazzo, owned by a group of Protestant churches, accommodates all visitors

The courtyard of the Istituto Gould, one of Florence's best-value places to stay

regardless of faith. Rooms are plain, clean and comfortable, and sleep up to five people. The location in Oltrarno is very good. Breakfast and dinner can be eaten here for a small supplement, or there are cafés nearby.
🛏 🍴 €

Camping Panoramico in Fiesole, a shady alternative outside the city centre

Around Florence
HOTEL
Villa Fiesole Hotel
Via Beato Angelico 35, 50014 Fiesole; 055 597 252; www.villafiesole.it
The hills of Fiesole can make for a calmer and cooler stay than central Florence. This friendly, welcoming hotel enjoys sweeping views of the city. There is a balcony for guests to enjoy, and a small pool. Regular buses go into town.
🛏 ✿ 🍴 ⊗ €€

B&Bs
Fiorenza
Via Grecchi 36, 50125 Florence; 055 232 2183; www.fiorenzabb.it
South of the Arno in a quiet, residential neighbourhood, Elena's B&B is tastefully decorated, with bright rooms, antique furniture and pretty fabrics. There is a secluded garden and beautiful patio. Elena herself is extremely welcoming.
🛏 ✿ €

La Martellina
Via della Martellina 19, 50061 Fiesole; 33 5768 4675; www.martellina-bb-florence.it
Housed in an old mill that dates back to the 13th century, this B&B is located in a small village around 5 km (3 miles) from Florence. It is possible to get there by bike on a track that runs along the Arno. The riverside garden makes this a really lovely get-away-from-it-all choice.
✿ €

Casa Palmira
Via Faentina, 50030 Polcanto; 055 840 9749; www.casapalmira.it
Located in the hills near Fiesole, this country B&B has been restored by Assunta and Stefano, who offer a warm welcome and delicious home-grown food. The decor is lovely and there is a wood-burning oven in the kitchen for pizza-making. They have a cot for families with babies and the kitchen is open to guests for self-catering.
✕ ✿ ⌣ €€

AGRITURISMO
Azienda Agricola Il Borghetto
Via Collina 23, Montefiridolfi, 50020 San Casciano Val di Pesa; 055 824 4442; www.borghetto.org
An attractive, family-run winery 20 km (13 miles) from Florence, Il Borghetto offers tasteful and relaxing accommodation in eight suites and rooms, plus cookery courses and tours of the vineyard and olive groves. There is plenty of space to roam in the sweeping grounds, which include an Etruscan ruin. A cottage with private patio is also available. The food is excellent.
✕ ✿ €€

CAMPING
Camping Michelangelo
Via Michelangelo 80, 50125; 055 681 1977; www.camping.it/toscana/michelangelo; open Apr–Oct
An attractive camp site located in an olive grove near the city, a 15-minute walk from the Ponte Vecchio. The location ensures it is very popular, so book well in advance. There is a snack bar with a terrace that has views over Florence, a playground, supermarket and laundry facilities.
🍴 ☕ ⟡ 🍴 €

Camping Panoramico
Via Peramonda 1, 50014 Fiesole; 055 599 069; www.florence camping.com
Just outside Fiesole, this wooded camp site has good facilities including a pool, and – as its name suggests – great panoramic views from its hillside perch. It is not quite as handy for Florence as Camping Michelangelo, but it is a good alternative if they have no space in the summer season.
✿ ⊗ €

Tuscany

Tuscany has long had a special place in the hearts of visitors. Its famous hill towns are fun for families to explore, with dramatic fortresses, ancient walls, hidden art treasures and perfect town squares. Olive groves and mountain ranges offer opportunities for hiking and horse-riding, and there are plenty of seasonal events from archery to wine festivals.

Below Typical Tuscan landscape with cypress trees and poppies

① Siena: Piazza del Campo and Duomo
A shell-shaped square and a zebra-striped cathedral

Siena, with its perfectly preserved medieval heart, is one of the prettiest cities in Italy. At its hub is the scallop-shaped Piazza del Campo, one of Europe's greatest medieval squares. Its nine segments slope down to the magnificent Gothic Palazzo del Pubblico, with a tall tower that has dizzying views over the tiled roofs of the city. A short stroll through narrow backstreets leads to the black-and-white-striped Duomo, its high façade decorated with wonderful statues and its interior graced with frescoes, carvings and inlaid marble floors.

A she-wolf suckling Romulus and Remus, whose son Senius founded Siena

Key Sights

Fonte Gaia

Loggia della Mercanzia
Sienese merchants carried out their business under cover of this handsome arcade built in 1417.

Palazzo Pubblico
The elegant town hall, finished in 1342, was frescoed by Simone Martini and Ambrogio Lorenzetti, who painted the *Allegory of Good and Bad Government* (1338).

Piazza del Campo

Torre del Mangia
The tall, skinny bell tower (1340) offers magnificent views of the city. Climb the 503 steps to the top and read the time on the sundial.

Palazzo Pubblico

Piazza del Campo
The historic and social hub of Siena, this lovely piazza is famous for the thrilling Palio horse race run here.

PIAZZA DEL MERCATO

PIAZZA DEL DUOMO

VIA DI CITTÀ

Torre del Mangia

Duomo

Museo dell'Opera del Duomo
Duccio's gleaming *Maestà*, paraded around the streets on its completion in 1311, is the masterpiece of this collection.

Duomo
Striped marble inside and out, the spectacular Romanesque-Gothic cathedral (1136–1382) has a carved pulpit by Nicola Pisano (1265–8). Its Piccolomini Library was frescoed by Pinturicchio (1509).

Letting off steam

Split your family into *contrade* (city neighbourhoods) and run your own Palio race around the Campo. In the real Palio, held twice a year on 2 July and 16 August, madcap bareback horse-riders race three times around the piazza. The whole town erupts into life with flag-waving, flag-throwing and horseback parades in medieval costume. Each *contrada* has its own emblem, depicted on its flag, and cheers wildly for its jockey.

Prices given are for a family of four

Eat and drink

Picnic: under €25; Snacks: €25–40; Real meal: €40–80; Family treat: €80 or more (based on a family of four)

PICNIC Pizzicheria de Miccoli (*Via di Città 93–5, 53100; 0577 289 184*) is the place to go for picnic supplies. Choose from an enticing array of cold meats, cheeses and olives – staff there will make up sandwiches based on your selection. It also sells a wide range of pesto. Enjoy your lunch by the Fonte Gaia in the Campo.

SNACKS Nannini Gelateria (*Banchi di Sopra 24, 53100; 0577 236 009*), founded in 1911, is Siena's best bet for a classic ice cream or cake.
REAL MEAL Il Carroccio (*Via del Casato di Sotto 32, 53100; 0577 41165*) is in a great central location and serves up authentic Sienese food in a relaxed environment.
FAMILY TREAT Cane e Gatto (*Via Pagliaresi 6, 53100; 0577 287 545*) offers fine dining in an intimate and welcoming restaurant, with a five-course Tuscan tasting menu.

The Lowdown

🌐 **Map reference** 5 D4
Address 53100 Siena.
Palazzo Pubblico/Torre del
Mangia: Piazza del Campo 1;
www.comunesiena.it. Duomo
and Museo dell'Opera del
Duomo: Piazza del Duomo;
www.operaduomo.siena.it

🚗 **Train** from Florence and San
Gimignano, bus to centre (*www.
trenitalia.it*). **Bus** from Florence
and Arezzo to central Viale
Federico Tozzi (*www.trainspa.it*)

ℹ️ **Visitor information** Piazza del
Campo 56; 0577 280 551;
www.terresiena.it; closed Sun

🕐 **Open** Palazzo Pubblico: daily
10am–5:30pm Nov–Feb, till
6pm Mar, till 7pm Apr–Oct;
Torre del Mangia: daily
10am–7pm Mar–mid-Oct, till
4pm mid-Oct–Mar. Duomo:
Mar–mid-Jun and Sep–Oct
10:30am–7:30pm Mon–Sat, till
8pm mid-Jun–Aug, Mar–Oct
1:30–6pm Sun, 10:30am–

6:30pm Mon–Sat, 1:30–5:30pm
Sun Nov–Feb; Museo dell'Opera
del Duomo: 9:30am–7:30pm
Mar–Oct; 10am–5pm Nov–Feb

💶 **Price** Palazzo Pubblico: €16–25,
under-11s free. Torre del
Mangia: €16–32, under-11s
free. Duomo: €12. Duomo and
Museo dell'Opera: €40

👫 **Skipping the queue** Book
ahead for Palazzo Pubblico
(0577 292 614; 50c reduction)
and Duomo (0577 286 300).

🚩 **Guided tours** www.guidesiena.it

👫 **Age range** 5 plus

⏱️ **Allow** At least 1 day

☕ **Café** In the Campo and around

🚻 **Toilets** Via del Casato di Sotto 14

Good family value?
Siena is not cheap if you visit all
the sights, but they are all worth
paying for – or pick and choose,
and enjoy the Campo for free.

Shopping

Shop for delicious Panforte di Siena
at **Antica Drogheria Manganelli**
(*Via di Città 71–73, 53100*); it makes
a lovely gift to take home. **Libreria
Senese** (*Via di Città 94, 53100*) sells
books in English. For marbled paper
and other lovely stationery go to
Il Papiro (*Via di Città 37, 53100*).

Find out more

DIGITAL Italian speakers can look
up Palio statistics and play games at
www.ilpalio.siena.it or find out more
at *www.ilpaliodisiena.eu*.

Next stop...

SAN DOMENICO Visit the church
of San Domenico, which dominates
the west side of the city on Piazza
San Domenico. Begun in 1226, it is
plain from the outside, but a chapel
houses the preserved head of
St Catherine (1347–80) in a gilded
tabernacle. The city's patron saint,
she had her first visions at the age
of 5 and devoted her life to healing
the sick. She is also patron saint of
Italy along with St Francis. The
Santuario e Casa di Santa Caterina
(*Costa di Sant'Antonio; 0577 247
393*) can also be visited.

*Antica Drogheria Manganelli, which
makes and sells its own panforte*

*The large brick church of San Domenico,
repository of St Catherine's head*

KIDS' CORNER

Siena Q&A
1 How many steps lead to the
top of the Torre del Mangia?
2 How does the bell tower tell
the time? Clue: it is not a clock.
3 What shape is the main piazza
in Siena?
4 How many times do the
horse-riders in the Palio race
around the Campo?
5 See how many animals you
can spot on *contrada*
(area) flags in the city.

Answers at the bottom of
the page.

DUMMY RACE
Look out for adults
sucking dummies
after the Palio, if their
contrada has won!
They say it has been
reborn, like a baby.

Bareback horse race
The Palio is one of the craziest
races you will ever see. The
jockeys are mostly from Sardinia
and are considered to be very
tough. There are few rules, with
jockeys whipping each other as
well as their horses, and bribes
openly changing hands. The
race is so fast that
riders often fall
off. A riderless
horse can still
win and make its
followers the happiest people
in town – until next time!

Answers: **1** There are 503 steps. **2** A
sundial. **3** The Piazza del Campo,
Siena's main square, is shaped like a
scallop shell, with nine segments – one
for each member of the medieval
Council of Nine. **4** Three. **5** There are
13: an eagle, a snail, a panther, a
tortoise, an owl, a unicorn, a ram, a
caterpillar, a dragon, a giraffe, a
porcupine, a wolf and a goose.

Delicate Gothic arches in the ruined cloister of the Abbazia di San Galgano

The Lowdown

🌐 **Map reference** 5 C4
Address Abbazia di San Galgano, 53012 Chiusdino; www. sangalgano.org

🚌 **Bus** D4 from Siena. **Car** 35 km (20 miles) southwest of Siena (well signposted)

🕐 **Open** Daily: Mar–Sep 9am–8pm, Oct–Apr 9am–6:30pm

💲 **Price** Free

👫 **Age range** All; 5 plus to appreciate the stories about the saint

⏱ **Allow** Half a day, including springs

🍴 **Eat and drink** *Real meal* Il Palazzetto (*Palazzetto, 53012; 0577 751 160*) serves decent local dishes as well as pizzas. *Family treat* Dai Galli (*Via Massetana 3/5, Loc Ciciano, 53010 Chiusdino; 0577 750 206*) cooks traditional Tuscan food, including a great wild boar stew and home-made ravioli.

🎭 **Festivals** Opera at the abbey (*www. festivalopera.it*): Jun–Aug.

② San Galgano
Abbey in the woods

The ruined Abbazia di San Galgano, surrounded by thick woodland, is one of the most romantic sights in the area. The high walls of the roofless abbey still give a good sense of what the Gothic building must have been like when it was consecrated in 1288, 70 years after French Cistercians started to build it in this remote spot near the tomb of St Galgano in 1218. The monks enjoyed a hundred years of tranquil prayer and prosperity based on the wool trade, before the Black Death, famine and corruption led to the monastery's decline. It was pillaged by the notorious English mercenary Sir John Hawkwood in the late 14th century and by 1397 the abbot was

its sole occupant. Ten minutes' walk uphill is the Romanesque Cappella di Montesiepi, a rotunda built in 1182–5, enclosing St Galgano's tomb and the saint's sword embedded in a stone. In a side chapel there are beautiful frescoes of the saint's life by Sienese painter Ambrogio Lorenzetti.

Letting off steam

The unspoiled **Val di Merse** around the abbey is good for cycling and riding, and the **Petriolo hot springs** on the River Farma are perfect for a relaxing soak in the woods (off the SS 223 Siena-Grosseto road).

③ Radda in Chianti
Wine flasks and stone shields

Chianti is a famous wine-producing region, and both the wine and the rolling, fertile landscapes that support the vines are very popular

with British, Dutch and German visitors and wine-lovers. The wine, traditionally bottled in a rounded *fiasco* (flask) encased in straw, has been produced here since at least the 13th century. By 1716 production was limited to the Lega del Chianti of Radda, Gaiole and Castellina plus Greve, still the heart of the Chianti Classico region. The area gets busy in high summer, but places such as Radda remain pleasant for a wander. The tiny town is centred on the main square, Piazza Ferrucci, with a tall, arcaded Palazzo Comunale encrusted with heraldic stone shields. Opposite is the church of San Niccolò, which has a 16th-century wooden crucifix.

The Lowdown

🌐 **Map reference** 5 D3
Address 53017 Radda in Chianti

🚌 **Bus** 125 from Siena. **Car** 15 km (10 miles) north of Siena

ℹ️ **Visitor information** Piazza del Castello, 53017; 0577 738 494

👫 **Age range** All

⏱ **Allow** 2 hours

🍴 **Eat and drink** *Real meal* Osteria Le Panzanelle (*Loc Lucarelli 29, 53017; closed Mon; 0577 733 511; www.osteria.lepanzanelle.it*) offers a short menu of good Tuscan staples. *Family treat* La Botte di Bacco (*Viale XX Settembre 23, 53017; 0577 739 008; www.ristorantela bottedibacco.it*) is a stone-built, wood-beamed and green-shuttered establishment serving fish, succulent home-made pasta and hearty meat dishes.

🎭 **Festivals** Radda nel Bicchiere (Radda in a Glass, Chianti Classico wine celebration; *www. raddanelbicchiere.com*): Jun. Festa del Perdono (street party with fireworks): last weekend Aug.

Sangiovese grapes, a major component of Chianti wine, near Radda in Chianti

Prices given are for a family of four

Stalls selling spices and honey at the Saturday morning market, Greve in Chianti

Letting off steam

Pick up a map of walks through vineyards and woods, ranging from 25 minutes to 3 hours, from the *enoteca* at **Castello di Volpaia**, a medieval hamlet and winery (*www.volpaia.com*) 2 km (1 mile) from Radda (Loc Volpaia).

④ Greve in Chianti

Explorer's town

Perhaps the prettiest of the Chianti villages, Greve is surrounded on all sides by vineyards. The local wines are much in evidence on the graceful main square, Piazza Matteotti. The square – in fact a triangle – is lined with porticoes and dominated by a statue of Italian explorer Giovanni da Verrazzano, who travelled the coast of North America in 1528 and ended up being eaten by cannibals in Guadeloupe. It is a pleasant place to hole up for a couple of days, taking a peek at the paintings in the church, sampling the wine and tasting the local produce at the

Locally produced plum and apple preserves at Greve in Chianti market

Saturday morning market, where in autumn, chestnuts, truffles and *porcini* mushrooms are piled high. A few stalls sell trinkets that may appeal to kids.

Letting off steam

Run three-legged races around the three-sided piazza, or head west out of Greve and take the lane that leads uphill through vineyards to **Montefioralle** (a steep haul, but it takes under an hour) for a wander round the tight spiral of streets that comprises the medieval village.

The Lowdown

- 🌐 **Map reference** 5 D3
  Address 50022 Greve in Chianti
- 🚌 **Bus** from Florence's Santa Maria Novella station (*www.sitabus.it*).
  Car 42 km (26 miles) north of Siena
- ℹ️ **Visitor information** Piazza Matteotti, Palazzo del Fiorino (1st floor), 50022; 055 854 5271
- 👫 **Age range** All
- 🕐 **Allow** Half a day
- 🍽️ **Eat and drink** *Real meal* Albergo Giovanni da Verrazzano (*Piazza Matteotti 20, 50022; www.ristoranteverrazzano.it*) is a long-established hotel in the heart of town with a restaurant. *Family treat* Enoteca Ristorante Il Gallo Nero (*Via Cesare Battisti 9, 50022; www.enoristorante gallonero.it*) serves local food, with meat cooked on an open wood fire.
- 🎪 **Festivals** Rassegna del Chianti Classico (celebration of local wine): Sep (*www.greve-in-chianti.com*)

⑤ Lucca
Historic walls and a tree-topped tower

Lucca is a little off the beaten track, but it is a joy to explore. Enclosed within a circle of high Renaissance walls, it is well preserved, with remarkable churches and teetering towers. The walls were built in 1504–1645, their defensive purpose still evident from their massive proportions. Historically one of the region's most affluent towns because of its silk trade, Lucca still has a pleasingly self-sufficient air. It can be seen in a day, but it is well worth staying longer to enjoy the laid-back pace.

Lion on the walls of Lucca

Key Sights

Casa di Puccini This is the birthplace of Giacomo Puccini (1858–1924), composer of the operas *Tosca* and *La Bohème*.

San Michele in Foro The extraordinary façade of this church has four tiers of columns decorated with carvings of people and mythological creatures.

Torre delle Ore The oldest tower in Lucca (1390), with a great view of the more famous Torre dei Guinigi, offers a leg-stretching climb to the top.

VIA CALDERIA
VIA SANT'ANDREA
PLAZA SAN MICHELE
VIA FILUNGO
VIA ROMA
VIA SANTA CROCE
VIA SANT'ANASTASIO
VIA BATTISTERO
PIAZZA ANTELMINELLI

Torre dei Guinigi and Anfiteatro Romano

Torre dei Guinigi Lucca's oddest sight is a city landmark: a medieval tower with large holm oaks sprouting from the top.

Via Fillungo This long street features enticing cafés and some beautiful Art Nouveau shop fronts.

San Martino An 11th-century cathedral with an ornate façade and tall campanile houses the marble tomb of Ilaria del Carretto, with a faithful dog at her feet.

The Lowdown

🌐 **Map reference** 5 B2
Address 55100 Lucca. Casa di Pucini: Corte San Lorenzo 8; 0583 359 154. San Martino: Piazza San Martino; 0583 957 068. Torre di Guinigi: Via Sant'Andrea 41; 0583 316 846. Torre delle Ore: Via Filungo; 0583 316 846. San Michele in Foro: Piazza San Michele

🚆 **Train** Regular service from Pisa and Florence to Lucca's station, just outside the walls

ℹ️ **Visitor information** Piazzale Verdi; 0583 583 110; www.comune.lucca.it/turismo

🕐 **Open** Casa di Puccini: Mar–Sep 10am–6pm, Mon–Sun; Oct–Feb 10am–1pm & 3pm –6pm Tue–Sun. San Martino: 9:30am–5:45pm daily (until 6:45pm Sat). Torre dei Guinigi: Nov–Feb 9:30am–4:30pm, Mar and Oct 9:30am–5:30pm, Apr–May 9:30am–6:30pm, Jun–Sep 9:30am–7:30pm daily. Torre delle Ore: same hours as Torre dei Guinigi, but closed Nov–Feb

💰 **Price** Casa di Puccini: €12. San Martino: free, Ilaria tomb €8. Torre dei Guinigi: €12.00. Torre delle Ore: same price, or €20 for both towers.

🚩 **Guided tours** Ask at the tourist office for tours inside the walls.

👫 **Age range** All, but climbing the towers may be a challenge for under 5s.

⏱️ **Allow** At least a day

🎏 **Festivals** Festa di San Paolino (patron saint of Lucca) with a Palio della Balestra (archery competition): 12 Jul

Good family value?
The main sights are inexpensive, the streets are fun to roam and the best sight of all – the walls – is free.

Prices given are for a family of four

Piazza del Mercato, the site of the ancient Roman amphitheatre, Anfiteatro Romano

Letting off steam

The ramparts of the **city walls** provide Lucca's main open space, a wide, shady, 4-km (2-mile) tree-lined circuit with bird's eye views of the streets and houses of the city. Ask at the tourist office about bike hire, or simply walk and play, stopping off at play areas and snack bars.

Eat and drink

Picnic: under €25; Snacks: €25–40 Real meal: €40–80; Family treat: €80 or more (based on a family of four)

PICNIC Il Mercatino *(Via San Paolino 23, 55100; 0583 55261)* is an old-fashioned food shop selling cheese and salami galore – great for making up a sandwich.
SNACKS Antico Caffè di Simo *(Via Fillungo 58, 5100; 0583 496 234, www.caffedisimo.it; closed Mon)* has a period interior and serves great coffees and pastries.
REAL MEAL Rusticanella 2 *(Via San Paolino 32, 55100; 0583 55383)* serves reliably good pizza and pasta dishes and is in a good location.
FAMILY TREAT Cantine Bernardini *(Palazzo Bernardini, Via del Suffragio 7, 55100; 0583 494 336, www.cantinebernardini.com)* has elegant dishes such as duck in orange and steak with black truffle sauce on the menu. The restaurant is located in a brick-vaulted cellar.

The unaltered 19th-century façade of the Antico Caffè di Simo on Via Fillungo

Shopping

Via Fillungo is Lucca's main shopping street for clothes and shoes and will appeal to teenagers, while younger children will find the markets entertaining. Try the **craft market** in Piazza San Giusto (last weekend of the month), which has ceramics and toys, or the Sunday **art market** in Piazzetta dell'Arancio (third weekend of the month).

Find out more

DIGITAL Go to *www.classicsforkids. com* to find out more about Puccini and listen to some of his music.

Mermaid from the elaborately carved façade of San Michele in Foro

Next stop...

MUSEO DEL FUMETTO Lucca's Comic Museum *(www.museo italianodelfumetto.it)* has great exhibitions of graphic art and organizes workshops for children.
ANFITEATRO ROMANO Almost none of the Roman amphitheatre remains; gradually the stone was all stolen, leaving just the arena-shaped Piazza del Mercato of today. This is, however, a fun space for kids to explore, with its medieval houses and intriguing archways.

The Leaning Tower and Duomo in Pisa's Campo dei Miracoli

⑥ Pisa

The teetering tower

Everyone has seen its photo a hundred times, but nothing can prepare for the sheer weirdness of the **Leaning Tower** (Torre Pendente) of Pisa. For the full effect, try climbing it! Work began on the infamous tower in 1173 and, with its shallow foundations on sandy soil, it had begun to lean by the time the third storey was added in 1274. The building work continued until 1350, when the bell chamber at the top was finally completed. At least the tilt allowed Pisan scientist Galileo to conduct his experiments on the velocity of falling objects, but by 1995 it was leaning 5.4 m (17 ft 6 in) off vertical and was dangerously unsafe. Engineering work, finished in 2000, has decreased the lean by 38 cm (14 in).

There is plenty more to see in Pisa's Campo dei Miracoli (Field of Miracles). The tower started life as a campanile for the Duomo, begun in 1064, with its four-tiered façade of creamy colonnades and intricate blind arches. The domed Battistero was begun on Romanesque lines in 1152, and finished a century later in a more ornate Gothic style. The fourth building on the square, the arcaded Camposanto (cemetery) is said to enclose soil brought by Crusaders from the Holy Land.

Letting off steam

If you are not worn out by climbing the tower, there is a grassy space to play and picnic on the **Campo dei Miracoli**.

⑦ Garfagnana

Rugged villages and forested mountains

The mountains of the Garfagnana are ideal for outdoor activities such as walking, horse-riding, lake swimming, climbing, and skiing in winter; they are best explored from the pretty walled town of **Barga**, whose ancient Duomo has a famous 13th-century pulpit. From here, be sure to take a trip to the spa town of **Bagni di Lucca**, where poets Byron and Shelley once bathed. The region also includes the protected **Parco Naturale delle Alpi Apuane**, where the towering peak of Monte Pisanino dominates.

Take cover

West of Barga, the **Grotta del Vento** (*Cave of the Wind; cross the River Serchio to Gallicano and follow signs to Fornovolasco; www. grottadelvento.com; hourly tours*) is great for kids to explore, with beautiful, long stalactites dripping down, deep green pools and echoing chambers. Take a jumper as it is cool inside.

The Lowdown

🌐 **Map reference** 5 B3
Address 56125 Pisa

🚗 **Train** to Pisa from Florence, then bus to the Campo dei Miracoli

ℹ️ **Visitor information** Piazza Arcivescovado 8, 56126; 050 42291; www.pisaturismo.it; open 10am–5pm daily; also a kiosk at the train station

🕐 **Open** Leaning Tower: daily, until 10:30pm Jun–Aug; Duomo and Camposanto: daily; Battistero: Apr–Sep daily

💶 **Price** Leaning Tower: €60–70. Duomo, Battistero and Camposanto: €8–18 for each sight

👫 **Skipping the queue** Visitor numbers are limited; book 15–45 days in advance, online only at www.opapisa.it (€2 booking fee).

👫 **Age range** 8 plus for the Leaning Tower

♿ **Allow** 2 hours

🍴 **Eat and drink** *Snacks* Cassio (*Piazza Cavallotti 14, 56125*) is a handy pizzeria and *tavola calda*. *Family treat* Osteria dei Cavalieri (*Via San Frediano 16, 56125; 050 580 858; www.osteriacavalieri. pisa.it*) offers a modern twist on traditional Tuscan food in an elegant 13th-century building.

🎉 **Festivals** Gioco del Ponte (Game of the Bridge – mock medieval battle): last Sat evening in Jun

The village of Vagli di Sotto on Lago di Vagli in the Parco Naturale delle Alpi Apuane

The Lowdown

🌐 **Map reference** 5 B2
Address 55051 Barga; 55022 Bagni di Lucca

🚗 **Train** from Lucca to Barga, then bus from station. **Car** 36 km (22 miles) from Lucca to Barga

ℹ️ **Visitor information** Piazza Salvo Salvi, Barga, 55051; 0583 72471; www.barganews.com

🚻 **Age range** Something for all ages

⏲️ **Allow** A couple of days or more

🏃 **Activities** Parco Naturale delle Alpi Apuane (Piazza delle Erbe 1, 55032 Castelnuovo Garfagnana; 0583 644 242; www.parks.it) visitor centre has details of activities in the area.

🍴 **Eat and drink** Snacks Ristorante Pizzeria da Vinicio (Ponte a Serraglio, 55022 Bagni di Lucca; 0583 87250, www.ristorantedavinicio.it) bakes thin and delicious pizza in Bagni di Lucca. Real meal Trattoria da Riccardo (Via Guglielmo Marconi 8, 55051 Barga; 0583 722 345; www.trattoriadariccardo.it; closed Tue) offers a simple but dependable menu of Garfagnana specialities.

🎭 **Festivals** Sagra del Pesce e Patate (Fish and Chips Festival) in Barga – descendants of 19th-century Bargan migrants to Scotland celebrate this classic dish: Jul

⑧ Parco di Pinocchio

Home of the wooden puppet

Pinocchio, the famous long-nosed wooden puppet who dreams of being a boy, was created by writer Carlo Lorenzini in 1881. This theme park in Collodi celebrates all things Pinocchio, with paths winding through gardens and a maze inspired by the puppet's adventures. Marionette shows and puppet-making workshops are held. Children can have their faces painted, enjoy stories in the wooden "fairy carriage" and take a trip on a merry-go-round where they are rowed by Venetian gondoliers.

Letting off steam

If there is steam left to vent after exploring the Parco di Pinocchio, head for the **Villa Garzoni**, where

Illustrations from Walt Disney's film version of Pinocchio, Parco di Pinocchio

Pinocchio toys piled high in the shop at the Parco di Pinocchio, Collodi

Pinocchio's author stayed as a child. Its formal terraced gardens come complete with a a bamboo forest and another maze to get lost in, as well as a butterfly house.

The Lowdown

🌐 **Map reference** 5 C2
Address Parco di Pinocchio, Via San Gennaro 3, 51014 Collodi Pescia, Tuscany; 0572 429 342; www.pinocchio.it

🚗 **Train** to Pescia; free bus from station to park. **Car** 15 km (10 miles) from Lucca to Collodi

🕐 **Open** 10am–6:30pm daily

💶 **Price** €38, children aged 3–14 €8; joint ticket to Villa Garzoni: €72, children €16

🚻 **Age range** All ages

⏲️ **Allow** Half a day

♿ **Wheelchair access** Yes

🍴 **Eat and drink** Real meal Osteria del Gambero Rosso (Via San Gennaro 3, 51014 Collodi Pescia; 0572 429 364; www.ristorantegamberorosso.it) is the park's modern restaurant, and serves tasty traditional Tuscan food. It has good children's menus.

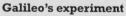

⑨ Montalcino

A fabulous fortress, and wine for the grown-ups

Montalcino has no outstanding art treasures, which has served to keep large numbers of tourists at bay. Even in summer it is easy to get a feel of rural Italian life here. It is at the heart of Brunello di Montalcino wine territory, and the locals are justly proud of their excellent red wines. The hilltop fortress with its outdoor café is well worth exploring, with steep towers and walkways that are a delight for children, while adults may enjoy sitting in one of the town's attractive cafés and watching life go by for a while.

The Fortezza wine shop sign

Key Sights

① **Museo Civico e Diocesano d'Arte Sacra** Just off Piazza Sant'Agostino, this museum features multi-coloured wooden sculptures of the Sienese school.

② **Palazzo Comunale** Montalcino's picturesque 13th-century town hall is decorated with carved coats of arms and features a tall, skinny medieval tower.

③ **Piazza del Popolo** The focal point of Montalcino's social life, featuring the venerable 19th-century Caffè Fiaschetteria Italiana.

④ **Fortezza** This fortress kept Florentines and Spaniards at bay and was the last, symbolic stronghold of medieval freedom. There is an *enoteca* (wine shop) in the grounds.

⑤ **Castello Banfi Estate** Located 15 km (9 miles) from Montalcino in a splendid medieval fortress, the estate offers tours of the hi-tech winery free of charge.

The Lowdown

🌐 **Map reference** 5 D4
Address 53024 Montalcino. Fortezza: Piazzale della Fortezza. Museo Civico: Via Ricasoli 21; *www.museisenesi.it*

🚗 **Train** to Buonconvento (10 km/6 miles away). **Bus** 114 from Buonconvento and Siena. **Car** 40 km (25 miles) south of Siena

ℹ️ **Visitor information** Via Costa del Municipio 1, 53024; 0577 849 331; *www.prolocomontalcino.it*; open 10am–1pm and 2–5:50pm daily in summer

🕐 **Open** Fortezza: Apr–Oct 9am–8pm Tue–Sun, Nov–Mar 9am–6pm Tue–Sun. Museo Civico: 10am–1pm and 2–5:50pm Tue–Sun

💲 **Price** Fortezza: €8–16, children €2. Museo Civico: €9–18, children €3; combined: family €12–24, children €4.50

👫 **Age range** 5 plus

🏃 **Activities** Summer theatre, jazz and medieval jousting in the Fortezza

⏱️ **Allow** Half a day

🎪 **Festivals** Opening of the hunting season: second Sun in Aug. Sagra del Tordo (Festival of the Thrush): last weekend in Oct

Good family value?
For a moderate price, the Fortezza makes a great playground, and the attractions of the Piazza del Popolo are free.

⑥ **Chiesa di Sant'Agostino** This beautiful but simple 13th-century church near the Fortezza has an elegant Romanesque façade.

Letting off steam

The vertiginous, pentagonal 14th-century **Fortezza** (fortress) sits at the top of the town, surveying the surrounding countryside. Stone steps and wooden ladders make it possible to run along the ramparts and climb the turrets, from where there is a bird's eye view of the town and the surrounding countryside. There is an outdoor café within the walls, where adults can enjoy a glass of the famous Brunello or Rosso di Montalcino while the children play.

The warm, cosy interior of the popular pizzeria, Pizza San Giorgio

Eat and drink

Picnic: under €25; Snacks: €25–40; Real meal: €40–80; Family treat: €80 or more (based on a family of four)

PICNIC Petto's Pizza *(Piazza Garibaldi 1, 53024; 0577 847 216)* is great for a thrifty lunch. Pick up a slice of their delicious pizza and some drinks and have an alfresco lunch at the Fortezza.
SNACKS Pizza San Giorgio *(Via San Saloni 10, 53024; 0577 848 507)* bakes a terrific range of pizzas in its oven, as well as some hearty Tuscan specialities.
REAL MEAL Osteria Bassomondo *(Via Basso Mondo, Castelnuovo dell'Abate, 53024; 0577 835 619),* handily placed near Sant'Antimo, serves delicious, plentiful antipastos and main dishes such as fresh pasta with *porcini* mushrooms.
FAMILY TREAT Il Re di Macchia *(Via Soccorso Saloni 21, 53024; 0577 846 116; closed Thu)* is one of Montalcino's best upmarket dining options and definitely worth a visit. Classic Tuscan dishes and handmade pastas are paired with Brunello wines by the friendly and knowledgeable owner, and the great selection of delicious homemade cakes will appeal to both children and adults.

A typical, pretty cobbled backstreet in quiet Montalcino

Shopping

Shopping in Montalcino means pretty much one thing: wine. As well as the superior **Enoteca la Fortezza** *(www.enotecalafortezza.com)* in the fortress, there are excellent wine shops dotted all around the town. **Souvenir shops** in the centre sell attractive painted ceramics, with some child-size bowls and mugs. The Friday market in the town can be fun for children and adults alike.

Find out more

DIGITAL Kids can find out about the ancient history of winemaking, from the Stone Age onwards, at *www.historyforkids.org/learn/food/wine.htm.*

Mythological two-bodied cat beast, one of the carved pillars at Sant'Antimo

Next stop...

SANT'ANTIMO One of the region's best sights, the 12th-century Romanesque abbey church of Sant'Antimo *(www.antimo.it)* is set in a valley 9 km (6 miles) south of Montalcino. Children can look out for the carved mythological beasts, including monsters, dragons and a cat-like creature with two bodies, and listen out for chanting monks.

⑩ Pienza
A perfect Renaissance city

Pienza – once known as Corsignano – was the birthplace of Aeneas Silvius Piccolomini in 1405. Having risen to become Pope Pius II in 1458 and attaining fame as a Humanist philosopher and scholar, the pope decided to remodel his home town and rename it Pienza in his own honour (Pienza comes from Pius). In just three years (1459–62), Florentine architect Bernardo Rossellino had built a brand new cathedral and papal palace set on a perfect Renaissance piazza, but at the pope's death construction stalled, and Pienza is now a small place with incongruously grand buildings. The **Palazzo Piccolomini** has a superb panorama from the loggia and arcaded courtyard at its rear. The **Duomo**, with six altarpieces of the *Madonna and Child* by leading Sienese painters of the day, has suffered from subsidence ever since it was built – look out for the cracks.

Letting off steam
Kids can have a run around the piazza and city walls or, for a slightly longer excursion, walk 1 km (half a mile) to the 11th-century Pieve (parish church) of old **Corsignano**,

Pienza's stout walls encircling a village of surprisingly grand buildings

where Aeneas Silvius was baptized. In contrast to Pienza's Renaissance rationalism, the Romanesque church is carved with symbols of medieval mysticism: mermaids with forked tails, dragons and dancers.

⑪ Monticchiello
High walls and a hilltop village

The intact and still forbidding walls that encircle the picturesque hamlet of Monticchiello attest to its origins, which go back at least as far as the 10th century. Studded with towers and rising to an impressive Rocca (fortress), the walls and the streets within give a strong sense of the medieval past, and are well worth exploring. The keep dates back to 1260, when the place was first fortified against attack from Siena. There is nothing much in the way of sights, but good restaurants makes

Pienza's famous sheep's cheese, Pecorino di Pienza

this atmospheric village an ideal stop-off on the walk from Montepulciano to Pienza (see below).

Letting off steam
The fortified walls of the village are great fun for kids to explore or, further afield, an old cross-country path leads 8 km (5 miles) from the gates of Monticchiello to **Montepulciano** (see p198). Alternatively, take a 6-km (4-mile) walk in the other direction to lunch in **Pienza**. The terrain is fairly easy and passes through lovely farmland, though the distances involved mean this is for older children only; take a picnic of *pecorino* sandwiches.

The Lowdown

🌐 **Map reference** 5 D4
Address 53026 Pienza. Palazzo Piccolomini and Duomo: Piazza Pio II; 0577 286 300/0578 748 502; *www.palazzopiccolominipienza.it*

🚌 **Bus** from Buonconvento (for train station) and Montepulciano

ℹ️ **Visitor information** Corso Rossellino 59, 53026 Pienza; 0578 749 905; *www.pienza.info*

🕐 **Open** Palazzo Piccolomini: Oct–Mar 10am–4:30pm Tue–Sun, Apr–Sep 10am–6:30pm; closed 7–14 Jan and 16–30 Nov

€ **Price** Palazzo Piccolomini: €24, under-5s free

👫 **Age range** All

⏱️ **Allow** 90 minutes

🍴 **Eat and drink** *Picnic* Shops sell local *pecorino* cheese. *Family treat* Ristorante Il Rossellino (*Piazza di Spagna 4, 53026 Pienza; 0578 749 064*) serves Tuscan dishes.

🎭 **Festivals** Pecorino cheese-rolling competition: first Sat & Sun of Sep

The Lowdown

🌐 **Map reference** 5 D4
Address 53026 Monticchiello

🚌 **Bus** Local services are sparse. **Car** or **bike** or are more practical.

ℹ️ **Visitor information** Corso Rossellino 59, 53026 Pienza; 0578 749 905; *www.pienza.info*

👫 **Age range** 8 plus for walks

⏱️ **Allow** 1–3 hours

🍴 **Eat and drink** *Real meal* Osteria La Porta (*Via del Piano 1, Monticchiello, 53026; 0578 755 163; www.osterialaporta.it*) has a great wine list and terrific food. *Family treat* La Taverna di Moranda (*Via di Mezzo 17, Monticchiello, 53020; 0578 755 050; www.tavernadimoranda.it*) includes stuffed pigeon, truffles and game on the menu.

🎭 **Festivals** Teatro Povero (renowned community theatre): Jul–Aug; *www.teatropovero.it*

Farmhouse ringed with cypress trees, Val d'Orcia

⑫ Val d'Orcia
Bathing pools for horses

Val d'Orcia was brought to the world's attention by Anglo-American writer Iris Origo's account of caring for refugee children in the valley in World War II, but has remained a backwater ever since. **San Quirico d'Orcia** is a little-known town that dates back to the Etruscan era. By the Middle Ages it was a stop on the Via Francigena pilgrim route to Rome. The town was endowed with an amazing 12th-century Collegiata (church), with sculpted lions supporting telamons (giant bearded figures). The Horti Leonini gardens were designed in the 15th century as a place for pilgrims to rest.

Known to the Romans, who enjoyed the warm thermal waters, the village of **Bagno Vignoni**

Natural sulphur spring feeding the pools at Bagno Vignoni

(5 km/3 miles away) was another stopping off point for pilgrims, to soothe their aching limbs. Lorenzo il Magnifico (1449–92), the greatest of Florence's ruling Medici family, eased his arthritis in the waters here, and it was the Medici who built the pools in the village – one for men, one for women and one for horses.

Across the valley are the fortified medieval villages of **Castiglione d'Orcia** and **Rocca d'Orcia**.

Letting off steam

Take a dip in the warm sulphur pools at **Bagno Vignoni** to relax tired little legs and for a breather from medieval history (*Piazza del Moretto 12; 0577 887 365; www. termebagnovignoni.it; open May–Oct 8am–1pm Mon–Sat*).

Thermal pool in Bagno Vignoni, built by the Medici family

The Lowdown

- 🌐 **Map reference** 5 D4
  Address 53027 San Quirico d'Orcia. 53027 Bagno Vignoni
- 🚌 **Buses** From Siena to San Quirico and Bagno Vignoni
- ℹ️ **Visitor information** Piazza Chigi 3, 53027 San Quirico d'Orcia; 0577 897 211
- 🚹 **Age range** All
- 🕐 **Allow** A day to explore the villages and thermal pools
- 🍵 **Eat and drink** *Snack* La Bottega di Cacio (*Piazza del Moretto 31, 53027 Bagno Vignoni, 0577 887477*) has cold meats and cheeses, Tuscan style. *Real meal* Trattoria Osenna (*Via Dante Alighieri 42, 53027 San Quirico d'Orcia; 0577 897 541*) serves great local food, with specials such as ravioli in wild boar sauce.
- 🎪 **Festivals** Festa del Barbarossa, Horti Leonini gardens, San Quirico d'Orcia (third weekend in Jun)

⑬ Montepulciano
Handsome hill town

One of Tuscany's highest and most lovely towns, Montepulciano dates back to the 4th century BC, when it was founded by the Etruscans. Today, adults may like to sample Montepulciano's famous Vino Nobile red wines, while the whole family will enjoy wandering around the medieval streets and exploring the town's wonderful mix of historic buildings. On Piazza Grande, the town's highest point, the 13th-century **Palazzo Comunale** is a Gothic town hall with a rusticated Renaissance front. Opposite, the **Duomo** contains a glittering triptych of the *Assumption of the Virgin* painted by Taddeo di Bartolo in 1401. Down the Via di Gracciano nel Corso is Palazzo Bucelli; built in 1648, its façade is studded with Etruscan carvings and cinerary urns.

Just outside the town, a steep walk downhill (and back up) leads to the splendid domed Santuario della Madonna di San Biagio, a classic example of Renaissance architecture known as the Tempio, built by Antonio da Sangallo il Vecchio between 1518 and 1580.

The Lowdown

- 🌐 **Map reference** 5 D4
  Address 53045 Montepulciano. Palazzo Comunale: Piazza Grand 1
- 🚌 **Bus** from Siena
- ℹ️ **Visitor information** Piazza Don Minzoni 1, 53045; 0578 757 341; www.prolocomontepulciano.it
- 🕐 **Open** Palazzo Comunale: Apr–Nov 10am–6pm daily; Duomo: 8:30am–1pm & 3–7pm daily
- 👫 **Age range** All for medieval streets, 11 plus for architecture
- ⏱ **Allow** 1 hour; more if wine-tasting is on the schedule
- 🍵 **Eat and drink** *Snacks* Caffè Poliziano (*Via Voltaia del Corso 27, 53045; 0578 758 615; www. caffepoliziano.it*) is a stylish Art Nouveau café – a lovely place for coffee and snacks. *Real meal* Gambe di Gatto (*Via dell'Opio nel Corso 3, 53045; 0578 757 431*) is run by a welcoming husband-and-wife team; one of the specialities is *tonno di Chianti*, a slow-cooked pork dish.
- 🎉 **Festivals** Bravío delle Botte (barrel-rolling race): last Sun in Aug

Campiglio d'Orcia, a small village clinging to the slopes of Monte Amiata

Letting off steam

Piazza Grande is a dramatic space to let off steam: run around the fountain, looking out for the lions and griffins that decorate it and, if the tall tower of the Palazzo Comunale is open, run up the stairs to look at the view: it is sometimes possible to see all the way to Siena.

⑭ Monte Amiata
Go wild in the chestnut groves

A volcanic mountain soaring to a height of 1,732 m (5,682 ft) Amiata, though long extinct, continues to supply hot thermal water to a number of springs. Its upper slopes are rich with chestnut, beech and, higher up, fir forests, with vineyards and olive groves on the lower slopes. A marked trail circles the mountain and it is possible to hike to its peak and even ski in winter.

The Lowdown

- 🌐 **Map reference** 5 D5
  Address 58037 Monte Amiata
- 🚌 **Bus** from Siena and Montalcino and between mountain villages
- ℹ️ **Visitor information** Via Adua 25, 53021 Abbadia S Salvatore; 0577 775 811; www.amiataturismo.it
- 👫 **Age range** All, from short walks in the woods for under-5s, to sturdier hikes for ages 8 plu
- 🏃 **Activities** Walking, cycling, horse-riding and swimming
- ⏱ **Allow** At least 1 day
- 🍵 **Eat and drink** *Snacks* Corsini Biscotti (*Via Marconi 2, 58033 Castel del Piano*), established in 1921, bakes mouthwatering pine-nut cakes, *panettone* and almond pastries. *Real meal* Al Barilotto (*Via Carolina 24, 58037 Santa Fiora; 0564 977 089; www. ristoranteilbarilotto.it*) serves traditional Tuscan food, with fabulous mushroom and truffle dishes in autumn.
- 🎉 **Festivals** Fiaccole della Notte di Natale, Abbadia San Salvatore (torchlit procession): Christmas Eve

The mountain is ringed by a host of attractive villages including little **Santa Fiora**, **Campiglio d'Orcia**, **Abbadia San Salvatore** – with a plain Romanesque abbey church and a perfect medieval centre – and **Arcidosso**, where Davide Lazzaretti, a millenarian prophet, campaigned for rural socialism before being gunned down by the Carabinieri in 1878. Every autumn these little places all host festivals celebrating the mountain's bounty of chestnuts, *porcini* mushrooms and truffles.

The attractive hill town of Montepulciano surrounded by Vino Nobile vineyards

Frescos showing the life of St Benedict in the Abbazia di Monte Oliveto Maggiore

Letting off steam

Either walking or cycling on Monte Amiata is a great way to explore, with the dense tree cover providing shade. The 29-km (18-mile) **Anello dell'Amiata** route circles the volcanic cone at around 1,100 m (3,600 ft) and is less challenging than the ascent to the summit. The mountain villages offer bike hire and a bus shuttles to the peak in summer. Horse-riding is an option, at the **Centro Equestre Ambasciador** near Arcidosso *(Loc Aiola, 58031; 339 183 6923; www. cavalloamiata.it)*, with treks for all the family. **Castel del Piano** has a swimming pool, and there is a thermal pool at **Bagni San Filippo** *(Via San Filippo 23, 53023; 0577 872 982; www.termesanfilippo.com; open 8:30am–7pm Wed–Mon, until 4:30pm Tue; €40; reduced rate after 3pm)*.

⑮ Monte Oliveto Maggiore

Abbey hidden in the woods

Hidden by tall cypresses, pines and oak trees, the Abbazia di Monte Oliveto Maggiore looks out over eroded chalk cliffs known as the Crete Senesi. It was built back in 1313 by Sienese merchants seeking a simpler life, who founded the Olivetan monastic order. The church has beautiful choir stalls made of inlaid wood and 36 frescoes in the cloister showing the life of St Benedict, by Luca Signorelli (1497) and Il Sodoma (1505) – look for St Benedict fixing a broken sieve.

Letting off steam

Walk through the woods to **Blessed Bernard's grotto** – not in fact a cave, but a chapel built on the spot where Giovanni Tolomei, one of the monastery's founders, gave it all up and lived a holy life as a hermit, changing his name to Bernardo after saintly Bernard of Clairvaux. He was himself made a saint in 2009.

The Lowdown

🌐 **Map reference** 5 D4
Address Monte Oliveto Maggiore, 53041 Loc Chiusure Asciano; *www. monteolivetomaggiore.it*

🚗 **Train** to Buonconvento, then taxi *(Lorenzetti: 0577 806 094)*; or to Asciano, then taxi *(Cassioli: 0577 718 273)*

ℹ️ **Visitor information** Corso Matteotti 18, 53041 Asciano; 0577 719 510

🕐 **Open** 9:15am–noon and 3:15–5pm daily, May–Sep closes 6pm

🚩 **Guided tours** 0577 718 567 to arrange a tour in English

👫 **Age range** Hold the interest of children aged 8 plus with stories from St Benedict's life and animal-spotting.

⏱️ **Allow** 1 hour

🍽️ **Eat and drink** *Snacks* La Torre *(by the gatehouse to the abbey; 0577 707 022; closed Tue)* is a decent café-restaurant serving Tuscan food, with good *antipasti* and *pecorino* cheese. *Real meal* Locanda d'Aceto *(Corso Matteotti 126, 53041 Asciano; 0577 719 220)*, a bright and friendly place in the nearest town, serves soup, pasta, grilled meats and chocolate lava cake.

16 San Gimignano
Medieval skyscrapers

From afar, San Gimignano looks like an old town from a Renaissance painting: a circle of 13th-century walls enclosing tall, teetering stone towers. This lovely sight would have been especially welcome for pilgrims on their way from northern Europe to Rome on the Via Francigena, who provided the town with much of its wealth. The medieval towers, built in a competitive surge, once numbered 72, but only 15 remain. The town is traffic-free and very popular with visitors.

Medieval iron hook on a wall

Key Sights

Palazzo del Popolo

Collegiata

Museo d'Arte Sacra

PIAZZA DEL DUOMO

PIAZZA DELLA CISTERNA

VIA SAN GIOVANNI

Palazzo del Popolo Still the town hall, it was begun in1288 and expanded in 1323; its Torre Grossa is the tallest tower in town at 54 m (177 ft).

Piazza della Cisterna Ringed by historic buildings, San Gimignano's second square is named for the impressive well at its centre.

Piazza del Duomo A spacious square in the heart of town, overlooked by the Duomo.

Palazzo Vecchio This palace has the town's oldest tower. Built in 1239, it set the rules for how high towers should be.

Museo Civico The gallery in the Palazzo del Popolo has a tranquil *Life of St Gimignano* by Taddeo di Bartolo.

Museo d'Arte Sacra This museum displays 14th-century painted wooden sculptures and Sienese paintings.

Via San Giovanni The main street is lined with shops selling olive oil, wine, salami and pretty ceramics.

Collegiata An 11th-century church with a fresco of the *Creation* by Bartolo di Fredi.

The Lowdown

🌐 **Map reference** 5 C3
Address 53037 San Gimignano. Museo Civico: Piazza Duomo. Museo d'Arte Sacra: Piazza Pecori. Collegiata: Piazza Duomo

🚗 **Train** to Poggibonsi, then bus (www.trenitalia.it). **Bus** from Siena and Certaldo, or Florence via Poggibonsi (www.trainspa.it); shuttle from the car park at Porta San Giovanni to centre

ℹ️ **Visitor information** Piazza del Duomo 1; 0577 940008; www.sangimignano.com

🕐 **Open** Museo Civico and Torre Grossa: daily Mar–Oct 9:30am–

7pm, Nov–Feb 10am–5:30pm. Museo d'Arte Sacra: Apr–Oct 9:30am–7:10pm Mon–Fri, 9:30am–5:10pm Sat, 12:30pm–5:10pm Sun, Nov–Mar 9:30am–4:40pm Mon–Sat, 12:30pm–4:40pm Sun. Collegiata: Apr–Oct 10am–7pm Mon–Fri, 10am–5pm Sat, 12:30pm–4:30pm Sun, Nov–Mar 10am–4:30pm Mon–Sat, 12:30pm–4:30pm Sun.

💶 **Price** Museo Civico and Torre Grossa (combined ticket): €20–30; Museo d'Arte Sacra: €20–30; Collegiata: €14–24

👫 **Skipping the queue** To avoid the crowds, start early in the day or visit in the late afternoon.

👫 **Age range** Children aged 5 plus will relish the steep streets, high walls, deep wells and intriguing alleyys, 11 plus the museums.

⏱️ **Allow** At least 3 hours

🚻 **Toilets** Behind the Palazzo Comunale in the Piazza Duomo

Good family value?
San Gimignano is a sight in itself; it makes a good day out without even visiting the paying attractions, but beware the cafés and shops!

Benches offering respite for weary legs outside the battlemented Rocca

Letting off steam
Uphill from the Piazza del Duomo, leaving the crowds behind, is the 14th-century **Rocca** (fortress). Within its battlemented walls are olive and fig trees, room to run around and picnic, and a great vantage point over the surrounding vineyards.

Eat and drink
Picnic: under €25; Snacks: €25–40; Real meal: €40–80; Family treat: €80 or more (based on a family of four)

PICNIC Pasticceria Lucia e Maria *(Via San Matteo 55; 0577 940 379)* is a little shop selling traditional pastries, *cantucci* biscuits and almond cake. The Rocca is a good location for a picnic.
SNACKS Gelateria di Piazza *(Piazza della Cisterna 4; www. gelateriadipiazza.com)* is a world champion *gelateria*. Tastebuds are tempted with flavours such as sparkling wine and pink grapefruit, blackberry and lavender and raspberry and rosemary.
REAL MEAL Il Trovatore *(Viale dei Fossi 17; 0577 942 240)* offers up great pizza, plus steak and other

Queues at Gelateria di Piazza, a world-champion ice-cream maker

more substantial dishes, all served by friendly waiters.
FAMILY TREAT Dulcisinfundo *(Vicolo degli Innocenti; 0577 941 919, www.dulcisinfundo.net)* prepares dishes such as home-made *gnocchi*, meatballs in tomato sauce with saffron potato puree, and pasta with a leek and mushroom sauce, in a nicely traditional setting.

Shopping
Very much geared to visitors, San Gimignano has lots of souvenir shops selling painted ceramics and knick-knacks. Its many delis sell olive oil, salami, the local wine – a white called Vernaccia – and saffron, a local speciality. Try one of the city's oldest delis, the **Antica Latteria** *(Via San Matteo 19)*.

Find out more
DIGITAL To find out more about medieval towers in Italy, visit *goeurope.about.com/od/italy/a/medieval_towers.htm*.

Torre dei Cugnanesi and view of Via San Giovanni from the Torre Grossa

Next stop...
MORE THINGS MEDIEVAL · Visit **San Gimignano 1300 Museum** *(www.sangimignano 1300.com)*, which brings the medieval town to life with a ceramic scale model of the city as it was, made by San Gimignanesi artisans and historians. For an excursion further afield, head 8 km (5 miles) southwest of San Gimignano to the ancient town of **Borgo di Castelvecchio** to see the remains of a 13th-century keep, a church, two mills and some houses, as well as the high encircling walls of this hamlet, which was abandoned at the beginning of the 17th century.

⑰ Volterra
Truly ancient clifftop city

Volterra is perhaps the most dramatic and unusual city in the region. Founded by the Etruscans in the 8th century BC, it is perched on a high plateau of volcanic rock and surrounded by medieval walls, some of which date back 2,400 years. The city's great antiquity is reflected in the **Museo Etrusco Guarnacci**, which is full of Etruscan artefacts, including a mysterious elongated human figure made of bronze, dating from around the 3rd century BC. Known as the "shadow of the evening", it was found by a farmer and used as a poker for the fire until someone realized its importance. Look out too for the alabaster cinerary urns with reclining portraits of the dead carved out of the soft, white stone, one portraying an unhappy-looking husband and wife. The streets of the town are still lined with alabaster workshops, as well as an Etruscan arch adorned with 6th-century BC carved stone heads, and a 13th-century Duomo.

Letting off steam

Children will love running up and down the rows of stone seats and playing hide and seek behind the columns of Volterra's 1st-century BC **Roman theatre**. Just outside the walls, it is still an impressive sight, with a two-tiered stage and tall columns made from Carrara marble. Baths were added in the 4th century AD, but in the Middle Ages it was used as a rubbish tip. It survived, hidden but intact, until the 1950s, when it was excavated.

The Lowdown

- 🌐 **Map reference** 5 C3
  Address 56048 Volterra
- 🚌 **Bus** from Florence or Siena to Poggibonsi or Colle Val d'Elsa (www.sitabus.it), then local bus (www.cpt.pisa.it); **car** is easier.
- ℹ️ **Visitor information** Piazza dei Priori 20; 0588 87257; www.volterratur.it; www.comune.volterra.pi.it
- 🕐 **Open** Museo Etrusco Guarnacci: mid-Mar–Nov daily 9am–7pm; Nov–mid-Mar daily 9am–1:30pm
- 💶 **Price** Museo Etrusco Guarnacci: €32–42
- 👫 **Age range** 5 plus
- ⏱️ **Allow** 2 hours
- 🍴 **Eat and drink** *Real meal* L'Antica Taverna (Via Sarti 18; 0588 87058; www.anticataverna volterra.it) offers full-blown meals, but is equally good for a quick pizza. *Family treat* La Vecchia Lira (Via Matteotti 19; 0588 86180; www.vecchialira.com) has self-service *tavola calda* for lunch and a cosy restaurant in the evening, with a good menu of fish, wild boar and steaks.
- 🎭 **Festivals** Medieval festival: mid-Aug for two weeks.

Hazy view from the hill town of Volterra over the surrounding plain

among them **Palazzo dei Priori**, decorated with *sgraffito* designs etched into the plaster. It houses the **Museo Civico**, with displays of Sienese painting and Etruscan pottery. The town is the birthplace of Arnolfo di Cambio, architect of Palazzo Vecchio in Florence.

Letting off steam

Children can stage their own siege of the **Porta Nuova**, a 15th-century fortress gate, with two big, round towers designed to repel attack from the Volterra road. To reach this dramatic model of defensive architecture, walk from the oldest part of town, Castello, across a

⑱ Colle di Val d'Elsa
A tale of two cities

Colle di Val d'Elsa is divided between a long, narrow old town, strung out along a ridge, and the more modern lower town below, filled with shops selling local crystalware. The upper town is lined with medieval-Renaissance palaces,

The Lowdown

- 🌐 **Map reference** 5 C3
  Address 53034 Colle di Val d'Elsa. Museo Civico: Via del Castello, 33
- 🚌 **Buses** from Siena and Florence (www.trainspa.it); **Train** to Poggibonsi, then local bus
- ℹ️ **Visitor information** Via Campana 43; 0577 922 791; www.collevaldelsa.net
- 🕐 **Open** Museo Civico: Apr–Oct 10am–noon and 4–7pm Tue–Sun; Nov–Mar 10am–noon and 3:30–6:30pm Sat and Sun
- 💶 **Price** Museo Civico: €12–22
- 👫 **Age range** 5 plus to wander the old streets and stage an attack on the Porta Nuova
- ⏱️ **Allow** 2 hours
- 🍴 **Eat and drink** *Real meal* Molino il Moro (Via della Ruota 2; 0577 920 862; www.molinoilmoro.it), set in an old stone mill in the lower town, dishes up good, seasonal standards. *Family treat* Arnolfo (Via XX Settembre 50; 0577 920 549; www.arnolfo.com) serves stylish Michelin-starred dishes in a 16th-century townhouse.

The medieval hill town of Volterra, one of Italy's oldest Etruscan settlements

narrow bridge and out through the elegant arched gateway of the Palazzo di Campana to the Borgo.

The high walls of the fortified village of Monteriggioni

⑲ Monteriggioni
Italy's prettiest village?

The striking high walls and towers of Monteriggioni make quite an impact on everyone who approaches. In the *Inferno*, Tuscan poet Dante Alighieri compares the "ring-shaped citadel… crowned with towers", to giants towering over an abyss. But there is nothing infernal about the fortified village today. It has a relaxed atmosphere, and its main square is a lovely spot to have something to eat before wandering around the walls, the Romanesque church of Santa Maria Assunta and craft shops. A venerable old town, it was built by the Sienese in 1213 as a defence against Florence, who repeatedly attacked but never breached the walls.

Letting off steam

The high and dramatic **walkway** around the remarkably intact ring of curtain walls, punctuated by 14 defensive towers and with two gateways (accessed via the tourist office on Piazza Roma), is the perfect place to let off steam: children with vivid imaginations can pretend to be medieval knights and defend the Sienese town from Florentine attackers.

The Lowdown

🌐 **Map reference** 5 C4
Address 53035 Monteriggioni

🚗 **Bus** from Siena on the San Gimignano route (www.trainspa.it)

ℹ️ **Visitor information** Piazza Roma 23; 0577 304 834; www.monteriggioniturismo.it

🕐 **Open** Walkway: Nov–Mar 10am–1:30pm and 2–4pm; Apr–Sep 9:30am–1:30pm and 2–7:30pm; Oct 9:30am–1:30pm and 2–6pm

🚹 **Age range** 5 plus

⏱️ **Allow** 2 hours

🍽️ **Eat and drink** *Snacks* The café at the top end of Piazza Roma, at the entrance to the village, makes fresh *panini* to eat on the square. *Real meal* Ristorante Il Pozzo (*Piazza Roma 2; 0577 304 127, www.ilpozzo. net*), by the well on Piazza Roma, dishes up bean soup, ravioli with truffles, stuffed pigeon, steak and rabbit.

🎪 **Festivals** Festa Medievale (medieval pageantry and food); first weekend of July

The upper town of Colle di Val d'Elsa overlooks the modern town below

⑳ Arezzo: Legend of the True Cross
Battle scenes and jousting

Affluent Arezzo is a centre for goldsmithery, but what brings visitors here in droves is one of Italy's greatest fresco cycles, Piero della Francesca's *Legend of the True Cross* (1452–66). Based on stories from medieval bestseller *The Golden Legend*, the cycle tells the tale of the cross that Christ was crucified on, the True Cross, in 12 episodes. The paintings, in the 13th-century church of San Francesco, combine perfect perspective with robust realism, vivid figures and lively battle scenes. In the town outside, narrow medieval lanes open out onto spacious Piazza Grande, the setting for an annual joust.

Buildings with coats of arms in Piazza Grande

Key Features

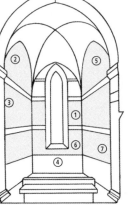

① **Raising the Cross**
Three men struggle to raise the heavy plank to bury it in the ground, on the orders of King Solomon, who has been told by the Queen of Sheba that the wood will be used to crucify the greatest king in the world.

② **Exaltation of the Cross**
Barefoot, hatless King Heraclius carries the cross to Jerusalem. The Oriental noblemen wear big hats of a type much admired by Piero's contemporaries.

③ **Discovery of the Cross**
Empress Helena, along with court ladies and a dwarf, watches as the True Cross is dug up. On the hilltop, Jerusalem looks like 15th-century Arezzo.

The Battle ⑦
The battle scene is full of horses' legs, colourful flags and pointing lances. Constantine (on a white horse behind the man in armour) goes into battle holding the cross.

④ **The True Cross** At the centre is a large image of Christ on the cross.

⑤ **The Death of Adam**
Adam and Eve are shown in old age. Their son Seth plants the seed of the Tree of Good and Evil (the True Cross), in his father's mouth.

⑥ **Constantine's Dream**
Emperor Constantine sleeps in a guarded tent the night before he goes into battle against Maxentius at Ponte Milvio. An angel appears to him in a dream and tells him to fight under the sign of the cross, presaging the conversion of Rome to Christianity.

The Lowdown

 Map reference 6 E3
Address San Francesco, Piazza San Francesco, 52100 Arezzo; 0575 20630; www.pierodellafrancesca.it

Train from Florence and Rome

i **Visitor information** Palazzo Comunale, Piazza della Libertà 1; 0575 401 945; www.turismo.provincia.arezzo.it

Open San Francesco and Casa Museo Vasari: 9am–6:30pm

Mon–Fri, 9am–3:30pm Sat, 1–5:30pm Sun

Price San Francesco: €16–26. Casa Museo Vasari: €4–14; EU under-18s free; combined ticket €24–38

Skipping the queue Visits to San Francesco are limited to 30 minutes and only 25 people are allowed into the chapel at a time; booking obligatory, online or by calling 0575 352 727.

Guided tours Audio tours to San Francesco can be picked up at the ticket office.

Age range The subject matter of Piero's painting is more accessible than that of many Renaissance artists, and children aged 8 plus may find the battle scenes, rearing horses and Renaissance fashions interesting.

Allow Half a day to see the frescoes and explore Arezzo

Shady avenues of the Passeggio del Prato park, an ideal picnic spot

Letting off steam

The **Passeggio del Prato**, a large open space at the top of town (a 20-minute walk from San Francesco) is perfect for ball games and picnics. At its centre is a Fascist-era monument to 14th-century scholar and poet Petrarch, whose birthplace is just outside the park entrance. Nearby, explore the ramparts of the **Fortezza Medicea**.

Eat and drink

Picnic: under €25; Snacks: €25–40; Real meal: €40–80; Family treat: €80 or more (based on a family of four)

PICNIC Antica Bottega Toscana *(Corso Italia 24; www. anticabottegatoscana.it)* is a picturesque deli crammed with ham, salami and cheese. They will make up sandwiches and also sell *panforte* and other sweets.
SNACKS Bar Caffè Vasari *(Piazza Grande 16; 0575 21945)* on the main square is a good option for a coffee, drink or snack.
REAL MEAL La Buca di San Francesco *(Via San Francesco 1; 0575 23 271)* has an attractive vaulted interior, charming service and Tuscan specialities.
FAMILY TREAT Le Chiavi d'Oro *(Via San Francesco 7, 52100; 0575 403 313, www.ristorantelechiavidoro.it; closed Mon)* is family-run and has

modern, stylish décor and food that both looks and tastes great, using local and seasonal ingredients. There is an English and Italian menu.

Shopping

Arezzo is a great place to buy gold jewellery, and antiques at the **antiques fair** held in Piazza Grande on the first Saturday and Sunday of the month. There is not much to buy with pocket money, but the stalls selling elaborate furniture, old prints, antique dolls and pretty crockery are fun to browse.

Traditional Tuscan food for sale at the Antica Bottega Toscana

Find out more

DIGITAL Little is known about the life of Piero della Francesca, who lived from around 1420 to 1492, but *www.artchive.com/artchive/P/piero. html* has a brief biography. The website *www.pierodellafrancesca.it* has educational games for children inspired by the frescoes.

Next stop...

AREZZO ATTRACTIONS The lovely old church of **Pieve di Santa Maria**, which backs onto Piazza Grande, dates back to the 12th century and features a Romanesque façade with carvings depicting the months of the year. Built in 1540, **Casa Vasari** (Via Ricasoli, 1), the home of famous Renaissance biographer, artist and architect Giorgio Vasari (1511–74), is richly decorated with his own frescoes and paintings.

Stalls at Arezzo's monthly antiques market in arcaded Piazza Grande

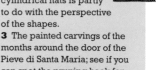

Good family value?
Piero della Francesca's frescoes are well worth the cost of entry, and there are no other costly attractions in Arezzo.

KIDS' CORNER

Look out for...

1 The battle flags in Piero's frescoes: the imperial eagle of Constantine, the venomous basilisk of Maxentius and the standards of Islam, with Moorish figures and crescent moons.
2 The hats of the Oriental noblemen in Piero's fresco of the Exaltation of the Cross; Piero's interest in these cylindrical hats is partly to do with the perspective of the shapes.
3 The painted carvings of the months around the door of the Pieve di Santa Maria; see if you can spot the pruning hook for February, flowers in bloom for April, vegetables being pulled up in November and a pig being slaughtered in December.
4 Vasari's frescoed self-portrait in his house: he is the bearded man in an oval painted frame.

FLY ON THE WALL

Most of what we know about Renaissance artists comes from Vasari's *Lives of the Most Excellent Painters, Sculptors and Architects*. Vasari mixed fact with gossip and good stories: he wrote that Giotto painted a fly that was so realistic his master Cimabue tried to swat it.

Jousting in Arezzo

Arezzo's Piazza Grande is the setting for one of Italy's most spectacular festivals, the Giostra del Saracino (Saracen's Joust; *www.giostradelsaracino.arezzo. it*), held on the first Sunday in September. Flags are unfurled from the windows, feasts are held in the streets and locals dress in medieval clothes. The main event is a jousting competition, where brave knights in armour on horseback score points by whacking an effigy of a Saracen king.

㉑ Cortona

An Etruscan chandelier, angelic and Futurist paintings

Roman poet Virgil claimed Cortona was "the mother of Troy and the grandmother of Rome", founded by the Greek mythological figure Dardanus, who later founded Troy (legend has it the Trojans went on to found Rome). Cortona is certainly as old as the Etruscans, who were here in 700 BC; Etruscan stonework can be seen in the walls of the steep, cobbled hill town. An Etruscan chandelier is on display at the **Museo dell'Accademia Etrusca**, alongside paintings by Futurist Gino Severini (1883–1966), who was born here. In the main square is the medieval Palazzo Comunale (town hall); narrow lanes lead off, inviting exploration. Walk along Via Ghibellini and Via Guelfi to get an idea of life in the town when it was ruled by the back-stabbing Casali family in the Middle Ages. Stop at the **Museo Diocesano** to see a *Deposition* by Luca Signorelli (1445–1523), a famous son of the town, and a glowing *Annunciation* (1430) by Florentine Fra Angelico.

Letting off steam

A good spot to run around and picnic with a view is the **Fortezza Medicea**, built by the Medicis after King Ladislaus of Naples captured Cortona and sold it to Florence in 1409. It is a stiff 30-minute walk up.

The town of Cortona looking out over the Val di Chiana

Enjoying coffee at a pavement café table in front of Cortona's Palazzo Comunale

Prices given are for a family of four

The Lowdown

- 🌐 **Map reference** 6 E4
  Address 52044 Cortona. Museo dell'Accademia Etrusca: Piazza Signorelli, 9, 52044, *www.cortonamaec.org*. Museo Diocesano: Piazza del Duomo 1, 52044; 0575 637 235

- 🚗 **Train** from Florence and Rome, then bus from station to centre (6 km/4 miles)

- ℹ️ **Visitor information** Palazzo Casali, Piazza Signorelli 9, 52044; 0575 637 223; www.turismo.provincia.arezzo.it

- 🕐 **Open** Museo dell'Accademia Etrusca and Museo Diocesano: daily Apr–Oct, Tue–Sun Nov–Mar

- 💰 **Price** Museo dell'Accademia Etrusca and Museo Diocesano: €14–22

- 👪 **Age range** Any for town, 8 plus for art and artifacts

- ⏱️ **Allow** Half a day

- 🍴 **Eat and drink** *Snacks* Pizzeria Fufluns (Via Ghibellina 3, 52044; 0575 604 140, www.fuflunssnc.it) dishes up pizza in a central location. *Real meal* Locanda al Pozzo Antico (Via Ghini 12, 52044; 0575 62091) is housed in a converted medieval building.

- 🎪 **Festivals** Giostra dell'Archidado (crossbow competition): May–Jun.

㉒ Monterchi

Pregnant Madonna

The pretty little hill hamlet of Monterchi has one big attraction: the *Madonna del Parto* (1460) by Piero della Francesca, a fresco of the pregnant Virgin Mary. Much has been written about her serene, melancholy expression: some people think her downcast eyes reflect knowledge of Christ's fate, but it is possible that she is a realistic portrayal of a weary mother-to-be. The mood is lightened by the symmetrical angels, who hold back the flaps of a tent to reveal the Madonna, the awning decorated with pomegranates to symbolize Christ's passion. Aside from the painting, Monterchi is a sleepy place, where it is pleasant to lunch outside on the leafy main square.

Letting off steam

Head for the sunflower fields of rustic **Toppole**, a 20-minute drive west of Monterchi and surrounded by marked paths, for a picnic.

The Lowdown

- 🌐 **Map reference** 6 E3
  Address 52035 Monterchi. Museo della Madonna del Parto: Via della Reglia 1, 52035; 0575 70713

- 🚗 **Car** from Arezzo (30 mins) or Sansepolcro (20 mins)

- 🕐 **Open** Museo della Madonna del Parto: daily

- 💰 **Price** Museo della Madonna del Parto: €14; pregnant women free

- 👪 **Age range** All

- ⏱️ **Allow** 30 minutes

- ♿ **Wheelchair access** Yes

- 🍴 **Eat and drink** *Snacks* An enoteca on the main square serves plates of local salami, ham and olives.

- 🎪 **Festivals** Monterchi Festival of classical music and jazz (www.monterchifestival.it): Jul–Aug

Piero della Francesca's Madonna della Misericordia, *Sansepolcro*

㉓ Sansepolcro

Famous paintings and fantastic restaurants

The smart little town of Sansepolcro was the birthplace of Piero della Francesca, some time around 1420. It is home to one of his most intriguing works, the *Resurrection*, displayed in the impressive **Museo Civico** in the 12th-century Palazzo dei Conservatori, where it was first painted. In the fresco, a solemn Christ bearing a flag arises from his tomb while four armoured Roman soldiers sleep. Also on display here is Piero's polyptych (a painting with many panels) of the *Madonna della Misericordia*, protecting her worshippers under a cape – look for the hooded member of the confraternity that commissioned the painting. Most visitors see little more of the town than this, but the *palazzi* along Via Matteotti, spacious squares and excellent restaurants make it worth stopping awhile.

Letting off steam

The large square, **Piazza Torre di Berta**, near the cathedral, is good for a run around, or make a circuit of the well-preserved **town walls**, never far away from the centre.

The Lowdown

- 🌐 **Map reference** 6 E3
  Address 52037 Sansepolcro. Museo Civico: Via Niccolò Aggiunti 65, 52037, *www.museocivicosansepolcro.it*
- 🚌 **Bus** from Arezzo and Città di Castello (*www.etruriamobilita.it*)
- ℹ️ **Visitor information** 0575 740 536; *www.sansepolcro.net*
- 🕙 **Open** Museo Civico: daily
- 💶 **Price** Museo Civico: €12–18
- 👫 **Age range** 8 plus
- 🕐 **Allow** Half a day
- ♿ **Wheelchair access** Yes
- 🍴 **Eat and drink** *Real meal* Albergo Ristorante da Ventura (*Via Niccolò Aggiunti 30, 52037; 0575 742 560; albergodaventura.it*) serves excellent Tuscan food including *ribollita* (vegetable and bread soup) and handmade pasta with white truffles. *Family treat* Ristorante Fiorentino (*Via Luca Pacioli 60, 52037; 0575 742 033; www.ristorantefiorentino.it*) also serves regional food; leave room for desserts.
- 🎉 **Festivals** Palio della Balestra (crossbow competition with pageantry): second Sun of Sep

The pretty town of Sansepolcro, founded around 1000 AD

Picnic under €25; **Snacks** €25–40; **Real meal** €40–80; **Family treat** €80 or more (based on a family of four)

Anghiari, perched on its hilltop balcony above the Valtiberina

㉔ Anghiari
Bird's eye view of a battle site

Anghiari is a delightfully pretty hill town, with steep, cobbled streets, traditional grocery stores, a weekly food market, and cosy cafés and restaurants. It sits high above the plain where the Battle of Anghiari was fought between the Florentines and the Milanese in 1440. The Florentines won in an almost bloodless battle, putting a stop to the Visconti family's ambitions in Tuscany forever. Leonardo da Vinci picked this dramatic event as his subject for the *Battle of Anghiari* frescoes in Palazzo Vecchio in Florence. The story of both battle and painting is told in the **Museo Statale di Palazzo Taglieschi**, housed in a Renaissance palazzo. Also described is how the fresco of the battle was lost due to a failed experiment with techniques. Luckily it was much copied, so we still have a good idea what it looked like. The museum also has a collection of 14th-century wooden statues, including a *Madonna and Child* by Jacopo della Quercia, and a more modern collection of Madonnas.

Letting off steam

A good-sized playground 15-minutes' walk from the main square at the top of the town has swings and roundabouts, as well as a playing field. Parents can take in the views of Anghiari's rooftops and the valley below over a coffee at the neighbouring café, Bar Cocomero, which specializes in fruit-based dishes and drinks.

Prices given are for a family of four

The Lowdown

- 🌐 **Map reference** 6 E3
  Address 52031 Anghiari; Museo Statale: Piazza Mameli, 16
- 🚌 **Bus** from Arezzo (www. etruriamobilità.it)
- ℹ️ **Visitor information** Via Matteotti 105; 0575 749 279
- 🕐 **Open** Museo Statale: Tue–Sat 8:30am–7pm, Sun 9am–7:30pm
- 💶 **Price** Museo Statale: €4 (children under 18 free)
- 🚻 **Age range** 5 plus
- ⏱️ **Allow** 90 minutes
- 🍴 **Eat and drink** *Real meal* La Pineta (Via Nova, 52031; 0575 788 400), a summer-only pizzeria and restaurant, has a super play area for kids. *Family treat* Da Alighiero (Via Garibaldi 8, 52031; 0575 788 040) serves ribollita (a thick local soup).
- 🎪 **Festivals** Palio della Vittoria (Battle of Anghiari parades): 29 Jun

㉕ La Verna
Mountain-top monastery

The monastery of La Verna sits on a steep and rocky crag in remote hills, surrounded by dense woodland. It is said that St Francis once saw in a vision that the crag had split when Christ died on the Cross. In 1213 the land here was given to the saint by local nobleman Count Orlando, and convention has it that this is where St Francis was marked with the stigmata in 1225; the painful nail wounds from the Crucifixion that appeared on his hands and feet hobbled the saint. The craggy monastery still draws pilgrims, plus visitors eager to see the painted terracotta reliefs by the Della Robbia workshop.

Letting off steam

The thick oak woodland around the monastery is crisscrossed with marked paths, one leading to the summit of **La Penna** and a chapel built on a precipitous rock. The park office at Chiusi della Verna (www. parcoforestecasentinesi.it) has maps.

A fresco by Giotto showing St Francis receiving the stigmata at La Verna

The monastery of La Verna, high in the mountains, still a place of pilgrimage

The arcaded streets of Poppi in the Casentino, pleasantly off the beaten track

The Lowdown
- **Map reference** 6 E3
- **Address** Santuario Francescano, Via del Santuario 45, 52010, Chiusi della Verna; 0575 5341; www.santuariolaverna.org
- **Car** from Arezzo (43 km/26 miles) and Bibbiena (27 km/15 miles)
- **Open** 6:30am–7:30pm daily, until 9:30pm in summer; chapel and museum shorter hours
- **Price** Free
- **Age range** All
- **Allow** Half a day
- **Eat and drink** *Picnic* Bring picnic food from Bibbiena and eat in the woods. *Real meal* La Verna's refectory offers decent meals, or Buca di Michelangelo (Via Roma 51, 52010, Caprese Michelangelo; 0575 793 921; www.bucadimichelangelo.it) serves Tuscan food in a dining room with mountain views, 18km (12 miles) south of La Verna.
- **Festivals** Festa della Stigmate: 17 Sep

26 Poppi
Explore a classic castle
Poppi is one of the most attractive hill towns of the Casentino, as the upper Valdarno is known. It has a remarkably intact medieval layout, with arcaded lanes punctuated by ancient churches, but the town is dominated by the battlemented 13th-century **Castello dei Conti Guidi**, built by the Guidi family who ruled here from 1000 to 1440. Modelled on the Palazzo Vecchio in Florence, its fairy-tale silhouette can be seen from afar, and it has a splendid courtyard and staircase emblazoned with coats of arms. It seems a grand structure for such a small place, but back in 1289 Poppi was at the heart of the action when Guelph-Florence fought Ghibelline Arezzo at the Battle of Campaldino, just outside the town. The events were recorded by young poet Dante Alighieri, fighting on the Guelph side. Florence won and Poppi fell under its control in 1440.

Letting off steam
Kids will love exploring the nooks and crannies, vertiginous staircases, wonky wooden landings and tall bell tower of the Castello dei Conti.

The Lowdown
- **Map reference** 5 D3
- **Address** 52014 Poppi; Castello dei Conti Guidi: 1, Piazza della Repubblica, 52014
- **Train** from Arezzo (hourly)
- **Visitor information** Via Cesare Battisti 13; 0575 529 682
- **Open** Castello dei Conti: daily Apr–Oct, Thu–Sun Nov–Mar
- **Price** Castello dei Conti: €8–16
- **Age range** Any
- **Allow** Half a day
- **Eat and drink** *Real meal* Antica Cantina (Via Lapucci 2; 0575 529 844; www.anticacantina.com) is set in a brick-vaulted wine cellar, and serves dishes such as rabbit stew. *Family treat* Albergo Ristorante Casentino (Piazza della Repubblica 6; 0575 529 090; www.albergocasentino.it) is in a lovely location facing the castle, with a leafy garden where Tuscan classics can be enjoyed.
- **Festivals** Festa del Fungo Porcino: 14–16 Aug

㉗ Pitigliano

Secret tunnels and hidden tombs

Pitigliano is an extraordinary place. Too remote to attract many visitors, the ancient city perches on a volcanic ridge, and is as deep as it is high: the soft tufa rock below was scooped out into chambers and tunnels by the Etruscans. Above ground, its narrow alleys invite exploration, opening onto views of tiled rooftops and verdant landscape. This unusual town is a good base for the Etruscan and medieval settlements of Sovana, Sorano and Saturnia, also famous for its thermal pools.

Water fountain in Pitigliano

Key Sights

① Jewish Ghetto
Pitigliano was known as Little Jerusalem for its thriving Jewish community until 1945. Visit the 1598 synagogue and a kosher butcher and baker.

② Duomo
The Romanesque building was restored in Baroque style, with a stucco façade and two altarpieces by local Rococo painter Francesco Zuccarelli (1702–88).

③ Museo Civico Archeologico
Housed in Palazzo Orsini, this small museum displays red and white geometric-patterned Etruscan vases, many from the nearby necropolis of Poggio Buco.

④ Museo Palazzo Orsini
Built in 1293 and upgraded in the Renaissance, the monumental palazzo houses a museum with displays of paintings, vestments and jewellery.

⑦ Aqueduct
A 16th-century aqueduct runs along the side of the town, crossing Via Cavour. The Palazzo Orsini gets its water supply from here.

⑤ Town Walls and Gates
Porta Sovana is the best preserved of the city's handsome gates, set in its forbiddingly intact walls.

⑥ Underground Tunnels and Caves
Pitigliano's tufa is riddled with tunnels and caves, which can be visited on tours.

Letting off steam

Piazza della Repubblica is a good place to have a run around; it is graced by a pair of fountains, as well as views of distant Monte Amiata and the wooded countryside. Then take a stroll up **Via Roma**, one of three main streets, past hidden arches and alleyways. Alternatively pick up a map and guide from the tourist office to the **Vie Cave**, Etruscan paths carved out of the rock.

Prices given are for a family of four

Fountain in Piazza della Repubblica, an oblong square in the heart of Pitigliano

Eat and drink

Picnic: under €25; Snacks: €25–40; Real meal: €40–80; Family treat: €80 or more (based on a family of four)

PICNIC Panificio del Ghetto (*Via Zuccarelli 66, 58017*) is a good bakery to try *sfratto* ("evicted"), which refers to the Jewish people of the city. The long pastry is filled with honey, nuts, orange and nutmeg.
SNACKS La Magica Torre (*Piazza Petruccioli 73, 58017; 0564 616 260; www.lamagicatorre.com*) is the

The Lowdown

- 🌐 **Map reference** 5 D5
  Address 58017 Pitigliano. Museo Civico Archeologico: Piazza della Fortezza Orsini; 0564 614 067. Museo Palazzo Orsini: Piazza della Fortezza Orsini; 0564 616 074

- 🚗 **Bus** from Siena, Florence and Grosseto (www.ramamobilita.it)

- ℹ️ **Visitor information** Piazza Garibaldi 51, 58017; 0564 617 111; open 9am–1pm and 4–7pm Tue–Sun; Comune di Pitigliano: Piazza Garibaldi 37, 58017; 0564 616 332; www.comune.pitigliano.gr.it

- 🕐 **Open** Museo Civico Archeologico: 10am–1pm, 4–7pm Easter–Nov; 10am–1pm, 3–6pm 26 Dec–6 Jan. Museo Palazzo Orsini 10am–1pm and 3–5pm Tue–Sun, until 7pm Apr–Sep, daily Aug

- 💶 **Price** Museo Civico Archeologico: €5–8; Museo di Palazzo Orsini: €6–12; under-8s free

- 🚩 **Guided tours** Ask at the tourist office for tours of underground Pitigliano and guided walks along the Vie Cave.

- 🚹🚺 **Age range** 5 plus for the unusual layout and dramatic appearance of the city

- ⏱️ **Allow** At least half a day; longer to explore Sorano, Sovana and Saturnia and relax in the thermal springs.

- 🚻 **Toilets** In Palazzo Orsini and café-bars

Good family value?
It is not necessary to visit any of the (not very expensive) paying sights to enjoy Pitigliano, and the Terme di Saturnia are free.

place to enjoy pizza in Pitigliano. Located in a rugged medieval bastion, with a flowery terrace and a vaulted stone interior, it offers pizza *al taglio* to take away home.
REAL MEAL Hostaria del Ceccottino (*Piazza San Gregorio VII 64, 58017; 0564 614 273; www.ceccottino.com*) is a popular restaurant serving excellent *crostini* and pumpkin *ravioli*, all washed down with the local white wine.
FAMILY TREAT Osteria Il Tufo Allegro (*Vicolo della Costituzione 5, 58017; 0564 616 192*) is an elegant, welcoming little restaurant hidden away down an alley; ask the genial staff for a look at their amazing wine cellar, deep below street level.

Find out more
DIGITAL Find out more about the Etruscans at *www.historyforkids.org/learn/romans/art/etruscans.htm* or *rome.mrdonn.org/etruscans.html*.

Osteria Il Tufo Allegro, a subterranean restaurant carved out of tufa

Cascades and pools at the Saturnia thermal spa

Next stop...
MUSEO ARCHEOLOGICO ALL'APERTO (*Via Cava del Gradone, SP127, 58017; 0564 614 067; open daily*). Just outside Pitigliano, this fun open-air museum combines reconstructions with an authentic 7th-century BC Etruscan necropolis.
SORANO (a 15-minute drive north of Pitigliano) tumbles, at times literally, down a steep tufa hillside.
SOVANA (also a 15-minute drive north of Pitigliano) is a perfectly preserved little *borgo*, which has an impressive 10th-century Duomo with an octagonal dome, and an Etruscan necropolis.
SATURNIA (a 30-minute drive north of Pitigliano) claims to be the oldest town in Italy, founded by the god Saturn. Its natural thermal baths, the **Terme di Saturnia**, have been in use since Etruscan times.

KIDS' CORNER

Be an archaeologist
The area around Pitigliano is crisscrossed by an extraordinary network of Etruscan paths hollowed out of the tufa, known as the Vie Cave, about 3 m (10 ft) wide, with walls as high as 20 m (66 ft), and some as long as a kilometre (half a mile), pitted by donkeys' hooves over hundreds of years. In some places trees form an arch over them, creating shady green "tunnels".

Not only are the Vie Cave fun to explore, but you may spot Etruscan tombs along the way. Hewn out of the rock walls, many have been converted into wine cellars and even garages. Pick up a map from the tourist office to help locate the paths and tombs.

GRAFFITI ARTISTS
The ancient walls of the Vie Cave around Pitigliano are scrawled with Etruscan graffiti. See if you can find any examples. Try to guess what they mean – no one is really sure!

Archaeologists *v* tomb raiders
The Etruscans must have been busy, because they produced heaps of exuberantly painted vases, lamps, elaborate jewellery and wall paintings, many of which can now be seen in museums. There are also plenty of tombs throughout the region, which were filled with objects for the dead to enjoy in the afterlife. You would be lucky to find an undiscovered one: most of the tombs have been emptied by archaeologists or by tomb raiders who sell the items on the thriving black market. Visit the fascinating Tomba Ildebranda near Sovana to find out more.

Where to Stay in Tuscany

Tuscan accommodation ranges from hotels and B&Bs to *agriturismi*. The best places are run by genial people who value good food and good company. Kids are welcomed with open arms. The summer period tends to be very busy so booking in advance is recommended.

AGENCY
To Tuscany Villas
www.to-tuscany.com
The most user-friendly of the many Tuscan villa websites has a good selection of properties listed (more than 300 farmhouses, cottages and castles). It specializes in family holidays and villas with private or shared pools.

Arezzo
Map 6 E3

HOTELS
Badia di Pomaio
Località Badia a Pomaio 4, 52100; 0575 371 407; www.hotelbadiadipomaioarezzo.it
Housed in a 17th-century building a 10-minute drive east of Arezzo, this hotel is surrounded by woodland, which guests are free to explore, and has a swimming pool in the grounds, as well as use of tennis courts and a football pitch down the road. There is a natural terrace from which to enjoy the view of the surrounding Tuscan hills and countryside. With traditional decor, the comfortable rooms have excellent facilities, and there are triple rooms for families.
€€

Graziella Patio Hotel
Via Cavour 23, 52100; 0575 401 962; www.hotelpatio.it
This hotel is just a couple of minutes walk away from the Basilica di San Francesco. Rooms are bright and reasonably attractive, with an Oriental theme and four-poster beds, though some are a little cramped. Massages and spa treatments are available.
€€

B&Bs
Antiche Mura
Piaggia di Murello 35, 52100; 0333 271 1628; www.antichemura.info
A sensitively converted mansion with bright rooms, the Antiche Mura is on a quiet street and has medieval walls. It is just a short walk away from the main sights in Arezzo.
€

Poggio del Drago
Map 5 D3
Località Poggio del Drago 18, Ponticino, 52041; 0575 446 372; www.poggiodeldrago.it
This gloriously named ("Dragon's Knoll") and very friendly B&B, 9 km (11 miles) west of Arezzo, is in a converted 19th-century rural stone building. The rooms are attractively decorated, and there is a swimming

The Baalbek suite with Oriental-style decor in the Graziella Patio Hotel, Arezzo

pool plus walking and cycling tracks in the extensive grounds, as well as fishing nearby. There is a suite for families, and children under 3 stay in their parents' room for free.
€

Tarussio
Via Isonzo 41, 52100; 0575 901035; www.bbtarussio.it
Located just west of the city centre, in a whitewashed villa, this B&B has wooden floors and modern bathrooms. One of the rooms is a triple. The welcoming owners will serve breakfast on the terrace.
€

AGRITURISMO
Rendola Riding Agriturismo
Map 5 D3
Rendola 66, Montevarchi, Arezzo, 52025; 055 970 7045, www.rendolariding.it
Riding lessons and tours for kids aged 12 and over are on offer at this organic farm in the Chianti hills. Accommodation is in a 17th-century farmhouse. Nearby trails allow riders to explore farmland, woodland and olive groves. There is a triple room for families.
€

Dining room of the Foresteria, a hostel in a converted convent with frescoes, Arezzo

Casa Cordati, housed in a historic 17th-century palazzo, Barga

HOSTEL
Foresteria
Via Bicchieraia 32, 52100; 0575 370 474, www.foresteriasanpierpiccolo.it
Run by a Protestant organization, Foresteria is housed in the converted convent of the church of San Pier Piccolo, which dates back to 1387. Complete with enchanting faded frescoes and a spacious courtyard, this is a very good bargain option for families in the centre of Arezzo. There is one triple room, as well as some singles and doubles.

€

Barga
Map 5 B2

B&Bs
Casa Fontana
Via di Mezzo 77, 55051; 349 684 2721; www.casa-fontana.com
This 18th-century townhouse consists of six attractive rooms with chestnut beams, whitewashed walls and shutters. There is a triple room, plus a family suite. The wine cellar has been converted into a breakfast room, which opens onto a private walled garden. The hospitable owners are full of advice to help visitors enjoy their stay in Barga.

€

Il Melograno Nano
Via Posta 25, Filecchio, 55051; 0583 171 3486; www.ilmelogranonano.com
Located just outside Barga, this eco-friendly B&B is a good rural option, with a lovely garden setting and an outdoor wood-fired oven. The decor is bright and colourful, and there is a well-priced triple room. The charming hosts make a good organic breakfast. Massage and other treatments are available.

€

SELF-CATERING
Casa Cordati
Via di Mezzo 17, 55051; 0583 723 450; www.casacordati.it
This 17th-century palazzo houses an art gallery showing contemporary art, but also rents out four simple rooms, including a very well-priced apartment with kitchen and living room, and a large room that sleeps four. There is access to a covered roof terrace, and a shady garden with sun loungers.

€

Gaiole in Chianti
Map 5 D3

B&B
Rocca di Castagnoli
53013 Gaiole in Chianti; 0577 731004; www.roccadicastagnoli.it
There are six rooms and seven apartments that can accommodate four to six people on this working vineyard, as well as a swimming pool and a well-equipped kitchen for self-catering. Many of the rooms have beamed ceilings, terracotta floors and wooden or wrought-iron beds.

€€

Greve in Chianti
Map 5 D3

HOTEL
Da Verrazzano
Piazza Matteotti 28, 50022; 055 853 189; www.ristoranteverrazzano.it
Set on the main square, this long-established hotel under the arcades is right in the heart of Greve. There are family rooms with three and four beds. Lunch and dinner can be taken at the excellent hotel restaurant, which also runs courses in Tuscan cooking.

€

Entrance to the Da Verrazzano hotel in the main square in Greve in Chianti

Lucca
Map 5 B2

HOTELS
Albergo San Martino
Via della Dogana 9, 55100; 0583 469 181; www.albergosanmartino.it
Located within the city walls, this small hotel has modern, well-furnished rooms. Near the Duomo, it is perfectly located for sightseeing – with the help of bikes available to rent. There are two suites that can accommodate families, comfortable communal areas and a laundry service.

€€

Alla Corte Degli Angeli
Via degli Angeli 23, 55100; 0583 46920; www.allacortedegliangeli.it
This charming city-centre hotel is near the Piazza Anfiteatro, within walking distance of all the sights. The 10 rooms are named after flowers, and have frescoed walls, preserving the character of the old building. There are bikes to rent and a babysitting service on request.

€€

Hotel Palazzo Alexander
Santa Giustina 48, 55100; 0583 583 571; www.hotelpalazzoalexander.it
This fabulous palazzo dates back to the 12th century and has been beautifully restored to keep its historic feel. The suites and family rooms all have modern bathrooms. Great service is provided and there is an opulent breakfast room.

€€

B&B
Da Elisa alle Sette Arti
Via Elisa 25, 55100; 0583 494 539; www.daelisa.com
Located close to the city walls near a canal, this homely little B&B in a 19th-century apartment building has frescoed ceilings and Art Deco furniture. There are triple rooms and larger family rooms, none of which are en-suite.

€

Price Guide
For a family of four per night in high season, in one or more rooms, inclusive of breakfast, service charges and any additional taxes such as VAT.
€ Under €200 €€ €200–350 €€€ over €350

Residenza Centro Storico
Corte Portici 16, 55100; 0583 490 748; www.inluccabedandbreakfast.com
Set in a great location inside the walls of Lucca, this B&B has very pretty rooms which feature white walls, old wooden furniture, roof beams and lovely fabrics. It has a triple room, a suite for four or five people and a cot for babies. Good breakfasts and a warm welcome.

 €

Il Seminario
Via del Seminario 5, 55100; 0583 954 488; www.luccabedandbreakfast.com
Two B&Bs, Il Seminario I and II, occupy an old palazzo, with nine rooms, and a tearoom with a garden where breakfast is served. Three excellent family rooms have beamed ceilings and terracotta-tiled floors, as well as kitchenettes.

€

HOSTEL
Ostello San Frediano
Via della Cavallerizza 12, 55100; 0583 469 957; www.ostellolucca.it
Lucca's bargain option is housed in a grand converted monastery a short walk away from the amphitheatre and city walls. It has a range of spacious family rooms sleeping three to six people, and roomy communal areas. There are basic meals on offer.

€

Dining room in Ostello San Frediano, a converted monastery, Lucca

Montalcino   Map 5 D4
HOTELS
Il Giglio Hotel and Restaurant
Via Soccorso Saloni 5, 53024; 0577 846 577; www.gigliohotel.com
An intimate, family-run hotel in the heart of Montalcino, Il Giglio has 12 bedrooms. Extra beds can be

added, or there are apartments. The terrace has great views over the countryside, and the restaurant serves good Tuscan food.

€

Hotel dei Capitani
Via Lapini 6, 53024; 0577 847 227; www.deicapitani.it
In a lovely location on the edge of Montalcino, Dei Capitani enjoys panoramic views of the countryside, as well as a large garden with a swimming pool, terrace and breakfast room. The rooms are plainly decorated but comfortable.

€€

Hotel Vecchia Oliviera
Porta Cerbaia, Angolo Via Landi 1, 53024; 0577 846 028; www.vecchiaoliviera.com
Located on the edge of town, Hotel Vecchia Oliviera has a swimming pool fringed with cypress trees and sweeping views from the garden. The hotel is housed in a converted olive oil mill. There is a triple room as well as a more expensive suite.

€€

B&B
Palazzina Cesira
Via Soccorso Saloni 2, 53024; 0577 846 055; www.montalcinoitaly.com
This wonderful home is located in a 13th-century, yellow ochre-coloured palazzo with high arched ceilings and tiled floors. The decor in the rooms is grand if idiosyncratic, and there are mini-suites for families. The lovely hosts make a delicious breakfast and are happy to advise on where to eat nearby.

€

Montepulciano   Map 5 D4
HOTELS
Meuble il Riccio
Via Talosa 21, 53045; 0578 757 713; www.ilriccio.net
A classic family-run Tuscan hotel set in a wonderful palazzo with an arcaded courtyard, Meuble il Riccio has an atmosphere that is more home than hotel. The comfortable rooms include a triple. Enjoy stunning views from the rooftop terrace and breakfasts that include delicious home-made cakes.

 €

Villa Cicolina
Via Provinciale 11, 53045; 0578 758620; www.villacicolina.it
This gorgeous 16th-century villa just north of Montepulciano has been converted into an elegant hotel, with formal gardens and a stunning pool. The rooms and suites have wooden and tiled floors and magnificent beamed ceilings. Two- or three-hour cooking classes are offered, teaching how to make Tuscan dishes.

€€€

B&B
Poggio Etrusco
Via del Pelago 11, Sant'Albino di Montepulciano, 53045; 0578 798 370; www.poggio-etrusco.com
A lovely traditional villa set among the olive groves of an organic farm, Poggio Etrusco has three elegant apartments and one double room. Two apartments sleep four, and the the B&B room can be joined to one of the apartments to accommodate a large family. There is a lovely swimming pool in the garden.

€€

Pisa   Map 5 B3
HOTELS
Hotel Alessandro della Spina
Via Alessandro della Spina 2/7/9, 56125; 050 502 777; www.hoteldellaspina.it
Located a short walk from the train station and the Arno, this hotel is housed in a modern building with marble and parquet floors. The rooms have traditional furnishings, with a triple for families. The very good breakfast buffet includes home-made bread and croissants.

€

Bologna Hotel
Via Mazzini 57, 56125; 050 502 120; www.hotelbologna.pisa.it
A comfortable four-star hotel just down the road from the train station serving the old town, Bologna Hotel is housed in a palazzo with rather old-fashioned decor, but the rooms are well equipped and include large triples and quadruples for families. The staff are friendly and there is a free shuttle bus service from the airport.

€

B&Bs

Michele Guest House

Via Vespucci 103, 56125; 333 601 1287; www.guest-house.it
Michele is a great host. As well as having ordinary doubles, this clean, reasonably priced B&B has a suite that can sleep four people. It is near the station, an easy walk into the town centre. There is no breakfast, but plenty of cafés are nearby.

€

Claudia Ferri

Via 2 Settembre 15/D, 56122; 050 533 868; www.bbclaudiaferri.it
Claudia's welcoming B&B is near the Arno, just outside the city centre. It has four rooms, one with four beds, a kitchenette and en-suite bathroom. Breakfast, with home-made cakes, can be eaten overlooking the pretty garden.

€€

CAMPING

Campeggio Torre Pendente

Viale delle Cascine 86, 56122; 050 561 704; www.campingtorrependente.it
Located within a short walk of the leaning tower, this camp site has a swimming pool to keep kids happy, plus a pizzeria and shop. There is also a communal kitchen for self-catering, and stationary caravans to rent. Bring mosquito repellent in summer.

€

Pitigliano   Map 5 D5

HOTELS

Albergo Guastini

Piazza F. Petruccioli 16/34, 58017; 0564 616 065; www.albergoguastini.it
In the heart of wonderful Pitigliano, this traditional hotel offers pretty good value for money. Rooms are plain but attractive, with marble and wood floors. They include some triples. The restaurant serves fine Maremma fare such as *pappardelle al cinghiale* (pasta with wild boar).

€

Valle Orientina

Valle Orientina, 58017; 0564 616 611; www.valleorientina.it
Located in the countryside 3 km (2 miles) from Pitigliano, this hotel has clean and spacious rooms.

Valle Orientina hotel in the countryside near Pitigliano

Enjoyable extras to keep kids happy include a tennis court, thermal pools and archery. Extra beds can be added to the double rooms.

€€

San Gimignano   Map 5 C3

HOTELS

Hotel Vecchio Asilo

Via delle Torri 4, 53030, Ulignano; 0577 950 032; www.vecchioasilo.it
This tastefully furnished hotel 7 km (4 miles) from San Gimignano has a helpful and welcoming host. There is a pretty garden and cut flowers in the rooms, all of which have tiled floors and simple rustic furniture. The excellent breakfast includes cake home-made daily.

€

Hotel L'Antico Pozzo

Via San Matteo 87, 53037; 0577 942 014; www.anticopozzo.com
A small, family-run hotel, L'Antico Pozzo is housed in a historic building in the centre of town. Some of the rooms are frescoed and all are nicely decorated. There are family rooms, and staff offer a babysitting service.

€€

SELF-CATERING

Fabio Apartments

Vicolo delle Vergini 2, corner Piazza del Duomo, 53037; 0127 959 0523; www.fabio-apartment-sangimignano.com
Down a side street in the middle of town, these two apartments have simple clean rooms and views of the towers. One can sleep four people, the other six, and both feature plain decor, with white walls and terracotta floors. Rental by the week.

€

Fattoria San Donato

Località San Donato 6, 53037; 0577 941 616; www.sandonato.it
These apartments are located in the restored medieval farm village of San Donato, 4 km (2 miles) south of San Gimignano. A pool, animals for kids to play with and horse-riding are nearby. Tuscan dinners and light lunches are home-cooked on request. Each apartment has a kitchenette.

€€

Entrance of Hotel L'Antico Pozzo in San Gimignano

AGRITURISMO

Il Borghetto di San Gimignano Agriturismo

Località Cortennano 21/23, 53037; 0577 941 780; www.ilborghettotuscanholidays.com
The attractive wood-beamed apartments here are painted in pastel colours. There's a swimming pool, pergola and extensive grounds with cypress trees. The owners do great home cooking for guests, but each apartment has a small kitchen for self-catering. Stays by the week.

€€

CAMPING

Campeggio Boschetto di Piemma

Località Santa Lucia 38c, 53037; 0577 907 134; www.sangimignanocamping.it
In a shady grove of holm oaks, with a good-sized swimming pool, a playground, tennis courts and an on-site pizzeria and restaurant, this camp site very near San Gimignano is a superb option for families, with plenty to keep kids entertained.

€

Key to symbols *see back flap*

San Quirico d'Orcia

Map 5 D4

HOTEL
Palazzo del Capitano
Via Poliziano 18, 53027; 0577 899 028; www.palazzodelcapitano.com;
In the medieval village of San Quirico, this gem has a walled garden and a spa. Cooking classes are offered. The suites can accommodate one or two extra beds to suit families.

🏖️ 🍴 €€

Entrance of Palazzo del Capitano hotel in San Quirico d'Orcia

---

Siena

Map 5 D4

HOTELS
Villa Elda
Via 24 Maggio, 10, 53100; 0577 247 927; www.villaeldasiena.it
Villa Elda offers views of the city centre, and it takes around 20 minutes to walk from here to Piazza del Campo. The lovely old Art Nouveau villa has very pleasant rooms decorated in pale colours, and there is a terrace garden where guests can breakfast on fresh fruit, croissants and coffee.

🏖️ €€

Campo Regio Relais
Via della Sapienza 25, 53100; 0577 222 073; www.camporegio.com
A distinctly classy option, this hotel offers stunning views of the Duomo from the terrace and rooms that feature gleaming wooden floors, prints on the walls and antique furnishings. The helpful staff operate a babysitting service and can organize child-friendly sightseeing tours with a private guide, as well as tickets to events such as the Palio.

There is one room with an extra bed or cot available on request (ask in advance).

🏖️ 🍴 🛒 €€€

Grand Hotel Continental Siena
Via Banchi di Sopra 85, 53100; 06 977 459, www.royaldemeure.com
As the name suggests, this is a grand option, in a city that has few upmarket, central hotels. The setting is a 17th-century balconied *palazzo*. It has 51 rooms, some frescoed, swathed in luxurious fabrics and furnished with antiques, and a gorgeous salon with 18th-century frescoes. This is the place to give kids a taste of the high life in historic style.

🍴 €€€

Palazzo Ravizza
Pian dei Mantellini 34, 53100; 0577 280 462; www.palazzoravizza.it/en
Located within an imposing Siena palazzo with frescoed ceilings and beamed bedrooms, this hotel also has a pretty garden terrace with country views where breakfast is served in summer. There is a useful English-language bookshop on site, and the suites can accommodate families.

🏖️ 🏖️ 🍴 €€€

B&Bs
Albergo Bernini
Via della Sapienza 15, 53100; 0577 289 047; www.albergobernini.com
Set in a building dating back to 1300, this family-run B&B has a wonderful terrace for breakfast, with a view of the Piazza del Campo and the Duomo. The 10 rooms (four of which are en-suite) are pleasant but simple, with tiled floors and some with air conditioning (but all with ceiling fans). It is reasonably priced for the central location.

☕ €

Antica Residenza Cicogna
Via dei Termini 67, 53100; 0577 285 613; www.anticaresidenzacicogna.it
This central B&B in a family-owned apartment is friendly and prettily furnished. Many of the rooms have daintily frescoed ceilings, and the communal breakfast area is very attractive. Given the decor and the location, this is a real bargain.

☕ 🏖️ €

La Coperta Ricamata
Via Garibaldi 46, 53100; 0577 43657; www.lacopertaricamata.it
The rooms in this early-20th-century villa are plain but tastefully decorated. There is also a mini-apartment which has a kitchenette, white walls, lovely old furniture, a dining area, chunky wooden beams and terracotta-tiled floors. The villa is located inside the city walls, a short walk away from the Piazza del Campo, and surrounded by a large garden.

🏖️ ☕ 🍽️ 🏖️ €

Palazzo Bruchi
Via Pantaneto 105, 53100; 0577 287 342; www.palazzobruchi.it
This wonderful old property is just 200 m (220 yards) from the Piazza del Campo in the heart of the medieval old town, about the best location one could hope for in Siena. There is a triple and a quadruple room, and all are decorated in attractive traditional style. Breakfast is served in a superb frescoed hall in high season.

🏖️ ☕ €

The terrace of Campo Regio Relais, with a view of Siena's Duomo

CAMPING
Campeggio Siena Colleverde
Strada di Scacciapensieri, 53100; 0577 332 545; www.campingcolleverde.com
Located a couple of kilometres (about a mile) from Siena, this camp site has panoramic views and a decent-sized pool, which will keep kids happy for hours. There is also a bar, a surprisingly good pizzeria and restaurant, and a small supermarket on site. There are small cabins to rent as well as tent pitches.

🏕️ ☕ 🏖️ 🍴 🛟

Emilia-Romagna

Situated north of Tuscany and Umbria, Emilia-Romagna has many attractive towns: the lively regional capital, Bologna, with its arcaded streets and delicious pasta; Ferrara, with its fantastic fortress; Parma, famed for its tasty cheese and ham; and Ravenna, gleaming with Byzantine frescoes. The coast around Rimini has long and sandy, if crowded, beaches.

Below Fontana di Nettuno, Piazza del Nettuno, Bologna

① Bologna
Porticoes and pasta

Bologna is a handsome city, its streets distinguished by porticoes that protect pedestrians from the elements – it has an amazing 45 km (28 miles) of these covered walkways. The city is home to the oldest university in Europe (founded in 1088), and the annual influx of students gives it a youthful zest. Bologna is also noted for its food, with markets and delis that are second to none – it is, of course, the home of *bolognese* pasta sauce. The *ragù* (meat sauce) is usually served with *tagliatelle* (ribbon pasta).

A Bolognese crest on a door

Key Sights

Abbazia di Santo Stefano A complex of four medieval churches, this includes the ancient Santi Vitale e Agricola, built from Roman stones in the 5th century.

Piazza Cavour This pretty medieval square is ringed by Bologna's distinctive porticoed buildings.

Palazzo Comunale The 13th-century town hall houses a museum devoted to muted still-life painter Giorgio Morandi (1890–1964).

Via Pescherie Vecchie The "street of the old fisheries" is lined with small food shops. Parallel Via Orefici is home to jewellers and goldsmiths.

San Giacomo Maggiore This 13th-century church on Piazza Rossini features a famous chapel with portraits of its Bentivoglio patrons.

VIA UGO BASSI
VIA RIZZOLI
VIA ZAMBONI
VIA SAN VITALE
VIA OREFICI
PIAZZA MAGGIORE
STRADA MAGGIORE
VIA D'AZEGLIO
VIA DELL'ARCHIGINNASIO
PIAZZA DI PORTA RAVEGNANA
VIA CASTIGLIONE
VIA SANTO STEFANO
VIA FARINI
PIAZZA CAVOUR
VIA GARIBALDI

Due Torri The 12th-century Torre degli Asinelli (climb up for a great view) and Torre Garisenda are the last surviving towers of the city's original 200 from the Middle Ages.

Piazza Maggiore The huge church of San Petronio and medieval civic buildings line this square. Next to it, Piazza del Nettuno has a dramatic fountain (1566) with bronze figures by Giambologna.

Abbazia di Santo Stefano

San Domenico Built in 1251, this church is dedicated to St Dominic. His very grand tomb has a Michelangelo angel on top of it.

The Lowdown

🌐 **Map reference** 5 D1
Address 40121 Bologna. Museo Morandi: Piazza Maggiore 6. Torre degli Asinelli: Porta Ravegnana. San Petronio: Piazza Maggiore. San Giacomo Maggiore: Piazza Rossini 1. San Domenico: Piazza di San Domenico. Abbazia di Santo Stefano: Via Santo Stefano 24

🚃 **Train** from northern Italian cities and regional towns in Europe

ℹ️ **Visitor information** Piazza Maggiore 1; 0512 39660; www.comune.bologna.it

🕐 **Open** Museo Morandi: 11am–6pm Tue–Fri (till 8pm Sat, Sun).

Torre degli Asinelli: 9am–6pm daily. San Petronio; San Giacomo Maggiore; San Domenico: daily. Abbazia di Santo Stefano: Mon–Fri

💶 **Price** Museo Morandi: €12–20, under-6s free; Wed free. Torre degli Asinelli: €12–22

🚩 **Guided tours** Walking, cycling gastronomic (ask at tourist office)

👫 **Age range** 8 plus

⏱️ **Allow** 1 day

Good family value?
For those old enough to enjoy a busy city without much green space, Bologna has plenty to offer.

Letting off steam

Kids can run around the **Fontana di Nettuno**, dominated by a huge bronze Neptune, in central Piazza del Nettuno. For vigorous exercise, take a 15-minute walk north of the centre to **Parco della Montagnola**; the beautiful, symmetrical gardens were created in 1806, with a pool at their centre. If it is hot or rainy, catch bus 20 from the Rizzoli stop by Piazza Maggiore to Villa Spada and walk 4 km (2 miles) up Via San Luca, under cover of the world's longest portico (666 arches), up to the **Santuario Madonna di San Luca**, a Baroque basilica on a wooded hill – or cheat and catch bus 58 up.

Eat and drink

Picnic: under €25; Snacks: €25–40; Real meal: €40–80; Family treat: €80 or more (based on a family of four)

PICNIC La Baita (*Via Pescherie Vecchie 3a, 40124; 051 223 940*), a fantastic, cavernous deli, sells fresh pasta, countless cheeses, ham and salami. There are hot and cold dishes to take away, or ask them to make up a sandwich.

SNACKS La Sorbetteria Castiglione (*Via Castiglione 44, 40124*) is the city's favourite ice cream – and sorbet – parlour and serves all the flavours imaginable, plus coffee and cakes.

REAL MEAL Trattoria da Pietro (*Via Falegnami 18a, 40121; 051 648 6240; www.trattoriadapietro.it; closed Sun*) is a traditional Bolognese eatery which serves superb *tortellini in brodo* (in broth) and filling dishes such as rabbit in lemon, wine and rosemary.

FAMILY TREAT Al Sangiovese (*Via Paglietta 12, Vicolo del Falcone, 40124; 051 583 057; www.alsangiovese.com*) is an excellent, intimate restaurant which cooks up tasty risotto, meat dishes and desserts such as *semifreddo* (literally "half-cold" – a mousse-like ice cream) with chocolate cream.

Shopping

Città del Sole (*Strada Maggiore 17, 40125, and Via San Felice 81, 40122; www.cittadelsole.com*) sells every toy and game under the sun, from traditional and educational toys to board games, video games and science packs. **Ta-Boo!** (*Via San Felice 24, 40122; www.ta-boo.it*) tempts with model kits of cars, ships, planes and space ships, from simple models to more sophisticated battery-powered ones.

The Fontana di Nettuno in Piazza del Nettuno, designed by Tommaso Laureti

The amazing La Baita deli and café, its counters piled high with cheese

Find out more

DIGITAL The website of the Museo di Palazzo Poggi (*see below*) has excellent films on the history of science, map-making and anatomy, and on fossils and ancient ruins.

A traditional puppet show in Piazza Maggiore, the vibrant heart of the city

Next stop...

MUSEO DI PALAZZO POGGI (*Via Zamboni 33, 40126; www.museopalazzopoggi.unibo.it; open Tue–Sun, children's workshops Sat pm and Sun am; €5*). Head for the marvellous Museo di Palazzo Poggi, a 15-minute walk from Piazza Maggiore, which displays the collections of Bologna's 18th-century Istituto delle Scienze, pretty much exactly as they were – an "encyclopedia of the senses" set against a frescoed background. Lifelike wax models of human anatomy from the 1700s are the highlight, but for the squeamish there are also maps and model ships.

ACROSS THE PLAINS The Via Emilia leads west across the flat Pianura Padana to **Modena**, **Reggio Emilia** and **Piacenza** (*see pp224–5*).
FAENZA To the east, Faenza gave its name to *faïence* white-glazed pottery; the town's chief attraction is the **Museo Internazionale delle Ceramiche** (*www.micfaenza.org*).

② Ferrara

Moats, cannons and dungeons

One of the region's greatest walled towns, Ferrara was ruled by the Este dynasty from the late 13th century until 1598. With its towers and battlements, the **Castello Estense** (begun 1385) dominates the town centre. The Este dynastic seat is a military masterpiece, with dungeons, moats and cannons, but the castle also has a Saletta dei Giochi (games room) decorated with scenes of wrestling and chariot-racing. Bronze statues of Nicolò III d'Este and one of his at least 27 children adorn the medieval Palazzo Comunale (town hall), while the Duomo (1135–1300) is decorated with reliefs of the *Last Judgment* above its central portal.

Letting off steam

If playing war games and family power struggles in the castle has not used up enough energy, hire a bike and pedal around the red-brick Renaissance walls of the **Herculean Addition**, 9 km (6 miles) in all, or continue into the flat countryside of the Po valley, crisscrossed with trails.

The façade of Ferrara cathedral, patterned with loggias and arcades

③ Ravenna

Glittering mosaics

Ravenna is unique among Italian cities for its treasure trove of glittering Byzantine mosaics. Now a sleepy backwater, the town and its port of Classe rose to power in the 1st century under Roman Emperor Augustus. It was made capital of the Western Empire in 402, just before the sack of Rome, retaining its role through invasion by Goths and Byzantine rule. In the 5th and 6th centuries churches and baptistries were built and decorated with stunning, shining mosaics. Head for **Sant'Apollinare Nuovo**, **San Vitale**, the **Battistero Neoniano** and the **Battistero degli Ariani** to see lambs and lions, as well as a bejewelled cast of human characters.

Letting off steam

Take the kids to the **Mirabilandia** (*www.mirabilandia.it*) theme park on the edge of town; catch the train to Lido di Classe, then a shuttle bus to the park. For a natural alternative, explore the extraordinary **Parco Delta del Po** wetlands reserve; drive 10 km (6 miles) north on the SS309 and park at the Oasi di Punte Alberete or Pineta di San Vitale, then follow paths from signboards.

Mosaic showing Empress Theodora inside the Basilica of San Vitale, Ravenna

The Lowdown

- 🌐 **Map reference** 3 D6
  Address 44121–44124 Ferrara. Castello Estenze: Largo Castello, 44121; 0532 299 233

- 🚗 **Train** from Bologna, then a 20-minute walk or bus 1, 2, 9 or 3c from the station

- ℹ️ **Visitor information** Castello Estense, Largo Castello, 44121; 0532 209 370; *www.ferrara terraeacqua.it*

- 🕐 **Open** Castello Estense: 9:30am–5:30pm Tue–Sun

- 💶 **Price** Castello Estense: €16–29, under-18s free

- 👫 **Age range** All

- 🏃 **Activities** The tourist office has a list of bike-hire outlets with bikes for children and toddler seats.

- ⏱️ **Allow** 1 day

- ☕ **Eat and drink** *Snacks* Antica Salumeria Marchetti (*Via Cortevecchia 35, 44121; 0532 204 800*) is a traditional deli that makes up great sandwiches. *Real meal* Il Mandolino (*Via del Volte 52, 44121; 0532 760 080; www. ristorantemandolino.it*) serves excellent pumpkin and ricotta-filled pasta.

- 🎪 **Festivals** Ferrara Balloons Festival (*www.ferrarafestival.it*): Sep

The Lowdown

- 🌐 **Map reference** 6 E1
  Address 48121–48125 Ravenna. Sant'Apollinare Nuovo: Via di Roma 48020. San Vitale: Via San Vitale 17 48121. Battistero Neoniano: Piazza del Duomo 48121. Battistero degli Ariani: Piazzetta degli Ariani 48121. Mirabilandia: Statale Adriatica SS16, km 162, Loc. Mirabilandia

- 🚗 **Train** from Bologna, Rimini, Ferrara and other regional towns

- ℹ️ **Visitor information** Via Salara 8/12, 48121; 0544 35404; *www. turismo.ravenna.it*

- 🕐 **Open** Sant'Apollinare Nuovo, San Vitale, Battistero Neoniano and Battistero degli Ariani: daily. Mirabilandia: weekends only Apr and Sep–Oct, daily May–Aug

- 💶 **Price** Sant'Apollinare Nuovo, San Vitale, Battistero Neoniano: €19–36, under-10s free. Battistero degli Ariani: free. Mirabilandia: €66–110, kids under 100 cm (3 ft 4 in) free

- 👫 **Age range** 5 plus

- 🏃 **Activities** Ask at the tourist office about bike share and bike hire.

- ⏱️ **Allow** A day

- ☕ **Eat and drink** *Snacks* Gastronomia Marchesini (*Via Mazzini 2, 48121; 0544 212 309*) sells excellent deli produce. *Real meal* Ristorante Bella Venezia (*Via Quattro Novembre 16, 48121; 0544 212 746; closed Sun and Jan*) serves local specialities.

- 🎪 **Festivals** Ravenna Festival (music; *www.ravennafestival.org*): Jun

Rimini beach, with well-equipped play areas and activities to keep children entertained

④ Rimini

A beach resort with a temple

Rimini is Europe's largest beach resort, with 15 km (9 miles) of sandy beach. A bathing establishment was first opened here in 1843, and Italians have been coming for their summer holidays ever since. The beaches are crowded but clean, and offer plenty of activities for kids.

Away from the seafront, the old town houses a great Renaissance monument, the **Tempio Malatestiano**. Originally a Franciscan church, in 1450 it was converted into a temple by architect Leon Battista Alberti and became a shrine to Sigismondo Malatesta (1417–68). A *condottiere* with a reputation for evil, Sigismondo commissioned the greatest artists of the age to glorify him: a fresco (1451) by Piero della Francesca in

Façade of the Tempio Malatestiano, designed by Alberti

the tempio shows Sigismondo kneeling before St Sigismund. The pope called it "a temple of devil-worshippers". Film buffs may want to visit the **Casa Museo Fellini** near the Roman Arch of Augustus (27 BC).

Letting off steam

The beach is the place to let off steam. Its shallow water is patrolled by lifeguards. There are areas of free public beach, or pay a small fee for parasols and showers. Hire a pedalo, windsurf, play volleyball or Frisbee galore; the tourist office has lots of information on activities.

The Lowdown

- 🌐 **Map reference** 6 F2
  Address 47921–47924 Rimini. Tempio Malatestiano: Via IV Novembre; 0541 51130. Casa Museo Fellini: Via Nigra 26; *www. federicofellini.it*
- 🚆 **Train** from Bologna, Ravenna and Pesaro to central station
- ℹ️ **Visitor information** Marina Centro: Piazzale Fellini 3, 47921; 0541 56902; *www.riminiturismo.it*
- 🕐 **Open** Tempio Malatestiano: daily. Casa Museo Fellini: daily
- 💲 **Price** Tempio Malatestiano: free. Casa Museo Fellini: free
- 🚻 **Age range** All
- ⏱️ **Allow** From 1 day to 1 week
- 🍴 **Eat and drink** *Real meal* Ristorante da Lele *(Via Lagomaggio 168, 47924; 0541 392 131)* serves pizza, pasta, seafood and fish. *Family treat* Ristorante dallo Zio *(Via Santa Chiara16, 47921; 0541 786 747)* serves fresh seafood.

Picnic under €25; **Snacks** €25–40; **Real meal** €40–80; **Family treat** €80 or more (based on a family of four)

⑤ Parma
Parma ham and parmesan cheese

A delightful and well-to-do town famed for Parma ham and parmesan cheese, Parma is stuffed with delis, café-bars and restaurants purveying these delicious foods. The town is a harmonious array of medieval buildings: most striking are the octagonal Baptistry with its soaring tiers of marble and the Romanesque Duomo. The town also boasts one of Europe's oldest universities, founded in the 11th century, plus a top opera house, and some terrific museums and galleries.

A stone lion guards a door of Parma's Duomo

Key Sights

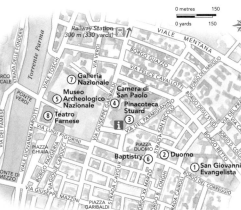

① San Giovanni Evangelista
The dome of this church has a fresco by Correggio of the Vision of St John (1520–22).

② Duomo
The 11th-century Duomo is famed for the trompe l'oeil *Assumption* (1526–30) in its cupola by painter Antonio da Correggio of Parma.

③ Pinacoteca Stuard
Art from the 14th to 19th centuries is housed here, including works by Spanish painter Goya (1746–1828).

④ Camera di San Paolo
Correggio frescoed the refectory of this ex-convent with mythological scenes.

⑤ Museo Archeologico Nazionale
The Palazzo della Pilotta houses a Roman Tabula Alimentaria, a bronze tablet listing dole payments made by landowners to poor children.

⑥ Baptistry
The octagonal baptistry (1196), next to the cathedral in Piazza Duomo, rises in beautifully carved tiers of pink and white marble.

⑦ Galleria Nazionale The gallery, inside the Palazzo della Pilotta, features works by Correggio and Parmigianino ("the little one from Parma"; 1503–40).

⑧ Teatro Farnese
The Palazzo della Pilotta includes this wooden theatre (1618–19), a restored copy of one built in Vicenza by the architect Andrea Palladio.

The Lowdown

🌐 **Map reference** 2 G4
Address 43121–43126 Parma. Teatro Farnese, Galleria Nazionale, Museo Archeologico Nazionale: Palazzo della Pilotta, Piazzale della Pilotta 15 43121; *www.artipr.arti.beniculturali.it.* Pinacoteca Stuard: Borgo del Parmigianino 2 43039. Camera di San Paolo 43121: Via Stretto Melloni Macedonio 3a; 0521 233 309

🚗 **Train** from Modena and Bologna or Piacenza and Milan, then 15-minute walk or bus 2, 8, 9 or 13 to centre

ℹ️ **Visitor information** Via Melloni 1a, 43121; 0521 218 889; *www.turismo.comune.parma.it*

🕐 **Open** Teatro Farnese, Galleria Nazionale and Camera di San Paolo: 9am–2pm Tue–Sun. Museo Archeologico Nazionale: 9am–1pm Tue–Sat, 3–5pm Sun (9:30am–12:30pm, 4–7pm Sun Jun–Jul and Sep, 9:30am–12:30pm Sun Aug). Pinacoteca Stuard: 9am–6:30pm Mon, Wed–Sat, 9am–1:20pm Sun

€ **Price** Galleria Nazionale: €12–18, under-18s free.

Museo Archeologico Nazionale: €5.80–9.60. Teatro Farnese, Pinacoteca Stuard and Camera di San Paolo: €6–12, under-18s free

👫 **Age range** 8 plus to engage with the art and architecture

⏱️ **Allow** At least 1 day

🚻 **Toilets** In museums and cafés

Good family value?
Parma is not an obvious option for families on a budget, as there are few free attractions, little green space, and eating is expensive.

Letting off steam

From the centre, head down to the Parma river and cross over Ponte Verdi to the spacious **Parco Ducale** (www.servizi.comune.parma.it/giardinoducale), a 20-minute walk. There is plenty of space to run around in these beautiful 18th-century gardens, graced with lavish fountains and formal Italianate flowerbeds.

The 18th-century gardens of Parco Ducale, with cooling fountains

Eat and drink

Picnic: under €25; Snacks: €25–40; Real meal: €40–80; Family treat: €80 or more (based on a family of four)

PICNIC The **market** on Piazza Ghiaia *(Wed and Sat)* is great for picnic food. On other days, pick up provisions at one of the *alimentari* (food shops) dotted around the old centre. Picnic in the Parco Ducale.

SNACKS Ristorante Pizzeria La Duchessa *(Piazza Garibaldi 1, 43121; 0521 235 962; closed Mon)* has a good location, good pizza and a range of other dishes too.

REAL MEAL Gran Caffè Orientale *(Piazza Garibaldi 19/o, 43121; 0521 285 819; www.grancaffeorientale. com)* sits grandly on one of Parma's main squares. It has a terrace and serves stylish dishes – at a price.

FAMILY TREAT Trattoria del Tribunale *(Vicolo Politi 5, 43121; 0521 285 527; www.trattoriadeltribunale.it)* serves delicious *antipasti* including *prosciutto crudo* (Parma ham), pumpkin *ravioli* (in season) and beef *al Barolo* (cooked in red wine), in an attractive setting.

Find out more

DIGITAL To find out more about the *alimenta*, the institution set up by Roman emperors Nerva and Trajan to feed poor children,

Belle Epoque entrance of the Gran Caffè Orientale on Parma's Piazza Garibaldi

governed by the Tabula Alimentaria, visit www.archeobo.arti.beniculturali.it/down load/parma/Veleia_rooms_en.pdf.

Next stop...

PUPPETS, CASTELLI AND HAM

Next to the Camera di San Paolo in Parma is a museum of traditional puppets, **Il Castello dei Burattini** (www.castellodeiburattini.it). In the hills 50 km (30 miles) west of Parma, the little village of **Castell'Arquato** overlooks the Arda valley. Eat in the central square and visit the Rocca Viscontea, a 14th-century fortress. Some 23 km (14 miles) south of Parma is Langhirano, the centre for Parma ham production. The town's warehouses open their windows to the mountain air to cure the meat, and there is a prosciutto museum for aficionados. Nearby is the dramatic 15th-century **Castello di Torrechiara**, with four blunt towers.

The imposing medieval Rocca Viscontea fortress in Castell'Arquato

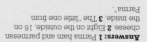

⑥ Modena
Fast cars, food and history

The handsome city of Modena has plenty of claims to fame: it is a producer of fast cars – Ferrari and Maserati both have their factories here; operatic tenor Luciano Pavarotti (1935–2007) was born and lived here; and balsamic vinegar is a Modenese delicacy. It is also a fine historic town: there has been a university here since 1175, and the wonderful Romanesque **Duomo**, carved with scenes by Wiligelmus and his pupils, was built in 1099. Its Torre Ghirlandina once housed the *Secchia*, a wooden bucket said to have been stolen from Bologna in 1325, sparking a war between the two rival cities. The **Palazzo dei Musei** houses an eclectic range of museums, including art collected by the Este dynasty who ruled Modena from 1288 to 1796. There is a portrait of Francesco I d'Este by Velazquez (1638), and a bust of him by Bernini (1651). The jewel of its Biblioteca Estense is the fabulously illuminated Borso d'Este Bible.

Petrolheads should head 20 km (12 miles) south of town to the **Galleria Ferrari** in Maranello, to see

Children participating in a mock battle at the Castello di Gropparello's fairy-tale park

vintage examples of the low-slung machines and a small exhibition of racing trophies and photos.

Letting off steam
The **Giardini Pubblici**, just beyond the Palazzo Ducale, are pleasant for a play. The **Parco di Piazza d'Armi Novi Sad**, near the station, is by the **Piscina Comunale Dogali** (*www.dogalisrl.it*), with a 50-m (164-ft) pool and a kids' pool (open-air in summer).

⑦ Piacenza
Horsey sculptures

Piacenza, on the western border of Emilia-Romagna, was settled by the Romans where the ancient Via Emilia met the River Po. Little visited, it offers a charming picture of provincial life. Piazza Cavalli is its main square, with two fine bronze equestrian statues created in the 1620s, their manes and tails blowing in the breeze and

hooves proudly raised. The dashing riders are Alessandro Farnese and his son Ranuccio, who ruled the town in the 16th century. Also on the piazza is the castellated red-brick Palazzo del Comune, dating back to 1280. The Duomo, with an octagonal cupola and campanile, was begun in 1122. The **Musei di Palazzo Farnese** incorporate the fine Pinacoteca (art gallery), which has Botticelli's beautiful *Madonna and Child with John the Baptist* (1483–7), and the Museo Archeologico. This has a bizarre Etruscan artefact: a bronze sheep's liver, used by priests to divine the future.

Letting off steam
Piazza Cavalli has room for a canter, or drive 30 km (19 miles) to the **Castello di Gropparello** for a medieval day out (*open daily; €22–52; book ahead; www.castellodigropparello.it*).

The Lowdown

- 🌐 **Map reference** 2 H5
  Address 41121–41126 Modena. Duomo: Corso Duomo, 41121. Palazzo dei Musei: Largo di Porta Sant'Agostino 337, 41121; *www.comune.modena.it/museoarte*. Galleria Ferrari: Via Dino Ferrari 43, Maranello 41053; *www.ferrari.com*

- 🚗 **Train** from Bologna and Parma, then 10-minute walk or bus 7, 11

- ℹ **Visitor information** Via Scudari 8, 41121; 059 203 2660; *www.turismo.comune.modena.it*

- 🕐 **Open** Duomo: daily. Palazzo dei Musei: Tue–Fri 9am–noon, Sat–Sun 10am–1pm and 3–6pm (May–Sep 4–7pm). Galleria Ferrari: 9:30am–6pm daily (May–Sep until 7pm)

- 💶 **Price** Palazzo dei Musei: free. Galleria Ferrari: €26–48

- 👫 **Age range** 8 plus

- ⏱ **Allow** Half a day

- 🍽 **Eat and drink** *Real meal* Pizzeria Quadrifoglio (*Via XXII Aprile 38, 41026; 059 670 191*) lets you design your own pizza. *Family treat* Trattoria Il Fantino (*Via Donzi 7, 41121; 059 223 646*) serves good local dishes.

Letting off steam at Modena's open-air swimming pool, the Piscina Comunale Dogali

The Lowdown

- **Map reference** 2 F4
  Address 29121–29122 Piacenza. Musei di Palazzo Farnese: Piazza Citadella 29; *www.musei. piacenza.it*
- **Train** from Bologna, Modena and Parma or Milan
- **Visitor information** Piazza Mercanti 7, 29121; 0523 32 93 24; *www.comune.piacenza.it*
- **Open** Musei di Palazzo Farnese: check ahead for opening hours.
- **Price** Musei di Palazzo Farnese: €12–21
- **Age range** 5 plus
- **Allow** 1 hour
- **Eat and drink** *Real meal* Le Tre Ganasce (*Via San Bartolomeo 62, 29121; 0523 499 133; closed Mon*) has classic dishes such as ravioli with spinach and ricotta. *Family treat* Antica Osteria del Teatro (*Via Verdi 16, 29121; 0523 323 777; closed Sun & Mon*) serves traditional dishes with a modern slant.

⑧ Reggio Emilia
Cheese town

This ancient and pretty town – known to the locals simply as Reggio – is well off the beaten track, but comes to life on market days (Tue and Fri) when the two main squares, Piazza Prampolini and Piazza San Prospero, are crammed with bargain hunters. The local food stalls are particularly good: take the chance to stock up on the cheese produced around here, Parmigiano-Reggiano, otherwise known as parmesan, and balsamic vinegar.

Once a Roman settlement on the Via Emilia, the old part of town has maintained a hexagonal shape delineated by its walls, but most of the buildings are from the 16th and 17th centuries. The Duomo, with an octagonal tower, has statues of Adam and Eve on its façade. The **Musei Civici** house Roman mosaics, medieval weapons, paintings and textiles, and include the Museo del Tricolore, which tells the story of how the Italian red, white and green flag was designed here in 1797. Reggio's most famous son, Ludovico Ariosto (1474–1533), author of the Renaissance epic poem *Orlando Furioso* (Frenzied Orlando), spent much of his youth at **Villa Il Mauriziano**, a little east of town.

Parmigiano-Reggiano (parmesan cheeses) maturing in a warehouse

Letting off steam

In town, head to the **Giardino Pubblico**, near the bus station. Further afield, the surrounding hills are popular for hikes – a good base is **Canossa**, 25 km (15 miles) southwest of Reggio. There are the remnants of a 10th-century castle here perched on a craggy outcrop. Not much is left, but it is a great romantic ruin for kids to discover.

The Lowdown

- **Map reference** 2 H5
  Address 42121–42124 Reggio Emilia. Musei Civici: Via Spallanzani 1; *www.municipio.re. it*. Villa Il Mauriziano: Via Louis Pasteur 11, San Maurizio, 42100; 0522 456 527
- **Train** from Bologna and Milan
- **Visitor information** Via Farini 1a, 42121; 0522 451 152
- **Open** Musei Civici: Tue–Fri 9am–12 noon, Sat–Sun 10am–1pm and 4pm–7pm, closed Mon. Villa Il Mauriziano: Mon–Fri 4–6pm
- **Price** Musei Civici and Villa Il Mauriziano: free
- **Age range** 8 plus
- **Allow** 2 hours
- **Eat and drink** *Snacks* Piccola Piedigrotta (*Piazza XXV Aprile 1, 42121; 0522 43492*) serves great pizza. *Real meal* Ristorante Canossa (*Via Roma 37, 42121, 42100; 0522 434 922*) has pumpkin pasta in season and a lively atmosphere.

Where to Stay in Emilia-Romagna

Prosperous Bologna caters well for families, with both modest and luxurious hotels, while for something more individual, B&Bs are a good option. Quiet, attractive Parma and Ferrara both offer a range of accommodation. Book in advance during the popular spring and autumn/winter seasons.

AGENCY
Iglu Villas
www.igluvillas.com
Large selection of family-friendly apartments and villas across Emilia-Romagna. Full holiday packages are also on offer.

Bologna
Map 5 D1

HOTELS
Hotel Il Guercino
Via Luigi Serra 7, 40129; 051 369 893; www.guercino.it
Well located in a residential area near the train station, this hotel has smart retro decor and a family room for four with kitchenette. Breakfasts are served on the terrace in summer.
€€

Hotel Porta San Mamolo
Vicolo del Falcone 6/8, 40124; 051 583 056; www.hotel-portasanmamolo.it
This is a good central option within walking distance of Piazza Maggiore, with plain decor, decent breakfasts and welcoming staff.
€€

Palazzo Loup
Via Santa Margherita 21, Loiano, 40050; 051 654 4040; www.palazzo-loup.it
Outside the city near Loiano, this old manor house has a lovely countryside setting, with pretty gardens and a pool. Its restaurant serves good Apennine specialities.
€€

Hotel Commercianti, a comfortable hotel in the heart of Bologna

Hotel Commercianti
Via de' Pignattari 11, 40124; 051 745 7511; www.art-hotel-commercianti.it
Just off Piazza Maggiore, this hotel offers every comfort. There is a suit of armour in the marble-floored reception. The rooms have large terraces and swish bathrooms.
€€€

B&Bs
Bologna nel Cuore
Via Ceasare Battisti 29, 40123; 051 269 442; www.bolognanelcuore.it
The rooms in this central apartment building are lovely. The owner, Maria, is attentive, and the bread and home-made jam for breakfast is delicious.
€

Ca' Fosca due Torri
Via Caprarie 7, 40125; 051 261 221; www.cafoscaduetorri.com
This gorgeous apartment has a lush rooftop garden. Its two double rooms can each fit another single, and the owner, Patrizia, makes great breakfasts and has two guest bikes.
€

Antica Residenza d'Azeglio
Via Massimo d'Azeglio 64, 40124; 051 644 7389; www.anticaresidenza dazeglio.it
Classic but colourful decor, a good location and a warm welcome from the hosts Agostino and Roberto. The green suite has a double bed and a lounge with a sofa bed.
€€

Ferrara
Map 3 D6

SELF-CATERING
Prisciani – ArtSuite
Piazza Repubblica 5, 44121; 0532 201 111; www.prisciani.com
These are smart modern apartments, each decorated by a different artist; added single beds are an option.
€€

Functional but central Hotel Button, a good family option in Parma

Parma
Map 3 B6

HOTELS
Hotel Button
Borgo della Salina, 7, 43121; 0521 208 039; www.hotelbutton.it
The spacious rooms in this traditional if plain hotel in the centre of the old town include quadruples and triples.
€€

Hotel Torino
Borgo Angelo Mazza 7, 43121; 0521281 046; www.hotel-torino.it
In the heart of Parma, this clean hotel does a good breakfast. Some rooms have balconies.
€€

B&Bs
Rubra Bed & Breakfast and Apartments
Strada Massimo d'Azeglio 48, 43121; 0521 289 140; www.bbrubra.com
A homely option, owned by friendly Max, this B&B has apartments that sleep three or four, and a terrace.
€

Kamiteo
Borgo Riccio da Parma 20, 43121; 335 624 0292; www.bbkamiteo.com
This comfortable B&B has bikes for guests. The attic room has a double bed and one or two singles.
€€

Price Guide
For a family of four per night in high season, in one or more rooms, inclusive of breakfast, service charges and any additional taxes such as VAT.

€ Under €200 €€ €200–350 €€€ over €350

Key to symbols *see back flap*

Umbria and Le Marche

Landlocked Umbria and little-known Le Marche make up one of Italy's most interesting areas, full of historic towns but less crowded than Tuscany. Set amid dramatic hilly countryside is Assisi, with its beautiful frescoes of St Francis, Orvieto's dazzling cathedral, ancient Spoleto, Urbino's ducal palace and hidden Ascoli Piceno, as well as beaches and mountains.

***Below** The façade of Orvieto's Duomo, a medieval masterpiece*

Urbino
p244

Assisi
p228

Orvieto
p240

Spoleto
p234

Ascoli Piceno
p248

① Assisi: Basilica di San Francesco
St Francis and the birds

With a dramatic hillside setting, a perfect medieval core and the remarkable Basilica di San Francesco, Assisi is one of the gems of Umbria. The basilica, with its stunning frescoes by the great painters Cimabue and Giotto, is one of the foremost Christian shrines in the world and receives vast numbers of visitors all year. Pope Gregory IX ordered the basilica's construction over St Francis's tomb soon after the saint's death in 1226; the basilica and frescoes were restored after an earthquake in 1997.

Portrait of St Francis by Cimabue

Key Features

Wooden choir
The ornate wooden choir is in Gothic Renaissance style, with pointed arches.

St Francis The simple painting of St Francis (1280) by Cimabue (1251–1302) captures the humility of the saint, who believed in respecting animals and birds as much as people (*see above right*).

The rose window
Above the main door of the church is a beautiful stained-glass window.

The façade The front of the church is plain compared with the interior. It is built in the Italian Gothic style, with pointed arches over the windows and doors.

Cappella di San Martino
The first chapel on the left was frescoed with scenes from the *Life of St Martin* (1315) by Sienese painter Simone Martini (1284–1344). Note the lovely sky-blue background.

The Life of St Francis
St Francis Preaching to the Birds is one of 28 panels of the *Life of St Francis* (1290–95), thought to be by Giotto (1267–1337).

Cappella di San Martino

Tomb of St Francis

Frescoes by Lorenzetti
Pietro Lorenzetti of Siena (1280–1348) painted the left transept of the lower church with frescoes, including a *Crucifixion* and a *Deposition* with a curious truncated cross.

Letting off steam

The spacious, traffic-free piazza around the basilica is good for a run around after the hush of the interior. Alternatively, follow signs to the Duomo and head up Via di Porta Perlici from Piazza San Rufino to the **Rocca Maggiore** fortress, easily spotted above the town. It is a steep 20-minute climb, but worth it for the views, and to explore the ramparts of this forbidding fortress.

It was built in the 12th century, but most of what visitors see now dates from 1367, with 15th-century towers.

Eat and drink

Picnic: under €25; Snacks: €25–40; Real meal: €40–80; Family treat: €80 or more (based on a family of of four)

PICNIC La Bottega del Pasticcere (*Via Portica 19, 06081; 075 812 392*) is a pretty pastry shop crammed

with Umbrian delicacies, as well as a wide selection of ice creams made with fresh ingredients.
SNACKS Café Duomo (*Piazza San Rufino 5, 06081; 075 813 794*) is a friendly local café offering pizza, sandwiches, pastries and *gelati* as well as coffee and drinks.
REAL MEAL Trattoria Pallotta (*Vicolo della Volta Pinta 3, 06081; 075 812 649; www.pallottaassisi.it*) is a cosy, centrally located *trattoria*.

Prices given are for a family of four

The Lowdown

- 🌐 **Map reference** 6 F4
  Address Piazza San Francesco, 06081 Assisi, Umbria; 075 819 901; www.sanfrancescoassisi.org
- 🚗 **Train** to Assisi's Stazione Santa Maria degli Angeli, then bus (tickets from the station kiosk)
- ℹ️ **Visitor information** Piazza del Comune, 06081; 075 819 0084; www.assisionline.com
- 🕐 **Open** Daily: upper church 8:30am–7pm, lower church 6am–7pm (until 6pm Nov–Mar)
- € **Price** Free
- 👪 **Skipping the queue** Visit early in the morning or late in the afternoon to avoid the crowds.
- 🚩 **Guided tours** English-language tours can be booked at www.sanfrancescoassisi.org/info_prenotazioni_modulovisite.htm

- 👫 **Age range** 5 plus. Even small children will respond to Giotto's enchanting fresco of St Francis Preaching to the Birds. Note, however, that a strict dress code is enforced and all visitors including children should cover up arms and legs, and that the custodians of the basilica aim for it to be as silent as possible.
- ⏱️ **Allow** Up to an hour in the basilica and a day in Assisi
- ♿ **Wheelchair access** Yes
- 🚻 **Toilets** Near the ticket office

Good family value?
Entry to the basilica, with its fine early Renaissance art, is free, but prices in the town's restaurants and cafés are higher than average.

Try the ravioli with artichokes and truffles, the bean and barley soup or the rabbit cacciatora (casserole). **FAMILY TREAT Ristorante Buca di San Francesco** (Vicolo Eugenio Brizi 1, 06083; 075 812 204; closed Mon) is an upmarket option serving fine Umbrian food.

A selection of freshly made ice cream flavours at La Bottega del Pasticcere

Find out more

DIGITAL For more on Giotto's life and work, see www.ibiblio.org/wm/paint/auth/giotto/. To read about the earthquake that shook Assisi in 1997 and the restoration of the frescoes, see www.news.bbc.co.uk/1/hi/entertainment/arts/2284161.stm.

Shopping

The souvenir shops near the basilica are worth a browse for kitsch animal figurines, Franciscan monk-shaped mugs and holographic Virgin Marys.

The 14th-century Rocca Maggiore, perched above the town

Next stop...

MORE SAINTS IN ASSISI Asissi has not one but two basilicas, the second one a pink-striped monument to St Clare, who gave up everything to be a disciple of St Francis. It also has its own cathedral, the Romanesque San Rufino, with a porphyry font where saints Francis and Clare were both baptized. **CITTÀ DI CASTELLO** An hour's drive north of Assisi, Città di Castello is one of Umbria's lesser-known gems, with art by Raphael and Ghirlandaio in its gallery. **CENTRO DELLE TRADIZIONI POPOLARI** In Garavelle, 2 km (1 mile) south of Assisi, is the excellent Centro delle Tradizioni Popolari (0758 552 119; closed Mon), a museum showcasing country life in the region, with rustic dances and activities for kids.

KIDS' CORNER

Look out for...
1 The tomb of St Francis (in the crypt). How did it go undiscovered until 1818?
2 St Francis Preaching to the Birds (in the nave), which shows the saint with birds clustered around him under a tree.
3 St Francis Giving his Cloak to a Poor Man and St Francis Renouncing his Worldly Goods (in the nave), which both show him giving away his clothes!

Answer at the bottom of the page.

TALE OF TWO ARTISTS
When the shepherd boy Giotto was 12, the painter Cimabue saw him do an amazingly lifelike drawing of a sheep on a rock. The older artist persuaded Giotto's father to let the boy study with him to become an artist.

St Francis, the animals and the birds
St Francis was born in Assisi in 1181. The son of a wealthy cloth merchant, as a young man he loved to dress up and party. Then one day, when he was out on his horse, he saw a leper. He nearly ran away, but felt ashamed, kissed the leper and gave him money. Eventually, St Francis gave all his money away and lived as a beggar, helping the poor and tending to sick people, animals and birds. His pure and simple life inspired many people. Today, Franciscan monks still wear a simple brown or grey habit.

Answer: 1 The tomb was sealed off so tomb-raiders from Assisi's arch-enemy Perugia would not find it.

② Perugia

Hidden alleys, chocolates and an Etruscan arch

Perched high on a hill above the Tiber Valley, Perugia is one of the most attractive towns in Italy. After a very bloody Middle Ages it became the quiet capital of Umbria. The town has steep medieval streets and a perfect town square, along with a wealth of great art in its gallery – and chocolate. The town's most famous export is Baci ("kisses"), chocolate-coated hazelnuts with a message in the wrapper, and pretty café windows are filled with chocolate confections.

The main street is wide Corso Vannucci, where smartly dressed Perugians take their passeggiata, or evening stroll. At its northern end, the huge Palazzo dei Priori (begun in 1293 and finished 150 years later) is unmissable, with rows of pointed windows, swallow-tail crenellations and a high belfry. An entrance at no. 25 gives access to the Collegio del Cambio, the moneychangers' guild, decorated in 1499 by local artist Perugino (real name Pietro Vannucci), Raphael's master. Through the palazzo's elaborate main entrance (1326) is the region's best art gallery, the **Galleria Nazionale dell'Umbria**. There is a sumptuous *Adoration of the Magi* (1473) here by Perugino; the kings wear clothes that would have been the height of fashion at the time of painting. Look out for pretty Gothic madonnas by Gentile da Fabriano and Fra Angelico, as well as

Palazzo dei Priori in Perugia, one of the largest town halls in Italy

Piero della Francesca's *St Anthony Polyptych* (1465–70), with an Annunciation scene at the top.

Around the corner in Piazza IV Novembre, look up to see the lion, emblem of the Guelph faction, and a griffin representing Perugia high on the wall of the palazzo. The piazza is dominated by the 25-sided pink and white marble fountain, Fontana Maggiore, designed in 1270 and decorated with carvings by Nicola and Giovanni Pisano, representing the entire medieval cosmology. Opposite, the Duomo houses the Santo Anello, said to be the Virgin Mary's wedding ring, a "mood" ring that changes colour according to the moral character of the wearer.

Ornate carvings by Nicola and Giovanni Pisano on Fontana Maggiore, Perugia

Perugia is studded with Etruscan remains, including the Etrusco-Roman **Arco di Augusto** (Arch of Augustus) at the bottom of Via Rocchi and the **Pozzo Etrusco** (Etruscan well) by the Duomo. This engineering marvel dates back to the 3rd century BC and is at least 35 m (115 ft) deep; it can be explored via an ancient alley. The 5th-century church of **Sant'Angelo**, just off Corso Garibaldi, is built on an Etruscan and Roman sacred site.

Corso Vannucci in Perugia, named after local painter Pietro Vannucci (Perugino)

Prices given are for a family of four

Letting off steam

Just 2 km (1 mile) west of town, the **Città della Domenica** theme park (*www.cittadelladomenica.it*) offers a change from medieval architecture and art: the grounds feature a mini-train, a zoo, a fairytale village, pony riding, a playground and a reptile house.

The Lowdown

🌐 **Map reference** 6 E4
Address 06121–06123 Perugia, Umbria; Galleria Nazionale dell'Umbria: Palazzo dei Priori, Corso Vannucci 19, 06123; *www.galleria nazionaleumbria.it*

🚗 **Train** from Florence, then minimetrò (*www.minimetrospa.it*)

ℹ️ **Visitor information** Corso Vanucci, 19, 06123; 075 573 6458; *www.perugiaonline.com*

🕐 **Open** Galleria Nazionale dell' Umbria: closed Mon; Pozzo Etrusco: daily; Sant'Angelo: closed Mon; Città della Domenica: daily Apr–Aug, weekends Sep–Oct

💶 **Price** Galleria Nazionale dell'Umbria: €13–19.50; Pozzo Etrusco: €5–10; Sant'Angelo: free; Città della Domenica: €29–49

👫 **Age range** 8 plus for museum

⏱️ **Allow** 1 day

🍽️ **Eat and drink** *Snacks* Pasticceria Sandri (*Corso Vannucci 32, 06123; 075 572 4112*) is one of the sights of Perugia, an early 19th-century café with frescoed ceilings and cake-filled windows. *Family treat* La Taverna (*Via delle Streghe 8, 06123; 075 572 4128*) is a serious but not stuffy eatery that serves Umbrian dishes with a modern, sophisticated twist.

🎉 **Festivals** Umbria Jazz Festival (*www.umbriajazz.com*): Jul

③ Gualdo Tadino

Ceramics, wolves and golden eagles

The historic hill town of Gualdo Tadino was hit by the earthquake that also rocked Assisi in 1997, but much has been done to restore its churches and other buildings. The town's wealth derives from ceramics: there are decorative tiles and signs embedded in the walls, and many little shops selling patterned bowls, plates and cups. The 13th-century Gothic Duomo has a grand façade and a rose window (1256) that miraculously survived the 1997 earthquake and an earlier one in 1751. In the imposing **Rocca Flea** (fortress), the **Museo Civico** displays some of the famous ceramics.

Letting off steam

In Gualdo Tadino itself, the paths and gardens of the Rocca Flea are good for a play. Further afield, the mountainous scenery of Umbria is seen at its best and wildest in the **Parco Regionale del Monte Cucco**, 8 km (5 miles) north of Gualdo Tadino. The park is home to wolves and golden eagles. As well as hiking and mountain-biking trails, there are opportunities for pony trekking and fishing. Alternatively, explore the **Grotta di Monte Cucco**, the world's fifth biggest cave system. The park visitor centre at Fossato di Vico (www.discovermontecucco.it) has maps and information.

Above A ceramic plate decorated in the Renaissance style from Gualdo Tadino
Below Gualdo Tadino's imposing Rocca Flea, looming over the little hill town

The Lowdown

🌐 **Map reference** 6 F4
Address 06023 Gualdo Tadino, Umbria; Rocca Flea and Museo Civico: Via della Rocca; 075 914 2445; www.roccaflea.com

🚂 **Train** from Assisi or Spoleto, then bus. **Bus** from Perugia and Gubbio, and to Fossato di Vico (www.apmperugia.it)

ℹ **Visitor information** Piazza Martiri della Libertà, 06023; 075 914 2445; open Fri–Sun

🕐 **Open** Rocca Flea and Museo Civico: Apr–May Thu–Sun, Jun–Sep Tue–Sun, Oct–Mar Fri–Sun

💲 **Price** Rocca Flea and Museo Civico: €10–20

👫 **Age range** Any

⏱ **Allow** 1 hour for the town, 1 day or more for the park

🍴 **Eat and drink** Snacks Hostaria da Baccus (Via Roberto Calai 32, 06023; 075 465 3062; closed Mon) serves good pizzas; full meals are available too.

🎪 **Festivals** Giochi de le Porte (archery and donkey races): last week of Sep.

④ Gubbio

A splendid civic palace and a dizzying funicular

Gubbio is a dramatic town, its medieval streets rising up a hillside backed by the wooded slopes of the Apennines. Founded by the ancient Umbrii way back in the 3rd century BC, it was developed by the Romans and flowered in the medieval period, when it was ruled by the dukes of Montefeltro. The town is dominated by the **Palazzo dei Consoli** (1332), the civic palace, which houses a Museo Civico and displays the Eugubine Tablets – seven slabs of bronze inscribed with texts in Etruscan and Latin. The palazzo fronts onto the aptly named Piazza Grande, with views of the town and the plains below. On the outskirts of Gubbio is a substantial **Roman theatre**, still used for summer plays and concerts.

Letting off steam

Follow signs to the **funicular**, which carries visitors swiftly up Monte Ingino for hikes and sensational views over the town. It is great fun, but the fragile-looking cages dangle from a cable, so travellers need a head for heights, and must be ready to jump quickly into a cage – the funicular does not stop or slow to pick up passengers. At the top, head for the Basilica di Sant'Ubaldo to see the *ceri* (see Kids' Corner).

⑤ Lake Trasimeno

Splash around in the lake

Italy's fourth largest lake is tranquil and mostly pretty (avoid the bleaker northern coast), and great for some summer swimming, sailing or windsurfing – it is about the only stretch of open water in Umbria. The lake is shallow, which means that in summer the water is always warm. Use the little resort town of Castiglione del Lago as a base. There are some nice sandy beaches, and the town sits scenically beside the water on a fortified promontory. Castiglione's castle, the **Rocca del Leone** (Fortress of the Lion), dates mostly from the 16th century, though parts date back to the 1250s. From the ramparts there are views across the lake.

Letting off steam

The waters of the lake are good for small children to swim and even try a bit of snorkelling, as the beach shelves very gently. For older children, Castiglione is the perfect place to try more challenging watersports, including windsurfing, sailing and waterskiing.

The Lowdown

🌐 **Map reference** 6 F4
Address 06024 Gubbio, Umbria. Palazzo dei Consoli: Piazza Grande, 06024; 075 927 4298; Roman theatre: Via Teatro Romano, 06024; 075 922 0992

🚌 **Bus** from Perugia or Fossato di Vico train station (www.apmperugia.it)

ℹ️ **Visitor information** Via Repubblica 6, 06024; 075 922 0790; www.comune.gubbio.pg.it

🕐 **Open** Palazzo dei Consoli: daily 10am–1pm and 3–6pm Apr–Oct, 10am–1pm and 2–5pm Nov–Mar. Roman theatre: daily 10:30am–7:00pm

💶 **Price** Palazzo dei Consoli: €10–13, schoolchildren €1.50, under-6s free. Roman theatre: €9

👫 **Age range** 8 plus

🕐 **Allow** Half a day

🍴 **Eat and drink** *Real meal* Grotta dell'Angelo (*Via Gioia 47, 06024; 075 927 1747; www.grottadellangelo.it*) is a hotel restaurant with stone walls, a log fire in winter and rustic cooking. It is very popular with locals, so book ahead. *Family treat* Locanda del Cantiniere (*Via Dante 30, 06024; 075 927 5999; www. locandadelcantiniere.it*) is an elegant place with subtle truffle-flavoured dishes.

🎭 **Festivals** Corsa dei Ceri (Race of the Candles); participants race each other through the town carrying immense wooden candles (see Kids' Corner): 15 May.

Gothic 14th-century Palazzo dei Consoli in Gubbio, housing a civic museum

The Lowdown

🌐 **Map reference** 6 E4
Address 06061 Castiglione del Lago. Rocca del Leone: 06061; 075 965 2484

🚂 **Train** to Castiglione del Lago

ℹ️ **Visitor information** Piazza Mazzini 10, 06061 Castiglione del Lago,; 075 965 2484

🕐 **Open** Rocca del Leone: Mar–Sep 9:30am–7pm daily; Nov–Mar 9:30am–5:30pm Fri–Mon

💶 **Price** €18

👫 **Age range** All

🕐 **Allow** 1 day

🍴 **Eat and drink** *Real meal* L'Acquario (*Via Vittorio Emanuele 69, 06061 Castiglione del Lago; 0759 652 432*) is a lakeside stalwart. *Family treat* Ristorante Monna Lisa (*Via del Forte 2, 06061 Castiglione del Lago; 075 951 071; www.ristorante monnalisa.com*) serves seafood.

🎭 **Festivals** Coloriamo i Cieli (kites and hot-air balloons): 27 Apr–1 May

Funicular at Gubbio, taking visitors up steep Monte Ingino – not for the faint-hearted

Prices given are for a family of four

View of Passignano on Lake Trasimeno from the boat heading to Isola Maggiore

⑥ Isola Maggiore
A ferry trip and lace-making

A half-hour crossing from Castiglione del Lago, Passignano sul Trasimeno or Tuoro Navaccia on the shores of Lake Trasimeno brings visitors to this charming little island with its medieval village, known for lace-making. Despite its name meaning "Greater Island", it is actually the middle-sized of the lake's three islands, and has just a 2 km (1 mile) circumference. It has a sleepy, tranquil air, in spite of the summer crowds. A cluster of houses lines Via Guglielmi, where holiday-makers sip coffee in the sun and enjoy fresh fish at the little restaurants. Above all, this is a pleasant street just to have a wander after the boat trip, but there is also a small museum where handmade lace can be bought. Otherwise, take a walk around the shores of the island, or head to the higher points to see the views. Visitors here are following in famous footsteps: St Francis of Assisi lived here as a hermit from 1211, and a Franciscan monastery was built here in 1328. Apart from other visitors, the island is very quiet – there are only 35 local inhabitants.

Letting off steam

Swim from Isola Maggiore, or from the tiny island of **Isola Polvese**, reached by ferry from San Feliciano on the mainland. Polvese is pretty and largely uninhabited, making it a great option for a get-away-from-it-all adventure.

The Lowdown

🌐 **Map reference** 6 E4
Address 06060 Isola Maggiore, Umbria

🚗 **Ferry** to Isola Maggiore from Castiglione del Lago, Passignano sul Trasimeno or Tuoro Navaccia and to Isola Polvese from San Feliciano (*around 20 crossings daily in summer, weekends only in winter; 075 827 157; www.umbriamobilita.it*)

👫 **Age range** All

⏱ **Allow** Half a day

☕ **Eat and drink** *Picnic* Take supplies from Castiglione del Lago and picnic on the island's shores. *Real meal* Ristorante e Albergo Da Sauro (*Via Guglielmi 1, 06060 Isola Maggiore; 075 826168, www.dasauro.it*) serves traditional cuisine and seafood.

Church of San Michele on Isola Maggiore, seen from Lake Trasimeno

⑦ Spoleto
Gleaming mosaics and a mighty aqueduct

Spoleto is a venerable city with a graceful cathedral, Roman remains, a gigantic fortress and enough back streets, arches and alleyways to occupy the most energetic of kids. Children also love to explore the medieval aqueduct, a history and engineering lesson in stone which is an easy stroll away from the upper fringes of the town, and leads to the sacred wooded hill of Monteluco. The lower part of Spoleto is much more modern, with the exception of the impressive San Gregorio Maggiore church, which dates back to Roman times.

Fontana del Mascherone

Key Sights

① San Gregorio Maggiore The atmospheric San Gregorio church in the lower town was founded in the 4th century and renovated in the 12th century. Parts of Roman buildings are visible in its stonework.

② Teatro Romano Built in the 1st century AD, the wide arc of stone seats that makes up the ancient Roman theatre is still used for concerts today.

③ Piazza del Mercato This square hosts a market (Mon–Sat mornings) in front of a pretty fountain with a clock tower above it. Nearby, on Piazza Campello, is the curious Fontana del Mascherone.

⑥ Museo Diocesano The gallery houses works by Filippino Lippi and Neri di Bicci's *Madonna della Neve* (Madonna of the Snow).

⑦ Duomo The cathedral (1198) has an attractive façade with glittering mosaics and a rocket-like tower. Inside are frescoes of the *Life of the Virgin* (1467–9) by Filippino Lippi.

④ Casa Romana In this Roman house, with wall frescoes and lovely black-and-white mosaic floors, it is possible to make out the bedrooms and bath.

⑤ Sant'Eufemia This 12th-century church shows the complex history of this ancient town: it was built over the remains of a Roman building and an 8th-century palace.

⑧ Rocca Albornoz The monolithic fortress looms dramatically over the city. It was built in 1359–70 by Cardinal Albornoz.

The Lowdown

🌐 **Map reference** 6 F5
Address 06049, Umbria

🚗 **Train** from Florence, Perugia and Rome, then shuttle bus from station to central Piazza della Libertà

ℹ **Visitor information** Piazza della Libertà 7–9, 06049; 0743 218 620

🕐 **Open** Teatro Romano: 10am–1pm and 3–5pm daily. Casa Romana: mid-Mar–mid-Oct 10am–8pm daily, until 6pm rest of year

Museo Diocesano: Apr–Oct 10am–1pm and 4–7pm Mon and Wed–Sat, 10am–12.30pm and 3–6pm Sun; Nov–Mar 10am–12.30pm and 3–6pm Mon and Wed–Sat, 11am–5pm Sun. Rocca Albornoz: daily

💶 **Price** Teatro Romano: free. Casa Romana: €6–10. Museo Diocesano: €7–12. Rocca Albornoz: €22–32

👪 **Skipping the queue** In high summer Spoleto gets very busy, so head for the sights early or late in the day; the aqueduct remains uncrowded even at busy times.

👫 **Age range** The cobbled streets and especially the aqueduct are fun for kids aged 5 plus.

⏱ **Allow** Half a day to stroll the alleys, see a couple of sights and walk to the aqueduct

Letting off steam

Walk (10 minutes) to the **Ponte delle Torri** aqueduct, its stone arches striding across the river valley. It is like an ancient playground and, once kids have run the length of it, they can explore the wooded slopes of **Monteluco**, the holy mountain. The more ambitious could walk (20 minutes) down through the woods to **San Pietro**, its façade hewn with mythological beasts, or up to 12th-century **San Giuliano** (1 hour's steep climb), with carved reliefs on its portal. Well-signed paths also lead to hermits' caves dotted around the mountain.

The 14th-century Ponte delle Torri, leading to Monteluco

Eat and drink

Picnic: under €25; Snacks: €25–40; Real meal: €40–80; Family treat: €80 or more (based on a family of four)

PICNIC Piazza del Mercato has some good delis and a market every morning except Sunday. There is often a van selling roast pork sandwiches. Picnic by the aqueduct.

Toilets In Museo Diocesano and in cafés

Festivals Festival dei Due Mondi (famous festival of theatre, dance, music held annually since 1958; *www.festivaldispoleto.it*) Jun–Jul

Good family value?
The old centre is a major draw, many of the attractions are free, including the aqueduct, and none of the museums are expensive.

SNACKS Osteria del Matto *(Vicolo del Mercato 3, 06049; 0743 225 506)*, located under an arch just off Piazza del Mercato, is a great spot to enjoy *antipasti* and the one pasta dish on the menu every day, in a homely setting.

REAL MEAL Cantina de' Corvi *(Piazzetta SS Giovanni e Paolo 10a, 06049; 0743 44 475; www.cantinadecorvi.it; closed Mon)*, set in a converted stable, serves treats such as *tagliatelle* (ribbon pasta) with black truffles and *cannelloni* (stuffed pasta rolls) with rabbit sauce.

FAMILY TREAT Ristorante Apollinare *(Via S Agata 14, 06049; 0743 223 256; www.ristoranteapollinare.it)* is a handsome traditional restaurant with a beamed ceiling just off the Piazza del Mercato, which produces elegantly presented local dishes.

Find out more

DIGITAL To find out more about Roman mosaics, and how to make mosaic patterns online, go to *www.rome.mrdonn.org/mosaics.html*.

Next stop…

SAN SALVATORE Just outside the town, San Salvatore is one of the oldest churches in the whole of Italy. It dates back to the 4th century, and is made from Roman materials, including columns and friezes. A compelling sight, it is a half-hour walk east of town, but not a particularly pleasant one – so it may be better to go by car.

The ancient church of San Salvatore with its recycled Roman columns

KIDS' CORNER

Look out for
1 The Rocca Albornoz, an impressive, huge fortress.
2 The sparkly mosaic on the cathedral façade – the Virgin Mary and St John the Baptist are asking Christ to help people.
3 The fresco in the cathedral showing the *Coronation of the Virgin* in a beautiful patterned, bejewelled gown.
4 A mosaic pavement in the cathedral of a huntsman blowing a horn, and his dog.
5 A carved figure of a violin player on the cathedral portal. reused in other buildings too.
6 The matrons' gallery in Sant'Eufemia, where women would sit apart from the men.

CHRISTIAN BONES

It is said that the bones of 10,000 Christian martyrs slain in the Roman amphitheatre are buried near to San Gregorio Maggiore. The church is dedicated to St Gregory of Spoleto, who was beheaded under the orders of Emperor Diocletian in AD 303.

Aqueduct engineering
Even today, the engineering of the Ponte delle Torri is impressive: its 10 arches span the wide valley of the river Tessino, and it is 230 m (755 ft) long and more than 70 m (230 ft) high. Some people think the aqueduct was built on the foundations of a Roman one, but its architect is thought to have been Il Gattapone (1300–1383), who also built the Rocca Albornoz. Primarily designed to carry water, it was also used as an escape route from the Rocca when it was under attack.

⑧ Norcia
Wild boar galore

The ancient Sabine settlement of Norcia is crammed with shops selling the hams and salamis, known as *norcineria*, for which this remote village in the shadow of the Monti Sibillini is famous all over Italy. The bristly heads of wild boar hang outside village shops, alongside strings of sausages, dangling cheeses and black truffles. As well as being renowned for its pork butchers, surgeons and *castrati* (male sopranos), Norcia was the birthplace of St Benedict (480–534), founder of Western Europe's first monastic order, the Benedictines.

The rather stark little town, described as *Frigida Nursia ("Cold Nurcia")* by Roman poet Virgil, has a surprisingly grand main square. Once the site of a Roman forum, Piazza San Benedetto is now dominated by the restored 13th-century Gothic façade of San Benedetto, the craggy 16th-century Castellina (fortress) and Palazzo Comunale (town hall), with a 15th-century portico. It is noticeable that there are no tall buildings in Norcia: it is prone to earthquakes (the most recent was in 1979) and there has been a law against buildings higher than two storeys since 1859.

Letting off steam
Walk around the 14th-century walls of Norcia or drive 30 km (20 miles) east to the isolated village of **Castelluccio**, above the plateau of the Piano Grande. In spring this vast meadow is carpeted with wildflowers. The village is a base for walking, hang-gliding, rafting and donkey- and pony- trekking on the plain and surrounding mountains.

The Gothic San Benedetto church on Piazza San Benedetto, Norcia

---

The Lowdown

- 🌐 **Map reference** 6 G5
  Address 06046 Norcia, Umbria
- 🚌 **Bus** from Spoleto, Assisi, Perugia and Foligno
- 👫 **Age range** All
- ⏱ **Allow** 1 hour for the town, 1 day to explore the Piano Grande around Castelluccio
- 🍽 **Eat and drink** *Picnic* Visitors to Norcia will not go hungry: the streets are lined with *alimentari* (grocery shops), which will make up *panini* with local ham, salami and cheese. *Family treat* Ristorante Vespasia *(Palazzo Seneca, Via Cesare Battisti 12, 06046; 0743 817 434; www.palazzoseneca.com)* is a very grand restored palazzo, which has been decorated in elegant style. The food is correspondingly sophisticated, excellent – and expensive.
- 🎊 **Festivals** Festa del Tartufo (Black Truffle Festival; www.neronorcia.it): second weekend in Feb.

---

⑨ Trevi and the Fonti del Clitunno
A perfectly perched hill town with its own sacred spring

From afar, the hill town of Trevi, cascading down a hillside of olive groves, appears to have emerged straight out of a Renaissance painting. It is called Trevi for the *tre vie* – three roads – that meet here. Famed for its olive oil, it is a lovely place to wander and explore the medieval walls. The 14th-century church of San Francesco is where a braying ass initially drowned out St Francis's preaching – but then fell silent at the saint's words.

Just south of Trevi are the Fonti del Clitunno, a sacred beauty spot in Roman times, described by Pliny the Younger in the 1st century AD. It was a must-see sight on the Grand Tour; Lord Byron wrote a description after his visit in 1816. Named after the pre-Roman river god Clitumnus, the springs bubble up into a little lake fringed with weeping willows. The only ancient building left is the 6th-century Tempietto del Clitunno, a pagan shrine and Christian sanctuary. The Classical style of its façade, with marble columns and pediment, belie the Byzantine frescoes inside: look for the angels.

Letting off steam
Besides the Fonti del Clitunno park, kids can run around Piazza Mazzini, the main square in Trevi.

Medieval Trevi, perched on a hilltop and surrounded by walls of Roman origin

The Lowdown

- 🌐 **Map reference** 6 F5
  Address 06039 Trevi, Umbria. Fonti del Clitunno: Via Flaminia 7, Loc Fonti del Clitunno, 06042 Campello sul Clitunno; 0743 521 141; www.fontidelclitunno.com
- 🚌 **Train** to Trevi, then bus to centre. **Bus** from Foligno (Società Spoletina; 0742 670 746). **Car** to Fonti del Clitunno, off Via Flaminia (SS3)
- ℹ **Visitor information** Piazza Mazzini 5, 06039; 0742 781 150; www.protrevi.com
- 🕐 **Open** Fonti del Clitunno: Nov–Feb 10am–1pm and 2–4:30pm, Mar and Oct 9am–1pm and 2–6pm, Apr and Sep 9am–7:30pm, May–Aug 8:30am–8pm
- 💰 **Price** Fonti del Clitunno: €6–12, under-10s free
- 👥 **Skipping the queue** Visit early or late, when it is less busy.
- 👫 **Age range** All
- ⏱ **Allow** 1 hour
- 🍽 **Eat and drink** *Real meal* Gustavo Ristorante Enoteca *(Via San Francesco 22a, 06039; 0742 78545; www.gustavo gustavino.it)* offers seasonal Umbrian food such as melted cheese with truffles. *Family treat* La Prepositura *(Via della Rocca, 06039; 0742 38541)* is a smart place in the town centre.
- 🎊 **Festivals** Palio, first Sun in Oct. Sagra del Sedano e della Salsiccia (celery and sausage fair), third Sun in Oct. Pageant, fourth Sun in Oct

A narrow cobbled street in the ancient hilltop town of Montefalco

⑩ Montefalco

Explore the falcon's mount

The name of this cobbled hill town – falcon's mount – indicates its position, high above the Spoleto valley, although according to legend it is actually named after the falcons of Holy Roman Emperor Frederick II. In 1249 he was all set to destroy the old town of Coccorone on this site when his falcons landed here and he decided to rename it Montefalco instead. The town is also known as the *ringhiera d'Umbria* (balcony of Umbria) – walk up to the arcaded Piazza del Comune and look across the valley to Assisi to see why. This tiny place was the birthplace of eight Italian saints, including St Chiara di Montefalco. The star exhibit of the Pinacoteca Comunale in the 14th-century ex-church of San Francesco is Benozzo Gozzoli's *Life of St Francis* (1452). The luminous fresco cycle shows the saint at work in his humble robes, the sky above him filled with bright angels. By contrast, creepy Sant' Agostino contains three mummified corpses, while just outside town is the church of **Santa Chiara di Montefalco**. After her death, the heart of this mystic visionary, St Clare of the Cross (1268–1308), was found to be branded with the sign of the cross.

Letting off steam

Explore the holm oak forests around the convent of **San Fortunato** (1 km/half a mile south of the Porta Spoleto gate), founded over a Roman basilica in the 5th century.

The Lowdown

- 🌐 **Map reference** 6 F5
  Address 06036 Montefalco, Umbria
- 🚗 **Train** to Foligno (15 km/10 miles away), then bus
- ℹ️ **Visitor information** Piazza del Comune, 06036; 0742 378 490; www.comune.montefalco.pg.it
- 🕐 **Open** Museo Chiesa di San Francesco: Tue–Sun 10:30am–1pm and 2–6pm, Jul–Aug until 7pm, Nov–Feb until 5pm
- 💶 **Price** Museo Chiesa di San Francesco: €6–12
- 👫 **Age range** 5 plus
- 🕐 **Allow** 1 hour
- ☕ **Eat and drink** *Real meal* Olevm (Corso Goffredo Mameli 55, 06036; 0742 379 057; www.olevm.it) is a cosy bistro with local dishes and a good wine list. *Family treat* Aurum (Piazza del Comune 19, 06036; 0742 379 357; www.hotelbontadosi.com), a stylish restaurant on the main square, serves exceptional food.

Admiring the view over the Spoleto valley from Montefalco

⑪ Spello

Roman statues and Renaissance art

With its network of steep, arched streets, Spello is a spellbinding little town, with plenty of scope for kids to run up and down its stepped passageways and peer down hidden alleys. The town has Roman origins: the Porta Consolare, which leads into the centre, is decorated with three timeworn Roman statues which are said to depict a family who expired after eating poisonous mushrooms. Make sure to explore the upper part of town, where there is a Roman arch, a lookout and the 14th-century Rocca (fortress), with views over a Roman amphitheatre.

The one unmissable sight, though, is the 12th-century church of Santa Maria Maggiore on Via Consolate, with a fresco cycle by the Perugian painter Pinturicchio (1454–1513), full of subtle details and colours – the *Annunciation* depicting the angel holding a lily and a dove above the Madonna's head is especially pretty.

Letting off steam

If climbing the steep streets to the Rocca is not enough, good walkers may want to continue to the summit of verdant **Monte Subasio** (three-hour round trip). Pick up a map at the tourist information office, and take water and snacks.

The Lowdown

- 🌐 **Map reference** 6 F5
  Address 06038 Spello, Umbria
- 🚗 **Train** from Perugia and Foligno to station in lower part of town
- ℹ **Visitor information** Piazza Matteotti 3, 06038; 0742 301 009; www.turismo.comune.spello.pg.it
- 👫 **Age range** 5 plus
- ⏱ **Allow** 1–2 hours
- 🍵 **Eat and drink** *Snacks* Enoteca Properzio (*Via Torri di Properzio 8a, 06038; 0742 301 688; www. enoteche.it; closed Wed*) is a lively little wine bar with good local food. *Real meal* Osteria del Buchetto (*Via Cappuccini, 06038; 0742 303 052; www. osteriadelbuchetto.it*) has views across to Assisi, giving it a magical feel on summer evenings, and the local food is delicious.
- 🎉 **Festivals** L'Infiorata (when the streets are carpeted with flower petal pictures and patterns): Jun

The steep, cobbled streets of Spello, brimming with brightly coloured flowers

⑫ Bevagna

Gruesome gargoyles and Roman remains

Wonderfully preserved, Bevagna is one of the most interesting Umbrian towns to wander through, with its ancient stone streets, Roman relics and two fine Romanesque churches, which sit on the central square, Piazza Silvestri. The façade of rugged old San Silvestro (1195) is partly composed of Roman stones, while San Michele (built a few years later) is decorated with eccentric gargoyles, birds and animals – fun for children to spot. Also on the square is grand Palazzo dei Consoli (1270), with its wide external staircase, and a 19th-century stone fountain completes the picture.

Explore the remains of the Roman amphitheatre: its circular walls were incorporated into the fabric of the medieval streets, and visitors who follow Via dell' Anfiteatro can discern the shape of the older structure – look out for the narrow tunnels that would have led under its stage. The Romans circled Bevagna with defensive walls, too, which were reinforced in the 12th and 13th centuries and still have lovely arched gates.

Letting off steam

Walk around the town walls, or enjoy an ice cream in **Piazza Silvestri** while spotting mythological beasts on the façade of San Michele and Roman stones on San Silvestro.

The Lowdown

- 🌐 **Map reference** 6 F5
  Address 06031 Bevagna, Umbria
- 🚗 **Bus** from Montefalco, Foligno (nearest train station) and Perugia (www.spoletina.com)
- ℹ **Visitor information** Via Santa Maria Laurentia 1, 06031; 0742 361 667
- 👫 **Age range** 5 plus
- ⏱ **Allow** 1–2 hours
- 🍵 **Eat and drink** *Real meal* La Trattoria di Oscar (*Piazza del Cirone 2, 06031; 0742 662 510*), near the main piazza, is an unpretentious little trattoria with a terrace, serving generous plates of healthy and tasty local food. *Family treat* Ottavius (*Via del Gonfalone 1, 06031; 0742 360 555*) has a strong wine list and a good menu of traditional dishes, with particularly good *gnocchi*.
- 🎉 **Festivals** Mercato delle Gaite (medieval processions and crossbow competitions; www. ilmercatodellegaite.com): Jun

Carved angel on the doorway of Romanesque San Michele, Bevagna

The impressive cascade of water at the Cascata delle Marmore, a Roman waterfall

⑬ Valnerina
Fortress hamlets and mighty mountains

The Valnerina (Little Valley of the Nera) forms the eastern border of Umbria. It is ruggedly beautiful, with wooded hillsides rising to high crags and twisting roads overlooked by stone villages. A little-visited part of Italy, the river valley, its hamlets, hidden monasteries and oak forests are well worth exploring – it is a wild place, with wolves still found roaming the high ridges.

A car is the only realistic way to reach the remote upper Valnerina, passing the rival feudal hamlets of **Arrone**, perched on a rock, and tiny **Polino** – both topped by defensive towers. Further up, **Ferentillo** is also guarded by twin citadels, but is best known for the surprising mummies in its church of Santo Stefano. Close by, the 8th-century Benedictine abbey of **San Pietro in Valle** is now

a hotel, but the church, with its Romanesque façade, ornate campanile and Byzantine frescoes, can be visited. Carry on up to **Scheggino**, crisscrossed by canals where crayfish and trout are farmed. Beyond is the ancient village of **Sant'Anatolia di Narco**, with an 8th-century BC necropolis, and the 12th-century church of San Felice di Narco, at the foot of medieval Castel San Felice, carved with reliefs of St Felice slaying a dragon. The road continues past Vallo di Nera, a picturesque village with cobbled streets, into the Monti Sibillini.

Letting off steam

The dramatic, man-made **Cascata delle Marmore** near Terni is the highest waterfall in Europe at 165 m (540 ft). Created in 271 BC by the Romans, the falls are now used to generate hydroelectric power. There is a steep path to the top of the waterfall (a 40-minute ascent).

KIDS' CORNER

Look out for…
1 The three Roman figures by the Porta Consolare in Spello.
2 The angel in the *Annunciation* in Spello's Santa Maria Maggiore, holding a lily for purity. The dove above Mary's head is a symbol of the baby Jesus.
3 Grinning gargoyles on the church of San Michele in Bevagna – take a sketchbook and draw them.
4 Traces of the Roman amphitheatre in Bevagna.

ST VALENTINE'S HEAD
St Valentine, the patron saint of lovers, was martyred in 273 at Terni. His mummified head was stolen in 1986. It was found under a bench at the Cascata delle Marmore!

The Romans in Umbria
The Romans are inescapable in this part of Umbria. The Via Flaminia, an ancient Roman road, passed through Spoleto and Spello on its way from Rome to Rimini on the Adriatic Coast, bringing with it trade and riches. It was opened in 220 BC and traces of it still remain, along with bridges and viaducts.

There are ancient Roman amphitheatres in Spello and Bevagna too. In Spello, the amphitheatre sat an amazing 15,000 people, a reminder that this tiny town – like many of the quiet backwaters of Umbria today – was once an important settlement.

Even in the countryside, the waterfalls of Marmore are a reminder of Roman building prowess (they were built to drain a malarial swamp).

The Lowdown

🌐 **Map reference** 6 F5
Address 06040, Umbria. San Pietro in Valle: Ferentillo, 05034 Terni. Cascata delle Marmore: 7 km (4 miles) along S209 Valnerina, 05100 Terni; www.marmorefalls.it

🚗 **Car** up SR209 from Terni, or via tunnel from Spoleto to the valley

ℹ️ **Visitor information** Via del Comune 1, 06040, Scheggino; 0743 613 232; www.lavalnerina.it

🕐 **Open** San Pietro in Valle: Mar Sat–Sun, Apr–Aug daily; Cascata delle Marmore: Feb–Dec daily, Jan Sat–Sun; check website for times of water release over the falls

💶 **Price** Cascata delle Marmore: €14–28, under-6s free

🚻 **Age range** All for the valley; the path up to the Cascata delle Marmore is very steep.

🕐 **Allow** 1 or more days

🍴 **Eat and drink** *Snacks* There are snack bars at the Cascata delle Marmore, and picnic sites at the top and bottom of the waterfall. *Real meal* Albergo Trattoria del Ponte (*Via di Borgo 5, 06040 Scheggino; 0743 61253*) is a little country restaurant across a footbridge over the river, specializing in river-caught fish and local truffles.

Picnic under €25; **Snacks** €25–40; **Real meal** €40–80; **Family treat** €80 or more (based on a family of four)

⑭ Orvieto: the Duomo
A stunning cathedral and a fun funicular

Set on a tufa plateau 300 m (984 ft) high, Orvieto is a dramatic sight – apparently unassailable; in fact the best way to reach the top of town is by its funicular, and then walk to the spectacular Duomo. One of the greatest of Italy's Romanesque-Gothic cathedrals, its exterior is patterned in stripes, its façade decked out with breathtaking carvings by the best sculptors of the age, its interior frescoed by Signorelli and other masters and decorated with beautiful paintings and stained glass.

Detail of bas-relief on the façade

Key Features

Cappella del Corporale

Frescoes by Signorelli
Luca Signorelli's great fresco cycle of the *Last Judgment* (1499–1504) in the Cappella Nuova shows some people getting into Heaven, others assigned to Hell.

Stained glass

The exterior
The cathedral is patterned with horizontal bands of white travertine and blue-grey basalt.

Adoration of the Magi

Main door

Façade
There is so much to see on the façade it is hard to take it all in: swirling pillars, glittering mosaics and countless sculpted Biblical scenes.

Adoration of the Magi
The Sanctuary, near the back of the church, was decorated with a lovely *Adoration of the Magi* in the 14th century; see how one of the kings kisses the baby Jesus's feet.

The rose window
Created by Andrea Orcagna in 1360, the rose window has Christ at the centre.

Main door
The big bronze doors bring things up to date: they were designed by sculptor Emilio Greco in 1970.

Stained glass
Head to the apse, at the rear of the church, to see the stained glass. There is a colourful scene showing Mary lying down with the swaddled baby Jesus and some oxen looking on.

Cappella del Corporale
This little chapel features a beautiful painting, the *Madonna dei Raccomandati* (1320), by Lippo Memmi. The Madonna shelters worshippers under her blue cloak.

Letting off steam
Climb the steps of the 42-m (137-ft) **Torre del Moro** – the tall tower with the clock face visible from all over town. It is a short stroll from the Duomo, at the far end of Via del Duomo where it meets wide Corso Cavour. The tower dates from the 12th century and the hours are still sounded on its 14th-century bell. From the top there are views of the whole of the town and the vineyards and hills beyond.

Prices given are for a family of four

Biblical reliefs by sculptor and architect Lorenzo Maitani on the Duomo façade

Eat and drink
Picnic: under €25; Snacks: €25–40; Real meal: €40–80; Family treat: €80 or more (based on a family of four)

PICNIC Carraro (*Corso Cavour 101, 05018; closed Wed*) is a great deli, which sells cheese, ham and salami, and will make up *panini*.
SNACKS Gelateria Pasqualetti (*Piazza del Duomo 14, 05018*), centrally located in the main square, scoops great ice cream within gazing distance of the cathedral.

The Lowdown

🌐 **Map reference** 6 F3
Address Duomo, Piazza Duomo 05018 Orvieto; 0763 343 592; www.orvietoturismo.it

🚗 **Train** from Rome, from Florence via Orte or Chiusi and from Perugia via Teróntola; **funicular** to high part of town

ℹ️ **Visitor information** Piazza Duomo 20, 05018; 0763 341 772; www.orvietoonline.com

🕐 **Open** Apr–Oct 9:30am–7:30pm Mon–Sat, 1–5:30pm Sun; Nov–Mar 9:30am–1pm, 2:30–5pm Mon–Sat, 2:30–5:30pm Sun

💲 **Price** £10–20, under-6s free

👥 **Skipping the queue** Visit early in the morning or late in the afternoon to avoid crowds.

🚩 **Guided tours** Ask at the tourist office opposite the Duomo.

👫 **Age range** The funicular will enliven the experience for kids. Signorelli's teeming *Last Judgment* may capture their imaginations and the carvings on the façade will interest older children. Parents of under-8s may spend much of their visit in Piazza Duomo and the streets of Orvieto.

⏱️ **Allow** 1 hour for the cathedral, half a day or a whole day for the rest of the city

♿ **Wheelchair access** Yes

🚻 **Toilets** In café-bars on Piazza Duomo.

Good family value?
The stunning exterior of the Duomo can be seen for free, and the streets of Orvieto provide plenty of diversion free of charge.

REAL MEAL Antica Cantina *(Piazza Monaldeschi 18–19, 05018; 0763 344 746; www.anticacantina orvieto.it)* is a bustling restaurant with outdoor tables under foliage. The food is traditional Umbrian.
FAMILY TREAT Duca d'Orvieto *(Via della Pace, 05018; 0763 344 663; www.ducadiorvieto.com; closed Wed and Sun eve)* has unassuming décor and cooks historical local dishes. Try barley and bean soup, fettuccine pasta with wild boar or truffle sauce, or chicken with wild fennel.

Shopping
Delicious food, including locally made salamis and cheeses, can be found at Orvieto's **market** (held on Thursday and Saturday mornings). The souvenir shops in and around the Piazza del Duomo sell pretty ceramics, wooden toys and other desirable objects to take home.

Antica Cantina restaurant, hung with historical prints of Orvieto

The remains of Orvieto's 5th-century BC Etruscan temple

Find out more
DIGITAL Read all about funicular railways at science.howstuffworks. com/engineering/civil/question512. htm, which explains how they work.

Next stop...
POZZO DI SAN PATRIZIO Dug out of the tufa and lined with brick, this deep well near the funicular has an unusual double-helix staircase of 248 steps each – one spiral leads down, another up – used to carry water by donkey. It was built by the paranoid Medici Pope Clement VII to survive a siege and designed by Renaissance architect Antonio Sangallo the Younger in the 1530s.
ETRUSCAN TEMPLE Next to the well are the remains of an Etruscan temple – Orvieto began as the wealthy Etruscan city of Velzna, sacked by the Romans in 280 BC.

⑮ Todi

Top of the world

This elegant little city with its wonderful architecture is one of the gems of Umbria. Its lofty location at more than 400 m (1,312 ft) ensures it has a "top of the world" feel, as well as stunning views of the valley below. Its historic and social centrepiece is Piazza del Popolo, a magnificent square lined with three 13th-century *palazzi* and a Duomo, approached up a steep flight of steps. The Palazzo del Capitano, linked to the adjacent, swallowtail-crenellated Palazzo del Popolo by a grand external stairway, contains the **Museo Etrusco-Romano**, whose highlight is a collection of Roman coins, and the **Pinacoteca Comunale**, with a glorious *Coronation of the Virgin* (1507–11) by Lo Spagna. At the top of town is the church of San Fortunato (1292), with its unfinished façade.

Letting off steam

Follow a lane from San Fortunato down to **public gardens** where there is a playground and a small fortress. The zigzag path continues down to Viale della Consolazione, where the serene Renaissance **Santa Maria della Consolazione** (1508–1607), designed by Bramante, stands. Its dome is an icon of Todi.

The Lowdown

🌐 **Map reference** 6 E5
Address 06059 Todi, Umbria. Museo Etrucsco-Romano and Pinacoteca Comunale: Palazzi Comunali, 06059

🚌 **Bus** from Orvieto, Perugia and other towns *(www.sitabus.it)*

ℹ **Visitor information** Piazza del Popolo 36, 06059; 075 894 5416

🕐 **Open** Museo Etrusco-Romano and Pinacoteca Comunale: Tue–Sun

💲 **Price** €7–14

👫 **Age range** All

⏱ **Allow** Half a day

🍴 **Eat and drink** *Real meal* Pane & Vino (*Via Augusto Ciuffelli 33, 06059; 075 894 5448*) offers traditional Umbrian cuisine with a twist. *Family treat* I Rossi Ristoro di Campagna (*Frazione Pesciano 42, 06059; 075 894 7079*) serves real home cooking such as *bruschetta*, truffle pasta and steaks.

🎉 **Festivals** Todi Art Festival (dance, drama and music): Aug–Sep.

Santa Maria della Consolazione outside Todi, built on a Greek cross plan

⑯ Amelia

Awesome city walls and Roman treasures

Ancient Roman writer Pliny the Elder claimed that Amelia, which had been dated back to the 12th century BC, was one of the oldest towns in Italia (as the peninsula was called then). It is certainly one of Umbria's most charismatic towns. The mighty Mura Poligonali (city walls) were built by the Umbri tribe in the 5th century BC from huge blocks fitted together without mortar. They are known as Cyclopean walls, as it was believed that only the mythical Cyclopes were strong enough to build them. Look out for the section near the Renaissance Porta Romana, where they are 8 m (26 ft) high and 3 m (10 ft) wide. Nearby, the **Museo Archeologico** in Palazzo Boccarini has Roman finds from the town,

The Lowdown

🌐 **Map reference** 6 E6
Address 05022 Amelia, Umbria. Museo Archeologico: Piazza Augusto Vera 10, 05022; 0744 978 120; *www.sistemamuseo.it*

🚌 **Bus** from Orvieto, Narni, Terni, and Orte. For nearest train connection see *www.atcterni.it*

🕐 **Visitor information** Via Roma 4, 05022; 0744 981 453

ℹ **Open** Museo Archeologico: Oct–Mar Tue–Sun Apr–Sep, Fri–Sun

💲 **Price** Museo Archeologico: €10–18

👫 **Age range** 5 plus

⏱ **Allow** 2 hours

🍴 **Eat and drink** *Snacks* Pizzeria Porcelli (*Via Farrattini, 05022; 0744 983 639; closed Tue*) has a long list of pizzas. *Real meal* In July and August, villages near Amelia open seasonal taverns serving excellent local food; ask at the tourist office for details.

🎉 **Festivals** Palio dei Colombi (jousting): late Jul–early Aug.

notably a bronze statue of Emperor Caligula's father, Germanicus. More Etruscan and Roman fragments are visible throughout the town, where a labyrinth of narrow streets spirals up past Renaissance *palazzi* to the Duomo. Close by is a dodecagonal (12-sided) tower built as a Torre Civica in 1050 using Roman stones.

Letting off steam

From the Porta Romana, leave the city and walk around the outside of the vast walls. The impressive scale of the walls are most evident here.

The pretty hill-town of Todi, surrounded by olive groves

Piazza Garibaldi, the principal square in Narni, with its 15th-century fountain

⑰ Narni

Ancient hotchpotch

The Romans called this town Narnia when they conquered it in 299 BC. Author C S Lewis plucked the name from an atlas for his *Chronicles of Narnia* (1950–56) because he liked the sound of it. Narni was once an important stop on the ancient Via Flaminia road, with its Ponte Augusto (27 BC) bridge crossing the Valnerina gorge. Today it has a web of narrow streets studded with Roman and medieval buildings. In Piazza Garibaldi is a 15th-century fountain carved with mythical beasts; the piazza was a Roman piscina (swimming pool) and steps lead down from the fountain into a medieval cistern. Inside the Duomo from 1047 is an even older (6th-century) chapel, with a

9th-century mosaic of Christ. In Piazza dei Priori is a pretty fountain from 1303. Overlooking it, the 13th-century **Palazzo del Podestà** displays a *Coronation of the Virgin* (1486) by Domenico Ghirlandaio, gleaming with gold leaf.

Letting off steam

Climb up to the **Rocca Albornoz**, a stern, battlemented fortress that must have been forbidding to invaders. It is surrounded by a park.

The Lowdown

- 🌐 **Map reference** 6 F6
  Address 05035 Narni, Palazzo del Podestà: Piazza dei Priori, 05035
- 🚗 **Train** to Narni Scalo from Orvieto, Todi and Terni, then bus into town
- ℹ️ **Visitor information** Piazza dei Priori 3, 05035; 0744 715 362
- 🕐 **Open** Palazzo del Podestà: daily
- 💶 **Price** Palazzo del Podestà: free
- 👪 **Age range** 5 plus
- ⏱️ **Allow** 2 hours
- 🍴 **Eat and drink** *Real meal* La Gallina Liberata (*Vicolo Belvedere 13, 05035; 349 254 3515*) serves simple local food. There is no menu, but diners will the enjoy *antipasti* and pasta with *ragù* (meat sauce). *Real meal* Ristorante Gattamelata (*Via Pozzo della Comunita 4, 05035; 0744 717 245; closed Mon*) has a range of menus to choose from – there is even a vegetarian option.
- 🎪 **Festivals** Festa di San Giovenale and Corsa all'Anello ("Ring Race"; torchlit procession and medieval jousting): 2nd Sun of May.

The square, majestic Rocca Albornoz fortress, dominating the Nera Valley

Picnic under €25; **Snacks** €25–40; **Real meal** €40–80; **Family treat** €80 or more (based on a family of four)

⑱ Urbino: Palazzo Ducale
The ideal Renaissance palace

The Palazzo Ducale in Urbino is unmissable, and its hill-town setting is pretty impressive too. From the east side the hulk of the palace appears forbidding, but the west side with its twin fairytale turrets, loggia and arches is beautiful. It was commissioned by soldier and nobleman Duke Federico da Montefeltro (1422–82), whose aim was that the palace, with its elegant architecture and wonderful paintings, should celebrate the ideals of the Renaissance.

A modern horse sculpture at the Palazzo Ducale

Key Features

The Flagellation by Piero della Francesca
In this famous painting the main scene, of Jesus being beaten, is in the background – but perspective draws the eye to it.

Duke Federico by Pedro Berruguete
The duke sits reading a book in full armour, with his grandly robed son at his side in this painting.

La Muta by Raphael
The name of this painting (1508) by Urbino-born Raffaello Sanzio means "silent lady". As mysterious as the *Mona Lisa*, she is thought be a portrait of a Florentine noblewoman.

The Flagellation by Piero della Francesca

Duke Federico by Pedro Berruguete

Studiolo

La Muta by Raphael

The west side
This side of the building is elaborate, with delicate towers and loggia – a contrast to the long plain east side of the palace which is decorated with round-arched windows.

Ideal City by Luciano Laurana
This 15th-century painting is so precise it looks like a computer-generated image. Notice the city has no people in it!

The library
Federico was a great reader and scholar, and built up one of the biggest libraries in Europe.

Studiolo This room was Federico's study. The inlaid wood makes it look as if it has cupboards full of interesting objects.

Cortile d'Onore At the heart of the palace a Renaissance courtyard designed by Laurana provides outside space and sunlight.

The Lowdown

🌐 **Map reference** 6 F3
Address Piazza Duca Federico 13, 61029, Urbino Le Marche; 0721 855 987; *www. palazzoducaleurbino.it*

🚗 **Bus** from Pesaro and Rimini (*www.adriabus.eu*).

ℹ️ **Visitor information** Piazza Duca Federico 35; 0722 2613; *www. urbinoculturaturismo.it*

🕐 **Open** 8:30am–2pm Mon, 8:30am–7:15pm Tue–Sun

💲 **Price** €10, under-18s free

👪 **Skipping the queue** The palace is a popular attraction, but Urbino is remote enough to discourage crowds.

👫 **Age range** Children aged 8 plus will get more from a visit

than younger children, but the intarsia animals in inlaid wood in the Studiolo and the story of Duke's nose *(see right)* may interest little ones.

⏱️ **Allow** At least 3 hours if the kids are old enough to last that long – there is lots to see.

♿ **Wheelchair access** Yes

☕ **Café** In Piazza della Repubblica

🛍️ **Shop** By the exit, selling guide books and postcards

🚻 **Toilets** On the ground floor

Good family value
The palace is free for kids, with lots of different areas to explore. They will be Renaissance buffs by the end of their trip.

Letting off steam

Head up to the top of the town where the **Giardini Pubblici** (public gardens) provide some green space and a playground. This is also the location of the **Fortezza Albornoz** (Viale B. Buozzi), a 16th-century fortress built by a cardinal, with views of the town and countryside.

Children's playground in Urbino's public gardens, at the top of town

Eat and drink

Picnic: under €25; Snacks: €25–40; Real meal: €40–80; Family treat: €80 or more (based on a family of four)

PICNIC Supermarket Margherita (Via Raffaello 37) stocks a vast range of meats and cheeses as well as fresh fruit and vegetables and other picnic provisions.

SNACKS Caffè Central (Piazza Repubblica), right in the centre of town, as the name suggests, is a lively place to stop for a coffee and a sandwich. Sit outside and watch the world go by while the kids play in the square.

REAL MEAL La Trattoria del Leone (Via Cesare Battisti 5; 0722 329 894), also located in the town centre, right under the church of San Francesco, is a traditional trattoria with good food and service.

FAMILY TREAT Vecchia Urbino (Via dei Varsari 3/5; 0722 4447; www.vecchiaurbino.it; closed Tue in winter) is an elegant but not stuffy place, with delicious local food, home-made pasta and plenty of truffles in season (for a price). Book ahead to guarantee a table.

Caffè Central on Piazza Repubblica, perfect for people-watching

Shopping

Bartolucci (Via Vittorio Veneto 23; www.bartolucci.com) sells beautifully crafted wooden toys, from Pinocchios to keyrings, clocks, swords and shields.

Amazing wooden motorbike and other hand-crafted toys at Bartolucci

Find out more

DIGITAL To find out more about Raphael, Urbino's most famous painter, see www.artchive.com/artchive/R/raphael.html.

Next stop...
CASTLES AND PAINTINGS

The **Casa Natale di Raffaello** on Via Raffaello (www.accademiaraffaello.it; open May–Sep 9am–1pm and 3pm–7pm, Sun closes 1pm, Oct–Apr closes 1pm) is where the artist Raphael was born in 1483. His father was a painter too, and the stone on which father and son mixed their pigments is on display, alongside a sweet Madonna and Child by Raphael. Afterwards travel back in time: head northwest to **San Leo** (see p246), the old capital of the craggy Montefeltro, passing **Sassocorvaro**, with its 15th-century fortress, the Rocca Ubaldinesca; **Macerata Feltria**, a medieval hill-town topped by a Malatesta castle; and **Piandimeleto**, with yet another castle, the 15th-century Castello dei Conti Oliva. Carry on further into the shadow of Monte Carpegna to **Pennabilli**, with its twin castles, and **Sant'Agata Feltria** with the Rocca Fregoso (fortress) on its crag.

Entrance to the Casa Natale di Raffaello, the house where Raphael was born

Colourful beach huts at the Adriatic Coast resort of Pesaro in Le Marche

⑲ Pesaro
Beside the seaside

The sprawling Adriatic Coast resort of Pesaro has some pretty Art Nouveau-style villas, a promenade lined with white stucco hotels and a jolly seaside atmosphere in summer. Look for the Villino Ruggieri (1908) on Piazzale della Libertà, decorated with organic floral motifs. The town has a medieval core, with the Rocca

The Lowdown

- 🌐 **Map reference** 6 F2
  Address 61100 Pesaro, Le Marche. Musei Civici: Piazza Toschi Mosca 29; 0721 387 295; www.museicivici pesaro.it. Casa Rossini: Via Rossini 34; 0721 387 357
- 🚗 **Train** from Milano, Bologna, Ancona, Lecce and Rome
- ℹ️ **Visitor information** Viale Trieste 164; 0721 69341; www. pesaroeurbino.info
- 🕐 **Open** Musei Civici: Jun–Sep 10am–1pm and 4–7:30pm Tue–Sat, 10am–1pm Sun, Oct–May 10am–1pm and 3:30–7pm Fri–Sun. Casa Rossini: Tue–Sun
- 💶 **Price** Musei Civici: €8. Casa Rossini: €8; combined ticket: €14; under-14s free
- 👫 **Age range** All
- ⏱️ **Allow** Half a day
- 🍽️ **Eat and drink** *Real meal* Bristolino *(Piazzale della Libertà 7; 0721 31609)* has good seafood. *Family treat* Restaurant Pizzeria Felici e Contenti *(Piazzetta Esedra Ciacchi; 0721 32 060; closed Tue)* serves pasta dishes.
- 🎭 **Festivals** Rossini Opera Festival *(www.rossinioperafestival.it)*: Aug

Costanza (fortress) built in 1478 by Laurana, architect of Urbino's ducal palace. The **Musei Civici** house a Renaissance masterpiece, Bellini's *Coronation of the Virgin* (1470), and a collection of glazed ceramics from the region. The city's other claim to fame is as birthplace of composer Gioacchino Rossini in 1792; the **Casa Rossini** displays memorabilia.

Letting off steam
Have a swim! The long, sandy town beach shelves gently into the sea, and has beach umbrellas for hire.

⑳ San Leo
A dramatic fortress

Rocky and formidable on its crag, San Leo's **Fortezza** looms over the village. The Romans built a fort here and it was added to piecemeal until Federico da Montefeltro decided to remodel it to withstand cannon fire in the 15th century. The result is an impressive structure which was not, however, unassailable: Lorenzo dei

Medici the Younger captured the castle in 1516, scaling the walls with ropes and ladders. It became a prison in the 18th century, housing the infamous necromancer the Conte di Cagliostro, who was kept in solitude for fear that the guards would catch his "evil eye".

At its foot is the village with its cobbled square and 9th-century Pieve (parish church), built with stones from a Roman temple. The Romanesque Duomo has columns from the temple, and pagan carvings are visible behind the altar.

Letting off steam
The square and grassy banks around the churches provide space to play – or do the visit in reverse and scale the castle after visiting the village.

The Lowdown

- 🌐 **Map reference** 6 E2
  Address 47865 San Leo, Emilia-Romagna; Fortezza: Via Giacomo Leopardi; 0541 926 967
- 🚌 **Bus** from Rimini (www.amrimini.it)
- ℹ️ **Visitor information** Piazza Dante 14, 47865; 0541 916 306; www. san-leo.it
- 🕐 **Open** Fortezza: 9am–5.15pm daily (until 6.15pm in winter)
- 💶 **Price** Fortezza: €16–26
- 👫 **Age range** All
- ⏱️ **Allow** 1 day
- 🍽️ **Eat and drink** *Snack* Osteria La Corte di Berengario II *(Via Michele Rosa 74; 0541 916 145; www.osterialacorte.it; closed Tue)* serves local favourites. *Real meal* Osteria Belvedere *(Via Toselli 19; 0541 916 361; www. belvederesanleo.it)* is rustic, family-run and serves steak.
- 🎭 **Festivals** San Leo Giullari (street art, jesters and juggling): late Jun

The cobbled main square of San Leo

Above *Palazzo Pubblico in San Marino*
Below *The distinctive red and green uniforms of the Palazzo's guards*

㉑ San Marino
A very tiny country

Little San Marino has the distinction of being a republic in its own right, in fact it is the smallest (60 sq km/ 23 sq miles) and oldest republic in the world – its constitution dates back to 1243. Travellers can get their passport stamped at the information office and buy one of the distinctive stamps of this tiny country. Children will enjoy the cable car from Borgomaggiore to the medieval citadel of San Marino, lined with souvenir stalls and phony sights – the Palazzo Pubblico was built in 1894, and has its own theatrical changing of the guards.

Letting off steam

Walk along the ridge to the three towers, the Rocca Guaita, Rocca Cesta and Rocca Montale, that look so dramatic from below. Then try a Torta Tre Monti (Three Tower Cake), layered and coated in chocolate.

The cable car going up to the citadel of San Marino

The Lowdown

🌐 **Map reference** 6 F2
Address 47031 San Marino, Repubblica di San Marino

🚌 **Bus** from Rimini (www.bus.it/ benedettini or www.bonellibus.it), then **Funivia** (cable car) every 15 minutes from 7:50am until early evening, until 1am Jun–Sep (www.aass.sm)

ℹ️ **Visitor information** Contrada del Collegio; 0549 882 914; www.visitsanmarino.com

🚻 **Age range** All

⏱️ **Allow** Half a day

🍴 **Eat and drink** *Real meal* Il Piccolo (Via del Serrone 17, 47031 Loc Murata; 0549 992 815) offers a warm welcome and serves good pizza and fish. *Family treat* La Fratta (Via Salita della Rocca 14, 0549 991 594; www.ristorante lafratta.com; closed Feb, Winter closed Wed) is a smart *trattoria* serving hearty food.

🎪 **Festivals** Medieval Festival (archery and jousting): Jul

Picnic under €25; **Snacks** €25–40; **Real meal** €40–80; **Family treat** €80 or more (based on a family of four)

㉒ Ascoli Piceno
Tall towers and a dolphin fountain

It is a mystery that the lovely town of Ascoli Piceno is not more visited. It is circled by old walls and has some interesting Roman remains, graceful squares, intriguing artisan shops, arcaded streets, tall medieval towers and enticing cafés and restaurants. There is a Baroque Duomo, an array of churches and a Museo Archeologico containing artefacts of the Piceni people, who founded the town long before Rome was built, including objects inscribed with curses against Roman invaders.

Ceiling detail, Anisetta Meletti café

Key Sights

① **Medieval towers** The city once had around 100 towers, but only a couple of these tall stone structures remain, in Via dei Soderini.

⑤ **Museo Archeologico** Find out more about the Piceni, who predated the Roman occupation of Ascoli, at this museum. Artefacts include Roman mosaics.

⑥ **Pinacoteca Civica** Located in the Palazzo Comunale, next to the Duomo, the town gallery features works by 15th-century artist Carlo Crivelli.

② **Loggia dei Mercanti** This little square with a loggia was the commercial heart of the city from the 16th century. There is a small daily market.

③ **San Francesco** The Gothic church of San Francesco is one of the town's most significant buildings, begun in 1258 but not completed until 1549.

④ **Piazza del Popolo** Dominated by the imposing 13th-century Palazzo del Popolo, this grand city square is the social hub of Ascoli. The shady loggias around the sides house cafés and shops.

⑦ **Duomo** Set on Piazza Arringo, the 12th-century Duomo has a Baroque façade and a glowing polyptych by Crivelli (1435–95).

⑧ **Roman remains** A bridge, the remains of a theatre and the 14th-century San Gregorio church, built around a Roman temple, are remnants of the town's Roman past.

The Lowdown

🌐 **Map reference** 6 G5
Address 63100 Le Marche. Museo Archeologico: Palazzo Panighi, Piazza Arringo, 63100; 0736 253 562. Pinacoteca Civica: Palazzo Comunale, Piazza Arringo, 63100; 0736 298 213

🚗 **Train** from San Benedetto del Tronto on the Adriatic Coast. **Car** 30 mins on motorway from the coast, or over 1 hour over the mountains from Norcia in Umbria

ℹ️ **Visitor information** Palazzo del Comune, Piazza Arringo 1, 63100; 0736 298 204

🕐 **Open** Museo Archeologico: 8:30am–7:30pm Tue–Sun. Pinacoteca Civica: Apr–Oct 10am–7pm daily, Sep–Mar 10am–5pm, Sat & Sun till 7pm

💶 **Price** Museo Archeologico: €8. Pinacoteca Civica: €26

👫 **Skipping the queue** Off the beaten track, so no queues!

👫 **Age range** All
🕐 **Allow** At least 1 day
🚻 **Toilets** In cafés and museums.
🎭 **Festivals** Palio della Quintana (jousting festival): Aug

Good family value?
The city is the main attraction here, and the paying attractions are relatively inexpensive; even *olive all'ascolana* make a cheap snack.

Children playing at the fountain in Piazza Arringo on a hot summer's day

Letting off steam

Have a run around broad, largely pedestrianized **Piazza Arringo**. The square is graced with an unusual fountain: water spurts from the mouths of two bronze horses with fishy tails, and the structure is topped by a playful dolphin.

Eat and drink

Picnic: under €25; Snacks: €25–40; Real meal: €40–80; Family treat: €80 or more (based on a family of four)

PICNIC Gastronomia Migllori *(Piazza Arringo 2, 63100; 0736 250 042; www.miglioriolive.it)* is a local institution; this café-deli serves fresh and delicious snacks to take away, as well as the town speciality, *olive all'ascolana*, deep-fried olives stuffed with veal.

SNACKS Anisetta Meletti *(Palazzo del Popolo, 63100; 0736 259 626)*, the town's most famous café, was built in 1907 and retains a wonderful Art Nouveau interior, with painted ceilings and gleaming ranks of bottles.

REAL MEAL Leopoldus Ristorante *(Via Vidacilio 18, 63100; 0736 258 857; www.leopoldus.it)* is a friendly, bustling restaurant with a brick-vaulted ceiling and rustic wooden tables. It serves excellent pizza, as well as pasta, meat and fish dishes.

FAMILY TREAT Trattoria Laliva *(Piazza della Viola 13, 63100; 0736 259 358; www.trattorialaliva.it)* is an informal and welcoming place for sampling *olive all'ascolana*, followed by *lasagna in bianco* (flat pasta sheets baked with a creamy white sauce) and a delicacy all their own: candied olives.

Shopping

Near Piazza Arringo, head to the little network of streets lined with artisan workshops selling ceramics, stationary and clothes.

Find out more

DIGITAL Play in your own jousting tournament after seeing the "knights" in action at the Quintana festival, at *www.agame.com/game/medieval-jousting.html*

Next stop…

MONTEFORTINO Head west into Umbria over the Monti Sibillini; turn right onto the SP37 into the village of Montefortino (one hour's drive; *www.montefortino.it*). This is a good base for walking and has a small gallery and some lovely rustic restaurants.

GOLA DELL'INFERNACCIO From Montefortino there is an easy walk (4 hours round trip) to the scarily named Gola dell'Infernaccio (Gorge of Hell), a beautiful limestone gorge.

PIANO GRANDE Keep on the SS4 towards Norcia, take the high pass over the Forca Canapine (1,500 m/ 4,920 ft; closed in winter) to the flower meadow of Piano Grande – a beautiful flat plain for walking.

A range of jam delicacies at Gastronomia Migliori

㉓ Macerata

A Renaissance town and a famous explorer

Set on a hill amid gentle Le Marche countryside, this vibrant university town with its laid-back atmosphere is a relaxed base for exploring the Chienti valley. In the centre, the vast Piazza della Libertà boasts an arcaded Loggia dei Mercanti (1505), while Corso Matteotti has several Renaissance *palazzi*. Vaster still is the colonnaded Arena Sferisterio, an open-air theatre built in the 1820s. In the **Pinacoteca Civica** (town art gallery) is a beautiful *Madonna and Child* by Carlo Crivelli (1435–95), a painter noted for his decorative style, while the Baroque Duomo has a monument to the town's famous explorer, Matteo Ricci, depicted in Chinese clothes with a long beard.

Head out of town to Corridonia, which has another Crivelli *Madonna* in its art gallery. To the west (22 km/ 14 miles) is Cingoli, a summer resort known as the Balcony of Le Marche for its views. Up the valley is Tolentino, where the Santuario di San Nicola has Giottesque frescoes (1310–25). Further up are pretty, walled San Ginesio, Sarnano spa, medieval San Severino Marche and hill-top Camerino, with its grand Renaissance Palazzo Ducale.

Memorial to 16th-century adventurer and scholar Matteo Ricci in Macerata

Letting off steam

East of Macerata (15 km/9 miles), the winding lanes of the medieval hill village **Morrovalle** offer plenty of scope to play hide and seek.

㉔ Monti Sibillini National Park

Brown bears and bike tracks

The limestone peaks of the Parco Nazionale dei Monti Sibillini are thickly forested and support an impressive range of exotic wildlife, including brown bears, wolves, golden eagles, porcupines and chamois. The park is rich in legends of enchantresses and devils, and its peaks, gorges and caves too cast a spell over visitors. The most attractive bases are Amandola and the hill village of Montefortino.

Letting off steam

The region is perfect for strenuous but rewarding mountain biking and long-distance hikes. Ambitious cyclists should attempt at least part of the **Grande Anello dei Sibillini** (Great Sibylline Ring; www.sibillini.net), 120 km (75 miles) of signed paths through the woods. Mountain refuges along the route provide shelter for overnight stops. Families with younger children can walk shorter sections of the route, or simply go looking for fields of wild flowers or chestnuts, depending on the season.

The Lowdown

🌐 **Map reference** 6 G5
Address 63021 Monti Sibillini National Park, Le Marche/Umbria

🚗 **Car** is the only practical way to get around this region.

ℹ **Visitor information** Casa del Parco, Palazzo Leopardi, Largo Duranti, 63047 Montefortino; 0736 859 491; www.sibillini.net

👫 **Age range** All

Activities Hire mountain bikes at Agricamp Picobello (*Contrada Cortaglie, 63853 Montelparo; www.agricamppico.com*).

⏱ **Allow** 1 day to 1 week

🍴 **Eat and drink** *Snack* Osteria del Nonno (*Località Ambro, 63044; 333 791 9961*) serves *girella*, a spiral lasagna filled with spinach and ricotta cheese and good meat dishes and wine. *Real meal* Da Benito (*Via Tenna 9, 63021; 0736 859 515*) serves seasonal dishes.

The Lowdown

🌐 **Map reference** 6 G4
Address 62100 Macerata, Le Marche. Pinacoteca Civica: Via Don Giovanni Minzoni 24, 62100

🚗 **Train** from Civitanova Marche on the Adriatic Coast line, then 10-minute walk or bus to centre

ℹ **Visitor information** Piazza della Libertà 12, 62100; 0733 234 807; www.provincia.mc.it

🕐 **Open** Pinacoteca Civica: daily

💲 **Price** Pinacoteca Civica: free

👫 **Age range** 11 plus

⏱ **Allow** 1 hour for Macerata, 2 days for a leisurely tour of the Chienti valley

🍴 **Eat and drink** *Snacks* Da Silvano (*Piaggia della Torre 15, 62100; 0733 260 216*) is a basic little pizzeria with a wood-fired oven. *Real meal* Ristorante Da Secondo (*Via Pescheria Vecchia 26/28, 62100; 0733 260 912*) serves delicious fried *antipasti*.

🎪 **Festivals** Sferisterio Opera Festival (*www.sferisterio.it*): Jul–Aug

Flowering poppy and mustard fields in the Monti Sibillini National Park

The historic little town of Amandola in amongst the Monti Sibillini

25 Amandola
Mountain refuge

The little village of Amandola is the best-equipped base for a stay in the Monti Sibillini National Park, with a couple of welcoming guesthouses (www.montisibillini.it/casa.html or www.palazzopecci.com) and simple restaurants. It was founded in the Middle Ages when local castle-dwellers decided to create a mini-federation. It is also a good place to learn more about the history and traditions of the region:

The Lowdown

- 🌐 **Map reference** 6 G5
  Address 63021 Amandola, Le Marche. Museo Antropogeografico: Chiostro di San Francesco, Largo Leopardi 4, 62020; 0736 848 598
- 🚗 **Car** is the easiest way to reach Amandola and the surrounding attractions.
- 🕐 **Open** Museo Antropogeografico: daily Jul and Aug only
- 💶 **Price** free
- 👫 **Age range** 8 plus
- ⏱ **Allow** 1 hour for the village, more for walks in the mountains
- ☕ **Eat and drink** *Real meal* Vecchio Moro sul Lago (Contrada Santo Stefano 14, 62020; 0736 847 575; www.vecchiomoro.it) is a lakeside restaurant serving good pizza and wine. *Family treat* Paradiso (Piazza Umberto I 7, 63021; 0736 847 468) offers traditional dishes.
- 🎭 **Festivals** Theatre Festival (mime and movement): first week of Sep

the **Museo Antropogeografico** in the ex-convent of San Francesco has displays on the legends and flora and fauna of the Monti Sibillini, as well as all manner of tools and household items used by the locals until not so long ago.

Letting off steam

For a play, head to pizzeria **Vecchio Moro sul Lago**, set beside a lake. For a hike, drive south to the walled village of Montemonaco (15 km/ 9 miles). From here a challenging 2-hour walk leads to the **Cave of the Sibyl** – where it is said an enchantress waits to lure travellers – or a 3-hour walk along a river leads to the **Gola dell'Infernaccio** (hellish gorge); both summer only.

Picturesque doorway in the back streets of Amandola

KIDS' CORNER

Sibyl the enchantress

Ever since medieval times, Italians have flocked to the Mountains of the Sibyl in search of the bewitching lady who gave them their name. An ancient Roman enchantress, she was said to be one of the wise women who prophesied Christ's birth – but turned nasty when she was not chosen to be his virgin mother. She has even been identified as Venus, the Roman goddess of love. In the 1490s, the pope threatened to excommunicate (throw out of the Church) anyone who went looking for her, but that did not stop people!

EDELWEISS, EDELWEISS

May–June is the best time to see wild flowers here: wild mustard, poppies, edelweiss and cornflowers. The peaks are covered in snow from October until May.

MACERATA'S MISSIONARY

Matteo Ricci was born into a noble family in Macerata in 1552. He became a Jesuit priest against his father's will and was sent on a mission to India and, later, China. He learned Chinese, and whilst living in the Portuguese-speaking city of Macau, he wrote a Portuguese-Chinese dictionary, and adopted Chinese customs. In 1601, Ricci was the first foreigner invited by the emperor to enter the Forbidden City in Beijing. He lived the rest of his life in China as a court scholar, took the name of Li Matou and dressed like a Buddhist monk. He died and was buried in Beijing.

Where to Stay in Umbria and Le Marche

Umbria has a wealth of accommodation choices for families, from luxurious country hotels with swimming pools and tennis courts to friendly city-centre B&Bs. A great family option in the region is an *agriturismo* (farm holiday), which gives a flavour of Italian rural life that will appeal to children.

AGENCY
Villa in Umbria
www.villainumbria.com
Run by a Dutch couple who live in Umbria, this agency has a good selection of private villas with swimming pool, farmhouses and apartments in the countryside and in town centres.

Ascoli Piceno
Map 6 G5

HOTEL
Albergo Piceno
Via Minucia 10, 63100; 0736 253 017; www.albergopiceno.it
Converted from a 17th-century palazzo close to the Duomo, this elegant boutique hotel has bright, comfortable rooms and friendly staff. Good breakfasts.
€€

HOSTEL
Ostello de Longobardi
Palazzetto Longobardo, Via Soderini 26, 63100; 0736 259 191
A fun option for kids, this hostel is based in one of the city's last two medieval towers, constructed in the 12th century. No breakfast, but there are plenty of cafés nearby.
€

Assisi
Map 6 F4

HOTELS
Hotel Alexander
Piazza Chiesa Nuova 6, 06081; 075 816 190; www.hotelalexanderassisi.it
This hotel is housed in a lovely old stone building done up in a modern style, but retaining old beams. Ask for a room with a view. Additional beds on request.
€€

Hotel La Terrazza
Fratelli Canonichetti, 06081; 075 812 368; www.laterrazzahotel.it
Just outside the city, this attractive modern hotel is well located for exploring Assisi and its countryside.

There is a lovely pool screened by olive trees, and the food in the attached restaurant is excellent.
€€

Hotel Giotto Assisi
Via Fontebella 41, 06082; 075 812 209; www.hotelgiottoassisi.it
Right in the old town, this hotel has fantastic views from its lovely roof terrace. The grand old building has ultra-traditional decor and a spa.
€€€

HOSTEL
Ostello della Pace
Via di Valecchie 4, 06081; 075 816 767; www.assisihostel.com
Assisi's hostel is a good budget option, a 20-minute walk from town through an olive grove. It has table tennis, bikes for hire and a kitchen.
€

Gubbio
Map 6 F4

HOTELS
Grotta dell'Angelo
Via Gioia 47, 06024; 075 927 1747; www.grottadellangelo.it
A small, family-run hotel, Grotta dell'Angelo is close to the funicular and Duomo. There is a great little

restaurant in the "grotta" (cave), where Umbrian classics are served to a mainly Italian clientele.
€

Hotel Bosone Palace
Via XX Settembre 22, 06024; 075 922 0688; hotelbosone.com
In a grand palazzo, with a sweeping stone staircase and antique frescoes, this hotel has 30 rooms, including two suites, plus family rooms that sleep four. Bicycles available to rent.
€€

Park Hotel ai Cappuccini
Via Tifernate, 06024; 075 9234; www.parkhotelaicappuccini.it
This grand hotel is set in spacious parkland within walking distance of the old town. It is housed in a 17th-century former monastery, with grand communal areas, elegant rooms and a large pool and spa.
€€€

B&B
Casa La Valle
Frazione Santa Cristina 27, 06024; 075 922 9767; www.casalavalle.it
An enchanting country B&B located 20 km (12 miles) south of Gubbio in the Tiber valley, in an old stone

The historic Hotel Bosone Palace in Gubbio, dating back to the 14th century

Courtyard of Park Hotel ai Cappuccini in a former monastery in Gubbio

house, Casa La Valle has an apartment for families and a third bed can be added to double rooms. Visitors have use of a pool nearby.

 €

Orvieto
Map 6 E5

B&Bs
Ripa Medici
Vicolo Ripa Medici 14, 05018; 328 746 9620; www.ripamedici.it
Located in the centre of Orvieto, this B&B has lovely country views and rustic decor. Sabrina, the owner, is very helpful and prepares delicious breakfasts. There are two rooms and a shared living room and kitchen.

€

Casa Selita
Strada di Porta Romana 8, 05018; 0763 344 218; www.casaselita.com
This family-owned old farmhouse is built on an ancient site, using Etruscan stones, hand-fired bricks and wooden floors. It is located just outside the Porta Romana, among olive groves.

€€

AGRITURISMO
Locanda Rosati
Località Buonviaggio 22, 61029; 0763 217 314; www.locandarosati.it
Beamed ceilings, quilts on the bed and wooden floors contribute to the rustic atmosphere at this attractive farm just outside Orvieto. It is very friendly, with home-cooked, organic food, which is superb.

€€

Perugia
Map 6 E4

HOTELS
Albergo Morlacchi
Via Leopoldo Tiberi 2, 06123; 075 572 0319; www.hotelmorlacchi.it
This welcoming guesthouse is within easy walking distance of the town's attractions. It also has a historic apartment nearby, which will sleep a family of four.

€

Le Torri di Bagnara
Strada Bruna 8, Località Solfagnano, 06123; 075 579 2001; www. letorridibagnara.it
Superb for nature lovers, this hotel is set on a hillside overlooking the Tiber valley, around 16 km (10 miles) north of Perugia. Guest rooms are in restored stone outhouses around a courtyard. It serves delicious local food and there is a swimming pool in the summer.

€€

AGRITURISMO
San Lorenzo della Rabatta
Località Cenerente, 06134; 075 690 764; www.sanlorenzodellarabatta.com
Set in a medieval hamlet 9 km (6 miles) from Perugia, in hilly surroundings, the picturesque ivy-covered stone buildings here have tasteful rooms and there is a decent-sized pool.

€€€

CAMPING
Il Rocolo
Strada Fontana la Trinità 1n, 06123; 075 518 1635; www.ilrocolo.it
This well-equipped camp site 6 km (4 miles) from Perugia is surrounded by olive trees, with its own snack bar and BBQ. It is a 15-minute ride into town from the bus stop outside.

€

Spoleto
Map 6 F5

HOTELS
Albergo La Macchia
Località Licina 11, 06049; 020 042 4054; www.albergolamacchia.it
Set in an olive grove a short bus ride from Spoleto, this hotel is a converted railway station. It serves great food, has a pool and the owners can arrange horse-riding.

€€

Hotel dei Duchi
Viale G. Matteotti 4, 06049; 0743 44541; www.hoteldeiduchi.com
Looking onto the Roman theatre, the Hotel dei Duchi is modern and well equipped, and has splendid views. There is a garden with mature trees where guests can eat in summer, and a bar with a view.

€€€

Hotel San Luca
Via Interna delle Mura 21, 06049; 0743 223 399; www.hotelsanluca.com
This hotel is set in a very grand mid-19th-century building around a pretty courtyard, with comfortable, modern rooms. Breakfast is served outside, under the olive trees.

€€€

SELF-CATERING
Pianciano
Località Silvignano, 06049; 333 250 5284; www.pianciano.it
With views down to Spoleto, these beautifully restored farm buildings feature a pool, playroom and table tennis. Cook in the kitchen, or order a gourmet dinner or pizzas.

€€

Urbino
Map 6 F3

HOTEL
Albergo Italia
Corso Garibaldi 32, 61029; 0722 2701; www.albergo-italia-urbino.it
On an arcaded street under the Palazzo Ducale, this is a convenient central option. Some rooms have views of the ducal palace. Breakfast is served on the terrace in summer.

€€

Reception area of Albergo Italia in the heart of Urbino

Price Guide
For a standard double room per night, incusive of breakfast, service charges and any additional taxes such as VAT and also a fourth line is added here.

€ Under €200 €€ €200–350 €€€ over €350

Rome and Lazio

Exuberant Rome is a city that brings history to life like no other – full of stories and tiny details that can give children a sense of the hurly-burly reality behind some of the most revered buildings and works of art in Western Europe. Imagine what it was like to attend a wild animal fight in the Colosseum, descend underground to hidden churches and run free in splendid Baroque piazzas, then escape to Lazio – the wonderfully varied region that surrounds Rome – for Etruscan cities of the dead, volcanic lakes and the spectacular coastline of Monte Circeo.

Highlights

Colosseum
The arena is where gladiators fought to the death and battled wild beasts in ancient times (see pp266–7).

Piazza Navona
The pulsing heart of Rome has extraordinary Baroque fountains, great cafés and an entertaining array of street vendors and caricature artists (see pp274–5).

Campo de' Fiori
It is easy to imagine medieval and Renaissance Rome in this vibrant piazza, with its lively fruit and vegetable market (see pp280–81).

Sistine Chapel
The most extraordinary work of art of the Renaissance tells the story of the creation with 336 lusciously dressed figures (see pp294–5).

St Peter's
The capital of Christendom is a sumptuously decorated basilica beneath a vast dome designed by Michelangelo (see p296).

Monte Circeo
This dramatic peninsula, ringed by sandy beaches, is rich in legends of the Odyssey (see pp310–11); from here it's a short hop to the lush gardens of Ninfa (see p312).

Left Visitors to the Baroque confection of the Trevi Fountain, tossing coins into the water to make sure they return to Rome **Above right** Plants wind over ruined towers and walls in the verdant gardens of Ninfa

The Best of
Rome and Lazio

Rome is a chaotic city with layers of history piled haphazardly one on top of the other. As well as famous sights, from the Colosseum to St Peter's, explore the city's maze of narrow streets, finding ancient Roman columns embedded in Renaissance palaces, Egyptian obelisks in Baroque fountains and dank pagan temples beneath flamboyant basilicas. Then head into Lazio, combining more culture with open countryside.

Culture vultures

Recreate a day in the life of an ancient Roman: shopping at **Trajan's Market** (see p270), bathing at the **Baths of Caracalla** (see p268) and gladiator-fighting at the **Colosseum** (see pp266–7). Get a sense of the splendour in which wealthy Romans lived by exploring the ruined palaces of the **Palatine** (see p268), then go to see the frescoes and mosaics from their luxurious homes in the **Museo Nazionale Romana** (see p270). Another day, head out of town to the ruins of **Ostia Antica** (see p302).

For the best, theatrical Baroque architecture, play among the fountains of **Piazza Navona** (see pp274–5), cross the **Ponte Sant'Angelo** (see p297) and visit **St Peter's** (see p296).

Rome and Lazio for free

Much of what is appealing about Rome is free: pedestrianized piazzas, elaborate fountains and mazes of alleys, and everyday spectacles such as a policeman on a tiny pedestal controlling the traffic or a shrine to the Madonna decorated with plastic roses. Entrance to churches is free, and on the last Sunday of the month so are many museums, including the Vatican Museums. There is no charge to swim in the lakes and sea in Lazio.

By season

Spring and autumn are the best seasons to visit Rome and Lazio: expect clear skies and sunshine, without the heat. **Holy Week** is a special time to visit, culminating in the pope's

Below Visitors approaching Rome's most majestic sight, the Colosseum, commissioned in AD 72 by Emperor Vespasian

Above *Sailing on Lake Bracciano, about an hour north of Rome* **Centre** *A street artist sketches a portrait in Piazza Navona, Rome* **Below** *A spouting lion at the base of the obelisk in Piazza del Popolo, Rome*

address on Easter Day. September and even October have the feel of late summer. Winter closes in during November, and at Christmas crib scenes are set up in churches and piazzas. From mid-December until 6 January there is a **Christmas market** in Piazza Navona. August can be swelteringly hot, but the **Roma Estate** summer arts festival puts on a series of outdoor events, with restaurants opening stalls on the banks of the Tiber. At the end of July, Trastevere holds the **Festival of Noantri**, with processions, street parties and fireworks. Head into Lazio for more seasonal festivals: Nemi's **strawberry festival** and the **Infiorata** at Genzano both take place in June.

In three days

Rome was not built in a day, but you can visit many of its highlights in three, and even see a bit of Lazio too. Spend at least a day at two of the city's ancient sites – the **Roman Forum** *(see p268)* and the **Colosseum** *(see p266–7)*. On day two, dedicate a morning to the art treasures of the **Galleria Borghese**. Let the kids run around in the vast **Villa Borghese** park *(see pp286–7)* afterwards or spend an hour or two outdoors at **Campo de' Fiori** *(see pp280–81)*. On your last day, take a trip out to Tivoli and stretch your legs at **Villa Adriana** (Hadrian's Villa – *see p302*) for a refreshing change of pace from the city.

Rome and Lazio

Ancient Roman roads lead out like the spokes of a bicycle wheel from Rome's compact historic centre. It is possible to avoid public transport and walk to most sights; engage kids by getting them to navigate from piazza to piazza. The attractions of Lazio – the region around Rome – from Etruscan cities of the dead to the stunning Monte Circeo National Park, can be reached by train and bus, but car may be easier.

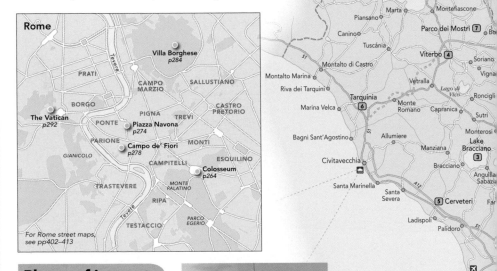

Rome

PRATI
CAMPO MARZIO
SALLUSTIANO
Villa Borghese *p284*
BORGO
PIGNA
TREVI
CASTRO PRETORIO
The Vatican *p292*
PONTE
Piazza Navona *p274*
PARIONE
MONTI
Campo de' Fiori *p278*
GIANICOLO
CAMPITELLI
ESQUILINO
Colosseum *p264*
TRASTEVERE
MONTE PALATINO
RIPA
PARCO EGERIO
TESTACCIO

For Rome street maps, see pp402–413

Castel Giorgio
Basc
Bolsena
571
Grádoll
Bagnoregio
Lago di Bolsena
Valentano
Montefiascone
Piansano
Marta
Canino
Parco dei Mostri [7]
Bo
Tuscánia
57
Viterbo [4]
Soriano
Montalto di Castro
Vigna
Montalto Marina
Vetralla
Lago di Vico
Roncigli
Riva dei Tarquini
Tarquinia [6]
Monte Romano
Capranica
Sutri
Marina Velca
Monterosi
Bagni Sant'Agostino
Allumiere
Lake Bracciano [3]
Manziana
Civitavecchia
Bracciano
Anguilla Sabázia
Santa Marinella
Santa Severa
[5] **Cerveteri**
Far
Ladispoli
Palidoro
Ostia Antica [2]
Lido di Castel Fusano

Places of interest

- **ROME** (see pp261–308)
- **DAY TRIPS FROM ROME**
  1 Tivoli
  2 Ostia Antica
  3 Lake Bracciano
  4 Viterbo
  5 Cerveteri
  6 Tarquinia
  7 Parco dei Mostri, Bomarzo
- **LAZIO**
  1 Monte Circeo National Park
  2 Sermoneta and Ninfa
  3 Sperlonga
  4 The Pontine Islands

0 kilometres   20
0 miles   20

The Cordonata steps leading up to Michelangelo's Piazza Campidoglio

Mar Tirre

Giacomo della Porta's Fontana del Nettuno (1574) in Piazza Navona, Rome

The astonishingly intact Colosseum, seen from the eastern end

The top of a grand Baroque fountain at the Villa d'Este pleasure gardens in Tivoli

Sand dunes at Torre Paola, at the southernmost end of Sabaudia beach in the Monte Circeo National Park

The Lowdown

🚗 **Air** to Rome Fiumicino or Ciampino airports (see p260). **Train** to Roma Stazione Termini. **Long-distance bus** to Stazione Tiburtina. **Metro** lines A and B, which intersect at Termini. **Bus and tram** Many bus and six tram routes connect all parts of Rome, three mini- buses navigate the historic centre and a hop-on hop-off bus (110) stops at the main sights. Tickets from train and metro stations, kiosks and tobacconists. Flat-fare ticket (valid 75 minutes) €1, children under 1 m (3 ft) free; one-day ticket €4; weekly ticket €16. Validate ticket on bus or tram.

ℹ️ **Visitor information** 060608; www.turismoroma.it; offices at airports and train station, and dotted around the city centre. **Roma Pass** gives unlimited travel on city transport for three days, free entry to two sights and reduced entry to others for €25 per adult; book on 060608 or at www.roma pass.it and collect at sight or tourist office.

🛒 **Supermarkets** Carrefour chain is everywhere in the region. **Markets** In Rome: Campo de'Fiori, Piazza San Cosimato, Piazza Vittorio Emanuele, Piazza Testaccio, Piazza delle Coppelle (all Mon–Sat am). In Lazio: Viterbo, San Felice Circeo, Sabaudia, Sermoneta and Sperlonga.

➕ **Pharmacies** Go to farmaturni. federfarmaroma.com/orario. aspx

🚻 **Toilets** Few public toilets; use the facilities in bars and cafés.

Rome and Lazio Airports

Rome has two major airports. Fiumicino, 30 km (17 miles) southwest of the city, is the main Italian hub for international flights and is also used by several Italian budget airlines. Ciampino, 15 km (9 miles) southeast of Rome, is used mainly by low-cost and charter flights. It is usually cheaper to fly to Ciampino, but Fiumicino has better facilities and more direct transport connections to Rome.

Rome Fiumicino

Fiumicino, also known as Leonardo da Vinci, is Italy's main international hub, with flights to and from most major European and international destinations, and the rest of Italy. It is the hub for Italian national carrier Alitalia, and all major international airlines that fly to Italy land here. Passengers flying to other Italian destinations may well transit here. The airport is also used by low-cost companies, including Air Italy, Blue Air, easyJet, Wind Jet and Wizz Air.

Fiumicino is a large airport, with four terminals – confusingly, 1, 2, 3 and 5 – with 1 devoted to Alitalia and 5 all flights to and from the United States and Israel. There are long walks to reach departure gates and between terminals – you may have to catch a shuttle train to your gate, or a shuttle bus between terminals, so allow plenty of time. If booking a flight with a connection at Fiumicino, allow around 2 hours for the transfer, to be reasonably sure that you – and your luggage – will not miss the connecting flight.

Following expansion, there are several large shopping zones, but most shops are fashion boutiques, with just a few bookshops and toy shops. There are plenty of eating options, from McDonald's to the Gelateria San Crispino, cafés and wine bars. However there are no play areas for children so – as on any journey with kids – come prepared with books, colouring pads and games, or an iPod or Nintendo DS (there is free Wi-Fi).

Fiumicino is well connected to central Rome. The Rome–Fiumicino Leonardo Express non-stop train takes passengers to Stazione Termini in 30 minutes, and the service is guaranteed even if there are public transport strikes (€14 per person). Regular commuter trains to Rome's Ostiense (for Testaccio and Aventino), Trastevere and Tiburtina stations take 50 minutes but cost less (€8 per person).

Concourse at Fiumicino Leonardo da Vinci Airport

Alternatively, COTRAL (€4.50 per person), SIT (€10 per person) and Terravision (€4 per person) buses all have frequent departures to the Stazione Termini area of Rome. The journey takes around 1 hour.

Authorized taxis are white and charge a flat rate of €40 to carry up to four passengers and baggage to anywhere in central Rome.

All major car hire companies, including Avis, Budget, easyCar, Europcar, Hertz, Maggiore and Sixt, have offices at the airport.

Should you have to overnight at the airport, there are two **Hilton hotels**: the Hilton Rome Airport Hotel is within walking distance of terminals, and the Hilton Garden Inn Rome Airport is connected by shuttle bus. Both have family rooms.

Ciampino

Ciampino handles almost exclusively low-cost and charter flights. EasyJet, Ryanair and Wizz Air are the main operators, with flights to Dublin in Ireland; Edinburgh, London Gatwick, London Stansted and Manchester in the UK; and many European cities. Despite recent growth, Ciampino is a small airport and easy to navigate. However it has only a handful of shops and cafés and no play areas.

The easiest way to reach Rome is by bus, as Ciampino train station is itself a bus trip away. ATRAL (€3.90 per person), SIT (€6 per person) and Terravision (€4 per person) buses all have frequent departures to the Stazione Termini area of Rome. The journey takes around 40 minutes.

Authorized taxis are white and charge a flat rate of €30 to carry up to four passengers and baggage to anywhere in central Rome.

Several major car hire companies, including Autoeuropa, Avis, Budget, Europcar, Hertz, Maggiore and Sixt, have offices at the airport.

There are no airport hotels, but the area around Stazione Termini has plenty of options. An alternative is **Villa Giulia** in Ciampino town, 3 km (2 miles) from the airport, which can be reached by local bus.

The Lowdown

Ciampino 06 65951; 06 6595 9515 (flight information); www.adr.it

Fiumicino 06 65951; 06 65643 (Alitalia); www.adr.it

Hilton hotels 06 65258; www.hilton.com

Villa Giulia www.hotelvillagiulia.com

Rome

It is all too easy to be overwhelmed by Rome; the trick is to be selective. If the kids already know about ancient Romans, start with the Colosseum. If they are younger, wander around Piazza Navona or Campo de' Fiori, look at market stalls and fountains, see the Pantheon's dome and the obelisk-topped elephant, and treat the family to Roman pizza and ice cream.

Below The majestic Arch of Constantine, in front of the Colosseum in Rome

Rome's Churches and Fountains

In the 16th and 17th centuries the Catholic Church was immensely rich and powerful. The greatest threat to its might was the wave of Protestantism sweeping through northern Europe, which rejected the pope in favour of plain churches and simple ceremonies. Rome responded by erecting scores of churches, palaces and fountains to glorify Catholicism – an astonishing Baroque building boom dominated by arch-rivals Bernini and Borromini.

Sant'Ivo alla Sapienza

A hexagonal church with a scalloped cupola and spiralling gold pinnacle, **Sant'Ivo alla Sapienza** (1642–60) is the most ingenious of architect Francesco Borromini's churches. The stunning interior is shaped like an exotic flower, with alternating scooped and sharply angled bays forming the "petals". The church took more than 20 years to build, spanning the reign of three highly influential popes from noble families: Urban VIII Barberini, Innocent X Pamphilj and Alexander VII Chigi. Borromini incorporated symbols from all of their aristocratic coats of arms in the decorations: look out for Barberini bees, Pamphilj doves with olive branches in their beaks, and the star and jelly-mould (actually a mountain) from the Chigi shield.

San Carlo alle Quattro Fontane

An enchanting church, with a curved façade and column capitals licked by curling fronds of foliage, **San Carlo alle Quattro Fontane** (see p290) was commissioned from Borromini in 1638. An octagonal courtyard leads to the oval church. Look carefully at the dome: the coffering of crosses, hexagons and octagons gets smaller towards the top, to create the illusion that the dome is higher than it is.

Sant'Andrea al Quirinale

Sant'Andrea al Quirinale (see p291) is possibly the most theatrical church in Rome. From 1658 to 1670, Gian Lorenzo Bernini combined architecture, painting and sculpture to depict the martyrdom and subsequent journey to heaven of St Andrew. The church is an oval set on its short axis, so that visitors are confronted by the high altar niche, where sculpted angels appear to be positioning a painting of the saint crucified on his diagonal cross. At first this seems to be all, but look up to find a statue of the saint floating on a cloud, as if he has just slipped through the gap in the broken pediment behind him on the way to heaven.

The Jesuit churches: Sant'Ignazio and Il Gesù

Sant'Ignazio (see p277) was built to celebrate the canonization of Ignatius Loyola, Spanish founder of

Below The oval dome of San Carlo alle Quattro Fontane, with illusionistic coffering to make it seem higher than it is

Above Baroque interior of Sant'Ignazio, Rome's most flamboyant church
Below Bernini's Fontana del Tritone

read their own Bibles in their own language, for example, instead of having priests read carefully selected extracts. By providing people with prayer books and making the nave light enough to read by, the Jesuits hoped to make Catholicism more popular. By the late 17th century, when the interior was decorated, the war was over, and the Catholic Church was riding on a wave of glory. In this mood, the ceiling was decorated with triumphant paintings and statues that ridicule Protestants and heretics. The theme continues in the Chapel of St Ignatius, dominated by a statue of the saint with a bald silver head. On either side is a group of statues including the *Triumph of Religion over Heresy*, showing a woman representing religion stamping on a fanged serpent symbolizing heresy; and *Barbarians Adoring the Faith*, in which a cute angel aims a sharp kick at an old Barbarian couple struggling to escape the heresy snake.

Santa Maria della Vittoria

With a splendid, candlelit interior, the 1620 Baroque church of **Santa Maria della Vittoria** (see p291) houses a dramatic Bernini sculpture, *The Ecstasy of St Teresa* (1646), set in the Cappella Cornaro. Marble statues of the Cornaro family watch from boxes as St Teresa swoons, struck by the arrow of a smiling angel.

Caravaggio

Michelangelo Merisi da Caravaggio was a rebellious, ground-breaking artist who rejected the idealism of the Renaissance in favour of realism and the dramatic use of light and shadow. He was commissioned to paint three scenes (1597–1602) from the life of St Matthew for the church

of **San Luigi dei Francesi**. The first shows Matthew being called by Jesus from the tax office, the light glinting on the rims of coins, and spotlighting the faces of the main characters. The second, bathed in a sickly green light, shows Matthew's martyrdom, watched by a screaming boy. Caravaggio's first attempt at the third scene was rejected by the priests of San Luigi, who objected to Matthew being shown with dusty feet; the artist had to paint a scrubbed-up version. The priests at **Sant'Agostino** were apparently less fussy: Caravaggio's *Madonna di Loreto* shows a Madonna with dirty toenails.

Bernini fountains

Bernini's **Fontana del Tritone** (see p291) on Piazza Barberini features a sea-god blowing a conch shell, supported by four goggle-eyed dolphins. It was commissioned by Pope Urban VII Barberini, and entwined in the dolphins' tails are the papal keys, the papal tiara and a shield featuring Barberini bees. There are more bees on Bernini's **Fontana delle Api** (se p291), across the piazza. Bernini's apogee is the **Fontana dei Quattro Fiumi** (see p274) in Piazza Navona, part of Pope Innocent X's grand redesign.

The Lowdown

the Jesuits, in 1626. An intellectual, all-male order, it used all its might to fend off the attack of Protestantism. Designed by Jesuit mathematician Orazio Grassi, the illusionistic interior with a ceiling by Andrea Pozzo is the most flamboyant in Rome.

Il Gesù was the first seat of the Jesuits in Rome. The interior, with a single, broad, well-lit nave, was the first of its kind, designed in 1568 at the height of the Thirty Years' War between Catholics and Protestants. The Protestant church was gaining followers by involving people more in church proceedings, letting them

Colosseum and around

The heart of ancient Rome is also one of the city's busiest zones. At the foot of the Capitoline Hill is the chaotic, traffic-choked Piazza Venezia, and skirting the Roman Forum from here to the Colosseum is multi-laned Via dei Fori Imperiali. Pedestrian traffic is intense too: this is a part of town where kids could easily get lost among gaggles of tourists. Fortunately the rewards of the Colosseum, Forum and Palatine Hill make it all worth while.

Places of Interest

SIGHTS

1. Colosseum
2. Baths of Caracalla
3. Forum and Palatine Hill
4. Capitoline Hill
5. Trajan's Market and Column
6. Museo Nazionale Romano
7. San Clemente

● EAT AND DRINK

1. Caffè Ivanhoe
2. Pizza Forum
3. Cavour 313
4. Ciuri Ciuri
5. Cristalli di Zucchero
6. La Bottega del Caffè
7. La Vecchia Roma
8. Pizzeria Chicco di Grano
9. Pizza Luzzi

● WHERE TO STAY

1. Hotel Grifo
2. Palazzetto degli Artisti
3. Hotel Artorius
4. Hotel Celio
5. Duca d'Alba
6. Lancelot
7. Hotel Forum
8. Radisson Blu
9. B&B Il Covo

Families strolling in Villa Celimontana on the Celian Hill

The remains of the Roman Forum with the Temple of Saturn (top right) and the Capitoline Hill behind

Exterior of the Colosseum, still remarkably intact nearly 2,000 years after its construction

Actors in period Roman costume outside the Colosseum

Ruins of Trajan's Market hint at past splendour

The Lowdown

🚗 **Bus** 75, 81, 85, 87, 117, 175, 673, 810 for the Colosseum. 40, 62, 63, 64, 95, 170 for Piazza Venezia. **Tram** 3 (Villa Borghese to Trastevere) stops at the Colosseum and Circo Massimo. **Metro** Colosseo, Circo Massimo, Cavour and Termini are all on Linea B

ℹ️ **Visitor information** Tourist Information Point Via Nazionale, near the Palazzo delle Esposizioni; *www.turismoroma.it*; 9:30am–7pm daily

🛒 **Supermarkets** Emmepiù, Viale Aventino 58, 00153. **Markets** Campo de' Fiori, Piazza Campo de' Fiori, 00186; fruit and veg: 6am–2pm Mon–Sat *(see pp280–81)*. Nuovo Mercato Esquilino, Via Principe Amedeo, 00185; fruit and veg: 9am–2pm Mon–Sat *(see p270)*

🎌 **Festivals** Festa di Santa Francesca Romana (9 Mar): cars, buses and trams are blessed at this saint's church in the Forum.

✚ **Pharmacies** Farmacia Repubblica di Cristina Ed Eliana Barletta: Piazza della Repubblica 67, 00185; 06 488 0410; open 8am–1pm and 3–7pm Mon–Fri, 8am–1pm Sat; call 06 228 941 or check the list displayed in any pharmacy window to find pharmacies open after hours.

🛝 **Nearest play area** Colle Oppio (entrance on Via Labicana, 00184). Villa Celimontana (entrance on Piazza della Navicella, 00184)

① Colosseum
Gladiatorial combat and wild beasts

The Romans' favourite entertainments were gory gladiatorial fights and bloody wild animal shows. Emperor Vespasian commissioned the Colosseum, Rome's first purpose-built blood-sports arena, in AD 72 and at the opening games in AD 80, 9,000 beasts and scores of gladiators were killed. Spectacles often began with wild animals performing circus tricks, and the gladiatorial combat would commence with comic battles, after which the real gladiators would fight each other to the death.

Bust of Vespasian

Key Features

Velarium A vast awning fixed to the upper storey could be hoisted to shade spectators from the sun.

Colonnade To stop flirting, women were segregated at the top behind a colonnade. Ringside seats were reserved for the emperor's retinue.

Vomitoria These were the exits from each numbered section of the seating tiers.

Entry routes The Colosseum could seat up to 55,000 people, who entered via 76 numbered arched entrances.

Columns Each floor had different columns – plain Doric ones at the bottom, then Ionic (with curled tops) and above that Corinthian, the most ornate, with acanthus-leaf decoration.

Network of tunnels Waiting animals were kept in cages under the arena floor, before being winched up in lifts.

Internal corridors The broad design made it easier for the large, unruly crowds to enter and get seated quickly.

Gladiatorial costume Gladiators wore ceremonial helmets and armour.

The Lowdown

 Map reference 21 B2
Address Piazza del Colosseo 1, 00184; 06 3996 7700; www.the-colosseum.net; archeoroma.beniculturali.it

Bus 60 from Piazza Venezia, 75 from Stazione Termini. **Tram** 3. **Metro** Colosseo (Linea B)

Open Daily 8:30am–5:30pm mid-Feb–end Mar, till 7:15pm end Mar–end Aug, till 7pm Sep, 9am–6:30pm Oct–Nov, end Nov–mid-Feb 8:30am–4:30pm

Price €24–48 (includes Forum and Palatine Hill), EU under-18s free. Underground and Third Tier additional €8. A 7-day Archeologia Card (€23.50 per person; reduced €13.50) adds entry to the Baths of Caracalla and Museo Nazionale Romano.

Skipping the queue Buy tickets at the Colosseum (queues are longest here), Forum or Palatine. Tickets can also be booked online at www.pierreci.it and printed at home or by calling 06 3996 7700 (€1.50 fee for advance booking), or buy a Roma Pass (see p259) and enter via a special turnstile.

Guided tours Audio guide (€5.50) or tour guide (€5)

Age range 5 plus

Activities Stage a gladiatorial combat in the arena!

Allow 45 minutes–1 hour

Wheelchair access Yes, to the arena; lifts to some upper levels

Café At the Roman Forum

Shop Souvenirs and guides

Toilets Near the entrance

Good family value?
The Colosseum's combination of gory history and space for exploring makes it one of the city's most child-friendly sights.

Prices given are for a family of four

Letting off steam

Head away from busy roads up Via Claudia to the **Celian Hill**, where animals destined for the Colosseum were kept in a zoo. The quietest of the city's seven hills, it has a shady park in the **Villa Celimontana** (Piazza della Navicella, 00184).

Peaceful Villa Celimontana on the Celian Hill, ideal for ball games and picnics

Eat and drink

Picnic: under €25; Snacks: €25–40; Real meal: €40–80; Family treat: €80 or more (based on a family of four)

PICNIC As there are no markets in the Colosseum area, buy a picnic at **Campo de' Fiori** *(see pp278–9)* before setting off and take it up to the pretty park at Villa Celimontana.
SNACKS Caffè Ivanhoe *(Via Ciancaleoni 50, 00184; closed Sun)* in the Monti area north of Via Cavour is a good place to escape the traffic and eat triple-decker *tramezzini* (classic sandwiches), stuffed *piadine* (flat bread) or *focaccia* (pizza-style bread).
REAL MEAL Pizza Forum *(Via San Giovanni in Laterano 34/38, 00184; 06 7759 1158; closed Tue)* on the Celian Hill offers speedy service and a fixed-priced kids' menu of pizza and *supplì al telefono* (deep-fried mozzarella-filled rice balls).
FAMILY TREAT Cavour 313 *(Via Cavour 313, 00184; 06 678 5496; www.cavour313.it; closed Mon)* is a family-friendly *enoteca* with great cheese and salami platters and an excellent wine list for the adults.

Chefs in action at one of Rome's rapid-service pizzerias

Find out more

DIGITAL For more on the Colosseum visit *www.videos. howstuffworks.com/history/ ancient-rome-videos.htm*, which has several excellent short videos for children, on topics ranging from the gladiatorial games to how the lifts winched the animals up from their cages below ground to the stage.
FILM Watch Audrey Hepburn and Gregory Peck ride past the Colosseum (and many other famous city sights) on a Vespa scooter in *Roman Holiday* (1953).

Take cover

A 5-minute walk away, **Rewind Rome** *(Via Capo d'Africa 5, 00184; 06 7707 6627; www.3drewind.com)* is Rome's most fun multi-media museum, with interactive scale models and the chance to dress up as an ancient Roman.
  Alternatively, catch tram 2 to Belle Arti for hands-on children's museum **Explora** *(www.mdbr.it; see p288)* or Villa Borghese's state-of-the-art **zoo** *(www.bioparco. it; see p286)*.

Next stop...

ROMAN FORUM AND PALATINE HILL Visit the gruesome **Mamertine Prison** beneath the 16th-century church of San Giuseppe dei Falegnami, in the

The Palatine Hill, home to some of Rome's most ancient ruins

Roman Forum *(see p268)*. Prisoners were thrown in through a hole in the roof and left to starve, or were garotted and dumped in the sewers. Continue on to the **Ludus Magnus**, ruins of the largest gladiatorial school and barracks in Rome, on Via San Giovanni in Laterano, at the foot of the Celian Hill.

View over the Roman Forum to the Colosseum

② Baths of Caracalla

Skin-scraping and perfume

In ancient Rome, going for a daily bath was not just a way of getting clean, but also a chance to meet people and catch up on gossip. The Baths of Caracalla had room for 1,600 people and, as well as the baths, there were gardens, cafés and a reading room.

Today it is possible to wander through the ruins of the main building, past hot steam baths (*laconiae*), two gyms (*palestrae*), two changing rooms (*apodyteriae*) with black and white mosaic floors, and a circular hot bath (*caldarium*). After soaking in the *caldarium*, bathers would have their skin scraped to remove dirt and dead skin, before being massaged and perfumed. Then they would move on to a lukewarm bath (*tepidarium*) and finally plunge into a chilly open-air swimming pool (*frigidarium*).

Mosaic floor tile at the Baths of Caracalla depicting Cupid and a sea monster

Prices given are for a family of four

Letting off steam

In summer, go for a refreshing dip at **All'Ombra del Colosseo**, an outdoor swimming pool that is set up in the Circo Massimo (*www.allombradelcolosseo.it; mid-Jun–early-Sep*).

Wisteria on the ruins of the Imperial Palace, Palatine Hill

The Lowdown

🌐 **Map reference** 21 C4
Address Via delle Terme di Caracalla 52, 00153; 06 3996 7700; *archeoroma.beneculturali.it*

🚗 **Bus** 118, 160, 628. **Tram** 3.
Metro Circo Massimo (Linea B)

🕐 **Open** 9am–2pm Mon, 9am–4:30pm Tue–Sun

💶 **Price** €12–24, EU under-18s free

👫 **Age range** All

⏱ **Allow** 30 minutes

♿ **Wheelchair access** Yes

🍴 **Eat and drink** *Picnic* Emmepiù (*Viale Aventino 58, 00153*) is a good place for supplies. Eat in the park that surrounds the baths. *Snacks* There are no eateries in this area, so take Metro Linea B to Cavour for tasty Sicilian treats at Ciuri Ciuri (*Via Leonina 18–20, 00184; 06 4544 4548*).

③ Forum and Palatine Hill

Chequerboards and mirror walls

The **Roman Forum** was like an Italian piazza today, an open space where people would meet to shop, gossip, play, listen to speeches or go to a temple. The huge Basilica Julia – now a pavement fringed with column stumps – was a law court; carved into its steps are chequerboards, where people played games between cases. Nearby, eight columns remain from the Temple of Saturn, focus of the Saturnalia winter festival, which had much in common with Christmas: schools closed, presents were given and special dinners were held.

At the other end of the Forum, the House of the Vestal Virgins has a beautiful courtyard with lily ponds and (headless) statues of the Vestals, whose job was to keep alight a sacred flame in the circular temple next door. Opposite are three temples converted into churches, including the Basilica of Constantine and Maxentius.

The **Palatine Hill** was home to the imperial family, and is still the loveliest of Rome's ancient sites. Palaces were frescoed, with bronze or marble floors and ivory doors – the *triclinium* (dining room) of the Domus Flavia still has a pink and yellow

The Lowdown

🌐 **Map reference** 21 A2–3
Address Forum: Largo Salaria Vecchia, 00186; Palatine Hill: Via di San Gregorio, 00184; 06 3996 7700; *archeoroma.beniculturali.it*

🚗 **Bus** 60, 75. **Metro** Colosseo (Linea B)

🕐 **Open** 8:30am–5pm mid-Feb–mid-Mar, till 5:30pm mid-Mar–end Mar, till 7:15pm end Mar–end Aug, till 7pm Sept, till 6:30pm Oct, till 4:30pm end Oct–mid-Feb

💶 **Price** €24–48, EU under-18's free

👫 **Skipping the queue** Buy tickets at the Palatine at *www.pierreci.it* or buy a Roma Pass (*see p259*).

👫 **Age range** 5 plus

⏱ **Allow** Half a day

♿ **Wheelchair access** Partial

🍴 **Eat and drink** *Snacks* Cristalli di Zucchero (*Via San Teodoro 88, 00186; 06 6992 0945*) is Rome's best *pasticceria*.

Farnese Gardens on the Palatine Hill, an ideal spot in which to take things easy

marble pavement. Emperor Domitian was so afraid of an assassin creeping up behind him that he had the walls of this palace lined with mirror-like selenite.

Letting off steam

Play hide and seek among the ruins and pavilions in the Palatine Hill's pretty **Farnese Gardens**.

④ Capitoline Hill
How long till the world ends?

The Capitoline Hill began as the fortified centre of ancient Rome, and was later home to its most important temples, including that of Juno Moneta, whose cackling geese saved the city in 390 BC by waking the sleeping guards as the Gauls attacked. The ramp up – called the Cordonata after the stone *cordoni*,

The Lowdown

- 🌐 **Map reference** 24 G6
  Address Piazza del Campidoglio, 00186; www.museicapitolini.org
- 🚌 **Bus** 64 from Termini
- 🕐 **Open** 9am–8pm Tue–Sun
- 💶 **Price** €17–30, EU 6–25s €10, EU under-6s free
- 👫 **Skipping the queue** Buy tickets online (€1 booking fee).
- 👫 **Age range** Campidoglio all ages; 8 plus for Capitoline Museums
- ⏱ **Allow** 1 hour
- ♿ **Wheelchair access** Yes; call ahead on 06 6710 2071 to use the lift.
- 🍴 **Eat and drink** *Picnic* Campo de' Fiori market (see pp280–81) is a good place to pick up supplies. Enjoy a picnic in the piazza. *Snacks* The Capitoline Museum Café has great views and serves *panini*, pizza and pasta.

or rope-like steps – was designed much later by Michelangelo, as was the Piazza del Campidoglio at its head. According to legend, when the last gold leaf flakes off the gilded bronze statue of Emperor Marcus Aurelius on a horse, the world will end; the original is now in the Capitoline Museums. Inside, look out for the Capitoline Wolf, an Etruscan bronze with twins Romulus and Remus added during the Renaissance, and the Infant Hercules, which shows Emperor Caracalla as a boy strangling a snake (he later killed his brother).

Letting off steam

Run around the spacious Piazza del Campidoglio, or up and down the Cordonata.

The Cordonata, leading up to the Piazza del Campidoglio

Trajan's Column, decorated with a carved frieze of the emperor's victories

⑤ Trajan's Market and Column

Retail therapy, Roman-style

The world's first shopping mall, **Trajan's Market** was a complex of 150 shops laid out on five levels. Built in the 2nd century AD, the shops sold everything from fish (kept alive in fresh- and salt-water tanks) to spices, fruit, wine and oil. The complex is well preserved, with a two-storey hall where free corn was distributed to the poor, a paved street with shops opening off it and a three-storey crescent housing more shops.

Behind the market is one of ancient Rome's most striking monuments, **Trajan's Column** (AD 106–113). It is 40 m (130 ft) high from the bottom of its pedestal to the top of the statue of Trajan, and is built of 19 marble drums. Winding around it 23 times is a carved frieze which would be 190 m (623 ft) long if it was unwound, showing detailed scenes from Trajan's victory over Dacia (Romania). Spot the difference between the smart Roman soldiers and the shaggy-haired Dacians, and look for a scene of Roman soldiers crossing the River Danube in rowing boats. Small square windows let in light to the spiral staircase inside (closed to the public).

Letting off steam

The area behind Trajan's Market, Monti, is a relaxed place for children – let them play in the attractive **Piazza Madonna dei Monti**, with a fountain in its centre.

The Lowdown

- 🌐 **Map reference** 21 A1
  Address: Via IV Novembre 94, 00187; *www.mercatiditraiano.it*
- 🚌 **Bus** 40 from Termini
- 🕐 **Open** 9am–7pm Tue–Sun
- 💲 **Price** €22–44, EU 6–25s €9, EU under-6s free
- 🎧 **Guided tours** Call 06 0608 to book (€3.50).
- 👫 **Age range** 5 plus
- ⏱ **Allow** 1 hour
- ♿ **Wheelchair access** Yes
- 🍴 **Eat and drink** *Snacks* La Bottega del Caffè *(Piazza Madonna dei Monti 5, 00187; 06 4741 578; open 8am–2am)* serves sandwiches, salads, pasta and desserts all day long. *Real meal* La Vecchia Roma *(Via Leonina 10, 00187; 06 474 5887)* is a friendly, traditional trattoria.

⑥ Museo Nazionale Romano

The painted garden

Take the lift to the top floor to see the incredible collection of ancient Roman frescoes and mosaics. Four frescoes of a garden with fruit trees, from the country villa of Emperor Augustus's wife, Livia, are displayed here. Look for the ripe, bursting pomegranate, birds, roses, poppies, camomile, periwinkle and violets.

Next, go to see mosaics found in a villa on the banks of the Tiber. Look for the boy riding the dolphin, and fragments of a mosaic showing an octopus, moray eel and lobster fighting. Archaeologists noticed that the fish are all seafish, but the boats are of a kind used only on rivers.

Take the lift to the basement to see an assortment of items from everyday Roman life: ivory dice and needles, tiny spoons for mixing make-up, a child-sized abacus, as well as the sad mummy of an eight-year-old girl and some of the objects that were buried with her.

Letting off steam

This area is full of traffic and unsavoury types – so head to Rome's biggest covered market, the **Nuovo Mercato Esquilini** *(Via Principe Amedeo 184; 7:30am–2pm daily)*, or to Monti *(see left)* instead.

The Lowdown

- 🌐 **Map reference** 17 C5
  Address: Palazzo Massimo, Largo di Villa Peretti 1, 00185; 06 3996 7700; *archeoroma.beniculturali.it*
- 🚌 **Bus** 40, 64 and countless others to Termini; **Metro** Termini (Linea A and B) or Repubblica (A)
- 🕐 **Open** 9am–7:45pm Tue–Sun
- 💲 **Price** €14–21, under-18s free; ticket valid three days for all of the museum's sites.
- 👫 **Age range** 5 plus
- ⏱ **Allow** 1 hour
- ♿ **Wheelchair access** Yes
- 🍴 **Eat and drink**: *Snacks* Caffè Ivanhoe *(see p267)* is great for sandwiches. *Real meal* Pizzeria Chicco di Grano *(Via degli Zingari 6, 00184; 06 4782 5033)* in Monti serves *crostini* and even mini-pizzas for babies.

The remains of Trajan's Market, ancient Rome's multi-storey shopping mall

Prices given are for a family of four

⑦ San Clemente
Time travel

Descend through layers of time, from a richly decorated 12th-century church to a simple 4th-century basilica and an ancient Roman temple. In the upper church, a golden mosaic shows Jesus amid spirals of acanthus leaves; the sheep represent the 12 faithful apostles. A chapel is dedicated to St Catherine of Alexandria, who was tortured by being tied to a spiked wheel and rolled down a hill, and gave her name to the Catherine Wheel firework. Frescoes by 15th-century Renaissance artists Masolino and Masaccio depict scenes from her life and martyrdom.

Steps lead down to the lower church, where a halo and baby have been added to a fresco of Byzantine Empress Theodora to make her into a Madonna. Another flight of steps descends to the dank 2nd-century Roman Mithraeum, where a stone altar shows the god Mithras killing a bull. Followers of the cult, which was imported from Persia, believed Mithras brought life to the world by

Mosaic from San Clemente, showing peasants tending animals

spilling a bull's blood, and had to undergo initiation ceremonies such as trials by ice, fire and thirst.

Letting off steam

The nearest park is rough-edged **Colle Oppio** (*Via Labicana, 00184*), but **Villa Celimontana** is just a 10-minute walk away (*see p267*).

The Lowdown

- 🌐 **Map reference** 21 C2
  Address Via di San Giovanni in Laterano, 00184; www.basilicasanclemente.com
- 🚗 **Bus** 85, 87, 186 **Tram** 3 **Metro** Colosseo (Linea B)
- 🕐 **Open** Upper church: 9am–7pm daily; excavations: 9am–noon, 3–6pm Mon–Sat, noon–6pm Sun and public hols
- 💶 **Price** Upper church: free; excavations: €17–20
- 👫 **Age range** 8 plus
- 🕐 **Allow** 30 minutes
- ♿ **Wheelchair access** To upper church only
- ☕ **Eat and drink** *Snacks* Pizza Luzzi (*Via San Giovanni in Laterano 88, 00184; 06 709 6332*) is a popular, lively pizzeria, with a view of San Clemente.

Above Statue in the courtyard of Museo Nazionale Romano **Below** Café near Nuovo Mercato Esquilini

Piazza Navona and around

The hustle and bustle and the magnificent Baroque fountains of Piazza Navona are near the city's best ice-cream parlours, while the Pantheon is a triumph of Roman engineering, its huge dome breaking all records. A great place to hunt down stone turtles, an Egyptian cat and an obelisk-carrying elephant, the area's twisting backstreets and hidden piazzas are strictly for exploring on foot; buses skirt the area on the main thoroughfares.

Piazza Navona and around

- Villa Borghese and Tridente *p284*
- The Vatican and Trastevere *p292*
- Piazza Navona
- Campo de' Fiori *p278*
- Colosseum *p264*

Places of Interest

SIGHTS
1. Piazza Navona
2. Pantheon
3. Piazza della Minerva
4. Sant'Ignazio

EAT AND DRINK
1. Lo Zozzone
2. Da Tonino
3. Trattoria
4. Piazza delle Coppelle
5. Caffè Sant'Eustachio
6. Giolitti
7. Da Ugo
8. Vitti
9. Gino

See also Piazza Navona pp274–5

SHOPPING
1. Al Sogno
2. Poggi

WHERE TO STAY
1. Hotel Parlamento
2. Hotel Due Torri
3. Hotel Navona
4. Hotel Portoghesi
5. Hotel Santa Chiara
6. Hotel Teatro Pace

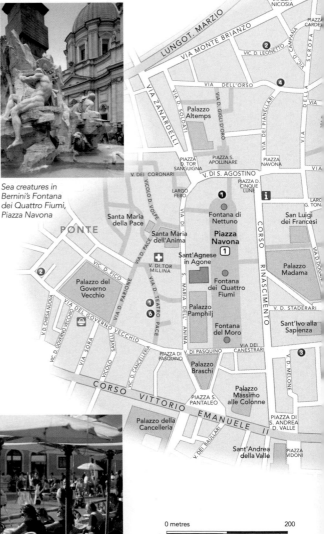

Sea creatures in Bernini's Fontana dei Quattro Fiumi, Piazza Navona

0 metres 200
0 yards 200

Pavement cafés on Piazza Navona

The Egyptian obelisk of Fontana dei Quattro Fiumi on Piazza Navona

The Lowdown

🚗 **Bus** 40 or 64 to Largo di Torre Argentina or Corso Rinascimento. Many others along Via del Corso and Corso Vittorio Emanuele II

ℹ️ **Visitor information** Tourist Information Point "Navona": Piazza delle Cinque Lune, 00100; 06 0608; *www.turismoroma.it*; open 9:30am–7pm daily

🏪 **Supermarket** Carrefour Express, Via del Governo Vecchio 119, 00100 **Markets** Campo de' Fiori, 00186; fruit and veg: 6am–2pm Mon–Sat *(see pp280–81)*. Piazza delle Coppelle, 00186; fruit and veg: 7am–1pm Mon–Sat

🎉 **Festivals** La Befana Christmas Market, Piazza Navona: 8 Dec–6 Jan

➕ **Pharmacies** Palermo, Via Tor Millina 6, 00186; 06 6880 1135; open 8am–1pm and 3–7pm Mon–Fri, 8am–1pm Sat. Call 06 228 941 or check the list in any pharmacy window to find pharmacies open after hours.

🛝 **Nearest play area** There are no dedicated play spaces for children in this area; Roman children use the piazzas as their playgrounds.

The illusionist pyrotechnics of the dome of Sant'Ignazio

① Piazza Navona
Tooth-pullers and fortune-tellers

Navona is Rome's most famous piazza, a cobbled oval dominated by
the Egyptian obelisk, cascading water and gleaming marble gods of the
Fontana dei Quattro Fiumi. Occupying an ancient Roman stadium, in the
Renaissance it hosted Carnival jousting and races. Pope Innocent X gave
it a facelift in the 17th century but astrologers continued to tell fortunes,
tooth-pullers to set up stalls and puppeteers to perform here.
Today tourists and locals mill about at all hours.

*Fontana di
Nettuno*

Key Sights

Fontana dei Quattro Fiumi
Bernini's fountain (1651) symbolizes
how Pope Innocent X (the dove)
triumphed over paganism (the
obelisk) and brought peace (an olive
branch) to the world (the four rivers).

**Sant'Agnese
in Agone**

Fontana del Moro
Bernini sculpted the Moor
wrestling with a dolphin at the
centre of this fountain.

Fontana di Nettuno
This fountain is a
19th-century work
showing sea-god
Neptune struggling
with a sea monster.

Pasquino
For over 500 years
Romans have been
attaching political or
social comments to
the "talking" statue
in Piazza di Pasquino.

Obelisk
In the centre of the
Baroque Fontana dei
Quattro Fiumi, this
Egyptian obelisk came
from the ancient
temple of Isis nearby.

Sant'Agnese in Agone
The church was built over the rooms
in which St Agnes was imprisoned.
Borromini's startling concave façade
(1657) was part of Pope Innocent X's
revamp of the piazza.

River giants, Fontana dei Quattro Fiumi
The great rivers are represented by giants.
The Nile has his face covered, Plate sits on
silver, Ganges holds an oar and Danube is
touching the papal coat of arms.

Prices given are for a family of four

The Lowdown

🌐 **Map reference** 16 G5-G6
Address Piazza Navona, 00186

🚌 **Bus** 46, 64, 87 and many more
to Largo di Torre Argentina

🕐 **Open** Sant'Agnese in Agone:
Tue–Sun

👫 **Skipping the queue** Go early in
the day to have it to yourself and
early evening to relax and stroll.

👫 **Age range** All ages

⏱ **Allow** 1 hour to see the
fountains and Sant'Agnese, eat
an ice cream or drink a coffee;
longer to let the kids run around
and watch street vendors and
caricature artists at work

♿ **Wheelchair access** Yes

☕ **Café** There are plenty of cafés
lining the piazza. One of the
best is Bar Tre Scalini (28–9
Piazza Navona, 00186; www.
trescalini.it), known for its rich
tartufo chocolate ice cream.

🚻 **Toilets** In the cafés surrounding
the piazza; buy an espresso or
water at the bar.

Good family value?
The cafés are expensive if you sit
down, but stand-up prices are
reasonable – and there's plenty of
space and free entertainment.

Street performer putting on a show for tourists in the piazza

Letting off steam

Stage races around the piazza, in ancient Roman or Renaissance style, dodging tourists and touts.

Eat and drink

Picnic: under €25; Snacks: €25–40; Real meal: €40–80; Family treat: €80 or more (based on a family of four)

PICNIC Campo de' Fiori market *(see pp280–81)* is a good place to stock up on fresh bread, fruit, cheese and cold cuts. Picnic on the piazza by the less crowded Fontana di Nettuno.

SNACKS Lo Zozzone *(Via del Teatro della Pace 32, 00186; 06 6880 8575; closed Sat pm and Sun)* doles out irresistible slices of crisp *pizza bianca*, slit open and filled with whatever takes your fancy. Sweet versions, such as ricotta and cherry, are also available. Devour on seats outside on a small alley.

REAL MEAL Da Tonino *(Via del Governo Vecchio 18, 00186; 06 687 7002)* is a cosy trattoria, hung with strings of plastic onions and packed with paper-covered tables. It serves gargantuan portions of pasta, followed by simple grilled steaks or veal stew with mushrooms and peas, all for next to nothing.

FAMILY TREAT Trattoria *(Via Pozzo delle Cornacchie 25, 00186; 06 6830 1427)*, a stylishly minimalistic restaurant, housed in a 17th-century palazzo, serves up exquisitely presented takes on traditional Sicilian dishes, with an emphasis on fresh fish and seafood.

Shopping

From 8 December until Epiphany (6 January), Piazza Navona is taken over by a Christmas market, known as the **Befana**. If you are inspired to paint or draw what you see in Piazza Navona or elsewhere in Rome, head to **Poggi**, a great art shop *(see p276)*. For year-round temptations, visit **Al Sogno** *(Piazza Navona 53, 00186; 06 686 4198)*, a fabulous toy shop, specializing in dolls and stuffed toy animals.

Find out more

DIGITAL For more on the Befana, go to www.kidscantravel.com/familyattractions/piazzanavona/funstuffkids/index.html

Outdoor seating at the historic Piazza Navona café, Bar Tre Scalini

Take cover

Duck into **Santa Maria della Pace** *(Vicolo dell'Arco della Pace 5, 00186, 06 686 1156)* to see four Raphael *Sibyls* and 16th-century carved portraits of twin sisters. The Bramante cloisters house a café.

Next stop...

FONTANA DELLE TARTARUGHE
Go to the Fontana delle Tartarughe in Piazza Mattei *(see p285)* to see Bernini working on a less monumental scale – designing tortoises! Or go and find other relics from the Temple of Isis *(see p276)*.

Art for sale in Piazza Navona, the centre of Roman social life for millennia

KIDS' CORNER

Look out for...
1 Which river god appears to be worried that the church of Sant'Agnese will collapse on top of him?
2 Can you see what is really frightening him?
3 Can you guess why the River Nile's head is covered with a cloth?
4 What is the River Ganges holding in his hand? Can you guess why?

Answers at the bottom of the page.

Bernini v Borromini
There was fierce rivalry between architects Bernini and Borromini. Borromini claimed that Bernini's obelisk was in danger of toppling over, while the river gods on Bernini's fountain are said to recoil in horror from Borromini's façade of Sant'Agnese in Agone.

CRACKING TOWERS
Borromini had a point *(see above)*. Bernini built two bell towers on St Peter's that were so high that the façade cracked, so the Pope ordered them to be demolished.

A Christmas witch
Italian kids get two lots of presents – on Christmas Day and on 6 January, when the Befana, an old lady with a long nose and black shawl, arrives on her broomstick bearing gifts. Just like Santa Claus she enters each house silently through its chimney and fills each child's sock – with presents for children who have been good and with lumps of coal for the naughty ones.

Answers: 1 The River Plate. **2** A snake. **3** Because the source of the Nile was unknown. **4** An oar, because the Ganges was easy to navigate.

The portico of the Pantheon, once home to a medieval fish market

The Lowdown

🌐 **Map reference** 16 G6
Address Piazza della Rotonda, 00186

🚌 **Bus** 46, 64, 87 and many others to Largo di Torre Argentina

🕐 **Open** 8:30am–7:30pm Mon–Sat; 9am–6pm Sun

💲 **Price** Free

🧑‍🤝‍🧑 **Age range** 5 plus

⏱ **Allow** 30 minutes

♿ **Wheelchair access** Yes

☕ **Eat and drink** *Picnic* Piazza delle Coppelle has a market; eat on the steps of Santa Maria sopra Minerva. *Snacks* Caffè Sant'Eustachio (*Piazza Sant'Eustachio 82, 00186; 06 6880 2048; www.sante ustachioilcaffe.it*) serves the best coffee in the city and has some tables outside.

② Pantheon
Pondering pumpkins

The Pantheon is the world's best-preserved Roman building, a brick cylinder fused to a huge dome that was said to have been designed by the goddess Cybele. In fact, the designer was probably Emperor Hadrian, allegedly inspired by contemplating a pumpkin in AD 128. Whatever the truth, stepping inside the Pantheon is an incredible experience, especially on a sunny day, with the sun streaming through the hole, or *oculus*, in the top.

The Pantheon was a temple to all gods, with statues of the 12 most important Olympian deities inside, including Venus wearing a pair of pearl earrings that Julius Caesar had given to Cleopatra. In 609 AD it was converted into a church after Christians complained of being assaulted by demons whenever they walked past. On the rare occasions when the building and the piazza are not full of visitors, there is indeed an overpowering, eerie stillness radiating from it.

The dome was originally covered with gilded bronze inside and out, but in AD 667 the bronze from the outside was stripped off and melted down into coins for Constantinople, and almost a thousand years later Bernini persuaded the pope to strip the inner ceiling to use it for the *baldacchino* inside St Peter's. In medieval Rome the portico of colossal granite columns sheltered a fish market.

Letting off steam

Adjacent **Piazza della Minerva** is good for a run around and to admire the stone elephant.

③ Piazza della Minerva
An elephantine tribute

Piazza della Minerva is home to one of Rome's most unusual monuments – a cheeky elephant sculpture made of marble, designed by Bernini in 1667, with a miniature granite obelisk taken from the Temple of Isis on its back.

Overlooking the sculpture of the elephant is the Gothic church of **Santa Maria sopra Minerva**, built in the 13th century on the site of a Roman temple to Minerva, goddess of wisdom. The church was the headquarters of the Inquisition – Galileo was put on trial here in 1633 – and inside is the tomb of head inquisitor Pope Paul IV (1555–9), who excommunicated Elizabeth I of England, confined Rome's Jews to the Ghetto, and disapproved so strongly of Michelangelo's *Last Judgment* that he called it a "stew of nudes". A gentler spirit, Florentine artist-monk Fra Angelico, who died in 1455, is buried in the church too.

Letting off steam

Start a Roman sketchbook: **Poggi** is a great art shop, 2 minutes' walk away (*Via Pie' di Marmo 38–9, 00186; www.poggi1825.it*). Nearby **Piazza di Montecitorio**, with an interesting obelisk in the centre, is another good square to run around.

Alfresco dining in Piazza della Minerva

Prices given are for a family of four

The Lowdown

- 🌐 **Map reference** 16 H6
  Address Piazza della Minerva, 00186
- 🚌 **Bus** 46, 64, 87 and many others to Largo di Torre Argentina
- 🕐 **Open** Santa Maria Sopra Minerva: 8am–7pm daily
- 👫 **Age range** Even toddlers will enjoy the elephant and obelisk.
- ⏱ **Allow** 30 minutes
- ♿ **Wheelchair access** Yes
- 🍴 **Eat and drink** *Snack* Giolitti (*Via Ufficio del Vicario 40, 00186; www.giolitti.it*) is a *belle époque* gelateria offering a wide range of ice creams. *Real meal* Da Ugo (*Via dei Prefetti 19, 00186; 06 687 3752; closed Sun*) is an old and inexpensive trattoria, which serves up huge portions of *bucatini all'amatriciana* (pasta with a bacon and tomato sauce) – perfect for sharing.

④ Sant'Ignazio
Virtual reality

Stepping inside the Jesuit church of Sant'Ignazio is like walking into a heavenly ballroom. This Baroque stunner, begun in 1626 to celebrate the canonization of Catholic zealot and founder of the Society of Jesus Ignatius of Loyola, is loveliest in the evenings when marble columns and pavements gleam, and polished brass glints in the lamplight. Go to the nave, and look for a star set into the pavement. Stand here, look up and get someone to put a coin in the nearby slot. The church will flood with light, and the roof will

The marble columns, polished brass, stucco and gilt of Sant'Ignazio

Bernini's elephant, Piazza della Minerva, a fun tribute to the artist's papal patron

seem to burst open to reveal a blue sky full of glamorous angels, shooting up to heaven where St Ignatius floats on a fluffy cloud – an astonishing feat of trompe l'oeil by Padre Andrea Pozzo, who created the illusion out of nothing but paint – aided by stucco and gilt.

Outside, pause to see how Filippo Raguzzini's elliptical Rococo piazza (1728–9) frames the church. Note the curvilinear design, theatrical setting and playful details.

Letting off steam

Five minutes' walk away, **Piazza San Lorenzo in Lucina** is a great place to have coffee while the children play (local families come here early evening). If it rains, walk 5 minutes down Via del Corso to the **Galleria Sordi**, a 19th-century shopping gallery full of high-street fashion.

The Lowdown

- 🌐 **Map reference** 16 H6
  Address Piazza di Sant'Ignazio, 00186
- 🚌 **Bus** 81 to Corso Rinascimento; 117, 492 to Via del Corso (Via Minghetti stop)
- 🕐 **Open** 7:30am–12:30pm, 3–7:15pm daily
- 👫 **Age range** 8 plus
  Allow 15 minutes
- ♿ **Wheelchair access** Yes
- 🍴 **Eat and drink** *Snacks* Vitti (*Piazza San Lorenzo in Lucina 33, 00186; 06 687 6304; www.caffevitti.com*) is a great café – it even does cooked breakfast with bacon and eggs. *Real meal* Gino (*Vicolo Rosini 4, 00186; 06 687 3434; closed Sun and Aug*) is the best trattoria in Rome for those seeking substantial fare. Popular with lunching MPs from Palazzo Montecitorio, its dishes include lamb and rabbit stew.

Campo de' Fiori and around

This area is the place to come for a gourmet street picnic amid haphazard fragments of history. Campo de' Fiori itself is a lively piazza with a daily market and some of the city's best bakeries and delis. It was the bustling – and at times rough – heart of Renaissance Rome and things can still get a little wild here at night, but by day there are plenty of cafés and bars, perfect for people-watching while the kids play. Elegant, quiet Piazza Farnese is a hop and a skip away.

Campo de' Fiori and around

Villa Borghese and Tridente *p284*

The Vatican and Trastevere *p292*

Piazza Navona *p272*

Campo de' Fiori

Colosseum *p264*

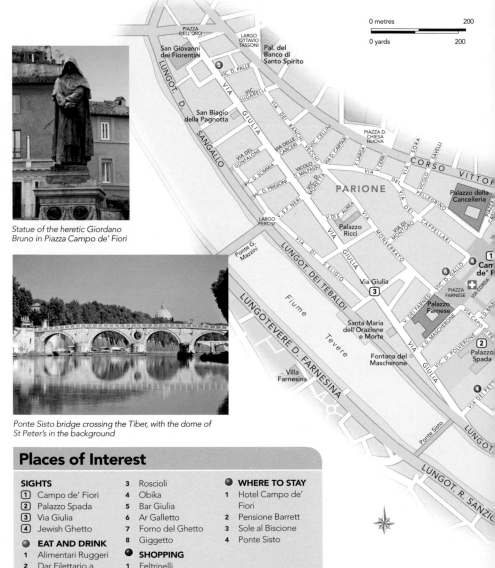

Statue of the heretic Giordano Bruno in Piazza Campo de' Fiori

Ponte Sisto bridge crossing the Tiber, with the dome of St Peter's in the background

Places of Interest

SIGHTS
1. Campo de' Fiori
2. Palazzo Spada
3. Via Giulia
4. Jewish Ghetto

● **EAT AND DRINK**
1. Alimentari Ruggeri
2. Dar Filettario a Santa Barbara

3. Roscioli
4. Obika
5. Bar Giulia
6. Ar Galletto
7. Forno del Ghetto
8. Giggetto

● **SHOPPING**
1. Feltrinelli

● **WHERE TO STAY**
1. Hotel Campo de' Fiori
2. Pensione Barrett
3. Sole al Biscione
4. Ponte Sisto

Stone bathtubs from Caracalla (see p268), now used as fountains in Piazza Farnese

The Lowdown

🚌 **Bus** 40, 46, 62, 64 to Largo di Torre Argentina. More buses run along the Lungotevere, Via Arenula and Corso Vittorio Emanuele II. **Taxi rank** In Largo di Torre Argentina

ℹ️ **Visitor information** Tourist Information Point "Navona": Piazza delle Cinque Lune, 00100; 06 0608; *www.turismoroma.it*; open 9:30am–7pm daily

🛒 **Supermarkets** Alimentari Ruggeri, Campo de' Fiori 1 (cnr Via dei Balestrari), 00186; 06 6880 1091; *www.ruggericampodefiori.com* **Markets** Campo de' Fiori, 00186; Mon–Sat 7am–2pm

➕ **Pharmacies** Giordani, Piazza Farnese 42, 00186; 06 6880 6684; open 8am–1pm and 3–7pm. Call 06 228 941 to find pharmacies open at night or weekends, or check the list in any pharmacy window.

🤸 **Nearest play area** Roman children play in the city's piazzas – Piazza Farnese is a good option in this area.

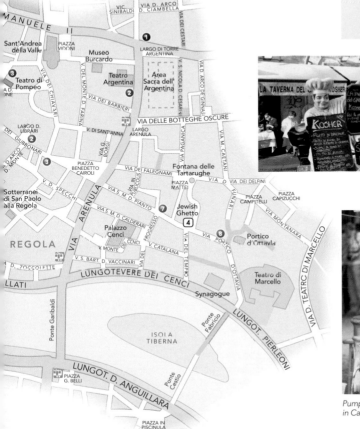

Restaurant signs advertising kosher food in the Jewish Ghetto

Pumpkins and strings of chillies for sale in Campo de' Fiori market

① Campo de' Fiori
Fruit, veg and murder most foul

Campo de' Fiori is home to central Rome's most appealing food market, its stalls surrounded by colourful houses with warped shutters and pigeons nestling on their sills. The neighbourhood also has a grisly history that kids will love: saunter the cobbled streets to find where Julius Caesar was murdered, where Giordano Bruno was burned at the stake for heresy, where painter Caravaggio killed his tennis opponent and where goldsmith Benvenuto Cellini murdered a business rival.

Madonna painting on the piazza

Key Sights

Giordano Bruno monument

Teatro di Pompeo

Palazzo della Cancelleria
This palace was built by Cardinal Raffaele Riario in the 15th century with the winnings of a single night's gambling.

Teatro di Pompeo
The theatre that stood on this site could seat 17,000 people. Behind it was the Curia, where the Roman Senate met and Brutus stabbed Julius Caesar.

Palazzo Farnese
It is closed to the public, but at night try to glimpse Annibale Carraci's allegorical frescoes of the loves of the gods through the lit-up first-floor windows.

Giordano Bruno monument
A statue marks the spot where the philosopher Bruno was burned at the stake for heresy in 1600. Caravaggio murdered his tennis rival here on the piazza too.

Street names
Streets around the Campo are named after the craftsmen that traditionally worked there: look for Via dei Cappellari (hat-makers), Via de' Giubbonari (jerkin-makers), Via dei Balestrari (crossbow-makers), Via dei Baullari (basket-makers) and Via dei Pettinari (comb-makers).

Campo de' Fiori market

Piazza Farnese
The two beautiful fountains in Piazza Farnese are made from gigantic stone bathtubs taken from the ancient Roman Baths of Caracalla (see p268).

Campo de' Fiori market
The name Campo de' Fiori means "field of flowers". In the Middle Ages it was a meadow, and a horse market was held here: look out for the horses' drinking fountain. Nowadays, stalls in the market sell seasonal fruit and vegetables, such as spiky purple artichokes and courgette flowers.

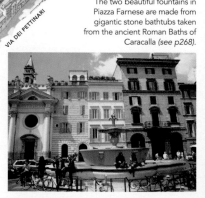

Prices given are for a family of four

The Lowdown

Map reference 23 C4–5
Address Campo de' Fiori, 00186

Bus 40, 46, 62, 64 along Corso Vittorio Emanuele II; 116 along Via dei Baullari

Skipping the queue Prepare to use your elbows to get served at the market stalls, as Romans don't really queue!

Age range The tastes, smells and bustle of the piazza will appeal to all ages.

Allow A morning or a couple of hours in the early evening

Wheelchair access Yes

Toilets In the cafés – buy an espresso or water at the bar.

Good family value
Nowhere in Rome could be better for a family to while away a morning – but get carried away at the delis and it may not be as cheap as expected.

Letting off steam

Stretch your legs in Campo de' Fiori or, if it gets hectic amid the market stalls, more tranquil Piazza Farnese.

Eat and drink

Picnic: under €25; Snacks: €25–40; Real meal: €40– 80; Family treat: €80 or more (based on a family of four)

PICNIC Alimentari Ruggeri *(Campo de' Fiori 1, 00186; 06 6880 1091; www.ruggericampodefiori.com)*, is a great deli, with a

Alimentari Ruggeri, purveyor of everything from olive oil to maple syrup

The elegant open space of Piazza Farnese, a quiet spot for a coffee

tantalizing selection of cheese, salami and ham, plus Marmite and peanut butter for the homesick.
SNACKS Dar Filettaro a Santa Barbara *(Largo dei Librai 88, 00186; 06 686 4018)* does a great takeaway alternative of a local speciality – *filetti di baccalà* (fried cod in batter).
REAL MEAL Roscioli (*Via dei Giubbonari 21–5, 00186; 06 687 5287; www.salumeriaroscioli.com*) uses top-quality ingredients to cook up what is said to be Rome's best *carbonara*, with organic eggs. The homemade cakes are delicious too.
FAMILY TREAT Obika (*Campo de' Fiori 26, 00186; 06 6880 2366; www.obika.it)* is a chic mozzarella bar with dishes such as tomato and basil soup with buffalo mozzarella.

Find out more

DIGITAL *www.eyewitnesshistory.com/caesar2.htm* has an eyewitness account of Caesar's murder.

Take cover

Visit the **Burcardo Theatre museum** *(Via del Sudario 44, 00186; 06 681 9471; open 9am–1:30pm, Mon–Fri; closed first 3 weeks in Aug)*, which covers 500 years of theatre history, and marvel at the comic masks.

Next stop...

PALATINE HILL Carry on, laden with picnic food, to the Palatine Hill – scene of more Imperial Roman murders *(see pp268–9)*.

Alternatively, cross the Tiber to Trastevere for another great fresh-produce market in **Piazza San Cosimato** *(see p293)*.

KIDS' CORNER

A Renaissance Harry Potter

Like Harry Potter and his friends, Giordano Bruno believed in the responsible and ethical use of magic – but suspicion and fear of the unknown was widespread, with many believing that philosophers and magicians communed with demons. Bruno did not help matters by telling the Inquisition he believed in extra-terrestrial life!

FOUL MURDER

Despite bad omens, Roman Emperor Julius Caesar went to a meeting in the Curia where he was attacked by senators, including his friend Brutus. His dying words were, "Et tu Brute?" ("Even you, Brutus?")

Look out for...

1 Find the remains of Pompey's Theatre and the Curia in the basement of Hotel Teatro di Pompeo (Largo del Pallaro) and at Ristorante Da Pancrazio (Piazza del Biscione).

2 Look out for the curved façades of buildings on Via Grottapinta, which follow the line of the old amphitheatre.

3 Look at the façade of the Palazzo della Cancelleria, which was built with limestone from the theatre; the red and grey columns in its courtyard are from the upper tiers.

4 Find the drinking fountains for horses and cattle in Campo de' Fiori, and the bathtubs from the Baths of Caracalla in Piazza Farnese.

② Palazzo Spada
Mermaids and monsters

Palazzo Spada (1540) is one of the most exuberantly decorated palaces in Rome. Look at its façade to find Mannerist statues of toga-wearing Romans, medallions, urns, ribbons and swags of flowers, all made of stucco, a kind of plaster. The courtyard is even better: try to find battling centaurs (half-man and half-horse), mermaids and sea monsters. On the right is what appears to be a long arcade flanked by columns. Look closely: the gallery is about a quarter of the length it appears to be, and the statue at the end quite tiny – the result of a crafty optical illusion by its creator, the architect Borromini.

The palazzo is named after its one-time owner, Cardinal Bernardino Spada, who was a keen art collector. As well as works by the likes of Caravaggio, he collected many paintings by female artists, including Artemisia Gentileschi, Lavinia Fontana and Sofonisba Anguissola. When she was only a young girl, Anguissola impressed Michelangelo with a drawing of a small boy crying – *Asdrubale Bitten by a Crab* (1554).

Letting off steam

Run riot in **Campo de' Fiori** next door, or browse for art books and music in the **Feltrinelli** bookshop, a 5-minute walk away *(Largo di Torre Argentina 11, 00186; 06 6866 3001; www.lafeltrinelli.it; open 10am–9pm daily).*

The Lowdown

- 🌐 **Map reference** 23 C5
  Address Piazza Capo di Ferro 13, 00186; 06 687 4893 (for ticket bookings 06 6832409); *www.galleriaborghese.it*
- 🚌 **Bus** 46, 56, 62, 64, 70, 81, 87 and 628 to Largo di Torre Argentina
- 🕐 **Open** 8:30am–7:30pm Tue–Sun
- 💶 **Price** €10–15, EU under-18s free
- 🧍 **Skipping the queue** Call 06 32810 or book tickets online.
- 🎫 **Guided tours** Call 06 855 5952.
- 👫 **Age range** 5 plus for the perspective, 8 plus for the gallery
- ⏱ **Allow** 45 minutes
- ♿ **Wheelchair access** Yes
- ☕ **Eat and drink** See Campo de' Fiori, *pp280–81*

The grotesque Mascherone fountain on Via Giulia, which once gushed with wine

③ Via Giulia
A cure for sore throats

Via Giulia is a broad, perfectly straight, cobbled street lined with Renaissance palaces and churches. It was laid out in the early 16th century on the orders of Pope Julius II, to link the centre of Rome with the new church of St Peter's (also commissioned by Julius), but money ran out and the pope died before the link could be completed with a bridge.

Approaching from Piazza Farnese, look out for an arch dripping with creepers. It was intended to be the first arch of a viaduct, designed by Michelangelo to link Palazzo Farnese with Villa Farnese on the other side of the Tiber, but never completed. Just below the arch is a weird, grotesque fountain, the Mascherone. On one

The ornate façade of Palazzo Spada, dotted with stucco swags and statues

The Lowdown

- 🌐 **Map reference** 23 A3–C5
  Address Via Giulia, 00186
- 🚌 **Bus** 46, 64, 87 and many others to Largo di Torre Argentina
- 👫 **Age range** Any, for a sore throat cure at San Biagio, and the gruesome skulls at Santa Maria
- ⏱ **Allow** 30 minutes
- ♿ **Wheelchair access** Yes
- ☕ **Eat and drink** *Snacks* Try Bar Giulia, aka Café Peru *(Via Giulia 84, 00186; 06 686 1310)*, where the barmen create fancy designs in the foam of cappuccino. *Real meal* Ar Galletto *(Piazza Farnese 102, 00186; 06 686 1714; closed Sun and Aug)* serves a hearty mixed antipasto of grilled vegetables, ham, salami and cheese, which makes a good lunch in itself. Sit on the terrace.

occasion the water dribbling from its mouth was replaced with wine.

Continuing, look out for a church decorated with grimacing skulls. This is Santa Maria dell'Orazione e Morte, whose priests had the sad job of collecting the corpses of poor people and giving them a Christian burial. Beyond is a huge orange building which was once the city prison, and the church of San Biagio della Pagnotta. San Biagio is believed to have the power to cure sore throats, and people still go to the church to be healed by holding two candles to their throat.

Take cover

Shelter in the neighbourly **Bar Giulia** in Via Giulia, or have a look inside one of the churches.

④ Jewish Ghetto
Jewish astrologers

In 1555 Pope Paul IV, one of the leaders of the Inquisition, confined Rome's Jews to one area. It was surrounded by a wall with five gates, which were opened at dawn and closed at sunset, and the inhabitants were forced to wear a yellow badge. Future popes banned Jews from all trades except selling old clothes and scrap iron, though some made a secret living reading horoscopes. The area is full of narrow streets and alleys and still has a strong Jewish presence, with a synagogue and restaurants serving Roman Jewish food such as crisp, deep-fried artichokes (*carciofi alla giudia*) and *pizza dolce*, a singed scone filled with candied fruit.

Not all the sights here are Jewish. On Piazza Mattei is the lovely 16th-century Fontana delle Tartarughe, with bronze tortoises, which were added in the 17th century and are usually attributed

Above Ruins of the Teatro di Marcello
Below Pretty Fontana delle Tartarughe, on Piazza Mattei in the Jewish Quarter

to Bernini, while the remains of the Teatro di Marcello stand at the end of Via Portico d'Ottavia.

Letting off steam
Look for twigs and let the kids play Pooh-sticks on **Ponte Fabricio**, Rome's oldest bridge.

The Ghetto's grand, lofty synagogue, built in 1901

The Lowdown

- 🌐 **Map reference** 24 E6
  Address Between Via del Portico d'Ottavia, Lungotevere dei Cenci, Via del Progresso and Via di Santa Maria del Pianto, 00186
- 🚌 **Bus** 46, 64, 87 and many others to Largo di Torre Argentina
- 🧍 **Age range** Any
- ⏱ **Allow** 1 hour
- ♿ **Wheelchair access** Yes
- 🍴 **Eat and drink** *Snacks* Forno del Ghetto (Vicolo Costaguti 31, 00186; 06 6880 3012; closed last 3 weeks in Aug) is great for warm almond biscuits and other sweet treats. *Real meal* Giggetto (Via del Portico d'Ottavia 21a, 00186; 06 686 1105; closed Tue) will provide heartier fare, with Roman Jewish specialities such as crisp, fried artichokes and roast lamb.

Villa Borghese and Tridente

There are few places in the world where it is possible to weave together a day in a park with high culture as easily as at the Villa Borghese. There's a zoo, some of the city's best art collections, and go-karts, bikes and roller skates to hire. Bring the Galleria Borghese to life with mythological tales, delve into the mysteries of the Etruscans at Villa Giulia or visit the hands-on museum Explora. Then run up and down the Spanish Steps, spot reliefs of Emperor Augustus's grandchildren and try to resist diving into the waters of the Trevi Fountain.

Egyptian lions spouting water in Piazza del Popolo, part of Giuseppe Valadier's grand design of the square (1816–20)

The temple of Aesculapius in the rowing lake, Villa Borghese gardens

Places of Interest

0 metres   500
0 yards   500

Fontana della Barcaccia at the foot of the Spanish Steps, Piazza di Spagna

The Lowdown

🚗 **Bus** 490, 495, 116, 52 and 53 for Villa Borghese; 117, 119 for Piazza del Popolo, Piazza di Spagna, Trevi Fountain and the Quirinale. **Tram 3** around Villa Borghese. **Metro** Spagna or Flaminio for Villa Borghese, Piazza del Popolo and Piazza di Spagna; Barberini for Trevi Fountain and the Quirinale (all Linea A)

ℹ️ **Visitor information** Tourist Info Point "Minghetti": Via Marco Minghetti, 00187; 060608; *www.turismoroma.it*; open 9:30am–7pm daily

🏪 **Supermarkets** Fratelli Fabbi, Via della Croce 27–8, 00187; *www.fabbi.it* and Salumeria Focacci, Via della Croce 45 are both superb delicatessens. **Markets** Via Bocca di Leone, 00187 (by the Spanish Steps), fruit and veg: Mon–Sat am

🎪 **Festivals** Azaleas on the Spanish Steps (Apr). Outdoor art show, Via Margutta (May). International Horse Show, Villa Borghese (May)

➕ **Pharmacies** Guarnacci, Via Flaminia 5–7, 00187. Ripetta, Via di Ripetta 255, 00186. Call 06 228 941 to find pharmacies open at night or weekends, or check the list displayed in any pharmacy window.

🛝 **Nearest play area** Casina Raffaello, Villa Borghese (see pp286–7)

Winged horse and Triton in the Trevi Fountain

① Villa Borghese
Mythological theme park

Villa Borghese is one of Rome's largest parks. It was created by Cardinal Scipione Borghese as a sort of 17th-century theme park, with ingenious fountains, exotic bird enclosures and a mechanical talking satyr with rolling eyes and a lolling head. The original attractions have all long gone – instead there are artificial ponds, mock temples, a children's play centre, a zoo and two fine museums, one devoted to the works of 17th-century sculptor Gianlorenzo Bernini, the other to Etruscan finds.

Statue, Galleria Borghese

Key Sights

① **Galoppatoio**
Catch a glimpse of the track where wealthy Romans ride their horses.

② **Casina Raffaello** There is a playground outside and activities and storytelling for young children inside.

Piazzale Flaminio entrance

③ **Villa Giulia** Rome's most important Etruscan collection includes a married couple smiling on their tomb. It also has a good café in a leafy conservatory.

④ **Boating lake and island**
This artificial lake features a temple on the island at its centre.

⑤ **Bioparco** Rome's small zoo emphasizes conservation and holds informative shows and workshops at the weekend.

Pincio Gardens entrance

Porta Pinciana entrance

⑧ **Cinema dei Piccoli**
The world's smallest purpose-built cinema, Cinema dei Piccoli has just 63 seats. It opened in 1934 with only a bedsheet for a screen and shows kids' movies in the afternoons.

⑥ **Galleria Nazionale d'Arte Moderna e Contemporanea**
This gallery houses a collection of 20th-century Italian art, with an elegant café that has both indoor and outdoor dining options.

⑦ **Galleria Borghese**
The gallery has a fine collection of sculptures by Bernini – he chose subjects from Greek mythology and Biblical tales that gave him the chance to show off his talents to the full.

The Lowdown

🌐 **Map reference** 17 A2
Address Entrances at Piazzale Flaminio, Porta Pinciana and from the Pincio Gardens, 00197. Villa Giulia: Piazzale di Villa Giulia 9; 06 322 6571. Bioparco: Piazzale del Giardino Zoologico 1, 06 360 8211, www.bioparco.it. Galleria d'Arte Moderna: Viale delle Belle Arti 131, 06 322 981, *www.gnam.beni culturali.it*. Galleria Borghese: Piazzale del Museo Borghese 5, 06 32810, *www.galleriaborghese.it*

🚗 **Bus** 52, 88, 95, 116, 490, 491 **Tram** 3, 19. **Metro** Flaminio, Spagna (Linea A)

Prices given are for a family of four

Letting off steam

Rent a go-kart, bike or roller skates from one of the huts by the Pincio Gardens entrance.

Eat and drink

Picnic: under €25; Snacks: €25–40; Real meal: €40–80; Family treat: €80 or more (based on a family of four)

PICNIC Salumeria Focacci (*Via della Croce 45, 00187*) sells salami, ham and cheese.

SNACKS Cinecaffè Casina delle Rose (*Casa del Cinema, Largo Marcello Mastroianni 1, 00187; 06 4201 6224; www.casadelcinema.it*) has tables under a portico and a lawn in front, which means kids can play while adults linger over lunch. It serves a delicious brunch on Saturdays and Sundays.

REAL MEAL Tramvì (*Explora,Via Flaminia 82, 00187; 06 3260 0432; www.tramvi.it; closed Mon, Sun dinner*), in the Explora museum (*see p200*), is by far the best place in the area for a decently priced lunch.

Elegant interior of Caffè delle Arti in the Galleria Nazionale d'Arte Moderna

Pony-riding in the park, perfect for kids inspired by the Galoppatoio

FAMILY TREAT Caffè delle Arti (*Galleria d'Arte Moderna, Via Gramsci 73, 131; 06 3265 1236*), in the modern art gallery, is perfect for an indulgent family brunch.

Shopping

The **Via del Corso** area and around is a paradise for teen fashionistas, with a range of shops selling clothes, jewellery and accessories.

Take cover

Duck into **Casina Raffaello** (*Viale della Casina di Raffaello, 00197; www.casinadiraffaello.it; closed Mon*), a wonderful children's play area and activity centre. Catch a film at **Cinema dei Piccoli** (*Viale della Pineta 15, 00197; www.cinemadeipiccoli.it*).

Next stop...

CERVETERI Visit the necropolis of this ancient Etruscan city of the dead (*see p304*).

🕐 **Open** Villa Giulia: 8:30am–7:30pm Tue–Sun. Bioparco: Jan–Mar & Oct–Dec 9:30am–4pm daily, March–Oct 9:30am–6pm (till 7pm Sat, Sun). Galleria d'Arte Moderna: 8:30am–7:30pm Tue–Sun. Galleria Borghese: 8:30am–7:30pm Tue–Sun

💶 **Price** Villa Giulia: €16–24, EU under-18's free. Bioparco: €25–46, children 1 m (3 ft) €10.50, under 1 m (3 ft) free. Galleria d'Arte Moderna: €16–24, EU under-18s free. Galleria Borghese: €21–28, EU under-18s €2

👨‍👩‍👧 **Skipping the queue** Booking essential for Galleria Borghese

🚩 **Guided tours** Galleria Borghese: audioguide €5; guided tours in English 9:10am and 11:10am, €6

👫 **Age range** 8 plus for galleries

⏱ **Allow** All day in summer, 1 hour for a gallery and a run in winter

♿ **Wheelchair access** Yes

☕ **Café** Villa Giulia, Casina Raffaello

🛍 **Shop** At Galleria Borghese

🚻 **Toilets** In the cafés

Good family value?

Pick and choose from a variety of free activities and paying sights to suit any budget.

② Explora
Check out the checkout

Rome's children's museum offers plenty to do, but is not so big as to be overwhelming. The emphasis is on hands-on activities and learning through play – there's a supermarket with working cash registers and weighing scales, a TV studio where kids can play at being a weather-person, and a waterplay area with pumps, hose pipes (and waterproof overalls). All the facilitators speak English, but most activities depend more on watching than listening.

Letting off steam

Explora has a café and a small adventure playground, or Villa Borghese is a 15-minute walk away.

The Lowdown

- 🌐 **Map reference** 16 G1
  Address: Via Flaminia 80/86, 00196; 06 361 3776; www.mdbr.it
- 🚗 **Bus** 88, 204, 490, 495 and others. **Tram** 2, 19. **Metro** Flaminio (Linea A)
- 🕐 **Open** Sessions begin at 10am, noon, 3pm and 5pm; closed Mon
- 💶 **Price** €20–28
- 👪 **Skipping the queue** Get there 30 minutes before each session.
- 👫 **Age range** 1 plus; adults only admitted with children.
- ⏱ **Allow** 1 hour 45 minutes: each shift consists of 30 minutes of free play followed by a science or art workshop, then more free play.
- ♿ **Wheelchair access** Yes
- 🍽 **Eat and drink** *Real meal* Tramvì, in the museum, serves simple pizza and pasta for kids along with more grown-up fare. Alternatively, bring a picnic to eat in Explora's garden.

The oval-shaped Piazza del Popolo with its obelisk, as seen from Pincio Gardens

③ Piazza del Popolo
Beheadings and horoscopes

Travellers arriving at the city through the gate here were awed by the Egyptian obelisk, or shocked by an execution in full swing (as seen by English poet Byron in 1817). Today it is a huge pedestrianized oval.

Just inside the gate is the church of **Santa Maria del Popolo**. Look inside for the tomb of Renaissance banker Agostino Chigi, in a chapel with his horoscope in its dome, and for a dramatic Bernini sculpture of *Daniel*, a lion licking his foot. Head to the Cerasi chapel for Caravaggio realism: *The Conversion of St Paul* shows the saint sprawled on the ground below a horse's rump.

Letting off steam

Above the piazza are **Pincio Gardens**, a great place to stroll, run around or take a rickshaw ride.

The Lowdown

- 🌐 **Map reference** 16 G3
  Address Piazza del Popolo, 00187
- 🚗 **Bus** 117, 119. **Tram** 2. **Metro** Flaminio (Linea A)
- 🕐 **Open** Santa Maria del Popolo: 7am–noon, 4–7pm Mon–Sat, 8am–1:30pm, 4:30–7:15pm Sun
- 👫 **Age range** Piazza del Popolo: 5 plus; Santa Maria: 8 plus
- ⏱ **Allow** 45 minutes
- ♿ **Wheelchair access** Yes
- 🍽 **Eat and drink** *Picnic* Fratelli Fabbi on Via della Croce (see p285) is useful for picnic supplies – eat in the Pincio Gardens. *Snack* Rosati (Piazza del Popolo 4/5a; www.rosatibar.it) is great for a quality hot chocolate and pastry.

④ Ara Pacis
Imperial children

The Altar of Peace, constructed under Emperor Augustus, is now encased in an ultramodern building of glass and travertine designed by New York-based architect Richard Meier. Creating a contemporary building in historic Rome was controversial, but look at the way Meier contrasts polished and uncut travertine (the stone from which most of Rome is built), and at the patterns made by the water wall.

The Ara Pacis itself was erected in 9 BC to celebrate the peace and prosperity Augustus had brought to the Roman Empire. Carved along its sides is a long procession of figures – they have been identified as members of Augustus's family and include several children. The

Children exploring how weighing scales and supermarket checkouts work at Explora

The Lowdown

- 🌐 **Map reference** 16 G4
  Address Lungotevere in Augusta, 00100; www.arapacis.it.
- 🚌 **Bus** 70, 81, 186; **Metro** Flaminio
- 🕐 **Open** 9am–7pm Tue–Sun
- 💶 **Price** €22–40, under-6s free
- 👫 **Age range** 5 plus
- ⏱ **Allow** 30 minutes
- ♿ **Wheelchair access** Yes
- 🍴 **Eat and drink** *Picnic* Salumeria Focacci and Fratelli Fabbi in Via della Croce (*see p285, 287*) sell tasty goodie. Picnic in Pincio Gardens. *Real meal* Dal Pollarolo (*Via di Ripetta 4–5, 00186; 06 361 0276; www.dalpollarolo1936.it; closed Thu and Aug*) serves *pasta alla checca*, with raw tomatoes, basil, capers, olives and fennel seeds, and crisp pizza.

sunken, overgrown brick cylinder visible from here is the Mausoleum of Augustus, where the emperor and his family were buried.

Letting off steam

There is space to run around and fountains to cool fingers and toes outside the Ara Pacis.

⑤ Piazza di Spagna

Sickly poets and Spanish Steps

This square is best known as the location of the Spanish Steps, built in the 18th century to link the piazza with the church of Trinità dei Monti. They were at the heart of the area

Frieze of the Emperor Augustus's family on the Ara Pacis, or Altar of Peace

where English Romantic poets John Keats (who died at no. 26, now the **Keats-Shelley House** museum), Percy Bysshe Shelley and Lord Byron chose to live. At the time, artists' models, dressed as saints, Madonnas and ancient Roman emperors, would wait here, hoping to attract a wealthy artist.

Take cover

Duck into **Sant'Andrea delle Fratte** church on the street of the same name, to see some heavenly carved angels by sculptor Bernini.

The ever-busy Spanish Steps, leading up to Trinità dei Monti

The Lowdown

- 🌐 **Map reference** 16 H4
  Address Piazza di Spagna, 00187; Keats-Shelley House: Piazza di Spagna 26, 00187; 06 678 4235; www.keats-shelley-house.org
- 🚌 **Bus** 116. **Metro** Spagna (Linea A)
- 🕐 **Open** Keats-Shelley House: 10am–1pm, 2–6pm Mon–Sat
- 💶 **Price** Keats-Shelley House: €9–16, 6–18s €3.50, under-6s free
- 👫 **Skipping the queue** Visit early to avoid the worst of the crowds.
- 👫 **Age range** All, for the buzz
- ⏱ **Allow** 30 minutes
- ♿ **Wheelchair access** Yes (not steps)
- 🍴 **Eat and drink** *Snacks* Babington's Tea Room (*Piazza di Spagna 26; babingtons.net*) is best for tea. *Real meal* Trattoria da Ugo al Gran Sasso (*Via di Ripetta 32; 06 321 4883; closed Sat*) is an amiable restaurant serving traditional local cuisine. Try the *bucatini all'amatriciana* (with a sticky tomato and bacon sauce).

⑥ Trevi Fountain
Dragon-tailed sea-horses

Despite being tucked away on a tiny piazza, the Fontana di Trevi is almost impossible to miss. The narrow streets and alleyways surrounding it are full of gaudy souvenir shops and takeaway pizzerias and, close to the fountain, filled with the sound of gushing water. Built between 1732 and 1762 in Rococo style, the Trevi Fountain is a travertine extravaganza showing the sea-god Neptune in a scallop-shell and two Tritons, one with an unruly "sea-horse" and one with a tame one. The water comes from an aqueduct, the Acqua Vergine, built in 19 BC to fill the city's first baths complex, and is fed by springs 22 km (14 miles) from the city.

The fountain sprang to world fame after it had a starring role in the 1950s film *La Dolce Vita* by Federico Fellini: glamorous film star Anita Ekberg, walking home at night through narrow streets with a stray cat on her head, comes across it and decides to go for a swim.

Take cover
Time Elevator Roma (2 minutes' walk away) turns the history of Rome into a multimedia experience, with a special-effects film telling the story.

Admiring crowds flocking to Rome's grandest fountain, the Trevi

The Lowdown

- 🌐 **Map reference** 17 A5
  Address Piazza di Trevi, 00187. Time Elevator Rome: Via SS Apostoli 20, 00187; www. timelevator.it
- 🚌 **Bus** 52, 53, 61, 62, 63, 80, 95, 116
- 🕐 **Open** Time Elevator Rome: 10:30am–7:30pm daily
- 💶 **Price** Time Elevator Rome: €24–38
- 👬 **Skipping the queue** In the evening the fountain is floodlit and less crowded.
- 👫 **Age range** All
- ⏲ **Allow** 20 minutes
- ♿ **Wheelchair access** Yes
- 🍽 **Eat and drink** *Snacks* San Crispino (*Via della Panetteria 42, 00187; www.ilgelatodisan crispino.it*) makes some of Rome's freshest *gelato*. *Real meal* Caffè Trevi e Tritone (*Galleria Alberto Sordi, Via del Corso; 06 678 0617; 8:30am–8:30pm daily*) serves light meals such as *pasta cacio e pepe*, with sheep's cheese and pepper.

⑦ The Quirinale
Baroque geometry and an ugly baby

The Quirinale Hill is the highest of the seven hills of Rome and there are great views of the city from Piazza del Quirinale. The monument in the centre of the square has two colossal statues of the patrons of horsemanship, Castor and Pollux, and their prancing horses, which are Roman copies of 5th-century BC Greek originals. The **Palazzo del Quirinale** was the official residence of the king following the unification of Italy in 1870. Since 1947, it has been the official home of the President of the Italian Republic. Many great architects worked on the palace before it assumed its present form in the 1730s. It contains 17th- and 18th-century art and has magnificent gardens.

A Triton struggles to control his "sea-horse" in the Trevi fountain

The Lowdown

- 🌐 **Map reference** 17 A5
  Address Piazza del Quirinale, 00187. Palazzo del Quirinale: Piazza del Quirinale, 06 46991. Sant' Andrea: Via del Quirinale 29. San Carlo: Via del Quirinale 23. Santa Maria: Via XX Settembre 17. Galleria Nazionale d'Arte Antica: Palazzo Barberini, Via Quattro Fontane 13, 06 482 4184, www.galleriaborghese.it
- 🚌 **Bus** 16, 36, 37, 38, 40, 60, 61, 62, 64, 70. **Metro** Barberini (Linea A)
- 🕐 **Open** Palazzo del Quirinale: 8:30am–noon Sun. Palazzo Barberini: Tue–Sun 8:30am–7:30pm
- 💶 **Price** Palazzo del Quirinale: €10–20, EU under-18s free; Galleria Nazionale d'Arte Antica : €10–15; EU under-18s free
- 👫 **Age range** 8 plus
- ⏲ **Allow** Half a day
- ♿ **Wheelchair access** Yes, but streets are steep and pavements narrow.
- 🍽 **Eat and drink** *Snacks* Caffetteria delle Scuderie del Quirinale (*Via XXIV Maggio 16, 00187; 06 3996 7500*) has good snacks. *Real meal* Hostaria Romana (*Via del Boccaccio 1, 00187; 06 474 5284; closed Sun*) serves classic dishes such as *spaghetti alla carbonara*.

If the jury's still out on Bernini versus Borromini after Piazza Navona (*see pp274–5*), three churches on the hill may decide the casting vote. **Sant'Andrea del Quirinale** (1658–72), known as the "Pearl of the Baroque", is Bernini's most theatrical church, an oval set on its short axis, so that the first thing people see as they enter the

Palazzo del Quirinale, official residence of the Italian president

high altar niche, in which statues of flying angels hold a painting of St Andrew being crucified on a diagonal cross. **San Carlo alle Quattro Fontane**, commissioned from rival Borromini in 1634, has a curved façade, an octagonal courtyard, and an oval dome designed to give the illusion that it is higher than it really is. **Santa Maria della Vittoria** is home to Bernini's most famous sculpture, the *Ecstasy of St Teresa* (1646) – an angel stands poised to shoot a fire tipped arrow into the ecstatic saint's heart, a show of divine love.

Inside the **Galleria Nazionale d'Arte Antica**, in Palazzo Barberini, a square staircase by Bernini leads up one side, an oval spiral staircase by Borromini up the other, to a fine collection of 13th–16th-century art. Filippo Lippi's *Madonna and Child* (c.1465) is notable for its ugly baby Jesus, with an idealized Madonna and angel disrupted by a couple talking anxiously. The gallery's most famous painting is Raphael's *La Fornarina* (c.1518), a semi-nude portrait of a young woman, traditionally identified as being the artist's girlfriend.

Take cover
Shelter in the **Scuderie del Quirinale** (*Via XXIV Maggio 16; www.scuderiequirinale.it*) on the south side of Piazza Quirinale. These were originally stables built for the pope's horses, but are now a gallery space with changing exhibitions and a café. The Scuderie del Quirinale often hosts kids' activities.

⑧ Santa Maria della Concezione
Deathly decor

Santa Maria della Concezione belonged (and still belongs) to the Capuchin order of monks, who were determined to make people confront the reality of death. In the 1630s, they dismantled thousands of skeletons belonging to their departed brothers and used the bones to decorate the walls of the church's labyrinthine underground chapels. Vertebrae were wired together to make sacred crowns, and clothed skeletons lie in niches constructed from pelvic bones.

Letting off steam
Five minutes' walk up Via Veneto and across a busy road are the open spaces and attractions of **Villa Borghese** park (*see pp286–7*).

Taking a stroll in the leafy expanses of Villa Borghese park

The Lowdown

- 🌐 **Map reference** 17 B4
  Address Via Veneto 27, 00187
- 🚗 **Bus** 52, 53, 63. **Metro** Barberini
- 🕐 **Open** 9am–noon, 3–6pm (closed Thu)
- 🚻 **Age range** 5 plus
- ⏱ **Allow** 20 minutes
- ♿ **Wheelchair access** Yes
- 🍴 **Eat and Drink** Snacks *Veneto* (*Via Veneto 120, 00187; closed Sun*) is a Dolce Vita-era classic for cakes and savouries. Real meal *Colline Emiliane* (*Via degli Avignonesi 22, 00184; 06 481 7538*) is a long-established eatery. Try the pumpkin-stuffed pasta.

The Vatican and Trastevere

The Vatican Museums – all 12 of them packed full of art and antiquities – can be overwhelming, so plan a visit carefully, with an early morning sprint to see the Sistine Chapel before anyone else arrives. Continue to St Peter's, where the highlight may be taking a lift to the roof to send a postcard from its very own post office. Further south, the Trastevere area is more fun, with traffic-free piazzas, delicious takeaway food and the Renaissance Villa Farnesina. Across the river is workaday Testaccio, site of the city's old slaughterhouse, and the peaceful Aventine Hill.

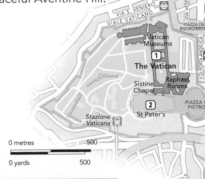

The Vatican
and Trastevere

Villa Borghese
and Tridente
p284

Piazza Navona
p272

The
Vatican and
Trastevere

Campo de' Fiori
p278

Colosseum
p264

A view of the Vatican from Piazza Garibaldi,
high up on the Janiculum hill

0 metres 500

0 yards 500

Bernini's Baroque
colonnade on Piazza
San Pietro

Places of interest

SIGHTS
1. The Vatican
2. St Peter's
3. Castel Sant'Angelo
4. Villa Farnesina
5. Santa Maria in Trastevere
6. Santa Cecilia in Trastevere
7. Testaccio
8. Aventine Hill
9. Piazza Bocca della Verità

EAT AND DRINK
1. Franchi Gastronomia
2. Alimentari Laurenti
3. Da Giovanni
4. Checco er Carrettiere
5. Hostaria da Osvaldo
6. Caffé Settimiano
7. Casa delle Donne
8. La Boccaccia
9. Frontoni
10. Volpetti Più

11. Tuttifrutti
12. La Dolce Roma
13. Sora Margherita

WHERE TO STAY
1. Adriatic
2. Hotel Santa Maria
3. Residenza Santa Maria
4. San Francesco
5. Foresteria Orsa Maggiore
6. Buonanotte Garibaldi

The lovely open space of Villa
Sciarra park, Trastevere

The brick cylinder of Castel Sant'Angelo and the Ponte Sant'Angelo

Taking a break in a streetside café in traffic-free Piazza Santa Maria, Trastevere

The Lowdown

🚗 For the Vatican: **Bus** 49, 62, 32, 81, 982, 492. **Metro** Ottaviano (Linea A). **Taxi rank** Viale Vaticano, in front of the Vatican Museums. For Trastevere: **Tram** 8 starting at Largo di Torre Argentina and running along broad, busy Viale di Trastevere

ℹ️ **Visitor information** Tourist Information Point "Castel Sant'Angelo" (Vatican): Piazza Pia, 00196. "Sonnino" (Trastevere): Piazza Sonnino, 00196; 060608; www. turismoroma.it; open 9:30am–7pm daily

🛒 **Supermarkets** Carrefour, Via Sebastiano Veniero 10a, 00100. Standa, Viale Trastevere 60, 00153 **Markets** Piazza San Cosimato, Trastevere; Piazza Testaccio

🎉 **Festivals** Papal Address, Piazza San Pietro (Christmas and Easter). Festa di San Pietro e Paolo (papal rites followed by a procession and firework display), Piazza San Pietro and around (29 Jun)

➕ **Pharmacies** Farmacia Vaticana, Porta Sant'Anna 1, 00120; 06 6989 0561; open 8am–1pm and 3pm–7pm Mon–Fri, 8am–1pm Sat. Call 06 228 941 to find pharmacies open at night or weekends, or check the list displayed in any pharmacy window.

🎯 **Nearest play area** Villa Sciarra: Via Calandrelli 23, 00100; bus 44, 75, 115

① The Vatican
Sprint or marathon?

The Vatican's complex of museums is the largest in the world. There are no fewer than 12 museums in all, not to mention the Sistine Chapel, Raphael Rooms and endless galleries – to see it all would mean walking over 7 km (4 miles). The main aim for most families will be to get to the Sistine Chapel before the children are tired, so that it makes an impact. Pick one of four colour-coded routes, ranging from a 90-minute sprint to a 5-hour marathon; a one-way system means no backtracking.

Roman funerary portrait

Key Features

① Room of the Animals
This room has ancient Roman statues of animals. The walls and floor are decorated with delightful mosaics, such as this pig with mushrooms.

② Pinacoteca
The art gallery has 15th–19th-century works, focussing mainly on the Renaissance.

■ **Lower floor** Greek, Roman and Egyptian collections, Renaissance art and the Sistine Chapel.

■ **Upper floor** More Greek and Roman sculpture, the Gallery of Maps and the Raphael Rooms.

⑦ Sistine Chapel
Michelangelo painted 366 figures on the ceiling of the chapel between 1508 and 1512, vividly illustrating the story of the Creation of the World, the Fall of Man and the Coming of Christ.

Prices given are for a family of four

③ Spiral staircase
This spectacular stairway leads down from the museums to the street level. It was designed by Giuseppe Momo in 1932.

Entrance

Inner garden

⑧ The Gallery of Maps
This gallery takes its name from the 40 frescoed maps of Italy on its walls. The collection is an important record of 16th-century history and cartography.

④ Gallery of the Candelabra
Once an open loggia, this gallery of Greek and Roman sculpture has a fine view of the Vatican Gardens.

⑤ Raphael Rooms
At the same time that Michelangelo was painting the Sistine, Raphael was at work redecorating a suite of rooms for Pope Julius. The most dramatic is *The Room of the Fire in the Borgo*.

⑥ Pio-Clementine Museum
This gallery contains the prize pieces of the Vatican's Greek and Roman collections. The ancient Roman copies of the Greek *Apollo del Belvedere* and *Venus of Cnidus* were considered to be paragons of male and female beauty.

⑨ Egyptian Museum
This collection contains finds from 19th- and 20th-century excavations in Egypt and statues that were brought over to Rome during Imperial times.

The Lowdown

- 🌐 **Map reference** 15 C4
  Address Viale Vaticano 100,
  00120 Città del Vaticano;
  06 6988 4947; www.
  museivaticani.va

- 🚗 **Bus** 49 or 32, 81, 982 to Piazza
  del Risorgimento. **Tram** 2.
  Metro Ottaviano (Linea A).
  Taxi rank in front of entrance

- 🕐 **Open** 9am–6pm (last entry
  4pm) Mon–Sat; 8:30am–2pm
  (last entry 12:30pm) last Sun of
  the month (check website)

- 💶 **Price** €30–46, 6–18s €8,
  under-6s and last Sun free

- 👪 **Skipping the queue** Buy
  your tickets in advance online
  and be there for the first entry
  at 8:30am.

- 🔫 **Guided tours** 2-hour guided
  tours are available in Italian or
  English; €62–100; book in
  advance online.

- 👫 **Age range** For under-11s, a
  visit to the Sistine Chapel will
  be enough.

- ⏱ **Allow** From an hour for the
  Sistine Chapel to a whole day
  for those with stamina.

- ♿ **Wheelchair access** Yes, with
  recommended itinerary; reserve
  a free wheelchair by emailing
  accoglienza.musei@scv.va

- 🍽 **Café** Self-service restaurant,
  pizzeria and café downstairs
  near Pinacoteca; Sistina coffee
  bar on stairs up to the chapel

- 🚻 **Toilets** By entrance, near main
  café, by the Raphael Rooms
  and outside the Sistine Chapel

Good family value?
The entry fee is expensive, but if
there's a flicker of interest from the
children it's money well spent –
they may thank you later.

Letting off steam

Take bus 115 up the **Janiculum Hill**
for the views, or walk 30 minutes to
shady **Orto Botanico** (see p298).

Eat and drink

*Picnic: under €25; Snacks: €25–40;
Real meal: €40–80; Family treat: €80 or
more (based on a family of four)*

PICNIC Franchi Gastronomia (Via
Cola di Rienzo 200, 00196; www.
franchi.it) has a great deli counter
and hot takeaway dishes.
SNACKS Alimentari Laurenti (Via
della Lungara 43, 00196) on the
road to Trastevere has slices of
pizza bianca and pizza rossa.
REAL MEAL Da Giovanni (Via della
Lungara 41, 00196; 06 686 1514;
closed Sun) is a tiny, traditional

trattoria serving very good-value,
simple dishes such as chickpea soup
or pasta with tomato sauce.
**FAMILY TREAT Checco er
Carrettiere** (Via Benedetta 10,
00153; 06 580 0985; closed Mon)
serves Roman specialities.

Find out more

DIGITAL Go to www.entertainment.
howstuffworks.com/arts/artwork/
sistine-chapel-michelangelo-
paintings1.htm for fun facts on the
Sistine Chapel and Michelangelo.

Next stop...

VILLA FARNESINA Visit this villa
(see p298) to see more of Raphael's
wonderful frescoes.

The inner garden (Giardino della Pigna) of the Vatican Museums

The grand entrance to St Peter's on Piazza San Pietro

② St Peter's

Bullet-proof Michelangelo and post office on the tiles

Fronted by immense, pincer-like colonnades designed by Bernini, St Peter's was built to impress the world with the awesome power of the Catholic Church. The approach from Via della Conciliazione is magnificent and the church holds hundreds of precious works of art.

St Peter was martyred and buried on this site in AD 64, and there has been a church here since the 4th century. In the early 16th century Pope Julius II realized that there was not enough room inside for the tomb he had commissioned from Michelangelo so he ordered the architect Bramante to replace the old church with a grand new basilica. The rebuilding of St Peter's cost the equivalent of £460m in

The interior of St Peter's Basilica, the largest church in the world

today's money and involved all the greatest artists and architects of the Roman Renaissance and Baroque – Bramante, Raphael, Michelangelo and Bernini – who disagreed with each other about the design.

The spectacular cupola, 136.5 m (448 ft) high, gives unity to the majestic interior of the basilica. It was designed by Michelangelo, though not finished in his lifetime. St Peter's was inaugurated in 1626.

The main sights in St Peter's
Take the lift or climb 320 steps to the **roof**, where there's a soft drinks machine, souvenir shop, post office and toilet. In the old days the *sanpietrini*, the workers responsible for maintaining the basilica, used to live up here with their families. From the roof, climb 200 steps to the dome for spectacular views – the superb symmetry of Bernini's colonnade is best appreciated from this vantage point.

Back on the ground, just inside the north door, is Michelangelo's **Pietà**, a sculpture of Mary holding the dying Christ. It has been protected by bullet-proof glass since the 1970s, when a mad geologist attacked it with a hammer.

Up near the high altar is Bernini's **baldacchino**, a kind of canopy on curly-wurly candy-cane columns, which stands above the tomb of St Peter. It was commissioned by Pope Urban VIII, a member of the Barberini family, and swarms with bees, their coat of arms. It also celebrated the survival of one of the pope's nieces and her baby after a difficult birth – look closely at the

Prices given are for a family of four

Swiss guards in official ceremonial uniform at St Peter's

column bases to see the faces of women suffering labour pains and, finally, a healthy baby.

In a vestibule to the right of the entrance porch is a **statue of Emperor Constantine** on a rearing horse. It represents the moment in AD 313, during the Battle of the Milvian Bridge, when Constantine had a vision of the cross and converted to Christianity.

Letting off steam
Take kids to play hide and seek in the shade of Bernini's colonnade on **Piazza San Pietro** and watch the changing patterns of columns, or head for the **Orto Botanico** (see p298) for a shady picnic.

The angel St Michael, by Raffaello da Montelupo, Castel Sant'Angelo

③ Castel Sant'Angelo

The escape of the jewel-thief

Castel Sant'Angelo is most theatrically approached across the Ponte Sant'Angelo, a pedestrian-only bridge adorned with silky marble statues of angels by Bernini. The castle itself is a massive brick cylinder on the banks of the Tiber that began life in AD 123 as a mausoleum for Emperor Hadrian, but was soon converted into a fortress and prison. Popes would retreat here in times of danger and, in 1527, during the Sack of Rome, goldsmith Benvenuto Cellini claimed to have defended the castle single-handed, and concealed the pope's jewels by sewing them into his clothes. He was later accused of having stolen the gems and locked in the prison, before escaping by shinning down the 25 m (82 ft) wall on a rope of knotted sheets.

Letting off steam

Head for the **Ponte Sant'Angelo** to appreciate the approach, while the kids get rid of excess energy by running up and down the bridge.

The Lowdown

🌐 **Map reference** 16 E5–6
Address Lungomare Castello 50, 00186; 06 681 9111; *www.castelsantangelo.com*

🚌 **Bus** 23, 62

🕐 **Open** Tue–Sun 9am–7:30pm

💶 **Price** €17–29, EU under-18s free

👪 **Age range** All

🤸 **Activities** In winter go ice skating in Piazza Adriana. In summer, kids' shows take place on the castle's terrace as part of the Estate Romana summer festival.

⏱ **Allow** 45 minutes

👆 **Guided tours** Book in advance by phone or fax on 06 855 5952.

♿ **Wheelchair access** Yes, but some rooms are inaccessible

☕ **Eat and drink** *Snacks* Caffetteria Castel Sant'Angelo (in the castle) is convenient for a quick drink and a snack, and has good views over the city. *Real meal* Hostaria da Osvaldo (*Via di Monte Giordano 61, 00184; 06 686 1014; closed Sun eve*), across the Ponte Sant'Angelo, is an old-fashioned, cosy *osteria* serving Puglian specialities such as breaded escalopes. Eat inside, or outside at one of three tables on a quiet street.

Castel Sant'Angelo from Ponte Sant'Angelo, flanked by Bernini angels

Picnic under €25; **Snacks** €25–40; **Real meal** €40–80; **Family treat** €80 or more (based on a family of four)

④ Villa Farnesina
Party palace

The apricot-washed Villa Farnesina, standing in its own grounds on the banks of the Tiber, was built in the early 16th century for a banking tycoon called Agostino Chigi. He loved to throw parties and had this villa built for banquets, to which he invited the city's greatest artists, writers, poets and philosophers. After Chigi died in 1520 the villa was abandoned and its statues, furniture and paintings were sold. Fortunately the best artworks – two loggias frescoed by Raphael – could not be moved.

Raphael began work in 1510, but kept running off to see his girlfriend, La Fornarina. Chigi kidnapped her and told Raphael that she had run away with another man to make him focus on his work, but the artist was so upset that he downed brushes. Chigi miraculously "found" the girlfriend and let her move into the villa. Despite this, the only painting Raphael completed was the famous *Triumph of Galatea*, showing a beautiful woman with strawberry blonde hair streaming in the wind. The rest of the frescoes, including one of the giant Polyphemus, were painted by his pupils.

The Lowdown

- 🌐 **Map reference** 23 B5
  Address: Villa Farnese, Via della Lungara 230, 00165; 06 6802 7268; www.villafarnesina.it. Orto Botanico: Largo Cristina di Svezia 24, 00165; 066 864 193
- 🚌 **Bus** 23, 280, 116
- 🕐 **Open** Villa Farnese: 9am–1pm Mon–Sat. Orto Botanico: 9am–5:30pm daily
- 💶 **Price** €10–16, under-14s free; Orto Botanico: €8–12, under-6s free
- 🚩 **Guided tours** Mon and Fri at noon; Sat at 11:30am, 12:30pm
- 🧍 **Age range** 8 plus
- ⏱ **Allow** 1 hour
- ♿ **Wheelchair access** Yes
- ☕ **Eat and drink** *Snacks* Caffè Settimiano (*Via di Porta Settimiana 1, 00165*) is good for sandwiches. *Real meal* Casa delle Donne (*Via Francesco di Sales 1, 00165*) serves organic meals. All are welcome at lunch; open only to women and children in the evenings.

The church of Santa Maria in Trastevere, famous for the mosaics on its façade

Letting off steam
Across the road is the **Orto Botanico**, with plenty of shade, and space to run around and picnic.

⑤ Santa Maria in Trastevere
The wise and the foolish girls

Piazza Santa Maria in Trastevere is a traffic-free square at the heart of this bustling neighbourhood, where according to legend, a miraculous fountain of oil bubbled up at the precise moment that Jesus was born. Whatever the truth, a church was built here and, although the present building dates from the 12th century, the original church may have been the first in Rome, dating way back to the 3rd century. Today, the most interesting thing about the church is its mosaics.

Three-dimensional fresco, Salone delle Prospettive, Villa Farnesina

On the façade a breastfeeding Madonna is flanked by 10 women holding lamps. Only five of the lamps are lit: they represent Jesus's story of the wise and the foolish virgins, a parable about being prepared – the wise virgins took supplies of oil with them, the foolish ones did not.

Inside, walk along the nave, lined with huge granite columns filched from the Baths of Caracalla (*see p268*), to see the mosaic in the apse that shows the *Virgin Mary as Bride of Christ*. Below are scenes from her life, including a realistic *Nativity of the Virgin* in which the nurse is checking the temperature of the bath water.

Letting off steam
Kids can play in the piazza outside the church while the adults recharge with a coffee.

The Lowdown

- 🌐 **Map reference** 20 F2
  Address Piazza Santa Maria in Trastevere, 00153
- 🚌 **Bus** 115, 125
- 🕐 **Open** 7:30am–8pm daily (no visiting during mass)
- 🧍 **Age range** 5 plus
- ⏱ **Allow** 30 minutes
- ♿ **Wheelchair access** Yes
- ☕ **Eat and drink** *Snacks* La Boccaccia (*Via Santa Dorotea 2, 00153*) bakes pizza by the slice, and Checco er Carettiere pasticceria next to the restaurant (*Via Benedetta 7, 00153; www.checcoercarettiere.it*) has delicious ice creams and cakes.

⑥ Santa Cecilia in Trastevere

The singing saint

The church of Santa Cecilia stands above the house in which the saint was martyred for her faith in the 3rd century. Locked in the steam room of her home to suffocate, she miraculously survived. When she still refused to renounce her Christianity, an axeman was sent to behead her, but Roman law permitted only three strokes and these again failed to kill her. She hung on, half dead, for another three days. The patron saint of music and an aristocrat, Cecilia is said to have sung throughout her ordeal in the steam room.

In 1599 her tomb was opened and there, wrapped in a gown shot with gold and a green silk veil, was her perfectly preserved body. On contact with air, her body began to disintegrate, but not before sketches had been made that sculptor Stefano Maderno used to create the statue of the saint (1600), lying with her head turned away to reveal her wounded neck. This can be seen in a niche below the high altar. There is also a fine 13th-century fresco of *The Last Judgment* by Pietro Cavallini in the singing gallery above the nave. Cecilia's house – beneath the church with the remains of a Roman tannery – is also well worth a visit.

Letting off steam

Piazza San Cosimato, with its lively daily market, is close at hand. Otherwise catch bus 44 or 75 to **Villa Sciarra** park *(Via Calandrelli 23,*

The 1725 façade and 12th-century bell tower of Santa Cecilia in Trastevere

00100), once owned by a Philadelphia heiress, with its monstrous Mannerist fountains.

The Lowdown

- 🌐 **Map reference** 20 G3
  Address Piazza di Santa Cecilia, 00153
- 🚌 **Bus** 23, 44, 280
- 🕐 **Open** 9:30am–1pm and 4–6pm daily
- 💶 **Price** Excavations of house: €5–10
- 👫 **Age range** 8 plus
- 🕐 **Allow** 20 minutes
- ♿ **Wheelchair access** Yes
- 🍴 **Eat and drink** *Snacks* Frontoni *(Viale Trastevere 52, 00153; 06 581 2436)* is a good-value *tavola calda* (snack bar) serving snacks such as pizza and *panini* and coffee during the day. *Real meal* Da Giovanni *(Via della Lungara 41, 00196; 06 686 1514, closed Sun)* serves up good-value meals in a traditional trattoria setting.

The Baroque interior of the basilica of Santa Cecilia in Trastevere

Picnic under €25; **Snacks** €25–40; **Real meal** €40–80; **Family treat** €80 or more (based on a family of four)

⑦ Testaccio
Pyramid piazza and pigs' trotters and tails

Bus 75 hops across the Tiber from Trastevere to Testaccio, a gutsy working-class neighbourhood which has become a fashionable place to live. There is a fantastic food market, while the ex-slaughterhouse (*mattatoio*) – once the area's main employer – has become a venue for concerts and art events.

The area is named after Monte Testaccio, a rubbish tip mound, made out of the shards of Roman amphorae that were dumped here in ancient times – their edges can be seen through the grass near its summit, while there are restaurants and bars on the slopes below.

The area's most extraordinary sight is a marble pyramid, rising from the traffic of Piazzale Ostiense. It was built in the late 1st century BC by a Roman called Gaius Cestius, whose main job was to organize parties for the emperor. At the time, spurred by the fame of Cleopatra, all things Egyptian were highly fashionable and Gaius decided to build himself a pyramid as a tomb.

Letting off steam

Piazza Testaccio has one of Rome's best markets, a good place to wander and graze – challenge the kids to try ready-to-eat pigs' trotters and tails or treat them to a "grated ice" with fruit syrup at the Chioschetto Testaccio Grattachecca on Via G Branca.

Parco Savello with umbrella pines and orange trees, on Aventine Hill

⑧ Aventine Hill
Through the keyhole

Although it is possible to walk from Testaccio to the Aventine, the roads are full of traffic, so it's better to make the hop by Metro. The Aventine is a lush, leafy twin-peaked hill where the sound of birdsong is louder than that of cars – at least once out of earshot of the traffic roaring around the ex-chariot-racing Roman stadium of Circus Maximus. At the foot of the hill is the **Roseto Comunale**, a lovely rose garden, and just above it the **Parco Savello**, a walled park with umbrella pines, orange trees and fabulous views of the city. Carry on to the beautiful church of **Santa Sabina**, with ancient sarcophagi in its porch, and a remarkable 5th-century carved wooden door. The luminous interior is an utterly simple early Christian

Stalls selling fresh fish at the market in Piazza Testaccio

basilica, with a flat wooden ceiling and a broad nave supported by columns from a Roman temple to Juno that once stood on the site. By the door is a black stone said to have been hurled at St Dominic by the devil (he missed).

At the end of Via Santa Sabina is the obelisk-fringed **Piazza dei Cavalieri di Malta**, designed by Piranesi, an artist best known for his nightmarish etchings of prisons. The keyhole in the door of the Priory of the Sovereign Order of Malta is famous for its telescopic view, in which a miniature St Peter's appears at the end of an avenue of trees.

Letting off steam

Go to **Parco Savello** (*Via di Santa Sabina, 00154*) for a picnic and play, but be sure to bring supplies as there are no shops on the Aventine.

⑨ Piazza Bocca della Verità

Medieval lie-detector

Kids may put up with the heavy traffic of Piazza Bocca della Verità in order to put their hands in the mouth of a medieval lie-detector, and see if it snaps shut if they do not tell the truth. The so-called Bocca della Verità, or Mouth of Truth, is actually a medieval drain cover in the portico of the church of Santa Maria in Cosmedin, carved with a bearded, slit-mouthed face, whose fame as a lie detector spread after it made an appearance in the 1953 film *Roman Holiday* with Audrey Hepburn and Gregory Peck.

The church itself is best seen in the evenings, when its interior is lit by candles. The pavement, choir and a twisting candlestick are all fine examples of a kind of mosaic work known as Cosmati – created from fragments of coloured marble, most of which came from the abandoned buildings of ancient Rome. On the other side of the piazza, stranded in a sea of traffic, are two exquisite Roman temples: the circular Temple of Hercules Victor and the tiny, rectangular Temple of Portunus. Both survived because they were converted into churches.

Letting off steam

To get away from the traffic cross the river into Trastevere and let the kids play around the octagonal, 15th-century fountain in beautiful **Piazza Santa Maria in Trastevere** (see p298). To cool off in summer head to **All'Ombra del Colosseo** outdoor swimming pool in the centre of **Circo Massimo** (see p268).

Above Bocca della Verità
Below Temple of Hercules Victor, in Piazza Bocca della Verità

The Lowdown

- 🌐 **Map reference** 20 H2
  Address Piazza Bocca della Verità 18, 00153
- 🚌 **Bus** 23, 44, 81, 95 and others
- 👫 **Age range** All
- ⏱ **Allow** 30 minutes
- ♿ **Wheelchair access** Yes
- ☕ **Eat and drink** *Snacks* La Dolce Roma (*Via Portico d'Ottavia 20b, 00186; open 8:30am–8pm Tue–Sat, 10am–1pm Sun*) serves sweet treats kids will love, such as American-style cakes and cookies. *Real Meal* Sora Margherita (*Piazza delle Cinque Scole 30; 06 687 4216; lunch only Mon–Thu, dinner too Fri–Sat, closed Sun*) in the Ghetto is the best option for a meal. This lively, old-fashioned trattoria has no menu, and serves hand-made pasta and deep-fried stuffed courgette flowers.

Day Trips from Rome

When Rome gets too much, it is quite easy to escape. The villas at Tivoli are perfect for a relaxed day out, while the ancient Roman remains of Ostia are far less crowded than any of the city centre's sites. To the north are the Etruscan necropolises of Cerveteri and Tarquinia, austere Viterbo and the mad monster park of Bomarzo. For a break from culture, head to Lake Bracciano for the simple pleasures of boating, swimming and picnicking.

Fontana dell'Ovato, also known as Tivoli Fountain, in Ville d'Este

① Tivoli
Pleasure palaces

The hill-town of Tivoli is the perfect place for a day trip with kids, with plenty of space to let off steam as well as lots to see. It has been a popular summer resort since the days of the Roman Republic, when Romans visited for the fresh water and sulphur springs and the beautiful surrounding countryside.

The **Villa d'Este** is the town's most famous sight and its water gardens, featuring many fountains, pools and water troughs, are the kind of thing Walt Disney might have designed had he been a Renaissance prince. The most dramatic feature is the huge Fontana dell'Organo (Organ Fountain), where millions of litres of water force air through the pipes. Children will love the grand Fountain of the Dragons.

Villa Adriana (Hadrian's Villa), just 5 km (3 miles) to the west, is easily visited in conjunction with a trip to Tivoli. Once a magnificent private retreat, it had a fire station, bath-houses, libraries, temples and theatres as well as a palace. Emperor Hadrian was so impressed by the architecture of Greece and Egypt he saw on his travels that he tried to reproduce it all here.

Among the rambling ruins of this vast complex is the Maritime Theatre, a round pool with an island in the middle surrounded by columns. Hadrian would retreat here to write and paint. A lovely spot for a picnic is the Vale of Tempe, named after the valley in Greece that was the legendary haunt of sun god Apollo and the Muses.

Letting off steam

Villa Gregoriana, also in Tivoli, is a wild contrast to the Villa d'Este. It is set in a lush wooded valley, perfect for letting the little ones run free.

The largest fountain in Ville d'Este (the Fontana del Nettuno), Tivoli

The Lowdown

- 🌐 **Map reference** 7 C2
  Address Villa Adriana: 00010 Tivoli, Lazio; 0774 530 203. Villa d'Este: 00019 Tivoli, Lazio; 0774 332 920; www.villadestetivoli.info
- 🚗 **Train** from Stazione Tiburtina (Metro Linea B) to Tivoli; then bus 4 to Villa Adriana. **Bus** COTRAL from Metro Ponte Mammolo (Linea B) to Tivoli
- 🕐 **Open** Villa Adriana: 9am–90 mins before sunset daily. Villa d'Este: 8:30am–1 hr before sunset daily
- 💶 **Price** Villa Adriana: €16–24, EU under-18s free. Villa d'Este: €14–22, EU under-18s free
- 👫 **Age range** All
- ⏱ **Allow** A day for both villas
- ♿ **Wheelchair access** Yes
- 🍽 **Eat and drink** *Picnic* Buy supplies in Via del Trevio, Tivoli. Picnic in the Villa d'Este gardens. *Real meal* Ristorante Sibilla *(Via della Sibilla 50, 00019 Tivoli, Lazio; 0774 335 281; www.ristorante sibilia.com)* has a nice terrace.

② Ostia Antica
A 20-seat toilet

The remains of the ancient port city of Ostia are a relaxing spot to stroll amid ancient history, their creeper-covered walls rising from long grass scattered with wild flowers in spring. Ostia was built on the coast in Republican times, but Tiber silt shifted the coast west, and it was abandoned in the 4th century AD. The site is now a good way inland from the sea.

Pick up a plan and head to the Baths of the Cisiarii, who were ancient Ostia's taxi drivers: mosaics show them driving citizens about town in wagons. The Piazzale delle Corporazioni was surrounded by port businesses – each one has a mosaic outside depicting its trade. Past a restored theatre, still used for

The Lowdown

- 🌐 **Map reference** 7 B3
  Address Viale dei Romagnoli 717, 00119 Ostia; 06 5635 8099; www. archeoroma.beniculturali.it
- 🚗 **Metro** Piramide (Linea B), then **train** from Porta San Paolo station
- 🕐 **Open** 8:30am–7:30pm Tue–Sun
- 💶 **Price** €13–19.50, under-18s free
- 👫 **Age range** Any
- ⏱ **Allow** Half a day
- ♿ **Wheelchair access** Partial
- 🍽 **Eat and drink** *Picnic* Bring supplies from Testaccio's excellent market *(see p300)*, conveniently close to the Porta San Paolo train station, and eat amid Ostia's ancient ruins.

The restored ancient Roman theatre at Ostia Antica

open-air concerts in summer, is the Thermopolium, a bar which served wine and snacks, with a marble counter and alfresco dining courtyard. Do not miss the *forica*, a 20-seat public toilet.

Take cover

Pop into the **museum**, where some wonderful reliefs evoke everyday life in the town, such as women selling fruit and vegetables. There is even one of a midwife helping a mother to give birth.

③ Lake Bracciano
Down by the lakeside

About 40 km (25 miles) northwest of Rome is Lake Bracciano, a large expanse of water filling a volcanic crater. Head for one of its resorts – **Bracciano**, **Trevignano** or **Anguillara** – or go to one of the lakeside restaurants to eat and

swim in peace: La Valletta, in Trevignano, has space to sunbathe and pedalos to hire.

The main town, Bracciano, on the east shore, is dominated by the 15th-century Castello Odescalchi, and there is swimming and boat hire at Lungolago Argenti – a 10-minute walk along Via del Lago.

Take cover

Duck into the beautiful **Castello Odescalchi** fortress for lake views, ancient sculptures, ceramics, medieval furniture, armour, frescoes and paintings.

The Lowdown

- 🌐 **Map reference** 7 B2
  Address Lake Bracciano, 00062 Lazio. Castello Odescalchi: Piazza Mazzini 14, 00062 Bracciano, Lazio; 06 9980 2379; *www.odescalchi.it*

- 🚗 **Train** from Stazione Ostiense to Bracciano, then local bus or taxi. **Boat** from Bracciano to Anguillara and Trevignano

- 🕐 **Open** Castello Odescalchi: summer 10am–noon, 3–6pm Tue–Sat, 9am–12:30pm, 3–6:30pm Sun; winter 10am–noon, 2–4pm Tue–Fri, 10am–noon, 2–5pm Sat, 10am–1pm, 2:30–5pm Sun

- 💶 **Price** Castello Odescalchi: €14–28, under-6s free

- 👫 **Age range** All

- ⏲ **Allow** Half a day

- ♿ **Wheelchair access** No

- ☕ **Eat and drink** *Picnic* Picnic on Lungolago Argenti. *Real meal* La Valletta (*Via Mincio 5, 00069 Trevignano Romano; 345 422 6866*) is good for lakeside dining, with fish or meat dishes.

View over tranquil Lake Bracciano from a tower of the Castello Odescalchi

Typical outdoor staircase in Viterbo, lined with elegant pot plants

④ Viterbo
Hot springs and dead saints

A walled medieval town (with an ugly modern periphery), Viterbo became the home of the popes during the 13th century, when battles in Rome between the Guelphs and Ghibellines made the capital city too dangerous. These days, its medieval core, ghoulish sights and free hot springs make Viterbo an appealing place for kids.

Wandering around the San Pellegrino quarter, a maze of narrow stone streets with arches and little piazzas with fountains, gives a great idea of life in a medieval town. Indications of how hazardous it must

have been are apparent in the Piazza della Morte, or Square of the Dead, named after the abandoned corpses of the poor that local monks would collect and bury here. The nearby Duomo has a splendid black and white striped belltower, while the **Museo della Macchina di Santa Rosa** is devoted to the annual festivities that celebrate the town's patron saint. Every 3 September, St Rose's corpse, dressed in a nun's habit, is paraded through town atop an illuminated wooden steeple 28 m (99 ft) high. At other times she can be seen at the **Museo della Casa di Santa Rosa**, next to the church.

Letting off steam
Just outside the city are the **Piscine Carletti**, natural thermal pools (free). A more luxurious option is the **Terme dei Papi** (*www.termedeipapi.it*).

⑤ Cerveteri
City of the dead

In the 9th century BC, Cerveteri was one of the most important towns of the Villanovan culture that preceded Etruscan civilization, and it stayed that way until the sun set on the Etruscans in the 3rd century BC. Today, only its cemetery survives, the vast Banditaccia necropolis where over 50,000 Etruscans were buried: a city of the dead, its streets of tombs were fitted out like homes with beds, furniture and painted walls. One of the most evocative visits is the Tomba dei Rilievi, with stone reliefs of cooking implements and pets.

Burial mounds at the Banditaccia necropolis, Cerveteri

Letting off steam
There is plenty of space for children to run around and play hide and seek at the necropolis.

The Lowdown

- 🌐 **Map reference** 7 B2
  Address 00052 Cerveteri, Lazio; Necropolis: 06 994 0001
- 🚃 **Train** from Rome Termini to Cerveteri-Ladispoli, then bus
- 🕐 **Open** 8:30am–1 hour before sunset Tue–Sun
- 💶 **Price** €12, under-18s free
- 👫 **Age** 5 plus
- ⏱ **Allow** 2 hours
- 🍵 **Eat and drink** *Snacks* Il Cavallino Bianco (*Piazza Risorgimento, 00052; 06 994 1507; closed Tue*) serves hearty local dishes. *Real meal* Le Ginestre (*Piazza Santa Maria, 00052; 06 995 1417; closed Mon*) has a traditional menu served in the elegant dining room or the courtyard.

Copy of a 5th century BC fresco of musicians, Tarquinia

⑥ Tarquinia
Dancing in the afterlife

Medieval Tarquinia's main attraction is the **Etruscan Museum**. Beautifully displayed in a Gothic-Renaissance palazzo, it has some wonderful tombs, decorated with lifelike sculptures of the deceased, while displays of gold jewellery, elaborate candlesticks and painted ceramics add details to the picture of how wealthy Etruscans lived. Tarquinia's **necropolis**, 2 km (1 mile) out of town, is worth a visit for its frescoed tombs. Designed to remind the dead of the pleasures of life, they include scenes of dancing and dining.

The Lowdown

- 🌐 **Map reference** 7 B1
  Address 01100 Viterbo, Lazio. Museo della Macchina di Santa Rosa: Via San Pellegrino 60, 01100; 0761 345 157; *www.facchinidisantarosa.it*. Museo della Casa di Santa Rosa (*Via Santa Rosa 33, 01100; 0761 342 887; www.monasterosantarosa.it*
- 🚃 **Train** from Rome Termini, Ostiense or Flaminio
- ℹ️ **Visitor information** Via Ascenzi 4, 01100 Viterbo; 0761 325 992
- 🕐 **Open** Museo della Macchina di Santa Rosa: Apr–Sep 10am–1pm and 3:30–7pm Wed–Sun, Oct–Mar 3–5:30pm Fri–Sun; Museo della Casa di Santa Rosa: 9:30am– noon and 4–6pm daily
- 💶 **Price** Free
- 👫 **Age** 5 plus
- ⏱ **Allow** A day, including hot springs
- 🍵 **Eat and drink** *Snacks* Schenardi (*Corso Italia 11, 01100*) is the place for ice cream. *Real meal* Enopizzeria da Lucio (*Via San Pellegrino 21, 01100; 0761 340 626; closed Tue*) is great for wood-fired pizza
- 🎉 **Festivals** Santa Rosa: 3 Sep.

Letting off steam

Lido di Tarquinia, 6 km (4 miles) away on the coast, is a popular seaside resort. Alternatively, follow signs 1 km (half a mile) south from the Lido to the **Saline** (salt marsh) nature reserve (www.parks.it).

The Lowdown

🌐 **Map reference** 7 A2
   Address Tarquinia 01016, Viterbo, Lazio. Etruscan Museum: Palazzo Vitelleschi, Piazza Cavour, 01016; 0766 856 036.

🚆 **Train** from Rome Termini

ℹ **Visitor information** Barriera San Giusto, 01016; 0766 849 282; www.tarquiniaturismo.it

🕐 **Open** Museum: 8:30am–7:30pm Tue–Sun. Necropolis: May–Sep 8:30am–one hour before sunset, Tue–Sun; Oct–Apr closes 2pm

€ **Price** Museum and necropolis combined ticket: €20

👫 **Age range** 5 plus

⏱ **Allow** A day, including the beach

🍴 **Eat and drink** *Real meal* La Cantina dell'Etrusco (*Via Menotti Garibaldi 13, 01016; 0766 225 755; www.vinoetrusco.it; closed Tue eve*) serves rustic dishes. Ambaradam (*Piazza Giacomo Matteotti 14, 01016; 0766 857 073*) offers twists on traditional fare.

⑦ Parco dei Mostri, Bomarzo
The world's first theme park?

The Monster Park, outside the forlorn little town of Bomarzo, is one of Lazio's top attractions, with cafés, a restaurant, a playground and even a football pitch for kids. Created in the 16th century by a hunchbacked Duke of Orsini, it was the world's first theme park. At the time the style of art known as Mannerism was at its height – full of distortions designed to break the rules of the Renaissance – and the sculptures here, far from capturing beauty, celebrate the grotesque. Most famous of all is a 6-m (20-ft) high screaming face, but there is also a life-size elephant crushing a Roman soldier, a giant tearing a man in two, and dragons, nymphs, mermaids and sphinxes.

Letting off steam

If the kids have any steam left after the Parco dei Monstri, head for the **Lago di Vico Natural Reserve** (*by car, drive back towards Viterbo and follow signs; www.riservavico.it*) for a wilderness walk and a picnic.

The Lowdown

🌐 **Map reference** 7 B1
   Address Parco dei Mostri, Loc Giardino, 01020 Bomarzo, Lazio; 0761 924 029; www.parcodeimostri.com

🚆 **Train** from Rome Termini or Ostiense to Viterbo, then bus

🕐 **Open** 8am–sunset daily

€ **Price** €34, under-3s free

👫 **Age range** All

⏱ **Allow** Half a day

🍴 **Eat and drink** *Snacks* Buy panini at the park cafés. *Real meal* Stop in Viterbo for a pizza.

Screaming Mannerist monster at the Parco dei Mostri, Bomarzo

Picnic under €25; **Snacks** €25–40; **Real meal** €40–80; **Family treat** €80 or more (based on a family of four)

Where to Stay in Rome

Capital city and popular tourist destination since the days of the Grand Tour, Rome has plenty of places to stay. There are classy old-fashioned hotels and simple *pensioni*, secluded B&Bs and stylish apartments. Most have large family rooms or extra beds, and many are surprisingly cheap.

AGENCY
Rental in Rome
www.rentalinrome.com
An apartment can be the best solution for families in Rome. This agency has a great selection of places, ranging from €80 to €250 a night, or splash out on an apartment with an indoor pool in Trastevere for €390 a night.

Campo de' Fiori

HOTELS
Hotel Campo de' Fiori   Map 23 D4
Via del Biscione 6, 00186; 06 6880 6865; www.hotelcampodefiori.com
This welcoming hotel has a roof terrace, where guests can picnic in the evenings. The rooms are small but comfortable and there are also four large apartments with kitchens on nearby Via de' Cappellari.
🛏 🗟 🍽   €

Pensione Barrett   Map 24 E5
Largo Argentina 47, 00186; 06 686 8481; www.pensionebarrett.com
Fascinating little hotel, with Roman walls from the Curia of Pompey, where Caesar was assassinated. The friendly owners provide coffee machines, cereal, milk and jams in the rooms, and fresh croissants daily.
❄   €

Sole al Biscione   Map 23 D4
Via del Biscione 76, 00186; 06 6880 6873; www.solealbiscione.it
A relaxed hotel just off Campo de' Fiori, with 60 rooms, half of which are triples and quads. Large family groups can take the whole attic floor, which has a double, two triples and a quad with a private roof terrace.
🛏 🗟   €

Ponte Sisto   Map 23 C6
Via dei Pettinari 64, 00186; 06 686 3100; www.hotelpontesisto.it
An elegant modern hotel in an ex-monastic complex just off Via Giulia, close to Campo de' Fiori and just across the Ponte Sisto bridge from Trastevere. An ideal base for enjoying Rome's atmospheric streetlife, with a quiet, shady inner courtyard to retreat to. Eleven family suites with two connecting rooms.
🛏 🗟   €€€

Colosseum

HOTELS
Hotel Grifo   Map 17 B6
Via del Boschetto 144, 00184; 06 487 1395; www.hotelgrifo.com
The owners here are sensitive to the needs of families and have original suggestions for activities for children. Rooms are simple, and include triples and quads, some with their own or shared terraces.
🛏 🗟   €

Palazzetto degli Artisti   Map 21 B1
Via Madonna dei Monti 108, 00184; 06 6992 4931; www.palazzettodegliartisti.com
Twenty contemporary rooms ranged over the five storeys of a palazzo in Monti. Friendly, and popular with families as there is no extra charge for children's beds in parents' rooms. Eight connecting rooms and a large roof terrace too.
🛏   €

Hotel Artorius   Map 17 B6
Via del Boschetto 13, 00184; 06 482 1196; 06 482 1196; www.hotelartorius.com
This mid-19th-century Monti palazzo has a sunny courtyard full of plants, with two resident parrots, where breakfast is served. Smart rooms, some with terraces.
🛏 🗟 ☕ 🍽   €€

Hotel Celio   Map 21 C2
Via dei Santi Quattro 35c, 00184; 06 7049 5333; www.hotelcelio.com
An excellent family choice in a quiet neighbourhood near the Colosseum, run by a couple with small children. There are toys in the cosy lounge, and rooms feature motifs from Roman mosaics. There is a miniature DVD cinema and a roof terrace with a paddling pool.
🗟   €€

Duca d'Alba   Map 21 B1
Via Leonina 14, 00184; 06 484 471; www.hotelducadalba.com
This pleasant hotel in the heart of Monti dates back to the 1940s. Six of the 27 rooms can have extra beds added. Tea is served every afternoon at 5pm, included in the price. Good deals in low season.
🛏 ☕   €€

A light and airy room in the Lancelot hotel, near the Colosseum

Lancelot   Map 21 C2
Via Capo d'Africa 47, 00184; 06 7045 0615; www.lancelothotel.com
A lovely, family-owned hotel with charming staff on a quiet street close to the Colosseum, which actively welcomes families. Four spacious family rooms, three with balconies, one with a terrace. Breakfast is served in a patio garden. Good half-board deal.
🛏 🗟 🍽   €€

Hotel Forum   Map 21 B1
Via Tor de' Conti 25, 00184; 06 679 2446; www.hotelforumrome.com
Staying in this charming hotel is almost like living in ancient Rome: the views over the Forum and Trajan's Market are spectacular. Children can have fun identifying monuments over breakfast, lunch or dinner in the rooftop restaurant.

Key to symbols *see back flap*

It is a former convent, and rooms are spacious. Twelve triples and eight connecting rooms.

€€–€€€

Radisson Blu
Map 18 E6

Via Filippo Turati 171, 00185; 06 444 841; www.radissonblu.com

The main attraction for families at this five-star hotel is the 20-m (66-ft) roof-top swimming pool and children's pool, but the rooms with raft beds inspired by Robinson Crusoe are lovely too. Takeaway breakfasts are available. Good public transport to centre.

€€€

B&B

B&B Il Covo
Map 17 B6

Via del Boschetto 91, 00184; 06 481 5871; www.bbilcovo.com

Il Covo has 20 rooms, including four triples and three quads, in several houses in Monti. All are in historic buildings with original features such as brick vaults and painted beams. Choose between room-only and B&B (breakfast in a local café-bar).

€

Piazza Navona

HOTELS

Hotel Parlamento
Map 24 F1

Via del Convertite 5, 00186; 06 6992 1000, www.hotelparlamento.it

This traditional hotel on the fourth floor of a palazzo close to Palazzo Montecitorio, seat of the Italian parliament, has a terrace and pleasant, pretty rooms. They include triples and quads, a room that can sleep up to five, and adjacent rooms that open onto a shared terrace.

€

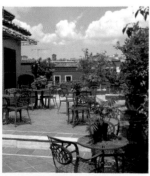

The terrace of the Hotel Parlamento, where breakfast is served

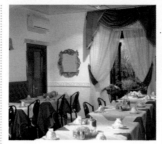

The dining room at Hotel Navona, a few paces from Piazza Navona

Hotel Due Torri
Map 23 D2

Vicolo del Leonetto 23, 00186; 06 6880 6956, www.hotelduetorriroma.com

An old-fashioned, higgledy-piggledy hotel close to Piazza Navona, whose rooms include four mini-apartments (with two rooms and a bathroom, but no kitchen). There is a relaxed common area with a shelf of books and a chess board, and a small breakfast room.

€€

Hotel Navona
Map 23 D3

Via dei Sediari 6, 00186; 06 686 4203; www.hotelnavona.com

A friendly, relaxed hotel across the road from Piazza Navona, run by a welcoming Italo-Australian family, with plenty of triples and quads. It is popular with school groups in term-time so can be a bit noisy.

€€

Hotel Portoghesi
Map 23 D2

Via del Portoghesi 1, 00186; 06 686 4231; www.hotelportoghesiroma.com

Another good *centro storico* option, this hotel's best feature is a roof terrace where breakfast is served. It is possible to get a key to the terrace in the evenings too, for a picnic meal. One triple room and two connecting rooms.

€€

Hotel Santa Chiara
Map 24 E4

Via Santa Chiara 21, 00186; 06 687 2979; www.albergosantachiara.com

Plenty of triples, along with three quads and an apartment for five with its own terrace (but no kitchen), make this a great family choice close to the Pantheon. Attentive staff help give the hotel an intimate feel, belying its real size: it has 100 rooms.

€€

Hotel Teatro Pace
Map 23 C3

Via del Teatro Pace 33, 00186; 06 687 9075; www.hotelteatropace.com

The most striking feature of this hotel is a tremendous spiral stone staircase coiling up through four storeys (there is no lift). There are three triple rooms (one with its own terrace) and all rooms have kettles so guests can make hot drinks.

€€

Vatican and Trastevere

HOTELS

Adriatic
Map 16 E4

Via Vitelleschi 25, 00193; 06 6880 8080; www.adriatichotel.com

A friendly and reasonably priced hotel that welcomes families, just three blocks from St Peter's, making it easy to see Piazza San Pietro after it empties and to be at the front of the queue for the Vatican Museums. There are four family rooms and several triples. There is also a roof garden where breakfast is served.

€

Hotel Santa Maria
Map 20 F2

Vicolo del Piede 2a, 00153; 06 589 4626; www.htlsantamaria.com

Tucked behind Piazza Santa Maria in Trastevere, with a pebbled court-yard surrounded by a frescoed portico, this hotel has a comfortable breakfast room and lounge with board games, and bikes for guests. All rooms but two have bath tubs, and several have bunk beds.

€€

Residenza Santa Maria
Map 20 G2

Via dell'Arco di San Calisto 20, 00153; 06 5833 5103; www.residenzasantamaria.com

There are six rooms in this hotel in a quiet Trastevere street. It has a breakfast room in an ancient water cistern and a covered courtyard with seats and sofa. All rooms are on the ground floor, and there are two quads with bunk beds.

€€

Price Guide

For a family of four per night in high season, in one or more rooms, inclusive of breakfast, service charges and any additional taxes such as VAT.

€ Under €200 **€€** €200–350 **€€€** over €350

San Francesco
Map 20 G3

*Via Jacopa de' Settesoli 7, 00153;
06 5830 0051; www.hotelsan
francesco.net*

Modern rooms, a stylish decked
roof terrace and a quiet location off
Viale Trastevere make this an
appealing left-bank choice.
Trastevere, with its vast choice of
eating and drinking places, is a
short walk away, and can also be
reached by electric minibus from
outside the hotel. Buses cross the
Tiber to Testaccio, too, a good
location for food shopping. Rooms
are small, but there are some triples
and extra beds can be added.
Varying prices mean it is possible to
pick up a double room for less than
€70 if demand is low.

€€

*The shady courtyard at Buonanotte
Garibaldi B&B*

B&Bs

**Foresteria Orsa Maggiore
(Casa Internazionale
delle Donne)**
Map 20 E1

*Via San Francesco di Sales 1a,
00165; 06 689 3753; www.
casainternazionaledelledonne.org*

This is a great place for mothers
travelling alone with children under
12 to stay. Set in the women's centre
in Trastevere, the 13 rooms are
simple, with terracotta-tiled floors
and beamed ceilings, and include
singles, doubles and rooms that
sleep four to eight people.
Breakfast, self-service lunches and
healthy, convivial (women-only)
dinners are served in a courtyard
shaded by an old magnolia tree.

€

Buonanotte Garibaldi
Map 20 E2

*Via Garibaldi 83, 00165; 06 583
0733; www.buonanottegaribaldi.com*

A jewel of a B&B, this was once the
studio of the owner, artist Luisa
Longo. It includes a room with a
terrace and another two that open
onto an enchanting, tree-shaded
courtyard hidden behind a high
stone wall. There is a stunning
beaded chandelier in the dashing
breakfast room and a comfortable
lounge furnished with the owner's
hand-made silks. Entertainment for
kids is provided by Tinto, the B&B's
tranquil dog. Double rooms only,
but extra beds can be added.

€€

Villa Borghese and
Tridente

HOTELS

Erdarelli
Map 17 A4

*Via Due Macelli 28, 00187; 06 679
1265; www.erdarelliromehotel.com*

A good, reasonably-priced, family-
run hotel halfway between the Trevi
Fountain and the Spanish Steps,
Erdarelli is ideally located for
sightseeing and leisurely evening
strolls in this part of town. Rooms
are basic but extremely clean and
some have balconies, but
air-conditioning is extra. There
are three family rooms.

€

Panda
Map 16 H4

*Via della Croce 35, 00187; 06 678
0179; www.hotelpanda.it*

A simple, friendly hotel in the heart
of the expensive Piazza di Spagna
area, the Panda is ideally located for
exploring the historic centre on
foot. Rooms are clean, and come
with or without bathroom. There
are six triples and five quads. There
is no breakfast, but the hotel has a
deal with the bar downstairs.

€

Hotel Fontanella
Borghese
Map 16 G4

*Largo Fontanella Borghese 84,
00186; 06 6880 9504; www.
fontanellaborghese.com*

There are two triples and two quads
in this gracious hotel in the historic
centre, within spitting distance of
the Ara Pacis and a short walk from
the Spanish Steps, Piazza del
Popolo and Piazza Navona.

Babysitting can be organized for
parents keen to enjoy a child-free
evening out.

€€

Hotel Julia
Map 17 B5

*Via Rasella 29, 00187; 06 488 1637;
www.hoteljulia.it*

This friendly hotel, in a 19th-century
palazzo on a quiet street near the
Trevi Fountain, has three rooms that
can sleep a family, as well as two
spacious, elegant apartments (with
kitchens), making it an excellent
family choice.

€€

Hotel Madrid
Map 17 A4

*Via Mario de Fiori 93–95, 00187;
06 699 1510, www.hotelmadrid
roma.com*

This hotel in the smart Piazza di
Spagna area, a short walk from the
Spanish Steps, has six tastefully
decorated suites that are ideal for
families of four or five. There is also
a fantastic roof terrace, where a
buffet breakfast is served, with
stunning views of the city.

€€

Hotel dei Borgognoni
Map 17 A5

*Via del Bufalo 126, 00186; 06 6994
1505; www.hotelborgognoni.it*

A smart and efficiently-run hotel
near Piazza di Spagna, Hotel dei
Borgononi has intelligently
designed rooms and bathrooms,
many of which have bath tubs. The
rooms are not huge, but four have
their own spacious terraces shaded
with orange trees. There is also a
communal terrace for guests where
drinks and snacks are served.

€€€

Locarno
Map 16 G3

*Via della Penna 22, 00186; 06 361
0841; www.hotellocarno.com*

An Art Nouveau jewel, Locarno is
on a quiet street a short walk from
Piazza del Popolo – well located for
excursions to the Pincio Gardens or
Villa Borghese park. In winter, a log
fire burns in the charming sitting
room, and in summer there is a roof
garden and a flower-filled patio.
More than a third of the rooms can
sleep three or four, making it an
excellent, if pricey, family choice,
and there is also a three-bedroom
apartment with a kitchen, ideal for
larger families.

€€€

Lazio

Inevitably Lazio's attractions pale in comparison with those of Rome. For more than a day trip, the south of the region has most to offer. Here, on the wild promontory of Monte Circeo, is a national park with ancient forest, wetlands, beaches and sea caves. Offshore is the tiny island of Ponza, and inland lie Sermoneta's medieval castle and the gardens of Ninfa.

Below *Fishing and pleasure boats at the wharf, Ponza*

Monte Circeo
p310

① Monte Circeo National Park
An ancient enchantress and Fascist futurism

The Monte Circeo National Park is the perfect antidote to the culture and chaos of Rome. According to legend, the jagged limestone promontory of Monte Circeo was originally an island, home to the enchantress Circe, who lived in a palace surrounded by woods where mountain wolves and lions roamed. Today, it is a diverse landscape with sandy dunes, forests, wetlands, sea caves and an offshore island to explore, along with futuristic towns built in the 1930s by Mussolini.

Pretty pot plant in San Felice Circeo

Key Sights

① The salt lakes
Four coastal salt lakes are linked to the sea by canals. Rare marsh turtles live here, and migrating birds pass by.

② Isola di Zannone
Take a boat trip to this island (2 km/1.2 miles away) and discover the fruit of the *corbezzolo* tree (see Kids' Corner).

③ Circeo promontory
Paths lead past Roman walls and boats visit the Grotta Guattari, where the skull of a Neanderthal man was found. Spot white-tailed eagles and ospreys here.

④ Sabaudia
Fascist propaganda claimed that this surreal seaside town was built in 253 days.

⑥ The dunes
There are more than 20 km (12 miles) of sandy dunes to choose from – making it easy to escape the crowds, even in summer.

⑤ San Felice Circeo
Stone houses cling to the mountainside of this pretty seaside village with a yacht marina. Take a boat trip to the Grotta della Maga Circe, reputed to be the cave home of the enchantress.

The Lowdown

🌐 **Map reference** 7 C4
Address Parco Nazionale del Circeo, 04017 San Felice Circeo

🚗 **Train** from Rome Termini to Priverno-Fossanova on the Roma–Napoli via Formia line, then bus (www.cotralspa.it) to Sabaudia. **Bus** from Sabaudia bus station to San Felice Circeo, past the visitor centre. **Car** 100 km (60 miles) south of Rome

ℹ️ **Visitor information** Via Carlo Alberto 107, 04016 Sabaudia; 0773 511 385; open 9am–1pm and 2:30–5pm daily. Porta del Parco, Piazza del Comune, 04016 Sabaudia; Porta del Parco, Piazza Lanzuisi, 04016 San Felice Circeo; 0773 547 770; www.parcocirceo.it

💶 **Price** Free; guided tour: €24, under-6s free

🏃 **Activities** The Istituto Pangea (www.istpangea.it) and the national park authorities offer a range of activities all year, some free: night visits to the park, boat trips to the Isola di Zannone, snorkelling and nature photography; special activities for children are listed on the website. All the guides are English-speaking.

👫 **Age range** All ages

⏱️ **Allow** With a car it could be a day trip from Rome; on public transport, at least a weekend, based in San Felice Circeo.

♿ **Wheelchair access** Partial; ask at the visitor centre.

Good family value?
This is an excellent destination for families in good weather; it is worth paying for a guided tour to get the most out of this natural wonderland.

Letting off steam

Download walk maps from *www. parcocirceo.it* or pick up information from the visitor centre on walks on the forested promontory (some are quite steep and precipitous for young children); or head down to the sandy beach at Sabaudia.

Sabaudia Beach, with Monte Circeo jutting out into the sea

Eat and drink

Picnic: under €25; Snacks: €25–40; Real meal: €40–80; Family treat: €80 or more (based on a family of four)

PICNIC Cheeses made from buffalo milk are the speciality around here. As well as mozzarella, try *caciotta di bufala pontina*, a semi-hard, mild cheese, sold from stalls along the road, along with olives from Gaeta. The **Conad** supermarket (*Via Monte Circeo 112, 04017; 4 km (2.5 miles) outside San Felice Circeo*) sells a good range of local cheeses along with fresh fruit and salad.
SNACKS Chez Louis (*Viale Tittoni 18, 04017 San Felice Circeo; 0773 540 893*) sells takeaway pizza. Follow it with a cooling ice cream on the seafront at **Picascia** (*Lungomare Europa 1, 04017 San Felice Circeo; 0773 540 102*).
REAL MEAL Profumi Toscani (*Piazza Vittorio Veneto 37, 04017 San Felice Circeo; 333 1702601, www.profumitoscani.it*) is run by a young couple, serving excellent

Tuscan food such as *ribollita* (a type of hearty soup), along with fabulous Chianina steaks. Children are welcome; they provide baby seats.
FAMILY TREAT Saporetti (*Via Lungomare di Sabaudia, km 32, 04016 Sabaudia; 0773 506 024*), the most famous of Sabaudia's beach establishments, has a bar for light meals as well as a restaurant, called Torre Paola, for more substantial dishes. Be here to watch the sun set.

Find out more

DIGITAL The national park website, *www.parks.it/parco.nazionale.it*, has an English version. To understand how this landscape of mountain and marsh was formed there is an informative flash animation at *earthquake.usgs.gov/ learn/glossary/?term=graben*

Take cover

The **Museo del Mare e della Costa** (*Piazza Verbania, 04016 Sabaudia; 0773 511 340*) tells the story of the coast, with finds that include a spine-chillingly huge tooth of a white shark, plus an aquarium. At the **Museo Malaria e la Sua Storia** (*Centro Culturale Polivalente, Viale Cavour 24, 04014 Pontinia; 0773 841 504*), 20 km (13 miles) away, find out about the history of malaria in the Pontine Marshes, which from Roman times until the 1930s were a mosquito-ridden no-man's land.

Next stop...

PONZA This jewel-like island (*see p313*), with its little fishing harbour and beaches, is part of the park, just a boat trip away. The most popular beach is Chiaia di Luna.

The little fishing harbour on the island of Ponza, off the coast of Monte Circeo

② Sermoneta and Ninfa

A medieval fairy tale

Crowned by a fairy-tale castle, **Sermoneta** is a medieval hill town of cobbled streets looking out over the Pontine plain. The view is clear for miles around, but the hilltop site and fortified **Castello Caetani**, with its portcullises, moats and drawbridges, were not enough to make the medieval inhabitants feel safe: in the Duomo is a painting of the Madonna holding the town in her hands for protection.

The town of **Ninfa**, 7 kilometres (4 miles) away, was sacked in 1382 and then abandoned as its inhabitants fled the malarial swamps for Sermoneta. Its ruined buildings, including a small castle, now stand among the waterfalls and lakes of an 18th-century botanical garden, created by the Caetani family.

The Lowdown

- 🌐 **Map reference** 7 C3
  Address Castello Caetani: Via della Fortezza 1, 04013 Sermoneta. Giardino di Ninfa: Via Provinciale Ninfina 68, 04013 Cisterna di Latina; *www. fondazionecaetani.org*
- 🚗 **Train** from Rome to Latina, then bus to Sermoneta (not Sun) or taxi (*0773 632 292*) to Ninfa. **Car** 85 km (53 miles) from Rome
- ℹ️ **Visitor information** Loggia dei Mercanti, 04013 Sermoneta; 0773 30312. Latina: 0773 695 404; *www.latinaturismo.it*
- 🕐 **Open** Castello Caetani: tours Apr–Sep Fri–Wed, Oct–Mar Sat and Sun. Ninfa: tours Apr–Oct first Sat and Sun of month; check website for extra days in summer.
- 💶 **Price** Castello Caetani: €10–20; Ninfa: €20–40, under-11s free for both sights
- 👫 **Age range** 5 plus
- ⏱️ **Allow** A full day
- 🍽️ **Eat and drink** *Real meal* Il Simposio al Corso (*Corso Garibaldi 33, 04013 Sermoneta; 339 284 6905; closed Mon*) reinvents medieval dishes, with garden tables in summer. The same owner's enoteca (*Via della Conduttura 2, 04013*) will also make up a picnic.
- 🎉 **Festivals** Strawberry Festival, Nemi: Jun. Infiorata, Genzano, Sun and Mon after Corpus Christi: Jun.

Ninfa castle, set among the beautiful gardens created by the Caetani family

Letting off steam

Climbing Sermoneta's castle and exploring Ninfa's garden offer some scope to let off steam, but both visits follow guided tours. Head instead for the **Lago di Nemi** (40 km/25 miles from Ninfa by car), a deep, blue volcanic lake surrounded by wooded hills. June is especially fun – there is a strawberry festival in Nemi, on one side of the lake, while Genzano, on the other side, carpets its streets with flowers in a festive Infiorata.

③ Sperlonga

Ancient Roman beach resort

Sperlonga is a pretty seaside town of narrow, whitewashed medieval streets and arched alleyways on a steep promontory, its coastline of cliffs punctuated by tiny beaches.

The old centre is traffic-free, which means adults can browse in its boutiques and sit at pavement bars while children amuse themselves.

Letting off steam

There is a short walk along the town's 2-km (1-mile) beach – turn off at the path marked "Lido Le Chiuse"– to the remains of Roman Emperor Tiberius's holiday villa, which has a grotto with a fishpond and a small museum with sculptures of the *Odyssey*. Natural caves in the nearby cliffs were converted by ancient Romans into places to dine and relax. Stop off for a run on the beach and cooling swim in the sea on the way.

The Lowdown

- 🌐 **Map reference** 7 D4
  Address Sperlonga 04029, Lazio
- 🚗 **Train** from Rome to Fondi, then connecting bus. **Car** 130 km (80 miles) from Rome
- ℹ️ **Visitor information** Via del Porto, Sperlonga 04029; 0771 557 341; open 9am–12pm, closed Sun
- 👫 **Age range** All
- ⏱️ **Allow** A day
- 🍽️ **Eat and drink** *Snacks* Tropical (*Via C Colombo 19, 04029; 0771 549 621*) has a beachside setting and is a great spot for lunchtime. pizza. *Real meal* L'Angolo (*Via Tiberio, 04029; 0771 548 808; www. langolosperlonga.it*) prides itself on its use of fresh produce, and serves pizza and delicious pasta. In summer eat in the garden or on the terrace.

Boats moored in the harbour at Sperlonga

The stunning Chiaia di Luna bay on the island of Ponza

④ The Pontine Islands

Volcanic crescents

The eruption of an ancient volcano created the five islands of the Pontine archipelago. Only two are inhabited: Ponza and Ventotene. Ponza, a hilly island shaped like a crescent moon, has a splendid fishing harbour and lots of bizarre rock formations, deposited by the volcano and sculpted into caves and arches by the sea. From the pastel-painted town it is a 10-minute walk to the beach of Chiaia di Luna, a crescent of sand backed by sheer cliffs, but beware, it catches the brunt of winds so the water can be very choppy. Near Ponza's other village, Le Forna, are a fabulous natural swimming pool and

A typical whitewashed Sperlonga street seen through an arched alleyway

Le Grotte di Pilato, three sea caves connected by ancient Roman tunnels, once used to store fresh fish for the inhabitants of the villa above (of which little now remains).

For centuries, **Ventotene** was a place of exile. A bleak, red rock, it has witnessed gruesome events: Emperor Caligula's mother starved herself to death and Emperor Nero had his wife Octavia murdered in her bath here – scant remains of her villa can be seen at Punta Eolo.

Letting off steam

Take a boat trip from Ponza's port to the uninhabited island of **Santo Stefano** and swim off the rocks.

The Lowdown

🌐 **Map reference** 7 C5
Address Ponza 04027 Lazio. Ventotene, 04020, Lazio

🚗 **Ferry** from Naples, Terracina, Anzio and Formia to Ponza; **hydrofoil** from Anzio, Formia and Ponza to Ventotene; www.ponza.it

ℹ️ **Visitor information** Via Molo Musco, Ponza 04027; 0771 80031; Via Roma 2, 04020 Ventotene; 0771 85257; www.ponza.it

⏱️ **Allow** At least 2 days

👫 **Age** Any with water confidence

☕ **Eat and drink** Picnic Get supplies at SIDIS (Via Chiesa Le Forna, 04027 Ponza) near the port. Real meal Ippocampo (Corso Carlo Pisacane 7, 04027 Ponza; 0771 809 852) serves good, fresh fish.

🎆 **Festivals** San Silverio, boat procession and fireworks: 9–23 Jun.

KIDS' CORNER

Ponza's strange rocks
Ponza's weird rock formations have reminded people of many different things. See if you can spot these – best seen on a boat trip round the island:
1 The Monk
2 The Mushrooms
3 The Castle
4 The Horseman
5 The arch that looks like a pair of baggy trousers.

STRAWBERRY STORIES
According to legend, when the goddess Venus's lover Adonis died, her tears turned into woodland strawberries.

Berry tasty!
Strawberries taste great straight out of the punnet, of course, but for something a little different try them with a few drops of balsamic vinegar or a sprinkling of black pepper – really! Alternatively, whip up some fresh ricotta with a fork, adding sugar to taste and some finely grated lemon or mandarin peel if you fancy; put a dollop of ricotta cream in a glass and top with strawberries… or dip the berries into the ricotta cream.

Emperor Tiberius
Tiberius was well known for his ability to eat and drink vast quantities of food and wine, and as a young soldier he was such a hard drinker that he was nicknamed Biberius (the drinker). On one occasion Biberius was dining in his villa's grotto when some huge rocks crashed down from the roof, crushing several guests, but he survived – perhaps the rocks bounced off his belly.

Picnic under €25; Snacks €25–40; **Real meal** €40–80; **Family treat** €80 or more (based on a family of four)

Where to Stay in Lazio

Overshadowed by Rome, Lazio has limited interesting accommodation.
The best places to stay are on the coast, around Monte Circeo National Park
at San Felice Circeo and Sabaudia, on the island of Ponza and north of the
capital at Tarquinia Lido. Some of the old towns have serviceable hotels, too.

AGENCIES
Immobiliare Magi
www.immobiliaremagi.com
This Italian and English website
offers flats, B&Bs and villas in
Ponza. Also mopeds and vespas
to rent.

Agenzia Maridea
www.marideaponza.it
Great villas and apartments all
over the island of Ponza.

Ponza
MAP 7 C5

HOTELS
Grand Hotel Chiaia di Luna
*Via Panoramica, 04027; 0771 801
134; www.hotelchiaiadiluna.com*
This four-star hotel offers fabulous
views over Ponza's harbour, the bay
of Chiaia di Luna and the island of
Palmarola. There is a poolside bar
and restaurant, a swimming pool
and a TV room. Trips around the
island, car hire and babysitting
services can be arranged at
reception. Guests can choose
from a range of rooms: the suites
include a large living room and a
terrace with panoramic views and
sunbeds. Families with two children
under 6 can opt to share a room.
€€€

Grand Hotel Santa Domitilla
*Via Panoramica, 04027; 0771 809
951; www.santadomitilla.com*
Luxurious choice for a family
wanting a big treat. Contemporary
and stylish (decorated with some
marvellous driftwood furniture), the
hotel is set in lush gardens 100 m
(330 ft) from Chiaia di Luna beach.
The most exciting feature is the
swimming pool, which extends
under the hotel into a series
of ancient Roman tunnels.
Accommodation is available for
families in several standard rooms
as well as in the five suites and four
junior suites. In low season there are
some fantastic deals. Open from
1 April to 1 October.
€€€

B&B
Casa Simonetta
*Via Calacaparra, 04027; 0771 808
512; www.casasimonetta.com*
Five minutes' walk from the shallow,
sheltered cove of Cala Fonte, this
spruce little family-run B&B has two
mini apartments, both with cooking
facilities, making it an ideal choice
for any family on a budget. There is
a studio suitable for a couple and
one small child, and a larger
apartment that sleeps 4–6 with two

bedrooms and a large kitchen.
Both have their own terrace, where
beautiful panoramic views of the
countryside can be enjoyed.
€

SELF-CATERING
TuristCasa
*Via Roma 2, 04027; 0771 809 886;
www.turistcasa.it*
Self-catering apartments and villas
to rent year-round. There are
properties all over the island,
ranging from tastefully furnished,
well-equipped family studios, to
ample villas. The website has
photos and details (in several
languages) of all properties, along
with locator maps. Prices range
from inexpensive to €2,000 for a
week in high season for a villa
sleeping six.
€€

Sabaudia
MAP 7 C4

HOTEL
Oasi di Kufra
*Lungomare di Sabaudia, 04016; 0773
5191; www.oasidikufra.it*
Set on the soft sandy dunes north of
Sabaudia, this is a good base for a
beach holiday, with apartments

The beachfront restaurant at Oasi di Kufra – a stunning setting for lunch or dinner

(with cooking facilities) as well as rooms. It also has the advantage of being open all year, and you can expect some good low season deals. Canoes and boat trips available, as well as children's activities in summer.

⊷ ❋ |◯| ⊟ ◑   €€

San Felice Circeo
MAP 7 C4

HOTELS
Giardino degli Ulivi
Via XXIV Maggio 13, 04017; 0773 548 034; www.giardinodegliulivi.eu
With views over the village to the sea, this charming hotel is set within a huge garden. There are six family rooms (with bunk beds). In July and August half-board or full-board is compulsory, but at €85 per person (€28 for children) for full-board, it is a good deal. The rest of the year, B&B for two adults and two children in a room is €100.

⊷ ◉ ⚑ |◯| €€

Punta Rossa
Via delle Batterie 37, 04017; 0773 548 085; www.puntarossa.it
A picturesque whitewashed cluster of buildings set in lovely grounds, right on the coast. There is a small hotel with family rooms, several apartments with sea views, and a secluded family chalet. Facilities include a restaurant, a sea-water pool carved into the rock, and a wellness centre. From June to August half-board is an option (including breakfast and lunch).

⊷ ◉ ⚑ |◯| ⊟   €€

Sermoneta
MAP 7 C3

HOSTEL
Ostello San Nicola
Via Matteotti 1, 04013; 0773 303 81; www.sannicola-hostel.com
A great option for families travelling on a budget, this unique hostel occupies a 13th-century priory in the heart of Sermoneta. There is accommodation for families in quad rooms with private facilities, and a walled garden with views out to the coast and the Pontine islands. There is a fully equipped kitchen. Breakfast is optional and costs €12.

⊷ ⚑ ⊟   €

Tarquinia
MAP 7 A2

HOTELS
La Torraccia
Viale Mediterraneo 45, 01016; 0766 86 43 75; www.torraccia.it
A modern, comfortable hotel set in pinewoods some 200 m (656 ft) from the sea. All rooms are decorated in bright primary colours with whitewashed walls, and each has a terrace. There is a garden terrace for breakfasts and a private beach just a short stroll away.

P ❋ ⚑ ◑   €

Hotel Tarconte
Via della Tuscia 19, 01016; 0766 856 141; www.hoteltarconte.it
This modern hotel is a good bet if your kids are interested in the Etruscans: there is an Etruscan tomb in the basement, and it is just five minutes' walk from the Etruscan museum. The hotel offers simple rooms and panoramic views. Good hearty food in the restaurant.

⊷ P ❋ |◯| ▤   €

AGRITURISMO
Podere Giulio Agriturismo
Strada Litoranea km 4,5, Loc. Piana di Spille, 01016; 0766 814 136; www.poderegiulio.it
Overlooking the sea, the family-run Giulio farm is set in unspoiled natural beauty. The converted farmhouse comprises 10 apartments, each tastefully decorated. For those who love sport, the farm offers sea fishing, bike-riding and horse-riding (by arrangement, 2 km/1 mile away). There is also a nearby golf course (3 km, 2 miles away).

⊷ |◯| ◉   €

Viterbo
MAP 7 B1

HOTELS
Roma
Via della Cava 26, 01100; 0761 226474; www.albergoromavt.com
This is a very simple, inexpensive little hotel in the medieval heart of town. The exterior is fabulous – a medieval palazzo – while the guest rooms are light, clean and spacious and include several family rooms (the nicest is "Celeste" with a double bed and bunk beds). Good deals can be arranged with local restaurants.

⊷ P   €

A restored priory dating to 1248 housing the Ostello San Nicola, Sermoneta

Hotel Mini Palace
Via Santa Maria della Grotticella 2b, 01100; 0761 390 742; www.minipalacehotel.com
Located a short walk from Porta Romana and the historic centre, this hotel is perfect for visitors looking for a quiet stay. The rooms are large, cosy and elegantly furnished, and the staff are very friendly. The hotel restaurant, Le Chandelier, is worth a try as it serves local dishes and wines.

⊷ P ❋ ⌇ |◯| €€

AGRITURISMO
Il Casaletto
Strada Grottana 9, Grotte Santo Stefano, 01026; 0761 367 077; www.ilcasaletto.it
Located 17 km (10.2 miles) from Viterbo in beautiful countryside, this farmhouse is a good option for families who want a taste of the outdoors. The apartments sleep up to six people and have a kitchen.

⊷ ◉ ⚑ |◯| ⊟   €

SELF-CATERING
Balletti Park
Via Umbria 2; 0761 3771; www.balletti.it
Set in vast grounds, this competitively priced hotel is ideal for families who want an active holiday. There is horse-riding, fishing, a football field, roller-skating, tennis, a swimming pool with water slides, duck ponds and lots of space to let off steam. There is accommodation for families in rooms and self-catering apartments.

⊷ ◉ ⚑ |◯| ⊟   €€

Price Guide
The following price ranges are based on one night's accommodation in high season for a family of four, inclusive of service charges and any additional taxes.
€ Under €200 €€ €200–350 €€€ over €350

The South
and the Islands

Italy's south and its islands make an ideal destination for a family holiday, with volcanoes, mountains, magnificent beaches, splendid Baroque towns and rustic villages, to say nothing of Pompeii and Herculaneum – Europe's best-preserved Roman towns. Sicily and Sardinia have intriguing ancient settlements and the food is outstanding too – with the south producing some of Italy's best fresh produce, oils and wine.

Highlights

Herculaneum and Pompeii
See Roman history come to life in ghost towns buried by an eruption of Mount Vesuvius in AD 79, then head to the Museo Archeologico Nazionale in Naples to see the objects found there *(see pp324–5 & p327)*.

Ischia
Snorkel from idyllic Sant'Angelo on this island in the Bay of Naples, exploring sea caves full of sea anemones *(see pp328–9)*.

Parco Nazionale d'Abruzzo
Track rare European wolves and bears in Abruzzo's vast national park *(see p337)*.

Matera
Explore this maze-like Basilicatan cave-town and experience troglodyte living in a luxury cave hotel *(see pp346–7)*.

Baroque towns
Marvel at the magnificent carved Baroque buildings of Lecce in Puglia *(see pp342–3)* or Siracusa *(see pp362–3)* and Noto *(see p364)* in Sicily.

Stromboli
This conical island in the Aeolian archipelago is an active volcano; trek to the summit or watch it erupt, like a firework display, from a boat *(see p361)*.

Left View of Isola Bella and Cape Sant'Andrea, off Taormina, Sicily *Above right* The ancient Greek Temple of Juno in the Valley of Temples near Agrigento in Sicily

The Best of the
South and the Islands

It would take a month or so to explore Italy's south and islands at leisure – it is far better to focus on a particular area. Puglia offers a mix of Baroque towns, little ports and architectural curiosities, while Sicily adds volcanoes to the mix. The ancient Roman remains of Herculaneum and Pompeii are must-see sights, and all around are stunning beaches. In high season, escape the heat and crowds by visiting the mountains of Abruzzo.

Short breaks

Puglia (see pp338–47) is a good destination for a week: take in the extraordinary mathematical puzzle of Castel del Monte and the Baroque carvings of Lecce; let the kids play hide and seek in the maze-like streets of whitewashed Ostuni; and see the conical dry-stone huts known as *trulli* in Alberobello. Then, take in the beaches of the **Gargano Peninsula** (see p340) or the rocky coast around the Salentine Peninsula, the heel of Italy's boot. The easiest small islands to reach are Sicily's **Egadi** group (see p357), close to the port (and airport) of Trapani.

Right The ornate Baroque façade of Santa Croce in Lecce, Puglia **Below** Mosaics in the ancient Roman House of Neptune and Amphitrite at Herculaneum, near Naples

Above Miles of beautiful beach and turquoise-blue sea of the Maratea Coast, seen out of season

Culture vultures

Ancient Greeks, Romans, Normans, Arabs (Saracens) and the Spanish have all ruled southern Italy, and all left their mark. See the ancient Greek temples at **Agrigento** *(see pp352–3)*, the old Roman towns of **Herculaneum** *(see pp324–5)* and **Pompeii** *(see p327)*, Frederick II's perplexing **Castel del Monte** *(see p341)* or the glorious Norman mosaics at **Monreale** *(see p355)*, and get lost in labyrinthine towns such as **Lucera** *(see p340)* and **Otranto** *(see p344)* that retain the layout of the Arab casbah. Italy's most flamboyant Baroque towns are to be found here: **Lecce**, in Puglia *(see pp342–3)*, and **Noto**, **Siracusa** and **Modica** in Sicily *(see pp362–5)*. Step back into prehistory amid the ancient *nuraghi* of **Sardinia** *(see pp370 and 376)*.

By season

Nowhere along the Italian coast is quiet in high summer, so in August either head to the cool mountains of Abruzzo's **Gran Sasso** *(see pp334–5)*

or enter into the Italian spirit, going to the beach after breakfast, home for lunch and a long siesta, then back to the beach in the late afternoon, followed by an evening stroll and late dinner – for kids too.

In spring and autumn almost anywhere in the south is lovely, though the mountainous parts of Abruzzo can still be very cold. These are the best times to visit popular destinations such as the **Amalfi Coast** *(see p330)*: the towns come into their own without the summer crowds, and there is great walking in the mountains behind.

The south is great for winter breaks, with crisp, sunny days and sea that is warm enough for swimming until Christmas. Carnival brightens up February throughout the south but especially in Sardinia.

The great outdoors

Top of the list for kids will be the volcanoes. It is possible to take a minibus most of the way up **Vesuvius** *(see p325)*, or walk on steaming, stinking fields of sulphur near the town of **Pozzuoli** *(see p326)*, outside Naples, and swim in seas heated by underwater fumaroles off the island of **Ischia** *(see pp328–9)*. Volcanic action is most likely to be found on the Sicilian island of **Stromboli** *(see p361)*; if the ascent is too tough, the nearby island of **Vulcano** *(see p361)* is easier to climb, with its eerie landscape of black rock and smoking vents. **Etna** *(see pp358–9)*, Europe's biggest volcano, is accessed by cable car and jeep, but the vast lava fields lower down may impress kids just as much. In winter the nursery slopes of Piano Provenzana on Etna are an ideal place to learn to ski or, in summer, have a watery adventure in the nearby Gola di Alcantara.

Left View of snow-capped, smoking Mount Etna, Europe's biggest volcano, from the coast at Giardini-Naxos in Sicily

The South and the Islands

If the entire Italian peninsula is a boot, southern Italy is a natty high-heeled ankle boot with a spur. Inland lie high mountains, vast plains and Europe's most dangerous volcano, while both Tyrrhenian and Adriatic coasts have spectacular stretches, notably the Amalfi coast and the Gargano peninsula. Offshore are the islands of Sicily and Sardinia, each with hilly, mountainous interiors where life has changed little in centuries. Sardinia is famous for its long, white sandy beaches, and Sicily too has an amazing coastline – and three active volcanoes.

The Lowdown

🚗 **Getting there and around**
Air to Naples or the many regional airports (see p322). **Ferry/hydrofoil** from Naples and the Amalfi Coast to Ischia and Capri; to Bari and Brindisi; to Reggio di Calabria; to Palermo, Messina and Trapani (Sicily); to Porto Torres, for Alghero, and Cagliari (Sardinia). **Car hire** from major firms at airports. **Train** Mainline to main towns (www.trenitalia.it); private trains in Puglia and Sicily. **Bus** Faster and more efficient than train in the south. For information, see entries.

🛒 **Supermarkets** See entries.
Markets Naples (Mon–Sat am). Trani (Tue am). Lecce (Mon and Fri). Palermo (Mon–Sat am). Siracusa (Mon–Sat am). Alghero (Mon–Sat am)

🎌 **Festivals** San Gennaro, Naples: 19 Sep. Festival of Snakes, Cocullo, Abruzzo: first week May. Festa della Madonna della Bruna, Matera: 2 Jul. Santa Rosalia, Palermo: second week Jul. Sant' Agata, Catania: 3–5 Feb. Santa Lucia, Siracusa: 13 Dec

🕐 **Opening hours** Shops close 1–4pm in winter, and 1–5pm in summer, and restaurants tend to open later in the evenings in the south, where all-day opening is rare.

➕ **Pharmacies** To find an all-night pharmacy check servizio notturno listings on pharmacy doors or in local papers.

🚻 **Toilets** Few and far between: some self-cleaning pay toilets in train stations. Elsewhere buy a drink in a café-bar to use the facilities.

Kite-flying competition on a sandy Sicilian beach

Ruins of the Teatro Greco at Taormina in eastern Sicily

The azure seas of the Amalfi Coast in Campania

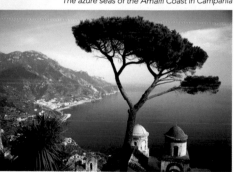

Places of Interest

CAMPANIA
1. Herculaneum
2. Naples
3. Pompeii
4. Ischia
5. Amalfi
6. Ravello
7. Capri

PUGLIA AND THE SOUTH
1. Gran Sasso and Campo Imperatore
2. Atri
3. Sulmona
4. L'Aquila
5. Trani
6. Alberobello
7. Lucera
8. Castel del Monte
9. Lecce
10. Ostuni
11. Otranto
12. Taranto
13. Matera
14. Maratea Coast
15. Tropea
16. Calabria's mountains

SICILY
1. Agrigento: Valley of the Temples
2. Villa Romana del Casale
3. Palermo
4. Monreale
5. Trapani
6. Erice
7. The Egadi Islands
8. Mount Etna
9. Catania
10. Taormina
11. The Aeolian Islands
12. Siracusa
13. Noto
14. Scicli
15. Modica

SARDINIA
1. Alghero
2. Bosa
3. Castelsardo
4. The Maddalena Islands
5. Cala Gonone
6. Cagliari
7. Su Nuraxi
8. Villasimius
9. Sant'Antioco and San Pietro
10. Sinis Peninsula

The South and the Islands Airports

Southern Italy is well provided with airports, serving both domestic and international flights. All have reasonable public transport connections to the nearest town, a range of car rental firms, and a café-bar where travellers can buy a coffee, drink, sandwich or pastry – but don't expect much more. None have a play area for children and only Naples Capodichino has a hotel, but all airports are close to town centres with hotels.

Naples Capodichino

Naples airport is served by major and low-cost airlines including Alitalia, Air Italy, Air One, British Airways, easyJet and Meridiana, with flights to most Italian cities and all major European destinations. A small airport, it is connected by regular Alibus buses with Naples and the port. Taxis from the stand in front of arrivals charge a flat rate for the city centre of €20.

Pescara Abruzzo

Pescara airport is served by Ryanair from London Stansted and other European cities. It is a very small airport, with modest facilities. Bus 38 leaves for Piazza della Repubblica every 15 minutes.

Bari Puglia

Bari airport is served by Alitalia, British Airways and Ryanair, with flights from London Gatwick, London Stansted and Italian cities. It is a small airport with modest facilities. Regular shuttle buses depart for Bari Centrale station.

Brindisi Salento

Brindisi airport is served by Alitalia and low-cost airlines including Air One, easyJet and Ryanair, with flights to London Stansted and Italian cities. A small airport with few facilities, it is connected by bus with the centre of Brindisi, and Lecce.

Reggio Calabria Aeroporto dello Stretto

Reggio Calabria airport is served by regular Alitalia and low-cost Blu-express flights from Rome and Milan, and less frequent flights from other Italian cities. It is a tiny airport, with regular buses into town. Some flights coincide with one of five daily direct hydrofoils to Messina and the Aeolian islands.

Catania, Sicily

Catania airport, 5 km (3 miles) south of the city, is Sicily's main airport. It is served by British Airways and easyJet flights from London Gatwick, and with major and low-cost airlines from most Italian cities and other European destinations. Regular buses depart for Catania Centrale station, and for Taormina, Palermo, Siracusa, Agrigento and Ragusa.

Palermo Falcone Borsellino, Sicily

Palermo airport serves Ryanair flights from London Stansted, and Italian destinations with Alitalia, Meridiana and Wind Jet. It is a small airport, connected by regular buses to Palermo Centrale station.

Trapani, Sicily

Trapani airport is served by Ryanair flights from Dublin and London Luton, plus other Italian and European cities. There are connecting buses to Trapani Centrale station, the port, Palermo and Agrigento.

Alghero, Sardinia

Alghero airport receives Thomson Airways flights from London Gatwick and Ryanair flights from London Stansted. Local buses depart hourly for the town (tickets from machines in the terminal),

The Lowdown

Alghero: 079 935 150; *www.aeroportodialghero.it*

Bari Puglia 080 580 1200; *www.aeroportidipuglia.it*

Brindisi Salento 080 580 1200; *www.aeroportidipuglia.it*

Cagliari 070 211211; *www.sogaer.it*

Catania 095 723 9111; *www.aeroporto.catania.it*

Naples Capodichino 081 789 6111; *www.gesac.it*

Olbia 0789 563 444; *www.olbiairport.it*

Palermo Falcone Borsellino 091 702 0111; *www.gesap.it*

Pescara Abruzzo 895 898 9512, 899 130 310; *www.abruzzo-airport.it*

Reggio Calabria Aeroporto dello Stretto 0965 640 517; *www.aeroportodellostretto.it*

Trapani 0923 842 502; *www.airgest.it*

For car rental firms, visit airport websites.

and there are direct services to Cagliari and in summer to resorts. Taxis to Alghero cost around €25.

Cagliari, Sardinia

Cagliari airport serves flights from London Heathrow on British Airways and London Stansted on easyJet, and flights from Italian cities. Bus to central Piazza Matteotti (tickets from airport shop). Taxis cost around €15.

Olbia, Sardinia

Olbia airport serves flights from London Gatwick and Bristol on easyJet, from London Heathrow on British Airways and from Edinburgh and Leeds-Bradford on Jet2.com. Regular buses (2 and 10) depart for central Piazza Regina Margherita (tickets from machine in terminal). Taxis cost around €20. In summer, there are direct buses to resorts and other Sardinian towns.

Naples Capodichino, with two terminals, one of the larger airports serving southern Italy

Campania

Campania is the start of Italy's south. Home to the ancient cities of Herculaneum and Pompeii, it also has a dramatic coastline and enticing islands, and has been a holiday destination since Roman times. Roman seaside villas abound, while the Amalfi Coast was later popular with Grand Tourists. Anarchic Naples is fascinating for children – in small doses.

Below Positano tumbling down the hillside to azure seas on the Amalfi Coast

① Herculaneum

The ghost town

In AD 79, no one in the towns of Herculaneum and Pompeii had any idea that Vesuvius was an active volcano, but in the early hours of 24 August, while most people were still sleeping, the eruption began. Pompeii was engulfed, but Herculaneum escaped until the next day, when it was blasted by the first of six massive avalanches of hot ash, stone and poisonous gases. The city was buried, and is now the best-preserved ancient Roman city in Italy.

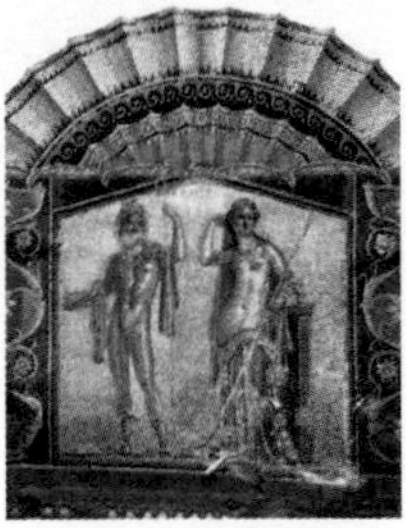

Mosaics in the House of Neptune and Amphitrite

Key Features

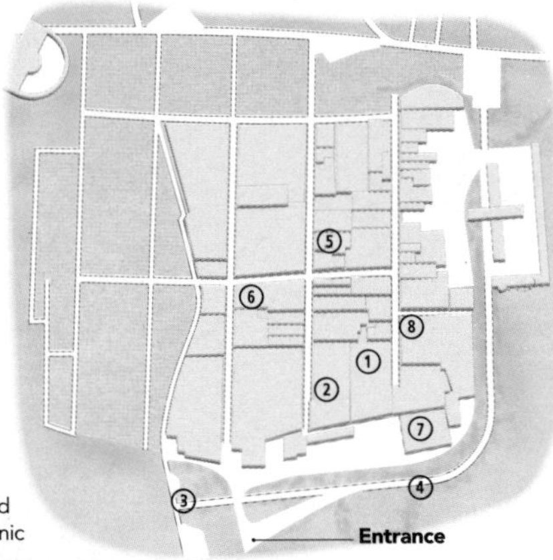

① House of the Stags This house gives an idea of the gracious style in which rich Herculaneans lived. In the courtyard are two sculptures of stags being attacked by dogs.

② House of the Mosaic Atrium This house has a famous mosaic floor with geometric patterns, as well as a portico and terrace.

③ Walkway The approach to the site is along a raised walkway; the town was buried beneath 20 m (66 ft) of volcanic deposits until its excavation.

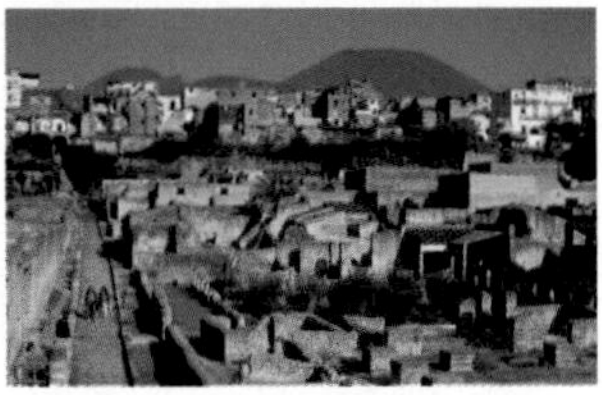

④ Boat House The remains of a wooden boat hurled onto the beach by one of the tidal waves that followed the eruption, and then covered by stone and ash, can be seen here. A coil of rope fused to a wooden plank and a leather cover with stitches visible along its seams were also found here.

⑤ House of Neptune and Amphitrite This house is named after the beautiful mosaic in the summer *triclinium (see above right and Kids' Corner)*. According to legend, Neptune carried Amphitrite off after he saw her dancing with nereids.

⑥ House of Latticework This is a characteristic example of an inexpensive Roman multi-family dwelling. Wood and reed laths can still be seen in the original crude tufa and lime masonry. Its *oecus* (living room) has decorative frescoes.

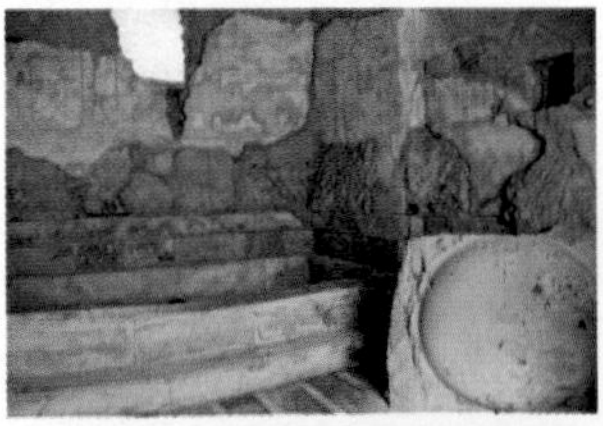

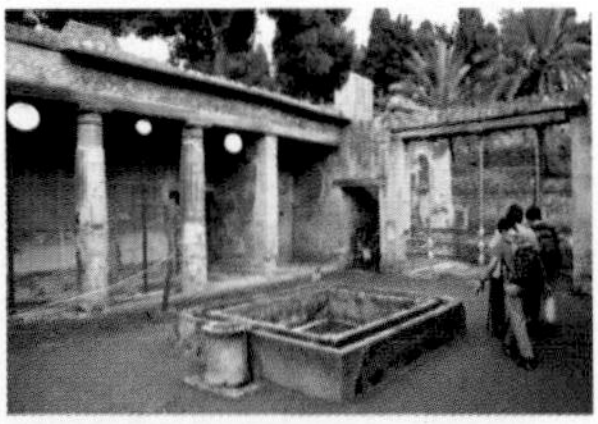

⑦ Suburban Baths Imagine what it must have been like to go to a Roman bath-house here. See how the heating system worked, with an oven below a water vat, and the tanks that held the hot, warm and icy-cold pools in the marble bathrooms.

⑧ House of the Relief of Telephus Colonnades surround the house's *atrium* (main hall), which has an *impluvium* to catch rainwater. The relief depicts Achilles and his mother, Thetis, aiding Mysian king Telephus in return for directions to Troy.

Prices given are for a family of four

The Lowdown

Map reference 8 F5
Address Corso Resina 187, 80056 Ercolano; 081 732 4311; *www.comune.ercolano.na.it*

Train (Circumvesuviana) from Naples Stazione Centrale to Ercolano Scavi

Visitor information Via IV Novembre 82, 80056; 081 788 1237; open 8am–6pm Mon–Sat

Open Daily: Apr–Oct 8:30am–7:30pm (last adm: 6pm), Nov–Mar 8:30am–5pm (last adm: 3:30pm)

Price €22, EU citizens aged 18–25 €5.50, under-18s free; joint with Pompeii (valid 3 days): €40, children free

Skipping the queue Herculaneum does not attract the crowds like Pompeii does, so just turn up.

Guided tours The excellent audio guide is popular with children and allows them to go at their own pace, €21.

Age range 5 plus to get to grips with ancient Roman life; Herculaneum is easier with a pushchair than Pompeii.

Allow 2 hours

Wheelchair access Yes

Café There is no café on site.

Toilets In the ticket office and just after the Boat House, at the top of Via del Mare

Good family value?
Entrance is not extortionate for such an important site. There is lots to see and do and children will learn a lot about everyday Roman history.

Letting off steam

Take a minibus from Ercolano Scavi train station to the **Mount Vesuvius** car park and climb (half an hour with older children) to the steaming lip of the volcano's crater. For younger children, there is a grassy patch to play in by the excavations' walkway.

The crater of Mount Vesuvius, the cavity created by successive eruptions

Eat and drink

Picnic: under €25; Snacks: €25–40; Real meal: €40–80; Family treat: €80 or more (based on a family of four)

PICNIC Alimentari De Luca (Via IV Novembre 4–6, 80056) is an old-fashioned deli close to the site entrance, selling excellent bread, local mozzarella, ham and salami. Find a triclinium (dining room) to picnic in amid the ruins.

SNACKS Filling pizza and panini are available from cafés all along Via IV Novembre and its cross street, Corso Italia. One option is **Italia Caffè e Pasticceria** (Corso Italia 17, 80056; 081 732 1499) for good coffee and pastries.

REAL MEAL La Fornacella (Via IV Novembre 90, 80056; 081 777 4861; closed Mon except public holidays) is a restaurant, pizzeria and tavola calda with some good, honest, local dishes such as pasta with beans, lentils or chickpeas – the cucina povera (poor cuisine) reflecting the historical poverty of the area.

Bird's-eye view of Herculaneum, showing the higher level of the modern town

FAMILY TREAT Viva Lo Re (Corso Resina 261, 80056; 081 739 0207; closed Sun eve and Mon) is a contemporary osteria with good wine and food, including melanzane alla parmigiana (oven-baked aubergines with parmesan), local sausages and costata di agnello (rack of lamb), followed by a great selection of cheeses.

Find out more

DIGITAL There is good background on Herculaneum and Pompeii at www.bbc.co.uk/history/ancient/romans/pompeii_rediscovery_01.shtml. Find out about Vesuvius at www.howstuffworks.com/european-history/mount-vesuvius
FILM The Secret of Vesuvius, an episode of the BBC Roman Mysteries series (available on DVD), brings the days around the eruption to life; go to www.bbc.co.uk/cbbc/romanmysteries/episodes/index.shtml for a full description.

Mount Vesuvius looming over the Bay of Naples

Take cover

The **Museo Archeologico Virtuale** (MAV, Via IV Novembre 44, 80056; www.museomav.it; open Tue–Sat 9am–5:30pm; €27), 5 minutes' walk from the ruins, is a virtual museum with interactive installations where you can make a virtual mosaic floor with footsteps or wave a hand to clear the virtual steam of a bath-house.

Next stop...

POMPEII If Herculaneum is a hit head to Pompeii, destroyed by the same eruption (see p327). It is 20 minutes away by Circumvesuviana railway, but the site is huge, with an amphitheatre, shops and houses, so don't attempt to do both in one day.

(see p327)

KIDS' CORNER

Look out for...

1 A loaf of bread stamped with its owner's name (in the House of the Stags). Dough prepared by slaves at home was taken to the bakery for baking, so loaves had to be named.
2 A statue of Hercules having a pee (also in the House of the Stags).
3 A marble counter with holes in it where vats of food were kept warm over hot coals (in the Big Tavern).
4 A luxurious gym (palestra) created in the old water cistern of the town, with a mosaic of swimmers and dolphins, and a table with lions' claw legs.
5 A shop (the Bottega) with amphorae in which wine was stored on wooden shelves.

HOUSE OF NEPTUNE AND AMPHITRITE

This is a beautiful house, with a summer dining room, or triclinium, decorated with a glass mosaic of the sea god Neptune and his wife, Amphitrite.

Men's and women's baths

The baths in the centre of town were divided into sections for men and women. In the men's area, spot the niches where bathers would hang their clothes, a circular frigidarium (cold room) and a tepidarium (warm room) with fantastic black and white mosaics of a sea god surrounded by octopuses, dolphins and squid. In the women's area, see the well from which water was drawn, and the furnace used to heat it.

The narrow, cobbled street of Spaccanapoli in the heart of Naples

② Naples

Christmas cribs and underground tunnels

Naples is the essence of southern Italy – a city of exuberant street life, anarchic traffic, superstitious religion and fabulous pizza. For adults, the chaotic city and its rich history can be fascinating, but families should make life easy by choosing a hotel in a safe, central location near the main sights and a metro station.

The Naples immortalized in a thousand photographs is along Via San Biagio dei Librai, better known as **Spaccanapoli** ①, a long, narrow, cobbled street, crisscrossed with even narrower streets and canopied with washing lines. For most children **Via San Gregorio Armeno** ② will be the highlight of the city: it is lined with workshops selling Christmas crib scenes, incorporating miniature fountains and glowing pizza ovens, as well as figurines, animals, fruit, vegetables, and mini trays of pizza.

Napoli Sotterranea offers fun tours through a maze of tunnels built by the ancient Greeks as water cisterns. Access to the water was via more than 10,000 wells, which for much of the city's history were used to chuck rubbish down – the floor is built on 5 m (15 ft) of garbage.

Naples sprawling around its bay, seen from the lower slopes of Vesuvius

Prices given are for a family of four

The Gothic **Duomo** ③ is dedicated to Naples' adored patron, St Gennaro, martyred at Pozzuoli under Roman Emperor Diocletian. A phial of his blood miraculously "liquefies" three times a year, bringing the city luck; its failure to do so in 1944 and 1980 was followed by an eruption of Vesuvius and an earthquake.

Visit the old-fashioned **Museo Archeologico Nazionale** ④ to see everyday items from Pompeii: on the top floor is a four-egg frying pan, wine glasses decorated with hearts, perfume bottles and a statuette of a crocodile. There are also some beautiful frescoes, splendid mosaics and body casts from both Pompeii and Herculaneum on display here.

Letting off steam

Take the metro from Museo (Linea 2), outside the archaeological museum, to **Pozzuoli**, a small port on a peninsula west of Naples. Kids will love looking at the boats here. Ten minutes' walk north of town is the **Solfatara** (open 8:30am–1 hour before sunset daily), where it is possible to walk into the hot, spongy, stinking fields of sulphur that occupy a volcanic crater.

The Lowdown

- 🌐 **Map reference** 8 E5–F5 **Address** 80121–80147 Naples. Napoli Sotterranea: Piazza San Gaetano 68, 80138; www.napoli sotterranea.org. Duomo: Via Duomo 149, 80138; 081 44 9097. Museo Archeologico Nazionale: Piazza Museo Nazionale 19, 80135; 06 3996 7050

- 🚗 **Train** from Rome or the south to Naples Stazione Centrale. **Metro** to Cavour or Museo (Linea B)

- ℹ️ **Visitor information** Stazione Centrale, Piazza Garibaldi, 80142; 081 268 779; www.naples.it

- 🕐 **Open** Napoli Sotterranea: tours noon, 2pm, 4pm Mon–Fri; 10am, 6pm Sat and Sun. Duomo: 9am–noon daily, 4:30–7pm Mon–Sat. Museo Archeologico Nazionale: 9am–7:30pm Wed–Mon

- 💶 **Price** Napoli Sotterranea: €40. Duomo: €20. Museo Archeologico Nazionale: €18, under-18s free

- 👪 **Age range** 5 plus

- ⏱️ **Allow** 2 days

- 🍴 **Eat and drink** Snacks Da Michele (Via Cesare Sersale 1/3, 80139; 081 553 9204) serves pizza. Real meal Da Dora (Via Ferdinando Palasciano 28, 80122; 081 680 519) is a great fish trattoria.

- 🎉 **Festivals** Festa di San Gennaro: 19 Sep

③ Pompeii
The buried city

The ancient Roman city of Pompeii, destroyed and preserved by the eruption of Vesuvius on 24 August 79 AD, is vast. Pick up a map and a guide from the ticket office, or download it from the website.

Highlights include the **House of the Tragic Poet**, with its *cave canem* (beware of the dog) mosaic at the entrance; the **House of the Faun**, with a delicate bronze statue of a dancing faun in its courtyard; and the **House of the Vettii**, with a fresco showing a young Hercules struggling with a snake. The **Teatro Grande** (theatre) is still used, while the amphitheatre had a capacity of 12,000 – over half the town's pre-volcano population.

The ancient Roman Teatro Grande at Pompeii, still used for performances

Letting off steam

From Pompei Scavi station, hop on a Circumvesuviana train to Castellammare di Stabia and take the cable-car to the top of **Monte Faita**, with amazing views over Vesuvius and the Bay of Naples, and plenty of room for the kids to let off steam.

The Lowdown

- 🌐 **Map reference** 8 F5
  Address Via Villa dei Misteri 2, 80045 Pompei; 081 857 5347; *www.pompeiisites.org*; entrances at Porta Marina, Piazza Esedra and Piazza Anfiteatro

- 🚍 **Train** (Circumvesuviana) from Naples Stazione Centrale to Pompei Scavi (for Porta Marina) or Pompei (for Piazza Anfiteatro)

- ℹ️ **Visitor information** Via Sacra 1, 80045; 081 850 7255

- 🕐 **Open** Nov–Mar 8:30am–5pm (last adm: 3:30pm), Apr–Oct until 7:30pm (last adm: 5:30pm)

- 💶 **Price** €22–33, under 18s free; combined ticket with Herculaneum (valid 3 days): €40–60, under-18s free with valid passport or ID

- 👫 **Skipping the queue** Avoid visiting in high summer, as there is no shade and thousands of tourists

visit every day, many on tour buses. If unavoidable, try to arrive at 8:30am to avoid the long queues and leave before midday to escape the heat.

- 🎧 **Guided tours** The ticket office has good audio guides; visit the interactive "World of Caius" (an 8-year-old Pompeiian boy) on the website before visiting.

- 👫 **Age range** 5 plus; the site requires stamina and the cobbles are hard going for pushchairs.

- ♿ **Allow** 2 hours

- ♿ **Wheelchair access** Not easy

- 🍴 **Eat and drink** *Snacks* Sgambati Bar at Pompei Scavi station or the on-site café for pizza, hot dogs, sandwiches, drinks and ice cream.

A well-preserved cobblestoned street outside the Temple of Venus in Pompeii

---

KIDS' CORNER

Pompeii Q&A

See if you can find the answers to these questions on your visit:
1 What warning did the owners of the House of the Tragic Poet give to guests?
2 How do you think the House of the Faun got its name?
3 What reptile is Hercules shown struggling with in a fresco here?
....
Answers at the bottom of the page.

SET IN STONE

The hot ash and poisonous gas from the volcano prevented oxygen from reaching organic matter. Instead of burning, foods such as bread, figs and walnuts turned to charcoal.

Pompeii AD 79

Pompeii was a busy town of some 20,000 people in AD 79. When Vesuvius erupted in the early hours of 24 August they were caught unawares. Hot ash and tiny volcanic stones known as lapilli rained down on the city; many people escaped, clutching pillows over their heads for protection. But at least 2,000 people were still in the city the next morning when, at about 7:30am, the city was buried in the burning fall-out from a massive surge-cloud. The hot pumice set around the dead Pompeiians like wet cement, leaving hollows where their bodies had been. Archaeologists later poured plaster into the cavities to make casts.

....

④ Ischia
Bubbling seas and shady spas

Ischia is the largest and most varied of the islands in the Bay of Naples. At its heart is an extinct volcano, which has blessed it with hot springs that bubble up through the sea or are tapped by leafy spas. Sant'Angelo is the most picturesque coastal village, with a cluster of whitewashed houses, a little port and its own islet. With its sandy beaches and variety of outdoor pursuits, Ischia is a perfect family destination.

Ceramic sea horse souvenir

Key Sights

① **Horse-riding** Aragona Arabians offers riding lessons, pony trekking in the woods of Cretaio Nature Reserve and a children's farm with llamas, skunks, owls and goats.

② **La Mortella** This exotic subtropical Mediterranean garden is one of the most beautiful in Europe.

③ **Forio** The historical centre of this pretty port town is well preserved. Outside it is the long sandy beach of Citara.

④ **Regno di Nettuno** Fun, exciting and inspiring snorkelling trips are run by two engaging marine biologists especially for children from the beach at Sant'Angelo.

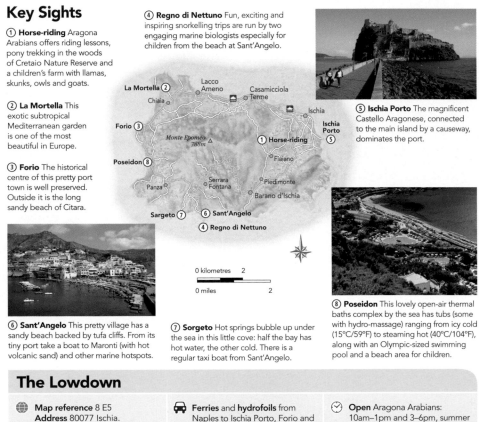

⑤ **Ischia Porto** The magnificent Castello Aragonese, connected to the main island by a causeway, dominates the port.

⑥ **Sant'Angelo** This pretty village has a sandy beach backed by tufa cliffs. From its tiny port take a boat to Maronti (with hot volcanic sand) and other marine hotspots.

⑦ **Sorgeto** Hot springs bubble up under the sea in this little cove: half the bay has hot water, the other cold. There is a regular taxi boat from Sant'Angelo.

⑧ **Poseidon** This lovely open-air thermal baths complex by the sea has tubs (some with hydro-massage) ranging from icy cold (15°C/59°F) to steaming hot (40°C/104°F), along with an Olympic-sized swimming pool and a beach area for children.

The Lowdown

🌐 **Map reference** 8 E5
Address 80077 Ischia. Aragona Arabians: Via Cretaio, 80070, Barano d'Ischia, www.aragona-arabians.com. Sant'Angelo: Serrana Fontana 80070. Regno di Nettuno: Via Regina Elena 75, 80070 Barano d'Ischia (HQ), 366 1270 197, www.nemoischia.it. Sorgeto: 80077. Poseidon: Via G. Mazzella 87, 80075 Forio, www.giardini poseidonterme. com. La Mortella: Via Francesco Calise 39, 80075 Forio, 081 986 220; www.lamortella.org

🚌 **Ferries** and **hydrofoils** from Naples to Ischia Porto, Forio and Casamicciola, and from Salerno, Sorrento and Pozzuoli; hydrofoils from Amalfi and Positano in summer; run by Alilauro (www.alilauro.it), Caremar (www.caremar.it), MedMar (www.medmargroup.it), Metro del Mare (www.metrodelmare.com), NLG (www.navlib.it) and SNAV (www.snav.it). **Bus** Good network of public buses. **Taxis** are plentiful.

ℹ️ **Visitor information** Via Sogliuzzo 72, 80077 Ischia Porto; 081 507 4231; www.infoischiaprocida.it

🕐 **Open** Aragona Arabians: 10am–1pm and 3–6pm, summer until 11pm, winter closed Mon. Regno di Nettuno: Apr–Nov. Poseidon: Apr–Oct 9am–7pm. La Mortella: Easter–Oct 9am–7pm Tue, Thu, Sat & Sun

👫 **Age range** All

👫 **Activities** Swimming, snorkelling, horse-riding, tree-climbing

⏱️ **Allow** A weekend to a week

Good family value?
Excellent destination for families in good weather, with lovely beaches and plenty of outdoor activities.

Letting off steam

Ischia's beaches are ideal for letting off steam, but for a strictly kid-oriented adventure, catch bus 6 from Ischia Porto to **Indiana Park** (Pineta di Fiaiano, 80070 Barano; 392 111 1121; www.ischia.indiana park.it; open Easter–Oct 10am–8pm daily), a tree-climbing park with rope routes and a small wooden playground for younger children.

Eat and drink

Picnic: under €25; Snacks: €25–40; Real meal: €40–80; Family treat: €80 or more (based on a family of four)

PICNIC Antica Macelleria di Francesco Esposto (Via delle Terme 2, 80077 Ischia Porto; 081 981 011) is a superb deli selling fresh bread, cheeses and hams.
SNACKS Bar Calise (Piazza degli Eroi, 80070 Ischia Porto; 081 991 270; www.barcalise.com) has a leafy terrace and makes the best pastries on the island. A stand opposite the Sant'Angelo bus stop sells orange juice squeezed to order, and bars all over the island sell zingari toasted sandwiches with Parma ham, mozzarella, tomato and basil.
REAL MEAL Dal Pescatore (Piazzetta Sant'Angelo, 80070 Sant'Angelo; 081 999 206; closed Jan and Feb) is a family-run café-bar on the port, with hand-made pasta, cakes and gremolate (sorbets).
FAMILY TREAT O'Pignatello (Piazza Santa Restituta, 80076, Lacco Ameno; 081 994 300), in Hotel Reginella o Pignatello, serves linguine all'astice (linguine with rock lobster) as a speciality, cooked in a deliciously concentrated and aromatic tomato sauce.

The lush terrace of Bar Calise in Ischia Porto, where the cakes are a draw

Sailing boats moored in pretty Casamicciola Harbour

Find out more

For more information about Ischia's sea look at the website of Regno di Nettuno, www.nemoischia.it, which has lots of good underwater videos.

Take cover

Ischia is a summer destination – boat trips, snorkelling, spas and other attractions only operate from Easter to October. **La Mortella** is the best rainy-day option, or catch a ferry back to Naples and visit the **Museo Nazionale Archeologico** (see p326).

The harbourside promenade, lined with cafés and bars, at Ischia Porto

Next stop...

PROCIDA The little island of Procida (20 minutes by Caremar or SNAV hydrofoil from Ischia Porto; www.infoischiaprocida.it) has a sleepy feel out of high season. Picturesque **Marina Corricella** is an enclosed fishing port with pastel-washed houses and a traffic-free quayside where kids can play and watch fishermen at work while adults lunch in one of the trattorias. The dark sandy beach of **Pozzo Vecchio**, where scenes from the film Il Postino were shot, is the island's most atmospheric strand.

Amalfi cascading down green, terraced slopes to the azure sea of the Amalfi Coast

⑤ Amalfi

Picturesque pastel town

Clinging precariously to plunging cliffs backed by mountains cloaked in rich vegetation, the **Amalfi Coast** (Costiera Amalfitana) is one of the most spectacular in Italy. A narrow corniche road snakes along it, jaw-dropping views alternating with tummy-lurching blind bends (driving it is not for the faint-hearted). There are no really good beaches, but this does not stop thousands of Italians from pouring in during the summer to lie shoulder to shoulder on narrow strips of gritty sand between the cliffs and the sea. With little flat land to build on, there is not much space in the towns either: houses are fused straight to the cliffs, and twisting in between them are tangles of stepped alleyways and tiny piazzas, meaning there are few places where children can really run around.

Amalfi was one of the most important maritime powers in Italy in the Middle Ages, trading with the Byzantine east. The world's oldest maritime code, the *Tavole Amalfitane*, originated here. There is an exotic air to its architecture: gleaming *Arabian Nights* domes and lots of intricate decoration, notably on the Duomo (9th–12th century), its façade a petrified embroidery of charcoal-grey, rose and creamy-white marble.

At the **Museo della Carta**, a paper museum in a working paper mill, children can try their hand at making paper. The 14th-century mill is the oldest in Europe, founded when paper was made of rags – a rag man used to go around town collecting old clothes – bleached in

animal urine, soaked and beaten to a pulp. A rectangular frame was dipped in to catch some of the stinking pulp and as soon as it set it was peeled off and left to dry. Try making a sheet of paper (*see Kids' Corner*) – though these days wood pulp (without urine) is used.

Letting off steam

Explore the coast by boat – Amalfi has plenty of trips to choose from, ranging from tiny beaches accessible only from the sea, to marvellous rock pinnacles and the emerald-hued waters of the **Grotta dello Smeraldo** sea cave (*boat from Pennello wharf; 9:30am–4pm; €40; or SS 163 highway; access by stairs or lift; €20*). Or head inland on a series of well-marked paths through river valleys and into the mountains; a walking guide is available in English from souvenir shops.

A family enjoying café life in Amalfi's Piazza del Duomo

The Lowdown

🌐 **Map reference** 8 F6
Address 84011 Amalfi. Museo della Carta: Via delle Cartiere 23, 84011; 0898 304 567; www.museodellacarta.it

🚗 **Train** to Vieste sul Mare for Amalfi on the Naples–Salerno line. **Bus** www.sitabus.it. **Ferry** from Naples, Sorrento and Salerno and to other Amalfi Coast towns (www.metrodelmare.net). **Cars** restricted in high summer

ℹ️ **Visitor information** Via delle Repubbliche Marinare, 84011, Amalfi; 089 871 107; www.amalfitouristoffice.it

🕐 **Open** Museo della Carta: Nov–Feb 10am–3:30pm, closed Mon, Mar–Oct till 6:30pm, closed Sun

🏷️ **Price** Museo della Carta: €8, under-5s free

👫 **Age range** 5 plus

⏱️ **Allow** A day with a boat trip

🍴 **Eat and drink** *Snacks* Cuoppo d'Amalfi (*Via Supportico dei Ferrari 10, 84011*) is a good place to try a *cuoppo* (cone) of deep-fried calamari, shrimps and anchovies; eat on the bench outside. *Real meal* Da Teresa (*Santa Croce beach; 0898 831 237*) is a fish restaurant. Hop on the free boat to get there.

⑥ Ravello

Coastal views

Ravello, high up in the mountains, is a tranquil and refined little town, with a huge piazza, two leafy gardens – **Villa Rufolo** and **Villa Cimbrone** – and an enticing network of stone paths where kids can run free. Villa Rufolo's gorgeous semi-tropical gardens, with fantastic views down to the coast, are all the lovelier for a ruined 11th-century palace. The Villa Cimbrone was laid out around another 11th-century villa (now a luxury hotel) and retains a private chapel and a cloister with barley sugar-twist columns and a relief of the seven vices, including a plump *Greed* and a yawning *Sloth*. The gardens include a vertigo-inducing terrace hanging over a cliff edge, from where there are truly dazzling views.

Letting off steam

Let the kids run wild in the gardens and along the stone paths; the Villa Cimbrone is the less child-friendly.

The Lowdown

- 🌐 **Map reference** 8 F6
  Address 84101 Ravello. Villa Rufolo: Piazza Duomo, 84101; www.villarufolo.it. Villa Cimbrone: Via Santa Chiara, 84101; www.villacimbrone.com
- 🚌 **Bus** from Amalfi
- ℹ️ **Visitor information** Via Roma, 84101; 089 857 096; www.ravello.it
- 🕐 **Open** Villa Rufolo: 9am–9pm daily. Villa Cimbrone: 9am–1 hour before sunset daily
- 💶 **Price** Villa Rufolo: €10. Villa Cimbrone: €12
- 👫 **Age range** 5 plus
- ⏱️ **Allow** Half a day
- 🍽️ **Eat and drink** Snacks Bar San Francesco (Via San Francesco, 84101; 089 857 166) serves real English tea with a toasted sandwich or omelette. Real meal Villa Amore (Via dei Fusco 5, 84101; 089 857 135; www.villaamore.it) is a great place for lunch with a fantastic view and a tiny lawn where kids can play.
- 🎊 **Festivals** Ravello Festival (classical music at Villa Rufolo; www.ravellofestival.com): Jul–Sep

⑦ Capri
Fashionable island

Capri, the most glamorous of all Italian islands, has been home to foreign politicians, artists and writers, including Alexandre Dumas and Oscar Wilde. A network of stone paths winds over the island, fringed by bougainvillea, plumbago and jasmine. Follow signs to Da Paolino restaurant from the port and then take Via Palazzo a Mare down to a sheltered turquoise bay overlooked by the ruined walls of the Villa Jovis, built by Emperor Tiberius, set on a cliff above. Alternatively, a boat service shuttles to the lido from the main port. Avoid the expense of hiring a sunbed and umbrella and head for a free stretch of sand; it is a safe place to swim or paddle. For more of an adventure head to the Faro (lighthouse) on Punta Carena at Anacapri, where there is exciting swimming in a rocky cove (accessed by little ladders) or lazy swimming in a pool (kids are welcome until 3pm) belonging to the Lido del Faro.

The ruins of Villa Jovis, Capri, from where Tiberius ruled the Roman Empire

Letting off steam

Go for a swim or climb the 800-step **Scala Fenicia**, crossing gardens and vineyards, from Capri to Anacapri.

The Lowdown

- 🌐 **Map reference** 8 E6
  Address 80073 Capri
- 🚌 **Hydrofoil** from Naples, Sorrento; run by Caremar (www.caremar.it), SNAV (www.snav.it), NLG (www.navlib.it), Neapolis (081 837 7577) or Ischia; run by Alilauro (www.alilauro.it). **Bus** from the port to Anacapri and **minibus** to the Faro
- ℹ️ **Visitor information** Capri town: Piazza Umberto I, 80073; 081 837 0686. Via Marina Grande: Banchina del Porto, 80073; 081 837 0634. Anacapri: Via G. Orlandi 19, 80073; 081 8371524
- 👫 **Age range** 3 plus
- ⏱️ **Allow** 1–2 days
- 🍽️ **Eat and drink** Snacks Bar Augusto (Via C. Colombo 20, 80073 Marina Grande) sells hot dogs and savoury pastries. Real meal Lido del Faro (Loc Punta Carena, 80073 Anacapri; 089 837 1798) serves artful, delicious food.

The lighthouse on the westernmost point of Capri at Punta Carena, Anacapri

Where to Stay in Campania

There is plenty of sophisticated, stylish accommodation in Campania, and some unexpected gems hidden away in backstreets and on hilltops away from the crowded city centres and beach resorts, with lush gardens and shady courtyards to relax in after a long day's sightseeing.

Atrani
Map 8 F6

SELF-CATERING
Dolce Vita in Amalfi
Via San Nicola 11, 84010; 347 973 3947; www.dolcevitainamalfi.com
These lovely bright apartments with terraces are run with flair and charm. Juice, chilled wine and Pansa bakery biscuits are served on arrival.
€€€

Capri
Map 8 E6

HOTEL
Villa Eva
Via La Fabbrica 8, Anacapri, 80071; 081 837 1549; www.villaeva.com
The Moorish-style main house has a tangle of terraced rooms, with views of the sea or semi-tropical gardens. There is a pool, where snacks can be ordered, and it is a 10-minute walk to the stunning Grotta Azzurra.
€€€

B&B
Casa di Anna
Via Palazzo a Mare 21, Capri (town) 80071; 081 837 7582
In a quiet location 5 minutes' walk from the Bagno Tiberio, this family-run B&B has a garden, a spacious lounge, two large bedrooms, a children's bedroom and a kitchen.
€

Ischia
Map 8 E5

HOTELS
Hotel Celestino
Via Chiaia di Rose, Sant'Angelo 80070; 081 999 529; www.hotelcelestino.it
This white and blue hotel brings Greek islands to mind. Most rooms have sea views and balconies. On the top floor three rooms open onto a spacious roof terrace.
€€

Providence
Via G Mazzella 108, 80075 Forio d'Ischia; 081 998 240; www.providence.it
Family-run and friendly, this hotel is perfect for families, with a big pool, and kids' activities in summer. Opt for B&B, rather than half board, and eat out in Forio's restaurants.
€€€

B&B
Casa Lora
Via Costa 16, 80075 Forio d'Ischia; 335 584 9988; www.casaloraischia.it
High up away from the crowds, this 18th-century house has a pool and a shady lemon grove with hammocks. Its seven rooms, two with kitchen, are all furnished with family heirlooms. There are sunset views and convivial dinners on the terrace.
€€€

Naples
Map 8 E5–F5

HOTELS
Costantinopoli 104
Via di Santa Maria di Costantinopoli 104, 80138; 081 557 1035; www.costantinopoli104.com
An oasis in the historic centre of Naples, a short walk from

Hotel Celestino in the fishing village of Sant'Angelo, Ischia

Spaccanapoli, this bijou designer hotel has a secluded courtyard, swimming pool and terrace.
€€€

Hotel Piazza Bellini
Via Santa Maria di Costantinopoli 101, 80138; 081 451 732; www.hotelpiazzabellini.com
In the centre of Naples, this hotel has spacious rooms, some of which have terraces and views of Vesuvius over the rooftops.
€€€

The pool and garden of the Hotel Costantinopoli 104 in Naples

Ravello
Map 8 F6

HOTELS
Villa Giordano
Via Trinità 14, 84010; 089 857 255; www.villagiordano.it
Ten of the 33 rooms at this Art Nouveau villa, with a shady garden and a pool, can sleep three or more.
€€

Villa Amore
Via del Fusco 5, 84010; 089 857 135; www.villaamore.it
In a charming villa, this lovely little hotel has fantastic views and a great restaurant. A triple and a quad open onto the small garden.
€€€

Key to symbols *see back cover flap*

Puglia and the South

Italy's "poor south" is off the beaten track and affordable, with a mild climate even in winter. The historic towns of Lecce, Matera and Trani are great for a quick shot of culture, while Puglia's weird conical stone huts, the *trulli*, may capture kids' imaginations. Throw in beaches, remote mountains and parks where wolves roam for an unusual family holiday.

Gran Sasso and Campo Imperatore *p334*
Trani *p338*
Matera *p346*
Lecce *p342*

Below *The sandy town beach in a secluded cove at Otranto in Puglia*

① Gran Sasso and Campo Imperatore

Step back in time

The Gran Sasso massif includes Corno Grande (2,912 m/9,521 ft), the highest peak in the Apennine mountain range that forms the spine of Italy. It is a wild place, peppered with fortified medieval hill villages whose wealth was built on the wool from sheep which grazed the rich upland pastures of the vast Campo Imperatore plain. Life up here was tough: as recently as the 20th century it was one of the poorest places in Europe. Today, this wild and beautiful region offers a wealth of outdoor activities.

Courtyard in Santo Stefano di Sessanio

Key Sights

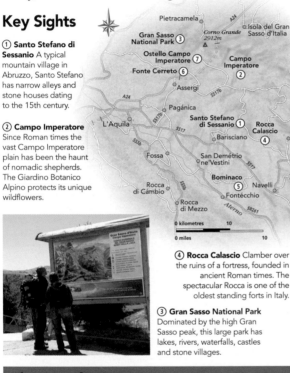

① **Santo Stefano di Sessanio** A typical mountain village in Abruzzo, Santo Stefano has narrow alleys and stone houses dating to the 15th century.

② **Campo Imperatore** Since Roman times the vast Campo Imperatore plain has been the haunt of nomadic shepherds. The Giardino Botanico Alpino protects its unique wildflowers.

③ **Gran Sasso National Park** Dominated by the high Gran Sasso peak, this large park has lakes, rivers, waterfalls, castles and stone villages.

④ **Rocca Calascio** Clamber over the ruins of a fortress, founded in ancient Roman times. The spectacular Rocca is one of the oldest standing forts in Italy.

⑤ **Bominaco** This village has two striking churches: San Pellegrino, with a giant St Christopher, and lovely Santa Maria Assunta.

⑥ **Fonte Cerreto** The hotels, restaurant and camp site here, set around a cable-car station, were built by Mussolini in the 1930s.

⑦ **Ostello Campo Imperatore** Fascist dictator Benito Mussolini was imprisoned in this grim hotel at the top of the cable-car route.

The Lowdown

Map reference 6 G6
Address Santo Stefano di Sessanio, 67020 L'Aquila, Abruzzo. Gran Sasso National Park: 67020 L'Aquila; *www.gransassolagapark.it.* Ostello Campo Imperatore: Loc Campo Imperatore, 67100 Assergi; 0862 400 000. Fonte Cerreto: 67100 L'Aquila; 0862 606 143. Bominaco: 67020 Caporciano, L'Aquila. Rocca Calascio: 67020 Calascio

Train to L'Aquila, Pescara or Sulmona *(www.trenitalia.com).* **Bus** to villages *(www.conoscereabruzzoturismo.it).* **Car** is much the easiest *(www.targarent.it)*

Visitor information Loc Fonte Cerreto, 67010 Assergi; *www.ilgransasso.it*

Open Bominaco: call ahead to request admission to churches (0862 93 764; tip expected). Giardino Botanico Alpino di Campo Imperatore: 15 Jun–15 Sep 10am–5:30pm daily. Fonte Cerreto: open Dec–Mar (for skiing) and Jun–Sep

Price Giardino Botanico Alpino di Campo Imperatore: free

Age range All

Activities Sextantio in Santo Stefano di Sessanio organizes truffle-hunting, pony-trekking and wolf-tracking tours *(www.sextantio.it)*; for information on skiing visit *www.ilgransasso.it*

Allow A long weekend in spring or summer, or in winter for skiing.

Good family value?
This little-known area of Italy will appeal to families in pursuit of outdoor activities – many are free.

Letting off steam

Run around **Santo Stefano**, or go for a hike on **Campo Imperatore**. There is an easy walk from Colle della Croce to an old hermitage at Acqua San Franco (1½-hour round trip). Take the road towards Passo delle Capannelle from Fonte Cerreto. After 13 km (8 miles) there is a dirt road to "Acqua San Franco". Park here and walk, following signs (closed Dec–May because of snow).

Wildflowers on the mountain plains of Campo Imperatore

Eat and drink

Picnic: under €25; Snacks: €25–40; Real meal: €40–80; Family treat: €80 or more (based on a family of four)

PICNIC I Sapori del Borgo *(Via Orto Pulcino, 67020 Santo Stefano di Sessano; 0862 89 117)* is a famous artisanal bakery selling delicious *fiadoni* (ricotta-stuffed pastries), a speciality of the Abruzzo region, and cakes.

SNACKS Tra Le Braccia di Morfeo *(Via Nazario Sauro, 67020 Santo Stefano di Sessano; 0862 899 110; closed Wed, open for dinner by reservation)* serves tasty finger food such as locally sourced cheeses and salami (and wine) for lunch in a welcoming atmosphere. On a cold day, try lentil soup, a local speciality, or ravioli with fresh ricotta.

REAL MEAL Locanda sul Lago *(Via del Lago, 67020 Santo Stefano di Sessano; 0862 899 019; www.lalocandasullago.it; closed Mon),*

Locanda Sotto gli Archi restaurant, Santo Stefano di Sessano

located on the edge of a small lake below the village, has great local food, including delicious lamb, cakes made to regional recipes and lemon sorbet.

FAMILY TREAT Locanda Sotto gli Archi *(Sextantio, Via Nazario Sauro, 67020 Santo Stefano di Sessano; 0862 899 110),* the Sextantio Hotel's stone-flagged, candlelit restaurant, is devoted to reviving ancient local dishes: try delicious home-made ravioli stuffed with tangy local sheep's cheese and fabulous lamb dishes.

Find out more

For more on regional flora, visit the website of the Giardino Botanico Alpino di Campo Imperatore: *www.giardinocampoimperatore.it.*

Take cover

Find out more about rural life in Abruzzo at the evocative **Museo delle Genti d'Abruzzo** in Pescara *(Via delle Caserme 22, 65127; 085 451 0026; www.gentidabruzzo.it; open daily in winter, closed Sun in summer; €12–18, under-4s free; free audioguide).* It has rooms devoted to spinning, weaving, music-making and sheep-herding. There are regular guided tours and activities for children, including drawing.

Statue of Ovid in Piazza XX Settembre in Sulmona, his birthplace

Next stop...

ATRI AND SULMONA Visit the beautiful towns of **Atri**, a cultural and artistic centre *(see p336)*, and **Sulmona**, where you can admire the jewels made by Renaissance goldsmiths *(see p336).*

KIDS' CORNER

Wildflowers and wild beasts

The Campo Imperatore is at its most beautiful from June to September, when it is covered with a haze of wildflowers, with some rare species unique to the high plain. Take a sketchbook and see if you can spot a yellow gentian *(Gentiana lutea)* or Apennine edelweiss *(Leontopodium nivale);* and an *Adonis distorta* at the Giardino Botanico Alpino. The Campo Imperatore is also home to the Apennine wolf, Apennine wildcat and almost-extinct Abruzzo chamois, but you have more chance of spotting wild boar, foxes, grass snakes, golden eagles and peregrine falcons.

MUSSOLINI'S ESCAPE

Mussolini was fed a diet of boiled onions, eggs, rice and grapes while imprisoned on Campo Imperatore in 1943. He was rescued by Germany's Nazi leader, Adolf Hitler, who sent an ace pilot in a tiny plane to pluck him out of his mountaintop eyrie.

Festival of witches

At the beginning of the 19th century, workers in Castel del Monte discovered a series of caves containing clothed skeletons sitting on cane chairs. The skeletons were immediately burnt as a health precaution, but their discovery inspired the town's biggest event of the year, a festival of witches, that takes place one night in mid-August, with locals acting out all manner of spooky scenarios. *(www.lanottedellestreghe.org)*

Thirteenth-century frescoes by painter Andrea de Litio in Atri's Duomo

② Atri

The Virgin Mary has a bath

Approaching Atri is like driving through the background of a Renaissance painting, with gently undulating hills planted with orderly olive groves giving way to a landscape of clay gullies known as *calanchi*, sculpted by rain into sleek ripples and folds. Within Atri's 13th-century **Duomo** is a marvellous fresco cycle of the *Life of the Virgin*, with natural scenery that creates the impression the New Testament happened in Atri: the *Birth of Mary* shows servants giving the newborn

baby Mary a bath, and the horror of the *Slaughter of the Innocents* is intensified by Herod and his men coolly observing the massacre from a Renaissance balcony.

A historical trail around town takes in the foundations of a Roman dye-works, spooky tunnels and the **Museo Etnografico**, which conjures up traditional peasant life.

Letting off steam

Run around in **Parco Comunale**, a shady park. Explore the *calanchi*, following the marked itinerary from town or at the **Riserva Naturale dei Calanchi di Atri** *(085 878 0088; www.riservacalanchidiatri.it)*, where guided walks depart from the visitor centre at Colle della Giustizia *(Jul–Aug: 6pm Tue and Sat, 9:30pm on full moon; reservation essential)*.

③ Sulmona

Land of sugared almonds

Overlooked by the bleak bulk of Monte Majella, Sulmona is a prosperous little provincial town that made its fortune from goldsmithery, wool and sugared almonds *(confetti)*. Although it sustained some damage in the 2009 earthquake *(see p337)*, it remains an atmospheric place, with a dark tangle of streets punctuated by small shops selling *confetti* and intricate gold jewellery. Its main street, Corso Ovidio, is named after its most illustrious citizen, the poet Ovid, who was born here in 43 BC.

Sulmona's most interesting building is the Santa Maria Annunziata, a Gothic-Renaissance palazzo adjoining a flamboyant Baroque church, established to take care of citizens from cradle to grave; its steps were once crowded with

Confetti (sugared almonds) in a typical flower design, a speciality of Sulmona

the sick and destitute seeking help. Inside the palace are several museums. The best, **Museo Civico**, is devoted to local costumes and transhumance (the practice of moving sheep to summer pastures) and has some fine jewellery made here during the Renaissance. In Piazza del Carmine the church of San Francesco della Scarpa gets its name ("St Francis of the shoe") from the fact that Franciscans wore shoes instead of monastic sandals. A fine Gothic aqueduct ends at a small 15th-century fountain, the Fontana del Vecchio, named for the bust of a chubby-cheeked old man on top.

Letting off steam

Piazza Garibaldi is a large square in which to let off steam. There is plenty of space to run around in the **Parco Nazionale della Majella**, 10 km (6 miles) east of Sulmona. It is named after sacred Monte Majella, where over 100 hermits made their retreat in caves in the Middle Ages. To visit, ask at the national park visitor centre in Pacentro *(www.parcomajella.it; open Apr–Sep 10:30am–1:30pm daily, Jun–Aug also 5–8:30pm)*.

The Lowdown

🌐 **Map reference** H E1
Address 64032 Atri, Abruzzo. Museo Etnografico: Piazza San Pietro 1, 64032; 085 87721. Duomo: Piazza Duomo, 64302

🚌 **Bus** from Pescara *(www.arpaonline.it)*

ℹ️ **Visitor information** Via D'Annunzio, 64025. Pineto (15 minutes' drive away); 085 949 1745; www.abruzzoturismo.it

🕐 **Open** Museo Etnografico: May–Sep 4:30–7:30pm Tue–Sun, Oct–Apr 10am–1pm Tue–Sat

💶 **Price** Museo Etnografico: €5

👫 **Age range** 8 plus for the frescoes and historical trail; younger kids may enjoy the *calanchi*.

⏱️ **Allow** 1 hour

☕ **Eat and drink** *Snacks* Gran Caffè *(Corso Adriano Elio 57, 64032; 085 87533)* serves great snacks. La Liquirizia Abruzzese *(Via San Domenico 37, 64032; 085 798 720)* sells local liquorice in pasta shapes. *Real meal* Locanda Duca d'Atri *(Via San Domenico 54, 64032; 085 879 7586; closed Mon)* cooks up local dishes such as pasta with ricotta, aubergine and tomato sauce.

The Lowdown

🌐 **Map reference** 8 E2
Address 67039 Sulmona, Abruzzo. Museo Civico: Santa Maria Annunziata, 67039.

🚆 **Train** www.trenitalia.it **Bus** from Rome, Pescara and L'Aquila. **Car** for national park

ℹ️ **Visitor information** Corso Ovidio 208, 67039; 0864 53 276

🕐 **Open** Museo Civico: 9am–4pm Tue–Sun

💶 **Price** Museo Civico: free

👫 **Age range** 5 plus

⏱️ **Allow** 2 hours, or a day with Monte Majella

☕ **Eat and drink** *Snacks* Locanda di Ovidio *(Piazza XX Settembre 15, 67039; 0864 300 070)*, selling pastries, salads and sandwiches, is one of several decent cafés on the piazza. *Real meal* Cesidio *(Piazza Solimo 25, 67039; 0864 52 724; closed Tue)* is a popular eatery serving home-made pasta.

🎭 **Festivals** Cocullo Snake Festival: first Thu in May; for information contact Cocullo tourist office *(0864 490 006; www.comune.cocullo.aq.it)*.

Piazza Garibaldi in Sulmona, with its mountain backdrop

④ L'Aquila
99 spouts

An ancient university town overlooked by the bulk of Gran Sasso, L'Aquila was founded in 1242 when, according to legend, the Holy Roman Emperor Frederick II drew together the populations from 99 local villages to form a new city. Each village built its own church, piazza and quarter, and one of the L'Aquila's best-loved sights is a medieval fountain with 99 spouts, the Fontana delle 99 Cannelle.

In April 2009 L'Aquila was devastated by an earthquake measuring 5.8 on the Richter scale. Since then much of the town's historic centre has been out of bounds, but there is a marked route through the centre (partly in tunnels), which is safe. There are many beautiful squares, *palazzi* and churches to discover.

One of the spouts of the Fontana delle 99 Cannelle in L'Aquila

Letting off steam
Kids can run around in the little **Villa Comunale** park, or head into the **Parco Nazionale d'Abruzzo** (1 hour's drive), one of the few places in Europe where the grey wolf (*Canis lupus*) and rare Apennine brown bear (*Ursus arctos marsicanus*) live in the wild – these animals usually keep well away from people. Wolves can also be seen close up at the national park visitor centres at Pescasseroli and Civitella Alfedena (www.parcoabruzzo.it), which also have information on walking routes.

The Lowdown

- 🌐 **Map reference** 7 D2
  Address 67100 L'Aquila, Abruzzo
- 🚗 **Train** to L'Aquila on the Roma–Sulmona line. **Bus** to L'Aquila's Collemaggio Bus Terminal near Porta Bazzano (www.arpaonline.it). **Car** 1 hour to the national park
- ℹ️ **Visitor information** The tourist office is currently located in a container at Parcheggio Stadio Rugby; bus 5 or 8 from the train station; 0862 410 808; www.abruzzoturismo.it; open Mon–Fri
- 👫 **Age range** Any for the fountain and park visitor centres, 8 plus for most national park walking routes
- 🕐 **Allow** 1 hour for L'Aquila; at least a day for the national park
- ☕ **Eat and drink** *Snacks* La Cantina del Boss (*Via Castello 3, 67100*) has great snacks (as well as a wide range of local and national wines). *Real meal* Ernesto (*Piazza Palazzo 22, 67100*) has a pretty courtyard for eating alfresco in summer. Its menu is a creative mix based on typical regional mountain dishes.

⑤ Trani
The cathedral of elephants

Trani is a beautiful port and fishing village built entirely of stone, with an unusually cosmopolitan air. One of the most important ports in medieval Italy, today it is the most immediately appealing of Puglia's coastal towns, and the perfect base for exploring the northern part of the region. Lovely at any time of the year, Trani bursts with activity in the evenings and at weekends, when locals pour into the excellent restaurants and wine bars around the port.

Detail of a bronze relief panel, Duomo

Key Sights

④ **San Pietro Martire** Originally a synagogue, this church was later dedicated to 13th-century St Peter Martyr, who preached against heresy.

⑤ **Giudecca** This is Trani's former Jewish ghetto. The street names echo the quarter's past, such as Via La Giudea and Via Cambio (street of the money-changers).

① **Duomo** Built at the time of the Crusades, the Duomo is dedicated to San Nicola Pellegrino. It consists of three churches: the main church is Norman, built over the Byzantine Santa Maria della Scala. This in turn was built on top of a Christian crypt. The façade is Romanesque, pierced by a rose window, decorated with two elephants and overlooked by a campanile that once doubled up as a watchtower.

② **Ognissanti** The Knights Templar, set up to protect pilgrims to the Holy Land, built Ognissanti with its amazing apse, carved with lions, griffins and gargoyles.

③ **The Port** Trani's fishing port is the most picturesque in Puglia. Get there in the morning to see the catch arrive, and fishermen may even let you climb aboard.

Prices given are for a family of four

The Lowdown

🌐 **Map reference** 9 D2
Address 70059 Trani, Puglia

🚗 **Train** from Bari (www.trenitalia.it). **Bus** from Bari or Foggia (www.sitabus.it)

ℹ️ **Visitor information** Piazza Trieste 10, 70059; 0883 588 830; www.viaggiareinpuglia.it

🕑 **Open** Duomo: 9am–8pm daily

👫 **Age range** All ages will enjoy the buzzy port atmosphere and old-town streets; the elephants on the Duomo may hold kids' attention briefly, but the churches are likely to appeal most to children over 11.

⏱️ **Allow** Half a day to visit the town, or use it as a base for the Gargano Peninsula's beaches (see p340) – returning in the evenings for dinner by the port.

🚻 **Toilets** In Villa Municipale park, or ask at bars.

Good family value?
Trani's old town and fishing port are cheap and cheerful places to wander and soak up the feel of southern Italy.

The shady Villa Municipale park with fountains, lovely for a stroll

Letting off steam

The **Villa Municipale** park above the port is well kept and has a great playground and a mini aquarium that kids will love. **Lido di Cocomero**, 15 minutes' walk away on Lungomare Cristoforo Colombo, is a pleasant beach. For an adventure, take the train to Bari and hop on the local Ferrovie del Sud Est train to Castellana Grotte (about 45 mins; www.fseonline.it) to visit the lovely **Grotte di Castellana** caves: the Grotta Bianca shimmers with white stalagmites and stalactites (15-minute walk from the train station; 0804 998 221; www.grottedicastellana.it; regular tours; €40–60).

Eat and drink

Picnic: under €25; Snacks: €25–40; Real meal: €40–80; Family treat: €80 or more (based on a family of four)

PICNIC De Marinis (Via Beltrami 32, 70059) is an all-round grocery shop with a good deli counter, located close to the port.
SNACKS Molo 4 (Via Statuti Marittimi 94, 70059) has outdoor tables with great views of the port and the Duomo perched by the sea. It serves a range of toasted flatbreads and sandwiches.

Corteinfiore restaurant, known for its antipasti and contemporary fish dishes

REAL MEAL Al Buco Preferito (Via Banchina al Porto 4, 70059; 0883 506 083) is a cosy pizzeria situated by the port serving delicious, crisp pizzas and good wine.
FAMILY TREAT Corteinfiore (Via Ognissanti 18, 70059; 0883 508 402; closed Mon; www. corteinfiore.it) offers fish dishes on a shady patio. Its range of antipasti make for a great lunch.

Find out more

Read all about the Crusades, including the role of the Knights Templar, at www.historyforkids.org/learn/medieval/history/highmiddle/secondcrusade.htm. There is a free Crusades game at www.online-games-zone.com/pages/strategy/swords-sandals-crusader.php.

Take cover

Dive into the **Duomo** if there is a rain shower, or if it looks like it is going to rain all day, drive up to extraordinary, octagonal **Castel del Monte** (45-minute drive; see p341).

The unique trulli buildings of Alberobello, a UNESCO World Heritage site

Next stop...

ALBEROBELLO, MOLFETTA AND LUCERA From Trani, head south to **Alberobello** and the beehive-shaped trulli houses (see p340). **Molfetta**, about 20 km (12 miles) to the south of Trani, has a fascinating historic centre on an island-like promontory dominated by two medieval towers. Visit the lively port and fishing harbour. There is also a lovely sandy beach, which is popular with locals. Alternatively, head north to the maze of souk-like streets of **Lucera** and the beaches of the **Gargano Peninsula** (see p340).

A street of whitewashed conical-roofed trulli *in Alberobello*

⑥ Alberobello
City of cones

The *trulli* of Puglia are the most peculiar of the region's – if not Italy's – rustic buildings, dotted across the Murgia dei Trulli, a rocky plateau terraced with olive groves and vineyards and grazed by goats. Cylindrical dry-stone huts with conical roofs, the *trulli* are often whitewashed and decorated with obscure religious, pagan or magical painted symbols. They are unique to Puglia and no-one is sure why they were built this way, but one theory is that they were quick to put up and pull down. Feudal lords had to pay taxes based on the number of people working for them and living on their land, so if word came that tax inspectors were on the prowl, the *trulli* could easily be dismantled – though what the inspectors made of the heaps of stone dotting the land is anyone's guess.

Most *trulli* have just one room – when more space was needed, a hole was knocked in the wall and an identical structure built next door. Originally they were both dwellings and store houses, but these days they are being snapped up as holiday homes; some are available to rent in and around Alberobello, the "*trullo* capital", where about 1,500 of these unusual beehive-shaped structures pack the narrow streets – housing souvenir shops, cafés and restaurants.

Letting off steam

The park on the corner of Via Indipendenza and Via Brigata Regina is good for a run around.

Prices given are for a family of four

The Lowdown

🌐 **Map reference 10 E3**
Address 70011 Alberobello, Puglia

🚃 **Train** Ferrovie del Sud-Est (FSE; *www.fseonline.it*) from Bari and Taranto via Martina Franca

ℹ️ **Visitor information** Via Monte Nero 3, 70011 Alberobello; 080 432 2060; open 10am–1pm and 2:30–5:30pm Mon–Sat, until 8:30pm Sun

👪 **Skip the queue** Visit out of season as it is very crowded in summer.

👫 **Age range** The *trulli* will appeal to young as well as older children.

⏱️ **Allow** 1 hour for Alberobello, more for the hinterland

🍽️ **Eat and drink** *Picnic* Pozzo Contino (*Via Brigata Regina 26, 70011; 080 432 3740*) is good for sandwiches – best eaten in the park across the road. *Real meal* L'Aratro (*Via Monte San Michele 25–9, 70011; 080 432 2789; closed Mon & 7–22 Jan*) is set inside a *trullo* and uses local produce to make great vegetable and cheese *antipasti*.

---

⑦ Lucera
Souk-like streets

Lucera is a lovely small town with a vivid, bustling centre. Frederick II, having forced the Saracens out of Sicily, resettled 20,000 of them here on the site of an old Roman town, with complete religious freedom. The vast **castle** on the outskirts was built in the early 14th century, when French invaders sacked the town, built a **cathedral** on the site of a mosque and ruined the Arab-influenced buildings. All that remains of

---

Lucera's Saracen past is its labyrinthine, souk-like layout, best appreciated by exploring narrow alleyways. The **Museo Civico** has Roman finds including a pair of small statues of muscled gladiators. On the edge of town is a Roman **amphitheatre** where 18,000 people once watched gladiatorial battles.

Letting off steam

Play in Lucera's alleys, or head for the **Gargano Peninsula**, with beaches to the north, a rocky coast to the east and a mountainous interior. The Baia di San Felice has a lovely beach.

A typical narrow winding street in the centre of Lucera

The Lowdown

🌐 **Map reference 9 B2**
Address 71036 Lucera, Puglia. Castle: Piazza Padre Angelo Cuomo, 71036. Cathedral: Piazza Duomo, 71036; 0881 547 041. Museo Civico: Via de Nicastri 74, 71036. Amphitheatre: Viale Augusto, 71036

🚃 **Train** from Foggia; to San Severo via Foggia for Gargano Peninsula (*www.ferroviedelgargano.com*)

ℹ️ **Visitor information** Piazza Nocelli 6, 71036; 0800 767 606; *www.comune.lucera.fg.it*

🕐 **Open** Castle: 9am–2pm Tue–Sun (till 6:45pm summer). Cathedral: 8am–noon, 5–8pm daily. Museo Civico: 9am–1pm Tue–Sun, 4–7pm Tue, Thu and Sat. Amphitheatre: 9am–2pm, 3:15–6:45pm Tue–Sun

👫 **Age range** 8 plus

⏱️ **Allow** 1 hour

🍽️ **Eat and Drink** *Real meal* Al Dragone (*Via Duomo 8, 71019 Vieste; 0884 701 212; closed Nov–Mar and Tue*) serves fish. *Family treat* Il Cortiletto (*Via de Nicastri 26, 71036; 0881 542 554; closed Sun eve, Mon lunch*) serves pasta.

The striking octagonal-shaped Castel del Monte

⑧ Castel del Monte

A mathematical conundrum

Octagonal Castel del Monte is the most extraordinary of all Puglia's castles, and outclasses all the other castles built by Frederick II. Begun by the Holy Roman Emperor known as Stupor Mundi (wonder of the world) in the 1240s, the castle is a high, isolated fortress built around an octagonal courtyard in two storeys of eight rooms. More mundane, but equally advanced, is Europe's first flushing toilet – it was flushed by the user pouring water into it, a system invented by the Arabs and adopted by Frederick. A mystery surrounds the castle's intended purpose, as there was little in the way of fortification – it may simply have been a hunting lodge, more palace than castle. The mathematical precision of its construction and the preoccupation with the number eight have led people to think that the castle is in

fact an enormous astrological calendar, but no one really knows the truth. After the defeat of Manfred, Frederick's illegitimate son, at the battle of Benevento in 1266, Manfred's sons and heirs were imprisoned here for over 30 years.

Letting off steam

There is a grassy space immediately outside the castle, or kids can play in the shade of 1,000-year-old olive trees in Andria while adults buy olive oil at **Lama di Luna Biomasseria** *(30 minutes' drive; Loc. Montegrosso, 73001 Andria; 0883 569 505; www.lamadiluna.com)*. For sea air, drive to **Trani** *(see pp338–9)*.

One of three rose windows of the Castel del Monte

The Lowdown

- 🌐 **Map reference** 9 C2
  Address Contrada Castel del Monte, 70031 Andria, Puglia; 0883 569 997; www.casteldelmonte.beniculturali.it
- 🚗 **Train** from Bari to Andria *(www.ferrovienordbarese.it)*, then minibus (Apr–Oct only)
- ℹ️ **Visitor information** Via Vespucci 114, 70031 Andria; 0883 592 283; www.proloco.andria.ba.it
- 🕐 **Open** Mar–Sep 10:15am–7:45pm, Oct–Feb 9am 6:45pm daily
- 💶 **Price** €6, under-18s free
- 👫 **Age range** All
- ⏲️ **Allow** 1 hour
- 🍴 **Eat and Drink** *Real meal* La Tradizione *(Via Imbriani 11–13, 70031 Minervino Murge; 0883 691 690; closed Thu)* has simple pasta. *Family treat* Antichi Sapori *(70031 Montegrosso di Andria; 0883 569 529)* serves superb traditional food using fine local produce – try one of the ricotta desserts.

⑨ Lecce
Cute cherubs and spooky dragons

Lecce's exuberant Baroque churches and *palazzi* – their golden façades a frolic of scrolls, curlicues, flowers, foliage, monsters, dragons, cherubs and angels – make carving stone look as easy as cutting butter. The perfect southern town, Lecce's beautiful historic centre is largely pedestrianized and its palaces and churches have been restored. There are plenty of stylish places to eat and drink, as well as hip hotels, along its cobbled streets.

Carved figure on the façade of Santa Croce

Key Sights

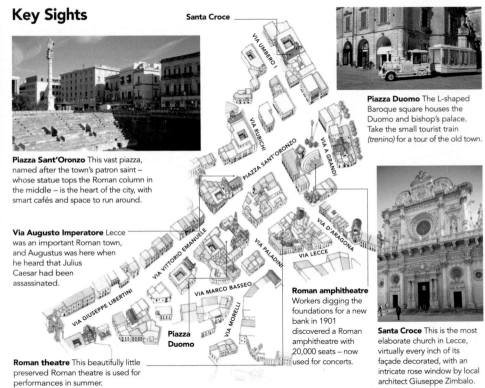

Santa Croce

Piazza Sant'Oronzo This vast piazza, named after the town's patron saint – whose statue tops the Roman column in the middle – is the heart of the city, with smart cafés and space to run around.

Via Augusto Imperatore Lecce was an important Roman town, and Augustus was here when he heard that Julius Caesar had been assassinated.

Roman theatre This beautifully little preserved Roman theatre is used for performances in summer.

Piazza Duomo The L-shaped Baroque square houses the Duomo and bishop's palace. Take the small tourist train *(trenino)* for a tour of the old town.

Roman amphitheatre Workers digging the foundations for a new bank in 1901 discovered a Roman amphitheatre with 20,000 seats – now used for concerts.

Santa Croce This is the most elaborate church in Lecce, virtually every inch of its façade decorated, with an intricate rose window by local architect Giuseppe Zimbalo.

The Lowdown

🌐 **Map reference** 10 G4
Address 73100 Lecce, Puglia. Roman Amphitheatre: Piazza Sant'Oronzo, 73100. Roman Theatre: Via del Teatro Romano, 73100. Santa Croce: Via Umberto I 3, 73100. Santa Chiara: Piazza Vittorio Emanuele II, 73100. Rosario: Via Libertini, 73100. San Matteo: Via dei Peroni, 73100

🚗 **Trains** from Brindisi *(www.tren italia.it)* and FSE trains from Martina Franca, Gallipoli

and Otranto via Maglie *(www. fseon line.it)*. **Bus** from Brindisi, Taranto and other regional towns *(www.cotrap.it)*. **Salento in Treno e Bus** to Santa Maria di Leuca via Gallipoli and Porto Cesareo (summer only) *(www. salentointrenoebus.it)*

ℹ️ **Visitor information** Via Libertini 76, 73100; 0832 245 497; www.salento4you.it; open 9am–1pm and 4:30–7:30pm Tue–Sun

👫 **Age range** All ages: 5 plus for monster-hunting on churches, 8 plus for Roman remains

🏃 **Activities** Pick up a bike from the bike-sharing scheme stand at Piazza Sant'Oronzo

⏱️ **Allow** Half a day for main sights to a week with trips to the coast

🚻 **Toilets** In cafés and bars

Good family value?
A fine architectural city, near the coast; free sights and great food.

Letting off steam

The **Villa Comunale** park in the historic centre of Lecce is full of avenues for running around. Alternatively, follow the Littoranea Otranto coast road through pinewoods, past dunes and rocky coves to the beach at **Roca Vecchia** (40 minutes' drive) and swim in a sheltered turquoise bay overlooked by soft cliffs honey-combed with 7th-century man-made caves.

Cliffs at Roca Vecchia, a beautiful bay for swimming

Eat and drink

Picnic: under €25; Snacks: €25–40; Real meal: €40–80; Family treat: €80 or more (based on a family of four)

PICNIC La Lupa (*Via della Arte di Cartapesta 25, 73100*), set on two floors of a Baroque palazzo, sells superb locally sourced salamis, hams, cheeses and *sott'olii* (vegetables preserved in oil). Follow the Littoranea Otranto coast road through pinewoods and walk down one of the tracks for a picnic on a sandy dune by the sea.

SNACKS Syrbar (*Via Giuseppe Libertini 67a, 73100; closed Mon in winter*), a laid-back café looking out on to Piazza Duomo, serves tasty snacks such as *crostini* with local cheese, ham and salami, or ricotta, marmalade and walnuts.

REAL MEAL Alle Due Corti (*Corte dei Giugni 1, 73100; 0832 242 223; closed Sun; www.alleduecorti.com*) is popular with locals and serves simple regional dishes such as delicious *taieddha* (oven-baked mussels, potatoes, tomatoes, onions and rice).

FAMILY TREAT L'Ideario di Liberrima (*Corte dei Cicala, 73100; 0832 245 524; www.liberrima.it*) is a hip *enoteca* (wine bar) in a bookshop, which serves *aperitivi*

with roast almonds, fresh ricotta and *crostini* with artichokes, as well as other local specialities.

Shopping

Lecce's main shopping streets are Via Vittorio Emanuele II and Via Trinchese. A Leccese speciality is *papier mâché*: see the heights this art form can reach at **Carta Pesta** (*Vico dei Pensini 1, 73100; 0832 241 170; www.france scacarallo.it*).

Find out more

DIGITAL Get a sneak preview of Lecce's stone gargoyles at *www. stonecarver.com/gargoyles/Lecce. html*. Children aged 11 plus may enjoy finding out how to recognize Baroque architecture at *www.ehow. com/how_2088770_recognize- baroque-architecture.html*.

Next stop...

CHIESA DEL ROSARIO, SAN MATTEO AND BARI To escape the heat, duck into the ornate **Rosario** in Lecce (also known as Chiesa di San Giovanni Battista), the most unusual of the churches built by Zimbalo brothers Giuseppe and Antonio, where plump cherubs swoop over lush fruit. Also check out the radical Baroque style of Lecce's **San Matteo**, with its elliptical nave. Then, head to Puglia's lively capital, **Bari**, and wander around the walled Città Vecchia (historic centre). Step inside the Basilica di San Nicola, one of Puglia's first great Norman churches. Visit the medieval Cattedrale, with its simple interior, and the Swabian castle.

The stylish L'Ideario di Liberrima café, bookshop and enoteca

⑩ Ostuni

The white city

Known as the "white city," Ostuni is a gorgeous little hill town, a beguiling tangle of dazzling whitewashed houses and cobbled streets. The coastline, 7 km (4 miles) away, has several marvellous coves and bays with good swimming beaches, but being inland has saved Ostuni from the excesses of tourism and it remains unspoilt. The maze of winding streets is traffic-free and perfect for family wanders, with stepped and arched alleyways that kids can climb and jump through.

There are some lovely palaces and churches on the walk along Via del Cattedrale to the **Duomo**, which has a huge and intricate rose window. The Rococo church of San Vito Martire holds a little **Museum of Prehistory** where the star exhibit is Delia, the 25,000-year-old skeleton of a pregnant woman from the Pleistocene era, whose skull is decorated with stones and beads.

Letting off steam

There are several good beaches near Ostuni, notably the sandy **Costa Merlata** beach, shared in high season with residents of the eponymous holiday village – which at least means there are toilets and a shop to pick up supplies (from Ostuni head to the coast at Marina di Ostuni, then south for about 5 km/3 miles; Costa Merlata is served by bus from Ostuni in the summer). Just a little further south is the enchanting rocky cove of **Baia di Santa Lucia**.

The Lowdown

- 🌐 **Map reference** 10 F4 **Address** 72017 Ostuni, Puglia. Museum of Prehistory: Via Cattedrale 15, 72017; *www. museiostunifasano.it*
- 🚆 **Train** from Brindisi, Bari or Lecce, then local bus or 2-km (1-mile) walk from station. **Bus** from Bari, Brindisi or Taranto
- ℹ **Visitor information** Corso Mazzini 8, 72017; 0831 301 268; open 8am–2pm daily, Jul and Aug also 4:30–10:30pm, Sep–Jun also 3:30–8pm; helpful InfoPoint, in the same office: 339 508 8036; *www.borgostuni.it*
- 🕑 **Open** Museum of Prehistory: 9:30am–noon Mon–Fri, also 3:30–6:30pm Thu
- 💲 **Price** Museum of Prehistory: free
- 👫 **Age range** All ages
- ⏱ **Allow** 1 hour plus beach time
- 🍴 **Eat and drink** *Snacks* Antica Osteria (*Via B Cairoli 1, 72017*) looks as it did a century ago and serves broth, tripe or mixed fried fish – all for a song. *Real meal* Osteria Piazzetta Cattedrale (*Largo Trinchera Francesco 72017; 0831 335 026*) uses local ingredients creatively; try the mixed *antipasti* for lunch.

⑪ Otranto

Tree of Life

Otranto, a whitewashed labyrinth clustering between castle and harbour, is a touristy town, but well worth a wander. Below the castle is the Romanesque **Cattedrale di Santa Maria Annunziata** with an incredible multi-coloured mosaic floor by a 12th-century monk of the *Tree of Life*, featuring Alexander the Great, the Queen of Sheba, serpents and mermaids. The **Basilica dei Santi Pietro e Paolo** is a tiny frescoed Byzantine chapel that survived the Turkish siege of 1480. Its side chapel contains drawers full of the bones of the 800 citizens of Otranto killed by the Turks.

The walls of the historic town of Otranto, seen from the port

From Otranto down to the cape at Santa Maria di Leuca the coastline is steep and rugged, the winding road passing one spectacular view of sheer cliffs and blue sea after another. **Capo d'Otranto**, 5 km (3 miles) south of Otranto, is the

The Lowdown

- 🌐 **Map reference** 10 G5 **Address:** 73028 Otranto, Puglia
- 🚆 **Train** or **bus** from Lecce to Otranto; **Salento in Treno e Bus** to Santa Cesarea Terme in summer. **Car** is the best way to explore the rest of the peninsula
- ℹ **Visitor information** Piazza Castello, 72017; 0836 801 436; *www.viaggiareinpuglia.it*; open 9am–1pm and 4–6pm Mon–Sat
- 🕑 **Open** Cattedrale di Santa Maria Annunziata and Basilica dei Santi Pietro e Paolo: daily
- 👫 **Age range** All ages
- ⏱ **Allow** 1 hour for Otranto, 1 day for the peninsula
- 🍴 **Eat and drink** *Snack* Boomerang (*13/14 Via Vittorio Emanuele II, 72017; 0836 802 619*) is self-service and has fresh *antipasti* and pasta. *Real meal* Da Sergio (*Corso Garibaldi 9, 72017; 0836 801 408; closed Wed*) serves good local fare.
- 🎉 **Festivals** Tarantella at Galatina: Jun 29. La Notte della Taranta: late Aug, Melpignano (*www. lanottedellataranta.it*).

Old Ostuni, the "white city," a maze of winding streets on a hillside

The seafront promenade at Taranto, a major port town, with views of the harbour

easternmost point on the Italian peninsula – it is the first place in Italy to see the sun rise, and is a popular place to welcome in the New Year. Climb up to the lighthouse and ruined 7th-century abbey here. The barren little seaside town of **Santa Maria di Leuca** was for generations the legendary southern end of the world, marked by the tiny church of Santa Maria de Finibus Terrae. Head to the town of **Galatina** nearby, a major Greek colony in medieval times. It has retained Greek customs and is the centre for the *tarantella*, a lively folk dance (*see Kids' Corner*).

Letting off steam

Vist the sandy beaches backed by dramatic sandstone cliffs just north of Otranto, or if you are feeling more adventurous, rent a boat at **Punta Ristola** and go swimming in the sea caves along the coast.

⑫ Taranto
Fresh fish and ancient jewels

Taranto is an old port in the shadow of a massive oil refinery. It is probably not a place to spend an entire holiday, but genuine southern Italian atmosphere, a state-of-the-art museum and the chance to eat good-value fresh fish and seafood make it well worth a visit. The old town, on an island strung like a bead on causeways between the industrial zone and the modern town, is an atmospheric, maze-like place full of Baroque houses held together by wooden braces. The 11th-century Duomo is dedicated

to the Irish saint Cathal (Cataldo in Italian). The **Museo Archeologico** in the new town has one of the best displays in Italy. Admire intricately carved medieval capitals up close and the amazing detail of 4th-century BC Greek gold jewellery. Other highlights among the Greek and Roman finds include a nutcracker in the form of two female hands and a multi-coloured terracotta of Aphrodite with a dove.

Letting off steam

Head for the **Lido Azzurro**, sign-posted about 2 km (1 mile) north of town along the SS106, where there is a long fine-sand beach.

The Lowdown

🌐 **Map reference** 10 E4
Address 74100 Taranto, Puglia. Museo Archeologico: Via Cavour, 74100; *www.museotaranto.org*

🚗 **Train** from Bari or Brindisi. **Bus** (direct) or train (via Martina Franca) from Lecce

ℹ **Visitor information** Corso Umberto I, 74100; 0994 532 397; *www.viaggiareinpuglia.it*

🕐 **Open** Museo Archeologico: 8:30am–7:30pm daily

👫 **Age range** 8 plus

⏱ **Allow** 2 hours

🍴 **Eat and drink** *Snacks* Caffè Tarentum (*Via Anfiteatro 97, 74100; closed Tue*) has typical almond-based sweets. *Real meal* Da Ugo al Orologio (*Largo San Nicola, 74100; 099 460 8736; closed Sat eve and Sun*) serves fresh fish at rock-bottom prices.

KIDS' CORNER

Turkish massacre
Otranto was a thriving port for Crusaders, pilgrims and traders in the Middle Ages, but in 1480 a Turkish fleet laid siege to the town, which held out for 15 days before capitulating. Nearly 12,000 people were killed in the fighting. Afterwards the Turks had the archbishop sawn in half, and the 800 survivors were taken up a hill to the west of town and beheaded. Their bones were saved in the basilica of SS Pietro and Paolo.

Giovanni be good!
Irish saint Cathal passed through Taranto on the way back from visiting the Holy Land in the 7th century. He was so shocked by the bad behaviour of the inhabitants that he stayed to teach them how to be good!

Dance the *tarantella*
Tarantism is a strange mental illness that appeared in the 16th century and was believed to be caused by the bite of the tarantula spider (*Lycosa tarantula*). Victims could cure themselves by dancing in a trance, the *tarantella*, often for days. At Galatina on the feast day of St Peter and St Paul (29 June), musicians and dancers gather at the chapel of St Paul for performances of the *tarantella*, while in late August there is an entire night of *tarantella* dancing at nearby Melpignano. You do not have to be bitten by a spider to dance your very own *tarantella*!

⑬ Matera
The town of the troglodytes

Matera is a town like no other. Built of the same soft creamy-gold tufa stone as the ravine that slices through it, the town is honeycombed with cave-dwellings (and cave-churches), known as the Sassi. Post-war, it was one of the poorest places in Italy, its starving people living in caves with no facilities; 15,000 people were rehoused in the 1960s in modern apartment blocks. Today, Matera has many boutique hotels and excellent restaurants.

Relief of a skull on the Chiesa del Purgatorio

Key Sights

① Chiesa del Purgatorio
The elliptical façade of the 17th-century Chiesa del Purgatorio is ghoulishly decorated with screaming skulls and skeletons.

② Convincinio Sant'Antonio
These four interlinked churches were used as wine cellars in the 18th century. There are wine spouts emerging from an altar.

③ Ruined Sassi Climb up steps from the Sassi di Matera Hotel through a series of unrestored Sassi, which retain stoves carved into the stone.

④ The Sassi The Sasso Caveoso and Sasso Barisano districts are reached by winding down from the Upper Town through a steep labyrinth of twisting stepped alleyways cut into the rock.

⑤ Madonna de Idris
The most theatrically sited of the *chiese rupestri* (cave-churches) soars above the Sassi, fused to conical Monte Errone. Inside are 14th-century frescoes.

⑥ Casa Grotta Visit this reconstructed Sasso dwelling, which was inhabited until the 1950s. Chickens were kept under the iron bed and the whole family ate out of one dish.

⑦ The upper town The heart of the upper town is Piazza Vittorio Veneto, a spacious square at its liveliest in the early evenings; stroll along Via San Biagio to see some lovely palazzos and churches.

The Lowdown

🌐 **Map reference** 9 D4
Address 75100 Matera, Basilicata. Chiesa del Purgatorio: Via Ridola, 75100. Convincinio Sant'Antonio: Vico Solitario, 75100. Madonna de Idris: Via Madonna dell'Idris, 75100. Casa Grotta: Vico Solitario 11, 75100; *www. casagrotta.it.*

🚗 **Train** Ferrovie Appulo Lucano (FAL) from Bari or from Potenza via Altamura (*www.fal-srl.it*; not Sun). **Bus** (*www.sitabus.it*) from Taranto, Metaponto or Potenza (for FS trains)

ℹ **Visitor information** Via de Viti de Marco 9, 75100; 0835 331 817; *www.aptbasilicata.it.* Sassi di Matera: Via Lanera 33, 75100; 0835 314 244; *www.sassidimatera.it*

🕙 **Open** Casa Grotta: 9:30am–dusk daily

💶 **Price** Casa Grotta: €6

🚩 **Guided tours** Pick up a self-guided map and itinerary from the tourist office or join a tour by Nuovi Amici dei Sassi (*Piazza Sedile 20; 0835 331 011).*

👫 **Age range** Fun for all ages, but there is no level ground. Watch toddlers on uneven steps.

⏱ **Allow** 1 day

🎭 **Festivals** Festa di Santa Bruna, Madonna statue carried on a *papier mâché* float, which is broken up by the crowds: 2 Jul

Good family value?
Strolling around the alleyways of the Sassi is fascinating and free.

The steep, twisting alleyways and old houses of the Sassi of Matera

Letting off steam

To explore the caves and *chiese rupestri* on the far side of the ravine, cross the river further up towards the Sasso Barisano into the **Parco della Murgia Materana** *(www.parcomurgia.it)*. Details of guided tours of the park and bus transfers from Matera can be found on *www.ceamatera.it*. Alternatively, on a hot day, drive to the **Lido di Metaponto** for a swim at the sandy beach.

Eat and drink

Picnic: under €25; Snacks: €25–40; Real meal: €40–80; Family treat: €80 or more (based on a family of four)

PICNIC Dal Buongustaio *(Piazza Vittorio Veneto 1, 75100; 0835 377 982)* is a good place to pick up local cheese, salami and ham for picnics.
SNACKS Caffè Tripoli *(Piazza Vittorio Veneto 17, 75100)* has delicious *gelato* and pastries.
REAL MEAL Il Cantuccio *(Via delle Beccherie 33, 75100; 0835 332 090)* is a family-run trattoria where prices are reasonable and the food

Fly's-eye view of Il Cantuccio, a friendly trattoria with unforgettable food

unforgettable: start with the mixed *antipasti*, the highlights of which are a fresh ricotta drizzled with sticky wine must and a *caponata* (cooked vegetable salad); and follow with a soup – in winter the broccoli, porcini and truffle soup is superb.
FAMILY TREAT Le Botteghe *(Piazza San Pietro Barisano 22, 75100; 0835 344 072)* is located in a vaulted room inside an old palace scooped into the tufa. Try the *antipasti*, which include a tasting plate with local vegetables and buffalo mozzarella. Alternatively, as the restaurant is known for its meat, consider skipping straight to a steak or locally raised lamb.

Shopping

Punto Catenella *(Via B Buozzi 20, 75100; 0835 319 476)* is a friendly shop selling embroidered drawstring bags and clothes items.

Find out more

DIGITAL There is some great, spooky black and white film footage that marvellously evokes how life once was in Matera at *www.legrottedellacivita.com.*

Next stop...

MASSAFRA There are lavishly frescoed cave-churches at Massafra, a little town 40 km (25 miles) to the southeast (just off the SS7 to Taranto). To visit them, call in at the tourist office in the centre of town *(Piazza Garibaldi 1, 74016, Massafra, Puglia; 0998 804 695)* and a guide will take you on a fascinating 90-minute walking tour of three of the best churches.

The beautiful Maratea Coast, seen from Marina di Maratea

⑭ Maratea Coast

Unspoilt rocky coastline

Stretching for just 30 km (19 miles), from Sapri (in Campania) to Tortora (in Calabria), the Maratea coast is unspoiled, with crystal water, sandy beaches, sheer cliffs punctuated with caves and five fishing villages that have developed into smart little resorts. The liveliest town is **Fiumicello**, which has some great places to stay and eat. **Marina di Maratea** is where wealthy Italians go to see and be seen, with a smart yacht marina and cafés and bars to match. The longest, and best known beaches are at Fiumicello and **Acquafredda**, but there are many smaller beaches to explore in between – and outside July and August there is a good chance of finding them deserted.

Letting off steam

If it is not too hot, make the hour's climb from Piazza Buraglia in Maratea town centre to the top of **Monte San Biagio** (624 m/2,050 ft). It is not a hard climb, but cannot be done with a pushchair. From the summit there are fabulous views over the Golfo di Policastro, and the chance to get a close-up look at the **Redentore**, or Redeemer, a giant marble Christ with arms outstretched. At the top, the **Santuario di San Biagio** occupies the site of a temple dedicated to Minerva and holds the relics of the saint. If it is too hot for climbing up the hill, go for a swim at **Macarro** beach just outside Maratea town, against a backdrop of maquis.

The Lowdown

🌐 **Map reference** 11 B1
Address Maratea, 85046, Basilicata

🚗 **Train** to Maratea, Acquafredda and Marina di Maratea on the Napoli–Reggio Calabria line (www.trenitalia.it). **Buses** to towns along the coast (all year). **Minibus** between Marina di Maratea, Fiumicello and Maratea (summer only). **Taxi** from Maratea train station to Fiumicello (5 minutes)

ℹ️ **Visitor information** Piazza del Gesù, Fiumicello, 85046 Maratea; 0973 876 908; www.discoverbasilicata.com

🧒 **Age range** All for beaches

🤸 **Activities** Boat trips to grottoes; ask at tourist office

⏱️ **Allow** At least a couple of days

☕ **Eat and drink** *Real meal* El Sol, *(Via Santa Venere 151, 85046 Fiumicello; 0973 876 920)* offers reasonably-priced pizza and seafood. *Family treat* Il Sacello, the restaurant of La Locanda delle Donne Monache, *(Via C Mazzei 4, 85046 Maratea; 0973 876 139; www.locanda monache.com)* serves excellent fish and seafood

🎉 **Festivals** Festa di San Biagio; (procession of saint's statue up Mt San Biagio): 2nd Sun in May

⑮ Tropea

The town of red onions

Famous throughout Italy for its red onions, Tropea is without a doubt the most spectacular of the coastal towns on the southern Tyrrhenian sea, fused atop a cliff towering high above its marvellous sandy beach. It is a thoroughly charming place, with a walkable historic centre where the Norman cathedral houses two unexploded bombs dropped by the Allies in World War II. The bird's-eye views from town are marvellous, stretching out over Santa Maria dell'Isola, a former medieval Benedictine sanctuary, to the active volcanic cone of Stromboli (see p361).

Letting off steam

Head to the town beach at Tropea or to **Capo Vaticano** (20 minutes' drive south; bus in summer), which has good beaches at Grotcelle and Tonicello. There is another lovely beach at **Briatico**, 16 km (10 miles) to the northeast.

The church of Santa Maria dell'Isola on top of a large rock outcrop facing Tropea

The Lowdown

🌐 **Map reference** 11 B4
Address 89861 Tropea, Calabria

🚗 **Trains** from Lamezia Terme, or from Reggio di Calabria via Rosarno (www.trenoitalia.it). **Buses** along the coast (summer only)

ℹ️ **Visitor information** Piazza Ercole, 89861 Tropea; 0963 61475; www.prolocotropea.eu

🧒 **Age range** All

🤸 **Activities** Boat trips to grottoes; ask at tourist office

⏱️ **Allow** 2 days with beaches

☕ **Eat and drink** *Snacks* Le Volpi e L'Uva *(Via Garibaldi 11, 89861 Tropea; 0963 61900)* is a friendly *enoteca* (wine bar), which has good savoury snacks. *Real meal* La Cantina del Principe *(Largo Galluppi 18, 89861 Tropea; 0963 609 399)* serves traditional local dishes in a converted wine cellar.

🎉 **Festivals** La Sagra della Cipolla Rossa (Red Onion Festival): Jul.

⑯ Calabria's mountains

Aspromonte and the Sila, if you dare

Calabria has two great mountain ranges, the Sila and Aspromonte. **Aspromonte**, the toe of Italy's boot, is a wild place, notorious as a stronghold of 'ndrangheta, the Calabrian mafia. Banditry exists, but the sensible traveller should have little to fear. Densely forested with oak and beech, and poorly sign-posted, much of it is traversed by rocky tracks passable only in an off-road vehicle. It is easy to get lost here. Although it is now a national park, there are no signs of tourism taking over the area, although the ski centre of **Gambarie** is popular with southerners seeking the snow. The fascinating, virtually abandoned Byzantine village of **Pentedattilo**, named for the five-fingered rock above it (from *penta*, meaning five, and *daktylos*, meaning fingers, in Greek) and accessible only from the Ionian coast, is worth a visit, especially for its amazing setting.

The **Sila** massif in the ball of Italy's foot has **La Fossiata**, a conservation area with well-marked walks and picnic spots. One of the most interesting hikes leads to an old brigand stronghold in the remote hamlet of **Longobucco**, at the bottom of a remote, narrow valley. The Sila is famous for its ancient pines, the Giganti della Sila, which can live for hundreds of years. The best base is the ski resort of **Camigliatello Silano**.

Letting off steam

There is no shortage of places to let off steam in the mountains, and there is a beach on the Tyrrhenian coast at

The atmospheric Aspromonte forest in winter

Scilla (legendary home of Scylla, who terrorized Odysseus). To take cover, drive to **Reggio di Calabria** (1 hour from Aspromonte, 3 hours from the Sila) to see the 5th-century BC *Riace Warriors* – 2.3-m (7-ft 6-in) bronzes attributed to Greek sculptor Phidias.

The Lowdown

- 🌐 **Map reference** 11 B5
  Address Calabria: 89057 Gambarie. 87052 Camigliatello Silano. *Riace Warriors*: Palazzo del Consiglio, Reggio di Calabria; www.bronzidiriace.org

- 🚗 **Bus** from Reggio di Calabria to Gambarie, and from Cosenza to Camigliatello Silano. **Car** useful

- ℹ️ **Visitor information** Piazzale Mangeruca, 89050 Santo Stefano in Aspromonte; 0965 743 295; www.parcoaspromonte.it. Casa del Forestiero, Via Roma, 87052 Camigliatello Silano; 0984 578 243; www.parcosila.it

- 🕐 **Open** *Riace Warriors*: 9am–7pm

- 🚻 **Age range** 5 plus for forest walks

- 🕑 **Allow** 1 day or more

- 🍽️ **Eat and drink** *Real meal* La Tavernetta (*Contrada Campo San Lorenzo, 87052 Camigliatello Silano; 0984 579 026*) serves local dishes, with wild mushrooms in season, as well as pasta and meat dishes.

Pentedattilo village, set against the five-fingered rock after which it is named

Where to Stay in Puglia and the South

Puglia and the South are significantly cheaper than northern Italy, and there are some fabulous places to stay, from the cone-shaped *trulli* of Alberobello in Puglia to the cave-dwellings of Matera in Basilicata, plus grand yet unpretentious *masserie* (farms) and charming, stylish B&Bs.

SELF-CATERING AGENCY
Trullidea
080 432 3860; www.trullidea.it
Trullidea offers self-catering accommodation in basic *trulli* (the beehive-shaped houses around Alberobello in Puglia) for both short and long stays.

Andria
Map 9 C2

B&B/AGRITURISMO
Lama di Luna
Loc Montegrosso, 70031; 0883 5695 0510; www.lamadiluna.com
This charming *masseria* (farm), run by its charismatic owner, is 10 km (6 miles) outside Andria on the road to Canosa di Puglia. Its minimalist but comfortable rooms occupy a single-storey 18th-century building that opens onto a garden, and there is a pool, free use of mountain bikes, and pizza on Wednesdays.
🛏 💲 🍴 ⊘ 🍽   €€€

Atri
Map 8 E1

B&B
L'Albero di Antonia
Via A Pacini 5, 64032; 340 928 7626; www.lalberodiantonia.it
This B&B 1 km (half a mile) outside Atri has four stylish rooms and a large garden. Children are welcome: there are friendly dogs and cats to play with, and the owners can organize horse-riding and bike hire.
🛏 💲   €

Lecce
Map 8 E1

B&Bs
Centro Storico
/Azzurretta
Via Vignes 2/b, 73100; 0832 242 727; www.bedandbreakfast.lecce.it
Two family-run B&Bs in one 16th-century building, with vaulted ceilings, balconies and a terrace. Guests at Azzurretta breakfast at Cin Cin bar on Piazza Sant'Oronzo.
🛏 💲   €

Arco Vecchio
Via Quinto Fabio Balbo 5, 73100; 083 243 620; www.arcovecchio.com
A spruce palazzo just off pleasant Via Paladini, with nine minimalist rooms and one suite with a fully equipped kitchen and a terrace.
🛏 💲 🍴   €

SELF-CATERING
Casa dei Mercanti
Piazza Sant'Oronzo 44, 73100; 0832 279 819; wwww.casadeimercanti.it
Nine smart, serviced apartments, with glossy parquet floors and modern furniture, overlooking Piazza Sant'Oronzo.
🛏 🍴   €

Sign at the entrance to boutique B&B Malía, in a 19th-century palazzo, Lecce

Malía
Via Paladini 33, 73100; 0832 307 573; www.maliabb.com.
A boutique B&B with an elegant sitting room, where breakfasts of fruit, bread baked in a wood-fired oven, home-made jams and fresh pastries are served. Two of the four rooms can have an extra bed added.
🛏 ☕ 🥤   €

CAMPING
Namastè
Via Novoli km 4.5, 73100; 0832 329 647; www.ostellolecce.it
Also a yoga centre, this campsite is accessible by bus 26 from Lecce train station, and is open year-round. There are also bungalows, and organic fruit grows on-site.
🛏 💲 ⛺ 📺 🍴 ◐ ☀ 🚶   €

A room at BB Trani 60, in a medieval house in the old ghetto of Trani

Matera
Map 9 DF

HOTEL
Sassi di Matera
Margaret Berg, Via Città 28, Sasso Barisano, 75100; 0835 332 744; www.sassidimatera.com
A sandstone honeycomb of caves transformed into luxury (heated) rooms. Breakfast is served in an old cave church or on the terrace.
🛏 💲 🍴   €€€

Santo Stefano di Sessanio
Map 6 G6

HOTEL
Sextantio
Via Principe Umberto, 67020; 0862 899 112; www.sextantio.it
A radical *albergo diffuso*, scattered among the medieval houses of a hill village. Bare plaster walls and stone floors warmed by under-floor heating.
🛏   €€€

Trani
Map 9 D2

B&B
BB Trani 60
Via La Giudea 60, 70059; 0883 954 763; www.bbtrani60.it
Three contemporary rooms and three mini-apartments with cooking facilities in a medieval house.
🛏 🍴   €

Price Guide
The following price ranges are based on one night's accommodation in high season for a family of four, inclusive of service charges and any additional taxes.

€ Under €200 €€ €200–350 €€€ over €350

Sicily

Sicily is a marvellous family destination, mild even in winter. The ancient Greeks left temples and theatres, the Romans a villa with magnificent mosaics, and there are numerous medieval and Baroque towns to explore, as well as small islands, fantastic beaches and three active volcanoes. And finally there is tantalizing food, from ice cream to fresh fish.

Below *The Greek theatre at Taormina, with views of Mount Etna*

Mount Etna
p358

Agrigento
p352

Siracusa
p362

① Agrigento: Valley of the Temples
Ivory furniture and tombs for pets

The well-preserved golden Greek temples of Agrigento, the ancient site of Akragas, are magnificently located on a ridge above a fertile valley that runs down to the sea. Founded in 581 BC, Akragas was one of Sicily's richest and most powerful Greek cities – visitors reported that its citizens had ivory furniture, abundant silver and gold, and even made elaborate tombs for their pets. A visit to the temples is ideal for families in February, when the almond trees are in blossom, and in spring, when the site is carpeted with wildflowers, but it can be very hot in summer.

Head of statue from Temple of Olympian Zeus

Key Sights

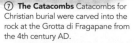

① Temple of Heracles This temple to the hero the Romans called Hercules had 38 columns, but only eight are still standing.

— Entrance

② Museo Archeologico The museum displays Greek and Roman finds such as vases, statues and sarcophagi. There is also a Telamon (pillar in the form of a male statue) from the Temple of Olympian Zeus.

③ Temple of Concord The world's best preserved Doric temple was converted into a Christian basilica in the 6th century AD.

④ Temple of Olympian Zeus Only a few ruins remain of what used to be the largest Doric temple ever built. It was supported by 38 giant Telamons.

⑤ Fortifications Along the ridge below the Temple of Hera are the massive blocks of the city's ancient fortifications.

⑥ The Kolymbetra From the Greek for "pool", this sunken garden with a stream running through it formed part of the city's irrigation system.

⑦ The Catacombs Catacombs for Christian burial were carved into the rock at the Grotta di Fragapane from the 4th century AD.

⑧ Temple of Hera Twenty-five of the temple's original 34 columns are still standing. Steps lead up to an altar where animals were sacrificed to the goddess Hera, known by the Romans as Juno.

Letting off steam

There is no shortage of space to run around in the **Valley of the Temples** – kids can even clamber over the ruins of the Temple of Heracles. It is a 30-minute drive to the stunning white cliffs of **Scala dei Turchi** (7 km/4 miles west of Porto Empedocle, following signs for Realmonte), where there are rocks to climb on and a beach. Alternatively, head further north to the unspoiled beaches at **Giallonardo**, near Siculiana (about

20 km/12 miles from Agrigento), and the **Torre Salsa** nature reserve (about 15 km/9 miles further north).

Eat and drink

Picnic: under €25; Snacks: €25–40; Real meal: €40–80; Family treat: €80 or more (based on a family of four)

PICNIC Via Bac Bac (off Via Atenea, 92100) is centrally located and has a fruit, vegetable and general grocery shop, handy for picnic provisions.

SNACKS Caffè Concordia (Piazza Pirandello 36/7, 92100; 0922 25894) serves sandwiches, ice creams and a

La Terra in Agrigento, serving delicious Sicilian dishes

Prices given are for a family of four

The Lowdown

🌐 **Map reference** 13 D5
Address Strada Panoramica
Valle dei Templi, 92100
Agrigento; 0922 621 611; www.
parcovalledeitempli.it, www.
valleyofthetemples.com

🚗 **Train** to Agrigento Centrale from
Palermo or Caltanissetta, with
connections from Catania (www.
trenitalia.com), then local bus 1,
2 or 3 from outside the station to
the main entrance. **Bus** from
Palermo (Sal; 0922 401 360),
Catania (Sais Autolinee; 0955
36168) and other towns. **Car**
from Palermo or Catania 2 hours

ℹ️ **Visitor information** Via
Empedocle, 92100 Agrigento;
0922 20391

🕐 **Open** 8.30am–7pm daily;
Temples of Concord, Hercules
and Hera also Sat and Sun
7:30pm–midnight, Mon–Fri
7:30pm–10pm Jul–Sep (entry at
the Temple of Hera entrance).
Museo Archeologico:
9am–7:30pm Tue–Sat,
9am–1:30pm Sun & Mon

€ **Price** Valley of the Temples:
€20, under-18s free;
Museo Archeologico: €16,
under-18s free; combined
ticket: €27

👫 **Skipping the queue** Get to the
site by 8am, or before 6:30pm
for evening tickets.

🚩 **Guided tours** Audio tour €5;
excellent guided tours in
English daily at 10:30am and
5:30pm, €56 plus entry fee
(book at www.
valleyofthetemples.com)

👫 **Age range** 5 plus

⏱️ **Allow** 2–4 hours

♿ **Wheelchair access** Partial

☕ **Café** By the main entrance and
the Temple of Hera

🚻 **Toilets** In the cafés.

Good family value?
It is well worth the cost of entry on
a mild day when it is pleasant to
roam, but on a hot day kids may
prefer to escape to the beach.

---

tempting selection of Sicilian
specialities including almond milk,
watermelon jelly and *cassata* (layers
of fruit juice- or liqueur-soaked
sponge, ricotta cheese, candied
fruit and vanilla cream, coated with
marzipan and iced).
REAL MEAL Osteria Expanificio
*(Piazza Sinatra 12, 92100; 0922 595
399; closed Sun and lunch in winter)*
has a terrace on a piazza and good
food. They will cook pasta for kids,
but watch out for extras, which will
be added to the bill.
FAMILY TREAT La Terra *(Via
Francesco Crispi 34, 92100; 0922
29742; closed Mon)* has a lovely
setting in the garden of playwright
Luigi Pirandello's former villa, with a
menu using seasonal Sicilian
produce. Children might like the fish
fillets in a potato crust, and the
mousse of Modica chocolate.

Find out more

DIGITAL On the British Museum
website, at www.ancientgreece.
co.uk/acropolis/challenge/cha_set.
html, kids can build themselves a
virtual Doric temple and learn about
classical Greek architecture. Older
children will find interesting

information about the history of the
Agrigento temples at www.valley
ofthetemples.com.

*Scala dei Turchi's white cliffs, a good
place to let off steam after Agrigento*

Next stop...
**TAORMINA, SIRACUSA AND
PALAZZUOLO ACREIDE** See
well-preserved Greek theatres at
Taormina (see p362), Siracusa and
Palazzuolo Acreide (see pp364–5).
The best archaeological museum
in Sicily is at Siracusa (Parco
Landolina, Via Teocrito 66, 96100
Siracusa; 0931 21243; open
9am–9pm Tue–Sun; €24). It houses
the huge quantity of finds from
all over the island, including
magnificent statues and
reconstructed temples.

② Villa Romana del Casale

Roman bikinis

The Villa Romana del Casale was a luxurious 3rd-century villa, built as a country retreat and hunting lodge for Maximianus Herculius, co-emperor with Diocletian from AD 285 to 310. He ruled Africa, and when it came to decorating his new home he brought mosaic artists from there to decorate it. The results were spectacular – the finest surviving set of mosaics in Italy, their African influence evident in the number of wild animals portrayed. Highlights include a circus scene showing a chariot race (with several crashes), 10 girl athletes dressed in bikinis and a 60-m (197-ft) long hunting scene featuring tigers, ostriches, elephants and a rhino being trapped and transported to the games at the Colosseum. Several rooms were designed for Maximianus's children: there is a scene showing a children's circus and a comic hunting scene showing hares and peacocks (a Roman delicacy) chasing children.

The Lowdown

- 🌐 **Map reference** 14 E4
  Address Piazza Armerina 94015; 0935 680 036; www. villaromanadelcasale.it
- 🚗 **Train** from Catania to Enna. **Bus** from Palermo or Enna to Piazza Armerina (www.interbus. it), then local bus (hourly 9am–noon and 3–6pm May–Sep) or taxi (€10; 0935 680 501) to the villa. **Car** 5 km (3 miles) from Piazza Armerina
- ℹ️ **Visitor information** Via Generale Muscara 13, 94015 Piazza Armerina; 0935 684 814; www. piazza-armerina.it
- 🕐 **Open** 10am–6pm daily
- 💶 **Price** £10–20, EU citizens under 18 free
- 👫 **Age range** 5 plus
- 🕐 **Allow** 1 hour
- ♿ **Wheelchair access** No
- 🍴 **Eat and drink** Picnic Supermercati Crai (Via Alessandro Manzoni 88, 94015 Piazza Armerina) stocks essentials. Real meal Ristorante Coccinella (Via Renato Guttuso 8, 94015 Piazza Armerina; 0935 682 374; www.ristorante coccinella. com) serves local specialities.

A mosaic from the Villa Romana del Casale of a hunting scene with a lion

Letting off steam

Just 150 m (150 yards) away, **Romaland** (Contrada Casale, 94015 Piazza Armerina; 0935 686 633; www.romaland.it; open 10am–5pm daily; €16) is an excellent ancient Roman theme park. Eat Roman food, try sports such as javelin and crossbow and watch gladiator fights. There is also a kids' park with ponies.

③ Palermo

Fountains, palaces and puppets

Palermo is Sicily's most exuberant and multi-layered city, packed with historical sights. Arabic cupolas, a fortified Norman cathedral, Byzantine mosaics, medieval and Baroque palazzi and voluptuous fountains jostle for space among vibrant street markets, fashion boutiques and anarchic traffic. Enjoying Palermo with kids takes planning. Perhaps the best way to start is with a walk down Via Alloro into the La Kalsa area. Renaissance Palazzo Abatellis houses the **Galleria Regionale** ①, a collection of medieval art that includes a 15th-century floor-to-ceiling *Triumph of Death* by an unknown artist and a marble bust by

The Lowdown

- 🌐 **Map reference** 13 C3
  Address 90121–90151 Palermo. Galleria Regionale: Via Alloro 4, 90133; 091 623 0011. Museo delle Marionette: Piazza Antonio Pasquauno 5, 90133; www. museo marionettepalermo.it. Palazzo dei Normanni: Piazza Indipendenza, 90129
- 🚗 **Train** to Stazione Centrale. **Bus** to Via P Balsamo. **AMAT** bus in the city (www.amat.pa.it).
- ℹ️ **Visitor information** Piazza Castelnuovo 34, 90141; 091 605 8351 Stazione Centrale; www.palermotourism.com
- 🕐 **Open** Galleria Regionale: 8:30am–6:30pm Tue–Sun; Museo delle Marionette: 9am–1pm and 2:30–6:30pm Mon–Sat, 10am–1pm Sun; Palazzo dei Normanni: 8:15am–5pm Mon–Sat
- 💶 **Price** Galleria Regionale: €16–32, EU citizens under-18s free. Museo delle Marionette: €16. Palazzo dei Normanni: €17–34, EU under-18s free
- 👫 **Age range** 5 plus
- 🕐 **Allow** One day
- 🍴 **Eat and drink** Snacks I Cuochini (Via R Settimo 68, 90132; Mon–Sat 8:30am–2:30pm) sells deep-fried goodies at 70c a portion. Real meal Trattoria Lo Bianco (Via E Amari 104, 90132; 091 585 816; closed Sun) is one of the cheapest places to eat a typical palermitano meal in town.
- 🎉 **Festivals** Santa Rosalia (fireworks and feasting): 11–15 Jul

Francesco Laurana of one-time queen of Sicily, Eleonora of Aragon. The **Museo delle Marionette** ② is nearby, with a fantastic collection of puppets showcasing the craft of puppetry in Sicily. A visit to the **Palazzo dei Normanni** ③ entering

A long stretch of sandy beach in Cefalù, a train-ride from Palermo

via the Cappella Palatina with its glittering gold mosaics, is like walking into a gilded jewel box.

Letting off steam

Play among the roots of the gigantic *Ficus magnolioides* trees in the **Giardino Garibaldi** or take a train to the beach at **Cefalù** (45 minutes).

④ Monreale

Skinny animals and stone snakes

The little hill-town of Monreale, 8 km (5 miles) from Palermo, is home to one of Italy's most glorious buildings, an exotic Arab-Norman **Duomo** founded in 1172. Its interior is covered with shimmering Byzantine mosaics. In the apse, a mosaic of Christ dominates – his head and shoulders alone are almost 20 m (66 ft) high and his arms and hands are curved as if to embrace the church. Mosaics along the nave tell the story of Creation in animated detail: God filling his world with water, light, animals and people; Adam and Eve; Abraham sacrificing Isaac; and skinny animals boarding a crowded Noah's ark.

The grand Arab-Norman cathedral in Monreale, famous for its golden mosaics

The Arabic influence on the cathedral is clearest in the cloisters, where more than 200 twin white marble columns sprout oriental-style pointed arches. Every capital is different, carved with a fantastic menagerie of winged beasts, birds and snakes, as well as flowers and foliage twined around Bible scenes.

Letting off steam

Climb up to the roof terraces or walk down to the convent grounds behind the cathedral for views along the fertile valley of the Conca d'Oro. Alternatively, take the kids to the mosaic school at **Istituto Statale d'Arte per il Mosaico** (Via Mulini 2; 091 640 2686), to watch students restoring mosaics.

The Lowdown

🌐 **Map reference** 13 C3
Address Duomo: Via Vittorio Emanuele, 90046

🚌 **Bus** 389 from Palermo's Piazza Indipendenza; 20-minute journey

ℹ️ **Visitor information** Piazza Vittorio Emanuele 1, 90046; 091 640 9589

🕐 **Open** Duomo: 8am–6:30pm Mon–Sat, 8am–12:30pm and 3–7pm Sun

💲 **Price** Free

👫 **Age range** 5 plus

⏱️ **Allow** 1 hour

🍴 **Eat and drink** *Picnic* Alimentari Ferraro (Via Roma 58, 90046) is a good source of local cheese, salami and olives, while Panificio Campanella (Piazza Duomo) sells *pane cunzato* (bread with tomatoes, anchovies and oil). *Family treat* Dietro l'Angolo (Via Piave 5, 90046; 091 640 4067; closed Tue) serves refined food and has spectacular views of the Conca d'Oro (the hill-backed plain that surrounds Palermo).

Picnic under €25; **Snacks** €25–40; **Real meal** €40–80; **Family treat** €80 or more (based on a family of four)

⑤ Trapani

A city built on salt

Africa seems very close in Trapani, its sun-scorched streets of cubic houses and sand-blown palm trees spread along a sickle-shaped peninsula to a Spanish fortress. A gutsy port, Trapani's fortune was made from tuna and salt. The salt pans are just south of town along the road to Marsala, where the **Museo del Sale** shows how a windmill transfers water from pool to pool and grinds the harvested salt. It is possible to sample dishes such as fish baked in salt in the museum's Trattoria del Sale.

The main streets of Trapani's historic centre have been pedestrianized, with plenty of places to eat and drink, making Trapani a fine, family-friendly town from which to begin or end a tour of Sicily's west, or a sojourn in the Egadi Islands.

There is a sandy beach in the middle of town and a traffic-free walkway above the beach, which runs down to the Spanish bastions and eventually continues to the Spanish Torre di Ligny at the end of the promontory.

Letting off steam

If kids tire of running up and down the traffic-free streets, there is a park, **Villa Margherita**, opposite the station. As well as the town **beach**, there are beaches along Lungomare Dante Alighieri. To get away from it all, head to the **Riserva Naturale dello Zingaro** (www.riservazingaro. it), a coastal nature reserve about 50 km (31 miles) away, with white sand and pebble beaches, secluded coves and bands of lush maquis (scrub) threading through dramatic limestone peaks, gullies and caves.

Museo del Sale, set in a restored windmill by the salt pans near Trapani

Prices given are for a family of four

The Lowdown

- 🌐 **Map reference** 13 B3
  Address 91100 Trapani.
  Museo del Sale: Via Chiusa Nubia, Paceco, 91021; 0923 867 142; wwwtrattoriadelsale.com
- 🚗 **Train** from Palermo to Stazione Centrale. **Bus** from Agrigento (www. autolineelumia.it), Palermo (www. segesta.it) and other towns to central bus station. **Hydrofoils** and **ferries** from Stazione Marittima to the Egadi Islands (www.siremar.it, www.usticalines.it)
- ℹ️ **Visitor information** Via Torrearsa, 91100; 0923 544 533; www. comune.trapani.it/turismo
- ⏰ **Open** Museo del Sale: 9am–7pm daily
- 👫 **Age range** All

- ⏱️ **Allow** Half a day for the town and salt museum plus a day for beaches and nature reserve
- ☕ **Eat and drink** *Snacks* Pizzeria Calvino (Via N Nasi 77, 91100; closed Tue) is a Trapani institution that has been making pizza since 1946. Try the local speciality, *rianata* with tomato, *pecorino* cheese and oregano, or sausages and potatoes roasted with onions in the pizza oven. *Real meal* Le Mura (Viale delle Sirene 15/19, 91100; 0923 872 622), on the seafront below the Bastione della Conca, serves lovely fish dishes.
- 🎭 **Festivals** Good Friday processions (wooden statues depicting the Passion are carried through streets), 2pm–midnight.

Cable car running from Trapani to Erice, making for a thrilling ride

⑥ Erice

Flying gondolas

Hill-top Erice is most excitingly approached by gondola cable car from Trapani – although there is a road. The medieval town perched on top of Monte San Giuliano is magical, the kind of place a fairy-tale princess might live. It is ringed by walls, its streets cobbled with the same grey stone from which its houses are built. It is, however, very popular, so avoid visiting in July and August and, to see Erice at its best, stay overnight.

Austere from the outside, many houses conceal exquisite courtyards. Climb the 108 steps of the bell-tower-cum-watchtower to the left of the Chiesa Madre for fine views of the town, mountains and coast, or head east from the Porta Trapani along Viale Conte Pepoli to the 12th-century Castello di Venere, fused to a crag, clad with ivy and incorporating chunks of a ruined

Greek temple to Aphrodite within its walls. There are more fantastic views from here.

Letting off steam

There are public gardens below the Castello di Venere. Alternatively, drive to the little-known **Monte Cofano coastal nature reserve** (www.parks.it), 30 km (18 miles) away, where a limestone headland juts out into the sea, sheltering sandy beaches and fostering rare flowers. In the 19th century, caves in the cliffs were inhabited by hermits famous for casting out demons.

The Lowdown

- 🌐 **Map reference** 13 B3
  Address 91016 Erice
- 🚗 **Funivia** (cable car) from Trapani. **Bus** 21 or 23 to the terminal from Piazza Vittorio Emanuele, Trapani
- ℹ️ **Visitor information** Via Guarrasi 1, 91016; 0923 869 388
- 👫 **Age range** All
- ⏱️ **Allow** 2 hours
- ☕ **Eat and drink** *Snacks* Le Rustichelle (Piazza Umberto I 13, 91016; 0923 869 716; open daily) has lots of tables outside and serves pizza, bruschetta, and a great selection of *arancini* (deep-fried, stuffed rice balls). *Real meal* La Pentolaccia (Via G F Guarnotti 17, 91016; 0923 869 099; closed Tue) is a friendly but elegant choice for delicious handmade pasta dishes, couscous and fish.
- 🎭 **Festivals** Good Friday processions

⑦ The Egadi Islands

Tuna and tufa

The Egadi Islands are the easiest of Sicily's islands to visit – Levanzo and Favignana are less than half an hour by hydrofoil from Trapani. The largest of the islands, **Favignana** (10 km/6 miles from end to end), is arid and rocky, covered with scrub and cacti, its sun-bleached, fortified farmhouses flat-roofed with towers and tiny windows. Ancient tufa quarries, some of them now home to exotic gardens, add a surreal note to the landscape, while the serrated coastline shelters coves of turquoise and indigo waters such as Cala Azzurra and Cala Rossa. The port town is a workaday place out of season, with a lively central piazza and abundant tuna shops (the island is famous for the fish).

Tiny **Levanzo** (4 km/2 miles long) has a single whitewashed village and a steep, rocky coastline riddled with caves, including the Grotta del Genovese, which has incised Palaeolithic drawings and Neolithic paintings of animals on its walls. There is also a lovely white pebble beach facing splintered offshore rocks (turn left on leaving the port).

Marettimo is the most remote of the islands. It has just one village of square white houses with blue shutters and cascades of pretty bougainvillea. There are lovely hikes amid limestone pinnacles here.

Letting off steam

All the islands have networks of clearly marked paths to explore. Those on Favignana and Levanzo are pretty level, and the white roads that crisscross Favignana are navigable with a three-wheel buggy. Marettimo is more mountainous. To cool off, take a boat trip from Cala Dogana to the Grotta del Genovese on Levanzo (339 741 8800; departs 10:30am, returns 3:30pm) or a boat tour around Favignana, departing from its port.

The Lowdown

- 🌐 **Map reference** 13 A3
  Address Favignana 91023
- 🚗 **Ferries** and **hydrofoils** from Trapani (Siremar: 0923 545 455; www.siremar.it or Ustica Lines: 0923 873 813; www.usticalines.it).
- ℹ️ **Visitor information** Piazza Madrice 78, Favignana, 91023; 0923 921 647; www.isoleegadi.it
- 👫 **Age range** All – the islands are a kids' paradise, but for Marettimo they will need to be walkers
- ⏱️ **Allow** Favignana and Levanzo make good day trips, while Marettimo is best explored by boat or on foot over a few days.
- 🍵 **Eat and drink** Picnic SMA (top of Via Roma, Favignana) is a supermarket selling picnic food and local ricotta. The Costanza bakery, also on Via Roma, makes some of the best bread in Sicily. Snacks Arte Pizza (Via Mazzini 16, off Piazza Madrice, Favignana; closed Wed) sells excellent take-away pizza. Restaurants tend to be overpriced here.

Whitewashed houses around the harbour on Levanzo, one of the Egadi Islands

Picnic under €25; **Snacks** €25–40; **Real meal** €40–80; **Family treat** €80 or more (based on a family of four)

⑧ Mount Etna
Nature's fireworks

Sicily straddles the European and African tectonic plates, whose jostlings are responsible for a chain of volcanoes, most famously Mount Etna – the highest in Europe. It has three main craters and more than a hundred smaller cavities from which lava flows. The spectacle of Etna in full eruption is unforgettable. At other times, take a cable car to the summit, or explore the solidified rivers and seas of lava and carbonized trees on the lower slopes. Picnic in the forests, walk to caves and ski.

Mount Etna erupting with clouds of smoke

Key Features

Eruptions At this point in history, eruptions in the central crater are rare, but they are frequent in the side vents, and here they create smaller secondary cones.

Principal craters These are called Trifoglietto I and II, and Mongibello.

Lowland landscapes The breakdown of volcanic material in the valley below Mount Etna has resulted in very fertile land, which supports almonds, olives, grapes, citrus fruits and vegetables below 1,000 m (3,280 ft).

Catania

Cable car

Zafferana Etnea

Valle del Bove A popular excursion is from the town of Zafferana Etnea to the Valle del Bove, the spectacular hollow whose shape was changed by eruptions in 1992.

Catania Situated between the Ionian Sea and the slopes of Mount Etna, Catania (see p360) has always had a close relationship with the volcano, and most of the city's buildings are made from black lava.

Cable car The cable car up Mount Etna leaves from Rifugio Sapienza. There is a jeep service from the top cable car station to the main crater, or it is a 4-hour trek.

The Lowdown

🌐 **Map reference** 14 G4
Address Catania Province. Etna Adventure: Parco Scarbaglio, Via Acque del Vescovo, 95010 Milo; 329 918 8187, www. etnaadventure.it

🚗 **Car** or guided **jeep** are easiest. **Bus** Daily from Catania to Rifugio Sapienza and back (www.azienda sicilianatrasporti.it) or bus from Taormina to Castiglione di Sicilia and Motta Camastra (0935 565 111; www.interbus.it). **Train** Circumetnea from Catania to Bronte and Maletto circles the base of Etna Mon–Sat (www. circumetnea.it). **Cable car** From

Rifugio Sapienza, with jeep link to main crater 9am–sunset, weather and eruptions permitting (www.funiviaetna.com).

ℹ️ **Visitor information** Via Etnea 107a, 95030 Nicolosi; 095 914 588; www.parcoetna.it; www. parks.it; www.comune.catania.it

🕐 **Open** Etna Adventure: 10am–8pm Jun–Sep, weather permitting

💶 **Price** Etna Adventure: €40–60, adults and children over 1 m 40 cm (4 ft 7in) €15; children 1 m 30 cm (4 ft 3 in) to 1 m 40 cm €12; children 1 m 10 cm (3 ft 7 in) to 1 m 30 cm €8; children aged 2–5 €5

👫 **Age range** 8 plus

Activities Etna Adventure arranges child-friendly activities and its refuges offer excursions. White-water rafting and wading can be organized at Gole di Alcantara (www.terralcantara.it)

⏱️ **Allow** 3 or 4 days

☕ **Café** At Etna Adventure, Rifugio Sapienza and Rifugio Citelli

Good family value?
Etna is a great place for families, with all the thrills of the volcano, a river gorge and Etna Adventure, but activities do not come cheap.

Delicious Sicilian ice creams on display at Pasticceria Conti Gallenti, Bronte

Letting off steam

Visit the excellent **Etna Adventure**, an adventure park with challenging Tarzan-like obstacle courses for adults and children (from age 2 and up). They also organize all manner of activities on and around Etna, including snowshoe trekking, white-water rafting, potholing and, for the timid, tours by jeep.

Eat and drink

Picnic: under €25; Snacks: €25–40; Real meal: €40–80; Family treat: €80 or more (based on a family of four)

PICNIC Alcantara Formaggi *(Via Federico II 105, 95012 Castiglione di Sicilia; 0942 984 268)*, a family-run artisan factory, is a good place to buy cheeses. Picnic by the Piccole Gole, at Etna Adventure, or along the road that climbs Etna from Linguaglossa, perhaps at Salto di Bove, where there is a house that sells home-made wine and honey.
SNACKS Pasticceria Conti Gallenti *(Corso Umberto 275, 95034 Bronte)* is a good place to taste ice cream, biscuits and other delicacies made of Etna pistachios.
REAL MEAL Turismo Rurale Parco Statella *(2 km/1 mile outside Randazzo on the SS187, direction Linguaglossa; 095 924 014; www.parcostatella.com)* is a family-run restaurant on a country estate. Their passion for wild mushrooms is evident in the signature dish, *zuppa dei funghi* (wild mushroom soup) served with hot *crostini*. Children can play in the grounds after lunch.
FAMILY TREAT Sine Tempore *(Hotel Federico Secondo, Via Maggiore Baracca 2, 95012 Castiglione di Sicilia; 0942 980 368)* uses local produce to fine effect in dishes such as handmade pasta with *porcini* mushrooms, wild fennel or pistachios and *involtini* of veal stuffed with Alcantara cheese.

View of Mount Etna at sunrise from the town of Taormina

Take cover

In cold weather, there is no cosier place to warm up with a hot drink than the mountain refuge **Rifugio Ragabo** *(Strada Mareneve, Pineta Bosco Ragabo, 95015 Linguaglossa; 095 647 841; www.ragabo.it)*.

Shopping

Pieces of lava, crystals and other volcanic souvenirs are for sale at the Rifugio Sapienza cable car station.

Find out more

DIGITAL The website *www.volcanolive.com* has links to webcams on Mount Etna. To learn more about how volcanoes erupt, visit *www.geo.mtu.edu/volcanoes*.

Next stop...
CASTIGLIONE DI SICILIA
The most alluring of Etna's towns, Castiglione di Sicilia has a ruined castle and a series of Byzantine frescoes in the church of San Nicola.

The medieval town of Castiglione di Sicilia, to the north of Mount Etna

⑨ Catania

An elephant and a bomb raid

Mount Etna looms high over Catania. A volcanic eruption in 1693 completely destroyed the city, and its centre was entirely reconstructed of Etna lava – even the streets and piazzas are paved with lava. The 18th-century rebuilding created imposing Baroque edifices, set on broad, straight streets and unevenly shaped squares, a precaution against earthquakes. Today it is a big, bustling and rather austere city, with a compact historic centre, perfect for a city day out.

Via Etnea slices through Catania, with Etna rising at one end. At the other end is Piazza Duomo, a large pedestrianized space with a lava monument of an elephant (Catania's emblem) in its centre. Black lava buildings trimmed with white limestone dominate: the Duomo's façade incorporates columns filched from the city's Roman amphitheatre (still visible 500 m/500 yards away on Piazza Stesicoro), while inside is the elaborately decorated chapel of the city's patron saint, Agatha, whose statue and relics are paraded through the city during the Festa di Sant'Agata (3–5 February). At the far end of the piazza, steps lead down to the Pescheria, where Catania's exuberant morning fish, fruit and vegetable market is held.

A wander along Via dei Crocifissi leads past the best of the city's black and white Baroque buildings. Back on Piazza Duomo, bus 1 or 4 goes to the train station, beyond which, housed in the former sulphur works of Le Ciminiere, is a superb arts complex. Its highlight is the **Museo Storico dello Sbarco in Sicilia 1943**, a tiny museum devoted to the Allied invasion of Sicily, where kids can experience a simulated bombing raid in a reconstructed Sicilian village.

Letting off steam

Piazza Duomo is fine for a quick run around. The centre's best park is **Villa Bellini**, further up Via Etnea, which has a playground. The gardens here also have lots of space for running free. For an outing, take the **Circumetnea train**, which circles Etna from its station at Via Caronda, at the northern end of Via Etnea by the Borgo metro station.

The Lowdown

🌐 **Map reference** 14 G4
Address 95121–95131 Catania. Museo Storico dello Sbarco in Sicilia 1943: Viale Africa, 95121; 095 533 540; www.provincia.ct

🚆 **Train** from Palermo, Messina, Siracusa and other towns to Stazione Centrale. **Long-distance bus** to Stazione Centrale (www.saisautolinee.it; www.azienda sicilianatrasporti.it; www.interbus.it). **City bus** 1/4, 4/7, 438 and 448 to Piazza Duomo (www.amt.ct.it). **Circumetnea** train and buses to Etna (www.circumetnea.it)

ℹ️ **Tourist information** Via Vittorio Emanuele 172, 95121 (near the Duomo); 800 841 042; www.aptcatania.it

🕐 **Open** Museo Storico dello Sbarco in Sicilia 1943: Tue–Sun 9:30am–12:30pm, Tue & Thu also 3–5pm

💶 **Price** Museo Storico dello Sbarco in Sicilia 1943: €8–10

👫 **Age range** 5 plus

⏱️ **Allow** 2 hours

☕ **Eat and drink** Snacks Internetteria (off Via Etnea at Via Penninello 44, 95124) serves good salads and sandwiches, and has tables outside on a traffic-free street. Real meal Antica Marina (Via Pardo 29, 95121; 095 348 197; closed Sun eve) is a homely trattoria in the heart of the fish market serving reasonably priced fresh fish dishes.

🎊 **Festival** Sant'Agata – street party, food stalls, fireworks and procession of St Agatha statue through Catania's streets: 3–5 Feb

The lava façade of Catania's Baroque Duomo, incorporating Roman columns

⑩ Taormina

Theatre with a view

Taormina is the most popular tourist destination in Sicily, a beguiling medieval hill town cascading with flowers, in an astonishing setting – with Etna soaring up behind and two fabulous bays spreading out below. The main pleasure of Taormina is wandering around its pedestrianized main street, Corso Umberto I, where sights include Gothic Palazzo Corvaja, a medieval clocktower and, inside the church of Santa Caterina, the remains of a Roman odeon, a small theatre for concerts and recitals.

The city's finest historical monument is even older – an ancient **Greek theatre** – with views of Etna, the Sicilian coast and across the Ionian Sea to Calabria. Finally, one of the most fun things to do in Taormina is to go down to the beach – a cable car sweeps down the hillside every 15 minutes from Via Pirandello.

Letting off steam

The **Giardino Pubblico**, below Corso Umberto I on Via Bagnoli Croce, is a lush park with pavilions, pagodas and a children's play area created in 1899 by a British woman, Florence Trevelyan, who settled in Taormina. Otherwise, hop on a cable car and head to the beach.

The popular beach in the Bay of Mazzarò, just below Taormina

The Lowdown

🌐 **Map reference** 14 G3
Address 98039 Messina

🚗 **Train** from Messina, Catania and Siracusa to station on coast way below town, then erratic bus or taxi (€15). **Bus** from Catania and Messina to central Via Pirandello. **Cable car** down to Mazzarò and beach from Via Pirandello

ℹ️ **Visitor information** Piazza Santa Caterina, Taormina, 98039; 0942 23243, www.gate2taormina.com; also in the train station

🕐 **Open** Teatro Greco (Via Teatro Greco, 98039; 0942 23220): 9am–1 hour before sunset daily

💶 **Price** Teatro Greco: €16–32

👫 **Age range** All

⏱️ **Allow** A day for town and beach

🍴 **Eat and drink** Snacks Vecchia Taormina (Vico Ebrei 3, 98039; 0942 625 589) is a bustling pizzeria in a little alley close to the Duomo, with tables outside. Real meal La Botte (Piazza San Domenico, 98039; 0942 24198) is a casual, cosy restaurant, popular with locals, that serves a wide selection of Sicilian dishes.

🎭 **Festivals** Classical drama in the Teatro Greco: Jun–Aug. Puppet shows, concerts, folk singing and dancing: Christmas and New Year

⑪ The Aeolian Islands

Volcanoes and donkeys

The seven islands of the Aeolian archipelago are volcanic in origin and include two active volcanoes. **Lipari** is the largest, but the best base for families is twin-peaked **Salina**. Its traffic-free seafront in the village of Lingua, overlooking shallow pebble beaches, is ideal for children. The island is well served by buses: take a trip to Pollara, where the film Il Postino was shot, set on the rim of a collapsed crater and a fine place to snorkel, and to the village of Leni, where a path leads down the mountain to the tiny port of Rinella, with a black sandy beach. There are great views of Europe's most active volcano, **Stromboli**, from Salina. To see the eruptions close up, either take a boat trip around the island or climb it – a tough three-hour ascent. Guided walks (guides obligatory above 400 m/ 1,312 ft) reach the

summit at sunset, with an hour to watch the explosions and a 2-hour descent through slippery ash – so it is only suitable for kids accustomed to trekking. **Vulcano**, the archipelago's second active volcano, is an easier climb – 45 minutes (with strong shoes) to the crater, surrounded by vents billowing stinking sulphurous fumes. The best walk on the islands is the circuit of the smallest, **Panarea**, with fantastic swimming in the beautiful bay of Cala Junco. To get a taste of real isolation, head to **Filicudi** and **Alicudi**. On the latter, the only transport is by donkey.

Letting off steam

Steps lead down to the beach from the piazza at Lingua, **Salina**, where parents can keep an eye on kids as they taste granita ice at the Bar Alfredo. In Santa Marina there is a tiny playground just off the piazza on the seafront piazza. Leni has a larger playground.

Fishing boats pulled up on the black lava beach of the volcanic island of Stromboli

The Lowdown

🌐 **Map reference** 14 G2
Address 98055 Lipari, other islands, 98050 Messina

🚗 **Hydrofoil** from Milazzo, Messina and Palermo; www.usticalines.it. **Car ferries** from Milazzo (www.tirrenia.it). **Bus** on Lipari, Salina and Vulcano

ℹ️ **Visitor information** Corso Vittorio Emanuele 202, 98055 Lipari; 090 988 0095; seasonal office in Santa Marina, Salina

🎒 **Activities** Stromboli guided walks: Magmatrek, Via Vittorio Emanuele, 98050; 090 986 5768; boat trips from the port

🍴 **Eat and drink** Snacks Da Alfredo (Piazza Marina Garibaldi, 98050 Lingua, Salina) is famous for its pane cunzato (Sicilian pizza) and granita (fruit or nut sorbets). Real meal Il Gambero (Piazza Marina Garibaldi, Locauta Lingua, 98050 Salina) serves pizzas and fish.

⑫ Siracusa
Hidden temples and secret fountains

Founded by Greeks from Corinth in 733 BC, ancient Syracuse became the most powerful city in the Western world, partly thanks to its safe, huge, but narrow-mouthed harbour. Traces of its glorious past can be seen in its archaeological park and museum, and dotted around its historic centre, Ortigia, an island where Baroque buildings of mellow golden sandstone twist and turn along a labyrinth of narrow medieval streets. Further traces of the ancient city survive in modern Siracusa.

Statue on the Duomo façade

Key Sights

① **Temple of Apollo** The ruins of this temple, dedicated to the god Apollo, dominate Ortigia's entrance. Dating back to the 6th century BC, it is the oldest Doric temple in Europe.

[Map showing: Museo Archeologico, Parco Archaeological della Neapolis ⑥, VIALE TEOCRITO, VIA TORINO, VIA MONTEGRAPPA, VIALE LUIGI CADORNA, VIA BASENTO, CORSO GELONE, RIVIERA DIONISIO, VIA PAOLO ORSI, VIALE ERMOCRATE, VIA ELORINA, CORSO UMBERTO I, VIA MALTA, Porta Marina Beach, Temple of Apollo ①, Hypogeum ②, Piazza del Duomo ③, Fonte Aretusa and Aquarium ⑤, Castello Maniace ④, ISOLA ORTIGIA. Scale: 0 metres 500, 0 yards 500]

⑥ **Parco Archeologico della Neapolis** A festival of classical Greek drama is held every May/June in the well-preserved ancient theatre. Also see the remains of a Roman amphitheatre and wander through the Latomie (ancient quarries) – the huge caves were used as prisons for centuries.

③ **Piazza del Duomo** The columns of an ancient Greek temple can be seen within the walls of the splendid cathedral. Also on this square is the church of Santa Lucia alla Badia, with a haunting painting by Caravaggio of the *Burial of St Lucy*.

⑦ **Museo Archeologico** Fragments of ancient temples are displayed alongside models and video reconstructions in this vast museum.

④ **Castello Maniace** There are great views of crashing waves from the ramparts of this Norman castle, built in the 13th century by Frederick II.

⑤ **Fonte Aretusa and Aquarium** This fountain on Largo Aretusa, facing the Porto Grande, is fed by a freshwater spring that bubbles up under the sea. Right next to it is an aquarium of tropical fish.

② **Hypogeum** Explore these ancient underground passages and water cisterns, used as bomb shelters during World War II.

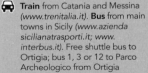

The Lowdown

🌐 **Map reference** 14 G5 **Address** 96100 Siracusa. Hypogeum: Palazzo Archivescovile, Piazza del Duomo. Aquarium: Largo Aretusa, next to the fountain. Parco Archeologico della Neapolis: Viale Paradiso. Museo Archeologio: Parco Landolina, Viale Teocrito 66

🚗 **Train** from Catania and Messina (www.trenitalia.it). **Bus** from main towns in Sicily (www.azienda sicilianatrasporti.it; www. interbus.it). Free shuttle bus to Ortigia; bus 1, 3 or 12 to Parco Archeologico from Ortigia

ℹ️ **Visitor information** Via Maestanza 33; 0931 464255

🕐 **Open** Duomo: 8am–noon, 4–8pm daily. Santa Lucia alla Badia: 11am–2pm, 3–7pm Tue–Sun. Hypogeum: 9am–1pm Tue–Sat. Castello Maniace: 10am–1:30pm Tue–Sun (military zone may be closed). Aquarium: 10am–10pm daily. Parco Archeologico della Neapolis: 9am–1 hour before sunset daily. Museo Archeologico: 9am–7pm Tue–Sat, 9am–1pm Sun (last entry 1 hour earlier)

💶 **Price** Hypogeum: €8–16, children free. Castello Maniace:

€8–16, children free; Aquarium: €14. Parco Archeologico: €16–45, EU citizens under 18 free. Museo Archeologico: same as Parco Archeologico

👪 **Skipping the queue** In May and June arrive at the Parco Archeologico at 9am. Book tickets for the classical theatre season well in advance

🚩 **Guided tours** Official guides to the Parco Archeologico wait in the ticket office.

🚻 **Age range** 5 plus for Parco Archeologico; 11 plus for Museo Archeologico

Letting off steam

Local kids play in pedestrianized **Piazza del Duomo**. Tiny **Porta Marina** beach is fine for a quick splash. Older children may prefer to swim off the rocks of the **Largo della Gancia**. The best beach is at **Arenella**, a 15-minute drive away (or bus 23 from Via Rubino). Take a boat up the River Ciane to see papyrus growing wild (from the bridge over the Ciane on SS115; €10 per person).

Horse-drawn carriage for sightseeing, Piazza del Duomo, Ortigia

Eat and drink

Picnic: under €25; Snacks: €25–40; Real meal: €40–80; Family treat: €80 or more (based on a family of four)

PICNIC Fratelli Burgio (Piazza Cesare Battista 4, 96100) has excellent bread, cheese, ham and salami. Settle down for a picnic on traffic-free Piazza del Duomo.

SNACKS Gran Caffè del Duomo (Piazza del Duomo 18–19, 96100; closed Mon) has cornetti filled with fresh ricotta and savoury pastries.

REAL MEAL Osteria da Seby (Via Mirabello 21, 96100; 0931 181 5619; closed Mon) is a self-service eatery with a great choice of vegetable dishes, plus pasta, grilled fish and meat. In the evening it turns into a proper little trattoria.

🕐 **Allow** 2 days

👫 **Toilets** At Parco Archeologico and museum, and in cafés

🎆 **Festivals** Santa Lucia (parades and fireworks): 13 Dec. Festa dell'Immacolata (processions, heralded by brass band parade at dawn): 29 Nov, 8 Dec. Classical theatre season (www. indafondazione.org): May–Jun

Good family value?
Siracusa's archaeological attractions are good value for EU families, but non-EU families may want to consider their kids' level of interest.

Outdoor café seating on Piazza del Duomo, Ortigia

FAMILY TREAT La Foglia (Via Capodieci 29, 96100; 0931 66233) offers bohemian chic and delicious dishes using local vegetables and legumes. Kids are welcome.

Shopping

Circo Fortuna (Lungomare Levante, Via dei Tolomei 20, 96100; 347 216 3374) creates quirky ceramics.

Find out more

DIGITAL The website www. historyforkids.org/learn/greeks/science/math/archimedes.htm has a fun page on local boy Archimedes.

Take cover

TEATRO DEI PUPI (Via della Giudecca 17–19, 96100; 0931 465 540; www.pupari.com) stages puppet performances. Find out more at the **Museo dei Pupi** (Piazza San Giuseppe, 96100), 2 minutes' away.

Next stop...

PALAZZOLO ACREIDE This Greek theatre, half an hour's drive from Siracusa, stages a Classical Theatre Festival every May (www. palazzolo-acreide.it).

VAL DI NOTO The cities of this region have more fine Baroque buildings (see p364–5).

RISERVA NATURALE L'OASI DI VENDICARI Explore marshlands and a lovely beach, 40 minutes' drive from Siracusa (see p364).

The Riserva Naturale l'Oasi di Vendicari, a protected area full of water birds

---

⑬ Noto

Apricot Baroque, flower carpets and the best ice cream in Italy

In 1693, an immense eruption of Etna, followed by an earthquake, flattened many towns in Sicily. All that was left of Noto was "a mountain of abandoned rocks," according to Giuseppe Lanza, the Sicilian-Spanish aristocrat who was given the job of rebuilding it. He decided to create a new town from scratch, 16 km (10 miles) away, and the people of Noto were furious – they had begun to rebuild among the ruins. But Lanza refused to listen to them, and even had the old town's surviving church demolished.

Rebuilt in Baroque style out of apricot-hued limestone, the new Noto was revolutionary, divided into an upper town for the people, and a monumental lower town, its broad avenues lined with political and religious buildings. The most lavish buildings are in the lower town: the magnificent **Duomo**, restored after the collapse of its dome in 1996; and

The Lowdown

🌐 **Map reference** 14 G6
Address 96017 Noto, Siracusa. Duomo: Via Cavour 88, 96017. Palazzo Villadorata: Via Corrado Nicolaci, 96017; 0931 835 005

🚌 **Bus** Interbus (www.interbus.it) from Catania and its airport; AST from Siracusa, Modica and Scicli (www.aziendasicilianatrasporti.it). **Train** Single-line, single-carriage from Siracusa to Gela, via Noto (www.ferroviedellasiciliasudest.it)

ℹ️ **Visitor information** Via Gioberti 13, 96017; 0931 572 156; www.pronoto.it

🕐 **Open** Palazzo Villadorata: 9am–1pm and 3–7pm Tue–Sun

💶 **Price** Palazzo Villadorata: €16

👫 **Age range** All

🕑 **Allow** A morning or afternoon

🍴 **Eat and drink** Snacks Costanzo (Via Spaventa 7, 96017; 0931 835 243; closed Wed) and Caffè Sicilia (Corso Vittorio Emanuele 125, 96017; 0931 837 582; closed Mon) are cafés that have made Noto famous for its ice cream: try flavours such as wild strawberry, jasmine and rose. Real Meal Enoteca Emily's Wine (Via Cavour 34, 96017; www.enotecanoto.com) serves snacks such as crostini with ricotta and honey.

Noto's Baroque Duomo, at the top of an impressive flight of steps

Palazzo Villadorata, its ornate balconies supported by stone horses, griffons, sirens and cherubs. On the third weekend in May, the streets are carpeted with flower-petal designs.

Letting off steam

The **Giardino Pubblico** at the eastern end of the main street is fine for a picnic. The **Riserva Naturale l'Oasi di Vendicari**, 10 km (6 miles) from Noto, is a coastal nature reserve with marked paths, salt lagoons and some of the best sandy beaches in Sicily. In March and October over 200 species of migratory birds can be spotted and the turtles that used to nest here until eaten almost to extinction are being encouraged back.

⑭ Scicli

Cave-dwellings, Baroque monsters and artists

Scicli is a fascinating small Sicilian town, spilling down from sheer limestone cliffs into three river valleys. The slow pace of life, and traffic-free zones including the magnificent Via Mormino Penna, lined with beautiful Baroque churches and palaces, make it an ideal family destination. Do not miss the monsters snarling on the façade of Palazzo Beneventano, down the street from the curvaceous church of San Bartolomeo; nor the tiny shacks behind the church, where craftsmen make all manner of domestic and garden implements out of scrap metal. There is also a fascinating marked itinerary to follow through the tangle of cave-dwellings and

higgledy-piggledy cottages built into the side of the gorge.

Scicli is also home to the renowned Gruppo di Scicli school of artists, and the **Chiaroscuro** cultural centre holds occasional, stimulating art workshops for kids, as well as concerts and other events. In May, a battle between the Saracens and Normans is re-enacted, while on 19 March, at the Festa di San Giuseppe, people playing the Holy Family are followed through the streets by a procession of horses adorned with flowers.

The Lowdown

🌐 **Map reference** 14 F6
Address Scicli 97018, Ragusa. Chiaroscuro: Via Alberto Mario 1, 97018; 0932 931 1940; www.tecnicamista.it

🚌 **Bus** AST from Siracusa, Modica, Ragusa, Sampieri and Catania (www.aziendasicilianatrasporti.it)

ℹ️ **Visitor information** Via Castellana 2, 97018; 3357 561 960

👫 **Age range** All

🏃 **Activities** Art workshops at Chiaroscuro cultural centre

🕑 **Allow** 2 hours

🍴 **Eat and drink** Picnic Supermercato DiMeglio (Via Cipro 6, 97018, Sampieri) is a block from the beach at Sampieri and sells fresh bread and a good range of cheeses, hams, salamis and olives. Real meal Ristorante Pomodoro (Corso Garibaldi 46, 97018; 0932 931 444) serves seasonal produce in a relaxed, family-run restaurant.

🚻 **Toilets** At Hotel Novecento bar

Monster-adorned balconies at Palazzo Beneventano in Scicli

The church of San Giorgio in Modica at the top of its 250 steps

Letting off steam
Kids can run safely on traffic-free **Via Mormino Penna**. A 10-minute drive from Scicli is tiny **Sampieri**, at the head of a fantastic 4 km (2 mile) beach. Further along the coast is the **Fiume Irminio nature reserve** (*www.parks.it/riserva.macchia.foresta.irminio*), with paths to beaches through bamboo and lentisk and, beyond, the ruins of the ancient Greek city of Kamarina in the dunes.

⑮ Modica
Chocolate and more Baroque
Modica is as well-known for its chocolate as for its Baroque architecture. The art of making chocolate was introduced to Sicily by the Spanish, who ruled the island in the 16th century. They had picked up the technique in their South American colonies, and the chocolate of Modica is still made in the traditional Aztec way, with pure cocoa and sugar. There is no cocoa butter, so Modica chocolate does not melt in the Sicilian sun! Sample it – flavoured with anything from chilli or sea salt to cinnamon and jasmine – at the famous **Antica Dolceria Bonajuto**, or watch it being made at the **Cooperativa Quetzal**, a charitable foundation dedicated to fair trade.

Modica itself occupies the valley formed by the river that used to flow through the city. In 1902 the river flooded (the high-water mark is still indicated with a line at the beginning of Corso Umberto I) and it was then channelled underground. Modica's two most impressive churches are the pretty **San Pietro**, just off Corso Umberto I, and **San Giorgio**, soaring above the lower town at the head of a theatrical flight of 250 steps.

Letting off steam
The limestone gorge of **Cava d'Ispica**, between Modica and Ispica, is honeycombed with caves and ancient tombs cut into the rock. Visit the **Parco Archeologico della Forza** to see cave-dwellings, cave-stables and cave-churches. The energetic can descend 3,300 steps to the valley floor (and back), as the inhabitants did to collect water!

The Lowdown

- 🌐 **Map reference** 14 F6
  Address Modica, 97015. Antica Dolceria Bonajuto: Corso Umberto I 159, 97015; *www.bonajuto.it*. Cooperativa Quetzal: Corso Umberto I 223, 97015; 032 066 374; *www.quetzalmodica.it*
- 🚗 **Bus** Interbus from Catania and airport; AST from Siracusa, Noto and Scicli. **Train** Single-track, single-carriage from Siracusa
- 👫 **Age range** All
- 🤸 **Activities** Chocolate-making; call Cooperativa Quetzal for details.
- ⏱ **Allow** 2 to 3 hours
- ☕ **Eat and drink** *Snacks* Caffè dell'Arte (*Corso Umberto I 114, 97015; 0932 943 257*) serves the best pastries in Modica. Children can have miniature cups of hot chocolate. *Real meal* Osteria dei Sapori Perduti (*Corso Umberto I 228, 97015; www.osteriadei saporiperduti.it*) has a menu in Sicilian dialect; the food is traditional rural fare.

Picnic under €25; **Snacks** €25–40; **Real meal** €40–80; **Family treat** €80 or more (based on a family of four)

Where to Stay in Sicily

Sicily has an abundance of places for families to stay, from simple beachside rooms to charming, family-run hotels, grand country retreats with heaps of space, and B&Bs set in caves and rambling *palazzi*. Perhaps the cream of the crop for children are *agriturismi* in farmhouses with gardens and animals.

AGENCY

Think Sicily
www.thinksicily.com
Lavish villas in stunning locations.
Sicily Cottages
www.sicilycottages.com
Affordable farmhouses and cottages in all regions of Sicily.

Aeolian Islands   Map 14 G2

HOTEL
Delfino
Via Marina Garibaldi 5, 98050 Lingua, Salina; 090 984 3024; www.ildelfinosalina.it
A restaurant on the traffic-free seafront at Lingua, with neat, comfortable rooms. Older rooms open onto the seafront, newer rooms have their own terraces. There are also rooms above sister restaurant Il Gambero, opening onto a terrace with stunning views.
€€

SELF-CATERING
A Cannata Rooms
Via Umberto I 13, 98050 Lingua, Salina; 090 984 3161; www.acannata.it
Self-catering accommodation scattered throughout Lingua.
€€

The Locanda di Terra B&B, with its shady garden, in Agrigento

Agrigento   Map 13 D5

B&Bs
Locanda di Terra
Via F. Crispi 34, 92100; 0922 22275
Beguiling family-run B&B in a 19th-century villa. Five spacious rooms, a shady garden, a sunny terrace and a common room. La Terra restaurant *(see p353)* is in its garden, and there is a babysitting service. Children stay half price.
€

Mille e una Notte
Via Garibaldi 46, 92100; 320 483 5856; www.milleeunanottebeb.it
Sensitively run B&B with spick-and-span rooms, all individually decorated (including two family rooms that sleep four and five), a small apartment with cooking facilities, and a courtyard where children can play. Breakfast is local pastries. Children under seven free.
€

Castiglione di Sicilia   Map 14 G3

HOTEL
Federico Secondo
Via Maggiore Baracca 2, 95012; 0942 980 368; www.hotelfedericosecondo.com
Castiglione's first ever hotel is a smart little place with a very nice restaurant. All rooms are large and comfortable. An excellent town base from which to explore Etna.
€€

Egadi Islands   Map 13 A3

HOTEL
Villa Antonella
Via Punta Marsala 20, 90123 Favignana; 0923 921 073; www.egadi.com
Simple, value-for-money rooms and a self-catering apartment a

10-minute walk from town, run by a friendly and obliging family, who will pick guests up from the port.
€

Erice   Map 13 B3

HOTEL
San Domenico
Via Tommaso Guerrasi 26, 91016; 0923 860 128; www.hotel-sandomenico.it
Sweet, family-run hotel in a medieval house in the heart of Erice, with toys in the sitting room, alongside robust, rustic antiques. Two sets of connecting rooms, and a triple. Breakfast is served in a tiny courtyard.
€€

Modica   Map 6 14 F6

HOTELS
Torre Dantona
Contrada Dantona, Marina di Modica, 97010; 0932 902 495; www.torredantona.it
Ask for a room in the former stables of this 17th-century farm, close to the fabulous beach at Sampieri. The hotel has rich green lawns, a kidney-shaped pool and relaxed, attentive staff. Food is sourced locally – much of it grown by the owners. Breakfasts include home-made cakes, biscuits and bread, and there are simple dishes for lunch and dinner.
€€

Casa Talia
Via Exaudinos 1, 97015; 0932 752 075; www.casatalia.it
Occupying a cluster of restored houses in the old Jewish Ghetto of Modica, Casa Talia is far removed from the bustle of the city centre, yet only five minutes' walk down a series of steps and alleyways to the Corso. It has a garden, and rooms are stylish and practical.

Hotel San Domenico in Erice, with sturdy antique furniture and a toy basket

Excellent breakfasts are served in a fascinating whitewashed room full of nooks and crannies, occupying a former cave cistern and stables.

€€€

B&B
Palazzo Il Cavaliere
Corso Umberto I 259, 97015; 0932 947 219; www.palazzoilcavaliere.it
A down-to-earth aristocratic family run this 18th-century palace as a B&B; do not be surprised to see the owner's children wandering the corridors mid-afternoon in their pyjamas! The setting is splendid and authentic: original Caltagirone tiled floors, frescoed ceilings and beautiful antique furniture. There are eight rooms, three of which open onto a courtyard – ideal for large families or several families travelling together. Excellent breakfasts are served.

€€

Monreale
Map 13 C3

HOTEL
Carrubella Park Hotel
Via Umberto I, 90046 ; 091 640 2187; www.carrubellaparkhotel.com
This charming, family-run hotel, has several rooms suitable for families and very friendly service. Guests are welcome to picnic in style on the lovely terrace, which has stunning views of the Conca d' Oro – perfect for families. Most of the rooms come with a balcony or terrace, also with pretty views. Lots of good choice at breakfast, including fruits and yogurts and cereals – perfect for fussy eaters.

€€

Mount Etna
Map 14 G4

HOTELS
Rifugio Ragabo
Pineta Bosco Ragabo, 95015 Linguaglossa; 095 647 841; www.ragabo.it
A simple, cosy, wooden *rifugio* hotel high up on Mount Etna – the perfect base for active holidays on the mountain in either winter snow or summer sun. All rooms have a TV and bathroom. The restaurant serves rustic *anitpasti* and meat dishes.

€

Parco Statella
2 km (1 mile) from Randazzo on the SS187 (direction Linguaglossa); 095 924 036; www.parcostatella.com
An 18th-century villa with extensive grounds, a paddock where horse-riding lessons are held, swings and a small football field. There are four mini-apartments and a suite that accommodates 6 available. A communal room has games and satellite television.The excellent restaurant serves traditional Sicilian dishes and fine local wines.

€€

Noto
Map 14 G6

B&Bs
Villa Fiorita
Via Principe Umberto 47, 96017; 0931 571 576; www.casafiorita.it.
Run by a friendly, easy-going family from Siracusa, Villa Fiorita has two comfortable mini-apartments, a larger, two-room apartment (all with kitchen), and another bedroom, set in a pretty, 18th-century house in Noto Alto. There are plenty of reasonably priced food shops

nearby, and if the children are not shy they can join local children playing in the piazza behind.

€

Montandon
Via Antonio Sofia 50, 96017; 339 524 4607; www.b-bmontandon.it
This B&B is first choice in Noto for families. Family-run, it is in a friendly street in the historic district of town, and has a huge walled garden with a couple of swings. There is also a little terrace for breakfast, where guests can prepare snacks and *aperitivi*, and make use of a barbecue. Each of the three large, light rooms has its own terrace and is air-conditioned.

€€

AGRITURISMI
Agriturismo Cala Mosche
Cala Mosche entrance, Riserva Naturale l'Oasi di Vendicari, 96017; 347 858 7319.
This agriturismo with six rooms and a restaurant is ideal for families, especially for children who need a lot of space to let off steam. Not only is there the *agriturismo's* own garden to run around in, but the whole of the Vendicari nature reserve and its unspoiled beaches are right on the doorstep. Many parents will feel they can give older children some freedom in the outdoors here.

€€

Fattoria Villa Rosa
Al Casale dei Mori, Contrada da Falconara, 96017 Noto Marina; 0931 812 909; www. alcasaledeimori.com
Comfortable *agriturismo* with 21 rooms (two with cooking facilities) housed in an enchanting creeper covered 18th-century farmhouse set in beautiful grounds. There is a pool, a playground, and excellent home-cooking in its restaurant. The farm's rabbits, chickens and goats (and cats and dogs) can be petted.

€€€

Palermo
Map 13 C3

B&B
Palazzo Pantaleo
Via Ruggero Settimo 74/h, 90141; 091 325 471; www.palazzopantaleo.it
In an excellent location in a quiet courtyard off the smart (and safe) shopping street of Via Ruggero Settimo, this B&B has large, light and well designed rooms. Extra beds can be added for families. There is also a kitchen where guests can make drinks and snacks, and one small self-catering apartment. Central Palermo's only pedestrianized street, Via Principe del Belmonte, is just across the road – a good place to wander with children.

€€

Scicli
Map 14 F6

HOTEL
Hotel Novecento
Via Duprè 11, 97018; 0932 843 817; www.hotel900.it
A gorgeous boutique hotel with friendly, helpful staff, occupying a Baroque palazzo in the heart of Scicli. Stairs of *pietra pece* – limestone naturally impregnated with swirls of petroleum, unique to this area – will intrigue geologically-minded children, while those with an artistic bent can see how local landscapes and beaches have inspired the artists of the Gruppo di Scicli, whose lithographs decorate every room. Excellent breakfasts include ricotta so fresh it is still hot; if children are interested to see how ricotta is made, the owners will be happy to arrange a visit to the cheese-maker.

€€€

Siracusa
Map 14 G5

HOTELS
Gutkowski
Lungomare Vittorini 26, 96100; 0931 465 861; www.guthotel.it
Chic simplicity and intelligent design make this hotel overlooking the sea on the eastern edge of Ortigia a good, restful choice in Siracusa's *centro storico*. It is worth booking well in advance to secure one of the rooms with a private

terrace. There is also a large communal terrace and café.

€€

Caol Ishka
Via Elorina, Contrada Pantanelli, 96100; 0931 69057; www.caolishka.it
Minimalist style coupled with ample grounds, a good swimming pool and a relaxed attitude to children, make this a great choice for any family. Its amenities and location make it easy to interweave lazy days by the pool and nearby beaches (and excursions along the river) with sightseeing forays into the heart of historic Siracusa, a mere 2 km (1 mile) away. Elegantly painted old farm buildings have been converted into chic rooms with spacious bathrooms. In summer there is a ferry direct from the nearby village of Isola across the bay to Ortigia. Children are made welcome in the elegant restaurant, and offered simple dishes that are not on the menu.

€€€

B&Bs
Giuggiulena
Via Pitagora da Reggio 35, 96100; 0931 468 142; www.giuggiulena.it
Belonging to the same owners as Palazzo del Sale *(see above right)*, Giuggiulena is a chic B&B in a clifftop villa above the sea, along the eastern seafront of Siracusa. There are balconies overlooking the water, and close by it is possible to swim in rocky coves or forage in rock pools, yet Ortigia is just a 15-minute walk away. Breakfasts are generous and delicious, and eaten on a balcony overhanging the sea.

€€

The elegantly simple breakfast room at Hotel Gutkowski in Siracusa

Palazzo del Sale
Via Santa Teresa 25, 96100; 0931 69558; www.palazzodelsale.it
This is a stylish but relaxed B&B set in a 19th-century palazzo and former salt-warehouse on a quiet street behind Piazza del Duomo. There are seven spacious rooms with wooden floors, designer beds and intriguing touches such as mirrors framed with driftwood and lamps with palm-bark shades. Breakfasts are superb, and the friendly service makes kids feel instantly at home.

€€€

One of the beautifully decorated rooms at the Palazzo del Sale in Siracusa

Taormina
Map 14 G3

HOTEL
Villa Belvedere
Via Bagnoli Croce 79, 98039; 0942 23791; www.villabelvedere.it
Good value – at least in Taormina – for its great pool, lush gardens and fantastic views, although the rooms are rather plain.

€€€

Trapani
Map 13 B3

HOTEL/SELF-CATERING
Tonnara di Bonagia
Map 6 C5
Piazza Tonnara di Bonagia, 91019 Valderice; 0923 431 111; www.tonnaradibonagia.it
Ten minutes' drive from Trapani and occupying the mellow buildings of an old tuna fishery, this is a perfect base for a pool- and beach-based summer holiday. There is an excellent swimming pool, and activities for children in summer. Paths lead to miniature rocky coves for those who prefer to swim in the sea. Accommodation in either hotel rooms or self-catering apartments.

€€€

Sardinia

At the heart of the Mediterranean, Sardinia has been visited
by most of the players in the power struggles of the past –
Phoenicians, Carthaginians, Romans, Spaniards, even
Admiral Nelson – and they have left behind a rich legacy.
But it is not all history: Sardinia has some of the best beaches
to be found anywhere, with fine sand and clear water.

Below Beautiful Romazzino beach, Costa Smeralda in northern Sardinia

Alghero
p370

Cagliari
p374

① Alghero

Medieval port with a Spanish past

Alghero is an ideal place for families, with myriad attractions from sea caves and beaches to ancient *nuraghe* buildings. Sardinia's oldest resort, the town has a huge range of places to stay and a tempting choice of eateries. In the largely traffic-free old town, the labyrinthine lanes are lined with tiny shops and cafés, and fishing boats are moored alongside glamorous yachts in the port – a reminder of when a mighty Spanish fleet docked here en route to flush out Algerian pirates in 1541.

Streetlamp in the old town

Key Sights

The Lowdown

Map reference 12 E2
Address 07041 Alghero. Nuraghe di Palmavera: *www.coopsilt.it*. Sella e Mosca Winery: 07041 I Piani; *www.sellaemosca.com*. Aquarium: Via 20 Settembre, 07041; *www.aquariumalghero.it*

Train from Sassari. **Bus** from other towns *(www.arstsardegna.it)*; bus AF or AP from station to centre. **Ferry** to Porto Torres

Visitor information Piazza Porta Terra 9, 07041; 079 979 054; *www.alghero–turismo.it*

Open Nuraghe di Palmavera: daily. Sella e Mosca Winery: Mon–Sat Jun–Sep. Grotta di Nettuno: daily. Aquarium: daily Apr–Oct, Sat–Sun Nov–Mar. Trenino Catalano *(336 691 836)* daily Apr–Oct

Price Nuraghe di Palmavera €12–20. Grotta di Nettuno €26–32. Aquarium: €44–60. Trenino Catalano: €10–20

Skipping the queue Avoid visiting in August.

Age range 5 plus

Activities Boat trips: Aquatica *(www.aquaticasardegna.it)*; to the Grotta di Nettuno: Navisarda *(www.navisarda.it)*. Bike hire: Cicloexpress *(www.cicloexpress.com)*

Allow At least two days

Toilets In café-bars

Festivals Festa di Sant Miquel: Sep

Good family value?
Alghero is a family-friendly place to wander, but the cost of attractions and activities adds up (and prices rise in August).

Prices given are for a family of four

① **Beaches** The best beaches are Le Bombarde and Lazzaretto, around 8 km (5 miles) northwest of town. Rent bikes from Cicloexpress by the port to get there.

② **Nuraghe di Palmavera** The ruins of this ancient palace 10 km (6 miles) northwest of town are surrounded by 50 circular huts and date from the 13th and 14th centuries BC.

③ **Sella e Mosca Winery** Tour the vineyards that grow the island's Cannonau grape at this winery, 11 km (7 miles) north of town. There is also a wine museum.

④ **Grotta di Nettuno** A deep cave gouged out of sheer cliffs west along the coast at Capo Caccia, Neptune's Grotto is accessible by boat from the port. Marvel at stalagmites resembling castles.

⑤ **Aquarium** Get face-to-face with exotic creatures of the deep, including huge sharks, turtles, piranhas and eels.

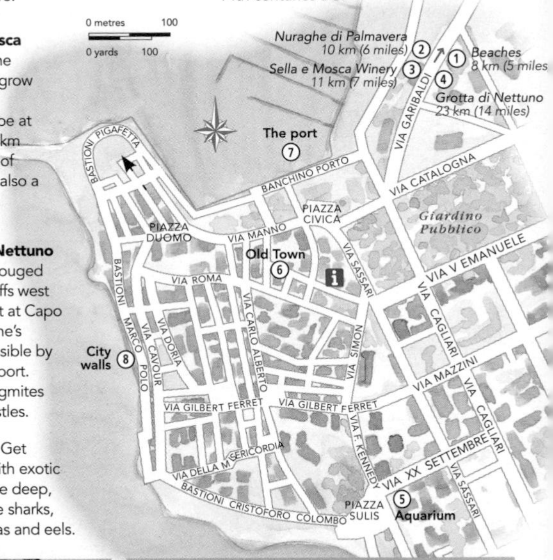

⑥ **Old Town** Tour the old town's narrow maze of lanes on the Trenino Catalano mini-train, from the port in summer.

⑦ **The port** Overlooked by the old city walls, the port is a hive of activity, where boat-tour operators offer trips along the coast to beaches.

⑧ **City walls** Alghero is enclosed within stout walls, which can be walked along, studded with seven watchtowers from the Spanish era.

Boats pulled up by the jetty on one of Alghero's sandy beaches

Letting off steam

Tracing the seafront north of the old town is a broad, car-free promenade, an ideal area for taking the sea air. It leads to **public beaches** as well as **private lidos** where a few euros give access to clean sand, parasols and showers, and pedalos can be rented. Further afield, on the slopes of Monte Timidone, is the **Parco Naturale Regionale di Porto Conte** (www.parcodiportoconte.it; open daily), a protected wildlife zone where miniature horses, white donkeys from the island of Asinara and wild boar graze amid pungent Mediterranean vegetation; take a bus for Capo Caccia to Tramariglio (20 km/12 miles), on the same peninsula as the Grotta di Nettuno.

Eat and drink

Picnic: under €25; Snacks: €25–40; Real meal: €40–80; Family treat: €80 or more (based on a family of four)

PICNIC There is a central **market** (off Via Sassari; Mon–Sat mornings) for the freshest fruit and vegetables, as well as a good selection of cheeses, olives and local bread. Cart the purchases to the *bastioni*, or city walls, where there are plenty of secluded benches overlooking the sea to enjoy an open-air feast.
SNACK Il Ghiotto (Piazza Civica 23, 07041; 079 974 820; open 7:30am–9pm, closes around midnight in summer) has a range of good-value buffet-style pasta, meat and seafood dishes, with tables inside and out. Delicious takeaway items are also available.
REAL MEAL Bella Napoli (Piazza Civica 29, 07041; 079 983 014; closed Nov–Dec, also Wed Jan–Apr and Oct), a bustling ristorante and pizzeria, offers generous portions

and a lively atmosphere. View the remains of an ancient *frantoio*, or olive-mill, inside.
FAMILY TREAT Nettuno (Via Maddalenetta 4, 07041; 079 979 774) is a popular pizzeria and ristorante overlooking the port, with balcony seating (booking essential). Fresh seafood is the speciality.

Shopping

L'Altra Isola (Via Maiorca 107, 07041; 079 975 171; www.altraisola. it; open Apr–Oct) sells wood and leather masks, colourful ceramics, intricate basketwork, eye-catching jewellery and patterned rugs.

Find out more

DIGITAL Go to www.neroargento. com for an amazing picture gallery of the *nuraghi* and, for virtual reconstructions, www.isolavirtuale.it/index.php/archeologia/52-nuragica.

Next stop...

DONKEY ISLAND Stintino, 55 km (35 miles) due north of Alghero, is the departure point for boat trips to the island of **Asinara**. Part of a national park, it is home to the small white donkeys (*asini*) for which the island is named (visits Easter–Sep; www.parcoasinara.org).

Il Ghiotto, a popular restaurant open late in summer

Take a stroll, or a row, down the River Temo in Bosa

② Bosa
Hilltop castle lookout

Along a wild, rocky stretch of coastline, 45 km (29 miles) south of Alghero, the town of Bosa sits a little way inland from the sea on the River Temo. The medieval town, with steep, traffic-free lanes, climbs up to the hilltop **Malaspina Castle**, which dates from the 12th century and affords grand views over the valley. Bosa Marina, 3 km (2 miles) downriver, has a first-class beach, overlooked by an old Spanish watchtower and ringed with cafés and restaurants. A little further inland from Bosa stands the solitary church of **San Pietro**, looking much as it must have done when it was finished in 1073.

Letting off steam

Piazza IV Novembre, at the end of Bosa's main drag, Corso Vittorio Emanuele, is a convenient space for a run around, but most kids will be champing at the bit to get to the beach at **Bosa Marina**, a 10-minute bus ride away.

The Lowdown

🌐 **Map reference** 12 F3
Address 08013 Bosa. Castello Malaspina: Via Ultimo Costa 14, 08013. San Pietro: 333 544 5675; www.castellodibosa.it

🚍 **Bus** from Alghero to Bosa (www.arst.sardegna.it)

🕐 **Open** Castello Malaspina: daily Apr–Oct, Sat–Sun Nov–Mar. San Pietro: Tue–Sun Apr–Oct

💶 **Price** Castello Malaspina: €6–10. San Pietro: €4–6; combined: €8–14

👫 **Age range** All

🕐 **Allow** 1 hour, more for beach

🍽 **Eat and drink** *Snacks* La Taverna (Piazza Carmine, 08013) makes simple *panini* and drinks. *Family treat* Sa Pischedda (Via Roma 8, 08013; 0785 373 065) has a merry atmosphere and outdoor seating.

🎊 **Festivals** Carnival and Holy Week: Feb/Mar/Apr. Festa dei Santi Pietro e Paolo (regatta to San Pietro): 29 Jun. Sagra di Santa Maria del Mare (boat parade of Madonna): first Sun of Aug. Sagra di Nostra Signora di Regnos Altos: second Sun of Sep

③ Castelsardo
A mighty elephant and a majestic castle

The Doria family of Genoa, a major contender in the medieval power struggles to control Sardinia, established their base at this town on the island's northern coast. The 12th-century **castle** they built on the town's highest promontory still stands, commanding majestic views of the coast, and today houses the **Museo dell'Intreccio**, displaying the basketwork for which the town is famous. A couple of ancient churches are nestled in the steep alleys below the castle, while the road east of town leads to one of Sardinia's iconic sights, the **Roccia dell'Elefante**, a wind-carved hunk of granite with an astonishing resemblance to a gnarled elephant.

Letting off steam

There is a green area of parkland below Castelsardo's cathedral and city walls on the seaward side, which is perfect for a run around, as well as an easy-to-reach crescent of beach west of the old centre, off Lungomare Anglona.

The distinctive Roccia dell'Elefante near Castelsardo, uncannily like an elephant

The Lowdown

🌐 **Map reference** 12 F2
Address 07031 Castelsardo. Castle and Museo dell'Intreccio: Via Marconi, 07031; 079 471 380

🚍 **Bus** from Sassari to Castelsardo (www.arst.sardegna.it)

🕐 **Open** Castle and Museo dell'Intreccio: daily Apr–Sep, Tue–Sun Oct–Mar

💶 **Price** Castle and Museo dell'Intreccio: €4–6

👫 **Age range** 5 plus for the town, all for the Roccia dell'Elefante

🕐 **Allow** 2 hours

🍽 **Eat and drink** *Snacks* Aragona (Via Manganella, 07031; 079 470 081) in the old quarter serves light meals. *Real meal* La Trattoria (Via Nazionale 20, 07031; 079 470 661) specializes in creamy *mazzafrissa* (a semolina pudding made with ewes' milk and honey).

🎊 **Festivals** Lunissanti (torch-lit procession): Mon before Easter

④ The Maddalena Islands
Island-hopping

Off Sardinia's northeastern coast, the Arcipelago della Maddalena includes some of Sardinia's most idyllic spots. Reached by regular ferry from the port of Palau, the main island, **Isola Maddalena**, has the only town, La Maddalena. A causeway carries a road to the neighbouring isle of **Caprera**, where the Italian revolutionary hero Giuseppe Garibaldi (1807–82) lived for many years (his tomb is here). A fascinating museum dedicated to his adventurous life, the **Compendio Garibaldino**, occupies his former home. Boat tours are available to explore the smaller islands, Santo Stefano, Spargi, Razzoli, Budelli and Santa Maria, all with secluded beaches.

Letting off steam

In La Maddalena, walk along the seafront west of the ferry port to reach **Cala Gavetta**, a marina for small boats where the town's main *passeggiata* (promenade) takes place. Local buses go from the centre to **beaches** on the northern and western coasts at Madonnetta, Cala Lunga and Spalmatore. The nearest is at Punta Tegge, 2 km (1 mile) southwest of town.

The Lowdown

🌐 **Map reference** 12 G1
Address 07024 La Maddalena, Isola Madalena. Compendio Garibaldino: 07024 Caprera; 0789 727 162; www.compendiogaribaldino.it

🚗 **Ferry** to La Maddalena from Palau (www.enermar.it; www.saremar.it; www.delcomar.it)

ℹ️ **Visitor information** Piazza Barone des Geneys, 07024 La Maddalena; 0789 736 321; www.comune.lamaddalena.ot.it

🕐 **Open** Compendio Garibaldino: 9am–8pm Tue–Sun

💶 **Price** Compendio Garibaldino: €10–15; under-18s free

👫 **Age range** All

⏱️ **Allow** 1 to 5 days

🍴 **Eat and drink** Snacks Vera Napoli (Via Tito Speri, 07024 La Maddalena; 0789 737 430; www.ristoranteveranapoli.com) offers good pizza and seafood. Family treat Trattoria da Bocchetta (Largo Matteotti 11, 07024 La Maddalena; 0789 737 437) serves fresh fish on the square.

⑤ Cala Gonone

Secret seaside hideaway

A steep, zigzagging road leads down a mountainside to Cala Gonone, a seaside hideaway sheltering a cluster of restaurants and hotels, and a choice of beaches. The best of these are reached by boat excursions from the harbour or, for the energetic, along a rough path running along the base of the cliffs. As well as the beaches, there are grottoes to explore, and opportunities for diving and other watersports.

A view of the harbour at La Maddalena, on Isola Maddalena, at dusk

Letting off steam

There is a sandy **beach** at the end of Lungomare Palmasera, or hike up to the mountain-top cave-village of **Tiscali** – Nuraghic buildings grouped in a vast cavern. It is best to go with a guide (list of guides from tourist office; 5-hour round trip; open daily; €10–14).

The Lowdown

🌐 **Map reference** 12 H3
Address 08020 Cala Gonone

🚌 **Bus** from Nuoro to Cala Gonone (www.arst.sardegna.it)

ℹ️ **Visitor information** Viale Bue Marino, 08020 Cala Gonone; 0784 93696; www.dorgali.it. Ask here about watersports and hikes.

👫 **Age range** All

⏱️ **Allow** At least 1 day, up to 1 week or more

🍴 **Eat and drink** Snacks Su Recreu (Via Vespucci, 08020; 0784 93135) is an excellent spot for breakfast or lunch with a shady terrace. Real meal Roadhouse Blues (Lungomare Palmasera 28, 08020; 0784 93187), across from the beach, has tasty burgers, pizza, seafood dishes and drinks.

The sandy beach and turquoise waters of Cala Gonone

Picnic under €25; **Snacks** €25–40; **Real meal** €40–80; **Family treat** €80 or more (based on a family of four)

⑥ Cagliari
Sardinia's walled capital city

Sardinia's capital, Cagliari presents an impressive sight, spreading up from the port to the old walled citadel on a hilltop. This historic quarter is the best place to wander with a family, with largely traffic-free streets and a glut of attractions. But the lower sections are also fun, not least arcaded Via Roma opposite the port, enlivened by pavement cafés, hawkers selling their wares and a steady parade of passers-by. There are Roman remains, underground vaults and botanical gardens too.

A 12th-century stone lion in the cathedral

Key Sights

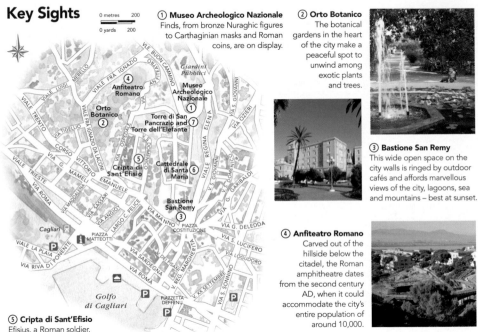

0 metres 200
0 yards 200

① **Museo Archeologico Nazionale**
Finds, from bronze Nuraghic figures to Carthaginian masks and Roman coins, are on display.

② **Orto Botanico**
The botanical gardens in the heart of the city make a peaceful spot to unwind among exotic plants and trees.

③ **Bastione San Remy**
This wide open space on the city walls is ringed by outdoor cafés and affords marvellous views of the city, lagoons, sea and mountains – best at sunset.

④ **Anfiteatro Romano**
Carved out of the hillside below the citadel, the Roman amphitheatre dates from the second century AD, when it could accommodate the city's entire population of around 10,000.

⑤ **Cripta di Sant'Efisio**
Efisius, a Roman soldier, was held in this cavernous underground vault before he was beheaded for his Christian beliefs; he later became the city's patron saint.

⑥ **Cattedrale di Santa Maria**
In the citadel is Cagliari's 13th-century cathedral. Members of the Savoy dynasty are buried here and a quartet of fierce marble lions guard the presbytery.

⑦ **Torre di San Pancrazio and Torre dell'Elefante**
These two medieval towers, one named after a tiny carved elephant, form part of the lofty walls around the old citadel. Climb to the top for superb views.

Letting off steam

Aside from the Orto Botanico and Bastione San Remy, Cagliari has a few areas of green space, most centrally the **Giardini Pubblici** (public gardens), just north of the archaeological museum off Viale Regina Elena. Outside town, take bus PF or PQ from Piazza Matteotti to the local beach resort of **Poetto** (a 15-minute ride), where some 5 km (3 miles) of golden sand stretches into the distance. Both the public beaches and the private lidos, which charge a few euros for a

Beachside café-bar in Poetto, with views of the Sella del Diavolo promontory

day's use of sun umbrellas and showers, offer windsurfing, pedalos to rent and beach sports.

Eat and drink

Picnic: under €25; Snacks: €25–40; Real meal: €40–80; Family treat: €80 or more (based on a family of four)

PICNIC I Sapori dell'Isola (*Via Sardegna 50, 09124; 070 666 342; closed Sun*), an *alimentari* (food shop) near the port, has an array of ham, cheese, olives and crusty fresh rolls. Take the picnic to Piazza del Carmine, a wide open space with benches near Piazza Matteotti.
SNACK Su Cumbidu (*Via Napoli 11, 09124; 070 660 017*) has a lively, sociable feel and up to five

Prices given are for a family of four

The Lowdown

🌐 **Map reference** 12 F5
Address Cagliari, 09122–09131;
Museo Archeologico: Piazza
Arsenale 1, 09123; *www.
archeocaor.beniculturali.it*. Orto
Botanico (070 675 3522) and
Anfiteatro Romano (*www.
anfiteatroromano.it*): Via Sant'
Ignazio da Laconi, 09123. Cripta
di Sant'Efisio: Via Sant'Efisio,
09124; 070 652 130. Cattedrale:
Piazza Palazzo 4, 09124; *www.
duomodicagliari.it*. Torre di San
Pancrazio and Torre dell'Elefante:
Piazza Indipendenza 8–13, 09124

🚗 **Train** from main towns (*www.
trenitalia.it*). **Bus** (*www.arst.
sardegna.it*) from all of Sardinia
to Piazza Matteotti; bus 7 to
citadel. **Ferry** from the mainland
and Sicily (*www.tirrenia.it*)

ℹ️ **Visitor information** Piazza
Matteotti, 09122; 070 669 255;
www.visit-cagliari.it

🕐 **Open** Museo Archeologico,
Anfiteatro Romano, Cripta di
Sant'Efisio & Torri: Tue–Sun. Orto
Botanico & Cattedrale: daily

💶 **Price** Museo Archeologico,
Cripta di Sant'Efisio & Cattedrale:
free. Orto Botanico: €4.
Anfiteatro Romano: €8. Torri €8.

👫 **Skipping the queue** Karalis
Card allows free transport and
entry to sights for one adult and
one child; valid 1 year, €30; from
tourist office and hotels (*www.
karaliscard.it*).

👫 **Age range** All

⏱️ **Allow** 1 to 2 days

🚻 **Toilets** On Salita Santa Chiara

Good family value?
Cagliari's old citadel is pleasant
to wander around, and sights are
not expensive. Restaurants are
cheaper than in the resorts.

---

fixed-price menus from €13 to €25,
all based on meat. The *antipasti*
are especially enticing.
REAL MEAL Il Serafino (*Via
Lepanto 6, 09124; 070 651 795;
closed Thu*), a family-friendly
trattoria, offers Sardinian specialities
such as *malloreddus* (gnocchi with a
meat sauce) and *seadas* (a pastry
filled with ricotta and drizzled with
honey). It has a relaxed air and
good-value menus.
FAMILY TREAT Il Gatto (*Viale
Trieste 15, 09124; 070 663 596;
closed Sat and Sun lunch*), a vaulted
pizzeria and restaurant off Piazza del
Carmine, has an innovative menu.
Its expertly prepared seafood dishes
and range of desserts are best.

Shopping
Isola (*Via Bacaredda 176, 09131;
070 492 756*) showcases a range of
Sardinian handicrafts, from jewellery

*A breezy outdoor café on the Bastione
San Remy*

and costumed dolls to hand-woven
carpets. There is also a **flea market**
on the Bastione San Remy (*every
Sun; not Aug*).

Find out more
DIGITAL To learn more about the
Phoenicians, visit *phoenicia.org* or
www.phoenician.org.

*The lovely sandy beach right next to the
ancient site of Nora*

Next stop...
PHOENICIANS AND ROMANS
The site of **Nora**, 40 km (25 miles)
south of Cagliari, has Phoenician
and Roman remains of a theatre,
baths and a temple, by a sandy
beach. A museum in nearby **Pula**
displays finds from the site (*open
daily; €11; www.coptur.net; bus to
Pula, and to Nora in summer*).

7 Su Nuraxi

A ruined city and a miniature island

Around 60 km (37 miles) north of Cagliari, outside the village of Barumini, lies Sardinia's greatest Nuraghic monument, **Su Nuraxi**, built between 1500 and 1300 BC, with additions right up to Roman times. It is dominated by a basalt central tower, with corridors leading to smaller towers, surrounded by dozens of prehistoric stone huts.

In Barumini itself, the remains of another Nuraghic complex lie inside the 17th-century palace of **Casa Zapata**. Also on display here are farming tools and *launeddas*, or Sardinian "triple pipes" – the island's traditional instrument.

A third attraction lies 1 km (half a mile) west of Barumini, towards Tuili: **Sardegna in Miniatura**, a miniature Sardinia showing all its most famous sights, including Su Nuraxi itself. The scale-model can be toured by boat and viewed from a tower.

Letting off steam

The archaeological site prohibits climbing on the stones and the only green space in the village is a tiny lawn inside Casa Zapata. However, there is plenty of scope for running around on the **Giara di Gesturi**, a plateau 5 km (3 miles) northwest of Barumini – follow the road up from Gesturi. This nature reserve of cork groves, rocky meadows and swampy ponds attracts migrating birds in spring. Buzzards can be spotted, too, and the small, shy ponies for which the plateau is most famous.

See all the best sights of Sardinia in miniature at Sardegna in Miniatura

8 Villasimius

Seaside and shipwrecks

Southern Sardinia's pre-eminent family resort, on the island's southeast corner, is a place to unwind. Surrounded by silky sands, the place bursts with energy in summer and is dead in winter, but has enough beaches, bars and restaurants for any season. Bikes and scooters can be rented to explore the lagoons and Spanish watchtowers scattered along the coast, and local outfits rent diving equipment to nose around the seabed. For landlubbers, the town's engaging **Museo Archeologico** displays local Carthaginian and Roman finds and items from a 16th-century Spanish shipwreck.

Letting off steam

Campu Longu, **Timi Ama**, **Simius** and the other beaches around Villasimius provide plenty of space for frolicking. For shadier recreation, head 15 km (9 miles) north to the **Foresta dei Minnimini**, a thickly wooded area planted in part by 19th-century convicts. The old prison quarters can still be seen at Castiadas, a tiny settlement on the forest's edge (www.castiadasonline.it).

The Lowdown

🌐 **Map reference** 12 H6
Address 09049 Villasimius. Museo Archeologico: Via A Frau 5, 09049; 070 793 0290

🚍 **Bus** from Cagliari to Villasimius (www.arst.sardegna.it)

ℹ️ **Visitor information** Piazza Giovanni XXIII, 09049; 070 793 0271; www.villasimiusweb.com

🕐 **Open** Museo Archeologico: Tue–Sun

💰 **Price** Museo Archeologico: €6–9

👫 **Age range** All

🏃 **Activities** Boat trips: Blu & Blu (www.blueblunoleggio.it)

⏱️ **Allow** A week for the beaches

🍽️ **Eat and drink** *Picnic* The market (Via Donatello, 09049; Sat am) is the place to pick up bread, olives, cheese and fruit for a feast on the beach. *Real meal* Tartana (Piazza Incani, 09049; 070 791 789) offers a choice of pastries, *panini* and pizzas, or delicous main meals served on the upstairs terrace.

Fishing boats tied up in the harbour at Calasetta, Sant'Antioco island

9 Sant'Antioco and San Pietro

Burial sites and secret beaches

Until they were dislodged by the Romans, the Carthaginians controlled Sardinia's southwestern corner from their base on the isle of **Sant'Antioco**, which they named Sulki. Today, the island is connected to the rest of Sardinia by a slender isthmus. A panoramic promontory

The Lowdown

🌐 **Map reference** 12 F4
Address 09021 Barumini. Su Nuraxi: Viale Su Nuraxi, 09021 Barumini; 070 936 8128; www.fondazionebarumini.it. Casa Zapata: Piazza Giovanni XXIII, 09021 Barumini; 070 936 8476; Sardegna in Miniatura: SP Las Plassas, 09021 Tuili; 070 936 1004; www.sardegnainminiatura.it

🚍 **Bus** from Cagliari to Barumini (www.arst.sardegna.it)

🕐 **Open** Su Nuraxi: daily. Casa Zapata: daily. Sardegna in Miniatura: daily

💰 **Price** Su Nuraxi and Casa Zapata: €20; Sardegna in Miniatura: €20

👫 **Age range** 5 plus, but bringing prehistoric stones to life is difficult.

🏃 **Activities** Guided nature walks in the Giara; call ahead to book (070 936 4277; www.parcodellagiara.it).

⏱️ **Allow** 1 day, more to explore the Giara di Gesturi

🍽️ **Eat and drink** *Snacks* Sardegna in Miniatura (SP Las Plassas, 09029 Tuili; 070 936 1004) has a good rustic-style restaurant on site, which offers fresh pasta and grills. Ask about special meal tickets at the site entrance. There is also a picnic area. *Real meal* Sa Lolla (Via Cavour 49, 09021 Barumini; 070 936 8419), in Barumini's backstreets, is a traditional trattoria which serves up dishes such as pasta with local wild mushrooms.

The beach at San Giovanni di Sinis on the Sinis Peninsula

at one end of Sant'Antioco is the location of a Carthaginian **tophet**, or burial site, dedicated to the gods Baal-Hammon and Tanit. Ancient pottery, jewellery and colourful mosaics are collected in the **Museo Archeologico** here. From Calasetta, at the north of the island, ferries cross to smaller **San Pietro**. Apart from the elegant town of Carloforte, it is a rugged spot, with a few scraps of beach and fantastic views from Capo Sandalo on its western tip.

Letting off steam

Head for the beach at **Maladroxia**, 5 km (3 miles) south of Sant'Antioco town, for some serious relaxation.

The Lowdown

- 🌐 **Map reference** 12 E6
  Address Sant'Antioco, 09017.
  San Pietro, 09014. Museo
  Archeologico and tophet:
  Piazza Insula Plumbea, 09017;
  www.archeotur.it

- 🚗 **Bus** from Cagliari to Sant'Antioco and Calasetta (www.arst. sardegna.it). **Ferry** from Calasetta to San Pietro (www.saremar.it)

- ℹ️ **Visitor information** Piazza Repubblica 41, Sant'Antioco 09017; 0781 82031

- 🕐 **Open** Museo Archeologico and tophet: 9am–1pm daily

- 💶 **Price** Museo Archeologico and tophet: €14–22

- 👫 **Age range** All

- ⏱️ **Allow** 1 to 2 days

- ☕ **Eat and drink** *Snacks* Compagnia del Moro (Lungomare Colombo 83, 09017 Sant'Antioco; 0781 840 671) is a mellow spot. *Real meal* Hostaria Caligola (Via Garibaldi 15, 09017 Sant'Antioco; 0781 83828; closed Wed) serves Roman-themed pizzas and meals.

- 🎭 **Festivals** Festa di Sant'Antioco: May. Girotonno, San Pietro: Jun

⑩ Sinis Peninsula
Underwater ruins

Halfway up Sardinia's west coast, the Sinis Peninsula is an area of lagoons and beaches. At its south is **Tharros**, founded by the Phoenicians in the 8th century BC and later settled by Carthaginians and Romans – much of it now underwater. Its stones were used to build the 5th-century church of San Giovanni di Sinis nearby.

Letting off steam

The best beaches are **Aruttas** and **Capo Mannu**, 12 km (8 miles) and 21 km (13 miles) up the coast.

The Lowdown

- 🌐 **Map reference** 12 E4
  Address 09070–09072 Oristano

- 🚗 **Train** or ARST **bus** (not Sun) from Cagliari to Oristano, then bus to Tharros and beaches (Jul–Aug)

- ℹ️ **Visitor information** Piazza Eleonora 19, 09170 Oristano; 0783 368 3210; www. oristanowestsardinia.it

- ☕ **Eat and drink** *Snacks* Abraxas (San Salvatore di Sinis, 09072; 347 132 5254) saloon bar serves salads and grilled meat. *Real meal* Il Caminetto (Via Cesare Battisti 8, 09072, Cabras; 0783 391 139) is renowned for its fish.

- 🎭 **Festivals** Corsa degli Scalzi (barefoot race): first weekend of Sep

A rocky shoreline near Calasetta, on the island of Sant'Antioco

Where to Stay in Sardinia

Family accommodation in Sardinia is excellent, ranging from grand hotels in lavish grounds to resort-style hotels by the sea; stylish modern hotels in the main cities to simple family-run places in small towns. Ask about family discounts and whether minimum stays and half- or full-board are mandatory.

AGENCIES
Rent-Sardinia
www.rent-sardinia.com
A wide choice of villas and apartments.

Sardinia Villa Collection
www.thesardiniavillacollection.com
Upmarket villas to rent.

Sardinian Villas
www.sardinianvillas.com
An easy-to-use website that lists family-friendly villas.

Alghero
Map 12 E2

HOTELS
Hotel Porto Conte
Località Porto Conte, 07041; 079 942 035; www.hotelportoconte.it; closed mid-Oct–mid-Apr
On an exquisite bay, this grand, family-friendly hotel has tennis courts, a pool and paddling pool and private beach. There are bikes to rent or it is a 20-minute bus journey into Alghero.
€€

Hotel Domomea
Via Vittorio Veneto 47, 07041; 079 973 2011; www.domomeagroup.com
In a quiet area of Alghero, close to the old centre, this hotel is popular with families. It has a rooftop pool and an airy interior with bright, modern decor. Bike hire is available.
€€€

Villa Las Tronas, on a rocky promontory just outside Alghero

Villa Las Tronas
Lungomare Valencia 1, 07041; 079 981 818; www.hotelvillalastronas.it
In its own grounds on a headland with lovely views, this castellated former royal residence from 1884 brims with character, and boasts two pools and a billiards room. It is a 10-minute walk by the sea to the centre of Alghero.
€€€

Bosa
Map 12 F3

HOTELS/SELF-CATERING
Corte Fiorita
Via Lungo Temo de Gasperi 45, 08013; 0785 377 058; www. hotel-bosa.it
An *albergo diffuso* – with buildings dotted around town – this hotel in old Bosa has a range of rooms in traditional settings, some with river views. Apartments are available too.
€

Isola Rossa
Località Campu e Mare, 08013 Bosa Marina; 0785 377 101; www. isolarossabosa.it
This hotel in family-friendly Bosa Marina has accommodating staff and clean rooms. The pool is small but the beach is a 10-minute walk away. Self-catering apartments are available. Dine outdoors in summer.
€

Cagliari
Map 12 F–G5

HOTELS
Hotel Chentu Lunas
Piazza Arcipelaghi, 09126; 070 389 539; www.chentulunas.it
With only eight rooms, this simple little hotel is next to Cagliari's beach and marina in Poetto. Its balconied rooms are neat and spotless, and the restaurant serves breakfast and basic meals. The bus stop for the centre is just outside.
€

T Hotel
Via dei Giudicati 66, 09131; 070 47400; www.thotel.it
A little out of the centre, but well connected to sights and beaches by bus, this is a stunning hotel, with lovely rooms and large bathrooms, sumptuous suites and two-level "maisonettes" that sleep four. There is a pool, formal restaurant, bistro and excellent buffet breakfasts.
€€

B&B
Sardinia Domus
Largo Carlo Felice 26, 09124; 070 659 783; www.sardiniadomus.it
Well-placed for Cagliari's centre and port, this smart B&B has spacious, modern rooms, all en-suite. Street-facing rooms are larger, brighter and slightly more expensive – but also noisier.
€

Cala Gonone
Map 12 H3

HOTELS
Hotel Miramare
Piazza dei Giardini 12, 08020; 0784 93140; www.htlmiramare.it; closed Nov–Mar
Ideally located for the beach, small port and centre of Cala Gonone, this hotel has a panoramic roof terrace and an excellent restaurant, with indoor and outdoor seating. It has cool, clean rooms with balconies; pay a little more for the ones at the front with views.
€

Cala Gonone Beach Village
Map 5 B1
Viale Bue Marino, 08020; 0784 93693; www.calagonone beachvillage.com; closed late Sep–late May
Despite the name, this hotel is nearly a kilometre (half a mile) inland, but the pool, kids' club and other facilities make up for it: the pool has children's areas and there

are tennis courts. All rooms have a patio or terrace. A shuttle "train" takes guests to the beach.

🚐 🏋️ 🍴 ⚓ ☉ €€

A children's play area at Cala Gonone Beach Village

Castelsardo
Map 12 F2

HOTELS
Hotel Baga Baga
Loc La Terra Bianca, 07031; 079 479 125; www.hotelbagabaga.it
This is the best place to stay around Castelsardo, 1 km (half a mile) out of town, with views of the old town and sea beyond. There are ten modern rooms, furnished in rustic style. Enjoy the panorama at breakfast, from the veranda or garden.

🏋️ 🍴 €

Hotel Corallo
Località Isola Rossa, 07038 Trinità d'Agultu; 079 694 055; www.hotelcorallosardegna.it
Opposite the fishing harbour of Isola Rossa, 20 km (12 miles) northeast of Castelsardo, this family-run hotel serves a buffet breakfast to guests as they watch the boats come and go. It has well-equipped rooms and sea-facing suites with balconies and spa pools. It is only a short walk to the local beach, or there are water taxis to ferry guests to the best beaches nearby.

🚐 🍴 ☉ €€€

A room with a sea-facing balcony at Hotel Corallo, near Castelsardo

La Maddalena
Map 12 G1

HOTEL/SELF-CATERING
Villa del Parco
Via Don Vico, 07024; 0789 720 026; www.villadelparco.com
A short walk from the centre of La Maddalena and 200 m (220 yards) from the sea, this modern, well-maintained hotel has rooms with kitchenettes, and apartments by the week. Dinghies can be rented to explore the archipelago, and diving and other trips arranged.

🚐 🏋️ 🍴 ☉ 🛏️ €€

Nora/Pula
Map 12 F6

HOTELS
Costa dei Fiori
09010 Santa Margherita di Pula; 070 924 5333; www.costadeifiori.it
This tasteful, palm-shaded resort hotel by the beach, 3 km (2 miles) from Nora, is custom-made for families, with a kids' club, tennis courts, table tennis and two pools. Boat trips and diving courses can be organized. Minimum three-night stay in high season. Shuttle buses run to Pula and Chia beach.

🚐 🏋️ 🍴 ☉ ⚓ €€

Nora Club Hotel
09010 Nora; 070 924 422; www.noraclubhotel.it
A small, friendly, family-run hotel 10 minutes' walk from the beach, the archaeological site of Nora and the holiday town of Pula, the Nora Club Hotel also has bikes for guests to get around on. Immaculate rooms overlook a gorgeous pool and lush garden.

🚐 🏋️ 📡 ☕ ⚓ €€

Sant'Antioco
Map 12 E6

HOTEL
Luci del Faro
Località Mangiabarche Calasetta, 09011; 0781 810 089; www.hotelucidelfaro.com; closed Nov–Mar
Off the beaten track, this hotel on the western coast of Sant'Antioco has 38 bright, airy rooms around a pool, and views over the sea. There is a rocky shore, and a sandy beach down the road easily reached by shuttle bus.

🚐 🏋️ 🍴 ☉ ⚓ €€

Sinis
Map 12 E4

HOTEL
Golf Hotel Is Arenas
Pineta Is Arenas, Narbolia, 09070; 0783 529 011; www.golfhotelisarenas.com
In dense pine woods on the coast, this hotel has minimalist chalets in its grounds. The fine-sand beach is often deserted, and there is a pool too. First-rate food. Minimum stay one week in summer.

🚐 🏋️ 🍴 ☉ ☉ €€

Stintino
Map 5 B1

HOTEL
Hotel Cala Reale
Località Ovile del Mercante, 07040; 0784 523 127; www.calareale.it; closed Oct–May
On the edge of Stintino, this hotel is near the glorious but often crowded beach of La Pelosa (reached by shuttle bus). Two pools and tennis courts provide on-site recreation. Minimum stay one week in summer.

🚐 🏋️ 📡 🍴 ☉ €€

Villasimius
Map 12 H6

HOTELS
Il Girasole
Via Masaccio 6, 09049; 070 791 496, www.ilgirasolehotel.com; closed early Nov–mid-Jan
Quiet and peaceful, 5 minutes' walk from the centre of Villasimius, this hotel has eight spacious double rooms, with terraces. The best beaches are a short bus ride away.

🏋️ ☉ €

Albaruja Hotel
Via Colombo, Costa Rei, Muravera, 09043; 070 991 557; www.albaruja.it; closed early Oct–Apr
Steps away from the pristine sands of the Costa Rei, 70 km (40 miles) east of Cagliari, this hotel is set in a luxuriant garden a short walk from restaurants and markets. Boat trips allow guests to explore the coast.

🚐 🏋️ ☉ 🛏️ ☉ €€

Price Guide
For a family of four per night in high season, in one or more rooms, inclusive of breakfast, service charges and any additional taxes such as VAT.

€ Under €200 €€ €200–350 €€€ over €200

Key to symbols *see back cover flap*

Aerial view of the scallop-shaped
Piazza del Campo in Siena, Tuscany

Area Maps

ITALY

Italy Maps

KEY TO MAPS 1–14

Motorway with junction	Ferry route	◇ Place of Interest
Dual carriageway	National border	▲ Summit
Road under construction	Regional border	✕ Pass
Main road	Urban area	
Other road	✈ Airport	**MAPS (1–14)**
Railway	⛴ Ferry port	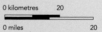

Rome City Maps

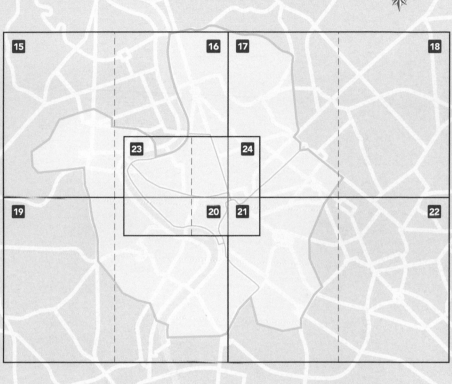

15	16	17	18
23	24		
19	20	21	22

0 kilometre 1

0 mile 1

KEY TO MAPS 15–24

- Major sight
- Place of interest
- Other building
- Train station
- M Metro station
- Tram stop

- ℹ Visitor information
- Play area
- Police station

MAPS (15–22)

0 metres 300

0 yards 300

- Pedestrian street
- Railway line
- City wall

MAPS (23–24)

0 metres 200

0 yards 200

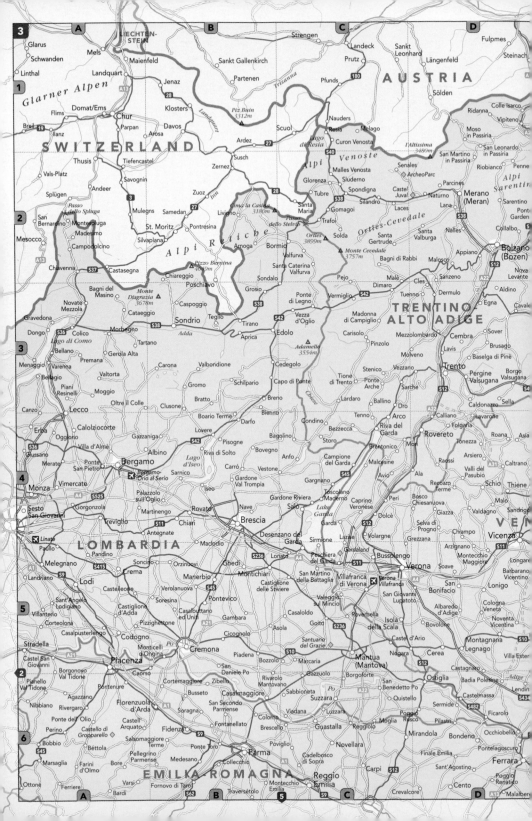

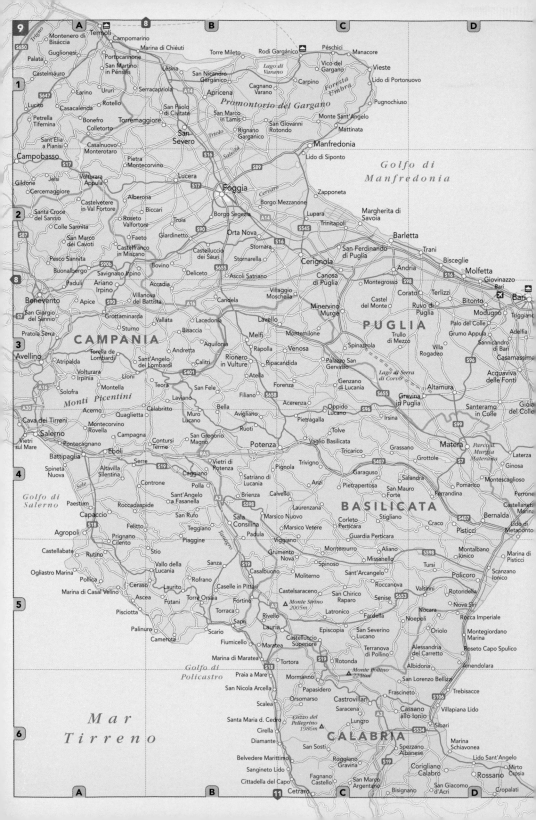

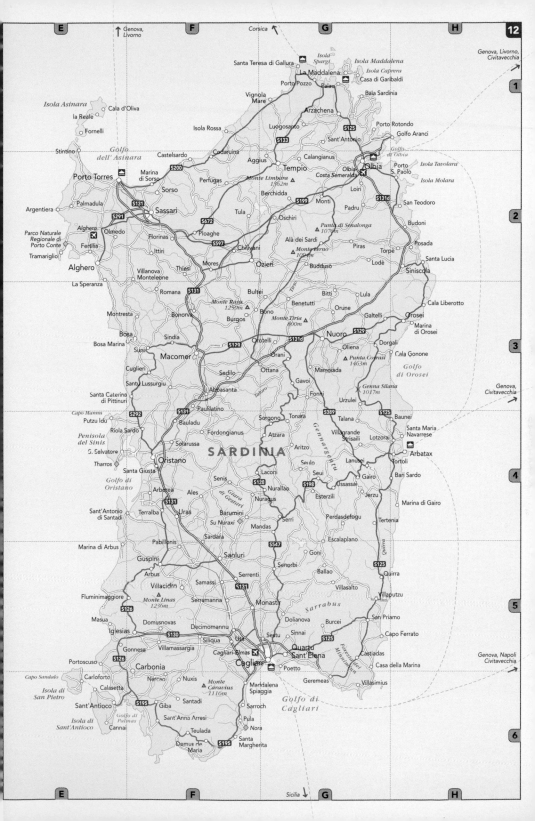

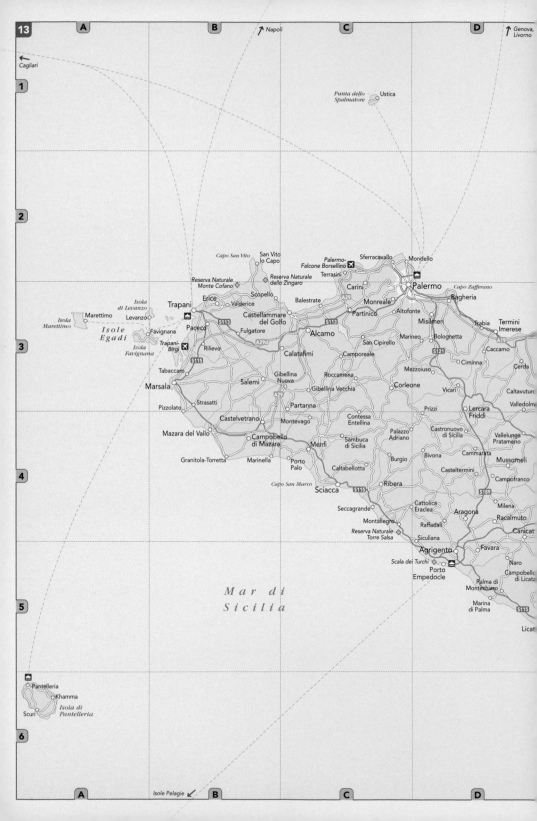

↑ Napoli

↑ Genova,
Livorno

← Cagliari

A **B** **C** **D**

1

Punta dello
Spalmatore ◇ ○ Ustica

2

Capo San Vito

San Vito
lo Capo
Reserva Naturale
Monte Cofano ◇
Reserva Naturale
dello Zingaro ◇

Sferracavallo
Mondello

Palermo-
Falcone Borsellino ✈

Terrasini

Palermo
🏛

Capo Zafferano

Marettimo
Isola
di Levanzo
Levanzo

Trapani
Erice
Valderice
Scopello
Balestrate

Carini
Monreale

Bagheria

Altofonte
Misilmeri
Trabia
Termini
Imerese

Isola
Marettimo

Isole
Egadi

Favignana
Paceco
Castellammare
del Golfo
Fulgatore

S113

Partinico
S113

Alcamo

San Cipirello
Marineo
Bolognetta

Caccamo
Cerda

3

Isola
Favignana
Trapani-
Birgi ✈
Rilievo

A294

Calatafimi
Camporeale
Mezzoiuso
Ciminna

S121

Caltavuturo

Tabaccaro
Salemi
Gibellina
Nuova
Roccamena

Corleone
Vicari

Cerda

Marsala
Gibellina Vecchia

A29

Prizzi
Lercara
Friddi
Valledolmo

Pizzolato
Strasatti
Partanna
Contessa
Entellina

Castronuovo
di Sicilia
Vallelunga
Pratameno

Mussomeli

S115

Castelvetrano
Montevago

Palazzo
Adriano
Cammarata

4

Mazara del Vallo
Campobello
di Mazara
Menfi
Sambuca
di Sicilia
Burgio
Bivona
Casteltermini
Campofranco

Granitola-Torretta
Marinella
Porto
Palo
Caltabellotta

Ribera
Cattolica
Eraclea
Milena
Racalmuto

Capo San Marco
Sciacca
S115
Seccagrande
Aragona

Canicat

Montallegro
Raffadali
Favara
Naro

Reserva Naturale
Torre Salsa ◇
Siculiana

S189

Campobello
di Licata

Agrigento

Scala dei Turchi ◇
Porto
Empedocle
🏛

Palma di
Montechiaro

5

Mar di
Sicilia

Marina
di Palma
S115

Licat

Pantelleria
🏛
Khamma

Scuri
Isola di
Pantelleria

6

A **B** **C** **D**

Isole Pelagie ↙

Selected Italy Town Index

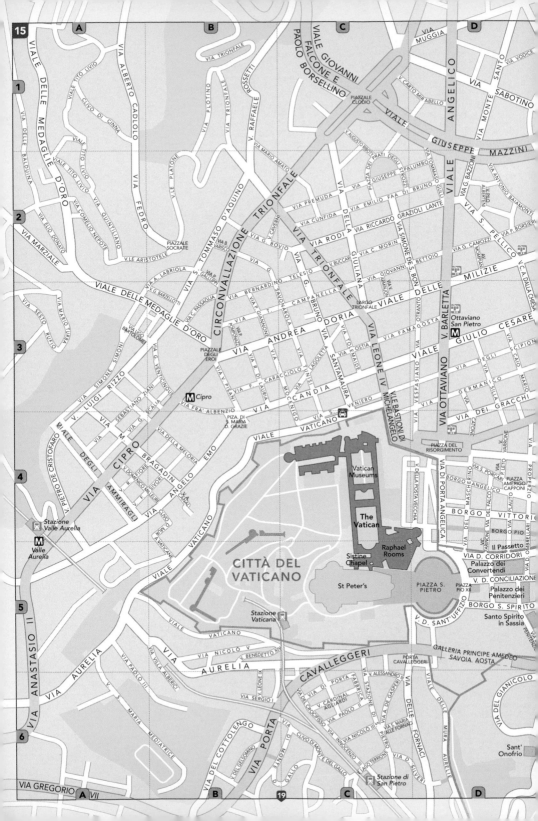

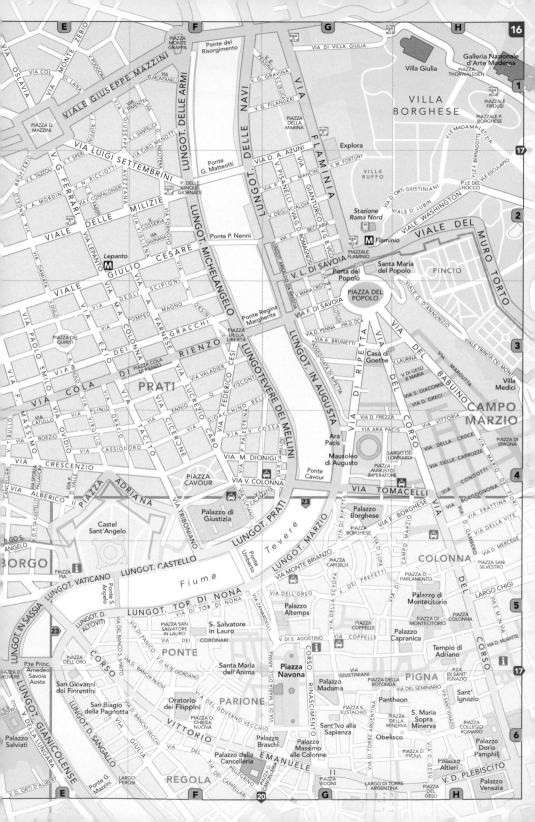

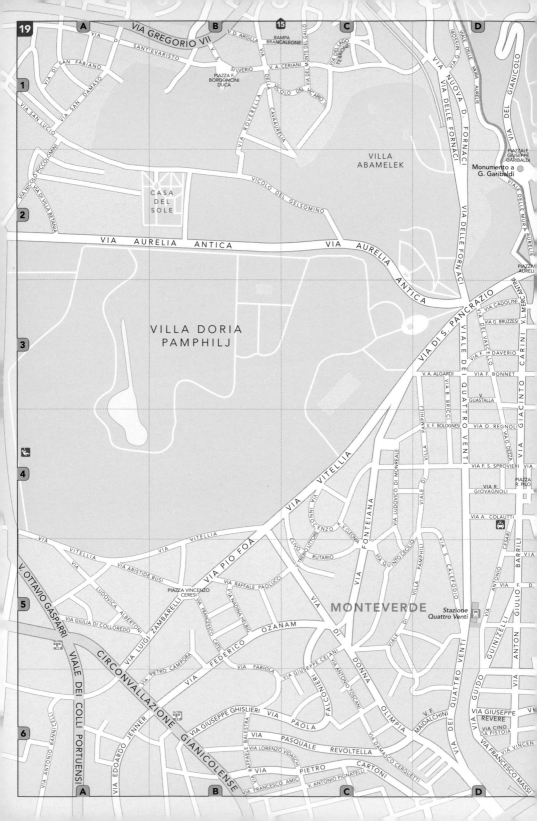

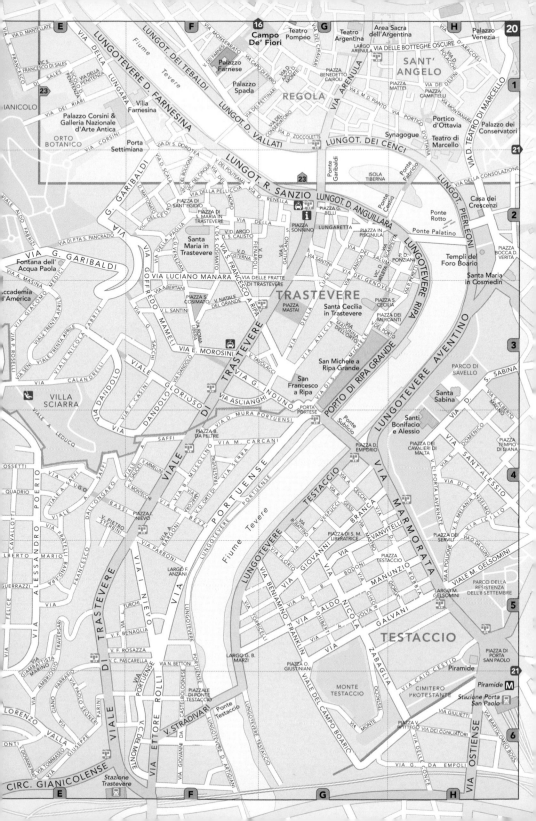

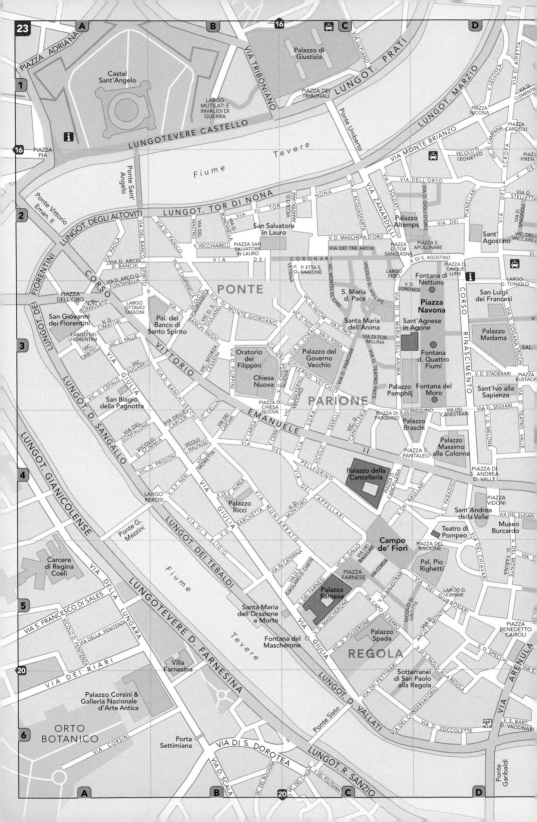

Rome Street Index

Index

Page numbers in **bold** type refer to main entries.

Acknowledgments

Dorling Kindersley would like to thank the following people whose help and assistance contributed to the preparation of this book.

Contributors

Gillian Arthur is a long term resident of Friuli-Venezia Giulia where she has her own company organizing wine and walking tours. She has collaborated on several travel books including Dorling Kindersley's *Back Roads Northern and Central Italy*. Gillian lives near Cividale del Friuli with her husband, daughter and dogs Lucy and Lola.

Ros Belford is co-author of *The Rough Guide to Italy* and author of Dorling Kindersley's *Eyewitness Travel Guide: Rome*. She has also written articles for magazines ranging from *National Geographic Traveler* to *Vogue*. Ros has two daughters and spends as much time as she can on the Aeolian island of Salina.

Lucy Ratcliffe is an award-winning travel writer and editor who has spent much of the last ten or more years living in and travelling around Milan and the Italian Lakes. Lucy currently shares her time between Bergamo and Barcelona, where she lives with her partner and two young children.

Born in England, Kate Singleton took a degree in Philosophy in Milan and has lived in Italy ever since. Over the years she has written for various publications in Italian and English, including *Il Giornale*, the *Wall Street Journal*, *The Sunday Times*, and the *International Herald Tribune*, for which she is still an occasional contributor.

Helena Smith is a writer, photographer and editor. She is a winner of the *Vogue* and *Independent on Sunday* writing competitions, and author of *The Rough Guide to Walks in London & Southeast England*. Helena has been around the world taking guidebook pictures, and when closer to home she blogs about food and her community at eathackney.com.

Celia Woolfrey is a travel writer and magazine journalist, whose work has appeared in numerous publications including Dorling Kindersley's *Back Roads Italy* and *Back Roads Northern and Central Italy*. She has also co-authored *The Rough Guide to Italy* since the first edition. Celia lives in London.

Additional Photography

Demetrio Carrasco; Judy Edelhoff; Philip Enticknap; Philip Gatward; Michelle Grant; Paul Harris and Anne Heslope; John Heseltine; Britta Jaschinski; Judith Miller/Biblion; Roger Moss; Rough Guides/Chris Hutty, /Dylan Reisenberger/James McConnachie/Martin Richardson; Kim Sayer; Tony Souter; Karen Trist; Christine Webb; Linda Whitwam; Celia Woolfrey.

Additional Design and Editorial Assistance

JACKET DESIGN Tessa Bindloss, Louise Dick
ICON DESIGN Claire-Louise Armitt
READERS Vincent Crump, Fiona Wild
FACT CHECKER John Murphy
PROOFREADER Anna Streiffert
INDEXER Helen Peters

Photography Permissions

DORLING KINDERSLEY would like to thank all the museums, galleries, churches and other sights that allowed us to photograph at their establishments. Aquario Genova; Bacilica Aquileia; Cappella Sarovegni; Gilberto Zedda at Comune di Milano; Dolonne Fun Park di Torino; Emanuela Travo at Galleria Nazionale di Palazzo Spinola; Peggy Guggenheim Collection, Venice; South Tyrol Museum of Archaeology; Messner Mountain Museum; Museo Nazionale del Cinema, Torino; Palazzo Reali di Torino; Triennale Design Museum; Stazione Zoologica Anton Dohrn; Carlo Zasio (Ufficio Stampa)/Press Office) at Ministero per i Beni e le Attività Culturali - Ministry of Cultural Heritage and Activities; Caol Ishka Hotel; Cinema dei Piccoli; Fondazione Idis-Città della Scienza; Hotel Raphaël – Roma; Carlo Anello at Museo Etnografico d'Atri; Susanna Cimino at Museo Galileo, Florence; Drssa Maria Laura Falsini (Archivio Fotografico) at Soprintendenza per I Beni Archeologici dell'Etruria Meridionale; Serena Del Giudice at Bioparco di Roma.

Picture Credits

a = above; b = below/bottom; c = centre;
f = far; l = left; r = right; t = top.

The publisher would like to thank the following for their kind permission to reproduce their photographs:
ACTV : 46bl. AEROPORTO DI VENEZIA MARCO POLO: 46cra.
AGRITURISMO VILLANOVA: 153cra. ALAMY IMAGES: The Art Archive/Collection Dagli Orti 65tl, 207tl, 208crb, 244crb, 271tc, 338tr; The Art Gallery Collection 228crb; David Ball 227b, 256b; Peter Barritt 66bl; Stephen Bisgrove 282tr; bobo 236bl; Carlo Bollo 279crb, 283bl; Marion Bull 357bl; Vittore Buzzi 334clb; Cephas Picture Library 94crb; charistoone-images 70tr; Caroline Commins 267cb; Peter Cook 255cr; CuboImages srl/Anania Carri 309b, /Angelo Tondini 234cra, /Bluered 84cr, 224br, 239tl, /Eddy Buttarelli 50bl, /Elio Lombardo 280cla, /Enrico Caracciolo 198tc, /Enrico Spanu 374cb, /Ghigo Roli 338cb, /Gimmi 210cb, /Marco Simonini 96br, /Nicola Iacono 322bl, 345tl, /Riccardo Lombardo 362cl; Ian Dagnall 371tl; Deco Images 266cb; Adam Eastland 294bl; EIGHTFISH 238tc; Greg Balfour Evans 333b, 360br, 363cla; F1online digitale Bildagentur GmbH 148clb; Michele Falzone 293c; Peter Forsberg 48crb; Gaertner 237tl; Carrie Garcia 297tl; Terry Harris 234clb; hemis.fr/René Mattes 301clb, /Stefano Torrione 228cb; Peter Horree 234crb, 294tr; Image Source/IS-200706 50tc; imagebroker/Alexander Pöschel 294bc, /Günter Lenz 243bl, /Norbert Eisele-Hein 94tr, /STELLA 373bl; Brian Jannsen 240clb; JLImages 268tl, 272bl; Rebecca Johnson 268c; Jon

Arnold Images Ltd/Alan Copson 217b; Maurice Joseph 248cb; Norma Joseph 248clb; Brenda Kean 295bl; John Kellerman 59bl; David Kilpatrick 346clb; Lautaro 248cla; Melvyn Longhurst 274clb; LOOK Die Bildagentur der Fotografen GmbH/Elan Fleisher 276bl, /Franz Marc Frei 284clb, /Jan Greune 157t, /Kay Maeritz 164c, /Konrad Wothe 250br, 340tl; Sabine Lubenow 79cb; David Lyons 209tl; MARKA/Claudio Ciabochi 235cl, /giovanni mereghetti 260cra, /pietro cappa 240bc; mauritius images GmbH/Rene Mattes 283tc; Steven May 70ca; Mayday 316-317; Nic Cleave Photography 2-3; nobleIMAGES 154-5; Peter I Noyce 233tl, 233bc; one-image photography 67bl; David Pearson 294ca; Chuck Pefley 61tr; Wiliam Perry 166crb; PhotoBliss 265c; Photoshot Holdings Ltd 276tl, 323b; PhotoStock-Israel/Talya Rosen 294br; Davide Piras 221tl; Christian Platzer 101tl; Robert Harding Picture Library Ltd/Godong 296cr; Robert Harding Productions 167bl; Grant Rooney 246tl; Ruby 244br; SAGAPHOTO.COM/Stephane Gautier 298tr; Alex Segre 293tl, 355tl; somewhere else 372cb; Spazio Foto Mereghetti 130cra; Stephen Roberts Photography 268bl; Tarek El Juan 139cb; Travel Division Images 269tl, 282bc; Travel Pictures 228cra; Travel Pictures/Pictures Colour Library 124br; Travelshots.com 73bl; Kirk Treakle 278clb; TTL Images 80tl; VIEW Pictures Ltd/Grant Smith 262b; Christine Webb 207bl, 249tl; Ken Welsh 163cl, 285tl; Tim E White 275tl; Wilmar Photography 280br. ALBERGHE I TO DELLA MARIANNA: 126tr. ALITALIA: 160cra. LES AMIS DU BOIS: 130tr, 131cla. ARCHEOPARC: 100bl. ARCHIVIO ANTONIO CALDERARA: Eraldo Misserini 141tl.B&B ARMELLINO: 127tr. BARTOLUCCI FRANCESCO SRL.: 245ca. BREK: 85ca. CA' POZZO INN: 75bc. CALA GONONE BEACH VILLAGE: 379tl. LA CAMOGLIESE: 152cb. CASA CORDATI: 213bl. CASA QUERINI: 74c. CASTELLO BANFI: 194bl. CASTELLO DI GROPPARELLO: 224tr. COMUNE DI BOLOGNA: 218cra. CORBIS: Fratelli Alinari 35tl; Arte & Immagini srl 244cl; Atlantide Phototravel/Guido Cozzi 5br, 40-1, /Massimo Borchi 16br; /Stefano Amantini 170br; Bettmann 266crb; Stefano Bianchetti 36clb; Massimo Borchi 362crb; The Gallery Collection 114tl; Image Source 380-1; Mark Karrass 161b; Jean-Pierre Lescourret 269bl; Araldo de Luca 286cb; René Mattes 181bl; Ocean 8-9; Gianni Dagli Orti 304bc; Sergio Pitamitz 222cr, 236tr; José Fuste Raga 254-5; Roger Ressmeyer 324clb, 358cra; Reuters 303bl; Steven Vidler 34clb; Wang Xingqiao 37tc; Bo Zaunders 119bc. COSTA EDUTAINMENT PH MERLOFOTOGRAFIA: 144cra, 144cl, 144cb. DREAMSTIME.COM: Aalexeev 311bl; Achilles 164ca; Artdirection 178tr; Bpperry 164br; Brians101 23bl; Caramaria 56tr; Chiakto 137clb; Mario Curcio 349bl; Sabrina Dvihally 321tc; Eg004713 178c; Exl01 82tl; Fabrizio Gattuso 335cla; Gkuna 186cla; Gmv 223bc; Walter Graneri 349tc; Miroslav Horovsky 328cr; Gabriela Insuratelu 48cra, 341bl; Javarman 51cr; Jenifoto406 346cra; Jojobob 210tr, 346tr; Jorisvo 222cl; Wendy Kaveney 25bl; Stanislav Kharchevskyi 329tc; Chiara Lozzi 313tl; Temistocle Lucarelli 312tc; Mbighin 137bl, Milla74 338bl; Mkistryn 210bc; Newphotoservice 211c; Paha_l 18bl; Philipzh 341tl; Propix 331bc; Robwilson39 19bl; Mubadda Rohana 15bl; Massimo Sala 108tr; Lex Schmidt 358tr; Sergey Skleznev 181tl; Michele Stefanile 334crb; Studio1a 110c; Piotr Tomczyk 17br; Aníbal Trejo 14bl; Raluca Tudor 180tl; Tupungato 24br, 171tl; Unknown1861 165bl; Gian Marco Valente 17bl; Vanbeets 1b; Zanico 223cla. EUROHOTEL: 128tr. FOTOLIA: averroe 356bl; Circumnavigation 50cr, 51cla; Rocco Di Biagio 30br; gaemau 358clb; Gary 112clb; Grischa

Georgiew 5tl; giemmephoto 237bc; Jörg Hackemann 33bl; Adriana Harakalova 18br; Living Legend 23br; Lsantilli 99bc; m.bonotto 222c; R Mazzonna 94clb; Moreno Novello 210cl; Michele Pautasso 117tc; Bill Perry 61bc; sergioboccardo 210crb; Moreno Soppelsa 117bl; soundsnaps 47b; Webpictureblog.com 377tl. FUNIVIA DELL'ETNA S.P.A.: 358crb. GETTY IMAGES: Alinari Archives/Reproduced with the permission of Ministero per i Beni e le Attività Culturali 172cl; The Bridgeman Art Library 35clb, 305bl, /Primavera c.1478 Sandro Botticelli 172cla, /Portraits of Duke Federico da Montefeltro (1422–82) Piero della Francesca 172clb; DEA/G. DAGLI ORTI 266tr, /M. BORCHI 231bl; Grant V. Faint 169bl; Iconica/Philip and Karen Smith 265tr; The Image Bank/Buena Vista Images 195tc; Photographer's Choice/Slow Images 273tr; Robert Harding World Imagery/Nico Tondini 176bc; SuperStock Annunciation by Leonardo da Vinci 172cr; Taxi/Ulf Sjostedt 185b. GOMBIT HOTEL SRL: 126bl. GRAZIELLA PATIO HOTEL: 212cra. HOTEL ANTICO DOGE: 76tr. HOTEL BOSONE PALACE: 252br. HOTEL CORALLO SARDEGNA: 379bl. HOTEL KRONE: 102clb. HOTEL LANCELOT: 306cr. HOTEL LOCANDA FIORITA: 74br. HOTEL MONTANA: 92cl. HOTEL NAVONA: 307tc. HOTEL OASI DI KUFRA: 314br. HOTEL PARLAMENTO: 307bl. HOTEL RELAIS VALLE ORIENTINA: 215tc.INFORMAZIONI E ACCOGLIENZA TURISTICA COMUNE DI PARMA: 225tc. L'ANTICO BORGO: 153cl. LAGACIO MOUNTAIN RESIDENCE: 103ca.MUSEO DI ARCHEOLOGIA LIGURE: 147bl. MUSEO PASSIRIA: 100cr. OSTELLO SAN NICOLA: 315tr. PALAZZO DEL SALE: 368cra. PARK HOTEL AI CAPPUCCINI: 253tl. PARKHOTEL HOLZNER: 102bc. PAV PARCO ARTE VIVENTE: 136br. PIZZA SAN GIORGIO: 195cla. PUR SÜDTIROL: 99cla. RELAIS CAMPO REGIO: 216crb. RISTORANTE PANE E VINO: 179clb. SARDEGNA IN MINIATURA: 376tc. SAT SOCIETA AEROPORTO TOSCANO SPA/PISA AIRPORT: 160bl. PHOTO SCALA, Florence: courtesy of the Ministero Beni e Att. Culturali 204cl, 204cr, 204crb, 266cl. SPAINI & PARTNERS: 133bl. TENUTA REGINA: 92cra. TERME MERANO: 98cla. VILLA LAS TRONAS HOTEL & SPA: 378BL. CHRISTINE WEBB: 196tr, 196bc, 199tl, 200clb, 201cb, 208tl, 208br, 220crb, 230tr, 230cb, 244c, 247tl, 247c.

Jacket images: Front: 4CORNERS: SIME/Massimo Ripani tc; PHOTOLIBRARY: tl; ROBERT HARDING PICTURE LIBRARY: Sylvain Grandadam b; SUPERSTOCK: imagebroker.net tr; Back: CORBIS: Atlantide Phototravel/Massimo Borchi tr; SUPERSTOCK: Belinda Images tc; F1 ONLINE tl; Spine: DORLING KINDERSLEY: Helena Smith t.

All other images © Dorling Kindersley
For further information see www.dkimages.com

SPECIAL EDITIONS OF DK TRAVEL GUIDES

DK Travel Guides can be purchased in bulk quantities at discounted prices for use in promotions or as premiums. We are also able to offer special editions and personalized jackets, corporate imprints, and excerpts from all of our books, tailored specifically to meet your own needs.
To find out more, please contact: (in the United States) **SpecialSales@dk.com;** (in the UK) **TravelSpecialSales@uk. dk.com;** (in Canada) DK Special Sales at **general@tourmaline.ca;** (in Australia) **business.development@ pearson.com.au**

Rome Transport Map

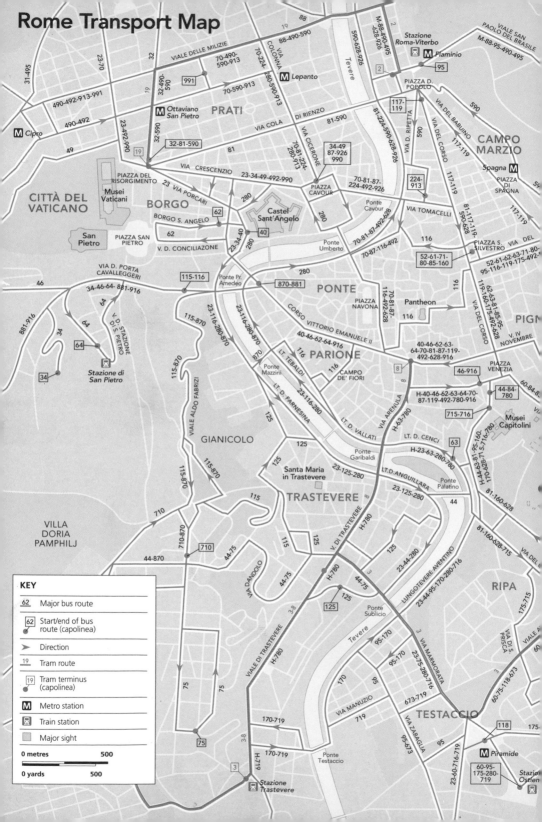

VIALE SAN PAOLO DEL BRASILE

Viale San
Paolo del Brasile

Stazione
Roma-Viterbo

M Flaminio

95

PIAZZA D.
POPOLO

VIALE DELLE MILIZIE

VIA COLONNA

M Lepanto

Tevere

VIA DEL BABUINO

590

CAMPO MARZIO

M Cipro

PRATI

VIA COLA DI RIENZO

M Ottaviano
San Pietro

VIA CICERONE

VIA D. RIPETTA

VIA DEL CORSO

Spagna M

PIAZZA DI SPAGNA

VIA CRESCENZIO

PIAZZA DEL RISORGIMENTO

VIA PORCARI

PIAZZA CAVOUR

Ponte Cavour

VIA TOMACELLI

CITTÀ DEL VATICANO

Musei Vaticani

BORGO

BORGO S. ANGELO

Castel Sant'Angelo

PIAZZA S. SILVESTRO

VIA DEL

San Pietro

PIAZZA SAN PIETRO

V. D. CONCILIAZONE

Ponte Umberto

VIA D. PORTA CAVALLEGGERI

Ponte Pr. Amedeo

280

PONTE

PIAZZA NAVONA

Pantheon

VIA DEL CORSO

VIA IV NOVEMBRE

PIGN

Stazione di San Pietro

V. D. STAZIONE D. S. PIETRO

CORSO VITTORIO EMANUELE II

PARIONE

Ponte Mazzini

LT. TEBALDI

CAMPO DE' FIORI

PIAZZA VENEZIA

PIAZZA VENEZIA

Musei Capitolini

VIALE ALDO FABRIZI

GIANICOLO

LT. D. FARNESINA

LT. D. VALLATI

LT. D. CENCI

Ponte Garibaldi

LT.D.ANGUILLARA

Santa Maria in Trastevere

TRASTEVERE

Ponte Palatino

VILLA DORIA PAMPHILJ

VIA DANDOLO

V. DI TRASTEVERE

LUNGOTEVERE AVENTINO

RIPA

VIALE DI TRASTEVERE

Ponte Sublicio

VIA MARMORATA

VIA ZABAGLIA

TESTACCIO

VIA MANUZIO

Ponte Testaccio

M Piramide

Stazione Ostien

Stazione Trastevere